COLONIAL DISCOURSE
AND
POST-COLONIAL THEORY
A Reader

COLONIAL DISCOURSE
AND
POST-COLONIAL THEORY
A Reader

edited and
introduced by

PATRICK WILLIAMS
AND
LAURA CHRISMAN

Columbia University Press
New York

Columbia University Press
New York
Introduction and section introductions and arrangement of
materials © Patrick Williams and Laura Chrisman 1994

Library of Congress Cataloging-in-Publication Data
Colonial discourse and post-colonial theory: a reader / edited and
introduced by Patrick Williams and Laura Chrisman.
      p.   cm.
   Includes bibliographical references.
   ISBN 0–231–10020–5
   ISBN 0–231–10021–3 (pbk.)
   1. Colonies.   2. Decolonization.   I. Williams, Patrick.
II. Chrisman, Laura.
JV51.C73   1994
325′.3–dc20   93–36929
                                                            CIP

Casebound editions of Columbia University Press books are
printed on permanent and durable acid-free paper.

∞

Printed and bound in Great Britain at the University Press,
Cambridge.

c 10 9 8 7 6 5 4 3 2 1
p 10 9 8 7 6 5 4 3

Contents

PART SIX: *Reading from Theory* 457

Preface

Even a few years ago, a book of this nature might well have seemed a rather strange proposition – not only because of a general lack of recognition of the importance of the field (or even a scepticism about whether such a field really existed), but also because of the apparent scarcity of texts from which one might construct such a collection. That this is not now the case, thanks on the one hand to a greater awareness and on the other to the remarkable output of people working in the post-colonial field in recent years, is obviously an occasion for some pleasure, though also, perhaps, for cautious reflection, as the rapid growth of post-colonial studies raises a number of worrying questions about academic trends – 'Is post-colonialism already, and merely, fashionable?', for instance – as well as issues which are familiar from feminism regarding the value – or not – of gaining access to the academy, and the ways in which institutions co-opt or incorporate radical movements. Beyond these issues, there are even larger and potentially more worrying questions of the relation of post-colonial studies to neo-colonial economies of power/knowledge, questions which we shall attempt to address in the Introduction to this volume.

A collection such as this always runs the risk of appearing somewhat arbitrary to the reader – 'Why this? Why not that?' – and it is as well, therefore, to say a little about the thinking behind the book, particularly in terms of selection, organisation and orientation. The texts included were chosen because of the range they represent. Chronologically, they include pieces written in the 1950s, and others written as recently as 1992. They represent a range of positions, or attitudes towards the questions at issue (and of course inclusion does not imply automatic editorial assent). It is not easy, even with the self-imposed limitations we worked within, to give a sense of the full scope of the debates in the post-colonial area, but we obviously hope that the collection goes some way towards that. The texts also represent a range of approaches to the topics and, concomitant with this, varying levels of complexity, since one aim of the book was to show that post-colonial theory does not have to be depressingly difficult. Finally, the pieces chosen represent what one might call a range of locations: metropolitan/overdeveloped world and colonial/developing world; academic/institutional and cultural/political.

The book is organised into thematic parts. The connections and cross-references between the theoretical and political concerns in different parts will allow readers to see the possibility of other maps of the post-colonial world, even to sketch in their own. The overall orientation of the book is towards accessibility: the introductions are conceived as points of access rather than sophisticated summations. This, together with the varying levels of difficulty of the texts, is in no way designed to water down the complexity of the debates; rather, it springs from a firm belief that unless a book of this nature is accessible and usable, it has little reason for existing.

As has already been hinted, although ideally we would like a collection such as this to be inclusive, we have necessarily had to proceed on the basis of all sorts of exclusions. This is not simply a question of the numbers of writers we would have liked to include (which was one reason why we decided on a limit of one piece per author), areas of current work such as radical geography had to be left out because of space constraints. A phrase such as post-colonialism will signify differently to someone working in international relations, sociology or development studies, and sadly it seemed impossible to us both to give a sense of the debates and to do justice to the wide range of disciplinary areas where post-colonialism is an important or emergent issue. Our decision to remain (broadly) within cultural theory therefore represents both our institutional location and the desire to produce a collection with some degree of internal coherence, while pointing to the great diversity of work being done in the post-colonial field. Cultural theory is – as the reader will perceive – a broad field, and an increasingly influential one, as evidenced by the fact that disciplines such as international relations, which previously regarded themselves as very distinct, are now increasingly using cultural theory to reorganise their methodologies.

The project was suggested, supported and shepherded by our editor Jackie Jones, who deserves all our thanks for getting us through. In addition, for suggestions, feedback and support, Laura would like to thank Elleke Boehmer and Benita Parry, as well as students and colleagues at the University of Sussex, especially Maria Balshaw, Ulele Burnham, Kadie Kanneh and Drew Milne. Patrick would like to thank Judith Still and Dave Murray for rapid response damage limitation, and Jen for endless patience and for feeding the cats.

Acknowledgements

The editors and publishers acknowledge with thanks permission granted to reproduce in this volume the following material previously published elsewhere. Every effort has been made to trace copyright holders, but if any have been inadvertently overlooked the publishers will be pleased to make the necessary arrangement at the first opportunity.

From Leopold Sedar Senghor, 'Negritude: A Humanism of the Twentieth Century' in *The Africa Reader: Independent Africa* (1990). Vintage, Random Century, London.

From the book *The Wretched of the Earth* by Frantz Fanon, Copyright © 1963 by Presence Africaine, copyright renewed 1991 by Presence Africaine. Used by permission of MacGibbon & Kee, an imprint of HarperCollins Publishers Limited and Grove/Atlantic Monthly Press. To order call 800–937–5557.

From Amilcar Cabral, 'National Liberation and Culture' in *Return to the Source: Selected Speeches of Amilcar Cabral*. Copyright © 1973 by PAIGC. Reprinted by permission of Monthly Review Foundation.

From Gayatri Chakravorty Spivak, 'Can the Subaltern Speak?' in Nelson, C. and Grossberg, L. (eds), *Marxism & the Interpretation of Culture* (1988). Reprinted by permission of Macmillan Press Ltd. and the University of Illinois Press.

From Homi Bhaba, 'Foreword: Remembering Fanon. Self, Psyche and the Colonial Condition' in *Black Skin, White Masks* (1986). Reprinted by permission of Pluto Press.

From *Orientalism* by Edward W. Said. Copyright © 1978 by Edward W. Said. Reprinted by permission of Routledge & Kegan Paul and Pantheon Books, a division of Random House, Inc.

From Dennis Porter, '*Orientalism* and its problems' in Barker, F. *et al.* (eds), *The Politics of Theory* (1983). Reprinted by permission of the author.

From Aijaz Ahmad, '*Orientalism* and after', in *In Theory: Classes, Nations, Literatures* (1992). Reprinted by permission of Verso.

From Aime Cesaire, *Discourse on Colonialism*. Copyright © 1972 by Monthly Review Press. Reprinted by permission of Monthly Review Foundation.

Reprinted from *The Consequences of Modernity* by Anthony Giddens with the permission of the publishers, Polity Press and Stanford University Press, and the author. © 1990 by the Board of Trustees of the Leland Stanford Junior University.

From Chandra Talpade Mohanty, 'Under Western Eyes: Feminist Scholarship and Colonial Discourses' in *Feminist Review*, no. 30, Autumn 1988. Reprinted by permission of the author.

From Jenny Sharpe, 'The Unspeakable Limits of Rape: Colonial Violence and Counter-Insurgency'. Reprinted from *Genders*, no. 10 (Spring 1991). By permission of the author and the University of Texas Press.

From Sara Suleri, 'Woman Skin Deep: Feminism and the Postcolonial Condition' in *Critical Inquiry*, no. 18, Summer 1992. Reprinted by permission of the author and the University of Chicago Press.

From Mae Gwendolyn Henderson, 'Speaking in Tongues: Dialogues, Dialectics & the Black Woman Writer's Literary Tradition', in Henry Louis Gates Jnr. (ed.), *Reading Black, Reading Feminist: A Critical Anthology* (1990). Meridian Press.

From Vijay Mishra and Bob Hodge, 'What is post(-)colonialism?' in *Textual Practice*, vol. 5, no. 3, 1991. Reprinted by permission of Routledge.

From Anne McClintock, 'The Angel of Progress: Pitfalls of the Term "Post-Colonialism"', in *Social Text*, 31/32, Spring 1992. Reprinted by permission of the author and *Social Text*.

From Ania Loomba, 'Overworlding the Third World', reprinted with permission from *Neocolonialism*, ed. Robert Young, *Oxford Literary Review* 13 (1991), pp. 164–6, 170–91, © 1991 *Oxford Literary Review*.

From Arjun Appadurai, 'Disjuncture and Difference in the Global Cultural Economy' from *Public Culture*, vol. 2, no. 2, Spring 1990. Reprinted by permission of the author and the University of Chicago Press.

From Teshome Gabriel, 'Towards a Critical Theory of Third World Films' in Pines, J. and Willeman, P. (eds), *Questions of Third World Cinema* (1989). Reprinted by permission of the author.

From Jean Franco, 'Beyond Ethnocentrism: Gender, Power & the Third World Intelligentsia', in Nelson, C. and Grossberg, L. (eds), *Marxism & the Interpretation of Culture* (1988). Reprinted by permission of Macmillan Press Ltd., the University of Illinois Press and the author.

From Deniz Kandiyoti, 'Identity and its Discontents: women & the nation' in *Millenium: Journal of International Studies*, vol. 20, no. 3, 1991. Reprinted by permission of the author and Millenium.

From Stuart Hall, 'Cultural Identity & Diaspora' in Jonathan Rutherford (ed.), *Identity: Community, Culture, Difference*, (1990). Reprinted by permission of the author.

From Paul Gilroy, 'Conclusion: urban social movements, 'race' and community' from *There Ain't No Black in the Union Jack* (1987). Reprinted by permission of Unwin Hyman.

From bell hooks, 'Postmodern blackness', in *Yearning. Race, Gender and Cultural Politics*. Copyright © 1991 by South End Press.

From *Morning Yet on Creation Day* by Chinua Achebe. Copyright © 1975 by Chinua Achebe. Used by permission of Doubleday, a division of Bantam Doubleday Dell Publishing Group, Inc. and David Bolt Associates.

From Ngũgĩ wa Thiong'o, 'The Language of African Literature', from *Decolonising the Mind* (1986). Reprinted by permission of James Currey.

From Rosemary Hennessy & Rajeswari Mohan, 'The Construction of Woman in Three Popular Texts of Empire: towards a critique of materialist feminism', in *Textual Practice*, vol. 3, no. 3, 1989. Reprinted by permission of Routledge.

From Patrick Williams, '*Kim* & Orientalism', in Mallett, P. (ed.), *Kipling Considered* (1989). Reprinted by permission of the author.

From Laura Chrisman, 'The Imperial Unconscious?: representations of imperial discourse', in *Critical Quarterly*, vol. 32, no. 3, 1990. Reprinted by permission of the author.

From Laura Mulvey, '*Xala*, Sembene Ousmane 1976: the carapace that failed', in *Third Text*, no. 16/17, Autumn/Winter 1991. Reprinted by permission of the author and Kala Press.

From Saree S. Makdisi, 'The Empire Renarrated: Season of Migration to the North and the Reinvention of the Present', in *Critical Inquiry*, no. 18, Summer 1992. Reprinted by permission of the author and the University of Chicago Press.

Colonial Discourse and Post-Colonial Theory: An Introduction

If one of the most spectacular events or series of events of the twentieth century was the dismantling of colonialism, in the shape of the European overseas empires, then one of the less immediately perceptible – but ultimately more far-reaching in its effects and implications – has been the continued globalising spread of imperialism. That such a differentiation between imperialism and colonialism might still be confusing to many people is not surprising, since in popular usage, but also in supposedly more specialist works, the two have frequently been employed interchangeably. J. A. Hobson's classic work *Imperialism*, published in 1902, seems to be at least partly responsible for an inability or disinclination to discriminate clearly between the two phenomena, which, though widespread among liberals, is not necessarily confined to them, nor indeed to obviously 'colonial' situations:

> A tendency to identify imperialism with colonialism is marked at both ends of the political spectrum in the United States: among liberals who reproduce Hobson's mistaken emphasis upon protectionist control of tropical markets and raw materials, and among adherents of the New Left who see corporate power lurking behind every bush, thus causing the US Government to intervene in Asian and Latin American countries so as to forestall or suppress national revolutions menacing the sources of corporate profit.[1]

In Britain, the term imperialism had never been a popular one – quite the reverse in fact, since it carried connotations of over-weening ambition and self-aggrandisement, the very antitheses of Britishness. The kind of confusion in political thinking outlined above was therefore compounded by a reluctance in certain quarters to think about imperialism. In academic circles it was, even relatively recently, quite acceptable for an historian (Ronald Hyam) to entitle his book *Britain's Imperial Century*[2] and then specifically refuse either to use the term imperialism or to discuss the phenomenon. That the suggested motive force behind colonial expansion was the export of surplus sexual energy, rather than the export of surplus capital (Hobson's liberal view), indicates some of the problems facing this type of analysis. Though the author's latest book offers merely the export of surplus energy, he still insists:

> Historians of empire have to come to terms with sex if only because it is there ... The expansion of Europe was not only a matter of 'Christianity and commerce', it was also a matter of copulation and concubinage. Sexual opportunities were often seized with imperious confidence.[3]

Quite so, though explanations of just where that 'imperious' confidence might originate, what combinations of power and ideology might legitimate it, indeed, in what sense, after the work of Michel Foucault (to whom even Hyam refers), we can any longer regard sex as simply 'there', are conspicuously absent.

Hyam's ideological foes are, interestingly enough, precisely the group who have made the most sustained and differentiated examination of imperialism, colonialism and neo-colonialism, namely Marxists. As Eric Hobsbawm has pointed out, the anti-imperialist work of Marxists has been met by 'anti-anti-imperialist' writings, though these are at best only partially convincing, since, as Hobsbawm says: 'All attempts to divorce the explanation of imperialism from the specific developments of capitalism in the late nineteenth century must be regarded as ideological exercises, though often learned and sometimes acute.'[4]

That intimate connection between economics and politics is one of the major contributions of Marxist thinking on the subject, and one which allows the most convincing distinctions between colonialism and imperialism to be drawn. In this view, colonialism, the conquest and direct control of other people's land, is a particular phase in the history of imperialism, which is now best understood as the globalisation of the capitalist mode of production, its penetration of previously non-capitalist regions of the world, and destruction of pre- or non-capitalist forms of social organisation. From its beginnings in the sixteenth century, capitalism has spread outward from its European heartland according to different rhythms and different pressures, by means of trade and conquest, economic forms of power as well as military, to the point where it now constitutes a truly global economy. The colonial phase, particularly the rapid acquisition of territories by European nations in the late nineteenth century (most famously in the 'Scramble for Africa'), represents the need for access to new (preferably captive) markets and sources of raw materials, as well as the desire to deny these to competitor nations.

Although critics of Marxist analyses of imperialism attempt to characterise them as rigid and outmoded (according to Hyam, Marxists are 'quietly recanting' in acknowledgement of this), such analyses have in fact continued to develop in response to the mutations of capitalism in the last one hundred and fifty years. The earliest stage of Marxist thinking is represented by Marx and Engels in the mid-nineteenth century, though Marx never used the term imperialism, which emerged as a semi-neologism in the context of late nineteenth-century 'New Imperialism' – a new phase, rather than the new phenomenon that it appeared to contemporary observers. The second stage comprises early twentieth-century efforts by Bukharin,

Rosa Luxemburg and Lenin to theorise the workings of monopoly capital as imperialism, particularly in Lenin's *Imperialism, the Highest Stage of Capitalism*, published in 1916 (though Lenin actually referred to imperialism as the 'latest stage', the alteration being made posthumously). The third stage, from the 1950s to the early 1970s, includes the influential work of Arghiri Emmanuel on dependency theory and Samir Amin on theories of unequal exchange. In the fourth and latest stage, much of the work of people like John Weeks and Christian Pailloix turns away from the dependency model to examine questions of multi-national capitalism and capitalist rivalry.

Beginning in 1947, the formal dissolution of colonial empires and the granting of independence to previously colonised countries followed various campaigns of anti-colonial resistance, usually with an explicitly nationalist basis. These took forms ranging from legal and diplomatic manoeuvres – opposing the colonisers on their ideological high ground of principles and procedures – to wars of independence, as in Kenya and Algeria in the 1950s – opposing the colonisers on what many would regard as the real ground of colonialism: military power. The ending of colonial rule created high hopes for the newly independent countries and for the inauguration of a properly post-colonial era, but such optimism was relatively short-lived, as the extent to which the West had not relinquished control became clear. This continuing Western influence, located in flexible combinations of the economic, the political, the military and the ideological (but with an over-riding economic purpose), was named neo-colonialism by Marxists, though the term was quickly taken up by leaders of newly or soon to be independent countries. Although the name apparently privileges the colonial, the process itself can be seen to be yet another manifestation of imperialism.

[margin note: S. Korea problematized by Japan's role.]

The persistence of neo-colonialist or imperialist practices in the contemporary world is a very obvious, perhaps the most serious, obstacle to any unproblematic use of the term post-colonial. As Anne McClintock points out in her reading 'The Angel of Progress' in this volume (see Part Four), the extent to which the formerly colonised countries can be considered post-colonial is both variable and debatable. The fact that the major imperialist nation, the United States, can intervene militarily in the Gulf against a country which it continued to arm and encourage up to the brink of hostilities, or under the guise of humanitarianism in Somalia, a country to which it had previously happily denied aid; the fact that it can do so while claiming the highest moral authority ('doing God's work', as President Bush put it in the case of Somalia); the fact that articles and editorials in respectable newspapers such as the *Sunday Telegraph* can call for the West to go back to Africa and sort out the mess into which their incompetent national governments have led them – all of these indicate how many of the attitudes, the strategies and even how much of the room for manoeuvre of the colonial period remain in place.

Like any other form of 'post-', the post-colonial carries with it at least a dual sense of being chronologically subsequent to the second term in the relationship and of – on the face of it – having somehow superseded that term. The first of these is reasonably uncontentious: the era of formal colonial control is over, apart from aberrations such as the Falklands/Malvinas. If temporal succession is not a particular problem, however, supersession may still be. Discussing post-structuralism, Derrida has said that if structuralism is viewed as 'an adventure of vision, a conversion in the way of putting a question to an object', then we are still very much within its sphere of influence. In the same way, if colonialism is a way of maintaining an unequal international relation of economic and political power (in the same way as Edward Said talks about Orientalism deploying a variety of strategies whose common factor is that they guarantee a position of superiority for the Westerner *vis-à-vis* the Orient), then no doubt we have not fully transcended the colonial. Perhaps this amounts to saying that we are not yet post-imperialist.

If there is a problem connected with calling some societies post-colonial because of the extent of their implication in contemporary capitalism, a different kind of problem arises about whether the historical relation of other societies to colonialism allows them to now be claimed as post-colonial. This is above all the case of the former white settler colonies – Canada, Australia, New Zealand. That these were not simply colonies was formally recognised at the time by Britain in granting them Dominion status. Economically and politically, their relation to the metropolitan centre bore little resemblance to that of the actual colonies. They were not subject to the sort of coercive measures which were the lot of the colonies, and their ethnic stratification was fundamentally different. Their subsequent history and economic development, and current location within global capitalist relations, have been very much in a metropolitan mode, rather than a (post-)colonial one. As such, their inclusion in the category of the post-colonial becomes something of a problem, though that has not prevented calls for just such an inclusion (indeed, there is an interesting correlation between the difficulty of the claim and the number of writers and critics working in the area of post-colonial studies in those countries who are making the claim). Clearly, this is not a matter for prescription, but it would seem that the argument for inclusion has not been won.

If texts exist in what – to be deliberately unfashionable – one could call a dialectical relationship with their social and historical context – produced by, but also productive of, particular forms of knowledge, ideologies, power relations, institutions and practices – then an analysis of the texts of imperialism has a particular urgency, given their implication in far-reaching, and continuing, systems of domination and economic exploitation. This involves an understanding of present circumstances as well as the ways in which these are informed by, perpetuate and differ from situations which preceded them, and the complex interrelation of history and the present moment provides the terrain on which colonial discourse analysis and post-colonial theory operate. History has, of course, been under debate – if not under siege – for some time now, from Hayden White's emphasis on historiography as subject to the rules of narrative discourse, to Robert Young's questioning of the totalising, even totalitarian, aspects of Enlightenment – and especially Marxist – models of history. That might seem like difficulty or complexity enough, but there is also the added problem of how to construe the contemporary.

Postmodernism represents a particular way – or rather a diversity of related ways – of understanding contemporaneity; post-colonialism works with different maps, chronologies, narratives and political agendas. The two are by no means entirely disjunct, however, and a recent attempt to consider their points of contiguity will be discussed later in this introduction.

Post-colonialism is far from being a unified field, as the title of this reader suggests, and it is necessary, therefore, to indicate some of the developments and divergences which have taken place. It is perhaps no exaggeration to say that Edward Said's *Orientalism*, published in 1978,[5] single-handedly inaugurates a new area of academic inquiry: colonial discourse, also referred to as colonial discourse theory or colonial discourse analysis. Michael Foucault has said that discursive constraints – the rules governing what can and cannot be said within the boundaries of a particular discourse – should be understood as productive as well as limiting; and certainly if we see *Orientalism* as setting out various discursive boundaries for colonial discourse analysis, then, judging from the work which has followed, they appear to have functioned much more as an incitement than as an impediment. Said's book is rather less concerned with drawing in territorial boundaries (which perhaps smacks too much of imperialist or Orientalist cartography) than it is with suggesting or opening up paths which others might follow. Some of these paths have been taken, with impressive results; others have not, or only belatedly. It is noteworthy that one of the most explicit invitations to further work contained in *Orientalism* – the moment when Said notes the lack of any systematic study of the relation between imperialism and culture – was not taken up, and it was left to Said himself to undertake that particular task, in his book *Culture and Imperialism*.[6] This is not to suggest that no important work has taken place – this reader alone disproves that – but that its focus has perhaps been the local rather than the global.

Work which has followed Said has drawn on other theories – psychoanalysis (in Homi Bhabha, for example), deconstruction (Gayatri Chakravorty Spivak), feminism (Chandra Mohanty), other forms of Marxism (Aijaz Ahmad) – and, as the different parts in this reader indicate, has diversified its areas of inquiry. *Orientalism* focused on what could be called colonial discourse – the variety of textual forms in which the West produced and codified knowledge about non-metropolitan areas and cultures, especially those under colonial control. Increasingly, however, as readings in the present collection make clear, both the point of origin of the theorising and of the texts studied have been more properly post-colonial, hence the need to signal both in the title of this reader. The division is one which it is no doubt necessary to keep in mind, but it is also one which is easily and frequently crossed: Gayatri Chakravorty Spivak, for instance, is very much a post-colonial critic (as the title of her latest book, *The Post-Colonial Critic*,[7] makes clear), while the texts and institutions she studies belong equally to the colonial and post-colonial periods. In addition, post-colonialism, although seen by some as a proper improvement, a more exact term, etc., is also a much debated, even strongly contested, concept, as readings such as those by Mishra and Hodge and Anne McClintock demonstrate (see Part Four). Gayatri Chakravorty Spivak has recently attacked post-colonialism as 'just totally bogus'[8] (while at the same time – and somewhat confusingly – seeming quite happy with the idea of post-coloniality). These are no mere terminological quibbles, however – names, as much as theories, can have political effects, but in the absence of any obvious – or, just as importantly, generally recognised – alternative, it seemed that the double title usefully signalled both the changes of emphasis and the areas of interest in the field.

One of the reasons for the success of *Orientalism* in encouraging similar or further research was no doubt its bringing together (some might say 'yoking together by violence') of two apparently very different areas: post-structuralism, in the shape of Foucault, and Western Marxism, in the shape of Gramsci. Although Dennis Porter's article in Part Two sees the attempt to align the two as fundamentally flawed, it could also be argued that Foucault's ideas and those of Gramsci come surprisingly close on a number of points, for example in moving away from a concept of society fixated on notions of the state, and most significantly in theories of power as located and exercised 'strategically' – in Foucault's phrase – at all levels of society. Theoretical and political tensions between post-structuralism and Marxism feature in a number of contemporary debates over post-colonial critical practices. For some post-structuralists, such as Robert Young, Marxism is part of the problem in post-colonial theory, whereas for someone like Gayatri Chakravorty Spivak it is an indispensable tool.

The question of agency constitutes another tension both within and around post-colonial theory. Post-structuralism in particular has criticised existing models of individual subjectivity, above all the bourgeois liberal concept of the autonomous individual, while post-modernist theory, in the shape of Jean-François Lyotard, has announced the end of 'les grands récits', the 'grand narratives' of the Enlightenment, which, among other things, promised emancipation, and provided the basis and legitimation for collective action and large-scale mobilisation. Politically speaking, post-structuralist attacks on bourgeois individualism are less problematic than attacks on Marxism (as one of the Enlightenment narratives), though both pose problems in terms of how one is to authorise and organise political action, and that in turn has implications for theory and practice in the post-colonial field. Another post-modernist theorist (and ex-Marxist), Jean Baudrillard, has rejected the disruptive potential of Marxism, claiming that such oppositional theory and practice is allowed for in advance by ruling ideologies. While in some sense this may be so at a conceptual level (though it sounds like nothing so much as a reworking of Frankfurt School theorist Herbert Marcuse's notion of 'repressive tolerance', where the state licences a degree of dissent in order to defuse anything more threatening), it fails to deal with the awkward fact that oppositional movements do occur – including Marxist ones – and do sometimes win.

If Said's *Orientalism* marks the point at which Western academic institutions formally recognised colonial discourse as an area of study, it must be pointed out that it was preceded by a number of academic texts from a German intellectual tradition which shared Said's concerns with the historical and theoretical relations between Western economic/political global domination and Western intellectual production. For these thinkers – Theodor Adorno and Max Horkheimer of the Frankfurt School, Walter Benjamin and Hannah Arendt – what prompted such concerns was the ascendancy of German fascism, Soviet totalitarianism (in the case of Hannah Arendt) and (in the case of the Frankfurt School) the 'totally administered society' of US capitalism. That twentieth-century Western fascism and totalitarianism were seen by these thinkers as the primary examples of dominatory philosophy/ economics does not render their theoretical insights any the less useful for a consideration of colonialism and imperialism, and much work remains to be done, reassessing and extending their contributions. Arendt's *The Origins of Totalitarianism* (1951), for example, contains a major and comprehensive account of the knowledge/power relations of nineteenth-century imperialism which in many ways anticipates Foucault's archaeological methods of investigation.[9] Whereas Foucault situates an epistemological break in *The Order of Things*,[10] in the Enlightenment of late eighteenth/early nineteenth-century Europe, and generalises the construction of 'man and his others' as objects of knowledge within this overall period, implying an ideological consistency that extends into the modernity of the twentieth century, Arendt qualifies such a sweeping characterisation by emphasising the crucial shifts within nineteenth-century intellectual formations.

Combining political, cultural and sociological theory with empirical investigation, Arendt explores the ways in which transformations of race-thinking, European nationalism and class structures engender the phenomenon of imperialism. Offering what might be termed an eclectic and singular Heideggerian-informed left-leaning cultural materialism, Arendt counters the economism of Lenin's description of imperialism as 'the highest stage of capitalism' by emphasising the transformations of class and state structures involved in colonialism's consolidation into imperialism, terming it instead 'the first stage in the political rule of the bourgeoisie'. For Arendt, aesthetic culture and philosophical idealism emerge as crucial components of imperialism's political self-legitimation. Whereas Said might see Europe's material relationship with, and discursive construction of, 'the Orient', as the paradigm of colonial/imperial structures, Arendt takes Europe's late-nineteenth-century scramble for Africa, and in particular, South Africa, as her historical and theoretical paradigm, in which all the contradictory relations of knowledge/power contained in imperialism have their fullest expression. (It is noteworthy that J. A. Hobson also rendered South Africa the chief example of imperialism's logic.) Although Arendt's reading of South Africa is marred by her own racism towards black African peoples, and although her reading of imperialism as a whole is restricted by the teleological scheme into which it is made to fit (imperialism features as the second stage in Western civilisation's descent into the final stage of evil, fascism) – nonetheless, her insights and methods offer an important resource for future colonial discourse theorisation.

Max Horkheimer and Theodor Adorno's *Dialectic of the Enlightenment* (1944) offers a critique of the epistemic violence of Enlightenment philosophy which precedes post-structuralist critiques by several decades. As Robert Young points out, the premise of this critique differs from that of post-structuralism in that for the Frankfurters, the dialectic is both part of the problem and part of the solution: it is only through using it against itself that society/philosophy can be emancipated from the domination and oppression (of self and other) brought on by the triumph of capitalism and an instrumental version of Enlightenment rationality. Not least of that text's contributions – and potential usefulness for post-colonial theorisations – is the way in which it constantly, and ambiguously, relates material *economic* processes with *philosophical* ones. Drawing on Georg Lukács's theorisation of the process and consequences of economic and social reification, Horkheimer and Adorno's analysis of the 'dialectic of Enlightenment' and its culmination in twentieth-century political authoritarianism and genocide links the violence of Enlightenment philosophy to the creation of capitalist commodification, the invention of 'exchange value' and its dominance over 'use value'.

One of Foucault's insights which is important for Said's project is the mutual implication of power and knowledge. In the context of *Orientalism*, Western power, especially the power to enter or examine other countries at will, enables the production of a range of knowledges about other cultures. Such knowledge in turn enables (legitimates, underwrites) the deployment of Western power in those other countries. Moreover, such is the power of Orientalist or colonialist knowledge that even those discourses or modes of representation which are not formally or ideologically aligned with it may be pulled in an Orientalist direction, or may simply be appropriated by Orientalism and utilised as if they were just another facet of its world view. Orientalism's enormous appetite for forms of knowledge – scientific, historical, geographical, linguistic, literary, artistic, anthropological – derives in part from its location within the period of the Enlightenment. The Enlightenment's universalising will to knowledge (for better or worse) feeds Orientalism's will to power. The latter then stands as an example of the production of knowledge as (certainly on balance, if not categorically) negative: stereotyping, Othering, dominatory. Colonial discourse analysis and post-colonial theory are thus critiques of the process of production of knowledge about the Other. As such, they produce forms of knowledge themselves, but other knowledge, better knowledge it is hoped, responsive to Said's central question: 'How can we know and respect the Other?' Nevertheless, they remain, potentially at least, vulnerable to the post-structuralist criticism of the way in which theories and concepts appropriate their objects of knowledge.

Robert Young's *White Mythologies: Writing History and the West* is a post-structuralist interrogation of Western Marxism's construction of history as he sees it. It also attempts to trace the possibility of another history, an alternative way of knowing the Other, and finds such a possibility in colonial discourse analysis.

Young examines Marxism's involvement in problematic Enlightenment processes, especially those which are linked to Hegelian concepts:

> Here it is not a question of suggesting that Hegel is somehow answerable for the excesses of capitalism or even socialism in the past two hundred years: rather what is at stake is the argument that the dominant force of opposition to capitalism, Marxism, as a body of knowledge itself remains complicit with, and even extends, the system to which it is opposed.[11]

What is not clear in this line of reasoning is whether this assumed conceptual complicity would automatically invalidate Marxism as an emancipatory political project, or whether, on analogy with Gayatri Chakravorty Spivak's notion of 'strategic essentialism', it would still be acceptable to Young to use Marxism for liberatory purposes though recognising all the while that it was complicit with the forces of domination. What *is* clearer is that for Young the potential other knowledges of colonial discourse analysis and post-colonial theory are necessarily partially disabled by their incorporation of Marxism – in the case of Said and Spivak, though not in that of Bhabha.

> For all the carefully constructed disparateness of her work, for all the discontinuities which she refuses to reconcile, Spivak's Marxism functions as an overall syncretic frame. It works, in fact, in exactly the same way as Jameson's – as a transcendentalising gesture to produce closure.[12]

For Robert Young, twentieth-century Western Marxism is blinkered by its adherence to a Hegelian interpretation of history in which history is construed as an absolutist and homogeneous evolutionary march of the world spirit, unfolding and creating itself through the dialectical incorporation of otherness, culminating in a total or totalitarian self-realisation. The corollary of this view of history-as-progress is a view of historical analysis termed historicism, which presupposes that history can become completely accessible to the modern historian, without mediation; all the contradictory and heterogeneous aspects of histories – including the history of the oppressed and colonised – are reconcilable with, or reducible to, historicist methods. This historicist approach, however, has been roundly criticised by a number of Marxists, among them the German critic Walter Benjamin, who proposed a model of 'historical materialism' to oppose historicism's delusions of grandeur.

Arguing (in 1940) that the study of history involves images as well as linearity, entailing a recognition of (and methodology predicated upon) discontinuity as well as continuity, Benjamin contends the following:

> [Historical materialism] involves not only the flow of thoughts, but their arrest as well. Where thinking suddenly stops in a configuration pregnant with tensions, it gives that

configuration a shock, by which it crystallizes into a monad. A historical materialist approaches a historical subject only where he encounters it as a monad. In this structure he recognizes the sign of a Messianic cessation of happening, or, put differently, a revolutionary chance in the fight for the oppressed past. He takes cognizance of it in order to blast a specific era out of the homogeneous course of history ... As a result of this method the life work is preserved in this work and at the same time cancelled; in the lifework, the era; and in the era, the entire course of history.[13]

Benjamin's notion of the historical monad, as that final sentence makes clear, is profoundly, if unusually, dialectical: the individual episode of oppressed history, its 'otherness' and singularity, is both 'preserved and cancelled' in and through its contemporary analysis. Benjamin develops this further in his notion of the contemporary study of the historical moment as based upon a frozen image:

An image is that in which the past and the now flash into a constellation. In other words: image is dialectic at a standstill. For while the relation of the present to the past is a purely temporal, continuous one, that of the past to the now is dialectical – isn't development but image, capable of leaping out.[14]

Benjamin's emphasis on the non-comprehensiveness of historical materialism *vis-à-vis* its subject, and on the self-reflexive situating of the contemporary historian or critic in dialectical/constellated relationship to her/his material, is not altogether remote from a Spivakian notion of the strategic and partial positioning of the critic in her/his relationship to, and selection of, historical moments. Indeed, Spivak's historical method could be described as a highly allegorical one, much as is Benjamin's. Benjamin's notion of contemporary history and historicism as proceeding on the modern principle of 'empty, homogeneous time' is also one which contemporary theorists of the nation/nationalism have taken much from. Benedict Anderson, for example, in *Imagined Communities: Reflections on the origins and spread of nationalism*, owes much to Benamin's concepts of modern temporality.[15] Benjamin's iconoclastic, imagistic approach to history, his notions of its discontinuities and fragments, also overlap significantly with Frantz Fanon's emphasis on the fragmentary and image-based history of the colonised.

There remains, of course, the question of whether any knowledge of theory is pure, whether Young's deconstructive moves are in the end any less appropriative of their objects of knowledge (Marxism, colonial discourse analysis) than the theories he criticises. Part of the problem lies in the assumption that theoretical 'purity' is possible; part of the problem lies in the assumption that 'purity', even if possible, is politically desirable. For Adorno and Horkheimer, for instance, these assumptions would be a major shortcoming in the operations of post-structuralism and some post-colonial theory. Such operations repeat the very way in which traditional philosophy (Enlightenment or otherwise) cuts itself off from a self-reflective consideration of its relationship to material and political power, deluding itself as to its pure and autonomous status, and thereby becomes all the more readily an instrument and mirror of social domination. As Adorno states elsewhere,

> ... the idea of the mastery of pure reason as a being-in-itself, separate from practice, subjects even the subject and turns it into an instrument toward purposes. A form of self-reflection of reason really of help would make its transition to *praxis*: this self-reflection would see through itself to its practical moment; instead of mistaking itself for the absolute, it would know that it is a kind of conduct. The anti-mythological aspect of progress cannot be thought without the practical act which seizes the delusion of the autarchy of spirit by the reins. Thus, progress is also not ascertainable through disinterested consideration.[16]

Adorno's comments arise from a complex meditation on the nature and theory of (social, historical and intellectual) 'progress', a concept which occupies an embattled position within and across a range of post-colonial and development theories. He argues (among other things) that

> progress means humanity emerges from its spellbound state no longer under the spell of progress as well, itself nature, by becoming aware of its own indigenousness to nature and by halting the mastery over nature through which nature continues its mastery. In this respect it could be said that progress only comes about at the point when it come to an end.[17]

In this conclusion, a notion of progress proves to be as indispensable as it is dangerous to human emancipation. The complex turns of Adorno's dialectic, in which Enlightenment traditions of identity-thinking are subjected to an immanent critique, suggest ways in which dialectical thinking can be a tool in challenging, not upholding, philosophical trends towards a totalising absolutism, founded on a notion of the fundamentally unstable, contradictory, interdependent, and mutually transformative relations between 'subject' and 'object', 'self' and 'other'.

Gayatri Chakravorty Spivak's critique of theoretical 'purity' overlaps in many ways with that of Adorno. Spivak would suggest that even those who do not go in for strategic essentialism do not thereby remain pure:

> You pick up the universal that will give you the power to fight against the other side, and what you are throwing away is your theoretical purity. Whereas the great custodians of the anti-universal are obliged therefore simply to act in the interest of a great narrative, the narrative of exploitation, while they keep themselves clean by not committing themselves to anything. In fact they are actually run by a great narrative even as they are busy protecting their theoretical purity by repudiating essentialism.[18]

In addition, she emphasises the implication of the intellectual in structures of power, and in a phrase reminiscent of Derrida's famous 'il n'y a pas de hors-texte' declares: 'I don't think there is a non-institutional environment'.[19] The result of this is not, however, that the post-colonial critic is disabled by such facts, rather that a constant awareness of the location of the individual and the circumstances of knowledge production must ensue.

The problem of history and debates over the purity of concepts and forms of knowledge occur in other guises. Just as for a number of years feminists have debated whether logic, rationality and theory could be considered somehow 'masculine' (produced by men, serving male needs, operating in a way which benefited men) and whether, therefore, feminists could or should be using them, so a number of post-colonial writers have queried both history as an essentially Western construct and the relevance of 'imported' Western theories such as Marxism and feminism in a non-Western context. Whether history becomes a problematic concept or not, the issue of periodising remains relevant to post-colonialism, and is of course something which it shares with post-modernism. In each case, the prefix suggests succession, temporal break, a new period (if not a new start); in each case, however, the idea of historical discontinuity has been challenged: post-modernism has been seen as simply the latest variant of modernism, and neo-colonialism has been suggested as a more appropriate term than post-colonialism. Although the suggestion is no doubt unpalatable to many, especially the supporters and celebrants of post-modernism, this pattern of an apparent newness masking an underlying continuity might be well-founded. Walter Benjamin described the process of commodity production as 'the always-new in the context of the ever-same', where the need for the commodity to present itself as always new, different, desirable, masked the underlying, unchanging nature of capitalist relations of production. To the extent, therefore, that both post-modernism and post-colonialism are bound up with the workings of contemporary capitalism, the one as its 'cultural logic', in Jameson's phrase, and the other as a specific form of its global ambitions, then their need to represent themselves as other than they are becomes readily comprehensible.

The connections between post-modernism and post-colonialism are the subject of a recent collection of essays, *Past the Last Post*.[20] Like the better-known volume *The Empire Writes Back*,[21] with which it shares a number of features, *Past the Last Post* presents a particular view of history and periodicity in relation to post-colonialism:

> Definitions of the post-colonial, of course, vary widely, but for me the concept proves most useful not when it is used synonymously with a post-independence historical period in once-colonised nations, but rather when it locates a specifically anti- or *post-*colonial *discursive* purchase in culture, one which begins in the moment that the colonising power inscribes itself onto the body and space of its Others and which continues as an often occluded tradition into the modern theatre of neo-colonialist international relations.[22]

This repeats the idea in *The Empire Writes Back* of a continuous post-coloniality, though a rather different kind of continuity to that proposed above. Foremost among the problems with such a view of post-colonialism is the sense of instantaneous resistance. Foucault's well-known formulation in *History of Sexuality*, 'Where there is power there is resistance', has been criticised for the picture of an apparently automatic oppositionality which it presents, but at least it makes sense in the context of Foucault's theories. This idea, on the other hand, of an unbroken history of automatic, effortless resistance by the colonised which is conjured up here ignores both the variety of cultural responses to European incursions and the material difficulties of co-ordinating and sustaining resistance. In addition, the sense of historical change disappears in the face of a seamless history of 'continuity of preoccupations', as *The Empire Writes Back* puts it. Seamlessness, continuity, the homogenisation of geographical, historical and cultural specificities of post-colonialism – these are among the more problematic aspects of the post-colonialism which *The Empire Writes Back* proposes.

Although their models of post-colonialism are similarly problematic, the authors of *Past the Last Post* part company with *The Empire Writes Back* over the question of post-modernism. In *The Empire Writes Back* post-modernism is something of an irrelevance in the post-colonial setting. The formerly colonised countries and their writers are discovered to be post-modernists and post-structuralists *avant la lettre*. The authors cite the idea of the 'shock of recognition' on the part of American writers and critics encountering European theories and practices and feeling that they had been writing and saying the same kind of thing all along. In this perspective, post-colonial critics could and should (although they don't because of the continuing hegemony of European ideas) ignore post-modernism and the rest and carry on doing what they are already doing. In *Past the Last Post*, post-modernism is something rather more threatening. Far from accepting a view, like that of Robert Young in *White Mythologies*, that 'Postmodernism can best be defined as European culture's awareness that it is no longer the unquestioned and dominant centre of the world',[23] the editors of *Past the Last Post* see it, on the contrary, as a determined attempt to retain the position and influence of global centrality. More than simply capitalism's cultural logic, it now sounds like the essence of capitalism itself:

> Post-modernism ... operates as a Euro-American western hegemony, whose global appropriation of time-and-place inevitably proscribes certain cultures as 'backward' and marginal while coopting to itself certain of their cultural 'raw' materials. Post-modernism is then projected onto these margins as normative, as a neo-universalism to which 'marginal' cultures may aspire, and from which certain of their more forward-looking products might be appropriated and 'authorised'.[24]

Their contention that post-modernism and post-structuralism exercise intellectual hegemony over the post-colonial world and post-colonial cultural production is obviously relevant to the problematically post-colonial former white settler colonies of Australia, Canada and New Zealand, but it is difficult to see anything of the same effects at work in the non-white post-colonial world. However contentious these arguments are, what they demonstrate is that the nature of these two major categories, post-modernism and post-colonialism, is still very much a subject of debate, and their intersections and divergences are going to require lengthy and careful delineation.

One effect of the success of *Orientalism* has been, simultaneously and somewhat paradoxically, to enable and to inhibit study of works by the earlier anti-colonial writers. Such study is enabled by the fact that *Orientalism*, and, to a greater or lesser extent, Said's subsequent work, indicates the existence and importance of a range of precursors, direct or indirect, and though Said's reading of colonial or post-colonial intellectuals has not gone uncriticised (by Aijaz Ahmad, for instance), it remains a useful pointer to significant topics. At the same time, in the move to 'get beyond' Said theoretically, historically or politically, the orientation – towards the post-colonial, towards the present or even the future – means at one level less attention is being paid to the earlier writers. It is notable that the work of Fanon is so far something of an exception to this neglect or marginalisation of the earlier theorists. Fanon is currently enjoying a remarkable vogue, so much so that the African-American critic Henry Louis Gates, Jr., has recently produced an article sceptical of the 'Critical Fanonism' he sees at large. Early African-American thinkers, such as W. E. B. du Bois and Alexander Crummel, have also recently received a certain amount of attention from academics, as witnessed by the work of Gates himself and Paul Gilroy.

Inclusion of earlier writers inevitably raises questions of nativism (at its most basic and contentious, the belief in an authentic ethnic identity, as in the Négritude movement, or the desire to return, after the catastrophe of colonialism, to an unsullied indigenous cultural tradition, as in various forms of cultural nationalism). Positions *vis-à-vis* nativism are frequently divided. Said, for example, dismisses it in his article 'Intellectuals in the post-colonial world' as 'one especially besetting hobble of most post-colonial work',[25] and suggests elsewhere that nativism is only the first stage of a process leading to full emancipation. Anthony Appiah has attacked probably the best-known African proponents of nativism, Chinweizu, Jemie and Madubuike, and their book, *Toward the Decolonization of African Literature*.[26] For Appiah, their type of cultural nationalism remains trapped in a position of counter-identification, which simply reverses the terms and the arguments of colonialism, as well as the trajectory it has traced out. 'Time and time again, cultural nationalism has followed the route of alternate genealogizing. We end up always in the same place; the achievement is to have invented a different past for it.'[27] Gayatri Chakravorty Spivak stands as evidence of the pull of a certain kind of covert nativism: although she does not believe that after 'the planned epistemic violence of the imperialist project' there is any possibility of recovering a (native) text which can 'answer one back', she nevertheless finds herself in the position of proposing an alternative conference title which, she later realises,

> nostalgically assumed that a critique of imperialism would restore the sovereignty for the lost self of the colonies so that Europe could, once and for all, be put in the place

of the other that it always was. It now seems to me that it is this kind of revisionary impulse that is allowing the emergence of the 'Third World' as a convenient signifier.[28]

The exiled South African critic Benita Parry, on the other hand, is concerned not to dismiss nativism, and her careful examination of Négritude, Césaire, Fanon, and the links between them, in a recent article, results in her at least being able to give, as the subtitle says, 'Two cheers for nativism'.[29] In Parry's view, Négritude offers more multiple and less essentialist positions than is usually assumed, as well as possibilities for anti-colonial resistance.

If nativism, as exemplified in the work of Edward Wilmot Blyden, for example, is one theoretical tenet of late nineteenth-/early twentieth-century anti-colonial discourse, then Enlightenment is another. This raises further questions about the denunciation of Enlightenment-as-imperialism as made by post-structuralists such as Robert Young. Taking just Southern and West Africa as examples, it can be seen that late nineteenth- and early twentieth-century nationalist black intellectuals, such as Sol Plaatje, S. M. Molema and Pixley Seme from South Africa, or James Africanus Horton and Joseph Casely-Hayford from West Africa, were engaged both in instrumentalising and immanently critiquing Enlightenment cultural forms (novels, newspapers, historiography, ethnography), political forms (parliamentary petitions, delegations), ethical and political emancipatory values (universal human equality, enfranchisement, self-government) in ways which require much critical attention today.[30]

Such an examination of early anti-colonial discourse needs to be accompanied by greater attention to mid- and late twentieth-century liberation theorists of the Third World. Thinkers such as C. L. R. James, George Padmore, Kwame Nkrumah, Jomo Kenyatta, Amilcar Cabral, Steve Biko, A. Sivanandan, have made significant contributions to the analysis of colonial and anti-colonial culture and politics; yet they tend to be overlooked by academics intent on identifying Frantz Fanon as the founding father of Third World liberationist discourse.[31]

There are two necessary components to such an examination: an historical theorisation of these intellectuals as crucial exponents of an anti-colonial subjectivity, one which goes beyond Fanon's own highly teleological and progressivist 'three stages' characterisation of anti-colonial intellectual development, or Bhabha's 'hybridity' and 'mimicry' models; and a consideration of the theoretical substance of these thinkers, their own potential contributions to a contemporary anti-colonial theory and analysis of colonial discourse.

There are many directions in which theories of colonial and post-colonial discourse could develop. This introduction has pointed to some already: the development of cultural materialist and dialectical/Frankfurtian Marxist methodologies, and the re-evaluation of Enlightenment philosophies. As this introduction has argued, future close critical analysis of early anti-colonial discourse is crucial and may necessitate a substantial revision of existing theoretical paradigms of anti- and post-colonial discourse. These revisions involve a reassessment of the relations between metropolitan, Western Enlightenment, nationalist and nativist strands in the discourses. They also involve, more generally, a theoretical reconsideration of the nature, function and evolution of militant anti-colonial intellectuals of the Third World.

At the same time, there is a danger that any such reassessment would repeat some of the shortcomings of existing theoretical analysis when it assumes that anti- and post-colonial discourses only emerge as a response to, and in (friendly or antagonistic) dialogue with, Western knowledge/power. Both of these assumptions need to be challenged. Viewed historically, emergent anti- and post-colonial cultural and theoretical discourse was formed as much through transnational dialogue with other Third World discourses and movements as it was through dialogue with the West. Early twentieth-century Black intellectuals, for instance – those directly involved in pan-Africanism, and those not directly involved too – were in often a three or four way transcultural intellectual and political dialogue: African-Americans such as Booker T. Washington and W. E. B. du Bois had an impact on black South African discourses, as did the Caribbean Marcus Garvey, and West African thinkers such as Joseph Casely-Hayford, and it would be surprising if the South African discourses did not also influence African-American, Caribbean and West African discourses. These patterns of cross-cultural fertilisation require both historical and conceptual discussion.

Furthermore, close analysis of these periods of discourse may have far-reaching consequences for the theorisation of the colonial and imperial discourses which were contemporary with these anti-colonial thinkers. 'Colonial discourse analysis' has concerned itself with, among other things, the ways in which the 'subaltern' native subject is constructed within these discourses. There has been a considerable debate about the extent to which this subaltern presence may carry a transgressive or oppositional weight, as witnessed in the different interpretations by Gayatri Spivak and Benita Parry of Jean Rhys's *Wide Sargasso Sea*.[32] Important as this work is, it still tends to position colonial/imperial subjectivity as having epistemological and ontological primacy; native or subaltern subjects feature as secondary 'subject-effects' allowed, according to the critic, greater or lesser degrees of oppositional power within the discourse of empire.

What has been less explored is the extent to which the subaltern may have played a constitutive rather than a reflective role in colonial and domestic imperial discourse and subjectivity. Rather than being that other onto which the coloniser projects a previously constituted subjectivity and knowledge, native presences, locations, and political resistance need to be further theorised as having a determining or primary role in colonial discourses, and in the attendant domestic versions of these discourses. In other words, the movement may have been as much from 'periphery' to 'centre' as from 'centre' to 'periphery'. In a number of material, institutional and discursive ways, the colonial scene quite literally preceded the metropolitan Western scene: the work of Gauri Viswanathan, for example, explores the ways in which the practice of English studies was first developed in India and then imported into the UK.[33] This has significant consequences for the ways in which colonial relations need to be rethought. The British working-classes were often characterised in racial terms borrowed from the contemporary practices of slavery, in the early nineteenth-century, and formal imperialism, in the late nineteenth-century. Again, this suggests that the relations between domestic and overseas versions of culture and authority are so complex as to need further analysis.

It cannot be assumed that the formidable resistances to colonial expansion, for example those of the Zulu against British and South African colonial powers in 1879, and those of the Shona and Ndebele in the 1890s – more successful than is often acknowledged – were quietly processed and anaesthetised by a triumphalist colonial discourse. There is a possibility that this resistance engendered defensiveness and fear within the colonial subject and that – as Rider Haggard's texts suggest – the colonised other came to serve as a template for self-construction, being a model of the martial power to which the colonist aspired.[34] That the colonial subject could be derivative from, as well as dominant over, the colonised, implies a set of dynamics which require further attention.

The conceptualisation of 'race', ethnicity and ethnic identity is a major concern both within and alongside post-colonial theory. For too long, though, ethnicity has been associated exclusively with people of colour, a property inherent in, conferred upon, or claimed by, peoples who have been subjected to colonialism and/or diaspora. This association – operative on popular, political and theoretical levels – has created some analytical anomalies. The power, valorisation and experience of 'whiteness' as a form of contemporary ethnicity needs serious theoretical and critical attention. So too does the experience and concept of 'mixed race', or 'mixed blood'. It is perhaps significant that both whiteness, and 'mixed-race', cast as 'Anglo-Saxonism' and as 'half-caste/hybrid' respectively, were eugenic concepts which held a strong theoretical and cultural currency within dominant Western intellectual production, throughout the nineteenth and early twentieth centuries. Having fallen officially into political and academic disrepute or disregard, these concepts are now due for re-examination.

In many respects, discussion of ethnicity is always also by implication a discussion of gender and sexuality. Women, as the biological 'carriers' of the 'race', occupy a primary and complex role in representations of ethnicity, popular and academic, Black and white, and it is women's exercise of their sexuality which is an often unacknowledged major concern underlying such representations. As Nira Yuval-Davis and Floya Anthias remark, the 'control of women and their sexuality is central to national and ethnic processes'.[35] The dynamics of gender and sexuality are, of course, central issues for both post-colonial and colonial discourse theory. If ethnicity is always-also, in some sense, concerned with gender, gender is always-also in some sense concerned with questions of labour and of the state. Labour, in that the construction of women within patriarchal discourse is inextricable from their construction as maternal, domestic and sexual labourers, whether the labour element be formally acknowledged or no. The state, because as Deniz Kandiyoti and Sara Suleri point out in this collection, the experience of national and post-colonial subjectivity for women is one that cannot be dissociated from the experience of legal and political definitions of subjectivity. Similarly, debates on the gender relations and discourses of colonial India, and particularly the function and practice of *sati*, testify to the importance of developing theoretical analysis of the state as a medium for cultural and political identity.

It is perhaps an unfortunate by-product of Foucauldianism that the precise relations between gender power and other forms of power, within both colonialism and post-coloniality, can be obscured. For some theorists and critics, colonial, imperial and indeed post-colonial or national discourses are largely allegories of gender contests. Similarly mechanistic notions ascribe to white colonial women an automatically oppositional position *vis-à-vis* dominant colonial powers, or, alternatively, an inescapable collusion with those same powers. As a number of the pieces in this collection suggest, these relations – and those of post-colonial women's discourse to post-colonial projects in general – are both more complex and more variable than such mechanistic notions allow.

This general introduction has been jointly written by Laura Chrisman and Patrick Williams. Parts 1, 3 and 5 are introduced and edited by Laura Chrisman; Parts 2, 4 and 6 are introduced and edited by Patrick Williams.

Notes

1. George Lichtheim, *Imperialism*, Penguin: Harmondsworth, 1974, p. 133.
2. Ronald Hyam, *Britain's Imperial Century, 1815–1914: A study of empire and expansion*, Longman: London, 1976.
3. *idem, Empire and Sexuality*, Manchester University Press: Manchester, 1990.
4. E. J. Hobsbawm, *The Age of Imperialism*, Weidenfeld & Nicolson: London, 1987, p. 73.
5. Edward Said, *Orientalism*, Routledge & Kegan Paul: London, 1978.
6. *idem, Culture and Imperialism*. Chatto & Windus: London, 1993.
7. Gayatri Chakravorty Spivak, *The Post-Colonial Critic: Interviews, strategies, dialogues*, ed. Sarah Harasym, Routledge: London, 1990.
8. *idem*, 'Neocolonialism and the secret agent of knowledge', *Oxford Literary Review*, 13, 1–2, 1991, p. 224.
9. Hannah Arendt, *The Origins of Totalitarianism*, Andŕe Deutsch: London, 1986.
10. Michel Foucault, *The Order of Things: An archaeology of the human sciences*, Tavistock: London, 1970.
11. Robert Young, *White Mythologies: Writing history and the West*, Routledge: London, 1990, p. 3.
12. *ibid.*, p. 173.
13. Walter Benjamin, 'Theses on the philosophy of history', in *Illuminations*, ed. and with an introduction by Hannah Arendt, trans. Harry Zohn, Fontana: London, 1973, pp. 262–3.
14. *idem*, 'Theoretics of knowledge; theory of progress', *The Philosophical Forum*, XV, 1–2, Fall–Winter 1983–4, p. 7.

15. Benedict Anderson, *Imagined Communities: Reflections on the origins and spread of nationalism*, Verso: London, 1983.

16. Theodor W. Adorno, 'Progress', *The Philosophical Forum*, XV, 1–2, Fall–Winter 1983–4, p. 63.

17. *ibid.*, p. 61.

18. Spivak, *The Post-Colonial Critic*, p. 12.

19. *ibid.*

20. Ian Adam and Helen Tiffin (eds), *Past the Last Post*, Harvester Wheatsheaf: Hemel Hempstead, 1991.

21. Bill Ashcroft, Gareth Griffiths and Helen Tiffin, *The Empire Writes Back: Theory and practice in post-colonial literatures*, Routledge: London, 1989.

22. Stephen Slemon, 'Modernism's last post', in Adam and Tiffin, *op. cit.*, p. 3.

23. Young, *op. cit.*, p. 19.

24. Adam and Tiffin, *op. cit.*, p. viii.

25. Edward Said, 'Intellectuals in the post-colonial world', *Salmagundi*, 70/71, Spring–Summer 1986.

26. Chinweizu, Jemie, Madubuike, *Toward the Decolonisation of African Literature*, KPI: London, 1985.

27. Anthony Appiah, 'Out of Africa: topologies of nativism, *Yale Journal of Criticism*, 1, 2, 1988, p. 170.

28. Gayatri Chakravorty Spivak, 'The Rani of Sirmur', in Francis Barker, Peter Hulme, Margaret Iversen and Diane Loxley (eds), *Europe and Its Others*, vol. 1, Proceedings of the Essex Sociology of Literature Conference, University of Essex: Colchester, 1984, p. 128.

29. Benita Parry, 'Resistance theory/theorising resistance or two cheers for nativism', in Peter Hulme (ed.), *Post-Colonial Theory and Colonial Discourse*, Manchester University Press: Manchester, 1993.

30. Sol T. Plaatje, *Native Life in South Africa*, Longman: Harlow, 1987, originally published 1916; *Mhudi*, Lovedale Press: Lovedale, 1930; S. M. Molema, *The Bantu Past and Present: An ethnographical and historical study of the native races of South Africa*, W. Green & Son Ltd: Edinburgh, 1920; Pixley Seme, 'The Regeneration of Africa', in Brian Filling and Susan Short (eds.), *The End of a Regime?*, Aberdeen University Press: Aberdeen, 1991, originally published 1906; James Africanus Horton, *West African Countries and Peoples, British and Native; with the Requirements Necessary for Establishing that Self-government recommended by the Committee of the House of Commons, 1865; and a Vindication of the African Race*, W. J. Johnson: London, 1868; Joseph Casely-Hayford, *Gold Coast Native Institutions: With thoughts upon a healthy imperial policy for the Gold Coast and Ashanti*, C. M. Phillips: London, 1903; *Ethiopia Unbound: Studies in race emancipation*, C. M. Phillips: London, 1911.

31. See the following. Steve Biko, *I Write What I Like*, Heinemann: London, 1979; Amilcar Cabral, *Return to the Source: Selected speeches of Amilcar Cabral*, Monthly Review Press: New York, 1973; C. L. R. James, *The C.L.R. James Reader*, ed. Anna Grimshaw, Basil Blackwell: Oxford, 1992; Jomo Kenyatta, *Facing Mount Kenya*, Mercury: London, 1964; George Padmore, *Pan-Africanism or Communism: The coming struggle for Africa*, Dobson: London, 1956; A. Sivanadan, *A Different Hunger: Writings on Black resistance*, Pluto Press: London, 1982.

32. Gayatri Chakravorty Spivak, 'Three Woman's Texts and a Critique of Imperialism', *Critical Inquiry*, 12, 1, 1985, pp. 262–80; Benita Parry, 'Problems in Current Theories of Colonial Discourse', *Oxford Literary Review*, 9, 1–2, pp. 27–58.

33. Gauri Viswanathan, *Masks of Conquest*, Faber: London, 1989.
34. H. Rider Haggard, *Nada the Lily*, Longmans, Green and Co: London, 1892. Also by the same author, *Cetywayo and His White Neighbours*, Trübner and Co: London, 1882.
35. Nira Yuval-Davis and Floya Anthias, (eds), Woman-Nation-State, MacMillan: London, 1989.

PART ONE

Theorising Colonised Cultures and Anti-Colonial Resistance

Introduction

Theorising the nature of colonised subjectivity and of cultural and political resistance raises a number of questions: the place of national and nationalist culture in relation to political liberation; the nature of colonialism's cultural impact on the psyches of the colonised and vice versa; essentialist and anti-essentialist views of cultural identity. These questions themselves generate concerns, such as the class and gender basis of colonial subjectification. For instance, is there 'a' colonised subject, and its binary opposite, 'a' coloniser subject, about whom theories can be produced, without regard for the socio-economic class of either party? For psychoanalytically-inclined theorists such as Homi Bhabha in this part, following the Frantz Fanon of *Black Skin, White Masks*, the answer may appear to be yes. The gendering of anti-colonial resistance and colonial subjectivity remains a crucial, problematic, theoretical and historical issue, as argued by Gayatri Chakravorty Spivak in this part, and Deniz Kandiyoti (see Part Five). Another set of questions concerns the nature of historical analysis of the colonised, the political and epistemological implications of modern intellectuals who have rendered themselves transparent and/or have claimed to be able to represent the subjectivity of the colonised Other. Further questions concern the definition and function of 'the nation', in whose name much of the resistance discussed here is undertaken.

All too often, as Ngũgĩ wa Thiong'o has suggested (see Part Five), theorisations of 'the' colonised subject can turn out to be theorisations of the petty-bourgeois or intellectual classes of the colonised, who take themselves to be identical with coloniality itself. Many of the readings in this part are concerned with an analysis of the cultural identity of the class of the colonised intellectual and nationalist leader, and with theorising his relation to the people he aspires to represent. Several of the contributors – Léopold Sédar Senghor, Frantz Fanon and Amilcar Cabral – are themselves examples of this class, combining political activism and intellectual production. As Gayatri Chakravorty Spivak forcefully argues, an awareness of the relation of the intellectual's inescapable implication in the politics of institutionalised knowledge-production and its corollary, processes of economic production, should inform that intellectual's theoretical project.

The philosophies of negritude, represented in this part by a speech given by Senghor, and subjected to critiques in the readings by Fanon and Cabral, stand as a highly influential example of black essentialist or nativist theory. Theories of black consciousness date from (at the least) the nineteenth-century work of West African-based Edward Wilmot Blyden, but through negritude in the 1940s and 1950s such theories achieved a more international audience and articulation. Though negritude, which spans West Africa to the diasporic Caribbean, is philosophically and historically particular to French colonisation, it has an anglophone counterpart of sorts in the movements of African, Caribbean and African-American pan-Africanism. By the time Senghor gave this speech to the first Festival of African Arts, in Dakar in 1966, he had been president of Senegal for the six years of its independence. Outlining the distinctiveness and value of a racialised black African culture, he pursues in fact a multiple strategy: Africa, he argues, has affinities with many of the philosophical, scientific and modernist aesthetic innovations of modern European discoveries, thereby undermining the opposition; at the same time, the 'essential' values of African culture, such as collectivity, dialogue and humanism, are venerated for their potential to resolve global conflict and introduce an alternative and compassionate world view.

Frantz Fanon, the Martiniquan-born psychiatrist and activist for the Algerian National Liberation Front, composed his influential essay 'On national culture' in 1959. It was originally delivered to an audience of the Second Congress of Black Artists and Writers in Rome. Later included in his 1961 book *The Wretched of the Earth*, the piece differs from the rest of that book in its relative abstraction. Among the reading's most noted features is its attack on negritude as a concept which mirrors the racialisation and continental dynamics of colonialism itself, and constitutes a metaphysical rather than a materialist politics. Fanon's own materialism, however, could be said to abandon him when it comes to the category of 'the nation', which serves as an unproblematic given (its origins in colonialism are not an issue) and as a transcendent value, much as 'Africa' serves Senghor. Fanon's thought pursues a complex and elusive course; at times, for example, 'culture' is definable as a kind of second-order aesthetic and critical commentary on – and morale-booster for – established political and social achievements; at other times, as in the last section of the reading, 'culture' seems to be defined anthropologically; and at others, it signifies the as-yet-unimaginable space of emancipated nationhood.

Fanon distinguishes 'culture' from pre-colonial aesthetic traditions and customs, and to the extent that he implies a certain class of the modern intelligentsia possesses a monopoly on cultural production, he could be said to have taken on board a romantic and francocentric notion of culture; the flipside, perhaps, of his nihilistic and absolutist perception of colonialism as having totally destroyed the possibility of culture itself within the communities it has colonised.

Amilcar Cabral, agronomist and Secretary-General of the African Party for the Independence of Guinea and the Cape Verde Islands (PAIGC), presents an interestingly contrasting theory of culture's role in national liberation movements, reflecting the differences between French and Portuguese forms of colonialism, as well as historical and political differences between the resistance movements of Algeria and Guinea-Bissau. His paper was originally delivered in 1970, as a memorial lecture for Eduardo Mondlane, in Syracuse University, New York. By this time, the national liberation movement in Guinea-Bissau and Cape Verde had been underway for at least seven years and was somewhat closer to success than Fanon's Algeria of his 1959 speech.

Whereas Fanon argues that it is 'the people', Cabral argues that it is 'popular culture' which forms the basis of the anti-colonial political struggle. Also, while for Fanon national culture cannot exist within the history and domination of colonialism, for Cabral the operations of national culture are in a dialectical relationship with history. Culture (this culture would, for Fanon, constitute 'tradition' or 'custom' rather than culture proper) continues throughout the period of domination, reflecting Cabral's view (and experience) of colonialism's power as never being total; colonialism's cultural hegemony, he argues, does not extend to the subaltern classes beyond the metropole. Unlike Fanon, Cabral theorises the relationship of cultural processes to the forces and relations of economic production. In a way, Cabral's greater attention to, and positive evaluation of, the strength and role of popular culture is the corollary of his holistic concern for the structures of the social totality in which culture functions; for Fanon, the sphere of politics alone constitutes that totality. Fanon's position represented here (which is not that of *The Wretched of the Earth* as a whole) leads him to a notion of 'the nation' which excludes consideration of the ways in which, as Cabral argues, the 'multiplicity of social and ethnic groups . . . complicates the effort to determine the role of culture in the liberation movement'. With respect to the coordinates of the national culture, Cabral fluctuates as much as does Fanon: such a culture features as a 'harmony', which preserves the differences of different social groups within it, and yet also as a 'unity'.

Indian-born, United States-based Gayatri Chakravorty Spivak provides an anti-foundationalist critique of the concept of a colonial subaltern subject accessible to and representable by disinterested intellectuals, a concept developed by, among others, the influential South Asian journal *Subaltern Studies*. Spivak's project combines the theoretical and political insights of Marxism, feminism and deconstruction, placing them in a non-dialectical dialogue. Theorising the production of blindspots as inevitable but contestable consequence of knowledge/power, she focuses on the figure of the subaltern South Asian woman, whose contradictory constructions and control by traditional patriarchal authority and by English colonialism, instanced in the history of *sati* (widow-burning), provide an illustration of the aporias of colonial discourse theory, and a challenge to both empiricist and idealist notions of 'the subaltern' subject's historical representability. Spivak's theme and scholarship can be seen to serve a double function; not only do they establish the complexity and material specificity of histories and historiographies of colonialism, but they also can be read allegorically, as a constellation of contemporary dynamics of global capitalism dependent upon the material labour and the discursive silencing of the subaltern woman.

Spivak's feminism produces a deconstruction of the coloniser/colonised polarity, pointing to the neglect of gender found in that conceptualisation. Indian-born, British-based critic Homi Bhabha also deconstructs that polarity, arguing not for the discontinuous social groups and narratives which such a binarism disguises or denies but for the psychoanalytic ambivalence which is constitutive of the identities of the coloniser and colonised subject alike. Taking up Fanon's critique of historicism, and his pursuit, in his 1952 *Black Skin, White Masks*, of a non-historicised approach to colonial subjectivity, Bhabha focuses on the spatialised and image-based dynamics of colonial subjectivity, founded on the politics of *dislocation* for both coloniser and colonised. Discussing the co-existence in Fanon's thought of Marxist/ Hegelian, existentialist/phenomenological and psychoanalytic methodologies, Bhabha argues for the irreducibility of the analysis of colonial subjectivity to any single theoretical paradigm.

1 □ *Negritude: A Humanism of the Twentieth Century*

Léopold Sédar Senghor

During the last thirty or so years that we have been proclaiming negritude, it has become customary, especially among English-speaking critics, to accuse us of *racialism*. This is probably because the word is not of English origin. But, in the language of Shakespeare, is it not in good company with the words humanism and socialism? Mphahleles[1] have been sent abut the world saying: 'Negritude is an inferiority complex'; but the same word cannot mean both 'racialism' and 'inferiority complex' without contradiction. The most recent attack comes from Ghana, where the government has commissioned a poem entitled 'I hate negritude' – as if one could hate oneself, hate one's being, without ceasing to be.

No, negritude is none of these things. It is neither racialism nor self-negation. Yet it is not just affirmation; it is rooting oneself in oneself, and self-confirmation: confirmation of one's *being*. Negritude is nothing more or less than what some English-speaking Africans have called the *African personality*. It is no different from the 'black personality' discovered and proclaimed by the American New Negro movement. As the American Negro poet, Langston Hughes wrote after the first world war: 'We, the creators of the new generation, want to give expression to our *black personality* without shame or fear. ... We know we are handsome. Ugly as well. The drums weep and the drums laugh.' Perhaps our only originality, since it was the West Indian poet Aimé Césaire who coined the word negritude, is to have attempted to define the concept a little more closely; to have developed it as a weapon, as an instrument of liberation and as a contribution to the humanism of the twentieth century.

But, once again, what is negritude? Ethnologists and sociologists today speak of 'different civilizations'. It is obvious that peoples differ in their ideas and their languages, in their philosophies and their religions, in their customs and their institutions, in their literature and their art. Who would deny that Africans, too, have a certain way of conceiving life and of living it? A certain way of speaking,

From Léopold Sédar Senghor, *The Africa Reader: Independent Africa*, Vintage, Random Century: London, 1970, pp. 179–92.

singing and dancing; of painting and sculpturing, and even of laughing and crying? Nobody, probably; for otherwise we would not have been talking about 'Negro art' for the last sixty years and Africa would be the only continent today without its ethnologists and sociologists. What, then, is negritude? It is – as you can guess from what precedes – *the sum of the cultural values of the black world*; that is, a certain active presence in the world, or better, in the universe. It is, as John Reed and Clive Wake call it, a certain 'way of relating oneself to the world and to others'.[2] Yes, it is essentially relations with others, an opening out to the world, contact and participation with others. Because of what it is, negritude is necessary in the world today: it is a humanism of the twentieth century.

'The Revolution of 1889'

But let us go back to 1885 and the morrow of the Berlin Conference. The European nations had just finished, with Africa, their division of the planet. Including the United States of America, they were five or six at the height of their power who dominated the world. Without any complexes, they were proud of their material strength; prouder even of their science, and paradoxically, of their *race*. It is true that at that time this was not a paradox. Gobineau, the nineteenth-century philosopher of racial supremacy, had, by a process of osmosis, even influenced Marx, and Disraeli was the great theoretician of that '*English race*, proud, tenacious, confident in itself, that no climate, no change can undermine'. (The italics are mine.) Leo Frobenius, the German ethnologist, one of the first to apprehend the rich complexity of African culture, writes in *The Destiny of Civilizations*: 'Each of the great nations that considers itself personally responsible for the "destiny of the world" believes it possesses the key to the understanding of the whole and the other nations. It is an attitude raised from the past.'

In fact, this attitude 'raised from the past' had begun to be discredited toward the end of the nineteenth century by books like Bergson's *Time and Free Will*, which was published in 1889. Since the Renaissance, the values of European civilization had rested essentially on discursive reason and facts, on logic and matter. Bergson, with an eminently dialectical subtlety, answered the expectation of a public weary of scientism and naturalism. He showed that facts and matter, which are the objects of discursive reason, were only the outer surface that had to be transcended by *intuition* in order to achieve a *vision in depth of reality*.

But the 'Revolution of 1889' – as we shall call it – did not only affect art and literature, it completely upset the sciences. In 1880, only a year before the invention of the word electron, a distinction was still being drawn between matter and energy. The former was inert and unchangeable, the latter was not. But what characterized both of them was their permanence and their continuity. They were both subject to a strict mechanical determinism. Matter and energy had, so to speak, existed from the beginning of time; they could change their shape, but not their substance. All we lacked in order to know them objectively in space and time were sufficiently accurate instruments of investigation and measurement.

Well, in less than fifty years, all these principles were to be outmoded and even rejected. Thirty years ago already, the new discoveries of science – quanta, relativity, wave mechanics, the uncertainty principle, electron spin – had upset the nineteenth-century notion of determinism, which denied man's free will, along with the concepts of matter and energy. The French physicist, Broglie, revealed to us the duality of matter and energy, or the wave-particle principle that underlies things; the Germany physicist, Heisenberg, showed us that objectivity was an illusion and that we could not observe facts without modifying them; others showed that, on the scale of the infinitely small as on that of the immensely great, particles act on one another. Since then, the physico-chemical laws, like matter itself, could no longer appear unchangeable. Even in the field, and on the scale, where they were valid, they were only rough approximations, no more than probabilities. It was enough to scrape the surface of things and of facts to realize just how much instability there is, defying our measuring instruments, probably because they are only mechanical: *material*.

It was on the basis of these discoveries, through a combination of logical coherence and amazing intuition, of scientific experiment and inner experience, that Pierre Teilhard de Chardin was able to transcend the traditional dichotomies with a new dialectic, to reveal to us the living, throbbing unity of the universe. On the basis, then, of the new scientific discoveries, Teilhard de Chardin transcends the old dualism of the philosophers and the scientists, which Marx and Engels had perpetuated by giving matter precedence over the spirit. He advanced the theory that the stuff of the universe is not composed of two realities, but of a single reality in the shape of two phenomena; that there is not matter and energy, not even matter and spirit, but spirit-matter, just as there is space-time. Matter and spirit become a 'network of relations', as the French philosopher Bachelard called it: energy, defined as a network of forces. In matter-spirit there is, therefore, only one energy, which has two aspects. The first, *tangential energy*, which is external, is material and quantitative. It links together the corpuscles, or particles, that make up matter. The other, *radial energy*, which is internal, is psychic and qualitative. It is centripetal force. It organizes into a complex the center-to-center relations of the internal particles of a corpuscle. Since energy is force, it follows that radial energy is the creative force, the 'primary stuff of things', and tangential energy is only a residual product 'caused by the interreactions of the elementary "centers" of the consciousness, imperceptible where life has not yet occurred, but clearly apprehensible by our experience at a sufficiently advanced stage in the development of matter' (Teilhard de Chardin). It follows that where life has not yet occurred the physico-chemical laws remain valid within the limitations we have defined above, while in the living world, as we rise from plant to animal and from animal to Man, the psyche increases in consciousness until it makes and expresses itself in freedom. 'Makes itself': that is, *realizes* itself, by means of – yet by transcending – material well-being through an increase of spiritual life. 'Realizes itself': by that I mean it

develops in harmonious fashion the two complementary elements of the soul: the
heart and the mind.

The Philosophy of Being

The paradox is only apparent when I say that negritude, by its ontology (that is,
its philosophy of being), its moral law and its aesthetic, is a response to the modern
humanism that European philosophers and scientists have been preparing since the
end of the nineteenth century, and as Teilhard de Chardin and the writers and artists
of the mid-twentieth century present it.

Firstly, African ontology. Far back as one may go into his past, from the northern
Sudanese to the southern Bantu, the African has always and everywhere presented
a concept of the world which is diametrically opposed to the traditional philosophy
of Europe. The latter is essentially *static*, *objective*, *dichotomic*; it is, in fact,
dualistic, in that it makes an absolute distinction between body and soul, matter and
spirit. It is founded on separation and opposition: on analysis and conflict. The
African, on the other hand, conceives the world, beyond the diversity of its forms,
as a fundamentally mobile, yet unique, reality that seeks synthesis. This needs
development.

It is significant that in Wolof, the main language of Senegal, there are at least three
words to translate the word 'spirit': *xel*, *sago*, or *degal*, whereas images have to be
used for the word 'matter': *lef* (thing) or *yaram* (body). The African is, of course,
sensitive to the external world, to the material aspect of beings and things. It is
precisely because he is more so than the white European, because he is sensitive to
the tangible qualities of things – shape, color, smell, weight, etc. – that the African
considers these things merely as signs that have to be interpreted and transcended
in order to reach the reality of human beings. Like others, more than others, he
distinguishes the pebble from the plant, the plant from the animal, the animal from
Man; but, once again, the accidents and appearances that differentiate these
kingdoms only illustrate different aspects of the same reality. This reality is *being*
in the ontological sense of the word, and it is life force. For the African, matter, in
the sense the Europeans understand it is only a system of signs which translates the
single reality of the universe: being, which is spirit, which is life force. Thus, the
whole universe appears as an infinitely small, and at the same time an infinitely
large, network of life forces which emanate from God and end in God, who is the
source of all life forces. It is He who vitalizes and devitalizes all other beings, all the
other life forces.

I have not wandered as far as might be thought from modern ontology. European
ethnologists, Africanists and artists use the same words and the same expressions
to designate the ultimate reality of the universe they are trying to know and to
express: 'spider's web', 'network of forces', 'communicating vessels', 'system of
canals', etc. This is not very different, either, from what the scientists and chemists

say. As far as African ontology is concerned, too, there is no such thing as dead matter: every being, every thing – be it only a grain of sand – radiates a life force, a sort of wave-particle; and sages, priests, kings, doctors and artists all use it to help bring the universe to its fulfilment.

For the African, contrary to popular belief, is not passive in face of the order – or disorder – of the world. His attitude is fundamentally ethical. If the moral law of the African has remained unknown for so long, it is because it derives, naturally, from his conception of the world: from his ontology – so naturally, that both have remained unknown, denied even, by Europeans, because they have not been brought to their attention by being re-examined by each new generation of Africans.

So God tired of all the possibilities that remained confined within Him, unexpressed, dormant, and as if dead. And God opened His mouth, and he spoke at length a word that was harmonious and rhythmical. All these possibilities expressed by the mouth of God *existed* and had the vocation *to live*: to express God in their turn, by establishing the link with God and all the forces deriving from Him.

In order to explain this *morality in action* of negritude, I must go back a little. Each of the identifiable life forces of the universe – from the grain of sand to the ancestor[3] – is, itself and in its turn, a network of life forces – as modern physical chemistry confirms: a network of elements that are contradictory in appearance but really *complementary*. Thus, for the African, Man is composed, of course, of matter and spirit, of body and soul; but at the same time he is also composed of a virile and a feminine element: indeed of several 'souls', Man is therefore a composition of mobile life forces which interlock: a world of solidarities that seek to knit themselves together. Because he exists, he is at once end and beginning: end of the three orders of the mineral, the vegetable and the animal, but beginning of the human order.

Let us ignore for the moment the first three orders and examine the human order. Above Man and based on him lies this fourth world of concentric circles, bigger and bigger, higher and higher, until they reach God along with the whole of the universe. Each circle – family, village, province, nation, humanity – is, in the image of Man and by vocation, a close-knit society.

So, for the African, living according to the moral law means living according to his nature, composed as it is of contradictory elements but complementary life forces. Thus he gives stuff to the stuff of the universe and tightens the threads of the tissue of life. Thus he transcends the contradictions of the elements and works toward making the life forces complementary to one another: in himself first of all, as Man, but also in the whole of human society. It is by bringing the complementary life forces together in this way that Man reinforces them in their movement towards God and, in reinforcing them, he reinforces himself; that is, he passes from *existing* to *being*. He cannot reach the highest form of being, for in fact only God has this quality; and He has it all the more fully as creation, and all that exists, fulfil themselves and express themselves in Him.

Dialogue

Ethnologists have often praised the unity, the balance and the harmony of African civilization, of black society, which was based both on the *community* and on the *person*, and in which, because it was founded on dialogue and reciprocity, the group had priority over the individual without crushing him, but allowing him to blossom as a person. I would like to emphasize at this point how much these characteristics of negritude enable it to find its place in contemporary humanism, thereby permitting black Africa to make its contribution to the 'Civilization of the Universal' which is so necessary in our divided but interdependent world of the second half of the twentieth century. A contribution, first of all, to international cooperation, which must be and which shall be the cornerstone of that civilization. It is through these virtues of negritude that decolonization has been accomplished without too much bloodshed or hatred and that a positive form of cooperation based on 'dialogue and reciprocity' has been established between former colonizers and colonized. It is through these virtues that there has been a new spirit at the United Nations, where the 'no' and the bang of the fist on the table are no longer signs of strength. It is through these virtues that peace through cooperation could extend to South Africa, Rhodesia and the Portuguese colonies, if only the dualistic spirit of the whites would open itself to dialogue.

In fact, the contribution of negritude to the 'Civilization of the Universal' is not of recent origin. In the fields of literature and art, it is contemporary with the 'Revolution of 1889'. The French poet Arthur Rimbaud (1854–1891), had already associated himself with negritude. But in this article I want to concentrate on the 'Negro revolution' – the expression belongs to Emmanuel Berl – which helped to stir European plastic art at the beginning of this century.

Art, like literature, is always the expression of a certain conception of the world and of life; the expression of a certain philosophy and, above all, of a certain ontology. Corresponding to the philosophical and scientific movement of 1889 there was not only a literary evolution – symbolism then surrealism – but another revolution, or rather revolutions, in art, which were called, taking only the plastic arts, nabism, expressionism, fauvism and cubism. A world of life forces that have to be *tamed* is substituted for a closed world of permanent and continuous substances that have to be *reproduced*.

Since the Greek *kouroi* (the term used for the statues of young men in classical Greek sculpture), the art of the European West had always been based on realism; the work of art had always been an imitation of the object: a *physeôs mimêsis*, to use Aristotle's expression: a corrected imitation 'improved', 'idealized' by the requirements of rationality but imitation all the same. The interlude of the Christian Middle Ages is significant insofar as Christianity is itself of Asian origin and strongly influenced by the African, St Augustine. To what will the artist then give expression? No longer to purely objective matter, but to his spiritual self: that is, to his inner self, his spirituality, and beyond himself to the spirituality of his age and of mankind. No longer by means of perspective, relief and chiaroscuro, but, as the

French painter Bazaine writes, 'by the most hidden workings of instinct and the sensibility'. Another French painter, André Masson, makes it more explicit when he writes: 'By a simple interplay of shapes and colors legibly ordered.' This interplay of shapes and colors is that of the life forces and which has been illustrated in particular by a painter like Soulages.

'Interplay of life forces': and so we come back to – negritude. As the French painter Soulages in fact once told me, the African aesthetic is 'that of contemporary art'. I find indirect proof of this in the fact that, while the consecration and spread of the new aesthetic revolution have occurred in France, the majority of its promoters were of Slav and Germanic origin; people who, like the Africans, belong to the mystical civilizations of the senses. Of course, without the discovery of African art, the revolution would still have taken place, but probably without such vigor and assurance and such a deepening of the knowledge of Man. The fact that an art of the subject and of the spirit should have germinated outside Europe, in Africa – to which ethnologists had not yet given its true place in world culture – was proof of the human value of the message of the new European art.

Over and above its aesthetic lesson – to which we shall return later – what Picasso, Braque and the other artists and early explorers of African art were seeking was, in the first place, just this: its human value. For in black Africa art is not a separate activity, in itself or for itself: it is a social activity, a technique of living, a handicraft in fact. But it is a major activity that brings all other activities to their fulfilment, like prayer in the Christian Middle Ages: birth and education, marriage and death, sport, even war. All human activities down to the least daily act must be integrated into the subtle interplay of life forces – family, tribal, national, world and universal forces. This harmonious interplay of life forces must be helped by *subordinating* the lower forces – mineral, vegetable and animal – to their relations with Man, and the forces of human society to its relations with the Divine Being through the intermediary of the Ancestral Beings.

A year or two ago I attended, on the cliffs of Bandiagara in the Mali Republic, an entertainment which was a microcosm of Dogon art.[4] Even though it was but a pale reflection of the splendors of the past, this 'play-concert' was an extremely significant expression of the Dogon vision of the universe. It was declaimed, sung and danced; sculptured and presented in costume. The whole of the Dogon universe was portrayed in this symbiosis of the arts, as is the custom in black Africa. The universe – heaven and earth – was therefore *represented* through the intermediary of Man, whose ideogram is the same as that of the universe. Then the world was *re-presented* by means of masks, each of which portrayed, at one and the same time, a totemic animal, an ancestor and a spirit. Others portrayed the foreign peoples: nomadic Fulani[5] and white Europeans. The aim of the entertainment was, by means of the symbiosis of the arts – poetry, song, dances, sculpture and painting, used as techniques of integration – to *re-create* the universe and the contemporary world, but in a more harmonious way by making use of African humor, which corrects distortions at the expense of the foreign Fulani and the white conquerors.

But this ontological vision was an entertainment – that is, an artistic demonstration – as well: a joy for the soul because a joy for the eyes and ears.

It was perhaps – indeed, it was certainly – this last aspect of the African aesthetic lesson that first attracted Picasso and Braque when, toward 1906, they discovered African art and were inspired by it. For my part, what struck me from the start of the Dogon 'play-concert', even before I tried to understand its meaning, was the harmony of form and movement, of color and rhythm, that characterized it. It is this harmony by which, as a spectator, I was moved; which, in the re-creation of reality, acts on the invisible forces whose appearances are only signs, subordinates them in a complementary fashion to one another and establishes the link between them and God through the intermediary of Man. By appearances I mean the attributes of matter that strike our senses: shape and color, timbre and tone, movement and rhythm.

I have said that these appearances are signs. They are more than that: they are meaningful signs, the 'lines of force' of the life forces, insofar as they are used in their pure state, with only their characteristics of shape, color, sound, movement and rhythm. Recently M. Lods, who teaches at the National School of Art of Senegal, was showing me the pictures his students intend exhibiting at the projected Festival of African Arts. I was immediately struck by the noble and elegant interplay of shape and color. When I discovered that the pictures were not completely abstract, that they portrayed ladies, princes and noble animals, I was almost disappointed. There was no need for me to be: the very interplay of colored shapes perfectly expressed that elegant nobility that characterizes the art of the northern Sudan.

This, then, is Africa's lesson in aesthetics: art does not consist in photographing nature but in taming it, like the hunter when he reproduces the call of the hunted animal, like a separated couple, or two lovers, calling to each other in their desire to be reunited. The call is not the simple reproduction of the cry of the Other; it is a complementarity, a *song*: a call of harmony to the harmony of union that enriches by increasing *Being*. We call it pure harmony. Once more, Africa teaches that art is not photography; if there are images they are rhythmical. I can suggest or create anything – a man, a moon, a fruit, a smile, a tear – simply by assembling shapes and colors (painting/sculpture), shapes and movement (dance), timbre and tones (music), provided that this assembling is not an aggregation, but that it is ordered and, in short, rhythmical. For it is rhythm – the main virtue, in fact, of negritude – that gives the work of art its beauty. Rhythm is simply the movement of attraction or repulsion that expresses the life of the cosmic forces; symmetry and asymmetry, repetition or opposition: in short, the lines of force that link the meaningful signs that shapes and colors, timbre and tones, are.

Before concluding, I should like to pause for a moment on the apparent contradiction that must have been noticed between contemporary European art (which places the emphasis on the subject) and African art (which places it on the object). This is because the 'Revolution of 1889' began by reacting, of necessity, against the superstition of the *object*; and the existentialist ontology of the African, while it it is based on the being-subject, has God as its pole-object; God who is the fullness of Being. What was noticed, then, was simply a nuance. For the contemporary European, and the African, the work of art, like the act of knowing, expresses the confrontation, the embrace, of subject and object: 'That penetration', wrote Bazaine, 'that great common structure, that deep resemblance between Man and the world, without which there is no living form'.

We have seen what constitutes for the African the 'deep resemblance between Man and the world'. For him, then, the act of restoring the order of the world by re-creating it through art is the reinforcement of the life forces in the universe and, consequently, of God, the source of all life forces – or, in other words, the Being of the universe. In this way, we reinforce ourselves at the same time, both as interdependent forces and as beings whose being consists in revitalizing ourselves in the re-creation of art.

Notes

1. The South African writer, Ezekiel Mphahlele, author, among other books, of *The African Image*, strongly disagrees with the concept of negritude.
2. *Léopold Sédar Senghor: Selected poems*, introduced and translated by John Reed and Clive Wake. See also *Léopold Sédar Senghor: Prose and poetry*, by the same authors.
3. In African religion, the ancestors are the essential link between the living and God. This is why they are surrounded by a complex ritual so as to ensure the maintenance of this link.
4. The Dogon are a West African tribe among whom wood sculpture has achieved a very remarkable degree of excellence.
5. The Fulani are a nomadic pastoral people found throughout West Africa.

2 □ *On National Culture*

Frantz Fanon

[. . .] In this chapter we shall analyse the problem, which is felt to be fundamental, of the legitimacy of the claims of a nation. It must be recognized that the political party which mobilizes the people hardly touches on this problem of legitimacy. The political parties start from living reality and it is in the name of this reality, in the name of the stark facts which weigh down the present and the future of men and women, that they fix their line of action. The political party may well speak in moving terms of the nation, but what it is concerned with is that the people who are listening understand the need to take part in the fight if, quite simply, they wish to continue to exist. [. . .]

Inside the political parties, and most often in offshoots from these parties, cultured individuals of the colonized race make their appearance. For these individuals, the demand for a national culture and the affirmation of the existence of such a culture represent a special battle-field. While the politicians situate their action in actual present-day events, men of culture take their stand in the field of history. Confronted with the native intellectual who decides to make an aggressive response to the colonialist theory of pre-colonial barbarism, colonialism will react only slightly, and still less because the ideas developed by the young colonized intelligentsia are widely professed by specialists in the mother country. It is in fact a commonplace to state that for several decades large numbers of research workers have, in the main, rehabilitated the African, Mexican and Peruvian civilizations. The passion with which native intellectuals defend the existence of their national culture may be a source of amazement; but those who condemn this exaggerated passion are strangely apt to forget that their own psyche and their own selves are conveniently sheltered behind a French or German culture which has given full proof of its existence and which is uncontested.

I am ready to concede that on the plane of factual being the past existence of an Aztec civilization does not change anything very much in the diet of the Mexican

From Frantz Fanon, *The Wretched of the Earth*, trans. Constance Farrington, Penguin: Harmondsworth, 1967, pp. 166–7, 168–71, 172–5, 178–83, 187–99.

peasant of today. I admit that all the proofs of a wonderful Songhai civilization will not change the fact that today the Songhais are under-fed and illiterate, thrown between sky and water with empty heads and empty eyes. But it has been remarked several times that this passionate search for a national culture which existed before the colonial era finds its legitimate reason in the anxiety shared by native intellectuals to shrink away from that Western culture in which they all risk being swamped. Because they realize they are in danger of losing their lives and thus becoming lost to their people, these men, hot-headed and with anger in their hearts, relentlessly determine to renew contact once more with the oldest and most pre-colonial springs of life of their people.

Let us go farther. Perhaps this passionate research and this anger are kept up or at least directed by the secret hope of discovering beyond the misery of today, beyond self-contempt, resignation and abjuration, some very beautiful and splendid era whose existence rehabilitates us both in regard to ourselves and in regard to others. I have said that I have decided to go farther. Perhaps unconsciously, the native intellectuals, since they could not stand wonder-struck before the history of today's barbarity, decided to go back farther and to delve deeper down; and, let us make no mistake, it was with the greatest delight that they discovered that there was nothing to be ashamed of in the past, but rather dignity, glory and solemnity. The claim to a national culture in the past does not only rehabilitate that nation and serve as a justification for the hope of a future national culture. In the sphere of psycho-affective equilibrium it is responsible for an important change in the native. Perhaps we have not sufficiently demonstrated that colonialism is not simply content to impose its rule upon the present and the future of a dominated country. Colonialism is not satisfied merely with hiding a people in its grip and emptying the native's brain of all form and content. By a kind of perverted logic, it turns to the past of the oppressed people, and distorts, disfigures and destroys it. This work of devaluing pre-colonial history takes on a dialectical significance today.

When we consider the efforts made to carry out the cultural estrangement so characteristic of the colonial epoch, we realize that nothing has been left to chance and that the total result looked for by colonial domination was indeed to convince the natives that colonialism came to lighten their darkness. The effect consciously sought by colonialism was to drive into the natives' heads the idea that if the settlers were to leave, they would at once fall back into barbarism, degradation and bestiality.

On the unconscious plane, colonialism therefore did not seek to be considered by the native as a gentle, loving mother who protects her child from a hostile environment, but rather as a mother who unceasingly restrains her fundamentally perverse offspring from managing to commit suicide and from giving free rein to its evil instincts. The colonial mother protects her child from itself, from its ego, and from its physiology, its biology and its own unhappiness which is its very essence.

In such a situation the claims of the native intellectual are no luxury but a necessity in any coherent programme. The native intellectual who takes up arms to defend his nation's legitimacy and who wants to bring proofs to bear out that legitimacy, who is willing to strip himself naked to study the history of his body, is obliged to dissect the heart of his people.

Such an examination is not specifically national. The native intellectual who decides to give battle to colonial lies fights on the field of the whole continent. The past is given back its value. Culture, extracted from the past to be displayed in all its splendour, is not necessarily that of his own country. Colonialism, which has not bothered to put too fine a point on its efforts, has never ceased to maintain that the Negro is a savage; and for the colonist, the Negro was neither an Angolan nor a Nigerian, for he simply spoke of 'the Negro'. For colonialism, this vast continent was the haunt of savages, a country riddled with superstitions and fanaticism, destined for contempt, weighed down by the curse of God, a country of cannibals – in short, the Negro's country. Colonialism's condemnation is continental in its scope. The contention by colonialism that the darkest night of humanity lay over pre-colonial history concerns the whole of the African continent. The efforts of the native to rehabilitate himself and to escape from the claws of colonialism are logically inscribed from the same point of view as that of colonialism. The native intellectual who has gone far beyond the domains of Western culture and who has got it into his head to proclaim the existence of another culture never does so in the name of Angola or of Dahomey. The culture which is affirmed is African culture. The Negro, never so much a Negro as since he has been dominated by the whites, when he decides to prove that he has a culture and to behave like a cultured person, comes to realize that history points out a well-defined path to him: he must demonstrate that a Negro culture exists.

And it is only too true that those who are most responsible for this racialization of thought, or at least for the first movement towards that thought, are and remain those Europeans who have never ceased to set up white culture to fill the gap left by the absence of other cultures. Colonialism did not dream of wasting its time in denying the existence of one national culture after another. Therefore the reply of the colonized peoples will be straight away continental in its breadth. In Africa, the native literature of the last twenty years is not a national literature but a Negro literature. The concept of Negro-ism, for example, was the emotional if not the logical antithesis of that insult which the white man flung at humanity. This rush of Negro-ism against the white man's contempt showed itself in certain spheres to be the one idea capable of lifting interdictions and anathemas. Because the New Guinean or Kenyan intellectuals found themselves above all up against a general ostracism and delivered to the combined contempt of their overlords, their reaction was to sing praises in admiration of each other. The unconditional affirmation of African culture has succeeded the unconditional affirmation of European culture. On the whole, the poets of Negro-ism oppose the idea of an old Europe to a young Africa, tiresome reasoning to lyricism, oppressive logic to high-stepping nature, and on one side stiffness, ceremony, etiquette and scepticism, while on the other frankness, liveliness, liberty and – why not? – luxuriance: but also irresponsibility.

The poets of Negro-ism will not stop at the limits of the continent. From America, black voices will take up the hymn with fuller unison. The 'black world' will see the light and Busia from Ghana, Birago Diop from Senegal, Hampaté Ba from the Sudan and Saint-Clair Drake from Chicago will not hesitate to assert the existence of common ties and a motive power that is identical. [...]

This historical necessity in which the men of African culture find themselves to racialize their claims and to speak more of African culture than of national culture will tend to lead them up a blind alley. Let us take for example the case of the African Cultural Society. This society had been created by African intellectuals who wished to get to know each other and to compare their experiences and the results of their respective research work. The aim of this society was therefore to affirm the existence of an African culture, to evaluate this culture on the plane of distinct nations and to reveal the internal motive forces of each of their national cultures. But at the same time this society fulfilled another need: the need to exist side by side with the European Cultural Society, which threatened to transform itself into a Universal Cultural Society. There was therefore at the bottom of this decision the anxiety to be present at the universal trysting place fully armed, with a culture springing from the very heart of the African continent. Now, this Society will very quickly show its inability to shoulder these different tasks, and will limit itself to exhibitionist demonstrations, while the habitual behaviour of the members of this Society will be confined to showing Europeans that such a thing as African culture exists, and opposing their ideas to those of ostentatious and narcissistic Europeans. We have shown that such an attitude is normal and draws its legitimacy from the lies propagated by men of Western culture. But the degradation of the aims of this Society will become more marked with the elaboration of the concept of Negro-ism. The African Society will become the cultural society of the black world and will come to include the Negro dispersion, that is to say the tens of thousands of black people spread over the American continents.

The Negroes who live in the United States and in Central or Latin America in fact experience the need to attach themselves to a cultural matrix. Their problem is not fundamentally different from that of the Africans. The whites of America did not mete out to them any different treatment from that of the whites that ruled over the Africans. We have seen that the whites were used to putting all Negroes in the same bag. During the first congress of the African Cultural Society which was held in Paris in 1956, the American Negroes of their own accord considered their problems from the same standpoint as those of their African brothers. Cultured Africans, speaking of African civilizations, decreed that there should be a reasonable status within the state for those who had formerly been slaves. But little by little the American Negroes realized that the essential problems confronting them were not the same as those that confronted the African Negroes. The Negroes of Chicago only resemble the Nigerians or the Tanganyikans in so far as they were all defined in relation to the whites. But once the first comparisons had been made and subjective feelings were assuaged, the American Negroes realized that the objective problems were fundamentally heterogeneous. The test cases of civil liberty whereby both whites and blacks in America try to drive back racial discrimination have very little in common in their principles and objectives with the heroic fight of the Angolan people against the detestable Portuguese colonialism. Thus, during the second congress of the African Cultural Society the American Negroes decided to create an American society for people of black cultures.

Negro-ism therefore finds its first limitation in the phenomena which take account of the formation of the historical character of men. Negro and African-Negro culture broke up into different entities because the men who wished to incarnate these cultures realized that every culture is first and foremost national, and that the problems which kept Richard Wright or Langston Hughes on the alert were fundamentally different from those which might confront Léopold Senghor or Jomo Kenyatta. In the same way certain Arab states, though they had chanted the marvellous hymn of Arab renaissance, had nevertheless to realize that their geographical position and the economic ties of their region were stronger even than the past that they wished to revive. Thus we find today the Arab states organically linked once more with societies which are Mediterranean in their culture. The fact is that these states are submitted to modern pressure and to new channels of trade while the network of trade relations which was dominant during the great period of Arab history has disappeared. But above all there is the fact that the political regimes of certain Arab states are so different, and so far away from each other in their conceptions, that even a cultural meeting between these states is meaningless.

Thus we see that the cultural problem as it sometimes exists in colonized countries runs the risk of giving rise to serious ambiguities. The lack of culture of the Negroes, as proclaimed by colonialism, and the inherent barbarity of the Arabs ought logically to lead to the exaltation of cultural manifestations which are not simply national but continental, and extremely racial. In Africa, the movement of men of culture is a movement towards the Negro-African culture or the Arab-Moslem culture. It is not specifically towards a national culture. Culture is becoming more and more cut off from the events of today. It finds its refuge beside a hearth that glows with passionate emotion, and from there makes its way by realistic paths which are the only means by which it may be made fruitful, homogeneous and consistent. [...]

If we wanted to trace in the works of native writers the different phases which characterize this evolution we would find spread out before us a panorama on three levels. In the first phase, the native intellectual gives proof that he has assimilated the culture of the occupying power. His writings correspond point by point with those of his opposite numbers in the mother country. His inspiration is European and we can easily link up these works with definite trends in the literature of the mother country. This is the period of unqualified assimilation. We find in this literature coming from the colonies the Parnassians, the Symbolists and the Surrealists.

In the second phase we find the native is disturbed; he decides to remember what he is. This period of creative work approximately corresponds to that immersion which we have just described. But since the native is not a part of his people, since he only has exterior relations with his people, he is content to recall their life only. Past happenings of the bygone days of his childhood will be brought up out of the depths of his memory; old legends will be reinterpreted in the light of a borrowed aestheticism and of a conception of the world which was discovered under other skies.

Sometimes this literature of just-before-the-battle is dominated by humour and by allegory; but often too it is symptomatic of a period of distress and difficulty, where death is experienced, and disgust too. We spew ourselves up; but already underneath laughter can be heard.

Finally, in the third phase, which is called the fighting phase, the native, after having tried to lose himself in the people and with the people, will on the contrary shake the people. Instead of according the people's lethargy an honoured place in his esteem, he turns himself into an awakener of the people; hence comes a fighting literature, a revolutionary literature, and a national literature. During this phase a great many men and women who up till then would never have thought of producing a literary work, now that they find themselves in exceptional circumstances – in prison, with the Maquis or on the eve of their execution – feel the need to speak to their nation, to compose the sentence which expresses the heart of the people and to become the mouthpiece of a new reality in action.

The native intellectual nevertheless sooner or later will realize that you do not show proof of your nation from its culture but that you substantiate its existence in the fight which the people wage against the forces of occupation. No colonial system draws its justification from the fact that the territories it dominates are culturally non-existent. You will never make colonialism blush for shame by spreading out little-known cultural treasures under its eyes. At the very moment when the native intellectual is anxiously trying to create a cultural work he fails to realize that he is utilizing techniques and language which are borrowed from the stranger in his country. He contents himself with stamping these instruments with a hall-mark which he wishes to be national, but which is strangely reminiscent of exoticism. The native intellectual who comes back to his people by way of cultural achievements behaves in fact like a foreigner. Sometimes he has no hesitation in using a dialect in order to show his will to be as near as possible to the people; but the ideas that he expresses and the preoccupations he is taken up with have no common yardstick to measure the real situation which the men and the women of his country know. The culture that the intellectual leans towards is often no more than a stock of particularisms. He wishes to attach himself to the people; but instead he only catches hold of their outer garments. And these outer garments are merely the reflection of a hidden life, teeming and perpetually in motion. That extremely obvious objectivity which seems to characterize a people is in fact only the inert, already forsaken result of frequent, and not always very coherent, adaptations of a much more fundamental substance which itself is continually being renewed. The man of culture, instead of setting out to find this substance, will let himself be hypnotized by these mummified fragments which because they are static are in fact symbols of negation and outworn contrivances. Culture has never the translucidity of custom; it abhors all simplification. In its essence it is opposed to custom, for custom is always the deterioration of culture. The desire to attach oneself to tradition or bring abandoned traditions to life again does not only mean going against the current of history but also opposing one's own people. When a people undertakes an armed struggle or even a political struggle against a relentless colonialism, the significance of tradition changes. All that has made up the technique of passive resistance in the past may, during this phase, be radically condemned. In an under-developed country during the period of struggle traditions are fundamentally unstable and are shot through by centrifugal tendencies. This is why the intellectual often runs the risk of being out of date. The peoples who have carried on the struggle are more impervious to demagogy; and those who wish to follow them reveal themselves as nothing more than common opportunists, in other words late-comers.

In the sphere of plastic arts, for example, the native artist who wishes at whatever cost to create a national work of art shuts himself up in a stereotyped reproduction of details. These artists, who have nevertheless thoroughly studied modern techniques and who have taken part in the main trends of contemporary painting and architecture, turn their back on foreign culture, deny it and set out to look for a true national culture, setting great store on what they consider to be the constant principles of national art. But these people forget that the forms of thought and what it feeds on, together with modern techniques of information, language and dress, have dialectically reorganized the people's intelligences and that the constant principles which acted as safeguards during the colonial period are now undergoing extremely radical changes.

The artist who has decided to illustrate the truths of the nation turns paradoxically towards the past and away from actual events. What he ultimately intends to embrace are in fact the cast-offs of thought, its shells and corpses, a knowledge which has been stabilized once and for all. But the native intellectual who wishes to create an authentic work of art must realize that the truths of a nation are in the first place its realities. He must go on until he has found the seething pot out of which the learning of the future will emerge.

Before independence, the native painter was insensible to the national scene. He set a high value on non-figurative art, or more often was specialized in still-lifes. After independence his anxiety to rejoin his people will confine him to the most detailed representation of reality. This is representative art which has no internal rhythms, an art which is serene and immobile, evocative not of life but of death. Enlightened circles are in ecstasies when confronted with this 'inner truth' which is so well expressed; but we have the right to ask if this truth is in fact a reality, and if it is not already outworn and denied, called in question by the epoch through which the people are treading out their path towards history.

In the realm of poetry we may establish the same facts. After the period of assimilation characterized by rhyming poetry, the poetic tom-tom's rhythms break through. This it a poetry of revolt; but it is also descriptive and analytical poetry. The poet ought, however, to understand that nothing can replace the reasoned, irrevocable taking up of arms on the people's side. Let us quote Depestre one more:

> The lady was not alone;
> She had a husband,
> A husband who knew everything,
> But to tell the truth knew nothing,
> For you can't have culture without making concessions.
> You concede your flesh and blood to it,
> You concede your own self to others;
> By conceding you gain
> Classicism and Romanticism,
> And all that our souls are steeped in.[1]

The native poet who is preoccupied with creating a national work of art and who is determined to describe his people fails in his aim, for he is not yet ready to make that fundamental concession that Depestre speaks of. The French poet René Char shows his understanding of the difficulty when he reminds us that 'the poem emerges out of a subjective imposition and an objective choice. A poem is the assembling and moving together of determining original values, in contemporary relation with someone that these circumstances bring to the front.'[2]

Yes, the first duty of the native poet is to see clearly the people he has chosen as the subject of his work of art. He cannot go forward resolutely unless he first realizes the extent of his estrangement from them. We have taken everything from the other side; and the other side gives us nothing unless by a thousand detours we swing finally round in their direction, unless by ten thousand wiles and a hundred thousand tricks they manage to draw us towards them, to seduce us and to imprison us. Taking means in nearly every case being taken: thus it is not enough to try to free oneself by repeating proclamations and denials. It is not enough to try to get back to the people in that past out of which they have already emerged; rather we must join them in that fluctuating movement which they are just giving a shape to, and which, as soon as it has started, will be the signal for everything to be called in question. Let there be no mistake about it; it is to this zone of occult instability where the people dwell that we must come; and it is there that our souls are crystallized and that our perceptions and our lives are transfused with light. [. . .]

The responsibility of the native man of culture is not a responsibility *vis-à-vis* his national culture, but a global responsibility with regard to the totality of the nation, whose culture merely, after all, represents one aspect of that nation. The cultured native should not concern himself with choosing the level on which he wishes to fight or the sector where he decides to give battle for his nation. To fight for national culture means in the first place to fight for the liberation of the nation, that material keystone which makes the building of a culture possible. There is no other fight for culture which can develop apart from the popular struggle. To take an example, all those men and women who are fighting with their bare hands against French colonialism in Algeria are not by any means strangers to the national culture of Algeria. The national Algerian culture is taking on form and content as the battles are being fought out, in prisons, under the guillotine and in every French outpost which is captured or destroyed.

We must not therefore be content with delving into the past of a people in order to find coherent elements which will counteract colonialism's attempts to falsify and harm. We must work and fight with the same rhythm as the people to construct the future and to prepare the ground where vigorous shoots are already springing up. A national culture is not a folklore, nor an abstract populism that believes it can discover the people's true nature. It is not made up of the inert dregs of gratuitous actions, that is to say actions which are less and less attached to the ever-present reality of the people. A national culture is the whole body of efforts made by a people in the sphere of thought to describe, justify and praise the action through which that people has created itself and keeps itself in existence. A national culture in under-developed countries should therefore take its place at the very heart of the struggle for freedom which these countries are carrying on. Men of African cultures who are still fighting in the name of African-Negro culture and who have called many congresses in the name of the unity of that culture should today realize that all their efforts amount to is to make comparisons between coins and sarcophagi.

There is no common destiny to be shared between the national cultures of Senegal and Guinea; but there *is* a common destiny between the Senegalese and Guinean nations which are both dominated by the same French colonialism. If it is wished that the national culture of Senegal should come to resemble the national culture of Guinea, it is not enough for the rulers of the two peoples to decide to consider their problems – whether the problem of liberation is concerned, or the trade-union questions, or economic difficulties – from similar view-points. And even here there does not seem to be complete identity, for the rhythm of the people and that of their rulers are not the same. There can be no two cultures which are completely identical. To believe that it is possible to create a black culture is to forget that niggers are disappearing, just as those people who brought them into being are seeing the break-up of their economic and cultural supremacy.[3] There will never be such a thing as black culture because there is not a single politician who feels he has a vocation to bring black republics into being. The problem is to get to know the place that these men mean to give their people, the kind of social relations that they decide to set up and the conception that they have of the future of humanity. It is this that counts; everything else is mystification, signifying nothing.

In 1959 the cultured Africans who met at Rome never stopped talking about unity. But one of the people who was loudest in the praise of this cultural unity, Jacques Rabemananjara, is today a minister in the Madagascan government, and as such has decided, with his government, to oppose the Algerian people in the General Assembly of the United Nations. Rabemananjara, if he had been true to himself, ought to have resigned from the government and denounced those men who claim to incarnate the will of the Madagascan people. The ninety thousand dead of

Madagascar have not given Rabemananjara authority to oppose the aspirations of the Algerian people in the General Assembly of the United Nations.

It is around the people's struggles that African-Negro culture takes on substance, and not around songs, poems or folklore. Senghor, who is also a member of the Society of African Culture and who has worked with us on the question of African culture, is not afraid for his part either to give the order to his delegation to support French proposals on Algeria. Adherence to African-Negro culture and to the cultural unity of Africa is arrived at in the first place by upholding unconditionally the people's struggle for freedom. No one can truly wish for the spread of African culture if he does not give practical support to the creation of the conditions necessary to the existence of that culture; in other words, to the liberation of the whole continent.

I say again that no speech-making and no proclamation concerning culture will turn us from our fundamental tasks: the liberation of the national territory; a continual struggle against colonialism in its new forms; and an obstinate refusal to enter the charmed circle of mutual admiration at the summit.

Reciprocal Bases of National Culture and the Fight for Freedom

Colonial domination, because it is total and tends to over-simplify, very soon manages to disrupt in spectacular fashion the cultural life of a conquered people. This cultural obliteration is made possible by the negation of national reality, by new legal relations introduced by the occupying power, by the banishment of the natives and their customs to outlying districts by colonial society, by expropriation, and by the systematic enslaving of men and women.

Three years ago at our first congress I showed that, in the colonial situation, dynamism is replaced fairly quickly by a substantification of the attitudes of the colonizing power. The area of culture is then marked off by fences and signposts. These are in fact so many defence mechanisms of the most elementary type, comparable for more than one good reason to the simple instinct for preservation. The interest of this period for us is that the oppressor does not manage to convince himself of the objective non-existence of the oppressed nation and its culture. Every effort is made to bring the colonized person to admit the inferiority of his culture which has been transformed into instinctive patterns of behaviour, to recognize the unreality of his 'nation', and, in the last extreme, the confused and imperfect character of his own biological structure.

Vis-à-vis this state of affairs, the native's reactions are not unanimous. While the mass of the people maintain intact traditions which are completely different from those of the colonial situation, and the artisan style solidifies into a formalism which is more and more stereotyped, the intellectual throws himself in frenzied fashion into the frantic acquisition of the culture of the occupying power and takes every opportunity of unfavourably criticizing his own national culture, or else takes refuge in setting out and substantiating the claims of that culture in a way that is passionate but rapidly becomes unproductive.

The common nature of these two reactions lies in the fact that they both lead to impossible contradictions. Whether a turncoat or a substantialist the native is ineffectual precisely because the analysis of the colonial situation is not carried out on strict lines. The colonial situation calls a halt to national culture in almost every field. Within the framework of colonial domination there is not and there will never be such phenomena as new cultural departures or changes in the national culture. Here and there valiant attempts are sometimes made to reanimate the cultural dynamic and to give fresh impulses to its themes, its forms and its tonalities. The immediate, palpable and obvious interest of such leaps ahead is nil. But if we follow up the consequences to the very end we see that preparations are being thus made to brush the cobwebs off national consciousness, to question oppression and to open up the struggle for freedom.

A national culture under colonial domination is a contested culture whose destruction is sought in systematic fashion. It very quickly becomes a culture condemned to secrecy. This idea of a clandestine culture is immediately seen in the reactions of the occupying power which interprets attachment to traditions as faithfulness to the spirit of the nation and as a refusal to submit. This persistence in following forms of cultures which are already condemned to extinction is already a demonstration of nationality; but it is a demonstration which is a throw-back to the laws of inertia. There is no taking of the offensive and no redefining of relationships. There is simply a concentration on a hard core of culture which is becoming more and more shrivelled up, inert and empty.

By the time a century or two of exploitation has passed there comes about a veritable emaciation of the stock of national culture. It becomes a set of automatic habits, some traditions of dress and a few broken-down institutions. Little movement can be discerned in such remnants of culture; there is no real creativity and no overflowing life. The poverty of the people, national oppression and the inhibition of culture are one and the same thing. After a century of colonial domination we find a culture which is rigid in the extreme, or rather what we find are the dregs of culture, its mineral strata. The withering away of the reality of the nation and the death-pangs of the national culture are linked to each other in mutual dependence. This is why it is of capital importance to follow the evolution of these relations during the struggle for national freedom. The negation of the native's culture, the contempt for any manifestation of culture whether active or emotional and the placing outside the pale of all specialized branches of organization contribute to breed aggressive patterns of conduct in the native. But these patterns of conduct are of the reflexive type; they are poorly differentiated, anarchic and ineffective. Colonial exploitation, poverty and endemic famine drive the native more and more to open, organized revolt. The necessity for an open and decisive breach is formed progressively and imperceptibly, and comes to be felt by the great majority of the people. Those tensions which hitherto were non-existent come into being. International events, the collapse of whole sections of colonial empires and the contradictions inherent in the colonial system strengthen and uphold the native's combativity while promoting and giving support to national consciousness.

These new-found tensions which are present at all stages in the real nature of colonialism have their repercussions on the cultural plane. In literature, for example, there is relative over-production. From being a reply on a minor scale to the dominating power, the literature produced by natives becomes differentiated and makes itself into a will to particularism. The intelligentsia, which during the period of repression was essentially a consuming public, now themselves become producers. This literature at first chooses to confine itself to the tragic and poetic style; but later on novels, short stories and essays are attempted. It is as if a kind of internal organization or law of expression existed which wills that poetic expression become less frequent in proportion as the objectives and the methods of the struggle for liberation become more precise. Themes are completely altered; in fact, we find less and less of bitter, hopeless recrimination and less also of that violent, resounding, florid writing which on the whole serves to reassure the occupying power. The colonialists have in former times encouraged these modes of expression and made their existence possible. Stinging denunciations, the exposing of distressing conditions and passions which find their outlet in expression are in fact assimilated by the occupying power in a cathartic process. To aid such processes is in a certain sense to avoid their dramatization and to clear the atmosphere.

But such a situation can only be transitory. In fact, the progress of national consciousness among the people modifies and gives precision to the literary utterances of the native intellectual. The continued cohesion of the people constitutes for the intellectual an invitation to go farther than his cry of protest. The lament first makes the indictment; then it makes an appeal. In the period that follows, the words of command are heard. The crystallization of the national consciousness will both disrupt literary styles and themes, and also create a completely new public. While at the beginning the native intellectual used to produce his work to be read exclusively by the oppressor, whether with the intention of charming him or of denouncing him through ethnical or subjectivist means, now the native writer progressively takes on the habit of addressing his own people.

It is only from that moment that we can speak of a national literature. Here there is, at the level of literary creation, the taking up and clarification of themes which are typically nationalist. This may be properly called a literature of combat, in the sense that it calls on the whole people to fight for their existence as a nation. It is a literature of combat, because it moulds the national consciousness, giving it form and contours and flinging open before it new and boundless horizons; it is a literature of combat because it assumes responsibility, and because it is the will to liberty expressed in terms of time and space.

On another level, the oral tradition – stories, epics and songs of the people, which formerly were filed away as set pieces – is now beginning to change. The storytellers who used to relate inert episodes now bring them alive and introduce into them modifications which are increasingly fundamental. There is a tendency to bring conflicts up to date and to modernize the kinds of struggle which the stories evoke, together with the names of heroes and the types of weapons. The method of allusion is more and more widely used. The formula 'This all happened long ago' is substituted by that of 'What we are going to speak of happened somewhere else, but it might well have happened here today, and it might happen tomorrow'. The example of Algeria is significant in this context. From 1952–3 on, the storytellers, who were before that time stereotyped and tedious to listen to, completely overturned their traditional methods of storytelling and the contents of their tales. Their public, which was formerly scattered, became compact. The epic, with its typified categories, reappeared; it became an authentic form of entertainment which took on once more a cultural value. Colonialism made no mistake when from 1955 on it proceeded to arrest these storytellers systematically.

The contact of the people with the new movement gives rise to a new rhythm of life and to forgotten muscular tensions, and develops the imagination. Every time the storyteller relates a fresh episode to his public, he presides over a real invocation. The existence of a new type of man is revealed to the public. The present is no longer turned in upon itself but spread out for all to see. The storyteller once more gives free rein to his imagination; he makes innovations and he creates a work of art. It even happens that the characters, which are barely ready for such a transformation – highway robbers or more or less anti-social vagabonds – are taken up and remodelled. The emergence of the imagination and of the creative urge in the songs and epic stories of a colonized country is worth following. The storyteller replies to the expectant people by successive approximations, and makes his way, apparently alone but in fact helped on by his public, towards the seeking out of new patterns, that is to say national patterns. Comedy and farce disappear, or lose their attraction. As for dramatization, it is no longer placed on the plane of the troubled intellectual and his tormented conscience. By losing its characteristics of despair and revolt, the drama becomes part of the common lot of the people and forms part of an action in preparation or already in progress.

Where handicrafts are concerned, the forms of expression which formerly were the dregs of art, surviving as if in a daze, now begin to reach out. Woodwork, for example, which formerly turned out certain faces and attitudes by the million, begins to be differentiated. The inexpressive or overwrought mask comes to life and the arms tend to be raised from the body as if to sketch an action. Compositions containing two, three or five figures appear. The traditional schools are led on to creative efforts by the rising avalanche of amateurs or of critics. This new vigour in this sector of cultural life very often passes unseen; and yet its contribution to the national effort is of capital importance. By carving figures and faces which are full of life, and by taking as his theme a group fixed on the same pedestal, the artist invites participation in an organized movement.

If we study the repercussions of the awakening of national consciousness in the domains of ceramics and pottery-making, the same observations may be drawn. Formalism is abandoned in the craftsman's work. Jugs, jars and trays are modified, at first imperceptibly, then almost savagely. The colours, of which formerly there were but few and which obeyed the traditional rules of harmony, increase in number and are influenced by the repercussion of the rising revolution. Certain ochres and blues, which seemed forbidden to all eternity in a given cultural area, now assert themselves without giving rise to scandal. In the same way the stylization of the human face, which according to sociologists is typical of very clearly defined regions, becomes suddenly completely relative. The specialist coming from the home country and the ethnologist are quick to note these changes. On the whole such changes are condemned in the name of a rigid code of artistic style and of a cultural life which grows up at the heart of the colonial system. The colonialist specialists do not recognize these new forms and rush to the help of the traditions of the indigenous society. It is the colonialists who become the defenders of the native style. We remember perfectly, and the example took on a certain measure of importance since the real nature of colonialism was not involved, the reactions of the white jazz specialists when after the Second World War new styles such as the be-bop took definite shape. The fact is that in their eyes jazz should only be the despairing, broken-down nostalgia of an old Negro who is trapped between five glasses of whisky, the curse of his race, and the racial hatred of the white men. As soon as the Negro comes to an understanding of himself, and understands the rest of the world differently, when he gives birth to hope and forces back the racist universe, it is clear that his trumpet sounds more clearly and his voice less hoarsely. The new fashions in jazz are not simply born of economic competition. We must without any doubt see in them one of the consequences of the defeat, slow but sure, of the southern world of the United States. And it is not utopian to suppose that in fifty years' time the type of jazz howl hiccupped by a poor misfortunate Negro will be upheld only by the whites who believe in it as an expression of nigger-hood, and who are faithful to this arrested image of a type of relationship.

We might in the same way seek and find in dancing, singing and traditional rites and ceremonies the same upward-springing trend, and make out the same changes and the same impatience in this field. Well before the political or fighting phase of the national movement an attentive spectator can thus feel and see the manifestation of new vigour and feel the approaching conflict. He will note unusual forms of expression and themes which are fresh and imbued with a power which is no longer that of invocation but rather of the assembling of the people, a summoning together for a precise purpose. Everything works together to awaken the native's sensibility and to make unreal and inacceptable the contemplative attitude, or the acceptance of defeat. The native rebuilds his perceptions because he renews the purpose and dynamism of the craftsmen, of dancing and music and of literature and the oral tradition. His world comes to lose its accursed character. The conditions necessary for the inevitable conflict are brought together.

We have noted the appearance of the movement in cultural forms and we have seen that this movement and these new forms are linked to the state of maturity of the national consciousness. Now, this movement tends more and more to express itself objectively, in institutions. From thence comes the need for a national existence, whatever the cost.

A frequent mistake, and one which is moreover hardly justifiable, is to try to find cultural expressions for and to give new values to native culture within the framework of colonial domination. This is why we arrive at a proposition which at first sight seems paradoxical: the fact that in a colonized country the most elementary, most savage and the most undifferentiated nationalism is the most fervent and efficient means of defending national culture. For culture is first the expression of a nation, the expression of its preferences, of its taboos and of its patterns. It is at every stage of the whole of society that other taboos, values and patterns are formed. A national culture is the sum total of all these appraisals; it is the result of internal and external extensions exerted over society as a whole and also at every level of that society. In the colonial situation, culture, which is doubly deprived of the support of the nation and of the state, falls away and dies. The condition for its existence is therefore national liberation and the renaissance of the state.

The nation is not only the condition of culture, its fruitfulness, its continuous renewal, and its deepening. It is also a necessity. It is the fight for national existence which sets culture moving and opens to it the doors of creation. Later on it is the nation which will ensure the conditions and framework necessary to culture. The nation gathers together the various indispensable elements necessary for the creation of a culture, those elements which alone can give it credibility, validity, life and creative power. In the same way it is its national character that will make such a culture open to other cultures and which will enable it to influence and permeate other cultures. A non-existent culture can hardly be expected to have bearing on reality, or to influence reality. The first necessity is the re-establishment of the nation in order to give life to national culture in the strictly biological sense of the phrase.

Thus we have followed the break-up of the old strata of culture, a shattering which becomes increasingly fundamental; and we have noticed, on the eve of the decisive conflict for national freedom, the renewing of forms of expression and the rebirth of the imagination. There remains one essential question: what are the relations between the struggle – whether political or military – and culture? Is there a suspension of culture during the conflict? Is the national struggle an expression of a culture? Finally, ought one to say that the battle for freedom, however fertile *a posteriori* with regard to culture, is in itself a negation of culture? In short is the struggle for liberation a cultural phenomenon or not?

We believe that the conscious and organized undertaking by a colonized people to re-establish the sovereignty of that nation constitutes the most complete and obvious cultural manifestation that exists. It is not alone the success of the struggle which afterwards gives validity and vigour to culture; culture is not put into cold storage during the conflict. The struggle itself in its development and in its internal progression sends culture along different paths and traces out entirely new ones for it. The struggle for freedom does not give back to the national culture its former value and shapes; this struggle which aims at a fundamentally different set of relations between men cannot leave intact either the form or the content of the people's culture. After the conflict there is not only the disappearance of colonialism but also the disappearance of the colonized man.

This new humanity cannot do otherwise than define a new humanism both for itself and for others. It is prefigured in the objectives and methods of the conflict. A struggle which mobilizes all classes of the people and which expresses their aims and their impatience, which is not afraid to count almost exclusively on the people's support, will of necessity triumph. The value of this type of conflict is that it supplies the maximum of conditions necessary for the development and aims of culture. After national freedom has been obtained in these conditions, there is no such painful cultural indecision which is found in certain countries which are newly independent, because the nation by its manner of coming into being and in the terms of its existence exerts a fundamental influence over culture. A nation which is born of the people's concerted action and which embodies the real aspirations of the people while changing the state cannot exist save in the expression of exceptionally rich forms of culture.

The natives who are anxious for the culture of their country and who wish to give to it a universal dimension ought not therefore to place their confidence in the single principle of inevitable, undifferentiated independence written into the consciousness of the people in order to achieve their task. The liberation of the nation is one thing; the methods and popular content of the fight are another. It seems to us that the future of national culture and its riches are equally also part and parcel of the values which have ordained the struggle for freedom.

And now it is time to denounce certain pharisees. National claims, it is here and there stated, are a phase that humanity has left behind. It is the day of great concerted actions, and retarded nationalists ought in consequence to set their mistakes aright. We, however, consider that the mistake, which may have very serious consequences, lies in wishing to skip the national period. If culture is the expression of national consciousness, I will not hesitate to affirm that in the case with which we are dealing it is the national consciousness which is the most elaborate form of culture.

The consciousness of self is not the closing of a door to communication. Philosophic thought teaches us, on the contrary, that it is its guarantee. National consciousness, which is not nationalism, is the only thing that will give us an international dimension. This problem of national consciousness and of national culture takes on in Africa a special dimension. The birth of national consciousness in Africa has a strictly contemporaneous connexion with the African consciousness. The responsibility of the African as regards national culture is also a responsibility with regard to African-Negro culture. This joint responsibility is not the fact of a metaphysical principle but the awareness of a simple rule which wills that every independent nation in an Africa where colonialism is still entrenched is an encircled nation, a nation which is fragile and in permanent danger.

If man is known by his acts, then we will say that the most urgent thing today for the intellectual is to build up his nation. If this building up is true, that is to say if it interprets the manifest will of the people and reveals the eager African peoples, then the building of a nation is of necessity accompanied by the discovery and encouragement of universalizing values. Far from keeping aloof from other nations, therefore, it is national liberation which leads the nation to play its part on the stage of history. It is at the heart of national consciousness that international consciousness lives and grows. And this two-fold emerging is ultimately the source of all culture.

Notes

1. René Depestre, 'Face à la nuit'.
2. René Char, 'Partage formel'.
3. At the last school prize-giving in Dakar, the president of the Senegalese Republic, Léopold Senghor, decided to include the study of the idea of Negro-ism in the curriculum. If this decision was due to an anxiety to study historical causes, no one can criticize it. But if on the other hand it was taken in order to create black self-consciousness, it is simply a turning of his back upon history which has already taken cognizance of the disappearance of the majority of Negroes.

3 □ *National Liberation and Culture*

Amilcar Cabral

When Goebbels, the brain behind Nazi propaganda, heard culture being discussed, he brought out his revolver. That shows that the Nazis – who were and are the most tragic expression of imperialism and of its thirst for domination – even if they were all degenerates like Hitler, had a clear idea of the value of culture as a factor of resistance to foreign domination.

History teaches us that, in certain circumstances, it is very easy for the foreigner to impose his domination on a people. But it also teaches us that, whatever may be the material aspects of this domination, it can be maintained only by the permanent, organized repression of the cultural life of the people concerned. Implantation of foreign domination can be assured definitively only by physical liquidation of a significant part of the dominated population.

In fact, to take up arms to dominate a people is, above all, to take up arms to destroy, or at least to neutralize, to paralyze, its cultural life. For, with a strong indigenous cultural life, foreign domination cannot be sure of its perpetuation. At any moment, depending on internal and external factors determining the evolution of the society in question, cultural resistance (indestructible) may take on new forms (political, economic, armed) in order fully to contest foreign domination.

The ideal for foreign domination, whether imperialist or not, would be to choose:

- either to liquidate practically all the population of the dominated country, thereby eliminating the possibilities for cultural resistance;
- or to succeed in imposing itself without damage to the culture of the dominated people – that is, to harmonize economic and political domination of these people with their cultural personality.

The first hypothesis implies genocide of the indigenous population and creates a void which empties foreign domination of its content and its object: the dominated

From Amilcar Cabral, *Return to the Source: Selected speeches of Amilcar Cabral*, Monthly Review Press: New York, 1973, pp. 39–56.

people. The second hypothesis has not, until now, been confirmed by history. The broad experience of mankind allows us to postulate that it has no practical viability: it is not possible to harmonize the economic and political domination of a people, whatever may be the degree of their social development, with the preservation of their cultural personality.

In order to escape this choice – which may be called the *dilemma of cultural resistance* – imperialist colonial domination has tried to create theories which, in fact, are only gross formulations of racism, and which, in practice, are translated into a permanent state of siege of the indigenous populations on the basis of racist dictatorship (or democracy).

This, for example, is the case with the so-called theory of progressive *assimilation* of native populations, which turns out to be only a more or less violent attempt to deny the culture of the people in question. The utter failure of this 'theory', implemented in practice by several colonial powers, including Portugal, is the most obvious proof of its lack of viability, if not of its inhuman character. It attains the highest degree of absurdity in the Portuguese case, where Salazar affirmed that Africa does *not exist*.

This is also the case with the so-called theory of apartheid, created, applied and developed on the basis of the economic and political domination of the people of Southern Africa by a racist minority, with all the outrageous crimes against humanity which that involves. The practice of apartheid takes the form of unrestrained exploitation of the labor force of the African masses, incarcerated and repressed in the largest concentration camp mankind has ever known.

These practical examples give a measure of the drama of foreign imperialist domination as it confronts the cultural reality of the dominated people. They also suggest the strong, dependent and reciprocal relationships existing between the *cultural situation* and the *economic* (and political) *situation* in the behaviour of human societies. In fact, culture is always in the life of a society (open or closed), the more or less conscious result of the economic and political activities of that society, the more or less dynamic expression of the kinds of relationships which prevail in that society, on the one hand between man (considered individually or collectively) and nature, and, on the other hand, among individuals, groups of individuals, social strata or classes.

The value of culture as an element of resistance to foreign domination lies in the fact that culture is the vigorous manifestation on the ideological or idealist plane of the physical and historical reality of the society that is dominated or to be dominated. Culture is simultaneously the fruit of a people's history and a determinant of history, by the positive or negative influence which it exerts on the evolution of relationships between man and his environment, among men or groups of men within a society, as well as among different societies. Ignorance of this fact may explain the failure of several attempts at foreign domination – as well as the failure of some international liberation movements.

Let us examine the nature of *national liberation*. We shall consider this historical phenomenon in in its contemporary context, that is, national liberation in opposition to imperialist domination. The latter is, as we know, distinct both in form and in content from preceding types of foreign domination (tribal, military-aristocratic, feudal and capitalist domination in the free competition era).

The principal characteristic, common to every kind of imperialist domination, is the negation of the *historical process* of the dominated people by means of violently usurping the free operation of the process of development of the *productive forces*. Now, in any given society, the level of development of the productive forces and the system for social utilization of these forces (the ownership system) determine the *mode of production*. In our opinion, the mode of production whose contradictions are manifested with more or less intensity through the class struggle is the principal factor in the history of any human group, the level of the productive forces being the true and permanent driving power of history.

For every society, for every group of people, considered as an evolving entity, the level of the productive forces indicates the stage of development of the society and of each of its components in relation to nature, its capacity to act or to react consciously in relation to nature. It indicates and conditions the type of material relationships (expressed objectively or subjectively) which exists among the various elements or groups constituting the society in question. Relationships and types of relationships between man and nature, between man and his environment. Relationships and type of relationships among the individual or collective components of a society. To speak of these is to speak of history, but it is also to speak of culture.

Whatever may be the ideological or idealistic characteristics of cultural expression, culture is an essential element of the history of a people. Culture is, perhaps, the product of this history just as the flower is the product of a plant. Like history, or because it is history, culture has as its material base the level of the productive forces and the mode of production. Culture plunges its roots into the physical reality of the environmental humus in which it develops, and it reflects the organic nature of the society, which may be more or less influenced by external factors. History allows us to know the nature and extent of the imbalances and conflicts (economic, political and social) which characterize the evolution of a society; culture allows us to know the dynamic syntheses which have been developed and established by social conscience to resolve these conflicts at each stage of its evolution, in the search for survival and progress.

Just as happens with the flower in a plant, in culture there lies the capacity (or the responsibility) for forming and fertilizing the seedling which will assure the continuity of history, at the same time assuring the prospects for evolution and progress of the society in question. Thus it is understood that imperialist domination, by denying the historical development of the dominated people, necessarily also denies their cultural development. It is also understood why imperialist domination, like all other foreign domination, for its own security, requires cultural oppression and the attempt at direct or indirect liquidation of the essential elements of the culture of the dominated people.

The study of the history of national liberation struggles shows that generally these struggles are preceded by an increase in expression of culture, consolidated progressively into a successful or unsuccessful attempt to affirm the cultural personality of the dominated people, as a means of negating the oppressor culture. Whatever may be the conditions of a people's political and social factors in practicing this domination, it is generally within the culture that we find the seed of opposition, which leads to the structuring and development of the liberation movement.

In our opinion, the foundation for national liberation rests in the inalienable right of every people to have their own history, whatever formulations may be adopted at the level of international law. The objective of national liberation is, therefore, to reclaim the right, usurped by imperialist domination, namely: the liberation of the process of development of national productive forces. Therefore, national liberation takes place when, and only when, national productive forces are completely free of all kinds of foreign domination. The liberation of productive forces and consequently the ability to determine the mode of production most appropriate to the evolution of the liberated people necessarily opens up new prospects for the cultural development of the society in question, by returning to that society all its capacity to create progress.

A people who free themselves from foreign domination will be free culturally only if, without complexes and without underestimating the importance of positive accretions from the oppressor and other cultures, they return to the upward paths of their own culture, which is nourished by the living reality of its environment, and which negates both harmful influences and any kind of subjection to foreign culture. Thus, it may be seen that if imperialist domination has the vital need to practice cultural oppression, national liberation is necessarily an act of *culture*.

On the basis of what has just been said, we may consider the national liberation movement as the organized political expression of the culture of the people who are undertaking the struggle. For this reason, those who lead the movement must have a clear idea of the value of the culture in the framework of the struggle and must have a thorough knowledge of the people's culture, whatever may be their level of economic development.

In our time it is common to affirm that all peoples have a culture. The time is past when, in an effort to perpetuate the domination of people, culture was considered an attribute of privileged peoples or nations, and when, out of either ignorance or malice, culture was confused with technical power, if not with skin colour or the shape of one's eyes. The liberation movement, as representative and defender of the culture of the people, must be conscious of the fact that, whatever may be the material conditions of the society it represents, the society is the bearer and creator of culture. The liberation movement must furthermore embody the mass character, the popular character of the culture – which is not and never could be the privilege of one or of some sectors of the society.

In the thorough analysis of social structure which every liberation movement should be capable of making in relation to the imperative of the struggle, the cultural characteristics of each group in society have a place of prime importance. For, while the culture has a mass character, it is not uniform, it is not equally developed in all sectors of society. The attitude of each social group toward the liberation struggle is dictated by its economic interests, but is also influenced profoundly by its culture. It may even be admitted that these differences in cultural levels explain differences in behavior toward the liberation movement on the part of individuals who belong to the same socio-economic group. It is at this point that culture reaches its full significance for each individual: understanding and integration into his environment, identification with fundamental problems and aspirations of the society, acceptance of the possibility of change in the direction of progress.

In the specific conditions of our country – and we would say, of Africa – the horizontal and vertical distribution of levels of culture is somewhat complex. In fact, from villages to towns, from one ethnic group to another, from one age group to another, from the peasant to the workman or to the indigenous intellectual who is more or less assimilated, and, as we have said, even from individual to individual within the same social group, the quantitative and qualitative level of culture varies significantly. It is of prime importance for the liberation movement to take these facts into consideration.

In societies with a horizontal social structure, such as the Balante, for example, the distribution of cultural levels is more or less uniform, variations being linked uniquely to characteristics of individuals or of age groups. On the other hand, in societies with a vertical structure, such as the Fula, there are important variations from the top to the bottom of the social pyramid. These differences in social structure illustrate once more the close relationship between culture and economy, and also explain differences in the general or sectoral behavior of these two ethnic groups in relation to the liberation movement.

It is true that the multiplicity of social and ethnic groups complicates the effort to determine the role of culture in the liberation movement. But it is vital not to lose sight of the decisive importance of the liberation struggle, even when class structure appears to be in embryonic stages of development.

The experience of colonial domination shows that, in the effort to perpetuate exploitation, the colonizer not only creates a system to repress the cultural life of the colonized people; he also provokes and develops the cultural alienation of a part of the population, either by so-called assimilation of indigenous people, or by creating a social gap between the indigenous elites and the popular masses. As a result of this process of dividing or of deepening the divisions in the society, it happens that a considerable part of the population, notably the urban or peasant *petite bourgeoisie*, assimilates the colonizer's mentality, considers itself culturally superior to its own people and ignores or looks down upon their cultural values. This situation, characteristic of the majority of colonized intellectuals, is consolidated by increases in the social privileges of the assimilated or alienated group with direct implications for the behavior of individuals in this group in relation to the liberation movement. A reconversion of minds – of mental set – is thus indispensable to the true integration of people into the liberation movement. Such reconversion – re-Africanization, in our case – may take place before the struggle, but it is completed only during the course of the struggle, through daily contact with the popular masses in the communion of sacrifice required by the struggle.

However, we must take into account the fact that, faced with the prospect of political independence, the ambition and opportunism from which the liberation movement generally suffers may bring into the struggle unconverted individuals. The latter, on the basis of their level of schooling, their scientific or technical knowledge, but without losing any of their social class biases, may attain the highest positions in the liberation movement. Vigilance is thus indispensable on the cultural as well as the political plane. For, in the liberation movement as elsewhere, all that glitters is not necessarily gold: political leaders – even the most famous – may be culturally alienated people. But the social class characteristics of the culture are even more discernible in the behavior of privileged groups in rural areas, especially in the case of ethnic groups with a vertical social structure, where, nevertheless, assimilation or cultural alienation influences are non-existent or practically non-existent. This is the case, for example, with the Fula ruling class. Under colonial domination, the political authority of this class (traditional chiefs, noble families, religious leaders) is purely nominal, and the popular masses know that true authority lies with and is acted upon by colonial administrators. However, the ruling class preserves in essence its basic cultural authority over the masses and this has very important political implications.

Recognizing this reality, the colonizer who represses or inhibits significant cultural activity on the part of the masses at the base of the social pyramid strengthens and protects the prestige and the cultural influence of the ruling class at the summit. The colonizer installs chiefs who support him and who are to some degree accepted by the masses; he gives these chiefs material privileges such as education for their eldest children, creates chiefdoms where they did not exist before, develops cordial relations with religious leaders, builds mosques, organizes journeys to Mecca, etc. And above all, by means of the repressive organs of colonial administration, he guarantees economic and social privileges to the ruling class in their relations with the masses. All this does not make it impossible that, among these ruling classes, there may be individuals or groups of individuals who join the liberation movement, although less frequently than in the case of the assimilated 'petite bourgeoisie'. Several traditional and religious leaders join the struggle at the very beginning or during its development, making an enthusiastic contribution to the cause of liberation.

But here again vigilance is indispensable: preserving deep down the cultural prejudices of their class, individuals in this category generally see in the liberation movement the only valid means, using the sacrifices of the masses, to eliminate colonial oppression of their own class and to re-establish in this way their complete political and cultural domination of the people.

In the general framework of contesting colonial imperialist domination and in the actual situation to which we refer, among the oppressor's most loyal allies are found some high officials and intellectuals of the liberal professions, assimilated people, and also a significant number of representatives of the ruling class from rural areas.

This fact gives some measure of the influence (positive or negative) of culture and cultural prejudices in the problem of political choice when one is confronted with the liberation movement. It also illustrates the limits of this influence and the supremacy of the class factor in the behavior of the different social groups. The high official or the assimilated intellectual, characterized by total cultural alienation, identifies himself by political choice with the traditional or religious leader who has experienced no significant foreign cultural influences.

For these two categories of people place above all principles or demands of a cultural nature – and against the aspirations of the people – their own economic and social privileges, their own *class interests*. That is a truth which the liberation movement cannot afford to ignore without risking betrayal of the economic, political, social and cultural objectives of the struggle.

Without minimizing the positive contribution which privileged classes may bring to the struggle, the liberation movement must, on the cultural level just as on the political level, base its action in popular culture, whatever may be the diversity of levels of cultures in the country. The cultural combat against colonial domination – the first phase of the liberation movement – can be planned efficiently only on the basis of the culture of the rural and urban working masses, including the nationalist (revolutionary) 'petite bourgeoisie' who have been re-Africanized or who are ready for cultural reconversion. Whatever may be the complexity of this basic cultural panorama, the liberation movement must be capable of distinguishing within it the essential from the secondary, the positive from the negative, the progressive from the reactionary in order to characterize the master line which defines progressively a *national culture*.

In order for culture to play the important role which falls to it in the framework of the liberation movement, the movement must be able to preserve the positive cultural values of every well-defined social group, of every category, and to achieve the confluence of these values in the service of the struggle, giving it a new dimension – the *national dimension*. Confronted with such a necessity, the liberation struggle is, above all, a struggle both for the preservation and survival of the cultural values of the people and for the harmonization and development of these values within a national framework.

The political and moral unity of the liberation movement and of the people it represents and directs implies achieving the cultural unity of the social groups which are of key importance for the liberation struggle. This unity is achieved on the one hand by total identification with the environmental reality and with the fundamental problems and aspirations of the people; and, on the other hand, by progressive cultural identification of the various social groups participating in the struggle.

As it progresses the liberation struggle must bring diverse interests into harmony, resolve contradictions and define common objectives in the search for liberty and progress. The taking to heart of its objectives by large strata in the population, reflected in their determination in the face of difficulties and sacrifices, is a great political and moral victory. It is also a cultural achievement of decisive importance for the subsequent development and success of the liberation movement.

The greater the differences between the culture of the dominated people and the culture of their oppressor, the more possible such a victory becomes. History proves that it is much less difficult to dominate and to continue dominating a people whose culture is similar or analogous to that of the conqueror. It could be contended that the failure of Napoleon, whatever may have been the economic and political motivations of his wars of conquest, resulted from his ignorance of this principle, or from his inability to limit his ambition to the domination of peoples whose culture was more or less similar to that of France. The same thing could be said about other ancient, modern or contemporary empires.

One of the most serious errors, if not the most serious error, committed by colonial powers in Africa may have been to ignore or underestimate the cultural strength of African peoples. This attitude is particularly clear in the case of Portuguese colonial domination, which has not been content with denying absolutely the existence of the cultural values of the African and his social position but has persisted in forbidding him all kinds of political activity. The people of Portugal, who have not even enjoyed the wealth taken from African peoples by Portuguese colonialism, but the majority of whom have assimilated the imperial mentality of the country's ruling classes, are paying very dearly today, in three colonial wars, for the mistake of underestimating our cultural reality.

The political and armed resistance of the people of the Portuguese colonies, as of other countries or regions of Africa, was crushed by the technical superiority of the imperialist conqueror, with the complicity of or betrayal by some indigenous ruling classes. Those elites who were loyal to the history and to the culture of the people were destroyed. Entire populations were massacred. The colonial kingdom was established with all the crimes and exploitation which characterize it. But cultural resistance of the African people was not destroyed. Repressed, persecuted, betrayed by some social groups who were in league with the colonialists, African culture survived all the storms, taking refuge in the villages, in the forests and in the spirit of the generations who were victims of colonialism. Like the seed which long awaits conditions favorable to germination in order to assure the survival of the species and its development, the culture of African peoples flourishes again today, across the continent, in struggles for national liberation. Whatever may be the forms of these struggles, their successes or failures, and the length of their development, they mark the beginning of a new era in the history of the continent and are both in form and in content the most important cultural element in the life of African peoples. The freedom struggle of African peoples is both the fruit and the proof of cultural vigor, opening up new prospects for the development of culture in the service of progress.

The time is past when it was necessary to seek arguments to prove the cultural maturity of African peoples. The irrationality of the racist 'theories' of a Gobineau or a Levy-Bruhl neither interests nor convinces anyone but racists. In spite of colonial domination (and perhaps even because of this domination), Africa was able to impose respect for her cultural values. She even showed herself to be one of the richest of continents in cultural values. From Carthage to Giza to Zimbabwe, from Meroe to Benin and Ife, from Sahara or Timbuktu to Kilwa, across the immensity and the diversity of the continent's natural conditions, the culture of African peoples is an undeniable reality: in works of art as well as in oral and written traditions, in cosmological conceptions as well as in music and dance, in religions and belief as well as in the dynamic balance of economic, political and social structures created by African man.

The universal value of African culture is now an incontestable fact; nevertheless, it should not be forgotten that African man, whose hands, as the poet said, 'placed the stones of the foundations of the world', has developed his culture frequently, if not constantly, in adverse conditions: from deserts to equatorial forests, from coastal marshes to the banks of great rivers subject to frequent flooding, in spite of all sorts of difficulties, including plagues which have destroyed plants and animals and man alike. In agreement with Basil Davidson and other researchers in African history and culture, we can say that the accomplishments of the African genius in economic, political, social and cultural domains, despite the inhospitable character of the environment, are epic – comparable to the major historical examples of the greatness of man.

Of course, this reality constitutes a reason for pride and a stimulus to those who fight for the liberation and the progress of African peoples. But it is important not to lose sight of the fact that no culture is a perfect, finished whole. Culture, like history, is an expanding and developing phenomenon. Even more important, we must take account of the fact that the fundamental characteristic of a culture is the highly dependent and reciprocal nature of its linkages with the social and economic reality of the environment, with the level of productive forces and the mode of production of the society which created it.

Culture, the fruit of history, reflects at every moment the material and spiritual reality of society, of man-the-individual and of man-the-social-being, faced with conflicts which set him against nature and the exigencies of common life. From this we see that all culture is composed of essential and secondary elements, of strengths and weaknesses, of virtues and failings, of positive and negative aspects, of factors of progress and factors of stagnation or regression. From this also we can see that culture – the creation of society and the synthesis of the balances and the solutions which society engenders to resolve the conflicts which characterize each phase of its history – is a social reality, independent of the will of men, the color of their skins or the shape of their eyes.

A thorough analysis of cultural reality does not permit the claim that there exist continental or racial cultures. This is because, as with history, the development of culture proceeds in uneven fashion, whether at the level of a continent, a 'race', or even a society. The coordinates of culture, like those of any developing phenomenon, vary in space and time, whether they be material (physical) or human (biological and social). The fact of recognizing the existence of common and particular features in the cultures of African peoples, independent of the colour of their skin, does not necessarily imply that one and only one culture exists on the continent. In the same way that from an economic and political viewpoint we can recognize the existence of several Africas, so also there are many African cultures.

Without any doubt, underestimation of the cultural values of African peoples, based upon racist feelings and upon the intention of perpetuating foreign exploitation of Africans, has done much harm to Africa. But in the face of the vital need for progress, the following attitudes or behaviors will be no less harmful to Africa: indiscriminate compliments; systematic exaltation of virtues without condemning faults; blind acceptance of the values of the culture, without considering what presently or potentially regressive elements it contains; confusion between what is the expression of an objective and material historical reality and what appears to be a creation of the mind or the product of a peculiar temperament; absurd linking of artistic creation, whether good or not, with supposed racial characteristics; and finally, the non-scientific or a scientific critical appreciation of the cultural phenomenon.

Thus, the important thing is not to lose time in more or less idle discussion of the specific or unspecific characteristics of African cultural values, but rather to look upon these values as a conquest of a small piece of humanity for the common heritage of humanity, achieved in one or several phases of its evolution. The important thing is to proceed to critical analysis of African cultures in relation to the liberation movement and to the exigencies of progress – confronting this new stage in African history. It is important to be conscious of the value of African cultures in the framework of universal civilization, but to compare this value with that of other cultures, not with a view of deciding its superiority or inferiority, but in order to determine, in the general framework of the struggle for progress what contribution African culture has made and can make, and what are the contributions it can or must receive from elsewhere.

The liberation movement must, as we have said, base its action upon thorough knowledge of the culture of the people and be able to appreciate at their true value the elements of this culture, as well as the different levels that it reaches in each social group. The movement must also be able to discern in the entire set of cultural values of the people the essential and the secondary, the positive and the negative, the progressive and the reactionary, the strengths and the weaknesses. All this is necessary as a function of the demands of the struggle and in order to be able to concentrate action on what is essential without forgetting what is secondary, to induce development of positive and progressive elements, and to combat with flexibility but with rigor the negative and reactionary elements; and finally, in order to utilize strengths efficiently and to eliminate weaknesses or to transform them into strengths.

The more one realizes that the chief goal of the liberation movement goes beyond the achievement of political independence to the superior level of complete liberation of the productive forces and the construction of economic, social and cultural progress of the people, the more evident is the necessity of undertaking a selective analysis of the values of the culture within the framework of the struggle for liberation. The need for such an analysis of cultural values becomes more acute when, in order to face colonial violence, the liberation movement must mobilize and organize the people, under the direction of a strong and disciplined political organization, in order to resort to violence in the cause of freedom – *the armed struggle for the national liberation.*

The negative values of culture are generally an obstacle to the development of the struggle and to the building of this progress. In this perspective, the liberation movement must be able, beyond the analysis mentioned above, to achieve gradually but surely as its political action develops the *confluence of the levels* of culture of the different social groups available for the struggle. The movement must be able to transform them into the national cultural force which undergirds and conditions the development of the armed struggle. It should be noted that the analysis of cultural reality already gives a measure of the strengths and weaknesses of the people when confronted with the demands of the struggle, and therefore represents a valuable contribution to the strategy and tactics to be followed, on the political as well as on the military plane. But only during the struggle, launched from a satisfactory base of political and moral unity, is the complexity of cultural problems raised in all its dimensions. This frequently requires successive adaptations of strategy and tactics to the realities which only the struggle is capable of revealing. Experience of the struggle shows how utopian and absurd it is to profess to apply without considering local reality (and especially cultural reality) plans of action developed by other peoples during their liberation struggles and to apply solutions which they found to the problems with which they were or are confronted.

It can be said that at the outset of the struggle, whatever may have been the extent of preparation undertaken, both the leadership of the liberation movement and the militant and popular masses have no clear awareness of the strong influence of cultural values in the development of the struggle, the possibilities culture creates, the limits it imposes, and, above all, how; and how much culture is for the people an inexhaustible source of courage, of material and moral support, of physical and psychic energy which enables them to accept sacrifices – even to accomplish 'miracles'. But equally, in some respects, culture is very much a source of obstacles and difficulties, of erroneous conceptions about reality, of deviation in carrying out duty, and of limitations on the tempo and efficiency of a struggle that is confronted with the political, technical and scientific requirements of a war.

The armed struggle for liberation, launched in response to the colonialist oppressor, turns out to be a painful but efficient instrument for developing the cultural level of both the leadership strata in the liberation movement and the various social groups who participate in the struggle.

The leaders of the liberation movement, drawn generally from the 'petite bourgeoisie' (intellectuals, clerks) or the urban working class (workers, chauffeurs, salary-earners in general) having to live day by day with the various peasant groups in the heart of the rural populations, come to know the people better. They discover at the grass roots the richness of their cultural values (philosophic, political, artistic, social and moral), acquire a clearer understanding of the economic realities of the country, of the problems, sufferings and hopes of the popular masses. The leaders realize, not without a certain astonishment, the richness of spirit, the capacity for reasoned discussion and clear exposition of ideas, the facility for understanding and assimilating concepts on the part of population groups who yesterday were forgotten, if not despised, and who were considered incompetent by the colonizer and even by some nationals. The leaders thus enrich their cultures – develop personally their capacity to serve the movement in the service of the people.

On their side, the working masses and, in particular, the peasants, who are usually illiterate and never have moved beyond the boundaries of their village or region, in contact with other groups, lose the complexes which constrained them in their relationships with other ethnic and social groups. They realize their crucial role in the struggle; they break the bonds of the village universe to integrate progressively into the country and the world; they acquire an infinite amount of new knowledge, useful for their immediate and future activity within the framework of the struggle, and they strengthen their political awareness by assimilating the principles of national and social revolution postulated by the struggle. They thereby become more able to play the decisive role of providing the principal force behind the liberation movement.

As we know, the armed liberation struggle requires the mobilization and organization of a significant majority of the population, the political and moral unity of the various social classes, the efficient use of modern arms and of other means of war, the progressive liquidation of the remnants of tribal mentality, and the rejection of social and religious rules and taboos which inhibit development of the struggle (gerontocracies, nepotism, social inferiority of women, rites and practices which are incompatible with the rational and national character of the struggle, etc.). The struggle brings about other profound modifications in the life of populations. The armed liberation struggle implies, therefore, a veritable forced march along the road to cultural progress.

Consider these features inherent in an armed liberation struggle: the practice of democracy, of criticism and self-criticism, the increasing responsibility of populations for the direction of their lives, literacy work, creation of schools and health services, training of cadres from peasant and worker backgrounds – and many other achievements. When we consider these features, we see that the armed liberation struggle is not only a product of culture but also a *determinant of culture*. This is without doubt for the people the prime recompense for the efforts and sacrifices which war demands. In this perspective, it behoves the liberation movement to define clearly the objectives of cultural resistance as an integral and determining part of the struggle.

From all that has just been said, it can be concluded that in the framework of the conquest of national independence and in the perspective of developing the economic and social progress of the people, the objectives must be at least the following: *development of a popular culture* and of all positive indigenous cultural values; *development of a national culture* based upon the history and the achievements of the struggle itself; constant promotion of the *political and moral awareness* of the people (of all social groups) as well as *patriotism*, of the spirit of sacrifice and devotion to the cause of independence, of justice, and of progress;

development of a technical, technological and *scientific culture*, compatible with the requirements for progress; development, on the basis of a critical assimilation of man's achievements in the domains of art, science, literature, etc., of a *universal culture* for perfect integration into the contemporary world, in the perspectives of its evolution; constant and generalized promotion of feelings of humanism, of solidarity, of respect and disinterested devotion to human beings.

The achievement of these objectives is indeed possible, because the armed struggle for liberation, in the concrete conditions of life of African peoples, confronted with the imperialist challenge, is an act of insemination upon history – the major expression of our culture and of our African essence. In the moment of victory, it must be translated into a significant leap forward of the culture of the people who are liberating themselves.

If that does not happen, then the efforts and sacrifices accepted during the struggle will have been made in vain. The struggle will have failed to achieve its objectives, and the people will have missed an opportunity for progress in the general framework of history.

4 □ Can the Subaltern Speak?

Gayatri Chakravorty Spivak

[...]

I

Some of the most radical criticism coming out of the West today is the result of an interested desire to conserve the subject of the West, or the West as Subject. The theory of pluralized 'subject-effects' gives an illusion of undermining subjective sovereignty while often providing a cover for this subject of knowledge. Although the history of Europe as Subject is narrativized by the law, political economy and ideology of the West, this concealed Subject pretends it has 'no geo-political determinations'. The much-publicized critique of the sovereign subject thus actually inaugurates a Subject. I will argue for this conclusion by considering a text by two great practitioners of the critique: 'Intellectuals and power: a conversation between Michel Foucault and Gilles Deleuze'.[1]

I have chosen this friendly exchange between two activist philosophers of history because it undoes the opposition between authoritative theoretical production and the unguarded practice of conversation, enabling one to glimpse the track of ideology. The participants in this conversation emphasize the most important contributions of French poststructuralist theory: first, that the networks of power/desire/interest are so heterogeneous, that their reduction to a coherent narrative is counterproductive – a persistent critique is needed; and second, that intellectuals must attempt to disclose and know the discourse of society's Other. Yet the two systematically ignore the question of ideology and their own implication in intellectual and economic history.

Although one of its chief presuppositions is the critique of the sovereign subject, the conversation between Foucault and Deleuze is framed by two monolithic and

From C. Nelson and L. Grossberg (eds.), *Marxism and the Interpretation of Culture*, Macmillan Education: Basingstoke, 1988, pp. 271–313.

anonymous subjects-in-revolution: 'A Maoist' (*FD*, p. 205) and 'the workers' struggle' (*FD*, p. 217). Intellectuals, however, are named and differentiated; moreover, a Chinese Maoism is nowhere operative. Maoism here simply creates an aura of narrative specificity, which would be a harmless rhetorical banality were it not that the innocent appropriation of the proper name 'Maoism' for the eccentric phenomenon of French intellectual 'Maoism' and subsequent 'New Philosophy' symptomatically renders 'Asia' transparent.[2]

Deleuze's reference to the workers' struggle is equally problematic; it is obviously a genuflection: 'We are unable to touch [power] in any point of its application without finding ourselves confronted by this diffuse mass, so that we are necessarily led . . . to the desire to blow it up completely. Every partial revolutionary attack or defense is linked in this way to the workers' struggle' (*FD*, p. 217). The apparent banality signals a disavowal. The statement ignores the international division of labor, a gesture that often marks poststructuralist political theory.[3] The invocation of *the* workers' struggle is baleful in its very innocence; it is incapable of dealing with global capitalism: the subject-production of worker and unemployed within nation-state ideologies in its Center; the increasing subtraction of the working class in the Periphery from the realization of surplus value and thus from 'humanistic' training in consumerism; and the large-scale presence of paracapitalist labor as well as the heterogeneous structural status of agriculture in the Periphery. Ignoring the international division of labor; rendering 'Asia' (and on occasion 'Africa') transparent (unless the subject is ostensibly the 'Third World'); reestablishing the legal subject of socialized capital – these are problems as common to much poststructuralist as to structuralist theory. Why should such occlusions be sanctioned in precisely those intellectuals who are our best prophets of heterogeneity and the Other?

The link to the workers' struggle is located in the desire to blow up power at any point of its application. This site is apparently based on a simple valorization of *any* desire destructive of *any* power. Walter Benjamin comments on Baudelaire's comparable politics by way of quotations from Marx:

> Marx continues in his description of the *conspirateurs de profession* as follows: '. . . They have no other aim but the immediate one of overthrowing the existing government, and they profoundly despise the more theoretical enlightenment of the workers as to their class interests. Thus their anger – not proletarian but plebian – at the *habits noirs* (black coats), the more or less educated people who represent [*vertreten*] that side of the movement and of whom they can never become entirely independent, as they cannot of the official representatives [*Repräsentanten*] of the party.' Baudelaire's political insights do not go fundamentally beyond the insights of these professional conspirators. . . . He could perhaps have made Flaubert's statement, 'Of all of politics I understand only one thing: the revolt', his own.[4]

The link to the workers' struggle is located, simply, in desire. Elsewhere, Deleuze and Guattari have attempted an alternative definition of desire, revising the one offered by psychoanalysis: 'Desire does not lack anything; it does not lack its object. It is, rather, the subject that is lacking desire, or desire that lacks a fixed subject; there is no fixed subject except by repression. Desire and its object are a unity: it is the machine, as a machine of a machine. Desire is machine, the object of desire also a connected machine, so that the product is lifted from the process of producing and something detaches itself from producing to product and gives a leftover to the vagabond, nomad subject.'[5]

This definition does not alter the specificity of the desiring subject (or leftover subject-effect) that attaches to specific instances of desire or to production of the desiring machine. Moreover, when the connection between desire and the subject is taken as irrelevant or merely reversed, the subject-effect that surreptitiously emerges is much like the generalized ideological subject of the theorist. This may be the legal subject of socialized capital, neither labor nor management, holding a 'strong' passport, using a 'strong' or 'hard' currency, with supposedly unquestioned access to due process. It is certainly not the desiring subject as Other.

The failure of Deleuze and Guattari to consider the relations between desire, power and subjectivity renders them incapable of articulating a theory of interests. In this context, their indifference to ideology (a theory of which is necessary for an understanding of interests) is striking but consistent. Foucault's commitment to 'genealogical' speculation prevents him from locating, in 'great names' like Marx and Freud, watersheds in some continuous stream of intellectual history.[6] This commitment has created an unfortunate resistance in Foucault's work to 'mere' ideological critique. Western speculations on the ideological reproduction of social relations belong to that mainstream, and it is within this tradition that Althusser writes: 'The reproduction of labour power requires not only a reproduction of its skills, but also at the same time, a reproduction of its submission to the ruling ideology for the workers, and a reproduction of the ability to manipulate the ruling ideology correctly for the agents of exploitation and repression, so that they, too, will provide for the domination of the ruling class "in and by words" [*par la parole*].'[7]

When Foucault considers the pervasive heterogeneity of power, he does not ignore the immense institutional heterogeneity that Althusser here attempts to schematize. Similarly, in speaking of alliances and systems of signs, the state and war-machines (*mille plateaux*), Deleuze and Guattari are opening up that very field. Foucault cannot, however, admit that a developed theory of ideology recognizes its own material production in institutionality, as well as in the 'effective instruments for the formation and accumulation of knowledge' (*PK*, p. 102). Because these philosophers seem obliged to reject all arguments naming the concept of ideology as *only* schematic rather than textual, they are equally obliged to produce a mechanically schematic opposition between interest and desire. Thus they align themselves with bourgeois sociologists who fill the place of ideology with a continuistic 'unconscious' or a parasubjective 'culture'. The mechanical relation between desire and interest is clear in such sentences as: 'We never desire against our interests, because interest always follows and finds itself where desire has placed it' (*FD*, p. 215). An undifferentiated desire is the agent, and power slips in to create the effects of desire: 'power . . . produces positive effects at the level of desire – and also at the level of knowledge' (*PK*, p. 59).

This parasubjective matrix, cross-hatched with heterogeneity, ushers in the unnamed Subject, at least for those intellectual workers influenced by the new hegemony of desire. The race for 'the last instance' is now between economics and power. Because desire is tacitly defined on an orthodox model, it is unitarily opposed to 'being deceived'. Ideology as 'false consciousness' (being deceived) has been called into question by Althusser. Even Reich implied notions of collective will rather than a dichotomy of deception and undeceived desire: 'We must accept the scream of Reich: no, the masses were not deceived; at a particular moment, they actually desired a fascist regime' (*FD*, p. 215).

These philosophers will not entertain the thought of constitutive contradiction – that is where they admittedly part company from the Left. In the name of desire, they reintroduce the undivided subject into the discourse of power. Foucault often seems to conflate 'individual' and 'subject';[8] and the impact on his own metaphors is perhaps intensified in his followers. Because of the power of the word 'power', Foucault admits to using the 'metaphor of the point which progressively irradiates its surroundings'. Such slips become the rule rather than the exception in less careful hands. And that radiating point, animating an effectively heliocentric discourse, fills the empty place of the agent with the historical sun of theory, the Subject of Europe.[9]

Foucault articulates another corollary of the disavowal of the role of ideology in reproducing the social relations of production: an unquestioned valorization of the oppressed as subject, the 'object being', as Deleuze admiringly remarks, 'to establish conditions where the prisoners themselves would be able to speak'. Foucault adds that 'the masses *know* perfectly well, clearly' – once again the thematic of being undeceived – 'they know far better than [the intellectual] and they certainly say it very well' (*FD*, pp. 206, 207).

What happens to the critique of the sovereign subject in these pronouncements? The limits of this representationalist realism are reached with Deleuze: 'Reality is what actually happens in a factory, in a school, in barracks, in a prison, in a police station' (*FD*, p. 212). This foreclosing of the necessity of the difficult task of counterhegemonic ideological production has not been salutary. It has helped positivist empiricism – the justifying foundation of advanced capitalist neocolonialism – to define its own arena as 'concrete experience', 'what actually happens'. Indeed, the concrete experience that is the guarantor of the political appeal of prisoners, soldiers and schoolchildren is disclosed through the concrete experience of the intellectual, the one who diagnoses the episteme.[10] Neither Deleuze nor Foucault seems aware that the intellectual within socialized capital, brandishing concrete experience, can help consolidate the international division of labor.

The unrecognized contradiction within a position that valorizes the concrete experience of the oppressed, while being so uncritical about the historical role of the intellectual, is maintained by a verbal slippage. Thus Deleuze makes this remarkable

pronouncement: 'A theory is like a box of tools. Nothing to do with the signifier'
(*FD*, p. 208). Considering that the verbalism of the theoretical world and its access
to any world defined against it as 'practical' is irreducible, such a declaration helps
only the intellectual anxious to prove that intellectual labor is just like manual labor.
It is when signifiers are left to look after themselves that verbal slippages happen.
The signifier 'representation' is a case in point. In the same dismissive tone
that severs theory's link to the signifier, Deleuze declares, 'There is no more
representation; there's nothing but action' – 'action of theory and action of practice
which relate to each other as relays and form networks' (*FD*, pp. 206–7). Yet an
important point is being made here: the production of theory is also a practice; the
opposition between abstract 'pure' theory and concrete 'applied' practice is too quick
and easy.[11]

If this is, indeed, Deleuze's argument, his articulation of it is problematic. Two
senses of representation are being run together: representation as 'speaking for', as
in politics, and representation as 're-presentation', as in art or philosophy. Since
theory is also only 'action', the theoretician does not represent (speak for) the
oppressed group. Indeed, the subject is not seen as a representative consciousness
(one re-presenting reality adequately). These two senses of representation – within
state formation and the law, on the one hand, and in subject-predication, on the
other – are related but irreducibly discontinuous. To cover over the discontinuity
with an analogy that is presented as a proof reflects again a paradoxical subject-
privileging.[12] *Because* 'the person who speaks and acts . . . is always a multiplicity',
no 'theorizing intellectual . . . [or] party or . . . union' can represent 'those who act
and struggle' (*FD*, p. 206). Are those who act and *struggle* mute, as opposed to
those who act and *speak* (*FD*, p. 206)? These immense problems are buried in the
differences between the 'same' words: consciousness and conscience (both *conscience*
in French), representation and re-presentation. The critique of ideological subject-
constitution within state formations and systems of political economy can now
be effaced, as can the active theoretical practice of the 'transformation of
consciousness'. The banality of leftist intellectuals' lists of self-knowing, politically
canny subalterns stands revealed; representing them, the intellectuals represent
themselves as transparent.

If such a critique and such a project are not to be given up, the shifting distinctions
between representation within the state and political economy, on the one hand, and
within the theory of the Subject, on the other, must not be obliterated. Let us
consider the play of *vertreten* ('represent' in the first sense) and *darstellen* ('represent' in the second sense) in a famous passage in *The Eighteenth Brumaire of
Louis Bonaparte*, where Marx touches on 'class' as a descriptive and transformative
concept in a manner somewhat more complex than Althusser's distinction between
class instinct and class position would allow.

Marx's contention here is that the descriptive definition of a class can be a
differential one – its cutting off and difference from all other classes: 'in so far as
millions of families live under economic conditions of existence that cut off their
mode of life, their interest, and their formation from those of the other classes and

place them in inimical confrontation [*feindlich gegenüberstellen*], they form a class'.[13] There is no such thing as a 'class instinct' at work here. In fact, the collectivity of familial existence, which might be considered the arena of 'instinct', is discontinuous with, though operated by, the differential isolation of classes. In this context, one far more pertinent to the France of the 1970s than it can be to the international periphery, the formation of a class is *artificial* and economic, and the economic agency or *interest* is impersonal because it is systematic and heterogeneous. This agency or interest is tied to the Hegelian critique of the individual subject, for it marks the subject's empty place in that process without a subject which is history and political economy. Here the capitalist is defined as 'the conscious bearer [*Träger*] of the limitless movement of capital'.[14] My point is that Marx is not working to create an undivided subject where desire and interest coincide. Class consciousness does not operate toward that goal. Both in the economic area (capitalist) and in the political (world-historical agent), Marx is obliged to construct models of a divided and dislocated subject whose parts are not continuous or coherent with each other. A celebrated passage like the description of capital as the Faustian monster brings this home vividly.[15]

The following passage, continuing the quotation from *The Eighteenth Brumaire*, is also working on the structural principle of a dispersed and dislocated class subject: the (absent collective) consciousness of the small peasant proprietor class finds its 'bearer' in a 'representative' who appears to work in another's interest. The word 'representative' here is not '*darstellen*'; this sharpens the contrast Foucault and Deleuze slide over, the contrast, say, between a proxy and a portrait. There is, of course, a relationship between them, one that has received political and ideological exacerbation in the European tradition at least since the poet and the sophist, the actor and the orator, have both been seen as harmful. In the guise of a post-Marxist description of the scene of power, we thus encounter a much older debate: between representation or rhetoric as tropology and as persuasion. *Darstellen* belongs to the first constellation, *vertreten* – with stronger suggestions of substitution – to the second. Again, they are related, but running them together, especially in order to say that beyond both is where oppressed subjects speak, act and know *for themselves*, leads to an essentialist, utopian politics.

Here is Marx's passage, using '*vertreten*' where the English use 'represent', discussing a social 'subject' whose consciousness and *Vertretung* (as much a substitution as a representation) are dislocated and incoherent: The small peasant proprietors 'cannot represent themselves; they must be represented. Their representative must appear simultaneously as their master, as an authority over them, as unrestricted governmental power that protects them from the other classes and sends them rain and sunshine from above. The political influence [in the place of the class interest, since there is no unified class subject] of the small peasant proprietors therefore finds its last expression [the implication of a chain of substitutions – *Vertretungen* – is strong here] in the executive force [*Exekutivgewalt* – less personal in German] subordinating society to itself.'

Not only does such a model of social indirection – necessary gaps between the source of 'influence' (in this case the small peasant proprietors), the 'representative' (Louis Napoleon), and the historical-political phenomenon (executive control) – imply a critique of the subject as *individual* agent but a critique even of the subjectivity of a *collective* agency. The necessarily dislocated machine of history moves because 'the identity of the *interests*' of these proprietors 'fails to produce a feeling of community, national links, or a political organization'. The event of representation as *Vertretung* (in the constellation of rhetoric-as-persuasion) behaves like a *Darstellung* (or rhetoric-as-trope), taking its place in the gap between the formation of a (descriptive) class and the nonformation of a (transformative) class: 'In so far as millions of families live under economic conditions of existence that separate their mode of life ... *they form a class*. In so far as ... the identity of their interests fails to produce a feeling of community ... *they do not form a class*.' The complicity of *Vertreten* and *Darstellen*, their identity-in-difference as the place of practice – since this complicity is precisely what Marxists must expose, as Marx does in *The Eighteenth Brumaire* – can only be appreciated if they are not conflated by a sleight of word.

It would be merely tendentious to argue that this texualizes Marx too much, making him inaccessible to the common 'man', who, a victim of common sense, is so deeply placed in a heritage of positivism that Marx's irreducible emphasis on the work of the negative, on the necessity for de-fetishizing the concrete, is persistently wrested from him by the strongest adversary, 'the historical tradition' in the air.[16] I have been trying to point out that the uncommon 'man', the contemporary philosopher of practice, sometimes exhibits the same positivism.

The gravity of the problem is apparent if one agrees that the development of a transformative class 'consciousness' from a descriptive class 'position' is not in Marx a task engaging the ground level of consciousness. Class consciousness remains with the feeling of community that belongs to national links and political organizations, not to that other feeling of community whose structural model is the family. Although *not* identified with nature, the family here is constellated with what Marx calls 'natural exchange', which is, philosophically speaking, a 'placeholder' for use value.[17] 'Natural exchange' is contrasted to 'intercourse with society', where the word 'intercourse' (*Verkehr*) is Marx's usual word for 'commerce'. This 'intercourse' thus holds the place of the exchange leading to the production of surplus value, and it is in the area of this intercourse that the feeling of community leading to class agency must be developed. Full class agency (if there were such a thing) is not an ideological transformation of consciousness on the ground level, a desiring identity of the agents and their interest – the identity whose absence troubles Foucault and Deleuze. It is a contestatory *replacement* as well as an *appropriation* (a *supplementation*) of something that is 'artificial' to begin with – 'economic conditions of existence that separate their mode of life'. Marx's formulations show a cautious respect for the nascent critique of individual and collective subjective agency. The projects of class consciousness and of the transformation of consciousness are discontinuous issues for him. Conversely, contemporary invocations of 'libidinal economy' and desire as the determining interest, combined with the practical politics of the oppressed (under socialized capital) 'speaking for themselves', restore the category of the sovereign subject within the theory that seems most to question it.

No doubt the exclusion of the family, albeit a family belonging to a specific class formation, is part of the masculine frame within which Marxism marks its birth.[18] Historically as well as in today's global political economy, the family's role in patriarchal social relations is so heterogeneous and contested that merely replacing the family in this problematic is not going to break the frame. Nor does the solution lie in the positivist inclusion of a monolithic collectivity of 'women' in the list of the oppressed whose unfractured subjectivity allows them to speak for themselves against an equally monolithic 'same system'.

In the context of type development of a strategic, artificial and second-level 'consciousness', Marx uses the concept of the patronymic, always within the broader concept of representation as *Vertretung*: the small peasant proprietors are therefore incapable of making their class interest valid in their proper name [*im eigenen Namen*], whether through a parliament or through a convention'. The absence of the nonfamiliar artificial collective proper name is supplied by the only proper name 'historical tradition' can offer – the patronymic itself – the Name of the Father: 'Historical tradition produced the French peasants' belief that a miracle would occur, that a man *named* Napoleon would restore all their glory. And an individual turned up' – the untranslatable '*es fand sich*' (there found itself an individual?) demolishes all questions of agency or the agent's connection with his interest – 'who gave himself out to be that man' (this pretense is by contrast, his only proper agency) 'because he carried [*trägt* – the word used for the capitalist's relationship to capital] the Napoleonic Code, which commands' that 'inquiry into paternity is forbidden'. While Marx here seems to be working within a patriarchal metaphorics, one should note the textual subtlety of the passage. It is the Law of the Father (the Napoleonic Code) that paradoxically prohibits the search for the natural father. Thus, it is according to a strict observance of the historical Law of the Father that the formed yet unformed class's faith in the natural father is gainsaid.

I have dwelt so long on this passage in Marx because it spells out the inner dynamics of *Vertretung*, or representation in the political context. Representation in the economic context is *Darstellung*, the philosophical concept of representation as staging or, indeed, signification, which relates to the divided subject in an indirect way. The most obvious passage is well known: 'In the exchange relationship [*Austauschverhältnis*] of commodities their exchange-value appeared to us totally independent of their use-value. But if we subtract their use-value from the product of labour, we obtain their value, as it was just determined [*bestimmt*]. The common element which represents itself [*sich darstellt*] in the exchange relation, or the exchange value of the commodity, is thus its value.'[19]

According to Marx, under capitalism, value, as produced in necessary and surplus labor, is computed as the representation/sign of objectified labor (which is rigorously distinguished from human activity). Conversely, in the absence of a theory of exploitation as the extraction (production), appropriation and realization of (surplus) value *as representation of labor power*, capitalist exploitation must be seen as a variety of domination (the mechanics of power as such). 'The thrust of Marxism', Deleuze suggests, 'was to determine the problem [that power is more diffuse than the structure of exploitation and state formation] essentially in terms of interests (power is held by a ruling class defined by its interests)' (*FD*, p. 214).

One cannot object to this minimalist summary of Marx's project, just as one cannot ignore that, in parts of the *Anti-Oedipus*, Deleuze and Guattari build their case on a brilliant if 'poetic' grasp of Marx's *theory* of the money form. Yet we might consolidate our critique in the following way: the relationship between global capitalism (exploitation in economics) and nation-state alliances (domination in geopolitics) is so macrological that it cannot account for the micrological texture of power. To move toward such an accounting one must move toward theories of ideology – of subject formations that micrologically and often erratically operate the interests that congeal the macrologies. Such theories cannot afford to overlook the category of representation in its two senses. They must note how the staging of the world in representation – its scene of writing, its *Darstellung* – dissimulates the choice of and need for 'heroes', paternal proxies, agents of power – *Vertretung*.

My view is that radical practice should attend to this double session of representations rather than reintroduce the individual subject through totalizing concepts of power and desire. It is also my view that, in keeping the area of class practice on a second level of abstraction, Marx was in effect keeping open the (Kantian and) Hegelian critique of the individual subject as agent.[20] This view does not oblige me to ignore that, by implicitly defining the family and the mother tongue as the ground level where culture and convention seem nature's own way of organizing 'her' own subversion, Marx himself rehearses an ancient subterfuge.[21] In the context of poststructuralist claims to critical practice, this seems more recuperable than the clandestine restoration of subjective essentialism.

The reduction of Marx to a benevolent but dated figure most often serves the interest of launching a new theory of interpretation. In the Foucault–Deleuze conversation, the issue seems to be that there is no representation, no signifier (Is it to be presumed that the signifier has already been dispatched? There is, then, no sign-structure operating experience, and thus might one lay semiotics to rest?); theory is a relay of practice (thus laying problems of theoretical practice to rest) and the oppressed can know and speak for themselves. This reintroduces the constitutive subject on at least two levels: the Subject of desire and power as an irreducible methodological presupposition; and the self-proximate, if not self-identical, subject of the oppressed. Further, the intellectuals, who are neither of these S/subjects, become transparent in the relay race, for they merely report on the nonrepresented subject and analyze (without analyzing) the workings of (the unnamed Subject irreducibly presupposed by) power and desire. The produced 'transparency' marks the place of 'interest'; it is maintained by vehement denegation: 'Now this role of referee, judge, and universal witness is one which I *absolutely refuse* to adopt.' One responsibility of the critic might be to read and write so that the impossibility of such interested individualistic refusals of the institutional privileges of power bestowed on the subject is taken seriously. The refusal of the sign-system blocks the way to a developed theory of ideology. Here, too, the peculiar tone of denegation is heard. To Jacques-Alain Miller's suggestion that 'the institution is itself discursive', Foucault responds, 'Yes, if you like, but it doesn't much matter for my notion of the apparatus to be able to say that this is discursive and that isn't ... given that my problem isn't a linguistic one' (*PK*, p. 198). Why this conflation of language and discourse from the master of discourse analysis?

Edward W. Said's critique of power in Foucault as a captivating and mystifying category that allows him 'to obliterate the role of classes, the role of economics, the role of insurgency and rebellion', is most pertinent here.[22] I add to Said's analysis the notion of the surreptitious subject of power and desire marked by the transparency of the intellectual. Curiously enough, Paul Bové faults Said for emphasizing the importance of the intellectual, whereas 'Foucault's project essentially is a challenge to the leading role of both hegemonic and oppositional intellectuals'.[23] I have suggested that this 'challenge' is deceptive precisely because it ignores what Said emphasizes – the critic's institutional responsibility.

This S/subject, curiously sewn together into a transparency by denegations, belongs to the exploiters' side of the international division of labor. It is impossible for contemporary French intellectuals to imagine the kind of Power and Desire that would inhabit the unnamed subject of the Other of Europe. It is not only that everything they read, critical or uncritical, is caught within the debate of the production of that Other, supporting or critiquing the constitution of the Subject as Europe. It is also that, in the constitution of that Other of Europe, great care was taken to obliterate the textual ingredients with which such a subject could cathect, could occupy (invest?) its itinerary – not only by ideological and scientific production, but also by the institution of the law. However reductionistic an economic analysis might seem, the French intellectuals forget at their peril that this entire overdetermined enterprise was in the interest of a dynamic economic situation requiring that interests, motives (desires) and power (of knowledge) be ruthlessly dislocated. To invoke that dislocation now as a radical discovery that should make us diagnose the economic (conditions of existence that separate out 'classes' descriptively) as a piece of dated analytic machinery may well be to continue the work of that dislocation and unwittingly to help in securing 'a new balance of hegemonic relations'.[24] I shall return to this argument shortly. In the face of the possibility that the intellectual is complicit in the persistent constitution of Other as the Self's shadow, a possibility of political practice for the intellectual would be to put the economic 'under erasure', to see the economic factor as irreducibly as it reinscribes the social text, even as it is erased, however imperfectly, when it claims to be the final determinant or the transcendental signified.[25]

II

The clearest available example of such epistemic violence is the remotely orchestrated, far-flung, and heterogeneous project to constitute the colonial subject as Other. This project is also the asymmetrical obliteration of the trace of that Other in its precarious Subject-ivity. It is well known that Foucault locates epistemic violence, a complete overhaul of the episteme, in the redefinition of sanity at the end of the European eighteenth century.[26] But what if that particular redefinition was only a part of the narrative of history in Europe as well as in the colonies? What if the two projects of epistemic overhaul worked as dislocated and unacknowledged parts of a vast two-handed engine? Perhaps it is no more than to ask that the subtext of the palimpsestic narrative of imperialism be recognized as 'subjugated knowledge', 'a whole set of knowledges that have been disqualified as inadequate to their task or insufficiently elaborated: naive knowledges, located low down on the hierarchy, beneath the required level of cognition or scientificity' (PK, p. 82).

This is not to describe 'the way things really were' or to privilege the narrative of history as imperialism as the best version of history.[26] It is, rather, to offer an account of how an explanation and narrative of reality was established as the normative one. To elaborate on this, let us consider briefly the underpinnings of the British codification of Hindu Law.

First, a few disclaimers: in the United States the third-worldism currently afloat in humanistic disciplines is often openly ethnic. I was born in India and received my primary, secondary and university education there, including two years of graduate work. My Indian example could thus be seen as a nostalgic investigation of the lost roots of my own identity. Yet even as I know that one cannot freely enter the thickets of 'motivations', I would maintain that my chief project is to point out the positivist-idealist variety of such nostalgia. I turn to Indian material because, in the absence of advanced disciplinary training, that accident of birth and education has provided me with a *sense* of the historical canvas, a hold on some of the pertinent languages that are useful tools for a *bricoleur*, especially when armed with the Marxist skepticism of concrete experience as the final arbiter and a critique of disciplinary formations. Yet the Indian case cannot be taken as representative of all countries, nations, cultures and the like that may be invoked as the Other of Europe as Self.

Here, then, is a schematic summary of the epistemic violence of the codification of Hindu Law. If it clarifies the notion of epistemic violence, my final discussion of widow-sacrifice may gain added significance.

At the end of the eighteenth century, Hindu law, insofar as it can be described as a unitary system, operated in terms of four texts that 'staged' a four-part episteme defined by the subject's use of memory: *sruti* (the heard), *smriti* (the remembered), *sastra* (the learned-from-another) and *vyavahara* (the performed-in-exchange). The origins of what had been heard and what was remembered were not necessarily continuous or identical. Every invocation of *sruti* technically recited (or reopened) the event of originary 'hearing' or revelation. The second two texts – the learned and the performed – were seen as dialectically continuous. Legal theorists and practitioners were not in any given case certain if this structure described the body of law or four ways of settling a dispute. The legitimation of the polymorphous structure of legal performance, 'internally' noncoherent and open at both ends, through a binary vision, is the narrative of codification I offer as an example of epistemic violence.

The narrative of the stabilization and codification of Hindu law is less well known than the story of Indian education, so it might be well to start there.[28] Consider the often-quoted programmatic lines from Macaulay's infamous 'Minute on Indian education' (1835): 'We must at present do our best to form a class who may be interpreters between us and the millions whom we govern; a class of persons, Indian in blood and colour, but English in taste, in opinions, in morals, and in intellect. To that class we may leave it to refine the vernacular dialects of the country, to enrich those dialects with terms of science borrowed from the Western nomenclature, and to render them by degrees fit vehicles for conveying knowledge to the great mass of the population.'[29] The education of colonial subjects complements their production in law. One effect of establishing a version of the British system was the development of an uneasy separation between disciplinary formation in Sanskrit studies and the native, now alternative, tradition of Sanskrit 'high culture'. Within the former, the cultural explanations generated by authoritative scholars matched the epistemic violence of the legal project.

I locate here the founding of the Asiatic Society of Bengal in 1784, the Indian Institute at Oxford in 1883, and the analytic and taxonomic work of scholars like Arthur Macdonnell and Arthur Berriedale Keith, who were both colonial administrators and organizers of the matter of Sanskrit. From their confident utilitarian-hegemonic plans for students and scholars of Sanskrit, it is impossible to guess at either the aggressive repression of Sanskrit in the general educational framework or the increasing 'feudalization' of the performative use of Sanskrit in the everyday life of Brahmanic-hegemonic India.[30] A version of history was gradually established in which the Brahmans were shown to have the same intentions as (thus providing the legitimation for) the codifying British: 'In order to preserve Hindu society intact [the] successors [of the original Brahmans] had to reduce everything to writing and make them more and more rigid. And that is what has preserved Hindu society in spite of a succession of political upheavals and foreign invasions.'[31] This is the 1925 verdict of Mahamahopadhyaya Haraprasad Shastri, learned Indian Sanskritist, a brilliant representative of the indigenous elite within colonial production, who was asked to write several chapters of a 'History of Bengal' projected by the private secretary to the governor general of Bengal in 1916.[32] To signal the asymmetry in the relationship between authority and explanation (depending on the race-class of the authority), compare this 1928 remark by Edward Thompson, English intellectual: 'Hinduism was what it seemed to be ... It was a higher civilization that won [against it], both with Akbar and the English.'[33] And add this, from a letter by an English soldier-scholar in the 1890s: 'The study of Sanskrit, "the language of the gods", has afforded me intense enjoyment during the last 25 years of my life in India, but it has not, I am thankful to say, led me, *as it has some*, to give up a hearty belief in our own grand religion.'[34]

These authorities are *the very best* of the sources for the nonspecialist French intellectual's entry into the civilization of the Other.[35] I am, however, not referring to intellectuals and scholars of postcolonial production, like Shastri, when I say that the Other as Subject is inaccessible to Foucault and Deleuze. I am thinking of the general nonspecialist, nonacademic population across the class spectrum, for whom the episteme operates its silent programming function. Without considering the map of exploitation, on what grid of 'oppression' would they place this motley crew?

Let us now move to consider the margins (one can just as well say the silent, silenced center) of the circuit marked out by this epistemic violence, men and women among the illiterate peasantry, the tribals, the lowest strata of the urban subproletariat. According to Foucault and Deleuze (in the First World, under the standardization and regimentation of socialized capital, though they do not seem to recognize this) the oppressed, if given the chance (the problem of representation cannot be bypassed here), and on the way to solidarity through alliance politics (a Marxist thematic is at work here), *can speak and know their conditions*. We must now confront the following question: on the other side of the international division of labor from socialized capital, inside *and* outside the circuit of the epistemic violence of imperialist law and education supplementing an earlier economic text, *can the subaltern speak?*

Antonio Gramsci's work on the 'subaltern classes' extends the class-position/class-consciousness argument isolated in *The Eighteenth Brumaire*. Perhaps because Gramsci criticizes the vanguardistic position of the Leninist intellectual, he is concerned with the intellectual's role in the subaltern's cultural and political movement into the hegemony. This movement must be made to determine the production of history as narrative (of truth). In texts such as 'The Southern question', Gramsci considers the movement of historical-political economy in Italy within what can be seen as an allegory of reading taken from or prefiguring an international division of labor.[36] Yet an account of the phased development of the subaltern is thrown out of joint when his cultural macrology is operated, however remotely, by the epistemic interference with legal and disciplinary definitions accompanying the imperialist project. When I move, at the end of this essay, to the question of woman as subaltern, I will suggest that the possibility of collectivity itself is persistently foreclosed through the manipulation of female agency.

The first part of my proposition – that the phased development of the subaltern is complicated by the imperialist project – is confronted by a collective of intellectuals who may be called the 'Subaltern Studies' group.[37] They *must* ask, Can the subaltern speak? Here we are within Foucault's own discipline of history and with people who acknowledge his influence. Their project is to rethink Indian colonial historiography from the perspective of the discontinuous chain of peasant insurgencies during the colonial occupation. This is indeed the problem of 'the permission to narrate' discussed by Said.[38] As Ranajit Guha argues,

> The historiography of Indian nationalism has for a long time been dominated by elitism – colonialist elitism and bourgeois-nationalist elitism ... shar[ing] the prejudice that the making of the Indian nation and the development of the consciousness – nationalism – which confirmed this process were exclusively or predominantly elite achievements. In the colonialist and neo-colonialist historiographies these achievements are credited to British colonial rulers, administrators, policies, institutions and culture; in the nationalist and neo-nationalist writings – to Indian elite personalities, institutions, activities and ideas.[39]

Certain varieties of the Indian elite are at best native informants for first-world intellectuals interested in the voice of the Other. But one must nevertheless insist that the colonized subaltern *subject* is irretrievably heterogeneous.

Against the indigenous elite we may set what Guha calls 'the *politics of the people*', both outside ('This was an *autonomous* domain, for it neither originated from elite politics nor did its existence depend on the latter') and inside ('it continued to operate vigorously in spite of [colonialism], adjusting itself to the conditions prevailing under the Raj and in many respects developing entirely new strains in both form and content') the circuit of colonial production.[40] I cannot entirely endorse this insistence on determinate vigor and full autonomy, for practical historiographic exigencies will not allow such endorsements to privilege subaltern consciousness. Against the possible charge that his approach is essentialist, Guha constructs a definition of the people (the place of that essence) that can be only an identity-in-differential. He proposes a dynamic stratification grid describing colonial social production at large. Even the third group on the list, the buffer group, as it were, between the people and the great macrostructural dominant groups, is itself defined as a place of in-betweenness, what Derrida has described as an '*antre*':[41]

elite {
1. Dominant foreign groups.
2. Dominant indigenous groups on the all-India level.
3. Dominant indigenous groups at the regional and local levels.
4. The terms "people" and "subaltern classes" have been used as synonymous throughout this note. The social groups and elements included in this category represent *the demographic difference between the total Indian population and all those whom we have described as the "elite."*

Consider the third item on this list – the *antre* of situational indeterminacy these careful historians presuppose as they grapple with the question, Can the subaltern speak? '*Taken as a whole and in the abstract* this ... category ... was *heterogeneous* in its composition and, thanks to the uneven character of regional economic and social developments, *differed from area to area*. The same class or element which was dominant in one area ... could be among the dominated in another. This could and did create many ambiguities and contradictions in attitudes and alliances, especially among the lowest strata of the rural gentry, impoverished landlords, rich peasants and upper-middle peasants all of whom belonged, *ideally speaking*, to the category of "people" or "subaltern classes."[42]

'The task of research' projected here is 'to investigate, identify and measure the *specific* nature and degree of the *deviation* of [the] elements [constituting item 3] from the ideal and situate it historically'. 'Investigate, identify, and measure the specific': a program could hardly be more essentialist and taxonomic. Yet a curious methodological imperative is at work. I have argued that, in the Foucault–Deleuze conversation, a postrepresentationalist vocabulary hides an essentialist agenda. In subaltern studies, because of the violence of imperialist epistemic, social and disciplinary inscription, a project understood in essentialist terms must traffic in a radical textual practice of differences. The object of the group's investigation, in the case not even of the people as such but of the floating buffer zone of the regional elite-subaltern is a *deviation* from an *ideal* – the people or subaltern – which is itself defined as a difference from the elite. It is toward this structure that the research is oriented, a predicament rather different from the self-diagnosed transparency of the first-world radical intellectual. What taxonomy can fix such a space? Whether or not they themselves perceive it – in fact Guha sees his definition of 'the people' within the master–slave dialectic – their text articulates the difficult task of rewriting its own conditions of impossibility as the conditions of its possibility.

'At the *regional and local levels* [the dominant indigenous groups] . . . if belonging to social strata hierarchically inferior to those of the dominant all-India groups still *acted in the interests of the latter and not in conformity to interests corresponding truly to their own social being*'. When these writers speak, in their essentializing language, of a gap between interest and action in the intermediate group, their conclusions are closer to Marx than to the self-conscious naiveté of Deleuze's pronouncement on the issue. Guha, like Marx, speaks of interest in terms of the social rather than the libidinal being. The Name-of-the-Father imagery in *The Eighteenth Brumaire* can help to emphasize that, on the level of class or group action, 'true correspondence to own being' is as artificial or social as the patronymic.

So much for the intermediate group marked in item 3. For the 'true' subaltern group, whose identity is its difference, there is no unrepresentable subaltern subject that can know and speak itself; the intellectual's solution is not to abstain from representation. The problem is that the subject's itinerary has not been traced so as to offer an object of seduction to the representing intellectual. In the slightly dated language of the Indian group, the question becomes, How can we touch the consciousness of the people, even as we investigate their politics? With what voice-consciousness can the subaltern speak? Their project, after all, is to rewrite the development of the consciousness of the Indian nation. The planned discontinuity of imperialism rigorously distinguishes this project, however old-fashioned its articulation, from 'rendering visible the medical and juridical mechanisms that surrounded the story [of Pierre Rivière]'. Foucault is correct in suggesting that 'to make visible the unseen can also mean a change of level, addressing oneself to a layer of material which had hitherto had no pertinence for history and which had not been recognized as having any moral, aesthetic or historical value'. It is the slippage from rendering visible the mechanism to rendering vocal the individual, both avoiding 'any kind of analysis of [the subject] whether psychological, psychoanalytical or linguistic', that is consistently troublesome (*PK*, pp. 49–50).

The critique by Ajit K. Chaudhury, a West Bengali Marxist, of Guha's search for the subaltern consciousness can be seen as a moment of the production process that includes the subaltern. Chaudhury's perception that the Marxist view of the transformation of consciousness involves the *knowledge* of social relations seems to me, in principle, astute. Yet the heritage of the positivist ideology that has appropriated orthodox Marxism obliges him to add this rider: 'This is not to belittle the importance of understanding peasants' consciousness or workers' consciousness *in its pure form*. This enriches our knowledge of the peasant and the worker and, possibly, throws light on how a particular mode takes on different forms in different regions, *which is considered a problem of second-order importance in classical Marxism*.'[43]

This variety of 'internationalist' Marxism, which believes in a pure, retrievable form of consciousness only to dismiss it, thus closing off what in Marx remain moments of productive bafflement, can at once be the object of Foucault's and Deleuze's rejection of Marxism *and* the source of the critical motivation of the Subaltern Studies group. All three are united in the assumption that there *is* a pure form of consciousness. On the French scene, there is a shuffling of signifiers: 'the unconscious', or 'the subject-in-oppression' clandestinely fills the space of 'the pure form of consciousness'. In orthodox 'internationalist' intellectual Marxism, whether in the First World or the Third, the pure form of consciousness remains an idealistic bedrock which, dismissed as a second-order problem, often earns it the reputation of racism and sexism. In the Subaltern Studies group it needs development according to the unacknowledged terms of its own articulation.

For such an articulation, a developed theory of ideology can again be most useful. In a critique such as Chaudhury's, the association of 'consciousness' with 'knowledge' omits the crucial middle term of 'ideological production': 'Consciousness, according to Lenin, is associated with a *knowledge* of the interrelationships between different classes and groups; i.e., a knowledge of the materials that constitute society. . . . These definitions acquire a meaning only within the problematic within a definite knowledge object – to *understand* change in history, or specifically, change from one mode to another, *keeping the question of the specificity of a particular mode out of the focus*.'[44]

Pierre Macherey provides the following formula for the interpretation of ideology: 'What is important in a work is what it does not say. This is not the same as the careless notation "what it refuses to say", although that would in itself be interesting: a method might be built on it, with the task of *measuring silences*, whether acknowledged or unacknowledged. But rather this, what the work *cannot* say is important, because there the elaboration of the utterance is carried out, in a sort of journey to silence.'[45] Macherey's ideas can be developed in directions he would be unlikely to follow. Even as he writes, ostensibly, of the literariness of the literature of European provenance, he articulates a method applicable to the social text of imperialism, somewhat against the grain of his own argument. Although the notion 'what it refuses to say' might be careless for a literary work, something like a collective ideological *refusal* can be diagnosed for the codifying legal practice of imperialism. This would open the field for a political-economic and multidisciplinary ideological reinscription of the terrain. Because this is a 'worlding of the world' on a second level of abstraction, a concept of refusal becomes plausible here. The archival, historiographic, disciplinary-critical and, inevitably, interventionist work involved here is indeed a task of 'measuring silences'. This can be a description of 'investigating, identifying, and measuring ... the *deviation*' from an ideal that is irreducibly differential.

When we come to the concomitant question of the consciousness of the subaltern, the notion of what the work *cannot* say becomes important. In the semioses of the social text, elaborations of insurgency stand in the place of 'the utterance'. The sender – 'the peasant' – is marked only as a pointer to an irretrievable consciousness. As for the receiver, we must ask who is 'the real receiver' of an 'insurgency'? The historian, transforming 'insurgency' into 'text for knowledge', is only one 'receiver' of any collectively intended social act. With no possibility of nostalgia for that lost origin, the historian must suspend (as far as possible) the clamor of his or her own consciousness (or consciousness-effect, as operated by disciplinary training), so that the elaboration of the insurgency, packaged with an insurgent-consciousness, does not freeze into an 'object of investigation', or, worse yet, a model for imitation. 'The subject' implied by the texts of insurgency can only serve as a counterpossibility for the narrative sanctions granted to the colonial subject in the dominant groups. The postcolonial intellectuals learn that their privilege is their loss. In this they are a paradigm of the intellectuals.

It is well known that the notion of the feminine (rather than the subaltern of imperialism) has been used in a similar way within deconstructive criticism and within certain varieties of feminist criticism.[46] In the former case, a figure of 'woman' is at issue, one whose minimal predication as indeterminate is already available to the phallocentric tradition. Subaltern historiography raises questions of method that would prevent it from using such a ruse. For the 'figure' of woman, the relationship between woman and silence can be plotted by women themselves; race and class differences are subsumed under that charge. Subaltern historiography must confront the impossibility of such gestures. The narrow epistemic violence of imperialism gives us an imperfect allegory of the general violence that is the possibility of an episteme.[47]

Within the effaced itinerary of the subaltern subject, the track of sexual difference is doubly effaced. The question is not of female participation in insurgency, or the ground rules of the sexual division of labor, for both of which there is 'evidence'. It is, rather, that, both as object of colonialist historiography and as subject of insurgency, the ideological construction of gender keeps the male dominant. If, in the context of colonial production, the subaltern has no history and cannot speak, the subaltern as female is even more deeply in shadow.

The contemporary international division of labor is a displacement of the divided field of nineteenth-century territorial imperialism. Put simply, a group of countries, generally first-world, are in the position of investing capital; another group, generally third-world, provide the field for investment, both through the comprador indigenous capitalists and through their ill-protected and shifting labor force. In the interest of maintaining the circulation and growth of industrial capital (and of the concomitant task of administration within nineteenth-century territorial imperialism), transportation, law and standarized education systems were developed – even as local industries were destroyed, land distribution was rearranged, and raw material was transferred to the colonizing country. With so-called decolonization, the growth of multinational capital, and the relief of the administrative charge, 'development' does not now involve wholesale legislation and establishing educational *systems* in a comparable way. This impedes the growth of consumerism in the comprador countries. With modern telecommunications and the emergence of advanced capitalist economies at the two edges of Asia, maintaining the international division of labor serves to keep the supply of cheap labor in the comprador countries.

Human labor is not, of course, intrinsically 'cheap' or 'expensive'. An absence of labor laws (or a discriminatory enforcement of them), a totalitarian state (often entailed by development and modernization in the periphery), and minimal subsistence requirements on the part of the worker will ensure it. To keep this crucial item intact, the urban proletariat in comprador countries must not be systematically trained in the ideology of consumerism (parading as the philosophy of a classless society) that, against all odds, prepares the ground for resistance through the coalition politics Foucault mentions (*FD*, p. 216). This separation from the ideology of consumerism is increasingly exacerbated by the proliferating phenomena of international subcontracting. 'Under this strategy, manufacturers based in developed countries subcontract the most labor intensive stages of production, for example, sewing or assembly, to the Third World nations where labor is cheap. Once assembled, the multinational re-imports the goods – under generous tariff exemptions – to the developed country *instead of selling them to the local market.*' Here the link to training in consumerism is almost snapped. 'While global recession has markedly slowed trade and investment worldwide since 1979, international subcontracting has boomed. ... In these cases, multinationals are freer to resist militant workers, revolutionary upheavals, and even economic downturns.'[48]

Class mobility is increasingly lethargic in the comprador theaters. Not surprisingly, some members of *indigenous dominant* groups in comprador countries, members of the local bourgeoisie, find the language of alliance politics attractive. Identifying with forms of resistance plausible in advanced capitalist countries is often of a piece with that elitist bent of bourgeois historiography described by Ranajit Guha.

Belief in the plausibility of global alliance politics is prevalent among women of dominant social groups interested in 'international feminism' in the comprador countries. At the other end of the scale, those most separated from any possibility of an alliance among 'women, prisoners, conscripted soldiers, hospital patients, and homosexuals' (FD, p. 216) are the females of the urban subproletariat. In their case, the denial and withholding of consumerism and the structure of exploitation is compounded by patriarchal social relations. On the other side of the international division of labor, the subject of exploitation cannot know and speak the text of female exploitation even if the absurdity of the nonrepresenting intellectual making space for her to speak is achieved. The woman is doubly in shadow.

Yet even this does not encompass the heterogeneous Other. Outside (though not completely so) the circuit of the *international* division of labor, there are people whose consciousness we cannot grasp if we close off our benevolence by constructing a homogeneous Other referring only to our own place in the seat of the Same or the Self. Here are subsistence farmers, unorganized peasant labor, the tribals and the communities of zero workers on the street or in the countryside. To confront them is not to represent (*vertreten*) them but to learn to represent (*darstellen*) ourselves. This argument would take us into a critique of a disciplinary anthropology and the relationship between elementary pedagogy and disciplinary formation. It would also question the implicit demand, made by intellectuals who choose a 'naturally articulate' subject of oppression, that such a subject come through history as a foreshortened mode-of-production narrative.

That Deleuze and Foucault ignore both the epistemic violence of imperialism and the international division of labor would matter less if they did not, in closing, touch on third-world issues. But in France it is impossible to ignore the problem of the *tiers monde*, the inhabitants of the erstwhile French African colonies. Deleuze limits his consideration of the Third World to these old local and regional indigenous elite who are, ideally, subaltern. In this context, references to the maintenance of the surplus army of labor fall into reverse-ethnic sentimentality. Since he is speaking of the heritage of nineteenth-century territorial imperialism, his reference is to the nation-state rather than the globalizing center: 'French capitalism needs greatly a floating signifier of unemployment. In this perspective, we begin to see the unity of the forms of repression: restrictions on immigration, once it is acknowledged that the most difficult and thankless jobs go to immigrant workers; repression in the factories, because the French must reacquire the "taste" for increasingly harder work; the struggle against youth and the repression of the educational system' (FD, pp. 211–12). This is an acceptable analysis. Yet it shows again that the Third World can enter the resistance program of an alliance politics directed against a '*unified* repression' only when it is confined to the third-world groups that are directly accessible to the First World.[49] This benevolent first-world appropriation and reinscription of the Third World as an Other is the founding characteristic of much third-worldism in the US human sciences today.

Foucault continues the critique of Marxism by invoking geographical discontinuity. The real mark of 'geographical (geopolitical) discontinuity' is the international division of labor. But Foucault uses the term to distinguish between exploitation (extraction and appropriation of surplus value; read, the field of Marxist analysis) and domination ('power' studies) and to suggest the latter's greater potential for resistance based on alliance politics. He cannot acknowledge that such a monist and unified access to a conception of 'power' (methodologically presupposing a Subject-of-power) is made possible by a certain stage in exploitation, for his vision of geographical discontinuity is geopolitically specific to the First World:

> This geographical discontinuity of which you speak might mean perhaps the following: as soon as we struggle against *exploitation*, the proletariat not only leads the struggle but also defines its targets, its methods, its places and its instruments; and to ally oneself with the proletariat is to consolidate with its positions, its ideology, it is to take up again the motives for their combat. This means total immersion [in the Marxist project]. But if it is against *power* that one struggles, then all those who acknowledge it as intolerable can begin the struggle wherever they find themselves and in terms of their own activity (or passivity). In engaging in this struggle that is *their own*, whose objectives they clearly understand and whose methods they can determine, they enter into the revolutionary process. As allies of the proletariat, to be sure, because power is exercised the way it is in order to maintain capitalist exploitation. They genuinely serve the cause of the proletariat by fighting in those places where they find themselves oppressed. Women, prisoners, conscripted soldiers, hospital patients, and homosexuals have now begun a specific struggle against the particular form of power, the constraints and controls, that are exercised over them. (*FD*, p. 216)

This is an admirable program of localized resistance. Where possible, this model of resistance is not an alternative to, but can complement, macrological struggles along 'Marxist' lines. Yet if its situation is universalized, it accommodates unacknowledged privileging of the subject. Without a theory of ideology, it can lead to a dangerous utopianism.

Foucault is a brilliant thinker of power-in-spacing, but the awareness of the topographical reinscription of imperialism does not inform his presuppositions. He is taken in by the restricted version of the West produced by that reinscription and thus helps to consolidate its effects. Notice the omission of the fact, in the following passage, that the new mechanism of power in the seventeenth and eighteenth centuries (the extraction of surplus value without extraeconomic coercion is its Marxist description) is secured *by means of* territorial imperialism – the Earth and its products – 'elsewhere'. The representation of sovereignty is crucial in those theaters: 'In the seventeenth and eighteenth centuries, we have the production of an important phenomenon, the emergence, or rather the invention, of a new mechanism of power possessed of highly specific procedural techniques ... which is also, I believe, absolutely incompatible with the relations of sovereignty. This new mechanism of power is more dependent upon bodies and what they do than the Earth and its products' (*PK*, p. 104).

Because of a blind spot regarding the first wave of 'geographical discontinuity', Foucault can remain impervious to its second wave in the middle decades of our own century, identifying it simply 'with the collapse of Fascism and the decline of Stalinism' (*PK*, p. 87). Here is Mike Davis's alternative view: 'It was rather the global logic of counter-revolutionary violence which created conditions for the peaceful economic interdependence of a chastened Atlantic imperialism under American leadership. . . . It was multi-national military integration under the slogan of collective security against the USSR which preceded and quickened the inter-penetration of the major capitalist economies, making possible the new era of commercial liberalism which flowered between 1958 and 1973.'[50]

It is within the emergence of this 'new mechanism of power' that we must read the fixation on national scenes, the resistance to economics, and the emphasis on concepts like power and desire that privilege micrology. Davis continues: 'This quasi-absolutist centralization of strategic military power by the United States was to allow an enlightened and flexible subordinancy for its principal satraps. In particular, it proved highly accommodating to the residual imperialist pretensions of the French and British . . . with each keeping up a strident ideological mobilization against communism all the while.' While taking precautions against such unitary notions as 'France', it must be said that such unitary notions as '*the* workers' struggle', or such unitary pronouncements as 'like power, resistance is multiple and can be integrated in global strategies' (*PK*, p. 142), seem interpretable by way of Davis's narrative. I am not suggesting, as does Paul Bové, that 'for a displaced and homeless people [the Palestinians] assaulted militarily and culturally . . . a question [such as Foucault's 'to engage in politics . . . is to try to know with the greatest possible honesty whether the revolution is desirable'] is a foolish luxury of Western wealth'.[51] I am suggesting, rather, that to buy a self-contained version of the West is to ignore its production by the imperialist project.

Sometimes it seems as if the very brilliance of Foucault's analysis of the centuries of European imperialism produces a miniature version of that heterogeneous phenomenon: management of space – but by doctors; development of administrations – but in asylums; considerations of the periphery – but in terms of the insane, prisoners and children. The clinic, the asylum, the prison, the university – all seem to be screen-allegories that foreclose a reading of the broader narratives of imperialism. (One could open a similar discussion of the ferocious motif of 'deterritorialization' in Deleuze and Guattari.) 'One can perfectly well not talk about something because one doesn't know about it,' Foucault might murmur (*PK*, p. 66). Yet we have already spoken of the sanctioned ignorance that every critic of imperialism must chart.

III

On the general level on which US academics and students take 'influence' from

France, one encounters the following understanding: Foucault deals with real history, real politics and real social problems; Derrida is inaccessible, esoteric and textualistic. The reader is probably well acquainted with this received idea. 'That [Derrida's] own work', Terry Eagleton writes, 'has been grossly unhistorical, politically evasive and in practice oblivious to language as "discourse" [language in function] is not to be denied.'[52] Eagleton goes on to recommend Foucault's study of 'discursive practices'. Perry Anderson constructs a related history: 'With Derrida, the self-cancellation of structuralism latent in the recourse to music or madness in Lévi-Strauss or Foucault is consummated. With no commitment to exploration of social realities at all, Derrida had little compunction in undoing the constructions of these two, convicting them both of a "nostalgia of origins" – Rousseauesque or pre-Socratic, respectively – and asking what right either had to assume, on their own premises, the validity of their discourses.'[53]

This paper is committed to the notion that, whether in defense of Derrida or not, a nostalgia for lost origins can be detrimental to the exploration of social realities within the critique of imperialism. Indeed, the brilliance of Anderson's misreading does not prevent him from seeing precisely the problem I emphasize in Foucault: 'Foucault struck the characteristically prophetic note when he declared in 1966: "Man is in the process of perishing as the being of language continues to shine ever more brightly upon our horizon." But who is the "we" to perceive or possess such a horizon?' Anderson does not see the encroachment of the unacknowledged Subject of the West in the later Foucault, a Subject that presides by disavowal. He sees Foucault's attitude in the usual way, as the disappearance of the knowing Subject as such; and he further sees in Derrida the final development of that tendency: 'In the hollow of the pronoun [we] lies the aporia of the programme.'[54] Consider, finally, Said's plangent aphorism, which betrays a profound misapprehension of the notion of 'textuality': 'Derrida's criticism moves us *into* the text, Foucault's *in* and *out*.'[55]

I have tried to argue that the substantive concern for the politics of the oppressed which often accounts for Foucault's appeal can hide a privileging of the intellectual and of the 'concrete' subject of oppression that, in fact, compounds the appeal. Conversely, though it is not my intention here to counter the specific view of Derrida promoted by these influential writers, I will discuss a few aspects of Derrida's work that retain a long-term usefulness for people outside the First World. This is not an apology. Derrida is hard to read; his real object of investigation is classical philosophy. Yet he is less dangerous when understood than the first-world intellectual masquerading as the absent nonrepresenter who lets the oppressed speak for themselves.

I will consider a chapter that Derrida composed twenty years ago: 'Of grammatology as a positive science' (*OG*, pp. 74–93). In this chapter Derrida confronts the issue of whether 'deconstruction' can lead to an adequate practice, whether critical or political. The question is how to keep the ethnocentric Subject from establishing itself by selectively defining an Other. This is not a program for the Subject as such; rather, it is a program for the benevolent *Western* intellectual.

For those of us who feel that the 'subject' has a history and that the task of the first-world subject of knowledge in our historical moment is to resist and critique 'recognition' of the Third World through 'assimilation', this specificity is crucial. In order to advance a factual rather than a pathetic critique of the European intellectual's ethnocentric impulse, Derrida admits that he cannot ask the 'first' questions that must be answered to establish the grounds of his argument. He does not declare that grammatology can 'rise above' (Frank Lentricchia's phrase) mere empiricism; for, like empiricism, it cannot ask first questions. Derrida thus aligns 'grammatological' knowledge *with the same problems* as empirical investigation. 'Deconstruction' is not, therefore a new word for 'ideological demystification'. Like 'empirical investigation ... tak[ing] shelter in the field of grammatological knowledge' obliges 'operat[ing] through "examples"' (*OG*, p. 75).

The examples Derrida lays out – to show the limits of grammatology as a positive science – come from the appropriate ideological self-justification of an imperialist project. In the European seventeenth century, he writes, there were three kinds of 'prejudices' operating in histories of writing which constituted a 'symptom of the crisis of European consciousness' (*OG*, p. 75): the 'theological prejudice', the 'Chinese prejudice' and the 'hieroglyphist prejudice'. The first can be indexed as: God wrote a primitive or natural script: Hebrew or Greek. The second: Chinese is a perfect *blueprint* for philosophical writing, but it is only a blueprint. True philosophical writing is 'independent[t] with regard to history' (*OG*, p. 79) and will sublate Chinese into an easy-to-learn script that will supersede actual Chinese. The third: that Egyptian script is too sublime to be deciphered. The first prejudice preserves the 'actuality' of Hebrew or Greek, the last two ('rational' and 'mystical', respectively) collude to support the first, where the center of the logos is seen as the Judaeo-Christian God (the appropriation of the Hellenic Other through assimilation is an earlier story – a 'prejudice' still sustained in efforts to give the cartography of the Judaeo-Christian myth the status of geopolitical history:

> The concept of Chinese writing thus functioned as a sort of *European hallucination.* ... This functioning obeyed a rigorous necessity. ... It was not disturbed by the knowledge of Chinese script... which was then available. ... A *"hieroglyphist prejudice"* had produced the same effect of *interested blindness.* Far from proceeding ... from ethnocentric scorn, the occultation takes the form of an hyperbolical admiration. We have not finished demonstrating the necessity of this pattern. Our century is not free from it; each time that ethnocentrism is precipitately and ostentatiously reversed, some effort silently hides behind all the spectacular effects to *consolidate an inside* and to draw from it some domestic benefit. (*OG*, p. 80; Derrida italicizes only 'hieroglyphist prejudice')

Derrida proceeds to offer two characteristic possibilities for solutions to the problem of the European Subject, which seeks to produce an Other that would consolidate an inside, its own subject status. What follows is an account of the complicity between writing, the opening of domestic and civil society, and the structures of desire, power and capitalization. Derrida then discloses the vulnerability of his own desire to conserve something that is, paradoxically, both ineffable and nontranscendental. In critiquing the production of the colonial subject, this ineffable, nontranscendental ('historical') place is cathected by the subaltern subject.

Derrida closes the chapter by showing again that the project of grammatology is obliged to develop *within* the discourse of presence. It is not just a critique of presence but an awareness of the itinerary of the discourse of presence in one's *own* critique, a vigilance precisely against too great a claim for transparency. The word 'writing' as the name of the object and model of grammatology is a practice 'only within the *historical* closure, that is to say within the limits of science and philosophy' (*OG*, p. 93).

Derrida here makes Nietzschean, philosophical and psychoanalytic, rather than specifically political, choices to suggest a critique of European ethnocentrism in the constitution of the Other. As a postcolonial intellectual, I am not troubled that he does not *lead* me (as Europeans inevitably seem to do) to the specific path that such a critique makes necessary. It is more important to me that, as a European philosopher, he articulates the *European* Subject's tendency to constitute the Other as marginal to ethnocentrism and locates *that* as the problem with all logocentric and therefore also all grammatological endeavours (since the main thesis of the chapter is the complicity between the two). *Not* a general problem, but a *European* problem. It is within the context of this ethnocentricism that he tries so desperately to demote the Subject of thinking or knowledge as to say that '*thought* is ... the blank part of the text' (*OG*, p. 93); that which is thought is, if blank, still *in the text* and must be consigned to the Other of history. That inaccessible blankness circumscribed by an interpretable text is what a postcolonial critic of imperialism would like to see developed within the European enclosure as *the* place of the production of theory. The postcolonial critics and intellectuals can attempt to displace their own production only by presupposing that *text-inscribed* blankness. To render thought or the thinking subject transparent or invisible seems, by contrast, to hide the relentless recognition of the Other by assimilation. It is in the interest of such cautions that Derrida does not invoke 'letting the other(s) speak for himself' but rather invokes an 'appeal' to or 'call' to the 'quite-other' (*tout-autre* as opposed to a self-consolidating other), of 'rendering *delirious* that interior voice that is the voice of the other in us'.[56]

Derrida calls the ethnocentrism of the European science of writing in the late seventeenth and early eighteenth centuries a symptom of the general crisis of European consciousness. It is, of course, part of a greater symptom, or perhaps the crisis itself, the slow turn from feudalism to capitalism via the first waves of capitalist imperialism. The itinerary of recognition through assimilation of the Other can be more interestingly traced, it seems to me, in the imperialist constitution of the colonial subject than in repeated incursions into psychoanalysis or the 'figure' of woman, though the importance of these two interventions *within* deconstruction should not be minimized. Derrida has not moved (or perhaps cannot move) into that arena.

Whatever the reasons for this specific absence, what I find useful is the sustained and developing work on the *mechanics* of the constitution of the Other; we can use it to much greater analytic and interventionist advantage than invocations of the *authenticity* of the Other. On this level, what remains useful in Foucault is the mechanics of disciplinarization and institutionalization, the constitution, as it were, of the colonizer. Foucault does not relate it to any version, early or late, proto- or post-, of imperialism. They are of great usefulness to intellectuals concerned with the decay of the West. Their seduction for them, and fearfulness for us, is that they might allow the complicity of the investigating subject (male or female professional) to disguise itself in transparency.

IV

Can the subaltern speak? What must the elite do to watch out for the continuing construction of the subaltern? The question of 'woman' seems most problematic in this context. Clearly, if you are poor, black and female you get it in three ways. If, however, this formulation is moved from the first-world context into the postcolonial (which is not identical with the third-world) context, the description 'black' or 'of color' loses persuasive significance. The necessary stratification of colonial subject-constitution in the first phase of capitalist imperialism makes 'color' useless as an emancipatory signifier. Confronted by the ferocious standardizing benevolence of most US and Western European human-scientific radicalism (recognition by assimilation), the progressive though heterogeneous withdrawal of consumerism in the comprador periphery, and the exclusion of the margins of even the center periphery articulation (the 'true and differential subaltern'), the analogue of class-consciousness rather than race-consciousness in this area seems historically, disciplinarily and practically forbidden by Right and Left alike. It is not just a question of a *double* displacement, as it is not simply the problem of finding a psychoanalytic allegory that can accommodate the third-world woman with the first.[1]

The cautions I have just expressed are valid only if we are speaking of the subaltern woman's consciousness – or, more acceptably, subject. Reporting on, or better still, participating in, antisexist work among women of color or women in class oppression in the First World or the Third World is undeniably on the agenda. We should also welcome all the information retrieval in these silenced areas that is taking place in anthropology, political science, history and sociology. Yet the assumption and construction of a consciousness or subject sustains such work and will, in the long run, cohere with the work of imperialist subject-constitution, mingling epistemic violence with the advancement of learning and civilization. And the subaltern woman will be as mute as ever.[57]

In so fraught a field, it is not easy to ask the question of the consciousness of the subaltern woman; it is thus all the more necessary to remind pragmatic radicals that such a question is not an idealist red herring. Though all feminist or antisexist projects cannot be reduced to this one, to ignore it is an unacknowledged political gesture that has a long history and collaborates with a masculine radicalism that renders the place of the investigator transparent. In seeking to learn to speak to (rather than listen to or speak for) the historically muted subject of the subaltern woman, the postcolonial intellectual *systematically* 'unlearns' female privilege. This systematic unlearning involves learning to critique postcolonial discourse with the best tools it can provide and not simply substituting the lost figure of the colonized. Thus, to question the unquestioned muting of the subaltern woman even within the anti-imperialist project of subaltern studies is not, as Jonathan Culler suggests, to 'produce difference by differing' or to 'appeal ... to a sexual identity defined as essential and privilege experiences associated with that identity'.[58]

Culler's version of the feminist project is possible within what Elizabeth Fox-Genovese has called 'the contribution of the bourgeois-democratic revolutions to the social and political individualism of women'.[59] Many of us were obliged to understand the feminist project as Culler now describes it when we were still agitating as US academics.[60] It was certainly a necessary stage in my own education in 'unlearning' and has consolidated the belief that the mainstream project of Western feminism both continues and displaces the battle over the right to individualism between women and men in situations of upward class mobility. One suspects that the debate between US feminism and European 'theory' (as theory is generally represented by women from the United States or Britain) occupies a significant corner of that very terrain. I am generally sympathetic with the call to make US feminism more 'theoretical'. It seems, however, that the problem of the muted subject of the subaltern woman, though not solved by an 'essentialist' search for lost origins, cannot be served by the call for more theory in Anglo-America either.

That call is often given in the name of a critique of 'positivism', which is seen here as identical with 'essentialism'. Yet Hegel, the modern inaugurator of 'the work of the negative', was not a stranger to the notion of essences. For Marx, the curious persistence of essentialism within the dialectic was a profound and productive problem. Thus, the stringent binary opposition between positivism/essentialism (read, US) and 'theory' (read, French or Franco-German via Anglo-American) may be spurious. Apart from repressing the ambiguous complicity between essentialism and critiques of positivism (acknowledged by Derrida in 'Of grammatology as a positive science'), it also errs by implying that positivism is not a theory. This move allows the emergence of a proper name, a positive essence, Theory. Once again, the position of the investigator remains unquestioned. And, if this territorial debate turns toward the Third World, no change in the question of method is to be discerned. This debate cannot take into account that, in the case of the woman as subaltern, no ingredients for the constitution of the itinerary of the trace of a sexed subject can be gathered to locate the possibility of dissemination.

Yet I remain generally sympathetic in aligning feminism with the critique of positivism and the defetishization of the concrete. I am also far from averse to learning from the work of Western theorists, though I have learned to insist on

marking their positionality as investigating subjects. Given these conditions, and as
a literary critic, I tactically confronted the immense problem of the consciousness
of the woman as subaltern. I reinvented the problem in a sentence and transformed
it into the object of a simple semiosis. What does this sentence mean? The analogy
here is between the ideological victimization of a Freud and the positionality of the
postcolonial intellectual as investigating subject.

As Sarah Kofman has shown, the deep ambiguity of Freud's use of women as a
scapegoat is a reaction-formation to an initial and continuing desire to give the
hysteric a voice, to transform her into the *subject* of hysteria.[61] The masculine-
imperialist ideological formation that shaped that desire into the 'daughter's
seduction' is part of the same formation that constructs the monolithic 'third-world
woman'. As a postcolonial intellectual, I am influenced by that formation as well.
Part of our 'unlearning' project is to articulate that ideological formation – by
measuring silences, if necessary – into the *object* of investigation. Thus, when
confronted with the questions, Can the subaltern speak? and Can the subaltern (as
woman) speak?, our efforts to give the subaltern a voice in history will be doubly
open to the dangers run by Freud's discourse. As a product of these considerations,
I have put together the sentence 'White men are saving brown women from brown
men' in a spirit not unlike the one to be encountered in Freud's investigations of the
sentence 'A child is being beaten'.[62]

The use of Freud here does not imply an isomorphic analogy between subject-
formation and the behaviour of social collectives, a frequent practice, often
accompanied by a reference to Reich, in the conversation between Deleuze and
Foucault. So I am not suggesting that 'White men are saving brown women from
brown men' is a sentence indicating a *collective* fantasy symptomatic of a *collective*
itinerary of sadomasochistic repression in a *collective* imperialist enterprise. There
is a satisfying symmetry in such an allegory, but I would rather invite the reader to
consider it a problem in 'wild psychoanalysis' than a clinching solution.[63] Just as
Freud's insistence on making the woman the scapegoat in 'A child is being beaten'
and elsewhere discloses his political interests, however imperfectly, so my insistence
on imperialist subject-production as the occasion for this sentence discloses my
politics.

Further, I am attempting to borrow the general methodological aura of Freud's
strategy toward the sentence he construed *as a sentence* out of the many similar
substantive accounts his patients gave him. This does not mean I will offer a case
of transference-in-analysis as an isomorphic model for the transaction between
reader and text (my sentence). The analogy between transference and literary
criticism or historiography is no more than a productive catachresis. To say that the
subject is a text does not authorize the converse pronouncement: the verbal text is
a subject.

I am fascinated, rather, by how Freud predicates a *history* of repression that
produces the final sentence. It is a history with double origin, one hidden in the
amnesia of the infant, the other lodged in our archaic past, assuming by implication
a preoriginary space where human and animal were not yet differentiated.[64] We are

driven to impose a homologue of this Freudian strategy on the Marxist narrative to explain the ideological dissimulation of imperialist political economy and outline a history of repression that produces a sentence like the one I have sketched. This history also has a double origin, one hidden in the manoeuverings behind the British abolition of widow sacrifice in 1829,[65] the other lodged in the classical and Vedic past of Hindu India, the *Rg-Veda* and the *Dharmaśāstra*. No doubt there is also an undifferentiated preoriginary space that supports this history.

The sentence I have constructed is one among many displacements describing the relationship between brown and white men (sometimes brown and white women worked in). It takes its place among some sentences of 'hyperbolic admiration' or of pious guilt that Derrida speaks of in connection with the 'hieroglyphist prejudice'. The relationship between the imperialist subject and the subject of imperialism is at least ambiguous.

The Hindu widow ascends the pyre of the dead husband and immolates herself upon it. This is widow sacrifice. (The conventional transcription of the Sanskrit word for the widow would be *sati*. The early colonial British transcribed it *suttee*.) The rite was not practiced universally and was not caste- or class-fixed. The abolition of this rite by the British has been generally understood as a case of 'White men saving brown women from brown men'. White women – from the nineteenth-century British Missionary Registers to Mary Daly – have not produced an alternative understanding. Against this is the Indian nativist argument, a parody of the nostalgia for lost origins: 'The women actually wanted to die.'

The two sentences go a long way to legitimize each other. One never encounters the testimony of the women's voice-consciousness. Such a testimony would not be ideology-transcendent or 'fully' subjective, of course, but it would have constituted the ingredients for producing a countersentence. As one goes down the grotesquely mistranscribed names of these women, the sacrificed widows, in the police reports included in the records of the East India Company, one cannot put together a 'voice'. The most one can sense is the immense heterogeneity breaking through even such a skeletal and ignorant account (castes, for example, are regularly described as tribes). Faced with the dialectically interlocking sentences that are constructible as 'White men are saving brown women from brown men' and 'The women wanted to die', the postcolonial woman intellectual asks the question of simple semiosis – What does this mean? – and begins to plot a history.

To mark the moment when not only a civil but a good society is born out of domestic confusion, singular events that break the letter of the law to instill its spirit are often invoked. The protection of women by men often provides such an event. If we remember that the British boasted of their absolute equity toward and noninterference with native custom/law, an invocation of this sanctioned transgression of the letter for the sake of the spirit may be read in J.D.M. Derrett's remark: 'The very first legislation upon Hindu Law was carried through without the assent of a single Hindu.' The legislation is not named here. The next sentence, where the measure is named, is equally interesting if one considers the implications of the survival of a colonially established 'good' society after decolonization: 'The recurrence of *sati* in independent India is probably an obscurantist revival which cannot long survive even in a very backward part of the country.'[66]

Whether this observation is correct or not, what interests me is that the protection of woman (today the 'third-world woman') becomes a signifier for the establishment of a *good* society which must, at such inaugurative moments, transgress mere legality, or equity of legal policy. In this particular case, the process also allowed the redefinition as a crime of what had been tolerated, known, or adulated as ritual. In other words, this one item in Hindu law jumped the frontier between the private and the public domain.

Although Foucault's *historical narrative*, focusing solely on Western Europe, sees merely a tolerance for the criminal antedating the development of criminology in the late eighteenth century (*PK*, p. 41), his *theoretical description* of the 'episteme' is pertinent here: 'The *episteme* is the "apparatus" which makes possible the separation not of the true from the false, but of what may not be characterized as scientific' (*PK*, p. 197) – ritual as opposed to crime, the one fixed by superstition, the other by legal science.

The leap of *suttee* from private to public has a clear and complex relationship with the changeover from a mercantile and commercial to a territorial and administrative British presence; it can be followed in correspondence among the police stations, the lower and higher courts, the courts of directors, the prince regent's court, and the like. (It is interesting to note that, from the point of view of the native 'colonial subject', also emergent from the feudalism–capitalism transition, *sati* is a signifier with the reverse social charge: 'Groups rendered psychologically marginal by their exposure to Western impact ... had come under pressure to demonstrate, to others as well as to themselves, their ritual purity and allegiance to traditional high culture. To many of them *sati* became an important proof of their conformity to older norms at a time when these norms had become shaky within.'[67]

If this is the first historical origin of my sentence, it is evidently lost in the history of humankind as work, the story of capitalist expansion, the slow freeing of labor power as commodity, that narrative of the modes of production, the transition from feudalism via mercantilism to capitalism. Yet the precarious normativity of this narrative is sustained by the putatively changeless stopgap of the 'Asiatic' mode of production, which steps in to sustain it whenever it might become apparent that the story of capital logic is the story of the West, that imperialism establishes the universality of the mode of production narrative, that to ignore the subaltern today is, willy-nilly, to continue the imperialist project. The origin of my sentence is thus lost in the shuffle between other, more powerful discourses. Given that the abolition of *sati* was in itself admirable, is it still possible to wonder if a perception of the origin of my sentence might contain interventionist possibilities?

Imperialism's image as the establisher of the good society is marked by the espousal of the woman as *object* of protection from her own kind. How should one examine the dissimulation of patriarchal strategy, which apparently grants the woman free choice as *subject*? In other words, how does one make the move from 'Britain' to 'Hinduism'? Even the attempt shows that imperialism is not identical with chromatism, or mere prejudice against people of colour. To approach this question, I will touch briefly on the *Dharmaśāstra* (the sustaining scriptures) and the *Rg-Veda* (Praise Knowledge). They represent the archaic origin in my homology of Freud. Of course, my treatment is not exhaustive. My readings are, rather, an interested and inexpert examination, by a postcolonial woman, of the fabrication of repression, a constructed counternarrative of woman's consciousness, thus woman's being, thus woman's being good, thus the good woman's desire, thus woman's desire. Paradoxically, at the same time we witness the unfixed place of woman as a signifier in the inscription of the social individual.

The two moments in the *Dharmaśāstra* that I am interested in are the discourse on sanctioned suicides and the nature of the rites for the dead.[68] Framed in these two discourses, the self-immolation of widows seems an exception to the rule. The general scriptural doctrine is that suicide is reprehensible. Room is made, however, for certain forms of suicide which, as formulaic performance, lose the phenomenal identity of being suicide. The first category of sanctioned suicides arises out of *tatvajnāna*, or the knowledge of truth. Here the knowing subject comprehends the insubstantiality or mere phenomenality (which may be the same thing as nonphenomenality) of its identity. At a certain point in time, *tat tva* was interpreted as 'that you', but even without that, *tatva* is thatness or quiddity. Thus, this enlightened self truly knows the 'that'-ness of its identity. Its demolition of that identity is not *ātmaghāta* (a killing of the self). The paradox of knowing of the limits of knowledge is that the strongest assertion of agency, to negate the possibility of agency, cannot be an example of itself. Curiously enough, the self-*sacrifice* of gods is sanctioned by natural ecology, useful for the working of the economy of Nature and the Universe, rather than by self-knowledge. In this *logically* anterior stage, inhabited by gods rather than human beings, of this particular chain of displacements, suicide and sacrifice (*ātmaghāta* and *ātmadāna*) seem as little distinct as an 'interior' (self-knowledge) and an 'exterior' (ecology) sanction.

This philosophical space, however, does not accommodate the self-immolating woman. For her we look where room is made to sanction suicides that cannot claim truth-knowledge as a state that is, at any rate, easily verifiable and belongs in the area of *sruti* (what was heard) rather than *smirti* (what is remembered). This exception to the general rule about suicide annuls the phenomenal identity of self-immolation if performed in certain places rather than in a certain state of enlightenment. Thus, we move from an interior sanction (truth-knowledge) to an exterior one (place of pilgrimage). It is possible for a woman to perform *this* type of (non)suicide.[69]

Yet even this is not the *proper* place for the woman to annul the proper name of suicide through the destruction of her proper self. For her alone is sanctioned self-immolation on a dead spouse's pyre. (The few male examples cited in Hindu antiquity of self-immolation on another's pyre, being proofs of enthusiasm and devotion to a master or superior, reveal the structure of domination within the rite.)

This suicide that is not suicide may be read as a simulacrum of both truth-knowledge and piety of place. If the former, it is as if the knowledge *in a subject* of its own insubstantiality and mere phenomenality is dramatized so that the dead husband becomes the exteriorized example and place of the extinguished subject and the widow becomes the (non)agent who 'acts it out'. If the latter, it is as if the metonym for all sacred places is now that burning bed of wood, constructed by elaborate ritual, where the woman's subject, legally displaced from herself, is being consumed. It is in terms of this profound ideology of the displaced place of the female subject that the paradox of free choice comes into play. For the male subject, it is the felicity of the suicide, a felicity that will annul rather than establish its status as such, that is noted. For the female subject, a sanctioned self-immolation, even as it takes away the effect of 'fall' (*pātaka*) attached to an unsanctioned suicide, brings praise for the act of choice on another register. By the inexorable ideological production of the sexed subject, such a death can be understood by the female subject as an *exceptional* signifier of her own desire, exceeding the general rule for a widow's conduct.

In certain periods and areas this exceptional rule became the general rule in a class-specific way. Ashis Nandy relates its marked prevalence in eighteenth- and early ninteenth-century Bengal to factors ranging from population control to communal misogyny.[70] Certainly its prevalence there in the previous centuries was because in Bengal, unlike elsewhere in India, widows could inherit property. Thus, what the British see as poor victimized women going to the slaughter is in fact an ideological battle-ground. As P. V. Kane, the great historian of the *Dharmasāstra*, has correctly observed: 'In Bengal, [the fact that] the widow of a sonless member even in a joint Hindu family is entitled to practically the same rights over joint family property which her deceased husband would have had ... must have frequently induced the surviving members to get rid of the widow by appealing at a most distressing hour to her devotion to and love for her husband' (*HD* II.2, p. 635).

Yet benevolent and enlightened males were and are sympathetic with the 'courage' of the woman's free choice in the matter. They thus accept the production of the sexed subaltern subject: 'Modern India does not justify the practice of *sati*, but it is a warped mentality that rebukes modern Indians for expressing admiration and reverence for the cool and unfaltering courage of Indian women in becoming *satis* or performing the *jauhar* for cherishing their ideals of womanly conduct' (*HD* II.2, p. 636). What Jean-François Lyotard has termed the '*différend*', the inaccessibility of, or untranslatability from, one mode of discourse in a dispute to another, is vividly illustrated here.[71] As the discourse of what the British perceive as heathen ritual is sublated (but not, Lyotard would argue, translated) into what the British perceive as crime, one diagnosis of female free will is substituted for another.

Of course, the self-immolation of widows was not *invariable* ritual prescription. If, however, the widow does decide thus to exceed the letter of ritual, to turn back is a transgression for which a particular type of penance is prescribed.[72] With the local British police officer supervising the immolation, to be dissuaded after a decision was, by contrast, a mark of real free choice, a choice of freedom. The ambiguity of the position of the indigenous colonial elite is disclosed in the nationalistic romanticization of the purity, strength and love of these self-sacrificing women. The two set pieces are Rabindranath Tagore's paean to the 'self-renouncing paternal grandmothers of Bengal' and Ananda Coomaraswamy's eulogy of *suttee* as 'this last proof of the perfect unity of body and soul'.[73]

Obviously I am not advocating the killing of widows. I am suggesting that, within the two contending versions of freedom, the constitution of the female subject *in life* is the place of the *différend*. In the case of widow self-immolation, ritual is not being redefined as superstition but as *crime*. The gravity of *sati* was that it was ideologically cathected as 'reward', just as the gravity of imperialism was that it was ideologically cathected as 'social mission'. Thompson's understanding of *sati* as 'punishment' is thus far off the mark:

> It may seem unjust and illogical that the Moguls, who freely impaled and flayed alive, or nationals of Europe, whose countries had such ferocious penal codes and had known, scarcely a century before suttee began to shock the English conscience, orgies of witch-burning and religious persecution, should have felt as they did about suttee. But the differences seemed to them this – the victims of their cruelties were tortured by a law which considered them offenders, whereas the victims of suttee were punished for no offence but the physical weakness which had placed them at man's mercy. The rite seemed to prove a depravity and arrogance such as no other human offense had brought to light.[74]

All through the mid and late-eighteenth century, in the spirit of the codification of the law, the British in India collaborated and consulted with learned Brahmans to judge whether *suttee* was legal by their homogenized version of Hindu law. The collaboration was often idiosyncratic, as in the case of the significance of being dissuaded. Sometimes, as in the general Sāstric prohibition against the immolation of widows with small children, the British collaboration seems confused.[75] In the beginning of the nineteenth century, the British authorities, and especially the British in England, repeatedly suggested that collaboration made it appear as if the British condoned this practice. When the law was finally written, the history of the long period of collaboration was effaced, and the language celebrated the noble Hindu who was against the bad Hindu, the latter given to savage atrocities:

> The practice of Suttee ... is revolting to the feeling of human nature. ... In many instances, acts of atrocity have been perpetrated, which have been shocking to the Hindoos themselves. ... Actuated by these considerations the Governor-General in Council, without intending to depart from one of the first and most important principles of the system of British Government in India that all classes of the people be secure in the observance of their religious usages, so long as that system can be adhered to without violation of the paramount dictates of justice and humanity, has deemed it right to establish the following rules. (*HD* II.2, pp. 624–5)

That this was an alternative ideology of the graded sanctioning of suicide as exception, rather than its inscription as sin, was of course not understood. Perhaps *sati* should have been read with martyrdom, with the defunct husband standing in for the transcendental One; or with war, with the husband standing in for sovereign or state, for whose sake an intoxicating ideology of self-sacrifice can be mobilized. In actuality, it was categorized with murder, infanticide and the lethal exposure of the very old. The dubious place of the free will of the constituted sexed subject as female was successfully effaced. There is no itinerary we can retrace here. Since the other sanctioned suicides did not involve the scene of this constitution, they entered neither the ideological battleground at the archaic origin – the tradition of the *Dharmaśāstra* – nor the scene of the reinscription of ritual as crime – the British abolition. The only related transformation was Mahatma Gandhi's reinscription of the notion of *satyāgraha*, or hunger strike, as resistance. But this is not the place to discuss the details of that sea-change. I would merely invite the reader to compare the auras of widow sacrifice and Gandhian resistance. The root in the first part of *satyāgraha* and *sati* are the same.

Since the beginning of the Puranic era (*c.* AD 400), learned Brahmans debated the doctrinal appropriateness of *sati* as of sanctioned suicides in sacred places in general. (This debate still continues in an academic way.) Sometimes the caste provenance of the practice was in question. The general law for widows, that they should observe *brahmacarya*, was, however, hardly ever debated. It is not enough to translate *brahmacarya* as 'celibacy'. It should be recognized that, of the four ages of being in Hindu (or Brahmanical) *regulative* psychobiography, *brahmacarya* is the social practice anterior to the kinship inscription of marriage. The man – widower or husband – graduates through *vānaprastha* (forest life) into the mature celibacy and renunciation of *samnyāsa* (laying aside).[76] The woman as wife is indispensable for *gārhasthya*, or householdership, and may accompany her husband into forest life. She has no access (according to Brahmanical sanction) to the final celibacy of asceticism, or *samnyāsa*. The woman as widow, by the general law of sacred doctrine, must regress to an anteriority transformed into stasis. The institutional evils attendant upon this law are well known; I am considering its asymmetrical effect on the ideological formation of the sexed subject. It is thus of much greater significance that there was no debate on this nonexceptional fate of widows – either among Hindus or between Hindus and British – than that the *exceptional* prescription of self-immolation was actively contended.[77] Here the possibility of recovering a (sexually) subaltern subject is once again lost and overdetermined.

This legally programmed asymmetry in the status of the subject which effectively defines the woman as object of *one* husband, obviously operates in the interest of the legally symmetrical subject-status of the male. The self-immolation of the widow thereby becomes the extreme case of the general law rather than an exception to it. It is not surprising, then, to read of heavenly rewards for the *sati*, where the quality of being the object of unique possessor is emphasized by way of rivalry with other females, those ecstatic heavenly dancers, paragons of female beauty and male pleasure who sing her praise: 'In heaven she, being solely devoted to her husband,

and praised by groups of *apsarās* [heavenly dancers], sports with her husband as long as fourteen Indras rule' (*HD* II.2, p. 631).

The profound irony in locating the woman's free will in self-immolation is once again revealed in a verse accompanying the earlier passage: 'As long as the woman [as wife: *stri*] does not burn herself in fire on the death of her husband, she is never released [*mucyate*] from her female body [*strisarīr* – i.e., in the cycle of births].' Even as it operates the most subtle general release from individual agency, the sanctioned suicide peculiar to woman draws its ideological strength by *identifying* individual agency with the supraindividual: kill yourself on your husband's pyre now, and you may kill your female body in the entire cycle of birth.

In a further twist of the paradox, this emphasis on free will establishes the peculiar misfortune of holding a female body. The word for the self that is actually burned is the standard word for spirit in the noblest sense (*ātman*), while the verb 'release', through the root for salvation in the noblest sense (*muc → moska*) is in the passive (*mocyate*), and the word for that which is annulled in the cycle of birth is the everyday word for the body. The ideological message writes itself in the benevolent twentieth-century male historian's admiration: 'The Jauhar [group self-immolation of aristocratic Rajput war-widows or imminent war-widows] practiced by the Rajput ladies of Chitor and other places for saving themselves from unspeakable atrocities at the hands of the victorious Moslems are too well known to need any lengthy notice' (*HD* II.2, p. 629).

Although *jauhar* is not, strictly speaking, an act of *sati*, and although I do not wish to speak for the sanctioned sexual violence of conquering male armies, 'Moslem' or otherwise, female self-immolation in the face of it is a legitimation of rape as 'natural' and works, in the long run, in the interest of unique genital possession of the female. The group rape perpetrated by the conquerors is a metonymic celebration of territorial acquisition. Just as the general law for widows was unquestioned, so this act of female heroism persists among the patriotic tales told to children, thus operating on the crudest level of ideological reproduction. It has also played a tremendous role, precisely as an overdetermined signifier, in acting out Hindu communalism. Simultaneously, the broader question of the consitution of the sexed subject is hidden by foregrounding the visible violence of *sati*. The task of recovering a (sexually) subaltern subject is lost in an institutional textuality at the archaic origin.

As I mentioned above, when the status of the legal subject as property-holder could be temporarily bestowed on the *female* relict, the self-immolation of widows was stringently enforced. Raghunandana, the late fifteenth-/sixteenth-century legalist whose interpretations are supposed to lend the greatest authority to such enforcement, takes as his text a curious passage from the *Rg-Veda*, the most ancient of the Hindu sacred texts, the first of the *Srutis*. In doing so, he is following a centuries-old tradition, commemorating a peculiar and transparent misreading at the very place of sanction. Here is the verse outlining certain steps within the rites for the dead. Even at a simple reading it is clear that it is 'not addressed to widows at all, but to ladies of the deceased man's household whose husbands were living'.

Why then was it taken as authoritative? This, the unemphatic transposition of the dead for the living husband, is a different order of mystery at the archaic origin from the ones we have been discussing: 'Let these whose husbands are worthy and are living enter the house with clarified butter in their eyes. Let these wives first step into the house, tearless, healthy, and well adorned' (*HD* II.2, p. 634). But this crucial transposition is not the only mistake here. The authority is lodged in a disputed passage and an alternate reading. In the second line, here translated 'Let these wives first step into the house', the word for first is *agré*. Some have read it as *agné*, 'O fire'. As Kane makes clear, however, 'even without this change Aparārka and others rely for the practice of *Sati* on this verse' (*HD* IV.2, p. 199). Here is another screen around one origin of the history of the subaltern female subject. Is it a historical oneirocritique that one should perform on a statement such as: 'Therefore it must be admitted that either the MSS are corrupt or Raghunandana committed an innocent slip' (*HD* II.2 p. 634)? It should be mentioned that the rest of the poem is either about that general law of *brahmacarya*-in-stasis for widows, to which *sati* is an exception, or about *niyoga* – 'appointing a brother or any near kinsman to raise up issue to a deceased husband by marrying his widow'.[78]

If P.V. Kane is the authority on the history of the *Dharmaśāstra*, Mulla's *Principles of Hindu Law* is the practical guide. It is part of the historical text of what Freud calls 'kettle logic' that we are unraveling here, that Mulla's textbook adduces, just as definitively, that the *Rg-Vedic* verse under consideration was proof that 'remarriage of widows and divorce are recognized in some of the old texts'.[79]

One cannot help but wonder about the role of the word *yonī*. In context, with the localizing adverb *agré* (in front), the word means 'dwelling-place'. But that does not efface its primary sense of 'genital' (not yet perhaps specifically *female* genital). How can we take as the authority for the choice of a widow's self-immolation a passage celebrating the entry of adorned wives into a dwelling place invoked on this occasion by its *yonī*-name, so that the extracontextual icon is almost one of entry into civic production or birth? Paradoxically, the imagic relationship of vagina and fire lends a kind of strength to the authority-claim.[80] This paradox is strengthened by Raghunandana's modification of the verse so as to read, 'Let them first ascend the *fluid* abode [or origin, with, of course, the *yonī*-name – *a rōhantu jalayōnimagné*], O fire [or of fire].' Why should one accept that this 'probably mean[s] "may fire be to them as cool as water" (*HD* II.2, p. 634)? The fluid genital of fire, a corrupt phrasing, might figure a sexual indeterminacy providing a simulacrum for the intellectual indeterminacy of *tattvajnāna* (truth-knowledge).

I have written above of a constructed counternarrative of woman's consciousness, thus woman's being, thus woman's being good, thus the good woman's desire, thus woman's desire. This slippage can be seen in the fracture inscribed in the very word *sati*, the feminine form of *sat*. *Sat* transcends any gender-specific notion of masculinity and moves up not only into human but spiritual universality. It is the present participle of the verb 'to be' and as such means not only being but the True, the Good, the Right. In the sacred texts it is essence, universal spirit. Even as a prefix it indicates appropriate, felicitous, fit. It is noble enough to have entered the most privileged discourse of modern Western philosophy: Heidegger's meditation on Being.[81] *Sati*, the feminine of this word, simply means 'good wife.'

It is now time to disclose that *sati* or *suttee* as the proper name of the rite of widow self-immolation commemorates a grammatical error on the part of the British, quite as the nomenclature 'American Indian' commemorates a factual error on the part of Columbus. The word in the various Indian languages is 'the burning of the *sati*' or the good wife, who thus escapes the regressive stasis of the widow in *brahmacrya*. This exemplifies the race-class-gender overdeterminations of the situation. It can perhaps be caught even when it is flattened out: white men, seeking to save brown women from brown men, impose upon those women a greater ideological constriction by absolutely identifying, *within discursive practice*, good-wifehood with self-immolation on the husband's pyre. On the other side of thus constituting the *object*, the abolition (or removal) of which will provide the occasion for establishing a good, as distinguished from merely civil, society, is the Hindu manipulation of female *subject*-constitution which I have tried to discuss.

(I have already mentioned Edward Thompson's *Suttee*, published in 1928. I cannot do justice here to this perfect specimen of true justification of imperialism as a civilizing mission. Nowhere in his book, written by someone who avowedly 'loves India', is there any questioning of the 'beneficial ruthlessness' of the British in India as motivated by territorial expansionism or management of industrial capital.[82] The problem with his book is, indeed, a problem of representation, the construction of a continuous and homogeneous 'India' in terms of heads of state and British administrators, from the perspective of 'a man of good sense' who would be the transparent voice of reasonable humanity. 'India' can then be represented, in the other sense, by its imperial masters. The reason for referring to *suttee* here is Thompson's finessing of the word *sati* as 'faithful' in the very first sentence of his book, an inaccurate translation which is nonetheless an English permit for the insertion of the female subject into twentieth-century discourse.[83])

Consider Thompson's praise for General Charles Hervey's appreciation of the problem of *sati*: 'Hervey has a passage which brings out the pity of a system which looked only for prettiness and constancy in woman. He obtained the names of satis who had died on the pyres of Bikanir Rajas; they were such names as: "Ray Queen, Sun-ray, Love's Delight, Garland, Virtue Found, Echo, Soft Eye, Comfort, Moonbeam, Love-lorn, Dear Heart, Eye-play, Arbour-born, Smile, Love-bud, Glad Omen, Mist-clad, or Cloud-sprung – the last a favourite name."' Once again, imposing the upper-class Victorian's typical demands upon 'his woman' (his preferred phrase), Thompson appropriates the Hindu woman as his to save against the 'system'. Bikaner is in Rajasthan; and any discussion of widow-burnings of Rajasthan, especially within the ruling class, was intimately linked to the positive or negative construction of Hindu (or Aryan) communalism.

A look at the pathetically misspelled names of the *satis* of the artisanal, peasant, village-priestly, moneylender, clerical and comparable social groups in Bengal, where *satis* were most common, would not have yielded such a harvest (Thompson's preferred adjective for Bengalis is 'imbecilic'). Or perhaps it would. There is no more dangerous pastime than transposing proper names into common nouns, translating them, and using them as sociological evidence. I attempted to reconstruct the names on that list and began to feel Hervey-Thompson's arrogance. What, for instance, might 'Comfort' have been? Was it 'Shanti'? Readers are reminded of the last line of T. S. Eliot's *Waste Land*. There the word bears the mark of one kind of stereotyping of India – the grandeur of the ecumenical Upanishads. Or was it 'Swasti'? Readers are reminded of the *swastika*, the Brahmanic ritual mark of domestic comfort (as in 'God Bless Our Home') stereotyped into a criminal parody of Aryan hegemony. Between these two appropriations, where is our pretty and constant burnt widow? The aura of the names owes more to writers like Edward FitzGerald, the 'translator' of the *Rubayyat of Omar Khayyam* who helped to construct a certain picture of the Oriental woman through the supposed 'objectivity' of translation, than to sociological exactitude. (Said's *Orientalism*, 1978, remains the authoritative text here.) By this sort of reckoning, the translated proper names of a random collection of contemporary French philosophers or boards of directors of prestigious southern US corporations would give evidence of a ferocious investment in an archangelic and hagiocentric theocracy. Such sleights of pen can be perpetuated on 'common nouns' as well, but the proper name is most susceptible to the trick. And it is the British trick with *sati* that we are discussing. After such a taming of the subject, Thompson can write, under the heading 'The psychology of the "*Sati*"', 'I had intended to try to examine this; but the truth is, it has ceased to seem a puzzle to me.'[84]

Between patriarchy and imperialism, subject-constitution and object-formation, the figure of the woman disappears, not into a pristine nothingness, but into a violent shuttling which is the displaced figuration of the 'third-world woman' caught between tradition and modernization. These considerations would revise every detail of judgments that seem valid for a history of sexuality in the West: 'Such would be the property of repression, that which distinguishes it from the prohibitions maintained by simple penal law: repression functions well as a sentence to disappear, but also as an injunction to silence, affirmation of non-existence; and consequently states that of all this there is nothing to say, to see, to know.'[85] The case of *suttee* as exemplum of the woman-in-imperialism would challenge and reconstruct this opposition between subject (law) and object-of-knowledge (repression) and mark the place of 'disappearance' with something other than silence and nonexistence, a violent aporia between subject and object status.

Sati as a woman's proper name is in fairly widespread use in India today. Naming a female infant 'a good wife' has its own proleptic irony, and the irony is all the greater because this sense of the common noun is not the primary operator in the proper name.[86] Behind the naming of the infant is *the* Sati of Hindu mythology, Durga in her manifestation as a good wife.[87] In part of the story, Sati – she is already called that – arrives at her father's court uninvited, in the absence, even, of an invitation for her divine husband Siva. Her father starts to abuse Siva and Sati dies in pain. Siva arrives in a fury and dances over the universe with Sati's corpse on his shoulder. Vishnu dismembers her body and bits are strewn over the earth. Around each such relic bit is a great place of pilgrimage.

Figures like the goddess Athena – 'father's daughters self-professedly uncontaminated by the womb' – are useful for establishing women's ideological self-debasement, which is to be distinguished from a deconstructive attitude toward the essentialist subject. The story of the mythic Sati, reversing every narrateme of the rite, performs a similar function: the living husband avenges the wife's death, a transaction between great male gods fulfills the destruction of the female body and thus inscribes the earth as sacred geography. To see this as proof of the feminism of classical Hinduism or of Indian culture as goddess-centered and therefore feminist is as ideologically contaminated by nativism or reverse ethnocentrism as it was imperialist to erase the image of the luminous fighting Mother Durga and invest the proper noun Sati with no significance other than the ritual burning of the helpless widow as sacrificial offering who can then be saved. There is no space from which the sexed subaltern subject can speak.

If the oppressed under socialized capital have no necessarily unmediated access to 'correct' resistance, can the ideology of *sati*, coming from the history of the periphery, be sublated into any model of interventionist practice? Since this essay operates on the notion that all such clear-cut nostalgias for lost origins are suspect, especially as grounds for counterhegemonic ideological production, I must proceed by way of an example.[89]

(The example I offer here is not a plea for some violent Hindu sisterhood of self-destruction. The definition of the British Indian as Hindu in Hindu law is one of the marks of the ideological war of the British against the Islamic Mughal rulers of India; a significant skirmish in that as yet unfinished war was the division of the subcontinent. Moreover, in my view, individual examples of this sort are tragic failures as *models* of interventionist practice, since I question the production of models as such. On the other hand, as objects of discourse analysis for the non-self-abdicating intellectual, they can illuminate a section of the social text, in however haphazard a way.)

A young woman of sixteen or seventeen, Bhuvaneswari Bhaduri, hanged herself in her father's modest apartment in North Calcutta in 1926. The suicide was a puzzle since, as Bhuvaneswari was menstruating at the time, it was clearly not a case of illicit pregnancy. Nearly a decade later, it was discovered that she was a member of one of the many groups involved in the armed struggle for Indian independence. She had finally been entrusted with a political assassination. Unable to confront the task and yet aware of the practical need for trust, she killed herself.

Bhuvaneswari had known that her death would be diagnosed as the outcome of illegitimate passion. She had therefore waited for the onset of menstruation. While waiting, Bhuvaneswari, the *brahmacārini* who was no doubt looking forward to good wifehood, perhaps rewrote the social text of *sati*-suicide in an interventionist way. (One tentative explanation of her inexplicable act had been a possible melancholia brought on by her brother-in-law's repeated taunts that she was too old to be not-yet-a-wife.) She generalized the sanctioned motive for female suicide by taking immense trouble to displace (not merely deny) in the physiological inscription of her body, its imprisonment within legitimate passion by a single male. In the immediate context, her act became absurd, a case of delirium rather than sanity. The displacing gesture – waiting for menstruation – is at first a reversal of the interdict against a menstruating widow's right to immolate herself; the unclean widow must wait, publicly, until the cleansing bath of the fourth day, when she is no longer menstruating, in order to claim her dubious privilege.

In this reading, Bhuvaneswari Bhaduri's suicide is an unemphatic, ad hoc, subaltern rewriting of the social text of *sati*-suicide as much as the hegemonic account of the blazing, fighting, familial Durga. The emergent dissenting possibilities of that hegemonic account of the fighting mother are well documented and popularly well remembered through the discourse of the male leaders and participants in the independence movement. The subaltern as female cannot be heard or read.

I know of Bhuvaneswari's life and death through family connections. Before investigating them more thoroughly, I asked a Bengali woman, a philosopher and Sanskritist whose early intellectual production is almost identical to mine, to start the process. Two responses: (a) Why, when her two sisters, Saileswari and Rāseswari, led such full and wonderful lives, are you interested in the hapless Bhuvaneswari? (b) I asked her nieces. It appears that it was a case of illicit love.

I have attempted to use and go beyond Derridean deconstruction, which I do not celebrate as feminism as such. However, in the context of the problematic I have addressed, I find his morphology much more painstaking and useful than Foucault's and Deleuze's immediate, substantive involvement with more 'political' issues – the latter's invitation to 'become woman' – which can make their influence more dangerous for the US academic as enthusiastic radical. Derrida marks radical critique with the danger of appropriating the other by assimilation. He reads catachresis at the origin. He calls for a rewriting of the utopian structural impulse as 'rendering delirious that interior voice that is the voice of the other in us'. I must here acknowledge a long-term usefulness in Jacques Derrida which I seem no longer to find in the authors of *The History of Sexuality* and *Mille Plateaux*.[89]

The subaltern cannot speak. There is no virtue in global laundry lists with 'woman' as a pious item. Representation has not withered away. The female intellectual as intellectual has a circumscribed task which she must not disown with a flourish.

Notes

1. Michel Foucault, *Language, Counter-Memory, Practice: Selected essays and interviews*, trans. Donald F. Bouchard and Sherry Simon, Cornell University Press: Ithaca, NY, 1977, pp. 205–17 (hereafter cited as *FD*). I have modified the English version of this, as of other English translations, where faithfulness to the original seemed to demand it.

It is important to note that the greatest 'influence' of Western European intellectuals upon US professors and students happens through collections of essays rather than long books in translation. And, in those collections, it is understandably the more topical pieces that gain a greater currency. (Derrida's 'Structure, sign and play' is a case in point.) From the perspective of theoretical production and ideological reproduction, therefore, the conversation under consideration has not necessarily been superseded.

2. There is an implicit reference here to the post-1968 wave of Maoism in France. See Michel Foucault, 'On Popular Justice: a discussion with Maoists', in *Power/Knowledge: Selected interviews and other writings 1972–77*, trans. Colin Gordon *et al.*, Pantheon: New York, p. 134 (hereafter cited as *PK*). Explication of the reference strengthens my point by laying bare the mechanics of appropriation. The status of China in this discussion is exemplary. If Foucault persistently clears himself by saying 'I know nothing about China', his interlocutors show toward China what Derrida calls the 'Chinese prejudice'.

3. This is part of a much broader symptom, as Eric Wolf discusses in *Europe and the People without History*, University of California Press: Berkeley, 1982.

4. Walter Benjamin, *Charles Baudelaire: A lyric poet in the era of high capitalism*, trans. Harry Zohn, Verso: London, 1983, p. 12.

5. Gilles Deleuze and Felix Guattari, *Anti-Oedipus: Capitalism and schizophrenia*, trans. Richard Hurley *et al.*, Viking Press: New York, 1977, p. 26.

6. The exchange with Jacques-Alain Miller in *PK* ('The Confession of the Flesh') is revealing in this respect.

7. Louis Althusser, *Lenin and Philosophy and Other Essays*, trans. Ben Brewster, Monthly Reivew Press: New York, 1971, pp. 132–3.

8. For one example among many see *PK*, p. 98.

9. It is not surprising, then, that Foucault's work, early and late, is supported by too simple a notion of repression. Here the antagonist is Freud, not Marx. 'I have the impression that [the notion of repression] is wholly inadequate to the analysis of the mechanisms and effects of power that is so pervasively used to characterize today' (*PK*, p. 92). The delicacy and subtlety of Freud's suggestion – that under repression the phenomenal identity of affects is indeterminate because something unpleasant can be desired as pleasure, thus radically reinscribing the relationship between desire and 'interest' – seems quite deflated here. For an elaboration of this notion of repression, see Jacques Derrida, *Of Grammatology*, trans. Gayatri Chakravorty Spivak, Johns Hopkins University Press: Baltimore, MD, 1976), pp. 88f. (hereafter cited as *OG*); and Derrida, *Limited inc.: abc*, trans. Samuel Weber, *Glyph*, 2, 1977, p. 215.

10. Althusser's version of this particular situation may be too schematic, but it nevertheless seems more careful in its program than the argument under study. 'Class *instinct*,' Althusser writes, 'is subjective and spontaneous. Class *position* is objective and rational. To arrive at proletarian class positions, the class instinct of proletarians only needs to be *educated*; the class instinct of the petty bourgeoisie, *and hence of intellectuals*, has, on the contrary, to be *revolutionized*' (*op. cit.*, p. 13).

11. Foucault's subsequent explanation (*PK*, p. 145) of this Deleuzian statement comes closer to Derrida's notion that theory cannot be an exhaustive taxonomy and is always formed by practice.

12. Cf. the surprisingly uncritical notions of representation entertained in *PK*, pp. 141, 188. My remarks concluding this paragraph, criticizing intellectuals' representations of subaltern groups, should be rigorously distinguished from a coalition politics that takes into account its framing within socialized capital and unites people not because they are

oppressed but because they are exploited. This model works best within a parliamentary democracy, where representation is not only not banished but elaborately staged.

13. Karl Marx, *Surveys from Exile*, trans. David Fernbach, Vintage Books: New York, 1974, p. 239.

14. *idem*, *Capital: A critique of political economy*, vol. 1, trans. Ben Fowkes, Vintage Books: New York, 1977, p. 254.

15. *ibid.*, p. 302.

16. See the excellent short definition and discussion of common sense in Errol Lawrence, 'Just plain common sense: the "roots" of racism', in Hazel V. Carby, *The Empire Strikes Back: Race and racism in 70s Britain*, Hutchinson: London, 1982, p. 48.

17. 'Use value' in Marx can be shown to be a 'theoretical fiction' – as much of a potential oxymoron as 'natural exchange'. I have attempted to develop this in 'Scattered speculations on the question of value', a manuscript under consideration by *Diacritics*.

18. Derrida's 'Linguistic circle of Geneva', especially pp. 143f., can provide a method for assessing the irreducible place of the family in Marx's morphology of class formation. In *Margins of Philosophy*, trans. Alan Bass, University of Chicago Press: Chicago, IL, 1982.

19. Marx, *Capital*, 1, p. 128.

20. I am aware that the relationship between Marxism and neo-Kantianism is a politically fraught one. I do not myself see how a continuous line can be established between Marx's own texts and the Kantian ethical moment. It does seem to me, however, that Marx's questioning of the individual as agent of history should be read in the context of the breaking up of the individual subject inaugurated by Kant's critique of Descartes.

21. Karl Marx, *Grundrisse: Foundations of the critique of political economy*, trans. Martin Nicolaus, Viking Press: New York, 1973, pp. 162–3.

22. Edward W. Said, *The World, The Text, The Critic*, Harvard University Press: Cambridge, MA, 1983, p. 243.

23. Paul Bové, 'Intellectuals at war: Michel Foucault and the analysis of power', *Sub-Stance*, 36/37, 1983, p. 44.

24. Carby *et al.*, *op. cit.*, p. 34.

25. This argument is developed further in Spivak, 'Scattered speculations'. Once again, the *Anti-Oedipus* did not ignore the economic text, although the treatment was perhaps too allegorical. In this respect, the move from schizo- to rhyzo-analysis in *Mille plateaux*, Seuil: Paris, 1980, has not been salutary.

26. See Michel Foucault, *Madness and Civilization: A history of insanity in the age of reason*, trans. Richard Howard, Pantheon Books: New York, 1965, pp. 251, 262, 269.

27. Although I consider Fredric Jameson's *Political Unconscious: Narrative as a socially symbolic act*, Cornell University Press: New York, 1981, to be a text of great critical weight, or perhaps *because* I do so, I would like my program here to be distinguished from one of restoring the relics of a privileged narrative: 'It is in detecting the traces of that uninterrupted narrative, in restoring to the surface of the text the repressed and buried reality of this fundamental history, that the doctrine of a political unconscious finds its function and its necessity' (p. 20).

28. Among many available books, I cite Bruse Tiebout McCully, *English Education and the Origins of Indian Nationalism*, Columbia University Press: New York, 1940.

29. Thomas Babington Macaulay, *Speeches by Lord Macaulay: With his minute on Indian education*, ed. G.M. Young, Oxford University Press, AMS Edition: Oxford, 1979, p. 359.

30. Keith, one of the compilers of the *Vedic Index*, author of *Sanskrit Drama in Its Origin, Development, Theory, and Practice*, and the learned editor of the *Krsnayajurveda* for Harvard University Press, was also the editor of four volumes of *Selected Speeches and Documents of British Colonial Policy* (1763 to 1937), of *International Affairs* (1918 to 1937), and of the *British Dominions* (1918 to 1931). He wrote books on the sovereignty of British dominions and on the theory of state succession, with special reference to English and colonial law.

31. Mahamahopadhyaya Haraprasad Shastri, *A Descriptive Catalogue of Sanskrit Manuscripts in the Government Collection under the Care of the Asiatic Society of Bengal*, Society of Bengal: Calcutta, 1925, vol. 3, p. viii.

32. Dinesachandra Sena, *Brhat Banga*, Calcutta University Press: Calcutta, 1925, vol. 1. p. 6.

33. Edward Thompson, *Suttee: A historical and philosophical enquiry into the Hindu rite of widow burning*, George Allen & Unwin: London, 1928, pp. 130, 47.

34. Holograph letter (from G. A. Jacob to an unnamed correspondent) attached to inside cover of the Sterling Memorial Library (Yale University) copy of Colonel G. A. Jacob (ed.) *Mahanarayana-Upanishad of the Atharva-Veda with the Dipika of Narayana*, The Government Central Books Department: Bombay, 1888, italics mine. The dark invocation of the dangers of this learning by way of anonymous aberrants consolidates the asymmetry.

35. I have discussed this issue in greater detail with reference to Julia Kristeva's *About Chinese Women*, trans. Anita Barrows, Marion Boyars: London, 1977, in 'French feminism in an international frame', *Yale French Studies*, 62, 1981.

36. Antonio Gramsci, 'Some aspects of the Southern question', *Selections from Political Writing: 1921–1926*, trans. Quintin Hoare, International Publishers : New York, 1978. I am using 'allegory of reading' in the sense developed by Paul de Man, *Allegories of Reading: Figural language in Rousseau, Nietzsche, Rilke, and Proust*, Yale University Press: New Haven, CT, 1979.

37. Their publications are: Ranajit Guha (ed.), *Subaltern Studies I: Writing on South Asian history and society*, Oxford University Press: New Delhi, 1982. Ranajit Guha (ed.) *Subaltern Studies II: Writings on South Asian History and Society*, Oxford University Press: New Delhi, 1983; and Ranajit Guha, *Elementary Aspects of Peasant Insurgency in Colonial India*, Oxford University Press: New Delhi, 1983.

38. Edward W. Said, 'Permission to narrate', *London Review of Books*, 16 February 1984.

39. Guha, *Studies*, I, p. 1.

40. *ibid.*, p. 4.

41. Jacques Derrida, 'The double session', in *Dissemination*, trans. Barbara Johnson, University of Chicago Press: Chicago, 1981.

42. Guha, *Studies*, I, p. 8 (all but the first set of italics are the author's).

43. Ajit K. Chaudhury, 'New wave social science', *Frontier*, 16–24, 28 January, 1984, p. 10 (italics are mine).

44. *ibid.*

45. Pierre Macherey, *A Theory of Literary Production*, trans. Geoffrey Wall, Routledge: London, 1978, p. 87.

46. I have discussed this issue in 'Displacement and the discourse of woman', in Mark Krupnick (ed.) *Displacement: Derrida and after*, Indiana University Press: Bloomington, IN, 1983, and in 'Love me, love my ombre, elle: Derrida's 'La carte postale', *Diacritics*, 14, 4, 1984, pp. 19–36.

47. This violence in the general sense that is the possibility of an episteme is what Derrida calls 'writing' in the general sense. The relationship between writing in the general sense and writing in the narrow sense (marks upon a surface) cannot be cleanly articulated. The task of grammatology (deconstruction) is to provide a notation upon this shifting relationship. In a certain way, then, the critique of imperialism is deconstruction as such.

48. 'Contracting poverty', *Multinational Monitor*, 4, 8, August 1983, p. 8. This report was contributed by John Cavanagh and Joy Hackel, who work on the International Corporations Project at the Institute for Policy Studies (italics are mine).

49. The mechanics of the invention of the Third World as signifier are susceptible to the type of analysis directed at the constitution of race as a signifier in Carby *et al.*, *op. cit.*

50. Mike Davis, 'The political economy of late-imperial America', *New Left Review*, 143, January–February 1984, p. 9.

51. Bové *op. cit.*, p. 51.

52. Terry Eagleton, *Literary Theory: An introduction*, University of Minnesota Press: Minneapolis, 1983, p. 205.

53. Perry Anderson, *In the Tracks of Historical Materialism*, Verso: London, 1983, p. 53.

54. *ibid.*, p. 52.

55. Said, *The World*, p. 183.

56. Jacques Derrida, 'Of an apocalyptic tone recently adapted in philosophy', trans. John P. Leavy, Jr., *Semia*, p. 71.

57. Even in such excellent texts of reportage and analysis as Gail Omvedt's *We Will Smash This Prison! Indian women in struggle*, Zed Press: London, 1980, the assumption that a group of Maharashtrian women in an urban proletarian situation, reacting to a radical white woman who had 'thrown in her lot with the Indian destiny,' is representative of 'Indian women' or touches the question of 'female consciousness in India' is not harmless when taken up within a first-world social formation where the proliferation of communication in an internationally hegemonic language makes alternative accounts and testimonies instantly accessible even to undergraduates.

   Norma Chincilla's observation, made at a panel on 'Third World feminisms: differences in form and content' (UCLA, 8 March, 1983), that antisexist work in the Indian context is not genuinely antisexist but antifeudal, is another case in point. This permits definitions of sexism to emerge only after a society has entered the capitalist mode of production, thus making capitalism and patriarchy conveniently continuous. It also invokes the vexed questions of the role of the '"Asiatic" mode of production' in sustaining the explanatory power of the normative narrativization of history through the account of modes of production, in however sophisticated a manner history is construed.

   The curious role of the proper name 'Asia' in this matter does not remain confined to proof or disproof of the empirical existence of the actual mode (a problem that became the object of intense maneuvering within international communism) but remains crucial even in the work of such theoretical subtlety and importance as Barry Hindess and Paul Hirst's *Pre-Capitalist Modes of Production*, (Routledge: London, 1975) and Fredric Jameson's *Political Unconscious*. Especially in Jameson, where the morphology of modes of production is rescued from all suspicion of historical determinism and anchored to a poststructuralist theory of the subject, the 'Asiatic' mode of production, in its guise of 'oriental despotism' as the concomitant state formation, still serves. It also plays a significant role in the transmogrified mode of production narrative in Deleuze and Guattari's *Anti-Oedipus*, in the Soviet debate, at a far remove, indeed, from these contemporary theoretical projects, the doctrinal sufficiency of the 'Asiatic' mode of production was most often doubted by producing for it various versions and nomenclatures of feudal, slave and communal modes of production. (The debate is presented in detail in Stephen F. Dunn, *The Fall and Rise of the Asiatic Mode of Production*, Routledge: London 1982.) It would be interesting to relate this to the repression of the imperialist 'moment' in most debates over the transition from feudalism to capitalism that have long exercised the Western Left. What is more important here is that an observation such as Chinchilla's represents a widespread hierarchization within third-world *feminism* (rather than Western Marxism), which situates it within the long-standing traffic with the imperialist concept-metaphor 'Asia'.

I should add that I have not yet read Madhu Kishwar and Ruth Vanita (eds.), *In Search of Answers: Indian women's voices from Manushi*, Zed Press: London, 1984.

58. Jonathan Culler, *On Deconstruction: Theory and criticism after structuralism*, Cornell University Press: Ithaca, NY, 1982, p. 48.

59. Elizabeth Fox-Genovese, 'Placing women's history in history', *New Left Review*, 133, May–June 1982, p. 21.

60. I have attempted to develop this idea in a somewhat autobiographical way in 'Finding feminist readings: Dante–Yeats', in Ira Konigsberg (ed.), *American Criticism in the Poststructuralist Age*, University of Michigan Press: Ann Arbor, MI, 1981.

61. Sarah Kofman, *L'Énigme de la femme: La Femme dans les textes de Freud*, Galilée: Paris, 1980.

62. Sigmund Freud. '"A child is being beaten": a contribution to the study of the origin of sexual perversions', *The Standard Edition of the Complete Psychological Works of Sigmund Freud*, trans. James Strachey *et al.*, Hogarth Press: London, vol. 17, 1955.

63. *idem*, '"Wild" psycho-analysis', *Standard Edition*, vol. 11.

64. *idem*, '"A child is being beaten"', p. 188.

65. For a brilliant account of how the 'reality' of widow-sacrifice was constituted or 'textualized' during the colonial period, see Lata Mani, 'The production of colonial discourse: sati in early nineteenth-century Bengal' (master's thesis, University of California at Santa Cruz, 1983). I profited from discussion with Ms Mani at the inception of this project.

66. J. D. M. Derrett, *Hindu Law Past and Present: Being an account of the controversy which preceded the enactment of the Hindu code, and text of the code as enacted, and some comments thereon*, A. Mukherjee & Co: Calcutta, 1957, p. 46.

67. Ashis Nandy, 'Sati: a nineteenth-century tale of women, violence and protest', in V. C. Joshi (ed.), *Rammohun Roy and the Process of Modernization in India*, Vikas Publishing House: New Delhi, 1975, p. 68.

68. The following account leans heavily on Pandurang Varman Kane, *History of Dharmasastra*, Bhandarkar Oriental Research Institute: Poona, 1963 (hereafter cited as *HD*, with volume, part and page numbers).

69. Upendra Thakur, *The History of Suicide in India: An introduction*, Munshi Ram Manohan Lal: New Delhi, 1963, p. 9, has a useful list of Sanskrit primary sources on sacred places. This laboriously decent book betrays all the signs of the schizophrenia of the colonial subject, such as bourgeois nationalism, patriarchal communalism and an 'enlightened reasonableness'.

70. Nandy, *op. cit.*

71. Jean-François Lyotard, *Le Différend*, Minuit: Paris, 1984.

72. *HD*, II.2, p. 633. There are suggestions that this 'prescribed penance' was far exceeded by social practice. In this passage below, published in 1938, notice the Hindu patristic

assumptions about the freedom of female will at work in phrases like 'courage' and 'strength of character'. The unexamined presuppositions of the passage might be that the complete objectification of the widow-concubine was just punishment for abdication of the right to courage, signifying subject status. 'Some widows, however, had not the courage to go through the fiery ordeal; nor had they sufficient strength of mind and character to live up to the high ascetic ideal prescribed for them [*brahmacarya*]. It is sad to record that they were driven to lead the life of a concubine or *avarudda stri* [incarcerated wife].' A. S. Altekar, *The Position of Women in Hindu Civilization: From prehistoric times to the present day*, Motilal Banarsidass: New Delhi, 1938, p. 156.

73. Quoted in Sena. *op. cit.*, 2, pp. 913–14.

74. Thompson, *op. cit.*, p. 132.

75. Here, as well as for the Brahman debate over *sati*, see Mani, *op. cit.*, pp. 71f.

76. We are speaking here of the regulative norms of Brahmanism, rather than 'things as they were'. See Robert Lingat, *The Classical Law of India*, trans. J. D. M. Derrett, University of California Press: Berkeley, 1973, p. 46.

77. Both the vestigial possibility of widow remarriage in ancient India and the legal institution of widow remarriage in 1856 are transactions among men. Widow remarriage is very much an exception, perhaps because it left the program of subject-formation untouched. In all the 'lore' of widow remarriage, it is the father and the husband who are applauded for their reformist courage and selflessness.

78. Sir Monier Monier-Williams, *Sanskrit–English Dictionary*, Clarendon Press: Oxford, 1899, p. 552. Historians are often impatient if modernists seem to be attempting to import 'feministic' judgments into ancient patriarchies. The real question is, of course, why structures of patriarchal domination should be unquestioningly recorded. Historical sanctions for collective action toward social justice can only be developed if people outside of the discipline question standards of 'objectivity' preserved as such by the hegemonic tradition. It does not seem inappropriate to notice that so 'objective' an instrument as a dictionary can use the deeply sexist-partisan explanatory expression: 'raise up issue to a deceased husband'!

79. Sunderlal T. Desai, *Mulla: Principles of Hindu law*, N. M. Tripathi: Bombay, 1982, p. 184.

80. I am grateful to Professor Alison Finley of Trinity College (Hartford, CT) for discussing the passage with me. Professor Finley is an expert on the *Rg-Veda*. I hasten to add that she would find my readings as irresponsibly 'literary-critical' as the ancient historian would find it 'modernist' (see note 79).

81. Martin Heidegger. *An Introduction to Metaphysics*, trans. Ralph Manheim, Doubleday Anchor: New York, 1961, p. 58.

82. Thompson, *op. cit.*, p. 37.

83. *ibid.*, p. 15. For the status of the proper name as 'mark', see Derrida, 'Taking chances'.

84. Thomspon, *op. cit.*, p. 137.

85. Michel Foucault, *The History of Sexuality*, vol. 1, trans. Robert Hurley, Vintage Books: New York, 1980, p. 4.

86. The fact that the word was also used as a form of address for a well-born woman ('lady') complicates matters.

87. It should be remembered that this account does not exhaust her many manifestations within the pantheon.

88. A position against nostalgia as a basis of counterhegemonic ideological production does not endorse its negative use. Within the complexity of contemporary political economy,

it would, for example, be highly questionable to urge that the current Indian working-class crime of burning brides who bring insufficient dowries and of subsequently disguising the murder as suicide is either a *use* or *abuse* of the tradition of *sati*-suicide. The most that can be claimed is that it is a displacement on a chain of semiosis with the female subject as signifier, which would lead us back into the narrative we have been unraveling. Clearly, one must work to stop the crime of bride-burning *in every way*. If, however, that work is accomplished by unexamined nostalgia or its opposite, it will assist actively in the substitution of race/ethnos or sheer genitalism as a signifer in the place of the female subject.

89. I had not read Peter Dews. 'Power and subjectivity in Foucault', *New Left Review*, 144, 1984, until I finished this essay. I look forward to his book on the same topic [Peter Dews, *The Logics of Disintegration: Post-structuralist thought and the claims of critical theory*, Verso: London, 1987]. There are many points in common between his critique and mine. However, as far as I can tell from the brief essay, he writes from a perspective uncritical of critical theory and the intersubjective norm that can all too easily exchange 'individual' or 'subject' in its situating of the 'epistemic subject'. Dews's reading of the connection between 'Marxist tradition' and the 'autonomous subject' is not mine. Further, his account of 'the *impasse* of the second phase of poststructuralism as a whole' is vitiated by his nonconsideration of Derrida, who has been against the privileging of language from his earliest work, the 'Introduction' in Edmund Husserl, *The Origin of Geometry*, trans. John Leavy, Nicholas Hays: Stony Brook, NY, 1978. What sets his excellent analysis quite apart from my concerns is, of course, that the Subject within whose History he places Foucault's work is the Subject of the European tradition (pp. 87–94).

5 □ Remembering Fanon: Self, Psyche and the Colonial Condition

Homi Bhabha

O my body make of me always a man who questions!
FRANTZ FANON, *Black Skin, White Masks*

In the popular memory of English socialism the mention of Frantz Fanon stirs a dim, deceiving echo. *Black Skin, White Masks, The Wretched of the Earth, Toward the African Revolution* – these memorable titles reverberate in the self-righteous rhetoric of 'resistance' whenever the English left gathers, in its narrow church or its Trotskyist camps, to deplore the immiseration of the colonized world. Repeatedly used as the idioms of simple moral outrage, Fanon's titles emptily echo a political spirit that is far from his own; they sound the troubled conscience of a socialist vision that extends, in the main, from an ethnocentric little Englandism to a large trade union internationalism. When that labourist line of vision is challenged by the 'autonomous' struggles of the politics of race and gender, or threatened by problems of human psychology or cultural representation, it can only make an empty gesture of solidarity. Whenever questions of race and sexuality make their own organizational and theoretical ethical demands on the primacy of 'class', 'state' and 'party' the language of traditional socialism is quick to describe those urgent, 'other' questions as symptoms of petty-bourgeois deviation, signs of the bad faith of socialist intellectuals. The ritual respect accorded to the name of Fanon, the currency of his titles in the common language of liberation, are part of the ceremony of a polite, English refusal.

There has been no substantial work on Fanon in the history of the *New Left Review*; one piece in the *New Statesman*; one essay in *Marxism Today*; one article in *Socialist Register*; one short book by an English author. Of late, the memory of Fanon has been kept alive in the activist traditions of *Race and Class*, by A. Sivanandan's stirring indictments of state racism. Edward Said, himself a scholar engagé, has richly recalled the work of Fanon in his important T. S. Eliot memorial

Foreword to Frantz Fanon, *Black Skin, White Masks*, Pluto Press: London, 1986, pp. vii–xxvi.

lectures, *Culture and Imperialism*. And finally, Stephan Feuchtwang's fine, far-reaching essay, 'Fanon's politics of culture' (*Economy and Society*) examines Fanon's concept of culture with its innovatory sights for a non-deterministic political organization of the psyche. Apart from these exceptions, in Britain today Fanon's ideas are effectively 'out of print'.

Memories of Fanon tend to the mythical. He is either revered as the prophetic spirit of Third World Liberation or reviled as an exterminating angel, the inspiration to violence in the Black Power movement. Despite his historic participation in the Algerian Revolution and the influence of his ideas on the race politics of the 1960s and 1970s, Fanon's work will not be possessed by one political moment or movement, nor can it be easily placed in a seamless narrative of liberationist history. Fanon refuses to be so completely claimed by events or eventualities. It is the sustaining irony of his work that his severe commitment to the political task in hand never restricted the restless, inquiring movement of his thought.

It is not for the finitude of philosophical thinking nor for the finality of a political direction that we turn to Fanon. Heir to the ingenuity and artistry of Toussaint and Senghor, as well as the iconoclasm of Nietzsche, Freud and Sartre, Fanon is the purveyor of the transgressive and transitional truth. He may yearn for the total transformation of Man and Society, but he speaks most effectively from the uncertain interstices of historical change: from the area of ambivalence between race and sexuality; out of an unresolved contradiction between culture and class; from deep within the struggle of psychic representation and social reality.

To read Fanon is to experience the sense of division that prefigures – and fissures – the emergence of a truly radical thought that never dawns without casting an uncertain dark. His voice is most clearly heard in the subversive turn of a familiar term, in the silence of a sudden rupture: '*The Negro is not. Any more than the white man.*' The awkward division that breaks his line of thought keeps alive the dramatic and enigmatic sense of the process of change. That familiar alignment of colonial subjects – Black/White, Self/Other – is disturbed with one brief pause and the traditional grounds of racial identity are dispersed, whenever they are found to rest in the narcissistic myths of Negritude or White cultural supremacy. It is this palpable pressure of division and displacement that pushes Fanon's writing to the edge of things; the cutting edge that reveals no ultimate radiance but, in his words, 'exposes an utterly naked declivity where an authentic upheaval can be born'.

The psychiatric hospital at Blida-Joinville is one such place where, in the divided world of French Algeria, Fanon discovered the impossibility of his mission as a colonial psychiatrist:

> If psychiatry is the medical technique that aims to enable man no longer to be a stranger to his environment, I owe it to myself to affirm that the Arab, permanently an alien in his own country, lives in a state of absolute depersonalization.... The social structure existing in Algeria was hostile to any attempt to put the individual back where he belonged.

The extremity of this colonial alienation of the person – this end of the 'idea' of the individual – produces a restless urgency in Fanon's search for a conceptual form appropriate to the social antagonism of the colonial relation. The body of his work splits between a Hegelian–Marxist dialectic, a phenomenological affirmation of Self and Other and the psychoanalytic ambivalence of the Unconscious, its turning from love to hate, mastery to servitude. In his desperate, doomed search for a dialectic of deliverance Fanon explores the edge of these modes for thought: his Hegelianism restores hope to history; his existentialist evocation of the 'I' restores the presence of the marginalized; and his psychoanalytic framework illuminates the 'madness' of racism, the pleasure of pain, the agonistic fantasy of political power.

As Fanon attempts such audacious, often impossible, transformations of truth and value, the jagged testimony of colonial dislocation, its displacement of time and person, its defilement of culture and territory, refuses the ambition of any 'total' theory of colonial oppression. The Antillean évolué cut to the quick by the glancing look of a frightened, confused, White child; the stereotype of the native fixed at the shifting boundaries between barbarism and civility; the insatiable fear and desire for the Negro: 'Our women are at the mercy of Negroes . . . God knows how they make love'; the deep cultural fear of the Black figured in the psychic trembling of Western sexuality – it is these signs and symptoms of the colonial condition that drive Fanon from one conceptual scheme to another, while the colonial relation takes shape in the gaps between them, articulated in the intrepid engagements of his style. As Fanon's text unfolds, the 'scientific' fact comes to be aggressed by the experience of the street; sociological observations are intercut with literary artefacts, and the poetry of liberation is brought up short against the leaden, deadening prose of the colonized world . . .

What is this distinctive *force* of Fanon's vision that has been forming even as I write about the division, the displacement, the cutting edge of his thought? It comes, I believe, from the tradition of the oppressed, as Walter Benjamin suggests; it is the language of a revolutionary awareness that 'the state of emergency in which we live is not the exception but the rule. We must attain to a concept of history that is in keeping with this insight.' And the state of emergency is also always a state of *emergence*. The struggle against colonial oppression changes not only the direction of Western history, but challenges its historicist 'idea' of time as a progressive, ordered whole. The analysis of colonial de-personalization alienates not only the Enlightenment idea of 'Man' but challenges the transparency of social reality, as a pre-given image of human knowledge. If the order of Western historicism is disturbed in the colonial state of emergency, even more deeply disturbed is the social and psychic representation of the human subject. For the very nature of humanity becomes estranged in the colonial condition and from that 'naked declivity' it emerges, not as an assertion of will nor as an evocation of freedom, but as an enigmatic questioning. With a question that echoes Freud's *what does woman want?*, Fanon turns to confront the colonized world. 'What does a man want?' he asks, in the introduction to *Black Skin, White Masks*, 'What does the black man want?'

To this loaded question where cultural alienation bears down on the ambivalence of psychic identification, Fanon responds with an agonizing performance of self-images:

> I had to meet the white man's eyes. An unfamiliar weight burdened me. In the white world the man of colour encounters difficulties in the development of his bodily schema.... I was battered down by tom-toms, cannibalism, intellectual deficiency, fetishism, racial defects.... I took myself far off from my own presence.... What else could it be for me but an amputation, an excision, a haemorrhage that spattered my whole body with black blood?

From within the metaphor of vision complicit with a Western metaphysic of Man emerges the displacement of the colonial relation. The Black presence ruins the representative narrative of Western personhood: its past tethered to treacherous stereotypes of primitivism and degeneracy will not produce a history of civil progress, a space for the *Socius*; its present, dismembered and dislocated, will not contain the image of identity that is questioned in the dialectic of mind/body and resolved in the epistemology of 'appearance and reality'. The White man's eyes break up the Black man's body and in that act of epistemic violence its own frame of reference is transgressed, its field of vision disturbed.

'What does the black man *want*?' Fanon insists, and in privileging the psychic dimension he changes not only what we understand by a *political* demand but transforms the very means by which we recognize and identify its *human agency*. Fanon is not principally posing the question of political oppression as the violation of a human 'essence', although he lapses into such a lament in his more existential moments. He is not raising the question of colonial man in the universalist terms of the liberal-humanist ('How does colonialism deny the Rights of Man?'); nor is he posing an ontological question about Man's being ('*Who* is the alienated colonial man?'). Fanon's question is not addressed to such a unified notion of history nor such a unitary concept of Man. It is one of the original and disturbing qualities of *Black Skin, White Masks* that it rarely historicizes the colonial experience. There is no master narrative or realist perspective that provide a background of social and historical facts against which emerge the problems of the individual or collective psyche. Such a traditional sociological alignment of Self and Society or History and Psyche is rendered questionable in Fanon's identification of the colonial subject who is historicized as it comes to be heterogeneously inscribed in the texts of history, literature, science, myth. The colonial subject is always 'overdetermined from without', Fanon writes. It is through image and fantasy – those orders that figure transgressively on the borders of history and the unconscious – that Fanon most profoundly evokes the colonial condition.

In articulating the problem of colonial cultural alienation in the psychoanalytic language of demand and desire, Fanon radically questions the formation of both individual and social authority as they come to be developed in the discourse of Social Sovereignity. The social virtues of historical rationality, cultural cohesion, the autonomy of individual consciousness assume an immediate, utopian identity with the subjects upon whom they confer a civil status. The civil state is the ultimate expression of the innate ethical and rational bent of the human mind; the social instinct is the progressive destiny of human nature, the necessary transition from Nature to Culture. The direct access from individual interests to social authority is objectified in the representative structure of a General Will – Law or Culture – where Psyche and Society mirror each other, transparently translating their difference, without loss, into a historical totality. Forms of social and psychic alienation and aggression – madness, self-hate, treason, violence – can never be acknowledged as determinate and constitutive conditions of civil authority, or as the ambivalent effects of the social instinct itself. They are always explained away as alien presences, occlusions of historical progress, the ultimate misrecognition of Man.

For Fanon such a myth of Man and Society is fundamentally undermined in the colonial situation where everyday life exhibits a 'constellation of delirium' that mediates the normal social relations of its subjects: 'The Negro enslaved by his inferiority, the white man enslaved by his superiority alike behave in accordance with a neurotic orientation.' Fanon's demand for a psychoanalytic explanation emerges from the perverse reflections of 'civil virtue' in the alienating acts of colonial governance: the visibility of cultural 'mummification' in the colonizer's avowed ambition to civilize or modernize the native which results in 'archaic inert institutions [that function] under the oppressor's supervision like a caricature of formerly fertile institutions', or the validity of violence in the very definition of the colonial social space; or the viability of the febrile, fantasmatic images of racial hatred that come to be absorbed and acted out in the wisdom of the West. These interpositions, indeed collaborations of political and psychic violence *within* civic virtue, alienation within identity, drive Fanon to describe the splitting of the colonial space of consciousness and society as marked by a 'Manichean delirium'.

The representative figure of such a perversion, I want to suggest, is the image of post-Enlightenment man tethered to, *not* confronted by, his dark reflection, the shadow of colonized man, that splits his presence, distorts his outline, breaches his boundaries, repeats his action at a distance, disturbs and divides the very time of his being. This ambivalent identification of the racist world – moving on two planes without being in the least embarrassed by it, as Sartre says of the anti-Semitic consciousness – turns on the idea of Man *as* his alienated image, not Self and Other but the 'Otherness' of the self inscribed in the perverse palimpsest of colonial identity. And it is that bizarre figure of desire, which splits along the axis on which it turns, that compels Fanon to put the psychoanalytic question of the desire of the subject to the historic condition of colonial man.

'What is often called the black soul is a white man's artefact,' Fanon writes. This transference, I've argued, speaks otherwise. It reveals the deep psychic uncertainty of the colonial relation itself; its split representations stage that division of 'body' and 'soul' which enacts the artifice of 'identity'; a division which cuts across the fragile skin – black and white – of individual and social authority. What emerges from the figurative language I have used to make such an argument are three conditions that underlie an understanding of the *process of identification* in the analytic of desire.

First: to exist is to be called into being in relation to an Otherness, its look or locus. It is a demand that reaches outward to an external object and, as J. Rose writes, 'it is the relation of this demand to the place of the object it claims that becomes the basis for identification'. This process is visible in that exchange of looks between native and settler that structures their psychic relation in the paranoid fantasy of boundless possession and its familiar language of reversal: 'when their glances meet he [the settler] ascertains bitterly, always on the defensive, "They want to take our place." It is true for there is no native who does not dream at least once a day of setting himself up in the settler's place.' It is always in relation to the place of the Other that colonial desire is articulated: that is, in part, the fantasmatic space of 'possession' that no one subject can singly occupy which permits the dream of the inversion of roles.

Second: the very place of identification, caught in the tension of demand and desire, is a space of splitting. The fantasy of the native is precisely to occupy the master's place while keeping his place in the slave's *avenging* anger. 'Black skins, white masks' is not, for example, a neat division; it is a doubling, dissembling image of being in at least two places at once which makes it impossible for the devalued, insatiable evolué (an abandonment neurotic, Fanon claims) to accept the colonizer's invitation to identity: 'You're a doctor, a writer, a student, you're *different*, you're one of *us*.' It is precisely in that ambivalent use of 'different' – to be different from those that are different makes you the same – that the Unconscious speaks of the form of Otherness, the tethered shadow of deferral and displacement. It is not the Colonialist Self or the Colonized Other, but the disturbing distance in between that constitutes the figure of colonial otherness – the White man's artifice inscribed on the Black man's body. It is in relation to this impossible object that emerges the liminal problem of colonial identity and its vicissitudes.

Finally, as has already been disclosed by the rhetorical figures of my account of desire and Otherness, the question of identification is never the affirmation of a pre-given identity never a self-fulfilling prophecy – it is always the production of an 'image' of identity and the transformation of the subject in assuming that image. The demand of identification – that is, to be *for* an Other – entails the representation of the subject in the differentiating order of Otherness. Identification, as we inferred from the illustrations above, is always the return of an image of identity which bears the mark of splitting in that 'Other' place from which it comes. For Fanon, like Lacan, the primary moments of such a repetition of the self lie in the desire of the look and the limits of language. The 'atmosphere of certain uncertainty' that surrounds the body certifies its existence and threatens its dismemberment.

Look a Negro. . . . Mama, see the Negro! I'm frightened. . . . I could no longer laugh, because I already know there were legends, stories, history and above all *historicity*. . . . Then assailed at various points, the corporal schema crumbled its place taken by a

racial epidermal schema. . . . It was no longer a question of being aware of my body
in the third person but in a triple person. . . . I was responsible for my body, for my
race, for my ancestors.

In reading *Black Skin, White Masks* it is crucial to respect the difference between
'personal identity' as all intimation of reality, or an intuition of being, and the
psychoanalytic problem of identification that, in a sense, always begs the question
of the subject – 'What does a man want?' The emergence of the human subject as
socially and psychically authenticated depends upon the *negation* of an originary
narrative of fulfilment or an imaginary coincidence between individual interest or
instinct and the General Will. Such binary, two-part, identities function in a kind
of narcissistic reflection of the One in the Other which is confronted in the language
of desire by the psychoanalytic process of identification. For identification, identity
is never an *a priori*, nor a finished product; it is only ever the problematic process
of access to an 'image' of totality. The discursive conditions of this psychic image
of identification will be clarified if we think of the perilous perspective of the concept
of the image itself. For the image – as point of identification – marks the site of
an ambivalence. Its representation is always spatially split – it makes *present*
something that is *absent* – and temporally deferred – it is the representation of a
time that is always elsewhere, a repetition. The image is only ever an *appurtenance*
to authority and identity; it must never be read mimetically as the 'appearance' of
a 'reality'. The access to the image of identity is only ever possible in the *negation*
of any sense of originality or plenitude, through the principle of displacement and
differentiation (absence/presence; representation/repetition) that always renders it a
liminal reality. The image is at once a metaphoric substitution, an illusion of
presence and by that same token a metonym, a sign of its absence and loss. It is
precisely from this edge of meaning and being, from this shifting boundary of
otherness within identity, that Fanon asks: 'What does a *black* man want?'

> When it encounters resistance from the other, self-consciousness undergoes the
> experience of desire. . . . As soon as I desire I ask to be considered. I am not merely here
> and now, sealed into thingness. I am for somewhere else and for something else. I
> demand that notice be taken of my negating activity in so far as I pursue something
> other than life . . . .
>   I occupied space. I moved towards the other . . . and the evanescent other, hostile but
> not opaque, transparent, not there, disappeared. Nausea.

From that overwhelming emptiness of nausea Fanon makes his answer: the Black
man wants the objectifying confrontation with otherness; in the colonial psyche
there is an unconscious disavowal of the negating, splitting moment of desire. The
place of the Other must not be imaged, as Fanon sometimes suggests, as a fixed
phenomenological point, opposed to the self, that represents a culturally alien
consciousness. The Other must be seen as the necessary negation of a primordial
identity – cultural or psychic – that introduces the system of differentiation which

enables the 'cultural' to be signified as a linguistic, symbolic, historic reality. If, as I have suggested, the subject of desire is never simply a Myself, then the Other is never simply an *It-self*, a font of identity, truth, or misrecognition.

As a principle of identification, the Other bestows a degree of objectivity but its representation – be it the social process of the Law or the psychic process of the Oedipus – is always ambivalent, disclosing a lack. For instance, the common, conversational distinction between 'the letter and spirit' of the Law displays the otherness of Law itself; the ambiguous grey area between 'Justice' and judicial procedure is, quite literally, a conflict of judgment. In the language of psychoanalysis, the Law of the Father or the paternal metaphor, again, cannot be taken at its word. It is a process of substitution and exchange that inscribes a normative, normalizing place for the subject; but that metaphoric access to identity is exactly the place of prohibition and repression, precisely a conflict of authority. Identification, as it is spoken in the *desire of the Other*, is always a question of interpretation for it is the elusive assignation of myself with a one-self, the elision of person and place.

If the differentiating force of the Other is the process of the subject's signification in language and society's objectification in Law, then how can the Other disappear? Can desire, the moving spirit of the subject, ever evanesce?

In his more analytic mode Fanon can impede the exploration of these ambivalent, uncertain questions of colonial desire. The state of emergency from which he writes demands more insurgent answers, more immediate identifications. At times Fanon attempts too close a correspondence between the *mise-en-scène* of unconscious fantasy and the phantoms of racist fear and hate that stalk the colonial scene; he turns too hastily from the ambivalences of identification to the antagonistic identities of political alienation and cultural discrimination; he is too quick to name the Other, to personalize its presence in the language of colonial racism – 'the real Other for the white man is and will continue to be the black man. And conversely.' These attempts, in Fanon's words, to restore the dream to its proper political time and cultural space can, at times, blunt the edge of Fanon's brilliant illustrations of the complexity of psychic projections in the pathological colonial relation. Jean Veneuse, the Antillean evolué, desires not merely to be in the place of the White man but compulsively seeks to look back and down on himself from that position. The White man does not merely deny what he fears and desires by projecting it on 'them'; Fanon sometimes forgets that paranoia never preserves its position of power for the compulsive identification with a persecutory 'They' is always an evacuation and emptying of the 'I'.

Fanon's sociodiagnostic psychiatry tends to explain away the ambivalent turns and returns of the subject of colonial desire, its masquerade of Western Man and the 'long' historical perspective. It is as if Fanon is fearful of his most radical insights: that the space of the body and its identification is a representational reality; that the politics of race will not be entirely contained within the humanist myth of man or economic necessity or historical progress, for its psychic affects questions such forms of determinism; that social sovereignty and human subjectivity are only realizable in the order of Otherness. It is as if the question of desire that emerged from the traumatic tradition of the oppressed has to be denied, at the end of *Black Skin, White Masks*, to make way for existentialist humanism that is as banal as it is beatific:

> Why not the quite simple attempt to touch the other to feel the other, to explain the other to myself . . . . At the conclusion of this study, I want the world to recognize, with me, the open door of every consciousness.

Such a deep hunger for humanism, despite Fanon's insight into the dark side of Man, must be an overcompensation for the closed consciousness or 'dual narcissism' to which he attributes the depersonalization of colonial man: 'There one lies body to body, with one's blackness or one's whiteness in full narcissistic cry, each sealed into his own particularity – with, it is true, now and then a flash or so.' It is this flash of 'recognition' in its Hegelian sense with its transcendental, sublative spirit – that fails to ignite in the colonial relation where there is only narcissistic indifference: 'And yet the Negro knows there is a difference. He wants it. . . . The former slave needs a challenge to his humanity.' In the absence of such a challenge, Fanon argues, the colonized can only imitate, never identify, a distinction nicely made by the psychoanalyst Annie Reich: 'It is imitation . . . when the child holds the newspaper *like* his father. It is identification when the child learns to read.' In disavowing the culturally differentiated condition of the colonial world in demanding '*Turn White or disappear*' – the colonizer is himself caught in the ambivalence of paranoic identification, alternating between fantasies of megalomania and persecution.

However Fanon's Hegelian dream for a human reality *in itself-for-itself* is ironized, even mocked, by his view of the Manichean structure of colonial consciousness and its non-dialectical division. What he says in *The Wretched of the Earth* of the demography of the colonial city reflects his view of the psychic structure of the colonial relation. The native and settler zones, like the juxtaposition of Black and White bodies, are opposed, but not in the service of 'a higher unity'. No conciliation is possible, he concludes, for of the two terms one is superfluous.

No, there can be no reconciliation, no Hegelian 'recognition', no simple, sentimental promise of a humanistic 'world of the You'. Can there be life without transcendence? Politics without the dream of perfectibility? Unlike Fanon, I think the *non-dialectical* moment of Manicheanism suggests an answer. By following the trajectory of colonial desire – in the company of that bizarre colonial figure, the tethered shadow – it becomes possible to cross, even to shift, the Manichean boundaries. Where there is no human *nature* hope can hardly spring eternal; but it emerges surely and surreptitiously in the strategic return of that difference that informs and deforms the image of identity, in the margin of Otherness that displays identification. There may be no Hegelian negation but Fanon must sometimes be reminded that the disavowal of the Other always exacerbates the 'edge' of identification, reveals that dangerous place where identity and aggressivity are twinned. For denial is always a retroactive process; a *half* acknowledgement of that

Otherness which has left its traumatic mark. In that uncertainty lurks the white masked Black man; and from such ambivalent identification – black skin, white masks – it is possible, I believe, to redeem the pathos of cultural confusion into a strategy of political subversion. We cannot agree with Fanon that 'since the racial drama is played out in the open the black man has no time to make it unconscious', but that is a provocative thought. In occupying two places at once – or three in Fanon's case – the depersonalized, dislocated colonial subject can become an incalculable object, quite literally, difficult to place. The demand of authority cannot unify its message nor simply identify its subjects. For the strategy of colonial desire is to stage the drama of identity at the point at which the black mask *slips* to reveal the white skin. At that edge, in between the Black body and the White body, there is a tension of meaning and being, or some would say demand and desire, which is the psychic counterpart to that 'muscular tension' that inhabits the native body:

> The symbols of social order – the police, the bugle calls in the barracks, military parades and the waving flags – are at one and the same time inhibitory and stimulating: for they do not convey the message 'Don't dare to budge', rather, they cry out 'Get ready to attack'.

It is from that tension – both psychic and political – that a strategy of subversion emerges. It is a mode of negation that seeks not to unveil the fullness of Man but to manipulate his representation. It is a form of power that is exercised at the very limits of identity and authority, in the mocking spirit of mask and image; it is the lesson taught by the veiled Algerian woman in the course of the Revolution as she crossed the Manichean lines to claim her liberty. In Fanon's essay 'Algeria Unveiled' the colonizer's attempt to unveil the Algerian woman does not simply turn the veil into a symbol of resistance; it becomes a technique of camouflage, a means of struggle – the veil conceals bombs. The veil that once secured the boundary of the home – the limits of woman – now masks the woman in her revolutionary activity, linking the Arab city and the French quarter, transgressing the familial and colonial boundary. As the 'veil' is liberated in the public sphere, circulating between and beyond cultural and social norms and spaces, it becomes the object of paranoid surveillance and interrogation. Every veiled woman, writes Fanon, became suspect. And when the veil is shed in order to penetrate deeper into the European quarter, the colonial police see everything and nothing. An Algerian woman is only, after all, a woman. But the Algerian *fidai* is an arsenal and in her handbag she carries her hand-grenades.

Remembering Fanon is a process of intense discovery and disorientation. Remembering is never a quiet act of introspection or retrospection. It is a painful re-membering, a putting together of the dismembered past to make sense of the trauma of the present. It is such a memory of the history of race and racism, colonialism and the question of cultural identity, that Fanon reveals with greater profundity and poetry than any other writer. What he achieves, I believe, is something far greater: for in seeing the phobic image of the Negro, the native, the colonized, deeply woven into the psychic pattern of the West, he offers the master and slave a deeper reflection of their interpositions, as well as the hope of a difficult, even dangerous, freedom: 'It is through the effort to recapture the self and to scrutinize the self, it is through the lasting tension of their freedom that men will be able to create the ideal conditions of existence for a human world.' Nobody writes with more honesty and insight of this lasting tension of freedom in which the self – the peremptory self of the present – disavows an image of itself as an originary past or an ideal future and confronts the paradox of its own making.

For Fanon, in *Black Skin, White Masks*, there is the intricate irony of turning the European existentialist and psychoanalytic traditions to face the history of the Negro which they had never contemplated, to face the reality of Fanon himself. This leads to a meditation on the experience of dispossession and dislocation – psychic and social – which speaks to the condition of the marginalized, the alienated, those who have to live under the surveillance of a sign of identity and fantasy that denies their difference. In shifting the focus of cultural racism from the politics of nationalism to the politics of narcissism, Fanon opens up a margin of interrogation that causes a subversive slippage of identity and authority. Nowhere is this slippage more visible than in his work itself where a range of texts and traditions – from the classical repertoire to the quotidian, conversational culture of racism – vie to utter that last word which remains unspoken. Nowhere is this slippage more significantly experienced than in the impossibility of inferring from the texts of Fanon a pacific image of 'society' or the 'state' as a homogeneous philosophical or representational unity. The 'social' is always an unresolved ensemble of antagonistic interlocutions between positions of power and poverty, knowledge and oppression, history and fantasy, surveillance and subversion. It is for this reason – above all else – in the twenty-fifth anniversary of his death, that we should turn to Fanon.

In Britain, today, as a range of culturally and racially marginalized groups readily assume the mask of the Black not to deny their diversity but to audaciously announce the important artifice of cultural identity and its difference, the need for Fanon becomes urgent. As political groups from different directions gather under the banner of the Black, not to homogenize their oppression but to make of it a common cause, a public image of the identity of otherness, the need for Fanon becomes urgent. Urgent, in order to remind us of that crucial engagement between mask and identity, image and identification, from which comes the lasting tension of our freedom and the lasting impression of ourselves as others.

> In the case of display . . . the play of combat in the form of intimidation, the being gives of himself, or receives from the other, something that is like a mask, a double, an envelope, a thrown-off skin, thrown off in order to cover the frame of a shield. It is through this separated form of himself that the being comes into play in his effects of life and death. (Jacques Lacan)

The time has come to return to Fanon; as always, I believe, with a question: How can the human world live its difference? how can a human being live Other-wise?

Note

Fanon's use of the word 'man' usually connotes a phenomenological quality of humanness, inclusive of man and woman and, for that very reason, ignores the question of gender difference. The problem stems from Fanon's desire to site the question of sexual difference within the problematic of cultural difference – to give them a shared origin – which is suggestive, but often simplifies the question of sexuality. His portrayals of White women often collude with their cultural stereotypes and reduce the 'desire' of sexuality to the desire for sex, leaving unexplored the elusive function of the 'object' of desire. .... [He] attempts a somewhat more complex reading of masochism but in making the Negro the '*predestined* depository of this aggression' (my emphasis) he again pre-empts a fuller psychoanalytic discussion of the production of psychic aggressivity in identification and its relation to cultural difference by citing the cultural stereotype as the predestined aim of the sexual drive. Of the woman of colour he has very little to say. 'I know nothing about her,' he writes in *Black Skin, White Masks*. This crucial issue requires an order of psychoanalytic argument that goes well beyond the scope of my foreword. I have therefore chosen to note the importance of the problem rather than to elide it in a facile charge of 'sexism'.

PART TWO
Theorising the West

Introduction

As mentioned in the Introduction to this volume, the publication in 1978 of Edward Said's *Orientalism* marked an undoubted turning point – although opinions differ about the nature of the change it enabled. For some, it was no more than a legitimation of the institutionalising of colonial discourse. For others, it offered genuinely novel and liberatory possibilities. Most of all, it made a certain kind of willed blindness, a refusal, all too common in academics, to contemplate the precise nature of the involvement of culture in processes of domination such as imperialism, all the harder to sustain. As a result, much of the criticism which the book attracted came from those whose habitual ways of seeing were fundamentally challenged.

The continuing reluctance, above all in certain sections of the Western academy, to examine the nature and role of the West can perhaps be explained in various ways. On the one hand, although they have been under sustained and increasing attack, Enlightenment notions of the progressive, world-historical role of the West have demonstrated a remarkable tenacity, and as members of that ideological state apparatus (in Althusser's phrase) which supposedly instantiates the benign superiority of the West, academics have the greatest ideological investment in continuing to regard the West in that light. On the other hand, the large-scale processes of identity constitution which Said discusses in *Orientalism*, though grounded in a separation of Self and Other, frequently involve more attention being paid to the nature of the Other than that of the Self. In this perspective, the identity formation of the West proceeds much more by listing – and denigrating – the characteristics of the Other than by explicitly enumerating those traits which make the West superior, though the negative classification of the non-Western 'them' allows the 'us' category to be silently filled with all the desirable traits which 'they' do not possess. This habit of lack of Self-scrutiny is one reason why criticism has tended to come from outside the geographical or disciplinary boundaries of the West, or at least from those places and positions which the West would regard as its margins.

One such margin in the twentieth century has been represented by those Marxist theories of colonialism and imperialism which were discussed in the Introduction to this volume. Located both within the academy (particularly in the case of post-war writers) and outside it (in the case of early thinkers such as Lenin, Bukharin and Rosa Luxemburg), they formed one of the few constant points of critique and theorising of the West. Important and influential though they have undoubtedly been, their impact in the area of literary and cultural study has hitherto been somewhat muted, not least because of their (perceived) economism and lack of attention to the 'superstructural' elements of imperialism.

Marxism is not, of course, merely, relentlessly, economistic. Nevertheless, it is significant that Said chooses the most famously anti-economistic of Marxists, Antonio Gramsci, as one of the two theorists on whom his analysis rests. Although some of the components of Said's critique may have been formulated earlier by others, a great deal of its power derives from his interdisciplinarity, his ability to bring previously disparate elements into what Walter Benjamin, in his 'Theses on the philosophy of history', called a 'constellation', a new and significant disposition of material which opens up the possibility for altered historical understanding. Said's approach allows powerful and previously unseen connections to be made. Certainly, the idea that reading *A Thousand and One Nights* or *Salammbô* might have profound and intimate links with political economy or imperial governance was novel for many and bordering on the outrageous for others. The shock effect of this particular constellation was to force the academy to abandon notions of the West as a benign or progressive force in world affairs, and to highlight the continuing power of sometimes centuries-old patterns of representation on everything from attitudes among the general public to policy decisions at the highest levels of government. A further effect of *Orientalism* was to inaugurate what became known as colonial discourse analysis, a name which, as mentioned in the Introduction to this volume, has its problems, but is still the preferred term for some. Although it is a very recent addition to the range of current theories, 'colonial discourse analysis is not merely a marginal adjunct to more mainstream studies, a specialised activity only for minorities or for historians of imperialism and colonialism, but itself forms the point of questioning of Western knowledge's categories and assumptions'.[1]

Despite the acknowledged importance of Said's work, the majority of responses to it have been of the 'yes, but . . .' variety, rather than attempts to utilise or extend his insights. Dennis Porter's article '*Orientalism* and its problems' is a fairly early response, though still more interesting than many which have followed. In keeping with many other commentators, Porter considers that Said constructs Orientalism as overly monolithic: 'the unified character of Western discourse on the Orient over some two millennia' – arguably the most common misrepresentation of Said. More perceptively, he identifies fundamental contradictions in *Orientalism* which he traces to Said's use of two theorists whose positions in Porter's eyes are incommensurable: Foucault and Gramsci. In particular, Porter feels that Said neglects the oppositional potential of Gramsci's theory of hegemony in terms of 'more directly counter-hegemonic writings or an alternative canon' – a failure caused by an overly homogenising model of textuality. To remedy this, Porter produces his own reading of Marco Polo's *Travels* (abridged below) and T. E. Lawrence's *Seven Pillars of*

Wisdom, the latter in particular being, on the face of it, an unlikely source of resistance to Orientalism.

If Porter's article represents the 'yes, but ...' approach to Said, then the Indian Marxist critic Aijaz Ahmad seems determined to remove even the qualified assent contained in the 'yes'. Ahmad is perhaps best known for his attack on Fredric Jameson over the manner in which the latter categorised Third World literature, and his criticisms of Said are even more controversial. Although *Orientalism* in particular antagonised numerous uncomprehending pundits, especially in the United States, Ahmad's is the most forthright assault on Said's work by any critic who might otherwise be regarded as being 'on the same side'. Ahmad's attack is launched in the name of Marxism, but of a very particular sort. He is, for instance, highly critical of what he sees as Western Marxism's excessive concern with 'cultural super-structures' as well as its 'distancing from political economy in favour of philosophy', and is even more dismissive of those approaches which appear to neglect Marxism, particularly post-structuralism and post-modernism. For Ahmad, Said's project is compromised by – among other things – his location within the metropolis and affiliation to its values. That this does not prevent Said from purportedly asserting 'the bad faith and imperial oppression of all European knowledges, beyond time and history' presumably only compounds his transgression. In one sense, Ahmad, in insisting that Said's work needs to be situated in its institutional context, and understood as emerging from various discourses, ideologies and forms of power/ knowledge, is doing no more to Said than Said has done to the colonial and post-colonial texts he analyses. In other ways, however, Ahmad's critique can seem excessively and pointlessly personalised, in a manner which detracts from its overall value.

The Martiniquan writer Aimé Césaire is best known as one of the founders of the 'negritude' movement of the 1940s and 1950s, (and, indeed, the first use of the term negritude occurs in Césaire's long poem 'Cahier d'un retour au pays natal', written in 1947). Historically, negritude's great value was its quality of resistance: its affirmation, in the face of racist denigration, of a range of positive qualities possessed by black people – as Césaire points out in the 'Cahier d'un retour', no race has the monopoly of beauty, intelligence or strength. Subsequently, however, negritude has been much criticised for its essentialist view of identity: the notion that these qualities are inherent in black people. A more outspoken and politically powerful form of resistance is represented by Césaire's *Discourse on Colonialism*, written in 1950. Surprisingly, in view of his long membership of the Communist Party, and time spent representing Martinique as a Communist deputy, Césaire's critique apparently owes nothing to Marxist theories of imperialism. That, in part at least, is due to the fact that he does not want to acknowledge any debt to a West which he sees as straightforwardly barbaric. Nevertheless, he chooses to oppose colonialism, particularly French colonialism, with a quintessentially French weapon: the literary-political-philosophical essay as polemical discourse. Indeed, the oratorical connotations of the French 'discours' accord well with Césaire's passionate mode of address. Although in the end it turns out to be a class-based analysis, much of Césaire's text is concerned with pointing out the moral bankruptcy of Europe – 'Europe is indefensible', as he says on the first page – in other words, vigorously contesting the putative superiority of the West on the very grounds on which that superiority is claimed. Among the contested areas is humanism, or 'pseudo-humanism' as Césaire terms it, and his scepticism here aligns him in different ways with Fanon, as well as with the post-structuralist critique of Robert Young. Although it may appear relatively untheoretical when placed alongside post-structuralist or later post-colonial analyses, Césaire's *Discourse*, in its directness and grounding in concrete examples, stands as a confirmation of Barthes's pronouncement 'Theory is not abstract, speculative. . . .'

Although writers like Césaire and Said feel able to view the West as a discrete entity, or in a very particular and circumscribed kind of relation (colonial, dominative, Other-constructing, etc.), such an option does not seem available to Anthony Giddens. Giddens regards the West itself as a more complex phenomenon, its relations with the rest of the world correspondingly complex, and the cause of this complexity is modernity. As he says elsewhere, modernity comprises:

> the institutions and modes of behaviour established first of all in post-feudal Europe, but which in the twentieth century increasingly have become world-historical in their impact. 'Modernity' can be understood as roughly equivalent to 'the industrialised world' so long as it be recognised that industrialism is not its only institutional dimension.[2]

Modernity for Giddens is 'inherently globalising', and while contemporary Marxists would locate the mechanism for that globalising process in the internal dynamic of capitalism, Giddens regards the latter as only one of a number of elements which go to make up globalisation. Modernity is of course a problematic concept, contested by critics of various persuasions, and the complexity of the modernity/ post-modernity debate resists easy summary.[3] In addition, a number of post-colonial critics have attempted various alignments of modernity/modernism/ colonialism and post-modernity/post-modernism/post-colonialism, most notably in the collection *Past the Last Post* which was discussed in the Introduction to this volume, though in this case multiplication of terms seemingly multiplies the problems which the authors face, rather than providing another Benjaminesque 'constellation' and enhanced understanding. To say this is, however, to acknowledge the complexity of the analytical task, rather than to criticise a particular failure.

Notes

1. Robert Young, *White Mythologies: Writing History and the West*, Routledge: London, 1990, p. 11.

2. Anthony Giddens, *Modernity and Self-Identity*, Polity Press; Cambridge, 1991, pp. 14–15.
3. For a full discussion of this dimension, readers are referred to Thomas Docherty (ed.), *Postmodernism: A Reader*, Harvester Wheatsheaf: Hemel Hempstead, 1992.

6 □ *From* Orientalism

Edward Said

[. . .]

II

I have begun with the assumption that the Orient is not an inert fact of nature. It is not merely *there*, just as the Occident itself is not just *there* either. We must take seriously Vico's great observation that men make their own history, that what they can know is what they have made, and extend it to geography: as both geographical and cultural entities – to say nothing of historical entities – such locales, regions, geographical sectors as 'Orient' and 'Occident' are man-made. Therefore as much as the West itself, the Orient is an idea that has a history and a tradition of thought, imagery and vocabulary that have given it reality and presence in and for the West. The two geographical entities thus support and to an extent reflect each other.

Having said that, one must go on to state a number of reasonable qualifications. In the first place, it would be wrong to conclude that the Orient was *essentially* an idea, or a creation with no corresponding reality. When Disraeli said in his novel *Tancred* that the East was a career, he meant that to be interested in the East was something bright young Westerners would find to be an all-consuming passion; he should not be interpreted as saying that the East was *only* a career for Westerners. There were – and are – cultures and nations whose location is in the East, and their lives, histories and customs have a brute reality obviously greater than anything that could be said about them in the West. About that fact this study of Orientalism has very little to contribute, except to acknowledge it tacitly. But the phenomenon of Orientalism as I study it here deals principally, not with a correspondence between Orientalism and Orient, but with the internal consistency of Orientalism and its

From Edward Said, *Orientalism*, Routledge & Kegan Paul: London, 1978, pp. 4–15, 201–11, 329, 343.

ideas about the Orient (the East as career) despite or beyond any correspondence, or lack thereof, with a 'real' Orient. My point is that Disraeli's statement about the East refers mainly to that created consistency, that regular constellation of ideas as the pre-eminent thing about the Orient, and not to its mere being, as Wallace Stevens's phrase has it.

A second qualification is that ideas, cultures and histories cannot seriously be understood or studied without their force, or more precisely their configurations of power, also being studied. To believe that the Orient was created, as I call it, 'Orientalized' – and to believe that such things happen simply as a necessity of the imagination, is to be disingenuous. The relationship between Occident and Orient is a relationship of power, of domination, of varying degrees of a complex hegemony, and is quite accurately indicated in the title of K. M. Panikkar's classic *Asia and Western Dominance*.[1] The Orient was Orientalized not only because it was discovered to be 'Oriental' in all those ways considered commonplace by an average nineteenth-century European, but also because it *could be* – that is, submitted to being – *made* Oriental. There is very little consent to be found, for example, in the fact that Flaubert's encounter with an Egyptian courtesan produced a widely influential model of the Oriental woman; she never spoke of herself, she never represented her emotions, presence or history. *He* spoke for and represented her. He was foreign, comparatively wealthy, male, and these were historical facts of domination that allowed him not only to possess Kuchuk Hanem physically but to speak for her and tell his readers in what way she was 'typically Oriental'. My argument is that Flaubert's situation of strength in relation to Kuchuk Hanem was not an isolated instance. It fairly stands for the pattern of relative strength between East and West, and the discourse about the Orient that it enabled.

This brings us to a third qualification. One ought never to assume that the structure of Orientalism is nothing more than a structure of lies or of myths which, were the truth about them to be told, would simply blow away. I myself believe that Orientalism is more particularly valuable as a sign of European-Atlantic power over the Orient than it is as a veridic discourse about the Orient (which is what, in its academic or scholarly form, it claims to be). Nevertheless, what we must respect and try to grasp is the sheer knitted-together strength of Orientalist discourse, its very close ties to the enabling socio-economic and political institutions, and its redoubtable durability. After all, any system of ideas that can remain unchanged as teachable wisdom (in academies, books, congresses, universities, foreign-service institutes) from the period of Ernest Renan in the late 1840s until the present in the United States must be something more formidable than a mere collection of lies. Orientalism, therefore, is not an airy European fantasy about the Orient, but a created body of theory and practice in which, for many generations, there has been a considerable material investment. Continued investment made Orientalism, as a system of knowledge about the Orient, an accepted grid for filtering through the Orient into Western consciousness, just as that same investment multiplied – indeed, made truly productive – the statements proliferating out from Orientalism into the general culture.

Gramsci has made the useful analytic distinction between civil and political society in which the former is made up of voluntary (or at least rational and noncoercive) affiliations like schools, families and unions, the latter of state institutions (the army, the police, the central bureaucracy) whose role in the polity is direct domination. Culture, of course, is to be found operating within civil society, where the influence of ideas, of institutions, and of other persons works not through domination but by what Gramsci calls consent. In any society not totalitarian, then, certain cultural forms predominate over others, just as certain ideas are more influential than others; the form of this cultural leadership is what Gramsci has identified as *hegemony*, an indispensable concept for any understanding of cultural life in the industrial West. It is hegemony, or rather the result of cultural hegemony at work, that gives Orientalism the durability and the strength I have been speaking about so far. Orientalism is never far from what Denys Hay has called the idea of Europe,[2] a collective notion identifying 'us' Europeans as against all 'those' non-Europeans, and indeed it can be argued that the major component in European culture is precisely what made that culture hegemonic both in and outside Europe: the idea of European identity as a superior one in comparison with all the non-European peoples and cultures. There is in addition the hegemony of European ideas about the Orient, themselves reiterating European superiority over Oriental backwardness, usually overriding the possibility that a more independent, or more skeptical, thinker might have had different views on the matter.

In a quite constant way, Orientalism depends for its strategy on this flexible *positional* superiority, which puts the Westerner in a whole series of possible relationships with the Orient without ever losing him the relative upper hand. And why should it have been otherwise, especially during the period of extraordinary European ascendancy from the late Renaissance to the present? The scientist, the scholar, the missionary, the trader or the soldier was in, or thought about, the Orient because *he could be there*, or could think about it, with very little resistance on the Orient's part. Under the general heading of knowledge of the Orient, and within the umbrella of Western hegemony over the Orient during the period from the end of the eighteenth century, there emerged a complex Orient suitable for study in the academy, for display in the museum, for reconstruction in the colonial office, for theoretical illustration in anthropological, biological, linguistic, racial and historical theses about mankind and the universe, for instances of economic and sociological theories of development, revolution, cultural personality, national or religious character. Additionally, the imaginative examination of things Oriental was based more or less exclusively upon a sovereign Western consciousness out of whose unchallenged centrality an Oriental world emerged, first according to general ideas about who or what was an Oriental, then according to a detailed logic governed not simply by empirical reality but by a battery of desires, repressions, investments and projections. If we can point to great Orientalist works of genuine scholarship like Silvestre de Sacy's *Chrestomathie arabe* or Edward William Lane's *Account of the Manners and Customs of the Modern Egyptians*, we need also to note that Renan's and Gobineau's racial ideas came out of the same impulse, as did a great many Victorian pornographic novels (see the analysis by Steven Marcus of 'The lustful Turk'[3]).

And yet, one must repeatedly ask oneself whether what matters in Orientalism is the general group of ideas overriding the mass of material – about which who could deny that they were shot through with doctrines of European superiority, various kinds of racism, imperialism and the like, dogmatic views of 'the Oriental' as a kind of ideal and unchanging abstraction? – or the much more varied work produced by almost uncountable individual writers, whom one would take up as individual instances of authors dealing with the Orient. In a sense the two alternatives, general and particular, are really two perspectives on the same material: in both instances one would have to deal with pioneers in the field like William Jones, with great artists like Nerval or Flaubert. And why would it not be possible to employ both perspectives together, or one after the other? Isn't there an obvious danger of distortion (of precisely the kind that academic Orientalism has always been prone to) if either too general or too specific a level of description is maintained systematically?

My two fears are distortion and inaccuracy, or rather the kind of inaccuracy produced by too dogmatic a generality and too positivistic a localized focus. In trying to deal with these problems I have tried to deal with [. . .] aspects of my own contemporary reality that seem to me to point the way out of the methodological or perspectival difficulties I have been discussing, difficulties that might force one, in the first instance, into writing a coarse polemic on so unacceptably general a level of description as not to be worth the effort, or in the second instance, into writing so detailed and atomistic a series of analyses as to lose all track of the general lines of force informing the field, giving it its special cogency. How then to recognize individuality and to reconcile it with its intelligent, and by no means passive or merely dictatorial, general and hegemonic context?

III

I mentioned [. . .] aspects of my contemporary reality: I must explain and briefly discuss [one of these] now, so that it can be seen how I was led to a particular course of research and writing.

[. . .] *The distinction between pure and political knowledge.* It is very easy to argue that knowledge about Shakespeare or Wordsworth is not political whereas knowledge about contemporary China or the Soviet Union is. My own formal and professional designation is that of 'humanist', a title which indicates the humanities as my field and therefore the unlikely eventuality that there might be anything political about what I do in that field. Of course, all these labels and terms are quite unnuanced as I use them here, but the general truth of what I am pointing to is, I think, widely held. One reason for saying that a humanist who writes about Wordsworth, or an editor whose specialty is Keats, is not involved in anything political is that what he does seems to have no direct political effect upon reality in the everyday sense. A scholar whose field is Soviet economics works in a highly charged area where there is much government interest, and what he might produce in the way of studies or proposals will be taken up by policy makers, government officials, institutional economists, intelligence experts. The distinction between 'humanists' and persons whose work has policy implications, or political significance, can be broadened further by saying that the former's ideological color is a matter of incidental importance to politics (although possibly of great moment to his colleagues in the field, who may object to his Stalinism or fascism or too easy liberalism), whereas the ideology of the latter is woven directly into his material – indeed, economics, politics and sociology in the modern academy are ideological sciences – and therefore taken for granted as being 'political'.

Nevertheless the determining impingement on most knowledge produced in the contemporary West (and here I speak mainly about the United States) is that it be nonpolitical, that is, scholarly, academic, impartial, above partisan or small-minded doctrinal belief. One can have no quarrel with such an ambition in theory, perhaps, but in practice the reality is much more problematic. No one has ever devised a method for detaching the scholar from the circumstances of life, from the fact of his involvement (conscious or unconscious) with a class, a set of beliefs, a social position, or from the mere activity of being a member of a society. These continue to bear on what he does professionally, even though naturally enough his research and its fruits do attempt to reach a level of relative freedom from the inhibitions and the restrictions of brute, everyday reality. For there is such a thing as knowledge that is less, rather than more, partial than the individual (with his entangling and distracting life circumstances) who produces it. Yet this knowledge is not therefore automatically nonpolitical.

Whether discussions of literature or of classical philology are fraught with – or have unmediated – political significance is a very large question that I have tried to treat in some detail elsewhere.[4] What I am interested in doing now is suggesting how the general liberal consensus that 'true' knowledge is fundamentally nonpolitical (and conversely, that overtly political knowledge is not 'true' knowledge) obscures the highly if obscurely organized political circumstances obtaining when knowledge is produced. No one is helped in understanding this today when the adjective 'political' is used as a label to discredit any work for daring to violate the protocol of pretended suprapolitical objectivity. We may say, first, that civil society recognizes a gradation of political importance in the various fields of knowledge. To some extent the political importance given a field comes from the possibility of its direct translation into economic terms; but to a greater extent political importance comes from the closeness of a field to ascertainable sources of power in political society. Thus an economic study of long-term Soviet energy potential and its effect on military capability is likely to be commissioned by the Defense Department, and thereafter to acquire a kind of political status impossible for a study of Tolstoi's early fiction financed in part by a foundation. Yet both works belong in what civil society acknowledges to be a similar field, Russian studies, even though one work may be done by a very conservative economist, the other by a radical literary historian. My point here is that 'Russia' as a general subject matter has political priority over nicer distinctions such as 'economics' and 'literary history', because political society in Gramsci's sense reaches into such realms of civil society as the academy and saturates them with significance of direct concern to it.

I do not want to press all this any further on general theoretical grounds: it seems to me that the value and credibility of my case can be demonstrated by being much more specific, in the way, for example, Noam Chomsky has studied the instrumental connection between the Vietnam War and the notion of objective scholarship as it was applied to cover state-sponsored military research.[5] Now because Britain, France and recently the United States are imperial powers, their political societies impart to their civil societies a sense of urgency, a direct political infusion as it were, where and whenever matters pertaining to their imperial interests abroad are concerned. I doubt that it is controversial, for example, to say that an Englishman in India or Egypt in the later nineteenth century took an interest in those countries that was never far from their status in his mind as British colonies. To say this may seem quite different from saying that all academic knowledge about India and Egypt is somehow tinged and impressed with, violated by, the gross political fact – and yet *that is what I am saying* in this study of Orientalism. For if it is true that no production of knowledge in the human sciences can ever ignore or disclaim its author's involvement as a human subject in his own circumstances, then it must also be true that for a European or American studying the Orient there can be no disclaiming the main circumstances of *his* actuality: that he comes up against the Orient as a European or American first, as an individual second. And to be a European or an American in such a situation is by no means an inert fact. It meant and means being aware, however dimly, that one belongs to a power with definite interests in the Orient, and more important, that one belongs to a part of the earth with a definite history of involvement in the Orient almost since the time of Homer.

Put in this way, these political actualities are still too undefined and general to be really interesting. Anyone would agree to them without necessarily agreeing also that they mattered very much, for instance, to Flaubert as he wrote *Salammbô*, or to H. A. R. Gibb as he wrote *Modern Trends in Islam*. The trouble is that there is too great a distance between the big dominating fact, as I have described it, and the details of everyday life that govern the minute discipline of a novel or a scholarly text as each is being written. Yet if we eliminate from the start any notion that 'big' facts like imperial domination can be applied mechanically and deterministically to such complex matters as culture and ideas, then we will begin to approach an interesting kind of study. My idea is that European and then American interest in the Orient was political according to some of the obvious historical accounts of it that I have given here, but that it was the culture that created that interest, that acted dynamically along with brute political, economic and military rationales to make the Orient the varied and complicated place that it obviously was in the field I call Orientalism.

Therefore, Orientalism is not a mere political subject matter or field that is reflected passively by culture, scholarship or institutions; nor is it a large and diffuse collection of texts about the Orient; nor is it representative and expressive of some nefarious 'Western' imperialist plot to hold down the 'Oriental' world. It is rather a *distribution* of geopolitical awareness into aesthetic, scholarly, economic, sociological, historical and philological texts; it is an *elaboration* not only of a basic geographical distinction (the world is made up of two unequal halves, Orient and Occident) but also of a whole series of 'interests' which, by such means as scholarly discovery, philological reconstruction, psychological analysis, landscape and sociological description, it not only creates but also maintains; it *is*, rather than expresses, a certain *will* or *intention* to understand, in some cases to control, manipulate, even to incorporate, what is a manifestly different (or alternative and novel) world; it is, above all, a discourse that is by no means in direct, corresponding relationship with political power in the raw, but rather is produced and exists in an uneven exchange with various kinds of power, shaped to a degree by the exchange with power political (as with a colonial or imperial establishment), power intellectual (as with reigning sciences like comparative linguistics or anatomy, or any of the modern policy sciences), power cultural (as with orthodoxies and canons of taste, texts, values), power moral (as with ideas about what 'we' do and what 'they' cannot do or understand as 'we' do). Indeed, my real argument is that Orientalism is – and does not simply represent – a considerable dimension of modern political-intellectual culture, and as such has less to do with the Orient than it does with 'our' world.

Because Orientalism is a cultural and a political fact, then, it does not exist in some archival vacuum; quite the contrary, I think it can be shown that what is thought, said, or even done about the Orient follows (perhaps occurs within) certain distinct and intellectually knowable lines. Here too a considerable degree of nuance and elaboration can be seen working as between the broad superstructural pressures and the details of composition, the facts of textuality. Most humanistic scholars are, I think, perfectly happy with the notion that texts exist in contexts, that there is such a thing as intertextuality, that the pressures of conventions, predecessors and rhetorical styles limit what Walter Benjamin once called the 'overtaxing of the productive person in the name of ... the principle of "creativity"', in which the poet is believed on his own, and out of his pure mind, to have brought forth his work.[6] Yet there is a reluctance to allow that political, institutional and ideological constraints act in the same manner on the individual author. A humanist will believe it to be an interesting fact to any interpreter of Balzac that he was influenced in the *Comédie humaine* by the conflict between Geoffroy Saint-Hilaire and Cuvier, but the same sort of pressure on Balzac of deeply reactionary monarchism is felt in some vague way to demean his literary 'genius' and therefore to be less worth serious study. Similarly – as Harry Bracken has been tirelessly showing – philosophers will conduct their discussions of Locke, Hume and empiricism without ever taking into account that there is an explicit connection in these classic writers between their 'philosophic' doctrines and racial theory, justifications of slavery, or arguments for colonial exploitation.[7] These are common enough ways by which contemporary scholarship keeps itself pure.

Perhaps it is true that most attempts to rub culture's nose in the mud of politics have been crudely iconoclastic; perhaps also the social interpretation of literature in my own field has simply not kept up with the enormous technical advances in detailed textual analysis. But there is no getting away from the fact that literary studies in general, and American Marxist theorists in particular, have avoided the effort of seriously bridging the gap between the superstructural and the base levels in textual, historical scholarship; on another occasion I have gone so far as to say that the literary-cultural establishment as a whole has declared the serious study of imperialism and culture off limits.[8] For Orientalism brings one up directly against that question – that is, to realizing that political imperialism governs an entire field of study, imagination and scholarly institutions – in such a way as to make its avoidance an intellectual and historical impossibility. Yet there will always remain the perennial escape mechanism of saying that a literary scholar and a philosopher, for example, are trained in literature and philosophy repectively, not in politics or ideological analysis. In other words, the specialist argument can work quite effectively to block the larger and, in my opinion, the more intellectually serious perspective.

Here it seems to me there is a simple two-part answer to be given, at least so far as the study of imperialism and culture (or Orientalism) is concerned. In the first place nearly every nineteenth-century writer (and the same is true enough of writers in earlier periods) was extraordinarily well aware of the fact of empire: this is a subject not very well studied, but it will not take a modern Victorian specialist long to admit that liberal cultural heroes like John Stuart Mill, Arnold, Carlyle, Newman, Macaulay, Ruskin, George Eliot and even Dickens had definite views on race and imperialism, which are quite easily to be found at work in their writing. So even a specialist must deal with the knowledge that Mill, for example, made it clear in *On Liberty and Representative Government* that his views there could not be applied to India (he was an India Office functionary for a good deal of his life, after all) because the Indians were civilizationally, if not racially, inferior. The same kind of paradox is to be found in Marx, as I try to show in this book. In the second place, to believe that politics in the form of imperialism bears upon the production of literature, scholarship, social theory and history writing is by no means equivalent to saying that culture is therefore a demeaned or denegrated thing. Quite the contrary: my whole point is to say that we can better understand the persistence and the durability of saturating hegemonic systems like culture when we realize that their internal constraints upon writers and thinkers were *productive*, not unilaterally inhibiting. It is this idea that Gramsci, certainly, and Foucault and Raymond Williams in their very different ways have been trying to illustrate. Even one or two pages by Williams on 'the uses of the Empire' in *The Long Revolution* tell us more about nineteenth-century cultural richness than many volumes of hermetic textual analyses.[9]

Therefore I study Orientalism as a dynamic exchange between individual authors and the large political concerns shaped by the three great empires – British, French, American – in whose intellectual and imaginative territory the writing was produced. What interests me most as a scholar is not the gross political verity but the detail, as indeed what interests us in someone like Lane or Flaubert or Renan is not the (to him) indisputable truth that Occidentals are superior to Orientals, but the profoundly worked over and modulated evidence of his detailed work within the very wide space opened up by that truth. One need only remember that Lane's *Manners and Customs of the Modern Egyptians* is a classic of historical and anthropological observation because of its style, its enormously intelligent and brilliant details, not because of its simple reflection of racial superiority, to understand what I am saying here.

The kind of political questions raised by Orientalism, then, are as follows: what other sorts of intellectual, aesthetic, scholarly and cultural energies went into the making of an imperialist tradition like the Orientalist one? How did philology, lexicography, history, biology, political and economic theory, novel-writing and lyric poetry come to the service of Orientalism's broadly imperialist view of the world? What changes, modulations, refinements, even revolutions take place within Orientalism? What is the meaning of originality, of continuity, of individuality, in this context? How does Orientalism transmit or reproduce itself from one epoch to another? In fine, how can we treat the cultural, historical phenomenon of Orientalism as a kind of *willed human work* – not of mere unconditioned ratiocination – in all its historical complexity, detail and worth without at the same time losing sight of the alliance between cultural work, political tendencies, the state and the specific realities of domination? Governed by such concerns a humanistic study can responsibly address itself to politics *and* culture. But this is not to say that such a study establishes a hard-and-fast rule about the relationship between knowledge and politics. My argument is that each humanistic investigation must formulate the nature of that connection in the specific context of the study, the subject matter, and its historical circumstances.

[...]

Latent and Manifest Orientalism

In Chapter One [of *Orientalism*, not reproduced here] I tried to indicate the scope of thought and action covered by the word *Orientalism*, using as privileged types the British and French experiences of and with the Near Orient, Islam and the Arabs. In those experiences I discerned an intimate, perhaps even the most intimate, and rich relationship between Occident and Orient. Those experiences were part of a much wider European or Western relationship with the Orient, but what seems to have influenced Orientalism most was a fairly constant sense of confrontation felt by Westerners dealing with the East. The boundary notion of East and West, the varying degrees of projected inferiority and strength, the range of work done, the kinds of characteristic features ascribed to the Orient: all these testify to a willed imaginative and geographic division made between East and West, and lived through during many centuries. In Chapter Two [not reproduced here] my focus narrowed a good deal. I was interested in the earliest phases of what I call modern Orientalism, which began during the latter part of the eighteenth century and the early years of the nineteenth. Since I did not intend my study to become a narrative chronicle of the development of Oriental studies in the modern West, I proposed instead an account of the rise, development and institutions of Orientalism as they were formed against a background of intellectual, cultural and political history until about 1870 or 1880. Although my interest in Orientalism there included a decently ample variety of scholars and imaginative writers, I cannot claim by any means to have presented more than a portrait of the typical structures (and their ideological tendencies) constituting the field, its associations with other fields, and the work of some of its most influential scholars. My principal operating assumptions were – and continue to be – that fields of learning, as much as the works of even the most eccentric artist, are constrained and acted upon by society, by cultural traditions, by worldly circumstance, and by stabilizing influences like schools, libraries and governments; moreover, that both learned and imaginative writing are never free, but are limited in their imagery, assumptions and intentions; and finally, that the advances made by a 'science' like Orientalism in its academic form are less objectively true than we often like to think. In short, my study hitherto has tried to describe the *economy* that makes Orientalism a coherent subject matter, even while allowing that as an idea, concept or image the word *Orient* has a considerable and interesting cultural resonance in the West.

I realize that such assumptions are not without their controversial side. Most of us assume in a general way that learning and scholarship move forward; they get better, we feel, as time passes and as more information is accumulated, methods are refined, and later generations of scholars improve upon earlier ones. In addition, we entertain a mythology of creation, in which it is believed that artistic genius, an original talent, or a powerful intellect can leap beyond the confines of its own time and place in order to put before the world a new work. It would be pointless to deny that such ideas as these carry some truth. Nevertheless the possibilities for work present in the culture to a great and original mind are never unlimited, just as it is also true that a great talent has a very healthy respect for what others have done before it and for what the field already contains. The work of predecessors, the institutional life of a scholarly field, the collective nature of any learned enterprise: these, to say nothing of economic and social circumstances, tend to diminish the effects of the individual scholar's production. A field like Orientalism has a cumulative and corporate identity, one that is particularly strong given its associations with traditional learning (the classics, the Bible, philology), public institutions (governments, trading companies, geographical societies, universities) and generically determined writing (travel books, books of exploration, fantasy, exotic description). The result for Orientalism has been a sort of consensus: certain things, certain types of statement, certain types of work have seemed for the Orientalist correct. He has built his work and research upon them, and they in turn have pressed hard upon new writers and scholars. Orientalism can thus be regarded as a manner of regularized (or Orientalized) writing, vision and study, dominated by imperatives, perspectives and ideological biases ostensibly suited to the Orient. The Orient is taught, researched, administered and pronounced upon in certain discrete ways.

The Orient that appears in Orientalism, then, is a system of representations framed by a whole set of forces that brought the Orient into Western learning, Western consciousness, and later, Western empire. If this definition of Orientalism seems more political than not, that is simply because I think Orientalism was itself a product of certain political forces and activities. Orientalism is a school of interpretation whose material happens to be the Orient, its civilizations, peoples and localities. Its objective discoveries – the work of innumerable devoted scholars who edited texts and translated them, codified grammars, wrote dictionaries, reconstructed dead epochs, produced positivistically verifiable learning – are and always have been conditioned by the fact that its truths, like any truths delivered by language, are embodied in language, and what is the truth of language, Nietzsche once said, but

> a mobile army of metaphors, metonyms, and anthropomorphisms – in short, a sum of human relations, which have been enhanced, transposed, and embellished poetically and rhetorically, and which after long use seem firm, canonical, and obligatory to a people: truths are illusions about which one has forgotten that this is what they are.[10]

Perhaps such a view as Nietzsche's will strike us as too nihilistic, but at least it will draw attention to the fact that so far as it existed in the West's awareness, the Orient was a word which later accrued to it a wide field of meanings, associations and connotations, and that these did not necessarily refer to the real Orient but to the field surrounding the word.

Thus Orientalism is not only a positive doctrine about the Orient that exists at any one time in the West; it is also an influential academic tradition (when one refers to an academic specialist who is called an Orientalist), as well as an area of concern defined by travelers, commercial enterprises, governments, military expeditions, readers of novels and accounts of exotic adventure, natural historians and pilgrims to whom the Orient is a specific kind of knowledge about specific places, peoples and civilizations. For the Orient idioms became frequent, and these idioms took firm hold in European discourse. Beneath the idioms there was a layer of doctrine about the Orient; this doctrine was fashioned out of the experiences of many Europeans, all of them converging upon such essential aspects of the Orient as the Oriental character, Oriental despotism, Oriental sensuality, and the like. For any European during the nineteenth century – and I think one can say this almost without qualification – Orientalism was such a system of truths, truths in Nietzsche's sense of the word. It is therefore correct that every European, in what he could say about the Orient, was consequently a racist, an imperialist, and almost totally ethnocentric. Some of the immediate sting will be taken out of these labels if we recall additionally that human societies, at least the more advanced cultures, have rarely offered the individual anything but imperialism, racism and ethnocentrism for dealing with 'other' cultures. So Orientalism aided and was aided by general cultural pressures that tended to make more rigid the sense of difference between the European and Asiatic parts of the world. My contention is that Orientalism is fundamentally a political doctrine willed over the Orient because the Orient was weaker than the West, which elided the Orient's difference with its weakness.

This proposition was introduced early in Chapter One, and nearly everything in the pages that followed was intended in part as a corroboration of it. The very presence of a 'field' such as Orientalism, with no corresponding equivalent in the Orient itself, suggests the relative strength of Orient and Occident. A vast number of pages on the Orient exist, and they of course signify a degree and quantity of interaction with the Orient that are quite formidable; but the crucial index of Western strength is that there is no possibility of comparing the movement of Westerners eastwards (since the end of the eighteenth century) with the movement of Easterners westwards. Leaving aside the fact that Western armies, consular corps, merchants and scientific and archaeological expeditions were always going East, the number of travelers from the Islamic East to Europe between 1800 and 1900 is minuscule when compared with the number in the other direction.[11] Moreover, the Eastern travelers in the West were there to learn from and to gape at an advanced culture; the purposes of the Western travelers in the Orient were, as we have seen, of quite a different order. In addition, it has been estimated that around 60,000 books dealing with the Near Orient were written between 1800 and 1950; there is no remotely comparable figure for Oriental books about the West. As a cultural apparatus Orientalism is all aggression, activity, judgment, will-to-truth and knowledge. The Orient existed for the West, or so it seemed to countless Orientalists, whose attitude to what they worked on was either paternalistic or candidly condescending – unless, of course, they were antiquarians, in which case the 'classical' Orient was a credit to *them* and not to the lamentable modern Orient. And then, beefing up the Western scholars' work, there were numerous agencies and institutions with no parallel in Oriental society.

Such an imbalance between East and West is obviously a function of changing historical patterns. During its political and military heyday from the eighth century to the sixteenth, Islam dominated both East and West. Then the center of power shifted westwards, and now in the late twentieth century it seems to be directing itself back towards the East again. My account of nineteenth-century Orientalism in Chapter Two stopped at a particularly charged period in the latter part of the century, when the often dilatory, abstract and projective aspects of Orientalism were about to take on a new sense of worldly mission in the service of formal colonialism. It is this project and this moment that I want now to describe, especially since it will furnish us with some important background for the twentieth-century crises of Orientalism and the resurgence of political and cultural strength in the East.

On several occasions I have alluded to the connections between Orientalism as a body of ideas, beliefs, clichés or learning about the East, and other schools of thought at large in the culture. Now one of the important developments in nineteenth-century Orientalism was the distillation of essential ideas about the Orient – its sensuality, its tendency to despotism, its aberrant mentality, its habits of inaccuracy, its backwardness – into a separate and unchallenged coherence; thus for a writer to use the word *Oriental* was a reference for the reader sufficient to identify a specific body of information about the Orient. This information seemed to be morally neutral and objectively valid; it seemed to have an epistemological status equal to that of historical chronology or geographical location. In its most basic form, then, Oriental material could not really be violated by anyone's discoveries, nor did it seem ever to be revaluated completely. Instead, the work of various nineteenth-century scholars and of imaginative writers made this essential body of knowledge more clear, more detailed, more substantial – and more distinct from 'Occidentalism'. Yet Orientalist ideas could enter into alliance with general philosophical theories (such as those about the history of mankind and civilization) and diffuse world-hypotheses, as philosophers sometimes call them; and in many ways the professional contributors to Oriental knowledge were anxious to couch their formulations and ideas, their scholarly work, their considered contemporary observations, in language and terminology whose cultural validity derived from other sciences and systems of thought.

The distinction I am making is really between an almost unconscious (and certainly an untouchable) positivity, which I shall call *latent* Orientalism, and the various stated views about Oriental society, languages, literatures, history, sociology, and so forth, which I shall call *manifest* Orientalism. Whatever change occurs in knowledge of the Orient is found almost exclusively in manifest Orientalism; the unanimity, stability and durability of latent Orientalism are more or less constant. In the nineteenth-century writers I analyzed in Chapter Two, the differences in their ideas about the Orient can be characterized as exclusively manifest differences, differences in form and personal style, rarely in basic content. Every one of them kept intact the separateness of the Orient, its eccentricity, its backwardness, its silent indifference, its feminine penetrability, its supine malleability; this is why every writer on the Orient, from Renan to Marx (ideologically speaking), or from the most rigorous scholars (Lane and Sacy) to the most powerful imaginations (Flaubert and Nerval), saw the Orient as a locale requiring Western attention, reconstruction, even redemption. The Orient existed as a place isolated from the mainstream of European progress in the sciences, arts and commerce. Thus whatever good or bad values were imputed to the Orient appeared to be functions of some highly specialized Western interest in the Orient. This was the situation from about the 1870s on through the early part of the twentieth century – but let me give some examples that illustrate what I mean.

Theses of Oriental backwardness, degeneracy and inequality with the West most easily associated themselves early in the nineteenth century with ideas about the biological bases of racial inequality. Thus the racial classifications found in Cuvier's *Le Règne animal*, Gobineau's *Essai sur l'inégalité des races humaines*, and Robert Knox's *The Races of Man* found a willing partner in latent Orientalism. To these ideas was added second-order Darwinism, which seemed to accentuate the 'scientific' validity of the division of races into advanced and backward, or European-Aryan and Oriental-African. Thus the whole question of imperialism, as it was debated in the late nineteenth century by pro-imperialists and anti-imperialists alike, carried forward the binary typology of advanced and backward (or subject) races, cultures and societies. John Westlake's *Chapters on the Principles of International Law* (1984) argues, for example, that regions of the earth designated as 'uncivilized' (a word carrying the freight of Orientalist assumptions, among others) ought to be annexed or occupied by advanced powers. Similarly, the ideas of such writers as Carl Peters, Leopold de Saussure and Charles Temple draw on the advanced/backward binarism[12] so centrally advocated in late-nineteenth-century Orientalism.

Along with all other peoples variously designated as backward, degenerate, uncivilized and retarded, the Orientals were viewed in a framework constructed out of biological determinism and moral-political admonishment. The Oriental was linked thus to elements in Western society (delinquents, the insane, women, the poor) having in common an identity best described as lamentably alien. Orientals were rarely seen or looked at; they were seen through, analyzed not as citizens, or even people, but as problems to be solved or confined or – as the colonial powers openly coveted their territory – taken over. The point is that the very designation of something as Oriental involved an already pronounced evaluative judgment, and in the case of the peoples inhabiting the decayed Ottoman Empire, an implicit program of action. Since the Oriental was a member of a subject race, he had to be subjected: it was that simple. The *locus classicus* for such judgment and action is to be found in Gustave Le Bon's *Les Lois psychologiques de l'évolution des peuples* (1894).

But there were other uses for latent Orientalism. If that group of ideas allowed one to separate Orientals from advanced, civilizing powers, and if the 'classical' Orient served to justify both the Orientalist and his disregard of modern Orientals, latent Orientalism also encouraged a peculiarly (not to say invidiously) male conception of the world. I have already referred to this in passing during my discussion of Renan. The Oriental male was considered in isolation from the total community in which he lived and which many Orientalists, following Lane, have viewed with something resembling contempt and fear. Orientalism itself, furthermore, was an exclusively male province; like so many professional guilds during the modern period, it viewed itself and its subject matter with sexist blinders. This is especially evident in the writing of travelers and novelists: women are usually the creatures of a male power-fantasy. They express unlimited sensuality, they are more or less stupid, and above all they are willing. Flaubert's Kuchuk Hanem is the prototype of such caricatures, which were common enough in pornographic novels (e.g. Pierre Louÿs's *Aphrodite*) whose novelty draws on the Orient for their interest. Moreover the male conception of the world, in its effect upon the practicing Orientalist, tends to be static, frozen, fixed eternally. The very possibility of development, transformation, human movement – in the deepest sense of the word – is denied the Orient and the Oriental. As a known and ultimately an immobilized or unproductive quality, they come to be identified with a bad sort of eternality: hence, when the Orient is being approved, such phrases as 'the wisdom of the East'.

Transferred from an implicit social evaluation to a grandly cultural one, this static male Orientalism took on a variety of forms in the late nineteenth century, especially when Islam was being discussed. General cultural historians as respected as Leopold von Ranke and Jacob Burckhardt assailed Islam as if they were dealing not so much with an anthropomorphic abstraction as with a religio-political culture about which deep generalizations were possible and warranted: in his *Weltgeschichte* (1881–1888) Ranke spoke of Islam as defeated by the Germanic-Romanic peoples, and in his 'Historische Fragmente' (unpublished notes, 1893) Burckhardt spoke of Islam as wretched, bare and trivial.[13] Such intellectual operations were carried out with considerably more flair and enthusiasm by Oswald Spengler, whose ideas about a Magian personality (typified by the Muslim Oriental) infuse *Der Untergang des Abendlandes* (1918–1922) and the 'morphology' of cultures it advocates.

What these widely diffused notions of the Orient depended on was the almost total absence in contemporary Western culture of the Orient as a genuinely felt and experienced force. For a number of evident reasons the Orient was always in the position both of outsider and of incorporated weak partner for the West. To the extent that Western scholars were aware of contemporary Orientals or Oriental movements of thought and culture, these were perceived either as silent shadows to be animated by the Orientalist, brought into reality by him, or as a kind of cultural and intellectual proletariat useful for the Orientalist's grander interpretative activity, necessary for his performance as superior judge, learned man, powerful cultural will. I mean to say that in discussions of the Orient, the Orient is all absence, whereas one feels the Orientalist and what he says as presence; yet we must not forget that the Orientalist's presence is enabled by the Orient's effective absence. This fact of substitution and displacement, as we must call it, clearly places on the Orientalist himself a certain pressure to reduce the Orient in his work, even after he has devoted a good deal of time to elucidating and exposing it. How else can one explain major scholarly production of the type we associate with Julius Wellhausen and Theodor Nöldeke and, overriding it, those bare, sweeping statements that almost totally denigrate their chosen subject matter? Thus Nöldeke could declare in 1887 that the sum total of his work as an Orientalist was to confirm his 'low opinion' of the Eastern peoples.[14] And like Carl Becker, Nöldeke was a philhellenist, who showed his love of Greece curiously by displaying a positive dislike of the Orient, which after all was what he studied as a scholar.

A very valuable and intelligent study of Orientalism – Jacques Waardenburg's *L'Islam dans le miroir de l'Occident* – examines five important experts as makers of an image of Islam. Waardenburg's mirror-image metaphor for late-nineteenth- and early-twentieth-century Orientalism is apt. In the work of each of his eminent Orientalists there is a highly tendentious – in four cases out of the five, even hostile – vision of Islam, as if each man saw Islam as a reflection of his own chosen weakness. Each scholar was profoundly learned, and the style of his contribution was unique. The five Orientalists among them exemplify what was best and strongest in the tradition during the period roughly from the 1880s to the interwar years. Yet Ignaz Goldziher's appreciation of Islam's tolerance towards other religions was undercut by his dislike of Mohammed's anthropomorphisms and Islam's too-exterior theology and jurisprudence; Duncan Black Macdonald's interest in Islamic piety and orthodoxy was vitiated by his perception of what he considered Islam's heretical Christianity; Carl Becker's understanding of Islamic civilization made him see it as a sadly undeveloped one; C. Snouck Hurgronje's highly refined studies of Islamic mysticism (which he considered the essential part of Islam) led him to a harsh judgment of its crippling limitations; and Louis Massignon's extraordinary identification with Muslim theology, mystical passion and poetic art kept him curiously unforgiving to Islam for what he regarded as its unregenerate revolt against the idea of incarnation. The manifest differences in their methods emerge as less important than their Orientalist consensus on Islam: latent inferiority.[15]

Waardenburg's study has the additional virtue of showing how these five scholars shared a common intellectual and methodological tradition whose unity was truly international. Ever since the first Orientalist congress in 1873, scholars in the field have known each other's work and felt each other's presence very directly. What Waardenburg does not stress enough is that most of the late-nineteenth-century Orientalists were bound to each other politically as well. Snouck Hurgronje went directly from his studies of Islam to being an adviser to the Dutch government on handling its Muslim Indonesian colonies; Macdonald and Massignon were widely sought after as experts on Islamic matters by colonial administrators from North Africa to Pakistan; and, as Waardenburg says (all too briefly) at one point, all five scholars shaped a coherent vision of Islam that had a wide influence on government circles throughout the Western world.[16] What we must add to Waardenburg's observation is that these scholars were completing, bringing to an ultimate concrete refinement, the tendency since the sixteenth and seventeenth centuries to treat the Orient not only as a vague literary problem but – according to Masson-Oursel – as 'un ferme propos d'assimiler adéquatement la valeur des langues pour pénétrer les moeurs et les pensées, pour forcer même des secrets de l'histoire.'[17]

I spoke earlier of incorporation and assimilation of the Orient as these activities were practiced by writers as different from each other as Dante and d'Herbelot. Clearly there is a difference between those efforts and what, by the end of the nineteenth century, had become a truly formidable European cultural, political and material enterprise. The nineteenth-century colonial 'scramble for Africa' was by no means limited to Africa, of course. Neither was the penetration of the Orient entirely a sudden, dramatic afterthought following years of scholarly study of Asia. What we must reckon with is a long and slow process of appropriation by which Europe, or the European awareness of the Orient, transformed itself from being textual and contemplative into being administrative, economic and even military. The fundamental change was a spatial and geographical one, or rather it was a change in the quality of geographical and spatial apprehension so far as the Orient was concerned. The centuries-old designation of geographical space to the east of

Europe as 'Oriental' was partly political, partly doctrinal and partly imaginative; it implied no necessary connection between actual experience of the Orient and knowledge of what is Oriental, and certainly Dante and d'Herbelot made no claims about their Oriental ideas except that they were corroborated by a long *learned* (and not existential) tradition. But when Lane, Renan, Burton, and the many hundreds of nineteenth-century European travelers and scholars discuss the Orient, we can immediately note a far more intimate and even proprietary attitude towards the Orient and things Oriental. In the classical and often temporally remote form in which it was reconstructed by the Orientalist, in the precisely actual form in which the modern Orient was lived in, studied or imagined, the *geographical space* of the Orient was penetrated, worked over, taken hold of. The cumulative effect of decades of so sovereign a Western handling turned the Orient from alien into colonial space. What was important in the latter nineteenth century was not *whether* the West had penetrated and possessed the Orient, but rather *how* the British and French felt that they had done it.

Notes

1. K. M. Panikkar, *Asia and Western Dominance*, George Allen & Unwin: London, 1959.
2. Denys Hay, *Europe: The emergence of an idea*, 2nd edn. Edinburgh University Press: Edinburgh, 1968.
3. Steven Marcus, *The Other Victorians: A study of sexuality and pornography in mid-nineteenth-century England*, 1966; reprint edn, Bantam Books: New York, 1967, pp. 200–19.
4. See my *Criticism Between Culture and System*, Harvard University Press: Cambridge, MA.
5. Principally in his *American Power and the New Mandarins: Historical and political essays*, Pantheon Books: New York, 1969, and *For Reasons of State*, Pantheon Books: New York, 1973.
6. Walter Benjamin, *Charles Baudelaire: A lyric poet in the era of high capitalism*, trans. Harry Zohn, New Left Books: London, 1973, p. 71.
7. Harry Bracken, 'Essence, accident and race', *Hermathena*, 116, Winter 1973, pp. 81–96.
8. In an interview published in *Diacritics*, 6, 3, Fall 1976, p. 38.
9. Raymond Williams, *The Long Revolution*, Chatto & Windus: London, 1961, pp. 66–7.
10. Friedrich Nietzsche, 'On truth and lie in an extra-moral sense', in *The Portable Nietzsche*, ed. and trans. Walter Kaufmann, Viking Press: New York, 1954, pp. 46–7.
11. The number of Arab travelers to the West is estimated and considered by Ibrahim Abu-Lughod in *Arab Rediscovery of Europe: A study in cultural encounters*, Princeton University Press: Princeton, NJ, 1963, pp. 75–6 and *passim*.
12. See Philip D. Curtin (ed.), *Imperialism: The documentary history of Western civilization*, Walker & Co: New York, 1972, pp. 73–105.

13. See Johann W. Fück, 'Islam as an historical problem in European historiography since 1800', in Bernard Lewis and P. M. Holt (eds.), *Historians of the Middle East*, Oxford University Press: London, 1962, p. 307.
14. *ibid.*, p. 309.
15. See Jacques Waardenburg, *L'Islam dans le miroir de l'Occident*, Mouton & Co: The Hague, 1963.
16. *ibid.*, p. 311.
17. P. Masson-Oursel, 'La Connaissance scientifique de l'Asie en France depuis 1900 et les variétés de l'Orientalisme', *Revue Philosphique*, 143, 7–9, July–September 1953, p. 345.

7 □ Orientalism *and its Problems*

Dennis Porter

My reading of Edward W. Said's important book *Orientalism*[1] has occurred in the context of an inquiry into travel literature and its modes of representation. I come to it preoccupied by such questions as the following: What are some of the principal forms that travel literature has taken? What techniques of reportage and representation does it employ? What happens when a writer encodes atomized features of an alien culture into the linguistic codes and conventional narrative forms of a culture of reference? Does a natural language itself set up subject/object relations that are also power relations? Are we so positioned by a given historical and geopolitical conjuncture that misrepresentation is a structural necessity or is there a place of truth?

From such a reading perspective, *Orientalism* is valuable for a number of reasons. Influenced both by Gramscian thought on hegemonic formations and by that Foucauldian discourse theory which is summed up in the concept of the episteme, Said's book delimits a field of inquiry in the West that it designates 'Orientalism' and defines as a relatively unified discourse that over the centuries has been virtually coterminous with Western consciousness of the East. Said makes it clear that he is concerned with the way in which the so-called Orient, from the Eastern Mediterranean to South East Asia, 'became known in the West as its great complementary opposite since antiquity' (p. 58). His focus is not therefore on a possible 'correspondence between Orientalism and the Orient, but with the internal consistency of Orientalism and its ideas about the Orient' (p. 5). Furthermore, Orientalism is variously defined as 'a Western style for dominating, restructuring, and having authority over the Orient' (p. 3), as a hegemonic Western discourse dependent on 'a distribution of geopolitical awareness into aesthetic, scholarly, historical and philosophical texts' (p. 120). Said's book has then the character of a Nietzschean genealogy which delimits a given field of inquiry in order to expose the multiple mystified relations between knowledge and power, culture and politics.

From Francis Barker, Peter Hulme, Margaret Iversen and Diane Loxley (eds.), *The Politics of Theory*, Proceedings of the Essex Sociology of Literature Conference, University of Essex: Colchester, 1983, pp. 179–82, 186–93.

In a discussion of the methodological problems raised by his study Said notes that he is not interested in 'a coarse polemic' nor a detailed and atomistic 'series of analyses', neither with 'the general group of ideas overriding the mass of material' nor 'the much more varied work produced by almost uncountable individual writers' (p. 8). In spite of the fact that he will focus on 'the British, French and American experience of the Orient taken as a unit' (p. 16), it is his intention to take account of 'individuality' as well as of the 'general and hegemonic context' (p. 9). Yet the methodological problems raised by Said's work are formidable and they appear in a particularly crucial form almost from the beginning.

From his introduction on, Said vacillates over the opposition between truth and ideology. On the one hand, he reaches the conclusion that there is no distinction between pure and political knowledge.[2] He even claims that 'all cultures impose corrections upon raw reality, changing it from free-floating objects into units of knowledge' (p. 67). On the other hand, in a discussion of representation he seems to imply, if only negatively, that a form of truth is obtainable; he comments for example that 'what is commonly circulated is not truth but representations' (p. 21), that there is perhaps a 'real' and consequently knowable Orient. It is on account of hegemonic discourse, therefore, that 'Truth ... becomes a function of learned judgement, not of the material itself' (p. 67).

Whereas the second set of propositions implies the existence of a place of truth, of the possibility of emergence from hegemonic discourse into a beyond of true knowledge, the first set denies the idea of any knowledge pure of political positioning. The contradiction is never fully resolved in Said's book in part because he deals in such problematic concepts as 'raw reality' and 'the material itself' without reference to an epistemology that legitimates them. Moreover, the important consequence from the point of view of this paper is that if one attempts to discover whether alternatives to Orientalism are possible, whether a knowledge as opposed to an ideology of the Orient can exist, Said is of no help in spite of the acknowledgement that such alternatives are a pressing need. He writes for example, 'Perhaps the most important task of all would be to undertake studies in contemporary alternatives to Orientalism, to ask how one can study other cultures and peoples from a libertarian, or a nonrepressive and nonmanipulative perspective' (p. 24).

If the first set of propositions, concerning the lack of distinction between pure and political knowledge, is true, then Orientalism in one form or another is not only what we have but all we can ever have.[3] If, on the other hand, as Said sometimes implies, truth in representation may be achieved, how can it be justified on the basis of a radical discourse theory which presupposes the impossibility of stepping outside of a given discursive formation by an act of will or consciousness? That this fundamental contradiction goes unresolved in Said's book is, I believe, due to the incomparability of the thought of Said's two acknowledged *maîtres*, Foucault and Gramsci, of discourse theory and hegemonic theory.[4]

On the one hand, in spite of the systematic periodization in which Foucault engages in such early works as *Madness and Civilization* and *The Order of Things*

– one remembers the tripartite schema of a pre-classical, a classical and a modern age – the emergence of such discourses is historically grounded in relatively perfunctory ways. Such discourses are posited as synchronic structures or period problematics that are embodied concurrently in verbal, social and material formations. But the whole question of process, of passage from one such problematic to the next, is left in abeyance. The concept of hegemony, on the other hand, derives precisely from Gramsci's effort to think the problem of the reproduction, by consent and not by force, of the existing power relations of bourgeois society as process. Because it is grounded in consciously interventionist thought, hegemony is able to posit such reproduction by consent as the result of ideological representation and of institutional manipulation within different social formations. Commenting on hegemony in *Marxism and Literature*,[5] Raymond Williams defined it as a form of practical consciousness that concerns not only 'the articulate upper levels of ideology' but also 'a whole body of practices and expectations, over the whole of our living: our senses and assignments of energy, our shaping perceptions of ourselves and our world' (p. 110). In the context of this paper, however, the most important feature of hegemony is that it always implies historical process. In Williams' words again: 'It has continually to be renewed, recreated, defended, and altered, challenged by pressures not at all its own' (p. 112). Such a sense of hegemony as process in concrete historical conjunctures, as an evolving sphere of superstructural conflict in which power relations are continually reasserted, challenged, modified, is absent from Said's book.

The problem is further compounded because, unlike Foucault, who posits not a continuous discourse over time but epistemological breaks between different periods, Said asserts the unified character of Western discourse on the Orient over some two millennia, a unity derived from a common and continuing experience of fascination with and threat from the East, of its irreducible otherness. He is thus led to claim a continuity of representation between the Greece of Alexander the Great and the United States of President Jimmy Carter, a claim that seems to make nonsense of history at the same time as it invokes it with reference to imperial power/knowledge. Accordingly, one important reason why Said apparently cannot suggest the form alternatives to Orientalism might take in the present is that his use of discourse theory prevents him from seeing any evidence of such alternatives in the past. In fact because he does not reflect on the significance of hegemony as process, he ignores in both Western scholarly and creative writing all manifestations of counter-hegemonic thought. Because Said is understandably eager to confront Western hegemonic discourse head on, he ignores Raymond Williams' warning that the reality of cultural process must always include 'the efforts and contributions of those who are in one way or another outside or at the edge of specific hegemony' (p. 113). The consequence is serious. The failure to take account of such efforts and contributions not only opens Said to the charge of promoting Occidentalism, it also contributes to the perpetuation of that Orientalist thought he set out to demystify in the first place. Thus although Said claims that what interests him as a scholar is the detail and that he intends to be attentive to individual voices, virtually no counter-hegemonic voices are heard. Even when he praises an occasional scholar for a rare objectivity, he does not show how within the given dominant hegemonic formation such an alternative discourse was able to emerge.

If one is attentive to the crucial contradiction that *Orientalism* embodies and to its failure to reflect on hegemony as process, then it is possible to see at least three kinds of alternatives to Orientalist discourse. First, the very heterogeneity of the corpus of texts among which Said discovers hegemonic unity raises the question of the specificity of the literary instance within the superstructure. Yet no consideration is given to the possibility that literary works as such have capacity for internal ideological distanciation that is usually absent from political tracts or statesmen's memoirs. Second, Said does not seem to envisage the possibility that more directly counter-hegemonic writings or an alternative canon may exist within the Western tradition. Third, the feasibility of a textual dialogue between Western and non-Western cultures needs to be considered, a dialogue that would cause subject/object relations to alternate, so that we might read ourselves as the others of our others and replace the notion of a place of truth with that of a knowledge which is always relative and provisional. At this stage in my thinking about travel literature and the methodological questions raised by *Orientalism*, I have only attempted to reflect on the first of the alternatives mentioned, namely the possibility of ideological distanciation within works of the Western literary canon and I shall limit myself to that in what follows.

Foucauldian discourse theory does not raise the possibility of the relative autonomy of aesthetic production. Unlike Althusserian thought it has nothing to say on the question of the specificity of the literary instance or on the overdetermination of literary artifacts. Both of these concepts have perhaps a distinctly old-fashioned sound for Essex conferees but I do not believe their explanatory power has been exhausted yet. In any case, in establishing the unity and continuity of Western discourse on the Orient, Said finds grist for his mill in a wide variety of written documents, from records of parliamentary debates and official reports to the memoirs of imperial pro-consuls, scholars' exhaustive tomes, travelers' tales, fiction and poetry. Yet although he is himself a literary scholar and critic, he adopts Foucault's strategy of making no qualitative distinctions between a variety of texts produced under a variety of historical conjunctures for a wide variety of audiences.[6] Such an approach has its usefulness and it is clearly important not to practice afresh that form of mystification which has traditionally distinguished among all written products a category of the literary and has then gone on to separate it from all other forms of textual production. If I use literary here, therefore, it is only to make a qualitative distinction between texts that are characterized by a self-interrogating density of verbal texture and those that offer no internal resistance to the ideologies they reproduce. I take the literary instance to signify all texts – traditionally literary, philosophical, historical, etc. – which are of sufficient complexity to throw ideological practices into relief and raise questions about their own fictionalizing processes. Such an approach will, I hope, show that there already exist within Orientalism itself alternative and only partially silenced counter-hegemonic voices that have expressed themselves differently at different historical moments.

The case is best made by means of specific examples and I have chosen for this brief demonstration two works from the hybrid products of travel literature, two works that were written almost seven hundred years apart, yet that from Said's point of view belong to a single Western tradition of discourse. The first is the thirteenth-century *Travels* of Marco Polo, a work that antedates the period of European exploration and colonial expansion which began with the Renaissance and continued into the early decades of our own century. The second is T. E. Lawrence's *Seven Pillars of Wisdom*, a work that is usually read as an arch-imperialist text written at a time when Western power and influence were still at their height. Said refers to both works. He mentions Marco Polo's *Travels* only once in order to situate the work in that Western tradition which goes back to Herodotus and Alexander the Great, and which visited, conquered and subdivided the Orient, breaking it down into the Near East or Levant and the Far East. T. E. Lawrence and his story of the Arab revolt are briefly referred to on a number of occasions but there is no extended discussion of Lawrence's work. In the remainder of this talk I will focus on each of these works in turn. [...]

The question raised by *The Travels* is [...] can one ever speak of a unified Western discourse even at a specific historical moment let alone across centuries of historical change? At the very least shouldn't one speak of a variety of national and class discourses that give rise to all manner of overdetermined cultural products? In short, isn't discourse theory in its pure form subject to the charge of essentialism and of being unsusceptible to historical grounding? Don't Marco Polo's *Travels* suggest that if one is looking for alternatives to Orientalism, they are already here from the beginning in the contradictory accounts of the various Easts that are embodied in the variety of literary texts centered in a variety of class discourses and the literary genres through which they achieved canonical expression, from the aristocratic *chansons de gestes* of the eleventh century down to the chronicle cum romance of a Venetian merchant adventurer?

Equally as much as Marco Polo's thirteenth-century work, T. E. Lawrence's *Seven Pillars of Wisdom* can only properly be read as a complexly determined cultural product of the early twentieth century. This modern work of close to seven hundred pages is characterized by a heterogeneity and fragmentariness comparable to its medieval predecessor. It suggests once again that the kind of 'typical encapsulations' to which Said refers are often, in fact, fields of ideological forces in a state of tension. The form of a journey that they typically take may begin with a departure and end with a return but such symbolic closure does not reduce the contradictory energies that traverse the work the reader reads. Lawrence's account of the Arab revolt and his part in it contains innumerable anecdotes, and events, descriptions of place and people, evocations of mood and attitude. His text is cross-hatched with historical, political, socio-economic, and psychological determinations that once again make the whole concept of Orientalism appear to be a counter-mystification.

The reasons why *The Seven Pillars of Wisdom* is resented not only by Arabs but by all those whose sensibilities have been heightened to racial doctrines by twentieth-century history is obvious enough. Because it tells the story of the Arab nationalist revolt against the Ottoman Empire from the point of view of a British army officer, it suggests that the prime mover in the cause of Arab unity and its leading military strategist was an Englishman. It promotes the myth that a white European male in a position of leadership is an essential ingredient if colored peoples are to pursue a national goal and be an effective fighting force. In other words, *Seven Pillars*, like Marco Polo's *Travels*, lends itself to a reading that relates it directly to the tradition of hegemonic Western discourse which Said has dubbed Orientalism. And there are, in fact, a great many passages that would support such a reading. The opening chapters in particular may serve to remind us that before he was commissioned as a liaison officer to Arabia, Lawrence had some experience as an 'Arabist' and had worked for two years as an archaeologist in Syria and Mesopotamia. It is no accident, therefore, if the authoritative voice which sketches in the history of the Middle East up to the outbreak of the First World War and comments on the racial and cultural characteristics of the peoples involved is the voice of Orientalist discourse as described by Said. Such a tradition allows Lawrence to refer unequivocally to the 'Semitic consciousness' and to assert the existence of an essence possessed in common by all Semites. In Lawrence's lexicon, it should be noted that Semite is virtually synonymous with Arab although it also includes Jews. Typically, Lawrence's assertions take the form of a proper noun or third person pronoun linked by the usually plural copula 'are' to an adjective or adjectival phrase. Sentences such as the following are typical: 'Semites had no half-tones in their register of vision. They were a people of primary colours, or rather of black or white, who saw the world always in contour. They were a dogmatic people, despising doubt, our modern crown of thorns. ... They were a limited, narrow-minded people, whose inert intellects lay fallow in incurious resignation' (p. 36)[7]. At such moments Lawrence shows no critical awareness of that nineteenth-century European discourse on race in general that is speaking through him, a discourse that transmitted the doctrine of national characteristics and fixed ethnic identities, of essences transmitted that were enabling or disabling for individual members of a given race. It is such a received wisdom that allows him to dismiss the Syrians as 'an ape-like people having much of the Japanese quickness but shallow' (p. 45).

The Seven Pillars of Wisdom is, then, an extreme case, a work apparently written from a position of privilege and authority – the privilege of race, class and gender – within the Western hegemonic world order. If such a work can be re-read, shown to be fissured with doubt and contradiction, it will confirm how under certain conditions Orientalist discourse, far from being monolithic, allows counter-hegemonic voices to be heard within it. If it is true that a given hegemonic order is reproduced in part through the mechanism of exposing succeeding generations to the literary canon, a reading that uncovers doubt and contradiction within a canonical work obviously raises the possibility of counter-hegemonic energies. In the case of *The Seven Pillars*, the reason why such a struggle can occur is that for a complex set of social and psychological causes, a particular background and training are brought into conflict with experience by a particular insertion into geo-political events. And it is within the space of the text that a literary sensibility such as Lawrence's transcribes the set of oppositions involved. Thus although the reader is frequently treated to passages of received Western wisdom such as those quoted above, such passages alternate with others in which Lawrence allows his own consciousness of contradiction to surface. At the same time he also often becomes so absorbed by the aesthetic problems posed by representation and by the play of words on the page that new possibilities emerge unbidden from their combinations. As a result, Western ideological representation may be perceived by an appropriately positioned reader to be both asserted and put into question. [...] I will briefly suggest how this occurs.

The most obvious quality of *The Seven Pillars of Wisdom*, like that of *The Travels*, is its generic heterogeneity. It combines the elements of a campaign diary, an autobiographical memoir, a travel book, a history and a romance with those of a modern epic in prose whose central subject is men at war in all their horror and heroism. Yet it is this heterogeneity that accounts for the work's strength. Because it follows no single model but shifts often within a single chapter from an historical and political text to autobiography and epic, there arise textual dissonances that constitute a challenge to Western hegemonic thought at a time when the narrator was an officer in the major enforcing apparatus of such thought, the British army. This challenge occurs at a number of levels and is best explained as a dual overdetermination, that of an author as well as of a text.

To begin with, it is obvious that Lawrence himself was no political *ingénu*, no Beau Geste. The politics of the Arab revolt are, in fact, right up front in the work's Introduction and opening chapters. Lawrence makes it very clear that the Arab war against domination by the Ottoman Empire was treated by the Western allies and by Germany as an extension of the European war into the Middle East. The Anglo-French purpose was to defeat Germany's allies, the Turks, in order to maintain their influence over the area and to keep open their strategic links with the Far East through the Suez canal. To this end, as Lawrence shows, elements in the British government and military establishment saw the usefulness of making common cause with the Arabs in a campaign against Turkey. Inserted into such a military and geopolitical conjuncture by historical forces beyond his control, Lawrence asserts how from the beginning his loyalties were divided. Insofar as a war between imperialist powers was in this case also an anticolonialist struggle of liberation, the war itself was subject to a double determination that Lawrence was forced to live. As an officer in the British army, he was committed to pursuing the war aims and colonial policies of the government he served. As companion in arms of the Arabs, he believed himself morally committed to the cause of Arab national independence. Thus Lawrence's Introduction, which situates its writer in the post-war peace conference at Versailles, is also his epilogue: it tells of the betrayal of Arab hopes to which Lawrence himself was a reluctant party – 'the only thing remaining was to refuse rewards for being a successful trickster' (p. 24).

The complexity of the narrator's persona, his aspirations and self-doubt, his sense of estrangement from his own culture, the sympathy for and distance from the Arab culture he shared for roughly two years, are part of the story Lawrence tells. What he does not tell, at least not directly, is the contradictions he was forced to live at other levels. Lawrence was constituted as a subject by a set of ideological formations and structures which are familiar and include an upper-middle-class family background, the Church of England, the public school, an Oxford college, a professorial mentor who was both an Arabist and a recruiter for the British Intelligence service, a British archaeological expedition to the Near East, and the British army itself. Thus Lawrence was first formed by a number of state ideological apparatuses, including finally that British archaeological school which took the ancient Near East as its province and object of knowledge, and transferred, as a consequence of the First World War, to serve in the army that helped keep the Middle East open to European scholarly penetration and intellectual control. The continuity between the two state apparatuses confirms, of course, Said's ideas on power/knowledge. On the basis of Lawrence's biography it is possible to reconstruct further the series of interpellations to which he would have been subject in the ideologically saturated discourses and social structures of the late Victorian and Edwardian school, drawing rooms and college common rooms as well as in the canonical texts of history, thought and literature that were the prescribed readings of all aspirants to functions within the higher cultural apparatus of the British imperial order of the time. Yet resistance to such constitution as imperial subject of an hegemonic world order is apparent both in the biographical data and in Lawrence's text itself.

Lawrence was himself sensitive to the contradiction already embodied in the notion of the 'amateur soldier'. To put on a uniform against one's will is to see oneself as a divided person, to reserve part of oneself from the commitment to soldiering and to establish a distance between one's role and one's self. In Lawrence's case the complexity of his situation was further heightened when he gave up British khaki for the costume of an alien culture. To wear the robes of a Bedouin Arab was to cease in part to be British even if it could not mean that he thereby became Arab.[8] Involved is a form of cultural transvestism that enhanced the ambiguities of an identity already subject to self-doubt.

The matter of Lawrence's illegitimacy or his homosexuality are not themselves at issue here. What is important, however, is a sensibility that for one reason or another was obviously deviant in relation to a Christian bourgeois mainstream that celebrated the virtues of patriarchy and of family. Unlike the campaign memoirs of generals from Caesar to Patton and Montgomery, therefore, *Seven Pillars of Wisdom* records movements of desire and aspiration along with military and political events; it is often deeply personal in its accents, managing among other things to suggest simultaneously the anguish and urgency of sex in the desert, where the only women available were the prostitutes of the rare settlements: 'In horror of such sordid commerce our youths began indifferently to slake one another's few needs in their own clean bodies – a cold convenience that, by comparison, seemed sexless and even pure. Later, some began to justify this sterile process, and swore that friends quivering together in the yielding sand with intimate hot limbs in supreme embrace, found there hidden in the darkness a sensual coefficient of the mental passion which was welding our souls and spirits in one flaming effort' (p. 28). The passage manages to be both passionate and impersonal, projecting desire on to others but participating in it through a celebratory prose that down to such a tender phrase as 'our youths' or the word 'clean' links it to a familiar, if underground, British homoerotic tradition. Warrant for such deviancy was, of course, an important element in male public school and Oxbridge culture at the time. The idealization of Greek art and thought gave a spiritual justification to the cult of youthful male beauty and of love between males as a higher, chaster bond than that which could exist between men and women.

If such passages as the above show how socio-biographical overdetermination comes to be expressed in Lawrence's text, they also combine with a wide variety of other and similar passages to suggest the kind of overdetermined cultural object that is *Seven Pillars of Wisdom* taken as a whole. As was noted earlier, Lawrence's work has as its model not a single literary genre but several. And it is in large part because the author shifts in his text from genre to genre that the work's contradictions emerge. They are present as a radical stylistic heterogeneity, as a variety of contents, as shifting authorial distance and point of view. If, as Althusser claimed in two familiar essays,[9] literary works are neither knowledge nor ideology but are significant because they use ideology as their raw material and transform it by putting it on display, then *Seven Pillars of Wisdom* is able to achieve this largely because of the radical disjunction between elements. Whether or not one swallows one's Althusser whole, however, it is clear that Lawrence's work does not easily submit to a reading founded on the mystifications of organic form.

It is a war story and a travel journal and the tale of a moral and political coming of age. Passages that reproduce a generalized Orientalist discourse alternate with those that recall the intensity and tedium of war, the confusions of sexual desire and spiritual yearning, and scenes of thrilling natural beauty. The late romantic pursuit of intense sensation for its own sake conflicts with the Victorian code of chivalry and service to country that was mediated by the public schools. The modern epic material of battles and preparation for battle, of Bedouin camps by night, of councils of war and the clash of wills and purposes, strategy and tactics, is joined to the romance theme of personal quest, of self-testing and self-discovery under the most extreme conditions. Moreover, the romance theme is joined to the peculiarly modern motif of the divided self, of the split between the public and the private, between the man of action and the man of anguish who suspects all causes along with his own motivations.

Lawrence's eclectic text employs, then, the narrative techniques and devices and echoes the themes and attitudes of a variety of genres of the western literary tradition from as far back as the Homeric epic – he was later to translate *The Odyssey* – and chivalric romance down through the Victorian poets and writers up to such contemporaries as Kipling and Conrad. Along with the campaign literature of

Caesar, Napoleon and others, one of the rare works he mentions reading by name is significantly enough the *Morte d'Arthur*. That Lawrence's work is a product of the literary instance, of the kind of textual self-interrogation which when read appropriately both reproduces and illuminates its ideological raw materials, is finally most obvious in certain passages of apparently realist reportage. A paragraph that describes Ashraf camel riders suggests the qualities of Lawrence's prose:

> They wore rusty-red tunics henna-dyed, under black cloaks, and carried swords. Each had a slave crouched behind him on the crupper to help him with rifle and dagger in the fight, and to watch his camel and cook for him on the road. The slaves, as befitted slaves of poor masters, were very little dressed. Their strong, black legs gripped the camels' woolly sides as in a vice, to lessen the shocks inevitable on their bony perches, while they had knotted up their rags of shirts into the plaited thong about their loins to save them from the fouling of the camels and their staling on the march. Semna water was medicinal, and our animals' dung flowed like green soup down their hocks that day. (p. 157)

On the level of the signified this is very obviously the Eastern other of Western ideological representation. The color of the costumes signify oriental brilliance, the weapons warlike ferocity, the slaves despotic practices. In the play of difference and identity by means of which we report back on the alien to our culture of reference, such a passage insists on Near Eastern difference. Yet the very vividness of this group portrait and the precision of its detailing are designed to reverberate in a reader's mind and body, both stimulating a *frisson nouveau* and communicating a shock of recognition. On the one hand, the passage is striking for the peculiar libidinal investments located in the particularity of the images. On the other hand, if this is the East, it is an East that recalls the heroic age of Greek epic; it is a reminder of the classical European past. The Near East here appears in the guise of an ally not an enemy, admired for the strength of its primary colors and the wholeness of its energies. The desert Arab becomes in part an expression of the age-old nostalgia for the supposed lost wholeness of the primitive world, a modern noble savage, who is different not only from the half-Europeanized and decadent Turk but also from city Arabs. From this point of view, the scene is implicitly noteworthy because it appears against the unstated background of a contemporary European muteness of tone, world-weariness and cynicism. Thus it is far from clear that in the implied contrast between Western civilization and Eastern barbarism – the traditional Orientalist trope – the good is on the European side. The hidden obverse of the Arabia of such a passage is after all European *fin-de-sièclisme* and world-weariness. It contrasts with other paragraphs that point to the duplicity of Western power politics and to Western industrial progress as the new Western barbarism.

Finally, perhaps the most significant feature of the passage is that it demonstrates how *Seven Pillars of Wisdom* is a self-conscious work of literature in a positive sense. One is made aware of the excess of signifier over signified. Because Lawrence is obviously preoccupied by the weight and shape of the paragraph on the page as an order of words, his attention is diverted from properly hegemonic questions. As a result, the passage illuminates the potential ideological irresponsibility of language wherever an eroticized phantasy is granted the freedom to indulge itself in a literary space. From the first line to the last, the passage displays its concern for phrasing and for energizing combinations of monosyllables and alliterative patterns, as well as for an arresting anal/oral simile. The foregrounding of words as signifiers releases forces that have a capacity for producing the unexpected.

The notion of new possibilities as inherent in previously untried combinations of words, as a Utopian potential emerging within the play of the poetic function of language, is perhaps best illustrated by a short sentence that comes soon after the passage just quoted: 'We got off our camels and stretched ourselves, sat down or walked before supper to the sea and bathed by hundreds, a splashing, screaming mob of fish-like naked men of all earth's colours' (p. 159). Such a sentence reminds us that we are in the presence of the literary instance because its significance is not in what it asserts, in any generalizing thought it expresses about East or West, but in a vision of a mingling where all previous categories break down. Further, its power is in the sharp impression of a scene which only exists as a newly invented verbal order but which nevertheless suggests a previously unrealized potential. And it is a potential for which there is no support in the dominant hegemonic discourse. The imagery of baptism and of a fresh emergence from the sea as a collectivity of races – 'fish-like naked men of all earth's colours' – amounts to a politically Utopian idea as well as a homoerotic phantasm. It is in any case an altogether unthinkable thought within the discourse of Orientalism as defined by Said.

In the light of all this the reason why Said is unable in the end to suggest alternatives to the hegemonic discourse of Orientalism is not difficult to explain. First, because he overlooks the potential contradiction between discourse theory and Gramscian hegemony, he fails to historicize adequately the texts he cites and summarizes, finding always the same triumphant discourse where several are frequently in conflict. Second, because he does not distinguish the literary instance from more transparently ideological textual forms he does not acknowledge the semi-autonomous and overdetermined character of aesthetic artifacts. Finally, he fails to show how literary texts may in their play establish distance from the ideologies they seem to be reproducing.

Notes

1. Vintage Books: New York, 1979. [Subsequent page references to all works cited are give in parentheses.]
2. Said's comment on this point seems incontrovertible: 'No one has ever devised a method for detaching the scholar from the circumstances of life, from the fact of his involvement (conscious or unconscious) with a class, a set of beliefs, a social position, or from the mere activity of being a member of a society' (p. 10).

3. Fredric Jameson has made the point in connection with historical writing: 'we need to take into account the possibility that our contact with the past will always pass through the imaginary and through its ideologies, will always in one way or another be mediated by codes and motifs of some deeper classification system of pensée sauvage, some properly political unconscious. 'Marxism and Historicism', *New Literary History*, Autumn 1979, p. 45.

4. I am thinking particularly of the early Foucault through *The Order of Things*, the Foucault who seems to have been most influential for Said during the time he was writing *Orientalism*.

   In this connection the problems raised by discourse theory have been touched on, among others, by Stuart Hall in 'Cultural studies and the Centre: some problematics and problems' and by Chris Weedon, Andrew Tolson and Frank Mort in 'Theories of language and subjectivity'. The former writes: 'Foucault, following the lead of Lévi-Strauss, though in a different way, directs attention to the internal relations and regularities of any field of knowledge. He remains agnostic about their general determining conditions and about their "truth". He examines them largely from a "topographical" or genealogical vantage point' (p. 57). Weedon, Tolson and Mort comment: 'However, the point of focus specified by discourse analysis – that is, the regularity of its organization and its field of effects – tends to militate against any examination of the interrelation between the emergence and continuity of a discourse and forms of resistance, struggle and contestation' (p. 214). *Culture, Media, Language*, Hutchinson: London, 1980.

5. Oxford University Press: Oxford, 1977.

6. As a literary scholar himself, Said is, of course, aware of textual complexity and qualitative difference between the variety of works he touches on: 'One need only remember that Lane's *Manners and Customs of the Modern Egyptians* is a classic of historical and anthropological observation because of its style, its enormously intelligent and brilliant details, not because of its simple reflection of racial superiority' (p. 15).

7. *The Seven Pillars of Wisdom*, Penguin: Harmondsworth, 1962.

8. 'In my case, the efforts for these years to live in the dress of Arabs, and to imitate their mental foundation, quitted me of my English self, and let me look at the West and its conventions with new eyes: they destroyed it all for me. At the same time I could not sincerely take on Arab skin: it was an affectation only' (p. 30).

9. 'A letter on art in reply to André Daspre' and 'Cremonini, painter of the abstract', in *Lenin and Philosophy and Other Essays*, Monthly Review Press: New York and London, 1971.

8 □ Orientalism *and* After

Aijaz Ahmad

[...]

V

Orientalism appeared in 1978, a rather precise point in the history of the world, in the history of the demographic composition and reorganization of the political conjuncture in the United States, and in the history of intellectual productions in the metropolitan countries generally.[1] Each of these aspects deserves some comment because all have some bearing on how books were being read, and how this book in particular intervened in intellectual history.

By 1978, the two great revolutionary decades, inaugurated – roughly speaking – by the onset of the Algerian War in 1954 and culminating in the liberation of Saigon in 1975, were over. The decisive turning point had come in Chile in 1973, with the defeat of *Unidad Popular*, but we did not know it then, because the liberation movements of Indochina and the Portuguese colonies in Africa were still in progress. The two revolutions of 1978–9, in Iran and Afghanistan, then made the shift unmistakable. The Khomeiniite takeover in Iran was one of those rare conjunctures in which the revolution and the counter-revolution were condensed in the same moment. In Afghanistan, the last country to have a revolution under a communist leadership, history now repeated itself, in Marx's famous phrase, both as tragedy and as farce. If the Iranian Revolution had signalled the decisive defeat of the Left in the Middle East and the rise to ideological hegemony of Islamic fundamentalism in that whole region, the history-as-tragedy-and-as-farce in Afghanistan was to contribute considerably to the collapse of what socialism there had ever been in the Comecon countries, helping to pave the way for perestroika first in the Soviet Union, then on a global scale. The savage destruction

From Aijaz, Ahmad, *In Theory: Classes, nations, literatures*, Verso: London, 1992, pp. 190–201, 202–3, 336.

of Baghdad in 1991, the worst since the Mongols sacked that city in the thirteenth century, was the gift of this global perestroika, making one recall Marx once more. As he famously put it in his correspondence on the Gotha Programme: capitalism does not lead necessarily to socialism, it may lead just as inexorably towards barbarism.

All that was to come later. What the end of the revolutionary decades did, however, was, first of all, to shift the entire balance within the metropolitan countries further to the Right. The Anglo-Saxon countries witnessed the rise to governmental power of the most reactionary ideologues, Reagan and Thatcher; movements for racial and social justice in the United States were beaten back, and the defeat of the miners' strike in Britain put an end to labour militancy there for years to come. Social Democracy itself was soon to be defeated in Germany and Scandinavia, while in Italy it submitted, under Craxi's leadership, to Christian Democracy, while the PCI retreated and was then, after 1976, decisively disorganized. Social Democracy did come to power in France, but survived by moving so far to the Right that it renounced even the autonomist positions of High Gaullism. For the backward capitalist zones, developments were far too numerous and too clearly rooted in histories of particular countries to be summarized in so short a space, but what happened in our own subcontinent is indicative. The Bhuttoite version of populist social democracy was first replaced, in 1977, by an Islamicist military dictatorship and then fleetingly reappeared in a farcical form under his daughter's regime. In Bangladesh, the progressive content of the liberation struggle was dissipated quickly, leading to a regime of right-wing military officers who had previously served in the Pakistan Army and had been trained at Fort Bragg in the United States; the widow of one of those officers is currently the Prime Minister. In India, communism has been contained in its regional locations; the social compact based on Gandhian ideas of religious tolerance has been increasingly under attack, sometimes in the name of Gandhi himself; Nehruvian models of parliamentary democracy, secularist polity, planned economy and non-aligned foreign policy have been emptied of their content, and a whole range of disorientations since the Emergency, dating back again to the mid 1970s, has moved the country and its entire political and social discourse cumulatively and decisively towards the Right.

This global offensive of the Right, global retreat of the Left, and retreat also of that which was progressive even in our canonical nationalism, is the essential backdrop for any analysis of the structure of intellectual productions and their reception in our time. Within this reorganized global conjuncture we have witnessed, in all the bourgeois countries, the ascent to dominance of an entirely new kind of intellectual within a formation which continued to call itself a Left. The characteristic posture of this new intellectual was that he or she would gain legitimacy on the Left by constantly and fervently referring to the Third World, Cuba, national liberation, and so on, but would also be openly and contemptuously anti-communist; would often enough not affiliate even with that other tradition which had also descended from classical Marxism, namely social democracy, nor be affiliated in any degree with any labour movement whatsoever, but would invoke an anti-bourgeois stance in the name of manifestly reactionary anti-humanisms enunciated in the Nietzschean tradition and propagated now under the signature of anti-empiricism, anti-historicism, structuralism and post-structuralism, specifically Lévi-Strauss, Foucault, Derrida, Glucksmann, Kristeva, and so on. It is in contrast to these reactionary anti-humanisms, across the whole spectrum of cultural theories that the rectitude in careers of people like Raymond Williams now seems so bracing.

I shall return to other kinds of determinations presently, but this matter of Nietzschean anti-humanism is of some crucial interest here, in part because of the way Said's treatment of Marx [...] stands in tense balance with Nietzsche's authority, invoked indirectly through Foucault, which structures the whole book around notions of representation and discourse. This surfaces openly in a crucial passage which I shall cite below; on two consecutive pages, meanwhile, we find two rather inconsistent statements, brief and stark. First:

> as this book has tried to show, Islam *has* been fundamentally misrepresented in the past. (p. 272).

But then, on the very next page, we find:

> My whole point about this whole system is not that it is a *mis*representation of some Oriental essence.

Now, the substitution of the term 'Oriental essence' in the latter sentence for the term 'Islam' in the former does suggest that what Orientalism misrepresents is Islam itself, not an 'essence'. In a much stronger way, however, the main issue in both sentences is (*mis*)representation, not Islam or 'essence', and what Said is actually doing is drawing closer to the Nietzschean idea that no true representation is possible because all human communications always distort the facts. What happens between these two sentences is that Said raises the key question: 'The real issue is whether there can be a true representation of anything.' In other words, is it possible to make true statements? There are powerful traditions, including the Nietzschean, which have denied such a possibility. There are other powerful traditions, including the Marxist, which have said that yes, true statements are possible. Said's equivocation on this key question is delivered in what appears to be a precise formulation – namely, that the line between a representation and a misrepresentation is always very thin. That appears to me to be not a personal but a discursive statement. I would suggest, in fact, that this statement belongs directly in the Nietzschean philosophical tradition, and that Edward Said, who is here in the midst of writing a history of Orientalism, is affiliating himself with a new kind of history-writing, which was emerging more or less at this time, which goes far beyond the empirical historian's usual interrogation of and scepticism about the available evidence and the accepted modes of interpretation; and enters the Nietzschean world of questioning not merely positivist constructions but the very facticity of facts, so that it will eventually force a wide range of historians around the globe – some of the Indian Subalternists, for example – to start putting the word 'fact' in quotation marks.

With this clarification in mind, we can now turn to page 203:

> [Orientalism's] objective discoveries – the work of innumerable devoted scholars who edited texts and translated them, codified grammars, wrote dictionaries, reconstructed dead epochs, produced positivistically verifiable learning – are and always have been conditioned by the fact that its truths, like any truths delivered by language, are embodied in language, and what is the truth of language, Nietzsche once said, but
>
> > a mobile army of metaphors, metonyms, and anthropomorphisms – in short, a sum of human relations, which have been enhanced, transposed, and embellished poetically and rhetorically, and which after long use seen firm, canonical and obligatory to a people: truths are illusions about which one has forgotten that this is what they are.

This image of language as the enemy of experience, this assertion that representation is always-already a misrepresentation, this shallow pathos about the impossibility of truthful human communication, is of course a familiar Romantic trope which has undergone much aggrandizement – first in those irrationalist philosophies of the late nineteenth century and the early twentieth which preceded the rise of fascism and then again, on a much wider scale, in the reactionary anti-humanisms which have dominated many strands in contemporary avant-gardist thought. In relation to the knowledge of history, then, this image of human communication as a ruse of illusory subjectivity precludes the possibility of truthful statement on the ground that evidence, the criterion of truthful statement in history-writing, is always-already prejudiced by the very nature of language itself. It is significant that these anti-humanisms have come to dominate so much of American scholarship on the eve of the unprecedented imperialist consolidations of the present decade.

That this form of irrationalism should surface so centrally in the very book which is doubtless the most influential among radically inclined cultural theorists today should give us, I believe, some pause, but it should also help us to grasp some aspects of its enthusiastic reception and extremely widespread influence. For in one range of formulations, Said's denunciations of the *whole* of Western civilization is as extreme and uncompromising as Foucault's denunciations of the Western episteme or Derrida's denunciations of the transhistorical Logos; nothing, nothing at all, exists outside epistemic Power, logocentric Thought, Orientalist Discourse – no classes, no gender, not even history; no site of resistance, no accumulated projects of human liberation, since all is Repetition with Difference, all is corruption – specifically Western corruption – and Orientalism always remains the same, only more so with the linear accumulations of time. The Manichaean edge of these visions – Derridean, Foucauldian, Saidian – is quite worthy of Nietzsche himself.

But this vision, in the case of *Orientalism*, gains further authority from the way it panders to the most sentimental, the most extreme forms of Third-Worldist nationalism. The book says nothing, of course, about any fault of our own, but anything we ourselves could remember – the bloodbath we conducted at the time of Partition, let us say – simply pales in comparison with this other Power which has victimized us and inferiorized us for two thousand five hundred years or more. So uncompromising is this book in its Third-Worldist passion that Marxism itself, which has historically given such sustenance to so many of the anti-imperialist movements of our time, can be dismissed, breezily, as a child of Orientalism and an accomplice of British colonialism. How comforting such visions of one's own primal and permanent innocence are one can well imagine, because given what actually goes on in our countries, we do need a great deal of comforting.

But it was not within the so-called 'Third World' that the book first appeared. Its global authority is in fact inseparable from the authority of those in the dominant sectors of the metropolitan intelligentsia who first bestowed upon it the status of a modern classic; while, perhaps paradoxically, its most passionate following in the metropolitan countries is within those sectors of the university intelligentsia which either originate in the ethnic minorities or affiliate themselves ideologically with the academic sections of those minorities. In Chapter 2 [of *In Theory*] I discussed the connection between the emergence of the category 'Third-World Literature' and the key changes that occurred in the patterns of immigration from the late 1960s onwards, with substantial numbers of Asian immigrants being based now among the petty-bourgeois and techno-managerial strata. Those who came as graduate students and then joined the faculties, especially in the Humanities and the Social Sciences, tended to come from upper classes in their home countries. In the process of relocating themselves in the metropolitan countries, they needed documents of their assertion, proof that they had always been oppressed. Books that connected oppression with class were not very useful, because *they* neither came from the working class nor were intending to join that class in their new country. Those who said that majority of the populations in Africa and Asia certainly suffered from colonialism, but that there were also those who benefited from it, were useless, because many of the new professionals who were part of this immigration themselves came from those other families, those other classes, which had been the beneficiaries; Said would pose this question of the beneficiaries of colonialism in very peculiar ways in his invocation of Ranajit Guha [. . .].

Among critiques that needed to be jettisoned, or at least greatly modified, were the Marxist ones, because Marxists had this habit of speaking about classes, even in Asia and Africa. What the upwardly mobile professionals in this new immigration needed were narratives of oppression that would get them preferential treatment, reserved jobs, higher salaries in the social position they already occupied: namely, *as* middle-class professionals, mostly male. For such purposes *Orientalism* was the perfect narrative. When, only slightly later, enough women found themselves in that same position, the category of the 'Third World female subaltern' was found highly serviceable. I might add that this latter category is probably not very usable inside India, but the kind of discourse *Orientalism* assembles certainly has its uses. Communalism, for example, can now be laid entirely at the doors of Orientalism and colonial construction; caste itself can be portrayed as a fabrication primarily of the Population Surveys and Census Reports – Ronald Inden literally does this,[2] and Professor Partha Chatterjee seems poised to do so.[3] Colonialism is now held responsible not only for its own cruelties but, conveniently enough, for ours too. Meanwhile, within the metropolitan countries, the emphasis on immigration was continually to strengthen. I have written on one aspect of it in relation to Salman Rushdie, but it is worth mentioning that the same theme surfaces with very major emphases in Said's latest essays, with far-reaching consequences for his own earlier positions, as we shall see.

The perspectives inaugurated in *Orientalism* served, in the social self-consciousness and professional assertion of the middle-class immigrant and the 'ethnic' intellectual, roughly the same function as the theoretical category of 'Third World Literature', arising at roughly the same time, was also to serve. One in fact presumed the other, and between the two the circle was neatly closed. If *Orientalism* was devoted to demonstrating the bad faith and imperial oppression of all European knowledges, beyond time and history, 'Third World Literature' was to be the narrative of authenticity, the counter-canon of truth, good faith, liberation itself. Like the bad faith of European knowledge, the counter-canon of 'Third World Literature' had no boundaries – neither of space nor of time, of culture nor of class; a Senegalese novel, a Chinese short story, a song from medieval India, could all be read into the same archive: it was all 'Third World'. Marx was an 'Orientalist' because he was European, but a Tagore novel, patently canonical and hegemonizing inside the Indian cultural context, could be taught in the syllabi of 'Third World Literature' as a marginal, non-canonical text, counterposed against 'Europe'. The homogenizing sweep was evident in both cases, and if cultural nationalism was the overtly flaunted insignia, invocation of 'race' was barely below the surface – not just with respect to the United States, which would be logical, but with reference to human history as such. Thus, if 'Orientalism' was initially posited as something of an original ontological flaw in the European psyche, Said was eventually to declare: 'in the relationship between the ruler and the ruled in the imperial or colonial or racial sense, race takes precedence over both class and gender ... I have always felt that the problem of emphasis and relative importance took precedence over the need to establish one's feminist credentials.'[4] That contemptuous phrase, 'establish one's feminist credentials', takes care of gender quite definitively, as imperialism itself is collapsed into a 'racial sense'. In a Nietzschean world, virtually anything is possible.

VI

Said's interventions since the initial publication of *Orientalism* have doubtless been prolific and diverse. *The Question of Palestine* and *Covering Islam*, as they came in quick succession thereafter, were explicitly conceived as volumes in a series inaugurated with *Orientalism*. *After the Last Sky* and *Blaming the Victims*, which came some years later, may also be considered as parts of that same integrated *œuvre*. Surrounding this impressive array of books are essays, articles and reviews on cognate themes in a great many periodicals, political journals and newspapers, not to speak of unpublished interventions in scholarly conferences and public forums of various kinds, including very effective television appearances, so numerous that they could easily fill two or three volumes. About *Orientalism*, I need not say more, and *Covering Islam* is undoubtedly Said's most forgettable book, so defensive is it about Islamicist kinds of politics and Khomeiniite kinds of criminalities (only after the sentencing of Salman Rushdie did Said begin to take public note of the terror which had by then enveloped tens of thousands within Iran). By contrast, the writings which deal directly with Palestine constitute not only the most enduring part of Said's work but also, by any standards, the most persuasive insertion of a national-liberation struggle into the American imagination, which is otherwise substantially formed by Zionist-colonial presumptions.

Almost equally extensive – though far more problematic and at times even disconcerting – are Said's publications in the field of literary and cultural studies. Central to this other work, of course, is his 1983 volume *The World, the Text, and the Critic*, which brings together essays written between 1969 and 1981. But there are also numerous other essays which have appeared in journals but have not yet been collected in a single volume; a few of these, too, have been included in volumes edited by others. The book includes at least two major pieces. 'Raymond Schwab and the romance of ideas' and 'Islam, philology and French culture: Renan and Massignon', which are thematically connected with *Orientalism*, even though some of the formulations in those essays are considerably different; the essay on Schwab, written much earlier but collected in a book more recently, makes very odd reading indeed, considering that the charitable view of Schwab's work which we find there has no analogue within *Orientalism* itself.[5] Two other essays in the book, which are in fact the best-known and the most influential – 'Criticism between culture and system' and 'Travelling theory' – were evidently written some time after *Orientalism* and are notable not so much for explicating Said's preference for Foucault over Derrida as for his partial distancing of himself from Foucault. This distancing is facilitated by his reliance on criticisms of Foucault which had been framed already by Poulantzas[6] and Chomsky, whom Said cites directly, and part of what Said now says about Foucault is uncannily similar to some points I have raised above about *Orientalism* itself. The following extract from 'Travelling theory', intended to express reservations about Foucault and his notion of Power, applies almost exactly to Said himself and his conception of Orientalism:

> Foucault's eagerness not to fall into Marxist economism causes him to obliterate the role of classes, the role of economics, the role of insurgency and rebellion in the societies he discusses. . . . The problem is that Foucault's use of the term *pouvoir* moves around too much, swallowing up every obstacle in its path, . . . obliterating change and mystifying its microphysical sovereignty . . . . Foucault's history is ultimately textual or rather textualized; its mode is one for which Borges would have an affinity . . . they [his archaeologies] make not even a nominal allowance for emergent movements, and none for revolutions, counterhegemony, or historical blocs.[7]

Since those two essays are only tangentially connected with the aspects of Said's work with which I am most concerned here, I shall not offer any reading of the remarkable ambivalences one finds in them; in any event, it is simply not possible within the space of one chapter – even an inordinately lengthy chapter such as this one – to give detailed accounts of each significant item in an output so substantial, distinctive and diverse.

This partial distancing from Foucault is in fact part of a number of shifts that have occurred in Said's more recent writings, which includes a retreat from the Nietzschean position of all representations being misrepresentations and admits, concomitantly, the possibilities of resistance from outside the colonial discourse. Meanwhile, his rereading of both Foucault and Derrida, and his many convergences with diverse postmodernist positions, then culminate in the insistence that the double task of responsible knowledge is to resist the pressures both of the dominant culture and of what would now increasingly be dubbed 'system', 'theory', 'grand theory', 'disciplinary knowledge' and several even more colourful epithets – referring frequently to Marxism in particular, but also to any other way of being-in-the-world which seeks to establish theoretical as well as narrative intelligibility of history as such, and then identifies collective agents (such as class, gender, nation) as bearers of resistance and political action. All such *systems* are rejected, in the characteristic postmodernist way, so that resistance can always only be personal, micro, and shared only by a small, determinate number of individuals who happen, perchance, to come together, outside the so-called 'grand narratives' of class, gender, nation.[8]

Ambivalences on this question are already notable in 'Travelling theory', but even more representative in all this is the essay 'Opponents, audiences, constituencies and community',[9] where Said first speaks derisively of 'the self-policing, self-purifying communities erected even by Marxist, as well as other disciplinary, discourses', and then goes on to specify what he considers to be a key project that needs to be posed against the 'disciplinary' character of Marxism, etc: 'to restore the nonsequential energy of lived historical memory and subjectivity . . . to tell other stories than the official sequential or ideological ones produced by institutional power'. I am not quite sure what this last formulation actually means, but it would not, I think, be unfair to say that the sense in which Marxism is said to be 'self-policing, self-purifying', as well as 'disciplinary', 'institutional' and 'ideological', applies inescapably to particular tendencies – notably the socialist tendencies – within feminism too. Meanwhile, theoretical eclecticism runs increasingly out of control: sweeping, patently poststructuralist denunciations of Marxism can be delivered in the name of Gramsci, using the terminology explicitly drawn from Althusser, and listing the names of communist poets like Aimé Césaire, Pablo Neruda and Mahmoud Darwish to illustrate the sites of resistance.

The largest shift, however, has been on the issue of nationalism. In the years immediately following the publication of *Orientalism*, Said's position was indistinguishable from straightforward Third-Worldist cultural nationalisms, and what we used to get was an unselfcritical narrative of European guilt, non-European innocence. This has shifted dramatically, beginning in about 1984 and growing increasingly more strident in rejecting nationalism, national boundaries, nations as such, so that one now has reason to be equally alarmed by the extremity of this opposite stance. Characteristically, though, the most sweeping statements about 'nation' and 'state' as 'coerceive identities' are frequently delivered alongside resounding affirmations of national liberation, of the Palestinian *intifada* in particular, and the right of the Palestinian people either to obtain a nation-state of their own or, alternatively, to live as coequals in a binational state. It is this growing ambivalence about nation and nationalism – combined with an even more surprising shift from a wholesale rejection of 'the West' to an equally wholesale assertion that the *only* authentic work that can be done in our time presumes (a) Third World origin, but combined with (b) metropolitan location – which should bear some scrutiny. The intellectual cited as an exemplary figure of our time in this latest construction, is, of course, Ranajit Guha, who is commended both for his initial origin in the Indian upper class and for his later location in the metropolitan university, but the autobiographical self-referentiality is quite unmistakable.[10] [. . .]

There had been, [. . .], no evidence until after the publication of [*Orientalism*] that Said had read any considerable number of non-Western writers. By contrast, references to principal figures of the counter-canon of 'Third World Literature' surface very regularly in his more recent writings, even though not even one of them has yet been treated with the hermeneutic engagement and informed reading that Said offers so often for scores of Western canonical figures; in the rare event that he actually refers to particular texts – as in the case of George Antonius or Ranajit Guha [. . .] – none receives the kind of detailed scrutiny which Said routinely accords to a wide range of European writers, from Swift to Renan to Schwab to Kipling. His engagement, both as activist and as scholar, with the Palestinian Liberation movement has been extended, meanwhile, to regular expressions of solidarity with anti-colonial movements in general, and a basic respect for figures associated with such movements. These partial gains in the range of engagements and sympathies stand, however, in peculiar and paradoxical relation with the freshly acquired but altogether irrepressible rage *against* the peoples, societies, national boundaries, reading communities and literatures of Asia, Africa and 'the Islamic world'; the enormous privileging of a handful of writers, strictly those who now live in the West, over those societies and literatures; and the conception of the 'Western centre' as the only site where 'contests over decolonization' can now take place. The enormity of this shift is puzzling. The continued American hostility towards the Arab world on the one hand, the sentencing of Rushdie by Ayatollah Khomeini on the other, combined with the failure of most people in Asia, Africa and the Arab world to do combat on Rushdie's behalf, seem to have given rise to an extraordinary fury against West and non-West alike, with the figure of the lonely writer in the Western city – and the uncommitted reader of novels in the same city – eventually emerging as the only figures of redemption.

Notes

1. Routledge & Kegan Paul: London, 1978. [Subsequent page references are given in parentheses in the main text.]
2. See my 'Between orientalism and anti-historicism; anthropological knowledge of India', *Studies in History*, 7, 1, 1991, for detailed comments on Ronald Inden's *Imagining India*, Oxford: Basil Blackwell, 1991.
3. See Partha Chatterjee, 'Caste and subaltern consciousness', in Ranajit Guha (ed.), *Subaltern Studies VI*, Oxford University Press: New Delhi, 1989.
4. 'Media, margins and modernity: Raymond Williams and Edward Said', Appendix to Raymond Williams, *The Politics of Modernism: Against the new conformists*, Verso: London, 1989, pp. 196–7. The transcript of that public discussion – and, indeed, the whole book – ends on that sentence about 'feminist credentials'.
5. This essay has also appeared as an introduction to Schwab's own *The Oriental Renaissance: Europe's rediscovery of India and the East, 1680–1880*, translation of *La Renaissance orientale* (1954) by Gene Patterson-Black and Victoria Reinking, Columbia University Press: New York, 1984.
6. In his last book, *State, Power, Socialism* (New Left Books: London, 1978; translation by Patrick Camiller of *L'État, le pouvoir, le socialisme*, published in Paris that same year), Poulantzas offers a critique of Foucault from a Marxist position but tries also to find common ground between the two. See, in particular, the section on 'Law' in Part One and the one entitled 'Towards a relational theory of power?' in Part Two. This critique, in the book that is theoretically the most eclectic in Poulantzas's overall *œuvre*, was probably not available to Said when he was writing *Orientalism*.
7. *The World, the Text and the Critic*, Faber: London, pp. 244–6. This distancing from Foucault was then to be repeated in the more recent essay 'Foucault and the imagination of power', in David Couzens Hoy (ed.), *Foucault: A critical reader*, Basil Blackwell: Oxford, 1989, which also says less than what is already there in Poulantzas.
8. This emphasis on 'resistance' outside the 'grand narratives' is not notably different from the one Foucault (partially aided by Deleuze) delineates in a great many places, including the two interviews published as the concluding chapters of Michel Foucault, *Language, Countermemory, Practice*, ed. Donald Bouchard, Cornell University Press: Ithaca, NY, 1977.
9. See Edward W. Said, 'Opponents, audiences, constituencies and community', *Critical Inquiry*, 9, 1982; reprinted in Hal Foster (ed.) *The Anti-Aesthetic: Essays in postmodern culture*, Bay Press: Port Townsend, WA, pp. 135–59.
10. Ranajit Guha, editor of the series 'Subaltern Studies' and author, most notably of *A Rule of Property for Bengal* (1963) and *Elementary Aspects of Peasant Insurgency in Colonial India* (1983), taught history for many years at Sussex University in Great Britain before moving in 1980 to the Australian National University, Canberra.

9 □ *From* Discourse on Colonialism

Aimé Césaire

A civilization that proves incapable of solving the problems it creates is a decadent civilization.

A civilization that chooses to close its eyes to its most crucial problems is a stricken civilization.

A civilization that uses its principles for trickery and deceit is a dying civilization.

The fact is that the so-called European civilization – 'Western' civilization – as it has been shaped by two centuries of bourgeois rule, is incapable of solving the two major problems to which its existence has given rise: the problem of the proletariat and the colonial problem; that Europe is unable to justify itself either before the bar of 'reason' or before the bar of 'conscience'; and that, increasingly, it takes refuge in a hypocrisy which is all the more odious because it is less and less likely to deceive.

Europe is indefensible.

Apparently that is what the American strategists are whispering to each other.

That in itself is not serious.

What is serious is that 'Europe' is morally, spiritually indefensible.

And today the indictment is brought against it not by the European masses alone, but on a world scale, by tens and tens of millions of men who, from the depths of slavery, set themselves up as judges.

The colonialists may kill in Indochina, torture in Madagascar, imprison in Black Africa, crack down in the West Indies. Henceforth the colonized know that they have an advantage over them. They know that their temporary 'masters' are lying.

Therefore that their masters are weak.

And since I have been asked to speak about colonization and civilization, let us go straight to the principal lie which is the source of all the others.

Colonization and civilization?

In dealing with this subject, the commonest curse is to be the dupe in good faith of a collective hypocrisy that cleverly misrepresents problems, the better to legitimize the hateful solutions provided for them.

From Aimé Césaire, *Discourse on Colonialism*, Monthly Review Press: New York, 1972, pp. 9–25.

In other words, the essential thing here is to see clearly, to think clearly – that is, dangerously – and to answer clearly the innocent first question: what, fundamentally, is colonization? To agree on what it is not: neither evangelization, nor a philanthropic enterprise, nor a desire to push back the frontiers of ignorance, disease and tyranny, nor a project undertaken for the greater glory of God, nor an attempt to extend the rule of law. To admit once for all, without flinching at the consequences, that the decisive actors here are the adventurer and the pirate, the wholesale grocer and the ship owner, the gold digger and the merchant, appetite and force, and behind them, the baleful projected shadow of a form of civilization which, at a certain point in its history, finds itself obliged, for internal reasons, to extend to a world scale the competition of its antagonistic economies.

Pursuing my analysis, I find that hypocrisy is of recent date; that neither Cortez discovering Mexico from the top of the great teocalli, nor Pizzaro before Cuzco (much less Marco Polo before Cambaluc), claims that he is the harbinger of a superior order; that they kill; that they plunder; that they have helmets, lances, cupidities; that the slavering apologists came later; that the chief culprit in this domain is Christian pedantry, which laid down the dishonest equations *Christianity = civilization, paganism = savagery*, from which there could not but ensue abominable colonialist and racist consequences, whose victims were to be the Indians, the yellow peoples and the Negroes.

That being settled, I admit that it is a good thing to place different civilizations in contact with each other; that it is an excellent thing to blend different worlds; that whatever its own particular genius may be, a civilization that withdraws into itself atrophies; that for civilizations, exchange is oxygen; that the great good fortune of Europe is to have been a crossroads, and that because it was the locus of all ideas, the receptacle of all philosophies, the meeting place of all sentiments, it was the best center for the redistribution of energy.

But then I ask the following question: has colonization really *placed civilizations in contact*? Or, if you prefer, of all the ways of *establishing contact*, was it the best?

I answer *no*.

And I say that between *colonization* and *civilization* there is an infinite distance; that out of all the colonial expeditions that have been undertaken, out of all the colonial statutes that have been drawn up, out of all the memoranda that have been despatched by all the ministries, there could not come a single human value.

First we must study how colonization works to *decivilize* the colonizer, to *brutalize* him in the true sense of the word, to degrade him, to awaken him to buried instincts, to covetousness, violence, race hatred and moral relativism; and we must show that each time a head is cut off or an eye put out in Vietnam and in France they accept the fact, each time a little girl is raped and in France they accept the fact, each time a Madagascan is tortured and in France they accept the fact, civilization acquires another dead weight, a universal regression takes place, a gangrene sets in, a center of infection begins to spread; and that at the end of all these treaties that have been violated, all these lies that have been propagated, all these punitive expeditions that have been tolerated, all these prisoners who have been tied up and 'interrogated', all these patriots who have been tortured, at the end of all the racial pride that has been encouraged, all the boastfulness that has been displayed, a poison has been instilled into the veins of Europe and, slowly but surely, the continent proceeds toward *savagery*.

And then one fine day the bourgeoisie is awakened by a terrific reverse shock: the gestapos are busy, the prisons fill up, the torturers around the racks invent, refine, discuss.

People are surprised, they become indignant. They say: 'How strange! But never mind – it's Nazism, it will pass!' And they wait, and they hope; and they hide the truth from themselves, that it is barbarism, but the supreme barbarism, the crowning barbarism that sums up all the daily barbarisms; that it is Nazism, yes, but that before they were its victims, they were its accomplices; that they tolerated that Nazism before it was inflicted on them, that they absolved it, shut their eyes to it, legitimized it, because, until then, it had been applied only to non-European peoples; that they have cultivated that Nazism, that they are responsible for it and that before engulfing the whole of Western, Christian civilization in its reddened waters, it oozes, seeps and trickles from every crack.

Yes, it would be worthwhile to study clinically, in detail, the steps taken by Hitler and Hitlerism and to reveal to the very distinguished, very humanistic, very Christian bourgeois of the twentieth century that without his being aware of it, he has a Hitler inside him, that Hitler *inhabits* him, that Hitler is his *demon*, that if he rails against him, he is being inconsistent and that, at bottom, what he cannot forgive Hitler for is not *crime* in itself, *the crime against man*, it is not *the humiliation of man as such*, it is the crime against the white man, the humiliation of the white man, and the fact that he applied to Europe colonialist procedures which until then had been reserved exclusively for the Arabs of Algeria, the coolies of India, and the blacks of Africa.

And that is the great thing I hold against pseudo-humanism: that for too long it has diminished the rights of man, that its concept of those rights has been – and still is – narrow and fragmentary, incomplete and biased and, all things considered, sordidly racist.

I have talked a good deal about Hitler. Because he deserves it: he makes it possible to see things on a large scale and to grasp the fact that capitalist society, at its present stage, is incapable of establishing a concept of the rights of all men, just as it has proved incapable of establishing a system of individual ethics. Whether one likes it or not, at the end of the blind alley that is Europe, I mean the Europe of Adenauer, Schuman, Bidault and a few others, there is Hitler. At the end of capitalism, which is eager to outlive its day, there is Hitler. At the end of formal humanism and philosophic renunciation, there is Hitler.

And this being so, I cannot help thinking of one of his statements: 'We aspire not to equality but to domination. The country of a foreign race must become once again a country of serfs, of agricultural laborers, or industrial workers. It is not a question of eliminating the inequalities among men but of widening them and making them into a law.'

That rings clear, haughty and brutal and plants us squarely in the middle of howling savagery. But let us come down a step.

Who is speaking? I am ashamed to say it: it is the Western *humanist*, the 'idealist' philosopher. That his name is Renan is an accident. That the passage is taken from a book entitled *La Réforme intellectuelle et morale*, that it was written in France just after a war which France had represented as a war of right against might, tells us a great deal about bourgeois morals.

The regeneration of the inferior or degenerate races by the superior races is part of the providential order of things for humanity. With us, the common man is nearly always a déclassé nobleman, his heavy hand is better suited to handling the sword than the menial tool. Rather than work, he chooses to fight, that is, he returns to his first estate. *Regere imperio populos*, that is our vocation. Pour forth this all-consuming activity onto countries which, like China, are crying aloud for foreign conquest. Turn the adventurers who disturb European society into a *ver sacrum*, a horde like those of the Franks, the Lombards, or the Normans, and every man will be in his right role. Nature has made a race of workers, the Chinese race, who have wonderful manual dexterity and almost no sense of honor; govern them with justice, levying from them, in return for the blessing of such a government, an ample allowance for the conquering race, and they will be satisfied; a race of tillers of the soil, the Negro; treat him with kindness and humanity, and all will be as it should; a race of masters and soldiers, the European race. Reduce this noble race to working in the *ergastulum* like Negroes and Chinese, and they rebel. In Europe, every rebel is, more or less, a soldier who has missed his calling, a creature made for the heroic life, before whom you are setting *a task that is contrary to his race* – a poor worker, too good a soldier. But the life at which our workers rebel would make a Chinese or a fellah happy, as they are not military creatures in the least. *Let each one do what he is made for, and all will be well.*

Hitler? Rosenberg? No, Renan.

But let us come down one step further. And it is the long-winded politician. Who protests? No one, so far as I know, when M. Albert Sarraut, the former governor-general of Indochina, holding forth to the students at the Ecole Coloniale, teaches them that it would be puerile to object to the European colonial enterprises in the name of 'an alleged right to possess the land one occupies, and some sort of right to remain in fierce isolation, which would leave unutilized resources to lie forever idle in the hands of incompetents'.

And who is roused to indignation when a certain Rev. Barde assures us that if the goods of this world 'remained divided up indefinitely, as they would be without colonization, they would answer neither the purposes of God nor the just demands of the human collectivity'?

Since, as his fellow Christian, the Rev. Muller, declares: 'Humanity must not, cannot allow the incompetence, negligence, and laziness of the uncivilized peoples to leave idle indefinitely the wealth which God has confided to them, charging them to make it serve the good of all.'

No one.

I mean not one established writer, not one academician, not one preacher, not one crusader for the right and for religion, not one 'defender of the human person'.

And yet, through the mouths of the Sarrauts and the Bardes, the Mullers and the Renans, through the mouths of all those who considered – and consider – it lawful to apply to non-European peoples 'a kind of expropriation for public purposes' for the benefit of nations that were stronger and better equipped, it was already Hitler speaking!

What am I driving at? At this idea: that no one colonizes innocently, that no one colonizes with impunity either; that a nation which colonizes, that a civilization which justifies colonization – and therefore force – is already a sick civilization, a civilization that is morally diseased, that irresistibly, progressing from one consequence to another, one repudiation to another, calls for its Hitler, I mean its punishment.

Colonization: bridgehead in a campaign to civilize barbarism, from which there may emerge at any moment the negation of civilization, pure and simple.

Elsewhere I have cited at length a few incidents culled from the history of colonial expeditions.

Unfortunately, this did not find favor with everyone. It seems that I was pulling old skeletons out of the closet. Indeed!

Was there no point in quoting Colonel de Montagnac, one of the conquerors of Algeria: 'In order to banish the thoughts that sometimes besiege me, I have some heads cut off, not the heads of artichokes but the heads of men.'

Would it have been more advisable to refuse the floor to Count d'Hérisson: 'It is true that we are bringing back a whole barrelful of ears collected, pair by pair, from prisoners, friendly or enemy.'

Should I have refused Saint-Arnaud the right to profess his barbarous faith: 'We lay waste, we burn, we plunder, we destroy the houses and the trees.'

Should I have prevented Marshal Bugeaud from systematizating all that in a daring theory and invoking the precedent of famous ancestors: 'We must have a great invasion of Africa, like the invasions of the Franks and the Goths.'

Lastly, should I have cast back into the shadows of oblivion the memorable feat of arms of General Gérard and kept silent about the capture of Ambike, a city which, to tell the truth, had never dreamed of defending itself: 'The native riflemen had orders to kill only the men, but no one restrained them; intoxicated by the smell of blood, they spared not one woman, not one child. . . . At the end of the afternoon, the heat caused a light mist to arise: it was the blood of the five thousand victims, the ghost of the city, evaporating in the setting sun.'

Yes or no, are these things true? And the sadistic pleasures, the nameless delights that send voluptuous shivers and quivers through Loti's carcass when he focuses his field glasses on a good massacre of the Annamese? True or not true?[1] And if these things are true, as no one can deny, will it be said, in order to minimize them, that these corpses don't prove anything?

For my part, if I have recalled a few details of these hideous butcheries, it is by no means because I take a morbid delight in them, but because I think that these heads of men, these collections of ears, these burned houses, these Gothic invasions, this steaming blood, these cities that evaporate at the edge of the sword, are not to be so easily disposed of. They prove that colonization, I repeat, dehumanizes even the most civilized man; that colonial activity, colonial enterprise, colonial conquest, which is based on contempt for the native and justified by that contempt, inevitably tends to change him who undertakes it; that the colonizer, who in order to ease his conscience gets into the habit of seeing the other man as *an animal*, accustoms himself to treating him like an animal, and tends objectively to transform *himself* into an animal. It is this result, this boomerang effect of colonization, that I wanted to point out.

Unfair? No. There was a time when these same facts were a source of pride, and when, sure of the morrow, people did not mince words. One last quotation; it is from a certain Carl Siger, author of an *Essai sur la colonisation* (Paris 1907):

> The new countries offer a vast field for individual, violent activities which, in the metropolitan countries, would run up against certain prejudices, against a sober and orderly conception of life, and which, in the colonies, have greater freedom to develop and, consequently, to affirm their worth. Thus to a certain extent the colonies can serve as a safety valve for modern society. Even if this were their only value, it would be immense.

Truly, there are stains that it is beyond the power of man to wipe out and that can never be fully expiated.

But let us speak about the colonized.

I see clearly what colonization has destroyed: the wonderful Indian civilizations – and neither Deterding nor Royal Dutch nor Standard Oil will ever console me for the Aztecs and the Incas.

I see clearly the civilizations, condemned to perish at a future date, into which it has introduced a principle of ruin: the South Sea islands, Nigeria, Nyasaland. I see less clearly the contributions it has made.

Security? Culture? The rule of law? In the meantime, I look around and wherever there are colonizers and colonized face to face, I see force, brutality, cruelty, sadism, conflict, and, in a parody of education, the hasty manufacture of a few thousand subordinate functionaries, 'boys', artisans, office clerks and interpreters necessary for the smooth operation of business.

I spoke of contact.

Between colonizer and colonized there is room only for forced labor, intimidation, pressure, the police, taxation, theft, rape, compulsory crops, contempt, mistrust, arrogance, self-complacency, swinishness, brainless élites, degraded masses.

No human contact, but relations of domination and submission which turn the colonizing man into a classroom monitor, an army sergeant, a prison guard, a slave driver, and the indigenous man into an instrument of production.

My turn to state an equation: colonization = 'thingification'.

I hear the storm. They talk to me about progress, about 'achievements', diseases cured, improved standards of living.

I am talking about societies drained of their essence, cultures trampled underfoot, institutions undermined, lands confiscated, religions smashed, magnificent artistic creations destroyed, extraordinary *possibilities* wiped out.

They throw facts at my head, statistics, mileages of roads, canals and railroad tracks.

I am talking about thousands of men sacrificed to the Congo-Océan.[2] I am talking about those who, as I write this, are digging the harbor of Abidjan by hand. I am talking about millions of men torn from their gods, their land, their habits, their life – from life, from the dance, from wisdom.

I am talking about millions of men in whom fear has been cunningly instilled, who have been taught to have an inferiority complex, to tremble, kneel, despair and behave like flunkeys.

They dazzle me with the tonnage of cotton or cocoa that has been exported, the acreage that has been planted with olive trees or grapevines.

I am talking about natural *economies* that have been disrupted – harmonious and viable *economies* adapted to the indigenous population – about food crops destroyed, malnutrition permanently introduced, agricultural development oriented solely toward the benefit of the metropolitan countries, about the looting of products, the looting of raw materials.

They pride themselves on abuses eliminated.

I too talk about abuses, but what I say is that on the old ones – very real – they have superimposed others – very detestable. They talk to me about local tyrants brought to reason; but I note that in general the old tyrants get on very well with the new ones, and that there has been established between them, to the detriment of the people, a circuit of mutual services and complicity.

They talk to me about civilization, I talk about proletarianization and mystification.

For my part, I make a systematic defense of the non-European civilizations.

Every day that passes, every denial of justice, every beating by the police, every demand of the workers that is drowned in blood, every scandal that is hushed up, every punitive expedition, every police van, every gendarme and every militiaman, brings home to us the value of our old societies.

They were communal societies, never societies of the many for the few.

They were societies that were not only ante-capitalist, as has been said, but also *anti-capitalist*.

They were democratic societies, always.

They were cooperative societies, fraternal societies.

I make a systematic defense of the societies destroyed by imperialism.

They were the fact, they did not pretend to be the idea; despite their faults, they were neither to be hated nor condemned. They were content to be. In them, neither the word *failure* nor the word *avatar* had any meaning. They kept hope intact.

Whereas those are the only words that can, in all honesty, be applied to the European enterprises outside Europe. My only consolation is that periods of colonization pass, that nations sleep only for a time, and that peoples remain.

This being said, it seems that in certain circles they pretend to have discovered in me an 'enemy of Europe' and a prophet of the return to the ante-European past.

For my part, I search in vain for the place where I could have expressed such views; where I ever underestimated the importance of Europe in the history of human thought; where I ever preached a *return* of any kind; where I ever claimed that there could be a *return*.

The truth is that I have said something very different: to wit, that the great historical tragedy of Africa has been not so much that it was too late in making contact with the rest of the world, as the manner in which that contact was brought about; that Europe began to 'propagate' at a time when it had fallen into the hands of the most unscrupulous financiers and captains of industry; that it was our misfortune to encounter that particular Europe on our path, and that Europe is responsible before the human community for the highest heap of corpses in history.

In another connection, in judging colonization, I have added that Europe has gotten on very well indeed with the local feudal lords who agreed to serve, woven a villainous complicity with them, rendered their tyranny more effective and more efficient, and that it has actually tended to prolong artificially the survival of local pasts in their most pernicious aspects.

I have said – and this is something very different – that colonialist Europe has grafted modern abuse onto ancient injustice, hateful racism onto old inequality.

That if I am attacked on the grounds of intent, I maintain that colonialist Europe is dishonest in trying to justify its colonizing activity *a posteriori* by the obvious material progress that has been achieved in certain fields under the colonial regime – since *sudden change* is always possible, in history as elsewhere; since no one knows at what stage of material development these same countries would have been if Europe had not intervened; since the technical outfitting of Africa and Asia, their administrative reorganization, in a word, their 'Europeanization', was (as is proved by the example of Japan) in no way tied to the European *occupation*; since the Europeanization of the non-European continents could have been accomplished otherwise than under the heel of Europe; since this movement of Europeanization *was in progress*; since it was even slowed down; since in any case it was distorted by the European takeover.

The proof is that at present it is the indigenous peoples of Africa and Asia who are demanding schools, and colonialist Europe which refuses them; that it is the African who is asking for ports and roads, and colonialist Europe which is niggardly on this score; that it is the colonized man who wants to move forward, and the colonizer who holds things back.

Notes

1. This is a reference to the account of the taking of Thuan-An which appeared in *Le Figaro* in September 1883 and is quoted in N. Serban's book, *Loti, sa vie, son oeuvre*. 'Then the great slaughter had begun. They had fired in double-salvos! and it was a pleasure to see these sprays of bullets, that were so easy to aim, come down on them twice a minute,

surely and methodically, on command. . . . We saw some who were quite mad and stood up seized with a dizzy desire to run. . . . They zigzagged, running every which way in this race with death, holding their garments up around their waists in a comical way . . . and then we amused ourselves counting the dead, etc.'

2. A railroad line connecting Brazzaville with the port of Pointe-Noire (trans. Joan Pinkham).

10 □ *From* The Consequences of Modernity

Anthony Giddens

The Globalising of Modernity

Modernity is inherently globalising – this is evident in some of the most basic characteristics of modern institutions, including particularly their disembeddedness and reflexivity. But what exactly is globalisation, and how might we best conceptualise the phenomenon? I shall consider these questions at some length here, since the central importance of globalising processes today has scarcely been matched by extended discussions of the concept in the sociological literature. [. . .] The undue reliance which sociologists have placed upon the idea of 'society' where this means a bounded system, should be replaced by a starting point that concentrates upon analysing how social life is ordered across time and space – the problematic of time-space distanciation. The conceptual framework of time-space distanciation directs our attention to the complex relations between *local involvements* (circumstances of co-presence) and *interaction across distance* (the connections of presence and absence). In the modern era, the level of time-space distanciation is much higher than in any previous period, and the relations between local and distant social forms and events become correspondingly 'stretched'. Globalisation refers essentially to that stretching process, in so far as the modes of connection between different social contexts or regions become networked across the earth's surface as a whole.

Globalisation can thus be defined as the intensification of worldwide social relations which link distant localities in such a way that local happenings are shaped by events occurring many miles away and vice versa. This is a dialetical process because such local happenings may move in an obverse direction from the very distanciated relations that shape them. *Local transformation* is as much a part of globalisation as the lateral extension of social connections across time and space. Thus whoever studies cities today, in any part of the world, is aware that what

From Anthony Giddens, *The Consequences of Modernity*, Polity Press: Cambridge, 1990, pp. 63–78, 183.

happens in a local neighbourhood is likely to be influenced by factors – such as world money and commodity markets – operating at an indefinite distance away from that neighbourhood itself. The outcome is not necessarily, or even usually, a generalised set of changes acting in a uniform direction, but consists in mutually opposed tendencies. The increasing prosperity of an urban area in Singapore might be causally related, via a complicated network of global economic ties, to the impoverishment of a neighbourhood in Pittsburgh whose local products are uncompetitive in world markets.

Another example from the very many that could be offered is the rise of local nationalisms in Europe and elsewhere. The development of globalised social relations probably serves to diminish some aspects of nationalist feeling linked to nation-states (or some states) but may be causally involved with the intensifying of more localised nationalist sentiments. In circumstances of accelerating globalisation, the nation-state has become 'too small for the big problems of life, and too big for the small problems of life'.[1] At the same time as social relations become laterally stretched and as part of the same process, we see the strengthening of pressures for local autonomy and regional cultural identity.

Two Theoretical Perspectives

Apart from the work of Marshall McLuhan and a few other individual authors, discussions of globalisation tend to appear in two bodies of literature, which are largely distinct from one another. One is the literature of international relations, the other that of 'world-system theory', particularly as associated with Immanuel Wallerstein, which stands fairly close to a Marxist position.

Theorists of international relations characteristically focus upon the development of the nation-state system, analysing its origins in Europe and its subsequent worldwide spread. Nation-states are treated as actors, engaging with one another in the international arena – and with other organisations of a transnational kind (intergovernmental organisations or non-state actors). Although various theoretical positions are represented in this literature, most authors paint a rather similar picture in analysing the growth of globalisation.[2] Sovereign states, it is presumed, first emerge largely as separate entities, having more or less complete administrative control within their borders. As the European state system matures and later becomes a global nation-state system, patterns of interdependence become increasingly developed. These are not only expressed in the ties states form with one another in the international arena, but in the burgeoning of intergovernmental organisations. These processes mark an overall movement towards 'one world', although they are continually fractured by war. Nation-states, it is held, are becoming progressively less sovereign than they used to be in terms of control over their own affairs – although few today anticipate in the near future the emergence of the 'world-state' which many in the early part of this century foresaw as a real prospect.

While this view is not altogether wrong, some major reservations have to be expressed. For one thing, it again covers only one overall dimension of globalisation as I wish to utilise the concept here – the international coordination of states. Regarding states as actors has its uses and makes sense in some contexts. However, most theorists of international relations do not explain *why* this usage makes sense; for it does so only in the case of nation-states, not in that of pre-modern states. The reason [is that] there is a far greater concentration of administrative power in nation-states than in their precursors, in which it would be relatively meaningless to speak of 'governments' who negotiate with other 'governments' in the name of their respective nations. Moreover, treating states as actors having connections with each other and with other organisations in the international arena makes it difficult to deal with social relations that are not between or outside states, but simply crosscut state divisions.

A further shortcoming of this type of approach concerns its portrayal of the increasing unification of the nation-state system. The sovereign power of modern states was not formed prior to their involvement in the nation-state system, even in the European state system, but developed in conjunction with it. Indeed, the sovereignty of the modern state was from the first *dependent upon the relations between states*, in terms of which each state (in principle if by no means always in practice) recognised the autonomy of others within their own borders. No state, however powerful, held as much sovereign control in practice as was enshrined in legal principle. The history of the past two centuries is thus not one of the progressive loss of sovereignty on the part of the nation-state. Here again we must recognise the dialectical character of globalisation and also the influence of processes of uneven development. Loss of autonomy on the part of some states or groups of states has often gone along with an *increase* in that of others, as a result of alliances, wars, or political and economic changes of various sorts. For instance, although the sovereign control of some of the 'classical' Western nations may have diminished as a result of the acceleration of the global division of labour over the past thirty years, that of some Far Eastern countries – in some respects at least – has grown.

Since the stance of world-system theory differs so much from international relations, it is not surprising to find that the two literatures are at arm's distance from one another. Wallerstein's account of the world system makes many contributions, in both theory and empirical analysis.[3] Not least important is the fact that he skirts the sociologists' usual preoccupation with 'societies' in favour of a much more embracing conception of globalised relationships. He also makes a clear differentiation between the modern era and preceding ages in terms of the phenomena with which he is concerned. What he refers to as 'world economies' – networks of economic connections of a geographically extensive sort – have existed prior to modern times, but these were notably different from the world system that has developed over the past three or four centuries. Earlier world economies were usually centred upon large imperial states and never covered more than certain regions in which the power of these states was concentrated. The emergence of capitalism, as Wallerstein analyses it, ushers in a quite different type of order, for the first time genuinely global in its span and based more on economic than political power – the 'world capitalist economy'. The world capitalist economy, which has its origins in the sixteenth and seventeenth centuries, is integrated through commercial and manufacturing connections, not by a political centre. Indeed, there exists a multiplicity of political centres, the nation-states. The modern world system is divided into three components, the core, the semi-periphery and the periphery, although where these are located regionally shifts over time.

According to Wallerstein, the worldwide reach of capitalism was established quite early on in the modern period: 'Capitalism was from the beginning an affair of the world economy and not of nation-states. . . . Capital has never allowed its aspirations to be determined by national boundaries.'[4] Capitalism has been such a fundamental globalising influence precisely because it is an economic rather than a political order; it has been able to penetrate far-flung areas of the world which the states of its origin could not have brought wholly under their political sway. The colonial administration of distant lands may in some situations have helped to consolidate economic expansion, but it was never the main basis of the spread of capitalistic enterprise globally. In the late twentieth century, where colonialism in its original form has all but disappeared, the world capitalist economy continues to involve massive imbalances between core, semi-periphery and periphery.

Wallerstein successfully breaks away from some of the limitations of much orthodox sociological thought, most notably the strongly defined tendency to focus upon 'endogenous models' of social change. But his work has its own shortcomings. He continues to see only one dominant institutional nexus (capitalism) as responsible for modern transformations. World-system theory thus concentrates heavily upon economic influences and finds it difficult satisfactorily to account for just those phenomena made central by the theorists of international relations: the rise of the nation-state and the nation-state system. Moreover, the distinctions between core, semi-periphery and periphery (themselves perhaps of questionable value), based upon economic criteria, do not allow us to illuminate political or military concentrations of power, which do not align in an exact way to economic differentiations.

I shall, in contrast, regard the world capitalist economy as one of four dimensions of globalisation [. . .] (see Figure 1).[5] The nation-state system is a second dimension; [. . .] although these are connected in various ways, neither can be explained exhaustively in terms of the other.

If we consider the present day, in what sense can world economic organisation be said to be dominated by capitalistic economic mechanisms? A number of considerations are relevant to answering this question. The main centres of power in the world economy are capitalist states – states in which capitalist economic enterprise (with the class relations that this implies) is the chief form of production. The domestic and international economic policies of these states involve many forms of regulation of economic activity, but [. . .] their institutional organisation maintains an 'insulation' of the economic from the political. This allows wide scope for the global activities of business corporations, which always have a home

Figure 1 The dimensions of globalisation

base within a particular state but may develop many other regional involvements elsewhere.

Business firms, especially the transnational corporations, may wield immense economic power, and have the capacity to influence political policies in their home bases and elsewhere. The biggest transnational companies today have budgets larger than those of all but a few nations. But there are some key respects in which their power cannot rival that of states – especially important here are the factors of territoriality and control of the means of violence. There is no area on the earth's surface, with the partial exception of the polar regions, which is not claimed as the legitimate sphere of control of one state or another. All modern states have a more or less successful monopoly of control of the means of violence within their own territories. No matter how great their economic power, industrial corporations are not military organisations (as some of them were during the colonial period), and they cannot establish themselves as political/legal entities which rule a given territorial area.

If nation-states are the principal 'actors' within the global political order, corporations are the dominant agents within the world economy. In their trading relations with one another, and with states and consumers, companies (manufacturing corporations, financial firms and banks) depend upon production for profit. Hence the spread of their influence brings in its train a global extension of commodity markets, including money markets. However, even in its beginnings, the capitalist world economy was never just a market for the trading of goods and services. It involved, and involves today, the commodifying of labour power in class relations which separate workers from control of their means of production. This process, of course, is fraught with implications for global inequalities.

All nation-states, capitalist and state socialist, within the 'developed' sectors of the world, are primarily reliant upon industrial production for the generation of the wealth upon which their tax revenues are based. The socialist countries form something of an enclave within the capitalist world economy as a whole, industry being more directly subject to political imperatives. These states are scarcely post-capitalist, but the influence of capitalistic markets upon the distribution of goods and labour power is substantially muted. The pursuit of growth by both Western and East European societies inevitably pushes economic interests to the forefront of the policies which states pursue in the international arena. But it is surely plain to all, save those under the sway of historical materialism, that the material involvements of nation-states are not governed purely by economic considerations, real or perceived. The influence of any particular state within the global political order is strongly conditioned by the level of its wealth (and the connection between this and military strength). However, states derive their power from their sovereign capabilities, as Hans J. Morgenthau emphasises.[6] They do not operate as economic machines, but as 'actors' jealous of their territorial rights, concerned with the fostering of national cultures, and having strategic geopolitical involvements with other states or alliances of states.

The nation-state system has long participated in that reflexivity characteristic of modernity as a whole. The very existence of sovereignty should be understood as something that is reflexively monitored, for reasons already indicated. Sovereignty is linked to the replacement of 'frontiers' by 'borders' in the early development of the nation-state system: autonomy inside the territory claimed by the state is sanctioned by the recognition of borders by other states. As noted, this is one the major factors distinguishing the nation-state system from systems of states in the pre-modern era, where few reflexively ordered relations of this kind existed and where the notion of 'international relations' made no sense.

One aspect of the dialectical nature of globalisation is the 'push and pull' between tendencies towards centralisation inherent in the reflexivity of the system of states on the one hand and the sovereignty of particular states on the other. Thus, concerted action between countries in some respects diminishes the individual sovereignty of the nations involved, yet by combining their power in other ways, it increases their influence within the state system. The same is true of the early congresses which, in conjunction with war, defined and redefined states' borders – and of truly global agencies such as the United Nations. The global influence of the UN (still decisively limited by the fact that it is not territorial and does not have significant access to the means of violence) is not purchased solely by means of a diminution of the sovereignty of nation-states – things are more complicated than this. An obvious example is that of the 'new nations' – autonomous nation-states set up in erstwhile colonised areas. Armed struggle against the colonising countries was very generally a major factor in persuading the colonisers to retreat. But discussion in the UN played a key role in setting up ex-colonial areas as states with internationally recognised borders. However weak some of the new nations may be economically and militarily, their emergence *as* nation-states (or, in many cases, 'state-nations') marks a net gain in terms of sovereignty, as compared to their previous circumstances.

The third dimension of globalisation is the world military order. In specifying its nature, we have to analyse the connections between the industrialisation of war, the flow of weaponry and techniques of military organisation from some parts of the world to others, and the alliances which states build with one another. Military alliances do not necessarily compromise the monopoly over the means of violence held by a state within its territories, although in some circumstances they certainly can do so.

In tracing the overlaps between military power and the sovereignty of states, we find the same push-and-pull between opposing tendencies noted previously. In the current period, the two most militarily developed states, the United States and the Soviet Union, have built a bipolar system of military alliances of truly global scope. The countries involved in these alliances necessarily accept limitations over their opportunities to forge independent military strategies externally. They may also forfeit complete monopoly of military control within their own territories, in so far as American or Soviet forces stationed there take their orders from abroad. Yet, as a result of the massive destructive power of modern weaponry, almost all states possess military strength far in excess of that of even the largest of pre-modern civilisations. Many economically weak Third World countries are militarily powerful. In an important sense there is no 'Third World' in respect of weaponry, only a 'First World', since most countries maintain stocks of technologically advanced armaments and have modernised the military in a thoroughgoing way. Even the possession of nuclear weaponry is not confined to the economically advanced states.

The globalising of military power obviously is not confined to weaponry and alliances between the armed forces of different states – it also concerns war itself. Two world wars attest to the way in which local conflicts became matters of global involvement. In both wars, the participants were drawn from virtually all regions (although the Second World War was a more truly worldwide phenomenon). In an era of nuclear weaponry, the industrialisation of war has proceeded to a point at which [...] the obsolescence of Clausewitz's main doctrine has become apparent to everyone.[7] The only point of holding nuclear weapons – apart from their possible symbolic value in world politics – is to deter others from using them.

While this situation may lead to a suspension of war between the nuclear powers (or so we all must hope), it scarcely prevents them from engaging in military adventures outside their own territorial domains. The two superpowers in particular engage in what might be called 'orchestrated wars' in peripheral areas of military strength. By these I mean military encounters, with the governments of other states or with guerrilla movements or both, in which the troops of the superpower are not necessarily even engaged at all, but where that power is a prime organising influence.

The fourth dimension of globalisation concerns industrial development. The most obvious aspect of this is the expansion of the global division of labour, which includes the differentiations between more and less industrialised areas in the world. Modern industry is intrinsically based on divisions of labour, not only on the level of job tasks but on that of regional specialisation in terms of type of industry, skills and the production of raw materials. There has undoubtedly taken place a major expansion of global interdependence in the division of labour since the Second World War. This has helped to bring about shifts in the worldwide distribution of production, including the deindustrialisation of some regions in the developed countries and the emergence of the 'Newly Industrialising Countries' in the Third World. It has also undoubtedly served to reduce the internal economic hegemony of many states, particularly those with a high level of industrialisation. It is more difficult for the capitalist countries to manage their economies than formerly was the case, given accelerating global economic interdependence. This is almost certainly one of the major reasons for the declining impact of Keynesian economic policies, as applied at the level of the national economy, in current times.

One of the main features of the globalising implications of industrialism is the worldwide diffusion of machine technologies. The impact of industrialism is plainly not limited to the sphere of production, but affects many aspects of day-to-day life, as well as influencing the generic character of human interaction with the material environment.

Even in states which remain primarily agricultural, modern technology is often applied in such a way as to alter substantially preexisting relations between human social organisation and the environment. This is true, for example, of the use of fertilisers or other artificial farming methods, the introduction of modern farming machinery, and so forth. The diffusion of industrialism has created 'one world' in a more negative and threatening sense than that just mentioned – a world in which there are actual or potential ecological changes of a harmful sort that affect everyone on the planet. Yet industrialism has also decisively conditioned our very sense of living in 'one world'. For one of the most important effects of industrialism has been the transformation of technologies of communication.

This comment leads on to a further and quite fundamental aspect of globalisation, which lies behind each of the various institutional dimensions that have been mentioned and which might be referred to as cultural globalisation. Mechanised technologies of communication have dramatically influenced all aspects of globalisation since the first introduction of mechanical printing into Europe. They form an essential element of the reflexivity of modernity and of the discontinuities which have torn the modern away from the traditional.

The globalising impact of media was noted by numerous authors during the period of the early growth of mass circulation newspapers. Thus one commentator in 1892 wrote that, as a result of modern newspapers, the inhabitant of a local village has a broader understanding of contemporary events than the prime minister of a hundred years before. The villager who reads a paper 'interests himself simultaneously in the issue of a revolution in Chile, a bush-war in East Africa, a massacre in North China, a famine in Russia'[8].

The point here is not that people are contingently aware of many events, from all over the world, of which previously they would have remained ignorant. It is that the global extension of the institutions of modernity would be impossible were it not for the pooling of knowledge which is represented by the 'news'. This is perhaps less obvious on the level of general cultural awareness than in more specific contexts. For example, the global money markets of today involve direct and simultaneous access to pooled information on the part of individuals spatially widely separated from one another.

Notes

1. Daniel Bell, 'The world and the United States in 2013', *Daedalus*, 116, 1987.
2. See, for example James N. Rosenthau, *The Study of Global Interdependence*, Pinter: London 1980.
3. Immanuel Wallerstein, *The Modern World System*, Academic Press: New York, 1974.
4. *idem*, 'The rise and future demise of the world capitalist system: concepts for comparative analysis', in his *The Capitalist World Economy*, Cambridge University Press: Cambridge, 1979, p. 19.
5. This figure (and the discussion which accompanies it) supersedes that which appears on p. 277 of *Nation-State and Violence, Vol. 2, A Contemporary Critique of Historical Materialism*, Polity: London, 1985.
6. H. J. Morgenthau, *Politics Among Nations*, Knopf: New York, 1960.
7. Clausewitz was a subtle thinker, however, and there are interpretations of his ideas which continue to insist upon their relevance to the present day.
8. Max Nordau, *Degeneration*, Fertig: New York, 1968, p. 39 (first published 1892).

PART THREE
Theorising Gender

Introduction

Theoretical considerations of gender in relation to colonial and post-colonial discourses cover an enormous range of issues and materials. For the sake of simplicity, we will divide this area into 'colonial' and 'post-colonial' categories here.

One theoretical approach to the gendering of colonialist discourse has what can be termed an ideological focus. This involves scrutiny of the ways in which imperialist and colonial discourse explicitly feature gender relations; considering, for example, how white femininity has been instrumentalised in dominant colonial and imperial discourses to signify the 'heart', or body, of Western civilisation. This discourse is nothing if not contradictory: for instance, while imperial and colonial discourse may argue that the status of women in any society is the measure of the stage of civilisation that has been reached by that society, it is equally prone to situating 'woman' as a biological universal category which in its function and in its status stands outside the evolutionary processes of cultural development. The mapping of the racial dynamics of sexuality is another aspect of ideological exploration: critics as diverse as Frantz Fanon and the African-American Angela Davis have explored the ways in which colonialism in practice as in ideology draws upon a mythology of the black male sexual threat to white femininity to legitimate itself.

Another focus of colonial discourse might be termed psychosexual, exploring the ways in which colonial and imperial discourse implicitly draws upon sexual paradigms to represent itself: to what extent does the conquest of, and domination over, the land and people of the colonies model itself upon the power relations of masculinity and femininity? To what extent can nineteenth-century colonialist discourse be analysed as corresponding to, or stemming from, a crisis within dominant masculinity, triggered by developments in feminist political and cultural identity of the nineteenth century? This latter is the argument underpinning the work of Sandra Gilbert and Susan Gubar in their recent *No Man's Land*.[1]

If these questions concern the possible ways in which discourses of colonialism and racial domination are gendered, there are also a number of questions concerning the *racialisation* of categories of gender within colonial and dominant metropolitan discourses. When Sigmund Freud described woman as 'the dark continent' – or when he dreamed of H. Rider Haggard's 1886 imperial fantasy *She* (a favourite also of Carl Jung) – he expressed a number of prevalent associations between femininity and the colonised Other, which occasion a number of questions about the ways in which psychoanalysis is theoretically and historically implicated in colonial and imperial structures of thought. (It should be noted that the French feminist thinker Hélène Cixous in her 'Laugh of the Medusa' continues the equation femininity = blackness, and extends it by rendering apartheid South Africa a metaphor for the oppression of women.[2]) Sander Gilman's *Difference and Pathology: Stereotypes of sexuality, race and madness* explores the connections made by nineteenth-century medical and popular discourses between blackness and femininity, including the ways in which white women could be featured as approximating black people in their lack of evolutionary development, their 'otherness' to the norms of white masculinity.[3]

As Gayatri Chakravorty Spivak points out (in Part One), there are a number of historical and theoretical questions to be asked concerning the relationship between colonial discourse and pre-colonial patriarchy, and the ways in which these construct or obliterate 'native' Black or Third World women. As Spivak points out elsewhere, in, for example, her 'Three women's texts and a critique of imperialism',[4] dominant (middle-class) Western feminism also has had an investment in the marginalisation of colonised women, at times instrumentalising them as the 'Other' in order to consolidate itself.

These tensions between white feminism and the colonised 'Other' are some of the issues explored by Chandra Talpade Mohanty and Jenny Sharpe in this part. Taking feminist scholarship in the social sciences as her subject, Chandra Talpade Mohanty explores the ways in which white feminism has constructed a monolithic 'third world woman' as its object of knowledge. Using E. M. Forster's *A Passage to India* (1922) as her focus and as an analytical springboard, Jenny Sharpe plots the ways in which white feminist readings of that novel have prioritised issues of gender over 'race' and colonialism, highlighted in the example of Azis's putative sexual attack on Adela Quested, an incident which in fact witnesses to the complex inextricability, not separability, of 'race' and gender. Arguing that this incident requires to be read in the light of nineteenth-century imperial/colonial constructions of white womanhood as sexually victimised by Indian manhood in the 1857 uprising, Sharpe urges a cultural materialist methodology as a way of getting beyond the impasses of an ahistorical idealist theorisation.

When it comes to anti-colonial, nationalist and post-colonial cultural and political projects, as Jean Franco (Part Four) and Deniz Kandiyoti (Part Five) point out, women's interests often continue to be subordinated to those of 'the nation' as it is defined in terms of masculinist ideology and material power. Just how to theorise post-colonial femininity and/or feminism is, as Sara Suleri points out in this part, an area of immense difficulty. Criticising the underlying ideological assumptions, and conclusions, of influential work by Chandra Talpade Mohanty, Trinh Minh-ha and bell hooks, Suleri suggests the academic professional conditions, the conceptual contradictions and political exclusivisms attached to their attempts to theorise on the basis of a personal identity politics and autobiography. She advocates instead a materialist feminist theory which locates the co-ordinates of post-colonial femininity within the axes of the institutions of the law and the state.

Materialism of a contrasting, if complementary kind, underlies Mae Gwendolyn Henderson's theorisation of African-American women's fiction. Her own methodology reflects the ideology of heterogeneity which, she argues, is the foundation of African-American women's writing. Combining the theories of the early twentieth-century Russian formalist Mikhail Bakhtin and the modern hermeneutical thinker German Hans-Georg Gadamer, Henderson attempts to 'account for racial difference within gender identity and gender difference within racial identity'. She argues that black women's writing is grounded upon both dialogism and dialectics: a 'dialogic relationship (not only) with an imaginary or generalised Other, but a dialogue with the aspects of "otherness" within the self'; a dialectics which emphasises 'those aspects of the self shared with others'. What emerges is a model of black women's literary production in which the literature is seen to be engaged simultaneously with 'hegemonic and ambiguously (non)hegemonic [black male] discourse', and is both adversarial and conciliatory.

Notes

1. Sandra M. Gilbert and Susan Gubar, *No Man's Land: The place of the woman writer in the twentieth century*, Yale University Press: New Haven, CT, 1989.
2. In Elaine Marks and Isabel de Courtivron (eds.), *New French Feminisms*, Schocken Books: New York, 1981.
3. Cornell University Press: Ithaca, NY, and London, 1985.
4. *Critical Inquiry*, 12, 1, 1985, pp. 262–80.

11 □ *Under Western Eyes: Feminist Scholarship and Colonial Discourses*

Chandra Talpade Mohanty

It ought to be of some political significance at least that the term 'colonization' has come to denote a variety of phenomena in recent feminist and left writings in general. From its analytic value as a category of exploitative economic exchange in both traditional and contemporary Marxisms (cf. particularly such contemporary scholars as Baran, Amin and Gunder-Frank) to its use by feminist women of colour in the US, to describe the appropriation of their experiences and struggles by hegemonic white women's movements,[1] the term 'colonization' has been used to characterize everything from the most evident economic and political hierarchies to the production of a particular cultural discourse about what is called the 'Third World.'[2] However sophisticated or problematical its use as an explanatory construct, colonization almost invariably implies a relation of structural domination, and a discursive or political suppression of the heterogeneity of the subject(s) in question. What I wish to analyse here specifically is the production of the 'Third World Woman' as a singular monolithic subject in some recent (western) feminist texts. The definition of colonization I invoke is a predominantly *discursive* one, focusing on a certain mode of appropriation and codification of 'scholarship' and 'knowledge' about women in the third world by particular analytic categories employed in writings on the subject which take as their primary point of reference feminist interests as they have been articulated in the US and western Europe.

My concern about such writings derives from my own implication and investment in contemporary debates in feminist theory, and the urgent political necessity of forming strategic coalitions across class, race and national boundaries. Clearly, western feminist discourse and political practice is neither singular nor homogeneous in its goals, interests or analyses. However, it is possible to trace a coherence of *effects* resulting from the implicit assumption of 'the west' (in all its complexities and contradictions) as the primary referent in theory and praxis. Thus,

From *Feminist Review*, 30, Autumn 1988, pp. 65–88.

rather than claim simplistically that 'western feminism' is a monolith, I would like to draw attention to the remarkably similar effects of various analytical categories and even strategies which codify their relationship to the Other in implicitly hierarchical terms. It is in this sense that I use the term 'western feminist'. Similar arguments pertaining to questions of methods of analysis can be made in terms of middle-class, urban African, and Asian scholars producing scholarship on or about their rural or working-class sisters which assumes their own middle-class culture as the norm, and codifies peasant and working-class histories and cultures as Other. Thus, while this article focuses specifically on western feminist discourse on women in the third world, the critiques I offer also pertain to identical analytical principles employed by third-world scholars writing about their own cultures.

Moreover, the analytical principles discussed below serve to distort western feminist political practices, and limit the possibility of coalitions among (usually white) western feminists and working-class and feminist women of colour around the world. These limitations are evident in the construction of the (implicitly consensual) priority of issues around which apparently *all* women are expected to organize. The necessary and integral connection between feminist scholarship and feminist political practice and organizing determines the significance and status of western feminist writings on women in the third world, for feminist scholarship, like most other kinds of scholarship, does not comprise merely 'objective' knowledge about a certain subject. It is also a directly political and discursive *practice* insofar as it is purposeful and ideological. It is best seen as a mode of intervention into particular hegemonic discourses (for example, traditional anthropology, sociology, literary criticism, etc.), and as a political praxis which counters and resists the totalizing imperative of age-old 'legitimate' and 'scientific' bodies of knowledge. Thus, feminist scholarly practices exist within relations of power – relations which they counter, redefine, or even implicitly support. There can, of course, be no apolitical scholarship.

The relationship between Woman – a cultural and ideological composite Other constructed through diverse representational discourse (scientific, literary, juridical, linguistic, cinematic, etc.) – and women – real, material subjects of their collective histories – is one of the central questions the practice of feminist scholarship seeks to address. This connection between women as historical subjects and the re-presentation of Woman produced by hegemonic discourses is not a relation of direct identity, or a relation of correspondence or simple implication.[3] It is an arbitrary relation set up in particular cultural and historical contexts. I would like to suggest that the feminist writing I analyse here discursively colonize the material and historical heterogeneities of the lives of women in the third world, thereby producing/representing a composite, singular 'third-world woman' – an image which appears arbitrarily constructed but nevertheless carries with it the authorizing signature of western humanist discourse.[4] I argue that assumptions of privilege and ethnocentric universality on the one hand, and inadequate self-consciousness about the effect of western scholarship on the 'third world' in the context of a world system dominated by the west on the other, characterize a sizable extent of western feminist work on women in the third world. An analysis of 'sexual difference' in the form of a cross-culturally singular, monolithic notion of patriarchy or male dominance leads to the construction of a similarly reductive and homogeneous notion of what I shall call the 'third-world difference' – that stable, ahistorical something that apparently oppresses most if not all the women in these countries. It is in the production of this 'third-world difference' that western feminisms appropriate and colonize the constitutive complexities which characterize the lives of women in these countries. It is in this process of discursive homogenization and systematization of the oppression of women in the third world that power is exercised in much of recent western feminist writing, and this power needs to be defined and named.

In the context of the west's hegemonic position today, of what Anouar Abdel-Malek calls a struggle for 'control over the orientation, regulation and decision of the process of world development on the basis of the advanced sector's monopoly of scientific knowledge and ideal creativity',[5] western feminist scholarship on the third world must be seen and examined precisely in terms of its inscription in these particular relations of power and struggle. There is, it should be evident, no universal patriarchal framework which this scholarship attempts to counter and resist – unless one posits an international male conspiracy or a monolithic, transhistorical power structure. There is, however, a particular world balance of power within which any analysis of culture, ideology and socio-economic conditions has to be necessarily situated. Abdel-Malek is useful here, again, in reminding us about the inherence of politics in the discourses of 'culture':

> Contemporary imperialism is, in a real sense, a hegemonic imperialism, exercising to a maximum degree a rationalized violence taken to a higher level than ever before – through fire and sword, but also through the attempt to control hearts and minds. For its content is defined by the combined action of the military – industrial complex and the hegemonic cultural centers of the West, all of them founded on the advanced levels of development attained by monopoly and finance capital, and supported by the benefits of both the scientific and technological revolution and the second industrial revolution itself.[6]

Western feminist scholarship cannot avoid the challenge of situating itself and examining its role in such a global economic and political framework. To do any less would be to ignore the complex interconnections between first- and third-world economies and the profound effect of this on the lives of women in *all* countries. I do not question the descriptive and informative value of most western feminist writings on women in the third world. I also do not question the existence of excellent work which does not fall into the analytic traps I am concerned with. In fact I deal with an example of such work later on. In the context of an overwhelming silence about the experiences of women in these countries, as well as the need to forge international links between women's political struggles, such work is both pathbreaking and absolutely essential. However, it is both to the *explanatory potential* of particular analytic strategies employed by such writing, and to their *political effect* in the context of the hegemony of western scholarship, that I want to draw attention here. While feminist writing in the US is still marginalized (except perhaps from the point of view of women of colour addressing privileged white women), western feminist writing on women in the third world must be considered in the context of the global hegemony of western scholarship – i.e. the production, publication, distribution and consumption of information and ideas. Marginal or not, this writing has political effects and implications beyond the immediate feminist or disciplinary audience. One such significant effect of the dominant 'representations' of western feminism is its conflation with imperialism in the eyes of particular third-world women.[7] Hence the urgent need to examine the *political* implications of our *analytic* strategies and principles.

My critique is directed at three basic analytical presuppositions which are present in (western) feminist discourse on women in the third world. Since I focus primarily on the Zed Press 'Women in the Third World' series, my comments on western feminist discourse are circumscribed by my analysis of the texts in this series.[8] This is a way of focusing my critique. However, even though I am dealing with feminists who identify themselves as culturally or geographically from the 'west', as mentioned earlier, what I say about these presuppositions or implicit principles holds for anyone who uses these analytical strategies, whether third-world women in the west, or third-world women in the third world writing on these issues and publishing in the west. Thus, I am not making a culturalist argument about ethnocentrism; rather, I am trying to uncover how ethnocentric universalism is produced in certain analyses. As a matter of fact, my argument holds for any discourse that sets up its own authorial subjects as the implicit referent, i.e. the yardstick by which to encode and represent cultural Others. It is in this move that power is exercised in discourse.

The first analytical presupposition I focus on is involved in the strategic location or situation of the category 'women' *vis-à-vis* the context of analysis. The assumption of women as an already constituted and coherent group with identical interests and desires, regardless of class, ethnic or racial location, implies a notion of gender or sexual difference or even patriarchy which can be applied universally and cross-culturally. (The context of analysis can be anything from kinship structures and the organization of labour to media representations.) The second analytical presupposition is evident on the methodological level, in the uncritical way 'proof' of universality and cross-cultural validity are provided. The third is a more specifically political presupposition, underlying the methodologies and the analytic strategies, i.e. the model of power and struggle they imply and suggest. I argue that as a result of the two modes – or, rather, frames – of analysis described above, a homogeneous notion of the oppression of women as a group is assumed, which, in turn, produces the image of an 'average third-world woman'. This average third-world woman leads an essentially truncated life based on her feminine gender (read: sexually constrained) and being 'third world' (read: ignorant, poor, uneducated, tradition-bound, religious, domesticated, family-oriented, victimized, etc.). This, I suggest, is in contrast to the (implicit) self-representation of western women as educated, modern, as having control over their own bodies and sexualities, and the 'freedom' to make their own decisions. The distinction between western feminist re-presentation of women in the third world, and western feminist self-presentation is a distinction of the same order as that made by some Marxists between the 'maintenance' function of the housewife and the real 'productive' role of wage-labour, or the characterization by developmentalists of the third world as being engaged in the lesser production of 'raw materials' in contrast to the real 'productive' activity of the first world. These distinctions are made on the basis of the privileging of a particular group as the norm or referent. Men involved in wage-labour, first-world producers and, I suggest, western feminists who sometimes cast third-world women in terms of 'ourselves undressed'[9], all construct themselves as the normative referent in such a binary analytic.

'Women' as Category of Analysis, or: We are all Sisters in Struggle

By women as a category of analysis, I am referring to the crucial presupposition that all of us of the same gender, across classes and cultures, are somehow socially constituted as a homogeneous group identifiable prior to the process of analysis. The homogeneity of women as a group is produced not on the basis of biological essentials, but rather on the basis of secondary sociological and anthropological universals. Thus, for instance, in any given piece of feminist analysis, women are characterized as a singular group on the basis of a shared oppression. What binds women together is a sociological notion of the 'sameness' of their oppression. It is at this point that an elision takes place between 'women' as a discursively constructed group and 'women' as material subjects of their own history.[10] Thus, the discursively consensual homogeneity of 'women' as a group is mistaken for the historically specific material reality of groups of women. This results in an assumption of women as an always-already constituted group, one which has been labelled 'powerless', 'exploited', 'sexually harassed', etc., by feminist scientific, economic, legal and sociological discourses. (Notice that this is quite similar to sexist discourse labelling women as weak, emotional, having math anxiety, etc.) The focus is not on uncovering the material and ideological specificities that constitute a group of women as 'powerless' in a particular context. It is rather on finding a variety of cases of 'powerless' groups of women to prove the general point that women as a group are powerless.[11]

In this section I focus on five specific ways in which 'women' as a category of analysis is used in western feminist discourse on women in the third world to construct 'third-world women' as a homogeneous 'powerless' group often located as implicit *victims* of particular cultural and socio-economic systems. I have chosen to deal with a variety of writers – from Fran Hosken, who writes primarily about female genital mutilation, to writers from the Women in International Development school who write about the effect of development policies on third-world women for both western and third-world audiences. I do not intend to equate all the texts that I analyse, nor ignore their respective strengths and weaknesses. The authors I deal with write with varying degrees of care and complexity; however, the *effect* of the representation of third-world women in these texts is a coherent one. In these texts women are variously defined as victims of male violence (Fran Hosken); victims of the colonial process (M. Cutrufelli); victims of the Arab familial system (Juliette Minces); victims of the economic development process (B. Lindsay and the – liberal – WID school); and finally, victims of the economic basis of *the* Islamic code (P. Jeffery). This mode of defining women primarily in terms of their *object status* (the way in which they are affected or not affected by certain institutions and systems) is what characterizes this particular form of the use of 'women' as a category of analysis. In the context of western women writing about and studying women in the third world, such objectification (however benevolently motivated) needs to be both named and challenged. As Valerie Amos and Pratibha Parmar argue quite eloquently, 'Feminist theories which examine our cultural practices as "feudal residues" or label us "traditional", also portray us as politically immature women who need to be versed and schooled in the ethos of western feminism. They need to be continually challenged.'[12]

Women as Victims of Male Violence

Fran Hosken, in writing about the relationship between human rights and female genital mutilation in Africa and the Middle East, bases her whole discussion and condemnation of genital mutilation on one privileged premise: the goal of genital mutilation is 'to mutilate the sexual pleasure and satisfaction of woman'.[13] This, in turn, leads her to claim that woman's sexuality is controlled as is her reproductive potential. According to Hosken, 'male sexual politics' in Africa and around the world 'share the same political goal: to assure female dependence and subservience by any and all means'. Physical violence against women (rape, sexual assault, excision, infibulation, etc.) is thus carried out 'with an astonishing consensus among men in the world'.[14] Here, women are defined systematically as the *victims* of male control – the 'sexually oppressed'. Although it is true that the potential of male violence against women circumscribes and elucidates their social position to a certain extent, defining women as archetypal victims freezes them into 'objects-who-defend-themselves', men into 'subjects-who-perpetrate-violence', and (every) society into a simple opposition between the powerless (read: women) and the powerful (read: men) groups of people. Male violence (if that indeed is the appropriate label) must be theorised and interpreted *within* specific societies, both in order to understand it better, as well as in order to effectively organize to change it.[15] Sisterhood cannot be assumed on the basis of gender; it must be forged in concrete historical and political praxis.

Women as Universal Dependants

Beverley Lindsay's conclusion to the book, *Comparative Perspectives on Third World Women: The impact of race, sex and class*, states: 'Dependency relationships, based upon race, sex and class, are being perpetuated through social, educational, and economic institutions. These are the linkages among Third World Women.'[16] Here, as in other places, Lindsay implies that third-world women constitute an identifiable group purely on the basis of shared dependencies. If shared dependencies were all that was needed to bind us together as a group, third-world women would always be seen as an apolitical group with no subject status! Instead, if anything, it is the *common context* of political struggle against class, race, gender and imperialist hierarchies that may constitute third-world women as a strategic group at this historical juncture. Lindsay also states that linguistic and cultural differences exist between Vietnamese and Black American Women, but 'both groups are victims of race, sex and class'. Again, Black and Vietnamese women are characterized and defined simply in terms of their victim status.

Similarly, examine statements like: 'My analysis will start by stating that all African women are politically and economically dependent.'[17] Or: 'Nevertheless, either overtly or covertly, prostitution is still the main if not the only source of work for African women.'[18] *All* African women are dependent. Prostitution is the only work option for African women as a *group*. Both statements are illustrative of generalisations sprinkled liberally through a recent Zed Press publication, *Women of Africa: Roots of oppression*, by Maria Rosa Cutrufelli, who is described on the cover as an 'Italian Writer, Sociologist, Marxist and Feminist'. In the 1980s is it possible to imagine writing a book entitled 'Women of Europe: Roots of oppression'? I am not objecting to the use of universal groupings for descriptive purposes. Women from the continent of Africa can be descriptively characterized as 'Women of Africa'. It is when 'women of Africa' becomes a homogeneous sociological grouping characterized by common dependencies or powerlessness (or even strengths) that problems arise — we say too little and too much at the same time.

This is because descriptive gender differences are transformed into the division between men and women. Women are constituted as a group via dependency relationships *vis-à-vis* men, who are implicitly held responsible for these relationships. When 'women of Africa' (versus 'men of Africa' as a group?) are seen as a group precisely because they are generally dependent and oppressed, the analysis of specific historical differences becomes impossible, because reality is always apparently structured by divisions between two mutually exclusive and jointly exhaustive groups, the victims and the oppressors. Here the sociological is substituted for the biological in order, however, to create the same — a unity of women. Thus, it is not the descriptive potential of gender difference but the privileged positioning and explanatory potential of gender difference as the *origin* of oppression that I question. In using 'women of Africa' (as an already constituted group of oppressed peoples) as a category of analysis, Cutrufelli denies any historical specificity to the location of women as subordinate, powerful, marginal, central, or otherwise, *vis-à-vis* particular social and power networks. Women are taken as a unified 'powerless' group prior to the historical and political analysis in question. Thus, it is then merely a matter of specifying the context *after the fact*. 'Women' are now placed in the context of the family, or in the workplace, or within religious networks, almost as if these systems existed outside the relations of women with other women, and women with men.

The problem with this analytical strategy is, let me repeat, that it assumes men and women are already constituted as sexual–political subjects prior to their entry into the arena for social relations. Only if we subscribe to this assumption is it possible to undertake analysis which looks at the 'effects' of kinship structures, colonialism, organization of labour, etc., on women who are defined in advance as a group. The crucial point that is forgotten is that women are produced through these very relations as well as being implicated in forming these relations. As Michelle Rosaldo argues, 'woman's place in human social life is not in any direct sense a product of the things she does (or even less, a function of what, biologically, she is) but the meaning her activities acquire through concrete social interactions.'[19] That women mother in a variety of societies is not as significant as the value attached to mothering in these societies. The distinction between the act of mothering and the status attached to it is a very important one – one that needs to be stated and analysed contextually.

Married Women as Victims of the Colonial Process

In Lévi-Strauss's theory of kinship structures as a system of the exchange of women, what is significant is that exchange itself is not constitutive of the subordination of women; women are not subordinate because of the *fact* of exchange, but because of the *modes* of exchange instituted, and the values attached to these modes. However, in discussing the marriage ritual of the Bemba, a Zambian matrilocal, matrilineal people, Cutrufelli in *Women of Africa* focuses on the fact of the marital exchange of women before and after western colonization, rather than the value attached to this exchange in this particular context. This leads to her definition of Bemba women as a coherent group affected in a particular way by colonization. Here again, Bemba women are constituted rather unilaterally as the victims of western colonization. Curtrufelli cites the marriage ritual of the Bemba as a multi-stage event 'whereby a young man becomes incorporated into his wife's family group as he takes up residence with them and gives his services in return for food and maintenance'.[20] This ritual extends over many years, and the sexual relationship varies according to the degree of the girl's physical maturity. It is only after the girl undergoes an initiation ceremony at puberty that intercourse is sanctioned, and the man acquires legal rights over the woman. This initiation ceremony is the most important act of the consecration of women's reproductive power, so that the abduction of an uninitiated girl is of no consequence, while heavy penalty is levied for the seduction of an initiated girl. Cutrufelli asserts that the effect of European colonization has changed the whole marriage system. Now the young man is entitled to take his wife away from her people in return for money. The implication is that Bemba women have now lost the protection of tribal laws. However, while it is possible to see how the structure of the traditional marriage contract (as opposed to the post-colonial marriage contract) offered women a certain amount of control over their marital relations, only an analysis of the political significance of the actual practice which privileges an initiated girl over an uninitiated one, indicating a shift in female power relations as a result of this ceremony, can provide an accurate account of whether Bemba women were indeed protected by tribal laws *at all times*.

However, it is not possible to talk about Bemba women as a homogeneous group within the traditional marriage structure. Bemba women *before* the initiation are constituted within a different set of social relations compared to Bemba women *after* the initiation. To treat them as a unified group, characterized by the fact of their 'exchange' between male kin, is to deny the specificities of their daily existence, and the differential *value* attached to their exchange before and after their initiation. It is to treat the initiation ceremony as a ritual with no political implications or effects. It is also to assume that in merely describing the *structure* of the marriage contract, the situation of women is exposed. Women as a group are positioned within a given structure, but there is no attempt made to trace the effect of the marriage practice in constituting women within an obviously changing network of power relations. Thus, women are assumed to be sexual–political subjects prior to entry into kinship structures.

Women and Familial Systems

Elizabeth Cowie, in another context,[21] points out the implications of this sort of analysis when she emphasizes the specifically political nature of kinship structures which must be analysed as ideological practices which designate men and women as father, husband, wife, mother, sister, etc. Thus, Cowie suggests, women as women are not simply *located* within the family. Rather, it is in the family, as an effect of kinship structures, that women as women are *constructed*, defined within and by the group. Thus, for instance, when Juliette Minces cites *the* patriarchal family as the basis for 'an almost identical vision of women' that Arab and Muslim societies have, she falls into this very trap.[22] Not only is it problematical to speak of a vision of women shared by Arab and Muslim societies, without addressing the particular historical and ideological power structures that construct such images, but to speak of the patriarchal family or the tribal kinship structure as the origin of the socio-economic status of women is again to assume that women are sexual–political subjects prior to their entry into the family. So while on the one hand women attain value or status within the family, the assumption of a singular patriarchical kinship system (common to all Arab and Muslim societies, i.e. over twenty different countries) is what apparently structures women as an oppressed group in these societies! This singular, coherent kinship system presumably influences another separate and given entity, 'women'. Thus all women, regardless of class and cultural differences, are seen as being similarly affected by this system. Not only are *all* Arab and Muslim women seen to constitute a homogeneous oppressed group, but there is no discussion of the specific *practices* within the family which constitute women as mothers, wives, sisters, etc. Arabs and Muslims, it appears, don't change at all. Their patriarchical family is carried over from the times of the Prophet Muhammad. They exist, as it were, outside history.

Women and Religious Ideologies

A further example of the use of 'women' as a category of analysis is found in cross-cultural analyses which subscribe to a certain economic reductionism in describing the relationship between the economy and factors such as politics and ideology. Here, in reducing the level of comparison to the economic relations between 'developed' and 'developing' countries, the question of women is denied any specificity. Mina Modares, in a careful analysis of women and Shi'ism in Iran, focuses on this very problem when she criticizes feminist writings which treat Islam as an ideology separate from and outside social relations and practices, rather than a discourse which includes rules for economic, social and power relations within society.[23] Patricia Jeffery's otherwise informative work on Pirzada women in purdah considers Islamic ideology as a partial explanation for the status of women in that it provides a justification for the purdah.[24] Here, Islamic ideology is reduced to a set of ideas whose internalization by Pirzada women contributes to the stability of the system. The primary explanation for purdah is located in the control that Pirzada men have over economic resources, and the personal security purdah gives to Pirzada women. By taking a specific version of Islam as *the* Islam, Jeffery attributes a singularity and coherence to it. Modares notes, '"Islamic Theology" then becomes imposed on a separate and given entity called "women". A further unification is reached: 'Women (meaning *all women*), regardless of their differing positions within societies, come to be affected or not affected by Islam. These conceptions provide the right ingredients for an unproblematic possibility of a cross-cultural study of women.'[25] Marnia Lazreg makes a similar argument when she addresses the reductionism inherent in scholarship on women in the Middle East and North Africa:

> A ritual is established whereby the writer appeals to religion as *the* cause of gender inequality just as it is made the source of underdevelopment in much of modernization theory. In an uncanny way, feminist discourse on women from the Middle East and North Africa mirrors that of theologians' own interpretation of women in Islam. . . .
>
> The overall effect of this paradigm is to deprive women of self-presence, of being. Because women are subsumed under religion presented in fundamental terms, they are inevitably seen as evolving in nonhistorical time. They have virtually no history. Any analysis of change is therefore foreclosed.[26]

While Jeffery's analysis does not quite succumb to this kind of unitary notion of religion (Islam), it does collapse all ideological specificities into economic relations, and universalizes on the basis of this comparison.

Women and the Development Process

The best examples of universalization on the basis of economic reductionism can be found in the liberal 'Women in Development' literature. Proponents of this school seek to examine the effect of development on third-world women, sometimes from self-designated feminist perspectives. At the very least, there is an evident interest in and commitment to improving the lives of women in 'developing' countries. Scholars like Irene Tinker, Ester Boserup, and Perdita Huston[27] have all written about the effect of development policies on women in the third world. All three women assume that 'development' is synonymous with 'economic development' or 'economic progress'. As in the case of Minces' patriarchal family, Hosken's male sexual control and Cutrufelli's western colonization, 'development' here becomes the all-time equalizer. Women are seen as being affected positively or negatively by economic development policies, and this is the basis for cross-cultural comparison.

For instance, Perdita Huston states that the purpose of her study is to describe the effect of the development process on the 'family unit and its individual members' in Egypt, Kenya, Sudan, Tunisia, Sri Lanka and Mexico. She states that the 'problems' and 'needs' expressed by rural and urban women in these countries all centre on education and training, work and wages, access to health and other services, political participation and legal rights. Huston relates all these 'needs' to the lack of sensitive development policies which exclude women as a group. For her, the solution is simple: improved development policies which emphasize training for women field-workers, use women trainees and women rural development officers, encourage women's cooperatives, etc. Here, again women are assumed to be a coherent group or category prior to their entry into 'the development process'. Huston assumes that all third-world women have similar problems and needs. Thus, they must have similar interests and goals. However, the interests of urban, middle-class, educated Egyptian housewives, to take only one instance, could surely not be seen as being the same as those of their uneducated, poor maids. Development policies do not affect both groups of women in the same way. Practices which characterize women's status and roles vary according to class. Women are constituted as women through the complex interaction between class, culture, religion and other ideological institutions and frameworks. They are not 'women' – a coherent group – solely on the basis of a particular economic system or policy. Such reductive cross-cultural comparisons result in the colonization of the specifics of daily existence and the complexities of political interests which women of different social classes and cultures represent and mobilize.

Thus it is revealing that for Perdita Huston women in the third-world countries she writes about have 'needs' and 'problems', but few if any have 'choices' or the freedom to act. This is an interesting representation of women in the third world, one which is significant in suggesting a latent self-presentation of western women which bears looking at. She writes, 'What surprised and moved me most as I listened to women in such very different cultural settings was the striking commonality – whether they were educated or illiterate, urban or rural – of their most basic values:

the importance they assign to family, dignity, and service to others.'[28] Would Huston consider such values unusual for women in the west?

What is problematical, then, about this kind of use of 'women' as a group, as a stable category of analysis, is that it assumes an ahistorical, universal unity among women based on a generalized notion of their subordination. Instead of analytically *demonstrating* the production of women as socio-economic political groups within particular local contexts, this analytical move – and the presuppositions it is based on – limits the definition of the female subject to gender identity, completely bypassing social class and ethnic identities. What characterizes women as a group is their gender (sociologically not necessarily biologically defined) over and above everything else, indicating a monolithic notion of sexual difference. Because women are thus constituted as a coherent group, sexual difference becomes coterminous with female subordination, and power is automatically defined in binary terms: people who have it (read: men), and people who do not (read: women). Men exploit, women are exploited. Such simplistic formulations are both historically reductive; they are also ineffectual in designing strategies to combat oppressions. All they do is reinforce binary divisions between men and women.

What would an analysis which did not do this look like? Maria Mies's work is one such example. It is an example which illustrates the strength of western feminist work on women in the third world and which does not fall into the traps discussed above. Maria Mies's study of the lace-makers of Narsapur, India, attempts to analyse carefully a substantial household industry in which 'housewives' produce lace doilies for consumption in the world market.[29] Through a detailed analysis of the structure of the lace industry, production and reproduction relations, the sexual division of labour, profits and exploitation, and the overall consequences of defining women as 'non-working housewives' and their work as 'leisure-time activity', Mies demonstrates the levels of exploitation in this industry and the impact of this production system on the work and living conditions of the women involved in it. In addition, she is able to analyse the 'ideology of the housewife', the notion of a woman sitting in the house, as providing the necessary subjective and socio-cultural element for the creation and maintenance of a production system that contributes to the increasing pauperization of women, and keeps them totally atomized and disorganized as workers. Mies's analyses show the effect of a certain historically and culturally specific mode of patriarchal organization, an organization constructed on the basis of the definition of the lace-makers as 'non-working housewives' at familial, local, regional, statewide and international levels. The intricacies and the effects of particular power networks are not only emphasized; they also form the basis of Mies's analysis of how this particular group of women is situated at the centre of a hegemonic, exploitative world market.

This is a good example of what careful, politically focused, local analyses can accomplish. It illustrates how the category of woman is constructed in a variety of political contexts that often exist simultaneously and overlaid on top of one another. There is no easy generalization in the direction of 'women' in India, or 'women in the third world', nor is there a reduction of the political construction of the exploitation of the lace-makers to cultural explanations about the passivity or obedience that might characterize these women and their situation. Finally, this mode of local, political analysis which generates theoretical categories from within the situation and context being analysed, also suggests corresponding effective strategies for organizing against the exploitations faced by the lace-makers. Here Narsapur women are not mere victims of the production process, because they resist challenge and subvert the process at various junctures. This is one instance of how Mies delineates the connections between the housewife ideology, the self-consciousness of the lace-makers and their inter-relationships as contributing to the latent resistances she perceives among the women:

> The persistence of the housewife ideology, the self-perception of the lace makers as petty commodity producers rather than as workers, is not only upheld by the structure of the industry as such but also by the deliberate propagation and reinforcement of reactionary patriarchal norms and institutions. Thus, most of the lace makers voiced the same opinion about the rules of *purdah* and seclusion in their communities which were also propagated by the lace exporters. In particular, the *Kapu* women said that they had never gone out of their houses, that women of their community could not do any other work than housework and lace work etc. but in spite of the fact that most of them still subscribed fully to the patriarchal norms of the *gosha* women, there were also contradictory elements in their consciousness. Thus, although they looked down with contempt upon women who were able to work outside the house – like the untouchable *Mala* and *Madiga* women or women of other lower castes, they could not ignore the fact that these women were earning more money precisely because they were *not* respectable housewives but workers. At one discussion, they even admitted that it would be better if they could also go out and do coolie work. And when they were asked whether they would be ready to come out of their houses and work in one place in some sort of a factory, they said they would do that. This shows that the *purdah* and housewife ideology, although still fully internalized, already had some cracks, because it has been confronted with several contradictory realities.[30]

It is only by understanding the *contradictions* inherent in women's location within various structures that effective political action and challenges can be devised. Mies's study goes a long way towards offering such an analysis. While there are now an increasing number of western feminist writings in this tradition,[31] there is also unfortunately a large block of writing which succumbs to the cultural reductionism discussed earlier.

Methodological Universalisms, or: Women's Oppression is a Global Phenomenon

Western feminist writings on women in the third world subscribe to a variety of methodologies to demonstrate the universal cross-culturul operation of male dominance and female exploitation. I summarize and critique three such methods below, moving from the most simple to the most complex methodologies.

First, proof of universalism is provided through the use of an arithmetic method. The argument goes like this: the more the number of women who wear the veil, the more universal is the sexual segregation and control of women.[32] Similarly, a large number of different, fragmented examples from a variety of countries also apparently add up to a universal fact. For instance, Muslim women in Saudi Arabia, Iran, Pakistan, India and Egypt all wear some sort of a veil. Hence, this indicates that the sexual control of women is a universal fact in those countries in which the women are veiled.[33] Fran Hosken writes: 'Rape, forced prostitution, polygamy, genital mutilation, pornography, the beating of girls and women, purdah (segregation of women) are all violations of basic human rights.'[34] By equating purdah with rape, domestic violence and forced prostitution, Hosken asserts its 'sexual control' function as the primary explanation for purdah, whatever the context. Institutions of purdah are thus denied any cultural and historical specificity and contradictions and potentially subversive aspects are totally ruled out. In both these examples, the problem is not in asserting that the practice of wearing a veil is widespread. This assertion can be made on the basis of numbers. It is a descriptive generalization. However, it is the analytic leap from the practice of veiling to an assertion of its general significance in controlling women that must be questioned. While there may be a physical similarity in the veils worn by women in Saudi Arabia and Iran, the specific meaning attached to this practice varies according to the cultural and ideological context. In addition, the symbolic space occupied by the practice of purdah may be similar in certain contexts, but this does not automatically indicate that the practices themselves have identical significance in the social realm. For example, as is well known, Iranian middle-class women veiled themselves during the 1979 revolution to indicate solidarity with their veiled working-class sisters, while in contemporary Iran mandatory Islamic laws dictate that all Iranian women wear veils. While in both these instances similar reasons might be offered for the veil (opposition to the Shah and western cultural colonisation in the first case, and the true Islamicization of Iran in the second), the concrete *meanings* attached to Iranian women wearing the veil are clearly different in the two historical contexts. In the first case, wearing the veil is both an oppositional and revolutionary gesture on the part of Iranian middle-class women; in the second case it is a coercive, institutional mandate.[35] It is on the basis of such context-specific differentiated analysis that effective political strategies can be generated. To assume that the mere practice of veiling women in a number of Muslim countries indicates the universal oppression of women through sexual segregation is not only analytically reductive, but also proves to be quite useless when it comes to the elaboration of oppositional political strategy.

Second, concepts like reproduction, the sexual division of labour, the family, marriage, household, patriarchy, etc., are often used without their specification in local cultural and historical contexts. These concepts are used by feminists in providing explanations for women's subordination, apparently assuming their universal applicability. For instance, how is it possible to refer to 'the' sexual division of labour when the *content* of this division changes radically from one environment to the next, and from one historical juncture to another? At its most abstract level, it is the fact of the differential assignation of tasks according to sex that is significant; however, this is quite different from the *meaning* or *value* that the content of this sexual division of labour assumes in different contexts. In most cases the assigning of tasks on the basis of sex has an ideological origin. There is no question that a claim such as 'women are concentrated in service-oriented occupations in a large number of countries around the world' is descriptively valid. Descriptively, then, perhaps the existence of a similar sexual division of labour (where women work in service occupations like nursing, social work, etc., and men in other kinds of occupations) in a number of different countries can be asserted. However, the concept of the 'sexual division of labour' is more than just a descriptive category. It indicates the differential *value* placed on 'men's work' versus 'women's work'.

Often the mere existence of a sexual division of labour is taken to be proof of the oppression of women in various societies. This results from a confusion between and collapsing together of the descriptive and explanatory potential of the concept of the sexual division of labour. Superficially similar situations may have radically different, historically specific explanations, and cannot be treated as identical. For instance, the rise of female-headed households in middle-class America might be construed as indicating women's independence and progress, whereby women are considered to have *chosen* to be single parents, there are increasing numbers of lesbian mothers, etc. However, the recent increase in female-headed households in Latin America,[36] where women might be seen to have more decision-making power, is concentrated among the poorest strata, where life choices are the most constrained economically. A similar argument can be made for the rise of female-headed families among Black and Chicana women in the US. The positive correlation between this and the level of poverty among women of colour and white working-class women in the US has now even acquired a name: the feminization of poverty. Thus, while it is possible to state that there is a rise in female-headed households in the US and in Latin America, this rise cannot be discussed as a universal indicator of women's independence, nor can it be discussed as a universal indicator of women's impoverishment. The *meaning* and *explanation* for the rise must obviously be specified according to the socio-historical context.

Similarly, the existence of a sexual division of labour in most contexts cannot be sufficient explanation for the universal subjugation of women in the workforce. That the sexual division of labour does indicate a devaluation of women's work must be shown through analysis of particular local contexts. In addition, devaluation of *women* must also be shown through careful analysis. In other words, the 'sexual division of labour' and 'women' are not commensurate analytical categories. Concepts like the sexual division of labour can be useful only if they are generated through local, contextual analyses.[37] If such concepts are assumed to be universally applicable, the resultant homogenisation of class, race, religious and daily material practices of women in the third world can create a false sense of the commonality of oppressions, interests and struggles between and amongst women globally. Beyond sisterhood there is still racism, colonialism and imperialism!

Finally, some writers confuse the use of gender as a superordinate category of organizing analysis with the universalistic proof and instantiation of this category. In other words, empirical studies of gender differences are confused with the analytical organization of cross-cultural work. Beverley Brown's review of the book *Nature, Culture and Gender* (1980) best illustrates this point.[38] Brown suggests that nature:culture and female:male are superordinate categories which organize and locate lesser categories (like wild/domestic and biology/technology) within their logic. These categories are universal in the sense that they organize the universe of a system of representations. This relation is totally independent of the universal substantiation of any particular category. Her critique hinges on the fact that rather than clarify the generalizability of nature:culture::female:male as superordinate organizational categories, *Nature, Culture and Gender*, the book construes the universality of this equation to lie at the level of empirical truth, which can be investigated through field-work. Thus, the usefulness of the nature:culture::female:male paradigm as a universal mode of the organization of representation within any particular socio-historical system is lost. Here, methodological universalism is assumed on the basis of the reduction of the nature:culture::female:male analytic categories to a demand for empirical proof of its existence in different cultures. Discourses of representation are confused with material realities, and the distinction between 'Woman' and 'women' is lost. Feminist work on women in the third world which blurs this distinction (a distinction which interestingly enough is often present in certain western feminists' self-representation) eventually ends up constructing monolithic images of 'Third World Women' by ignoring the complex and mobile relationships between their historical materiality on the level of specific oppressions and political choices on the one hand and their general discursive representations on the other.

To summarize: I have discussed three methodological moves identifiable in feminist (and other academic) cross-cultural work which seeks to uncover a universality in women's subordinate position in society. The next and final section pulls together the previous sections, attempting to outline the political effects of the analytical strategies in the context of western feminist writing on women in the third world. These arguments are not against generalization as much as they are for careful, historically specific generalizations responsive to complex realities. Nor do these arguments deny the necessity of forming strategic political identities and affinities. Thus, while Indian women of different backgrounds might forge a political unity on the basis of organizing against police brutality towards women,[39] an *analysis* of police brutality must be contextual. Strategic coalitions which construct oppositional political identities for themselves are based on generalization and provisional unities, but the analysis of these group identities cannot be based on universalistic, ahistorical categories.

The Subject(s) of Power

This last section returns to an earlier point about the inherently political nature of feminist scholarship, and attempts to clarify my point about the possibility of detecting a colonialist move in the case of a structurally unequal first/third-world relation in scholarship. The nine texts in the Zed Press 'Women in the Third World' series that I have discussed[40] focused on the following common areas in discussing women's 'status' within various societies: religion, family/kinship structures, the legal system, the sexual division of labour, education and, finally, political resistance. A large number of western feminist writings on women in the third world focus on these themes. Of course, the Zed texts have varying emphases. For instance, two of the studies, *Women of Palestine* (1982) and *Indian Women in Struggle* (1980), focus explicitly on female militancy and political involvement, while *Women in Arab Society* (1980) deals with Arab women's legal, religious and familial status. In addition, each text evidences a variety of methodologies and degrees of care in making generalizations. Interestingly enough, however, almost all the texts assume 'women' as a category of analysis in the manner designated above. Clearly this is an analytical strategy which is neither limited to these Zed Press publications, nor symptomatic of Zed Press publications in general. However, in the particular texts under question, each text assumes 'women' have a coherent group identity within the different cultures discussed, prior to their entry into social relations. Thus, Omvedt can talk about 'Indian Women' while referring to a particular group of women in the State of Maharashtra, Cutrufelli about 'Women of Africa' and Minces about 'Arab Women' as if these groups of women have some sort of obvious cultural coherence, distinct from men in these societies. The 'status' or 'position' of women is assumed to be self-evident because women as an already constituted group are *placed* within religious, economic, familial and legal structures. However, this focus on the position of women whereby women are seen as a coherent group across contexts, regardless of class or ethnicity, structures the world in ultimately binary, dichotomous terms, where women are always seen in opposition to men, patriarchy is always necessarily male dominance, and the religious, legal, economic and familial systems are implicitly assumed to be constructed by men. Thus, both men and women are always seen as preconstituted whole populations, and relations of dominance and exploitation are also posited in terms of whole peoples – wholes coming into exploitative relations. It is only when men and women are seen as different categories or groups possessing different *already constituted* categories of experience, cognition and interests as *groups* that such a simplistic dichotomy is possible.

What does this imply about the structure and functioning of power relations? The setting up of the commonality of third-world women's struggles across classes and cultures against a general notion of oppression (primarily the group in power – i.e. men) necessitates the assumption of something like what Michel Foucault calls the 'juridico-discursive' model of power,[41] the principal features of which are: 'a negative relation' (limit and lack); an 'insistence on the rule' (which forms a binary system); a 'cycle of prohibition'; the 'logic of censorship'; and a 'uniformity' of the apparatus functioning at different levels. Feminist discourse on the third world which assumes a homogeneous category – or group – called 'women' necessarily operates through such a setting up of *ordinary* power divisions. Power relations are structured in terms of a unilateral and undifferentiated source of power and a cumulative reaction to power. Opposition is a generalized phenomenon created as a response to power – which, in turn, is possessed by certain groups of people. The major problem with such a definition of power is that it locks all revolutionary struggles into binary structures – possessing power versus being powerless. Women are powerless, unified groups. If the struggle for a just society is seen in terms of the move from powerless to powerful for women as a *group*, and this is the implication in feminist discourse which structures sexual difference in terms of the division between the sexes, then the new society would be structurally identical to the existing organization of power relations, constituting itself as a simple *inversion* of what exists. If relations of domination and exploitation are defined in terms of binary divisions – groups which dominate and groups which are dominated – surely the implication is that the accession to power of women as a group is sufficient to dismantle the existing organization of relations? But women as a group are not in some sense essentially superior or infallible. The crux of the problem lies in that initial assumption of women as a homogeneous group or category ('the oppressed'), a familiar assumption in western radical and liberal feminisms.[42]

What happens when this assumption of 'women as an oppressed group' is situated in the context of western feminist writing about third-world women? It is here that I locate the colonialist move. By contrasting the representation of women in the third world with what I referred to earlier as western feminism's self-presentation in the same context, we see how western feminists alone become the true 'subjects' of this counter-history. Third-world women, on the other hand, never rise above the debilitating generality of their 'object' status.

While radical and liberal feminist assumptions of women as a sex class might elucidate (however inadequately) the autonomy of particular women's struggles in the west, the application of the notion of women as a homogeneous category to women in the third world colonizes and appropriates the pluralities of the simultaneous location of different groups of women in social class and ethnic frameworks; in doing so it ultimately robs them of their historical and political *agency*. Similarly, many Zed Press authors, who ground themselves in the basic analytic strategies of traditional Marxism, also implicitly create a 'unity' of women by substituting 'women's activity' for 'labour' as the primary theoretical determinant of women's situation. Here again, women are constituted as a coherent group not on the basis of 'natural' qualities or needs, but on the basis of the sociological 'unity' of their role in domestic production and wage labour.[43] In other words, western feminist discourse, by assuming women as a coherent, already constituted group which is placed in kinship, legal and other structures, defines third-world women as subjects *outside* of social relations, instead of looking at the way women are constituted as women *through* these very structures. Legal, economic, religious and familial structures are treated as phenomena to be judged by western standards. It is here that ethnocentric universality comes into play. When these structures are defined as 'underdeveloped' or 'developing' and women are placed within these structures, an implicit image of the 'average third-world woman' is produced. This is the transformation of the (implicitly western) 'oppressed woman' into the 'oppressed third-world woman'. While the category of 'oppressed woman' is generated through an exclusive focus on gender difference 'the oppressed third-world woman' category has an additional attribute – the 'third-world difference'! The 'third-world difference' includes a paternalistic attitude towards women in the third world.[44] Since discussions of the various themes identified earlier (e.g. kinship, education, religion, etc.) are conducted in the context of the relative 'underdevelopment' of the third world (which is nothing less than unjustifiably confusing development with the separate path taken by the west in its development, as well as ignoring the unidirectionality of the first/third-world power relationship), third-world women as a group or category are automatically and necessarily defined as: religious (read 'not progressive'), family oriented (read 'traditional'), legal minors (read 'they-are-still-not-conscious-of-their-rights'), illiterate (read 'ignorant'), domestic (read 'backward') and sometimes revolutionary (read 'their-country-is-in-a-state-of-war; they-must-fight!'). This is how the 'third-world difference' is produced.

When the category of 'sexually oppressed women' is located within particular systems in the third world which are defined on a scale which is normed through Eurocentric assumptions, not only are third-world women defined in a particular way prior to their entry into social relations, but since no connections are made between first- and third-world power shifts, it reinforces the assumption that people in the third world just have not evolved to the extent that the west has. This mode of feminist analysis, by homogenizing and systematizing the experiences of different groups of women, erases all marginal and resistant modes of experiences.[45] It is significant that none of the texts I reviewed in the Zed Press series focuses on lesbian politics or the politics of ethnic and religious marginal organizations in third-world women's groups. Resistance can thus only be defined as cumulatively reactive, not as something inherent in the operation of power. If power, as Michel Foucault has argued recently, can really be understood only in the context of resistance,[46] this misconceptualization of power is both analytically as well as strategically problematical. It limits theoretical analysis as well as reinforcing western cultural imperialism. For in the context of a first/third-world balance of power, feminist analyses which perpetrate and sustain the hegemony of the idea of the superiority of the west produce a corresponding set of universal images of the 'third-world woman', images like the veiled woman, the powerful mother, the chaste virgin, the obedient wife, etc. These images exist in universal ahistorical splendour, setting in motion a colonialist discourse which exercises a very specific power in defining, coding and maintaining existing first/third-world connections.

To conclude, then, let me suggest some disconcerting similarities between the typically authorizing signature of such western feminist writings on women in the

third world, and the authorizing signature of the project of humanism in general —
humanism as a western ideological and political project which involves the necessary
recuperation of the 'East' and 'Woman' as Others. Many contemporary thinkers like
Foucault, Derrida, Kristeva, Deleuze and Said have written at length about the
underlying anthropomorphism and ethnocentrism which constitutes a hegemonic
humanistic problematic that repeatedly confirms and legitimates (western) Man's
centrality.[47] Feminist theorists like Luce Irigaray, Sarah Kofman, Hélène Cixous
and others have also written about the recuperation and absence of woman/women
within western humanism.[48] The focus of the work of all these thinkers can be
stated simply as an uncovering of the political *interests* that underlie the binary logic
of humanistic discourse and ideology whereby, as a valuable recent essay puts it, 'the
first (majority) term (Identity, Universality, Culture, Disinterestedness, Truth,
Sanity, Justice, etc.), which is, in fact, secondary and derivative (a construction), is
privileged over and colonizes the second (minority) term (difference, temporality,
anarchy, error, interestedness, insanity, deviance, etc.), which is in fact, primary
and originative'.[49] In other words, it is only in so far as 'Woman/Women' and 'the
East' are defined as *Others*, or as peripheral that (western) Man/Humanism can
represent him/itself as the centre. It is not the centre that determines the periphery,
but the periphery that, in its boundedness, determines the centre. Just as feminists
like Kristeva, Cixous, Irigaray and others reconstruct the latent anthropomorphism
in western discourse, I have suggested a parallel strategy in this article in uncovering
a latent ethnocentrism in particular feminist writings on women in the third
world.[50]

As discussed earlier, a comparison between western feminist self-presentation and
western feminist representation of women in the third world yields significant
results. Universal images of 'the third-world woman' (the veiled woman, chaste
virgin, etc.), images constructed from adding the 'third-world difference' to 'sexual
difference', are predicated on (and hence obviously bring into sharper focus)
assumptions about western women as secular, liberated and having control over
their own lives. This is not to suggest that western women *are* secular and liberated
and have control over their own lives. I am referring to a *discursive* self-
presentation, not necessarily to material reality. If this were a material reality there
would be no need for feminist political struggle in the west. Similarly, only from the
vantage point of the west is it possible to define the 'third world' as underdeveloped
and economically dependent. Without the overdetermined discourse that creates the
third world, there would be no (singular and privileged) first world. Without the
'third-world woman', the particular self-presentation of western women mentioned
above would be problematical. I am suggesting, in effect, that the one enables and
sustains the other. This is not to say that the signature of western feminist writings
on the third world has the same authority as the project of western humanism.
However, in the context of the hegemony of the western scholarly establishment in
the production and dissemination of texts, and in the context of the legitimating
imperative of humanistic and scientific discourse, the definition of 'the third-world
woman' as a monolith might well tie into the larger economic and ideological praxis

of 'disinterested' scientific inquiry and pluralism which are the surface
manifestations of a latent economic and cultural colonization of the 'non-western'
world. It is time to move beyond the ideological framework in which even Marx
found it possible to say: They cannot represent themselves; they must be
represented.

Notes

1. See especially the essays in Cherrie Moraga and Gloria Anzaldua (eds.), *This Bridge is
   Called My Back: Writings by radical women of color*, New York: Kitchen Table Press,
   1983; Barbara Smith (ed.), *Home Girls: A black feminist anthology*, Kitchen Table
   Press: New York, 1983; Gloria Joseph and Jill Lewis, *Common Differences: Conflicts
   in black and white feminist perspectives*, Beacon Press: Boston, MA, 1981; and Cherrie
   Moraga, *Loving in the War Years*, South End Press: Boston, MA, 1984.
2. Terms like 'third' and 'first' world are very problematical both in suggesting over-
   simplified similarities between and amongst countries labelled 'third' or 'first' world, as
   well as implicitly reinforcing existing economic, cultural and ideological hierarchies. I use
   the term 'third world', with full awareness of its problems, only because this is the
   terminology available to us at the moment. The use of quotation marks is meant to
   suggest a continuous questioning of the designation 'third world'. Even when I do not
   use quotation marks, I mean to use the term critically.
3. I am indebted to Teresa de Lauretis for this particular formulation of the project of
   feminist theorizing. See especially her introduction to her *Alice Doesn't: Feminism,
   semiotics, cinema*, Indiana University Press: Bloomington, 1984; see also Sylvia Winter,
   'The politics of domination', unpublished manuscript.
4. This argument is similar to Homi Bhabha's definition of colonial discourse as
   strategically creating a space for a subject peoples through the production of knowledge
   and the exercise of power (Homi Bhabha, 'The other question – the stereotype and
   colonial discourse', *Screen*, 24, 6, 1983, p. 23). The full quote reads: '[colonial discourse
   is] an apparatus of power . . . an apparatus that turns on the recognition and disavowal
   of racial/cultural/historical differences. Its predominant strategic function is the creation
   of a space for a "subject peoples" through the production of knowledges in terms of
   which surveillance is exercised and a complex form of pleasure/unpleasure is incited. It
   [i.e. colonial discourse] seeks authorization for its strategies by the production of
   knowledges by colonizer and colonized which are stereotypical but antithetically
   evaluated.'
5. Anouar Abdel-Malek, *Social Dialectics: Nation and revolution*, State University of New
   York Press: Albany, 1981, esp. p. 145.
6. *ibid.*, pp. 145–6.
7. A number of documents and reports on the UN International Conferences on Women,
   Mexico City 1975, and Copenhagen 1980, as well as the 1976 Wellesley Conference on
   Women and Development attest to this. Nawal el Saadawi, Fatima Mernissi and Mallica
   Vajarathon in 'A critical look at the Wellesley Conference' (*Quest*, IV, 2, Winter 1978,
   pp. 101–7) characterize this conference as 'American-planned and organized', situating
   third-world participants as passive audiences. They focus especially on the lack of self-
   consciousness of western women's implication in the effects of imperialism and racism

in their assumption of 'international sisterhood'. Amos and Parmar characterize Euro-American feminism which seeks to establish itself as the only legitimate feminism as 'imperial' (Valerie Amos and Pratibha Parmar, 'Challenging imperial feminism', *Feminist Review*, 17, 1984).

8. The Zed Press 'Women in the Third World' series is unique in its conception. I choose to focus on it because it is the only contemporary series of books I have found which assumes that 'women in the Third World' is a legitimate and seperate study of research. Since 1985, when this essay was first written, numerous new titles have appeared in the Zed 'Women in the Third World' series. Thus I suspect that Zed has come to occupy a rather privileged position in the dissemination and construction of discourses by and about third-world women. A number of books in this series are excellent, especially those which deal directly with women's resistance struggles. In addition, Zed Press consistently publishes progressive, feminist, anti-racist and anti-imperialist texts. However, a number of texts written by feminist sociologists, anthropologists and journalists are symptomatic of the kind of western feminist work on women in the third world that concerns me. Thus an analysis of a few of these particular texts in this series can serve as a representative point of entry into the discourse I am attempting to locate and define. My focus on these texts is therefore an attempt at an internal critique: I simply expect and demand more from this series. Needless to say, progressive publishing houses also carry their own authorizing signatures.

9. Michelle Rosaldo's term: 'The use and abuse of anthropology: reflections on feminism and cross-cultural understanding', *Signs*, 5, 3, 1980, pp. 389–412, esp. p. 392.

10. Elsewhere I have discussed this particular point in detail in a critique of Robin Morgan's construction of 'women's herstory' in her introduction to Morgan (ed.), *Sisterhood is Global: The international women's movement anthology*, Anchor Press/Doubleday: New York; Penguin: Harmondsworth, 1984. (See Chandra Mohanty, 'Feminist encounters: locating the politics of experience', *Copyright* 1, 'Fin de siècle 2000', 1987, pp. 30–44, esp. pp. 35–7.)

11. My analysis in this section of the paper has been influenced by Felicity Eldhom, Olivia Harris and Kate Young's excellent discussions ('Conceptualising women', *Critique of Anthropology*, 'Women's issue', 3, 1977). They examine the use of the concepts of 'reproduction' and the 'sexual division of labour' in anthropological work on women, suggesting the inevitable pull towards universals inherent in the use of these categories to determine 'women's position'.

12. Valerie Amos and Pratibha Parmar, 'Challenging imperial feminism', *Feminist Review*, 17, 1984, p. 7.

13. Fran Hosken, 'Female genital mutilation and human rights', *Feminist Issues*, 1, 3, 1981, pp. 3–24, esp. p. 11. Another example of this kind of analysis is Mary Daly's *Gyn/Ecology*. Daly's assumption in this text, that women as a group are sexually victimized, leads to her very problematic comparison between the attitudes towards women witches and healers in the west, Chinese foot binding, and the genital mutilation of women in Africa. According to Daly, women in Europe, China and Africa constitute a homogeneous group as victims of male power. Not only does this label (sexual victims) eradicate the specific historical realities which lead to and perpetuate practices like witch-hunting and genital mutilation, but it also obliterates the differences, complexities and heterogeneities of the lives of, for example, women of different classes, religions and nations in Africa. As Audre Lorde pointed out, women in Africa share a long tradition of healers and goddesses that perhaps binds them together more appropriately than their

victim status. However, both Daly and Lorde fall prey to universalistic assumptions about 'African women' (both negative and positive). What matters is the complex, historical range of power differences, commonalities and resistances that exist among women in Africa which construct African women as 'subjects' of their own politics. See Mary Daly, *Gyn/Ecology: The metaethics of radical feminism*, Beacon Press: Boston, MA, 1978, pp. 107–312, and Audre Lorde, 'An open letter to Mary Daly', in Cherrie Moraga and Gloria Anzaldua (eds.), *This Bridge Called My Back: Writings by radical women of color*, New York: Kitchen Table Press, 1983.

14. Hosken, *op. cit.*, p. 14.
15. See Eldhom *et al.*, *op. cit.*, for a good discussion of the necessity to theorize male violence within specific societal frameworks, rather than to assume it as a universal fact.
16. Beverley Lindsay (ed.), *Comparative Perspectives of Third World Women: The impact of race, sex and class*, Praeger: New York, 1983, esp. pp. 298, 306.
17. Maria Ross Cutrufelli, *Women of Africa: Roots of oppression*, Zed Press: London, 1983, esp. p. 13.
18. *ibid.*, p. 33.
19. Michelle Rosaldo, 'The use and abuse of anthropology; reflections on feminism and cross-cultural understanding', *Signs*, 5, 3, 1980, p. 400.
20. Cutrufelli, *op. cit.*, p. 43.
21. Elizabeth Cowie, 'Woman as sign', *m/f*, 1, 1978, pp. 49–63.
22. Juliette Minces, *The House of Obedience: Women in Arab society*, Zed Press: London, 1980, esp. p. 23.
23. Mina Modares, 'Women and Shi'ism in Iran', *m/f*, 5–6, 1981, pp. 62–82.
24. Patricia Jeffery, *Frogs in a Well: Indian women in purdah*, Zed Press: London, 1979.
25. Modares, *op. cit.*, p. 63.
26. Marnia Lazreg, 'Feminism and difference: the perils of writing as a woman on women in Algeria', *Feminist Issues*, 14, 1, 1988, p. 87.
27. These views can also be found in differing degrees in collections like: Wellesley Editorial Committee (ed.), *Women and National Development: The complexities of change*, University of Chicago Press: Chicago, 1977, and *Signs*, Special Issue, 'Development and the sexual division of labor', 7, 2, Winter 1981. For an excellent introduction to WID issues see ISIS, *Women in Development: A resource guide for organization and action*, New Society Publishers: Philadelphia, PA, 1984. For a politically focused discussion of feminism and development and the stakes for poor third-world women, see Sita Sen and Caren Grown, *Development Crises and Alternative Visions: Third world women's perspectives*, Monthly Review Press: New York, 1987.
28. Perdita Huston, *Third World Women Speak Out*, Praeger: New York, 1979, p. 115.
29. Maria Mies, *The Lace Makers of Narsapur: Indian housewives produce for the world market*, Zed Press: London, 1982.
30. *ibid.*, p. 157.
31. See essays by Vanessa Maher, Diane Elson and Ruth Pearson, and Maila Stevens in Kate Young, Carol Walkowitz and Roslyn McCullagh (eds.), *Of Marriage and the Market: Women's subordination in international perspective*, CSE Books: London, 1981; and essays by Vivian Mota and Michelle Mattelart in June Nash and Helen I. Safa (eds.), *Sex and Class in Latin America: Women's perspectives on politics, economics and the family in the third world*, Bergin & Garvey: South Hadley, MA, 1980. For examples of excellent self-conscious work by feminists writing about women in their own historical and geographical locations, see Lazreg, *op. cit.*, on Algerian women; Gayatri

Chakravorty Spivak's 'A literary representation of the subaltern: a woman's text from the third world', in her *In Other Worlds: Essays in cultural politics*, Methuen: London and New York, 1987, and Lata Mani's essay 'Contentious traditions: the debate on *sati* in colonial India', *Cultural Critique*, 7, Fall 1987, pp. 119–56.

32. Ann Deardon (ed.), *Arab Women*, Minority Rights Group Report No. 27: London, 1975, pp. 4–5.

33. *ibid.*, pp. 7, 10.

34. Hosken, *op. cit.*, p. 15.

35. For a detailed discussion of these instances see Azar Tabari, 'The enigma of the veiled Iranian women', *Feminist Review*, 5, 1980.

36. Olivia Harris, 'Latin American women – an overview', in Harris (ed.), *Latin American Women*, Minority Rights Group Report No. 57: London, 1983, pp. 4–7. Other MRG reports include Deardon, *op. cit.*, and Rounaq Jahan (ed.), *Women in Asia*, Minority Rights Group Report No. 45 : London, 1980.

37. See Eldhom *et al.*, *op. cit.*, for an excellent discussion of this.

38. Beverly Brown, 'Displacing the difference – review *Nature, Culture and Gender*', *m/f*, 8, 1983 . Marilyn Strathern and Carol McCormack (eds.), *Nature, Culture and Gender*, Cambridge University Press: Cambridge, 1980.

39. For a discussion of this aspect of Indian women's struggles, see Madhu Kishwar and Ruth Vanita, *In Search of Answers: Indian women's voices from Manushi*, Zed Press: London, 1984.

40. List of Zed Press publications: Patricia Jeffery, *Frogs in a Well: Indian women in purdah*, 1979; Latin American and Caribbean Women's Collective, *Slaves of Slaves: The challenge of Latin American women*, 1980 ; Gale Omvedt, *We Shall Smash This Prison: Indian women in struggle*, 1980; Juliette Minces, *The House of Obedience: Women in Arab society*, 1980; Bobby Siu, *Women of China: Imperialism and women's resistance 1900–1949*, 1981; Ingela Bendt and James Downing, *We Shall Return: Women of Palestine*, 1982; Maria Rosa Cutrufelli, *Women of Africa: Roots of oppression*, 1983; Maria Mies, *The Lace Makers of Narsapur: Indian housewives produce for the world market*, 1983; Miranda Davis (ed.), *Third World/Second Sex: Women's struggles and national liberation*, 1983.

41. Michel Foucault, *Power/Knowledge*, Pantheon: New York, 1980, pp. 134–45.

42. For succinct discussion of western radical and liberal feminisms, see Hester Eisenstein, *Contemporary Feminist Thought*, G. K. Hall & Co.: Boston, MA, 1983, and Zillah Eisenstein, *The Radical Future of Liberal Feminism*, Longman: New York, 1981.

43. See Donna Haraway, 'A manifesto for cyborgs: science, technology and socialist feminism in the 1980s', *Socialist Review*, 80, 1985, pp. 65–108, esp. p. 76.

44. Amos and Parmar, *op. cit.*, p. 9, describe the cultural stereotypes present in Euro-American feminist thought: 'The image is of the passive Asian woman subject to oppressive practices within the Asian family, with an emphasis on wanting to "help" Asian women liberate themselves from their role. Or there is the strong, dominant Afro-Caribbean woman, who despite her "strength" is exploited by the "sexism" which is seen as being a strong feature in relationships between Afro-Caribbean men and women.' These images illustrate the extent to which *paternalism* is an essential element of feminist thinking which incorporates the above stereotypes, a paternalism which can lead to the definition of priorities for women of colour by Euro-American feminists.

45. I discuss the question of theorizing experience in my 'Feminist encounters', *op. cit.*, and in Chandra Mohanty and Biddy Martin, 'Feminist politics: what's home got to do with

it?', in Teresa de Lauretis (ed.), *Feminist Studies/Critical Studies*, Indiana University Press: Bloomington, IN, 1986.

46. This is one of Foucault's central points in his reconceptualization of the strategies and workings of power networks. See *History of Sexuality Volume One*, Random House: New York, 1978, and *Power/Knowledge*.

47. Michel Foucault, *History of Sexuality* and *Power/Knowledge*; Jacques Derrida, *Of Grammatology*, John Hopkins University Press: Baltimore, MD, 1974; Julia Kristeva, *Desire in Language*, Columbia University Press: New York, 1980; Edward Said, *Orientalism*, Random House: New York, 1978; and Giles Deleuze and Felix Guattari, *Anti-Oedipus: Capitalism and schizophrenia*, Viking: New York, 1977.

48. Luce Irigaray, 'This sex which is not one' and 'When the goods get together', in Elaine Marks and Isabel de Courtivron (eds.), *New French Feminisms*, Schocken Books: New York, 1981; Hélène Cixous, 'The laugh of the Medusa', in *ibid*. For a good discussion of Sarah Kofman's work, see Elizabeth Berg, 'The third woman', *Diacritics,* Summer 1982, pp. 11–20.

49. William V. Spanos, 'Boundary 2 and the polity of interest: humanism, the "center elsewhere", and power', *Boundary 2*, XII, 3/XIII, 1, Spring/Fall 1984.

50. For an argument which demands a *new* conception of humanism in work on third-world women, see Lazreg, *op. cit.* While Lazreg's position might appear to be diametrically opposed to mine, I see it as a provocative and potentially positive extension of some of the implications that follow from my arguments. In criticizing the feminist rejection of humanism in the name of 'essential Man', Lazreg points to what she calls an 'essentialism of difference' within these very feminist projects. She asks: 'To what extent can western feminism dispense with an ethics of responsibility when writing about "different" women? The point is neither to subsume other women under one's own experience nor to uphold a separate truth for them. Rather, it is to allow them to *be* while recognizing that what they are is just as meaningful, valid, and comprehensible as what "we" are. ... Indeed, when feminists essentially deny other women the humanity they claim for themselves, they dispense with any ethical constraint. They engage in the act of splitting the social universe into "us" and "them", "subjects" and "objects"' (pp. 99–100).

   This essay by Lazreg and an essay by S. P. Mohanty entitled 'Us and them: on the philosophical bases of political criticism', *The Yale Journal of Criticism*, 2, 2, March 1989, suggest positive directions for self-conscious cross-cultural analyses, analyses which move beyond the deconstructive to a fundamentally productive mode in designating overlapping areas for cross-cultural comparison. The latter essay calls not for a 'humanism' but for a reconsideration of the question of the 'human' in a post-humanist context. It argues that (1) there is no necessary 'incompatibility between the deconstruction of western humanism' and such 'a positive elaboration' of the human; and moreover that (2) such an elaboration is essential if contemporary political–critical discourse is to avoid the incoherencies and weaknesses of a relativist position.

12 □ *The Unspeakable Limits of Rape: Colonial Violence and Counter-Insurgency*

Jenny Sharpe

Jenny Sharpe teaches colonial and postcolonial studies in the English department at the University of California at Los Angeles. She is the author of *Allegories of Empire: The figure of woman in the colonial text.*

E. M. Forster's *A Passage to India* reenacts in the drama surrounding a rape the fears and fantasies of an imperial nation over the intermingling of two races, the colonizer and the colonized.[1] Adela Quested, who is English, accuses the educated Muslim, Dr Aziz, of sexually assaulting her in one of the Marbar Caves. By reading Aziz's 'crime' as 'the unspeakable limit of cynicism, untouched since 1857' (*PI*, p. 7), the English residents of Chandrapore place the alleged rape within the racial memory of the Mutiny, also known as the Sepoy Rebellion.[2] Eighteen fifty-seven has entered the colonial records as nothing less than the barbaric attack of mutinous Sepoys on innocent women and children. Yet, as one of the largest anti-British uprisings, 1857 is also known to Indian nationalists as the First War of Independence. During the 1920s when Forster was finishing his novel, Vinayak Savarkar's *Indian War of Independence of 1857* – a highly polemical book written to rouse Indians into armed struggle against the British – was widely circulated despite its proscription.[3] The memory of 1857 was thus a site of historical contention during those volatile years of early decolonization. I take from Forster's presentation of Adela's attack within the frame of 1857 the license to read his novel as a narrative that reveals the limits of an official discourse on native insurgency. It is a discourse that racializes colonial relations by implicating rebellion in the violence of rape.[4]

A Passage to India holds up for public scrutiny the racialization of imperial discourse by generating its narrative desire through the indeterminate status of the rape. Since the reader is not privy to what happened in the caves, she or he is faced

From *Genders*, 10, Spring 1991, pp. 25–46.

with the contradictory evidence of Adela's accusation and Aziz's denial. The accuracy of Adela's judgment is undermined during the trial when, upon interrogation, she suddenly withdraws the charge. Forster's staging of the court scene around the reversal of a rape charge disrupts the taken-for-grantedness of the racially motivated assumption that 'the darker races are physically attracted by the fairer, but not *vice versa*' (*PI*, pp. 218–19). The roles of assailant and victim are now dramatically reversed as the novel reveals the 'real crime' of imperialism to be an abuse of power that can only lead to its demise. Yet we are never told whether the attempted rape was real or imagined, and the question of what happened in the Marabar Caves continues to intrigue readers of the novel. Whereas early inquiries investigated the mystery for what it revealed about Forster's narrative technique or Indian metaphysics, recent criticism has shifted the terms of the debate toward issues of race and gender.

I situate my own reading of the rape in *A Passage to India* within the current effort of feminist theory to account for the heterogeneous text of women's history. As we attempt to pry apart the singularity of a female tradition, we often presume 'race' to be a unified and homogeneous field of otherness. By treating race as a transhistorical category, we thus fail to dislodge the dominant discourses that wrench racial (and sexual) constructions out of history and present them as essentializing categories of difference. The demand on contemporary feminism, then, is to disrupt the taken-for-grantedness of such categories through an excavation of the histories that produce racial and sexual difference. In response to this demand, I trace the signification of rape in Forster's novel to the historical production of a colonial discourse on the native assault of English women in India. Upon making this move, however, I do not wish to suggest that literature and history are repetitions of each other. While the historical records produce a racial memory that is silently constitutive of Anglo-Indian fiction, the familiar plots of such fictions render India 'imaginable' for historical narration. In this regard, my interest in *A Passage to India* lies in the particularly strategic role it has played in establishing the terrain for recent revisions of the Raj.

A replaying of the last days of the Raj in the ongoing drama of movies like *Gandhi*, *The Jewel in the Crown* and *A Passage to India* exhibits a nostalgia for Empire even as it masquerades as self-criticism. Forster's critical look at imperialism presents a problem that is particularly vexing for feminists. Upon questioning whether the real crime is Adela's accusation or Aziz's assault, *A Passage to India* sets up an opposition between 'the English woman' and the 'Indian man'. If one decides, in keeping with the novel's anti-imperialist theme, that the crime lies in a system capable of reducing an Indian man to his pathological lust for white women, then even the slightest hint of an actual rape cannot be entertained. Conversely, a defense of Adela's fear of assault brings with it a condemnation of the Indian patriarchy and Aziz's objectification of women as sex objects. The ambiguities surrounding the alleged rape thus force the critic to defend either the native man or the white woman against his or her opponent. It is this either/or decision (but never both) that has divided an anticolonial criticism of *A Passage to India* along gender lines.

Critical opinion tends to favor Adela's hallucination as the most likely explanation for what happened in the caves. Offering her sexual repression as evidence, such accounts discredit Adela's charge against Aziz as not only mistaken but also misguided. Even those readings that critically engage the problems of colonial representation treat Adela's cry of rape as an expression of her desire.[5] Although *A Passage to India* does suggest the imaginary nature of the attack, it does not provide sufficient evidence for presupposing that Adela's musings on Aziz's handsome appearance should translate into a sexual fantasy of rape. In his screen adaptation of the novel, David Lean legitimates this common reading by adding a scene which eliminates any doubt that, on at least one other occasion, the unattractive Adela suffered a bout of sexual hysteria. The scene shows Adela leaving the safety of the European compound to venture out on bicycle alone. She chances upon an ancient Hindu temple, whose sexually explicit carvings arouse her curiosity and interest. The threatening aspect of her sexual arousal is figuratively represented in the aggressive monkeys that swarm over the statues and scare her away. Adela returns to Chandrapore breathless, pale and sweating. Having just broken off her engagement to Ronny Heaslop, she now says she will marry him. His query – 'What happened?' and her response – 'Nothing' – are emblematic of the film's message regarding the cave scene. In a flashback of Adela staring at Aziz's silhouetted shape looming in the cave's entrance, Lean repeats the image of her pale and frightened face after her encounter with the monkeys. The conclusion to be drawn is so obvious that the film does not find it necessary to provide further elaboration.

A masculinist reading of the mystery in the cave (such as Lean's) is based on the 'common knowledge' that frigid women suffer from sexual hysteria and that unattractive women desire to be raped. This interpretation works backward from the imaginary rape, positing the effect of an effect as its cause. The argument consequently produces its own tautology: Adela hallucinated the rape because she was sexually repressed, the proof of which lies in her hallucination. Feminist criticism of *A Passage to India* has dismantled this tautology by revealing the 'making into meaning' of its assumptions. Rather than discounting the imaginary nature of the attack, feminists respond to the critical verdict against Adela by retracing her hallucination to a 'first cause' of patriarchal authority rather than sexual hysteria. Elaine Showalter, for instance, reads the hallucination in terms of Adela's apprehensions about committing herself to a loveless marriage that is nothing short of 'legalized rape'.[6] In 'Periphrasis, power, and rape in *A Passage to India*', Brenda Silver also links the imaginary rape to the gender roles suggested by marriage. Since Adela enters the cave disturbed about her forthcoming marriage to Ronny Heaslop, argues Silver, she is forced to acknowledge her social status as a sex object and thus to confront 'the material and psychological reality of what it means to be rapable'.[7]

Although they are correct to situate the alleged rape within the larger frame of women's oppression, Showalter and Silver fail to address the historical production of the category of rape within a system of *colonial* relations. Feminist criticism has thus replaced the masculinist tautology with another one. The feminist tautology goes something like this: Adela experiences the conditions of rape because she is objectified as a woman, the proof of which lies in her experience of rape. What does it mean for an English woman's experience of her oppression to be staged as a scenario in which she is the potential object of a native attack? In other words, how does the feminist critic negotiate the either/or opposition between the colonial female and the colonized male that the novel sets up? I would begin by insisting that Adela's confrontation of 'what it means to be rapable' is framed by racial tensions that cannot be understood as simply another form of patriarchal violence.

What is immediately noticeable about the representation of gender roles in *A Passage to India* is the fracture between Adela's social positioning and that of Anglo-Indian women.[8] From the early pages of the novel there are suggestions that colonial women are protectively cloistered behind an anachronistic code of chivalry and honor. 'Windows were barred lest the servants should see their mem-sahibs acting' the narrator informs us, 'and the heat was consequently immense' (*PI*, p. 24). Fielding's refusal to behave chivalrously toward English women 'would have passed without comment in feminist England' (*PI*, p. 62), we are told, but not in Anglo-India. Unfamiliar with their customs, Adela is surprised that club members have chosen to perform *Cousin Kate*, a play Showalter reminds us is 'a mildly anti-feminist comedy'.[9] Thus establishing an opposition between the emancipated women of England and the stalled liberation of the *memsahibs*, *A Passage to India* plots Adela's movement from one side of the East–West divide to the other.

It is not just that Adela enters the cave contemplating a marriage that will subsume her identity into that of her husband. More importantly, she recognizes the danger of assuming the Anglo-Indians' racist assumptions about India and its inhabitants. 'Well, by marrying Mr Heaslop, I shall become what is known as an Anglo-Indian,' she says to Aziz as they make their way toward the caves:

> He held up his hand in protest. 'Impossible. Take back such a terrible remark.' 'But I shall, it's inevitable. I can't avoid the label. What I do hope to avoid is the mentality. Women like – She stopped, not quite liking to mention names; she would boldly have said 'Mrs Turton and Mrs Callendar' a fortnight ago. (*PI*, p. 145).

Adela's inability to identify Mrs Turton and Mrs Callendar as the insensitive imperialists that they are demonstrates her new-found loyalty to Anglo-Indian women. Her transformation into a *memsahib* was already under way the moment she agreed to marry Heaslop. 'She was labeled now' (*PI*, p. 94), she thought to herself at the time. If the label is inevitable, the mentality is inescapable. A disregard for Indians to the degree of rendering them invisible is an offence that Anglo-Indian women repeatedly commit.[10] By the time Adela enters the cave, her self-consciousness about what it means to be an Anglo-Indian is forgotten. After presuming that Aziz has more than one wife by virtue of being a Muslim, Adela is oblivious to having offended him and, being so wrapped up in her own thoughts, she is not even aware of his presence. 'Quite unconscious that she had said the wrong thing, and not seeing him, she also went into the cave, thinking with half her mind "sight-seeing bores me", and wondering with the other half about marriage' (*PI*, p. 153). Only half of Adela's mind is on thoughts of marriage, the other expresses a boredom with Aziz's elaborate efforts to show her 'the real India'. Her divided mind reveals a tension between the Anglo-Indian woman's double positioning in colonial discourse – as the inferior sex but superior race. It is a contradiction that must be addressed in any discussion of the sexual assault.

When Adela emerges from the cave accusing Aziz of rape, she consolidates the identity she would rather deny. That is to say, she reconfirms the colonizer's racist assumption that, given the slightest opportunity, the native will revert to his barbaric ways. In her haste to escape she flees through cacti, lodging thousands of minuscule spines into her flesh. Her mutilated condition confirms the violence of the attack, but it also reduces her sensibility to her tortured body. 'Everything now was transferred to the surface of her body, which began to avenge itself, and feed unhealthily' (*PI*, p. 193). Her fellow expatriates react to the news of the assault from within their code of honor and chivalry: they treat Adela as a mere cipher for a battle between men. 'Miss Quested was only a victim, but young Heaslop was a martyr; he was the recipient of all the evil intended against them by the country they had tried to serve; he was bearing the sahib's cross' (*PI*, p. 185). The age-old equation of female chastity with male honor is reinscribed within the language of the colonial civilizing mission. By virtue of that mission, the white man reenacts a Christian allegory of self-sacrifice so that the weaker races might be raised into humanity.[11] The objectification of Adela into a passive victim denies her an entry into the grand narrative of the white man's burden even as that victimage reaffirms the self-sacrifice of the men who serve the colonial mission. *She* cannot save the natives from their depravity, but neither can she save herself. Adela the *memsahib*, the Anglo-Indian woman, has strayed far from the borders of 'feminist England'. She may have entered the caves with some semblance of her former identity, but she emerges a violated body bearing the visible signs of the native's ingratitude.

A Passage to India consciously invokes, in its animation of a sexual assault that transforms Adela into a sign for the victimage of imperialism, a nineteenth-century colonial discourse of counter-insurgency. During the 1857 uprisings, a crisis in colonial authority was managed through the circulation of 'the English Lady' as a sign for the moral influence of colonialism. A colonial discourse on rebellious Sepoys raping, torturing and mutilating English women inscribed the native's savagery onto the objectified body of English women, even as it screened the colonizer's brutal suppression of the uprisings. When the Anglo-Indians of Chandrapore read 'rape' as 'the unspeakable limit of cynicism, untouched since 1857', they are not only associating the attack in the cave with the racial memory of those earlier 'unspeakable' acts, but also reproducing its effects.

Feminist explications of *A Passage to India*, however, tend to ignore the racial memory that forms the historical frame to its theme of interracial rape. Silver, for instance, does not allude to a colonial past but, rather, a history that demystifies the myth of the black rapist in the American South. Her discussion of 'the Negro' in the place of 'the Indian' suggests a continuity between the divergent histories of slavery and imperialism.[12] To read racial stereotypes in terms of the discontinuous histories of colonial conquest, slavery and imperialism is to see that the selection of certain attributes for exaggeration has to do with the ideological sanction they provide. In her careful documentation of lynching, Ida B. Wells reveals that the fearful stereotype of 'the Negro rapist' sanctioned the upsurge in violence against black men, women and children that was aimed at reversing their political and economic gains.[13] Her evidence is reinforced in Eugene Genovese's observation that 'the violence-provoking theory of the superpotency of that black superpenis, while whispered about for several centuries, did not become an obsession in the South until after emancipation, when it served the purposes of racial segregationists.'[14] The myth of the black rapist presupposes even as it reproduces the Negro's lustful bestiality. The Oriental male, by contrast, is constructed as licentious, not lustful, duplicitous rather than bestial.

In the absence of its colonial constructions, Silver discusses racial codes on a level of generality that reduces out geopolitical differences. It is an absence that permits her to write the condition of both the black rapist and the colonized under the name of 'woman'. By understanding rape to be a discourse of power that objectifies colonial women and colonized men alike, she suggests that Aziz is figuratively raped by the accusation of rape. 'When spoken of as Indian within the discourse of English and Indian, sahib and native,' she writes, 'he himself [Aziz] is objectified; he enters the "category" of woman and becomes rapable.'[15] Although Silver expresses that she is 'aware of feeling privileged as a *woman*, to speak to and for third-world women (and in this case third-world men as well),[16] it is her problematical reading of third-world men as occupying the space of first-world women that permits the latter to serve as a model for all oppressed peoples. Since she *is* attentive to the dangers of substituting gender for race, I do not dismiss her essay as misinformed. Rather, I regard her informed reading as symptomatic of the persistent difficulty Anglo-American feminism has with dislodging the (white) woman as a privileged signifier for 'otherness'. It is a privilege that can be unlearned, but only through an attention to the historical production of our categories for class, race and gender relations. If feminism has anything to teach us, it is that an official history has produced a category of 'woman' that keeps women, to invoke Sheila Rowbotham, hidden from history. By deploying 'rape' as a master trope for the objectification of English women and natives alike, Silver produces a category of 'Other' that keeps the colonized hidden from history.

I submit reports on the 1857 uprisings as the beginnings of a racial discourse on brown-skinned men sexually assaulting white women in India. Since, as Edward Said reminds, beginnings are always strategically posited to enable a critical enterprise,[17] I initiate my discussion of the rape in *A Passage to India* with 1857 so as to demonstrate that 'what it means to be rapable' does have a history. When viewed historically, the category of rape can be seen to be so invested with the value of the 'English Lady' that its metaphoric extension to Indian men is foreclosed in literature written prior to decolonization. By reconstructing the historical production of a colonial discourse of rape, I hope to show that Aziz cannot enter the category of 'woman' and become rapable.

The 'Reality Effect of Historical Fictions

> Give full stretch to your imagination – think of everything that
> is cruel, inhuman, infernal and you cannot then conceive
> anything so diabolical as what these demons in human form
> have perpetrated.
>
> *Lahore Chronicle Extra*, June 17, 1857

> Manufacturers of gup [gossip], as it was termed, had a lively
> time, and imagination was freely called into play; yet
> imagination and fiction, with every advantage, were beaten by
> the truth, for I remember no story, however horrible, that
> equaled the realities of Cawnpore.
>
> Mrs Muter, *Travels and Adventures*

May 10, 1857, has been set down in colonial records as the most infamous day in
Anglo-Indian history. For the first time in their hundred-year stay in India, the
British faced rebellions on a scale that threw the authority of their rule into crisis.
A strange and horrifying tale took hold of the colonial imagination, spreading
throughout Anglo-India and all the way back to England. Mutineers, the story
went, are subjecting 'our countrywomen' to unspeakable torments. Natives, the
story continued, are systematically raping English women and then dismembering
their ravished bodies. Long before the British army regained control over its Indian
territories, the tales of terror were discredited as having little or no historical basis.
'Fortunately the actual occurrence of these horrors was seldom proved,' reports Pat
Barr in her apologia for Anglo-Indian women, 'but they served to inflame public
opinion in England and Anglo-India – particularly because the principal victims
were said to have been women. The press in both countries waxed hysterical [*sic*]
in demands for more severe punitive measures to be taken, and the rituals of
revenge-killing were enacted even in the nurseries and schoolrooms of the
homeland.'[18] Thus was the British reading public invited to share the terror of the
white settlers, and their revenge, as letters, stories and eyewitness reports slowly
made their way Irom India.

Our perception of 1857 has been colored by the years of myth-making that have
gone into popularized narrations of the revolt. The accounts of white settlers in a
state of exhaustion, terror and confusion have since been sealed with the stamp of
authenticity that guarantees all eyewitness reports. The rebellion was not quite the
military insurrection that its designated name of 'Mutiny' suggests. Although
initiated by Sepoy mutineers at Meerut, the uprisings included a heterogeneous
cross-section of the North Indian population that extended far beyond the military
ranks.[19] Nor was it simply a case of Sepoys suddenly turning against their colonial
masters and slaughtering British officers and their families. The battles were far
more protracted, involving maneuvers and countermaneuvers between the British

and relatively autonomous native factions for control of disparate regions. Rebels (sometimes armed with heavy artillery) lay siege to colonial towns, while loyal soldiers were marched from one part of the country to another to reclaim fallen territories. Anglo-Indian communities trapped within towns were often cut off from food, water, medicine and other necessary supplies. The East India Company, then entrusted with colononial administration, was unable to restore law and order for the good part of two years. Most Europeans, including women and children, suffered the 'mutilation' of bullet wounds or else 'fell victim' to diseases contracted during the long sieges. They did not, as was commonly believed, die at the sadistic hands of roving bands of *badmashes*. This latter belief, however, was reiterated and reproduced in literature, paintings and lithographs depicting leering Sepoys with their swords raised over the heads of kneeling women and children. The primary referent for the popular image of the Sepoy was the Cawnpore massacre.

Upon retreating from Cawnpore before an approaching British army, the Hindu rebel leader Nana Sahib ordered that his two hundred hostages, all of them women and children, be executed. The British army subsequently preserved Bibighar (the house in which the women were killed) with its dried blood and rotting remains as a kind of museum for passing troops to visit. Locks of hair from the dead women's heads were carried off as mementos and passed from hand to hand as the fetish objects of an erotic nightmare. Thus began the mythic invention of the dying women's torments, as soldiers covered the walls with bloody inscriptions in the hands of the 'ladies' directing their men to avenge their horrible deaths.[20] Nana Sahib has since been vilified in colonial historiography for having committed the unforgivable crime of desecrating English womanhood. Barr exhibits a predictable understanding of the Cawnpore massacre when she writes that there, 'one of the most revered of Victorian institutions, the English Lady, was slaughtered, defiled and brought low'.[21] The occurrence of even one massacre such as Cawnpore endowed all the tales of terror with their reality effect. British magistrates who were entrusted with investigating the stories, however, could find no evidence of systematic mutilation, rape and torture at Cawnpore or anyplace else.

Anglo-Indian descriptions of the tortures drew on a stockpile of horrors culled from the great works of Western civilization. The Bible, Homer, Virgil, Dante and Shakespeare all provided the Mutiny narratives with their charged plots of martydom, heroism and revenge. The familiar and easily recognizable plots thus enabled the British to make sense of what was an incomprehensible event – impossible to comprehend because anticolonial insurgency had previously been unthinkable. Yet, it is the details concerning the crimes against English women that gave the familiar plots their historical efficacy. Although the British and Anglo-Indian presses claimed the stories to be 'too foul for publication',[22] they disclosed fragments of information in hints and innuendo that prompted their readers to search their imagination for the awful deaths. The following editorial, which appeared in a London newspaper during the early stages of the Mutiny, establishes the 'fact' that women and children were killed by first declaring little knowledge of events, then appealing to the imagination as a privileged source of information, before finally reporting what has only been heard: 'others, and amongst them a large number of women and children, fell into the hands of the infuriate crew, thirsting for the blood of the infidel, and frenzied with *bhang*. We know little of the exact scenes which transpired, and imagination hesitates to lift the veil from them. We hear, however, that about 50 helpless women and children who had hid themselves in the palace on the outbreak were subsequently discovered, and the whole murdered in cold blood.'[23] As the mystery that imagination will reveal from behind the veil of ignorance, rumor has already been declared a truth.

The press tended to rely on the personal testimonies of people, many of whom were not present at the scenes they described. Attempts to establish the sources of stories proved that, as is the case with rumor, their origins were unknown.[24] Upon further questioning, so-called eyewitnesses admitted that what they 'saw' did not happen in their town but elsewhere, in the next town perhaps.[25] Some English readers did question the validity of the reports, while others, more sympathetic to the plight of the rebels, protested the brutal methods used for quelling the uprisings.[26] The general tenor of the editorials and letters, however, exhibits a desire to transform rumor and hearsay into fact and information. The invented stories could be explained – and Barr does – as a terror-induced response to the discovery that rebels did not spare the lives of European women. Yet, the Victorian male's horror over anticolonial insurrection invading the sanctity of his home does not sufficiently account for the sexualization of the women's deaths.

The sensationalist accounts, which are to be found in private letters, news reports and published narratives, all circulate around a single, unrepresentable center: the rape of English women. Upon declaring the crime 'unspeakable', the reports offer a range of signification that has the same effect as the missing details. In other words, they 'speak' a discourse of rape. After sorting through innumerable colonial reports, I was struck by a common narrative structure many of them shared. A particularly notorious version of this plot appears in a letter from a clergyman that was first published in the London *Times*. It tells of forty-eight 'delicately nurtured ladies', most of them girls, who were 'violated' and kept for 'base purposes' for a week. The letter goes on to describe the women being paraded naked through the streets of Delhi, publicly raped by 'the lowest of the people', before being submitted to a slow death by dismemberment.[27] Karl Marx, reporting on India for the *New York Daily Tribune*, points out that the story came from 'a cowardly parson residing at Bangalore, Mysore, more than a thousand miles, as the bird flies, distant from the scene of the action'.[28] The clergyman's letter has also been identified as fictitious in an 1858 publication representing the attempt of one Edward Lecky to provide a 'credible history' to the rebellions.[29] Variations on the basic structure of, in this case, an invented story – the humiliation, sexual assault, torture and death of English women – recur again and again in Mutiny accounts. Its plotting belongs to a discourse of rape, a specifically sexual form of violence which has as its aim an appropriation of women as 'the sex'.[30] This appropriation takes place through the objectification of women as sexualized, eroticized and ravaged bodies.

The narratives that stage the deaths of English women as a public spectacle constitute a violent appropriation of their bodies. As the following words of Sir Colin Campbell demonstrate, these stories bypass the mutilation of men to give a step-by-step account of the crimes perpetrated against women. What is noteworthy about this particular account is that the agent of torture is missing; it could be any native or every one. We will later see why no Indian – male, female, young or old – escapes suspicion. The details concerning the disfiguration of English women have the effect of reducing them to their mutilated bodies. A construction of the women as 'the sex' is visible in the necessity to subject both their primary and secondary sexual organs to attack. In this narrator's hierarchy of tortures, the 'most horrible' mutilation is the loss of identity through an effacement of the facial features. By the time Campbell has finished with his account, there is nothing left to the English woman but her brutalized body:

> Tortures the most refined, outrages the most vile, were perpetrated upon men, women and children alike. Men were hacked to pieces in the presence of their wives and children. Wives were stripped in the presence of their husband's eyes, flogged naked through the city, violated there in the public streets, and then murdered. To cut off the breasts of the women was a favourite mode of dismissing them to death; and, most horrible, they were sometimes scalped – the skin being separated round the neck, and then drawn over the head of the poor creatures, who were then, blinded with blood, driven out into the blazing streets. To cut off the nose, ears and lips of these unhappy women (in addition, of course to the brutal usage to which they were almost invariably submitted), was merciful.[31]

The scene is staged in a manner that forces us to view the women's rape and mutilation through the 'husband's eyes.' We do not know what it means for the women to see their husbands killed, even though men are included among the victims. We are here reminded of the line from *A Passage to India* that depicts an Anglo-Indian response to news of Adela's assault: '[the wife] was only a victim, but [the husband] was a martyr; he was the recipient of all the evil intended against them by the country they had tried to serve' (*PI*, p. 185). Forster's words can be read as an indictment of narratives like Campbell's that formulate the assault of English women as an indirect attack on colonial men. The mutilations described, then, reenact a sexual nightmare that fixates on the bodies of not just women, but *women who belong to English men*.

The unacknowledged terror of the rape and mutilation stories is to be found in the element of doubt the uprisings introduced to the language of racial superiority. This terror can be read in the absence of narratives that objectify English men through descriptions of their mutilated bodies. The reports hold no elaborate details concerning the torture of men and certainly no mention of the male sexual organ being removed. Such a fragmentation of the male body would allocate English men to the objectified space of 'the class of women'[32] – a status denying British power at the precise moment that it needed reinforcing. Once an English man has been struck down, then anything is possible; in death his mortality is revealed and sovereign status brought low. A focus on the slaughter of defenseless women and children displaces attention away from the image of English men dying at the hands of native insurgents. Through an animation of 'women and children,' the fiction of racial superiority could be upheld even as the seriousness of the revolt recognized.

The Mutiny reports transform Anglo-Indian women into an institution, the 'English Lady' by selectively drawing on the Victorian ideal of womanhood. This transformation permits a slippage between the violation of English women as the object of rape and the violation of colonialism as the object of rebellion. The value of the 'English Lady' – her self-sacrifice, moral influence and innocence – is thus extended to the social mission of colonialism. Because of its close association with her moral worth, the category of rape is reserved for English women alone. The rape of Indian women is not directly revealed in the information of the reports. It is revealed, however, in their repeated disavowals that, unlike the treacherous Sepoys, English soldiers did not rape enemy women. In even the most telling accounts, which are to be found in private correspondences rather than published narratives, the rape of Indian women remains unacknowledged: 'We advanced to the village and the general gave it up to the tender mercies of the 84th, as he said, to do as they liked with. They did clear it with a vengeance, for in 5 minutes there was not one *live* nigger in the village'.[33] What happens to Indian women when subjected to the 'tender mercies' of British soldiers is predictably missing from this report. In the place of that absent narrative, we have representations of Indian women inciting mutineers to rape and torture.

Contrary to stereotypical colonial constructions of Indian women as passive, the Mutiny narratives explicitly describe them as 'active instigators of the Sepoys in their worst atrocities'.[34] A particularly notorious actor in these crimes is the woman warrior: characterized as a hag or a she-fiend, she is nearly always dreadful in appearance. The most famous of these women warriors, the Rani of Jhansi (whom the British called 'the Jezebel of India'), is uncharacteristically noted for her handsome looks but then also her lasciviousness.[35] The British officer responsible for her death said of her: 'The Indian Mutiny has produced but one man, and that man was a woman.'[36] In the following account which appeared in the *Bombay Times*, the Rani is positioned in a decidedly masculine role. As the one who orders her men to rape, humiliate and torture their female victims, she exercises a power of speech that is capable of violating English womanhood:

Shortly after, the whole of the European community, men, women, and children, were forcibly brought out of their homes; and in the presence of the Ranee, stripped naked. Then commenced a scene unparalleled in historical annals. She, who styles herself 'Ranee,' ordered, as a preliminary step, the blackening of their faces with a composition of suet and oil, then their being tied to trees at a certain distance from each other; and having directed the innocent little children to be hacked to pieces before the eyes of their agonized parents, she gave the women into the hands of the rebel sepoys, to be dishonoured first by them, and then handed over to the rabble. The maltreatment these poor creatures had received was enough to kill them, and several died ere the whole of the brutal scene had transpired; but those who still lingered were put to death with the greatest cruelty, being severed limb from limb. The death the men were subject to was by no means so intensely cruel as that which our countrywomen received at the hands of their ravishers.[37]

The difficulty of representing a stereotypically passive Indian woman as an active agent is overcome by the double move of racially positioning her victims as lowly natives and sexually positioning the Rani as the one who directs the rape and torture. Before the Rani can exercise her will over the lives (and deaths) of the Europeans in this narration, she must first break their code of racial superiority. The English are consequently transformed into natives through a darkening of their faces. Yet, even in an instance of gender role reversal such as this, the report saves English men from objectification through mutilation. But more importantly, this account banishes into the realm of impossibility the rape of Indian women captured by an avenging army.

It would be difficult for a British reading public to envision the rape of native women after being presented with the image of the Rani directing the sexual brutalization of English women (an action that semantically positions the Sepoys in a passive role). According to the Mutiny reports, the native woman is not rapable. The closest the official discourse comes to depicting such rape is in the description of *English* women with their blackened faces. In this masquerade of race and gender roles, we are presented with the fantastic image of the Rani as the native woman who is behind the rape of other 'native' women. What we see in the making is a more explicitly race-oriented idiom that is being put into place through a semiosis of 'woman'.

Since it articulates the contradictions of gender and race *within the signifying system of colonialism*, the sexual discourse of rape is overdetermined by colonial relations of force and exploitation.[38] It is helpful, when unpacking a colonial economy of signs, to consider Elizabeth Cowie's important insight into the cultural production of women as not only exchange objects but also as signs.[39] According to Cowie, the exchange of women that reproduces their social roles of wife, mother, etc. constitutes a transaction that also produces value for a particular signifying system. In the case of the Mutiny reports, I would argue that the display of the violated bodies of English women produces the 'English Lady' as a sign for a colonial moral influence under threat of native violation. The signifier may be 'woman' but its signified is the value of colonialism that she represents. This might explain why despite the narrative energy going into a discourse on the English woman, stories of the women themselves escape the narrations. Since the signifying function of woman-as-victim in the Mutiny reports depends on her social role of wife and her restriction to the 'innocent' space on the domestic sphere, the English woman's access to colonial power is denied. There exists, as a consequence, a fracture between the colonial woman's positioning within the Mutiny reports as passive victim or violated body and her own sense of 'self'.

What is striking about the English women who narrate their Mutiny experiences is their reliance upon a language of colonial authority.[40] As they express their horror and fears in personal diaries, journals and letters they do not always respond to the threat of rape and torture from within their socially constructed gender role. In other words, they do not necessarily turn to their husbands for protection. There are, of course, the Harriet Tytlers who write of keeping poison nearby and instructing their husbands to avenge their deaths.[41] But there are also the wives of officers and civil servants who claim to have scared off hostile villagers by speaking to them authoritatively. These women were not always successful and some of them were killed for attempting to intimidate the rebels with commanding voices. By appealing to their own sense of authority under conditions that did not always guarantee its success, however, these women demonstrate a modicum of faith in their ability to command the natives. An official history negates the Anglo-Indian woman's access to colonial power, for her value to colonialism resides in her status of 'defenseless victim' alone. In this regard, as feminists, we should not similarly efface European women's agency by constructing them as the victims of colonial relations that are patriarchal alone.[42]

We see, in the invented stories of rape and mutilation, colonial power relations being written on the bodies of women. Their savaged remains display a fantasy of the native's savagery that screens the 'barbarism' of colonialism. Presupposing their women to inhabit a domestic sphere that was safe from colonial conflict, Anglo-Indian men responded as good soldiers, fathers and husbands to the stories of rebels executing their women and children. They reasserted claim over what was rightfully theirs by protecting the victims and punishing the offenders. And the honor of the victim was often defended by making the punishment fit or (as was more often the case) exceed the crime. After the British regained control over Cawnpore, they forced captured rebels to lick floors clean of dried blood before hanging them. It was also common practice to tie mutineers to the front of cannons and explode their bodies into minuscule pieces. The roads down which an avenging army marched were lined with the dead bodies of Indian men, women and children dangling from the trees as a message to the populace about the consequences of rebellion. Upon recapturing Delhi, the British army was reported to have massacred anywhere from twenty-five thousand to thirty thousand of its inhabitants. The response of revenge for the dishonor of English women thus not only reestablished a claim of lawful (sexual) ownership but also enforced violent strategies of counterinsurgency.

Mutiny historiography understands the brutality with which the uprisings were suppressed as the uncontrollable rage of Victorian men responding to the desecration of their women. When posited as a cause, the rape and mutilation of English women explains British reprisals as the aberrant response of otherwise civilized men driven mad at the thought of their tormented women. Thus adhering to the logic of colonialism as a civilizing influence, this explanation reconfirms the morality of the civilizers. By reading the sexualization of insurgency in the reports as *the effect of a violence already sanctioned by the structures of colonialism*, we see that the discourse of rape in fact normalizes repressive measures against anticolonial insurgency. Almost immediately after the outbreak of the Mutiny in May, an act giving summary powers to officers was passed. It was superseded by a more extreme Act of June 6th. 'Under that last Act,' records Sir George Campbell in his memoirs 'such powers were given wholesale to all and sundry, and barbarities were committed with a flimsy pretext of legality.'[43] The campaign of terror was thus already under way long before the news of Cawnpore (the massacre occurred on July 15) reached the ears of British soldiers.[44] What confirmed the atrocities against English women were the punishments that supposedly reflected them. Conducted as highly ritualized and publicized spectacles designed to maximize native terror, British retribution against rebels served as its own model for the torture and mutilation the army was ordered to quell.[45] 'My object', Brigadier-General Neill, one of the more infamous avenging officers, admits, 'is to inflict a fearful punishment for a revolting, cowardly, barbarous deed, and to strike terror into these rebels.'[46] The narratives of sexual violence cleared a space for what Neill, alluding to the punishment he administered, calls a 'strange law'.[47] His words reveal a discourse of power that violently enforced colonial law in the name of English women. What I am suggesting is that the sexual signification of the Mutiny reports sanctioned the use of colonial force and violence *in the name of* moral influence. During the course of the nineteenth century the 'English Lady' came to be invested increasingly with the self-sacrifice of colonialism, its ideological mission that was silently underpinned by apparatuses of force.

The sexual nightmare of rape and mutilation remained fixed within the British imagination throughout the nineteenth century, forming an historical memory of 1857 as the savage attack of brown-skinned fiends on defenseless women and children. It was possible by the end of the nineteenth century, to relive the 'heroic myth' of British martyrdom by making a pilgrimage to all the major sites where Europeans had been killed.[48] One site of particular mythic proportion was Cawnpore, where a plaque was placed on the well into which Nana Sahib threw the dead bodies of his hostages. Its inscription appropriately captures the racial memory produced about the Mutiny: 'Sacred to the perpetual memory of a great company of Christian people, chiefly women and children.'[49] This inscription, like the imaginary ones on the English women's bodies, was a spectacular sign of Indian savagery to be read by future generations. The tales of sexual violence consequently screened the even more savage methods used to ensure that natives knew their proper place *as well* as the vulnerability of colonial authority. It is here, in the memory of 1857 as the violent attack of natives on English women, that we are to find a historical explanation for the plotting of rape in *A Passage to India*.

The 'Ideological Effect' of Literary Plots

> The Mutiny – that nightmare of innumerable savage hands
> suddenly upraised to kill helpless women and children – ...
> has been responsible for deeds that would have been
> impossible to Englishmen in their right frame of mind.
>   Thompson, *The Other Side of the Medal*

> They had started speaking of 'women and children' – that
> phrase that exempts the male from sanity when it has been
> repeated a few times.
>
> Forster, *A Passage to India*

Due to the highly charged nature of its 'atrocities', the Mutiny not only haunts Anglo-Indian novels as a terrifying memory but is also silently constitutive of their stories. Anglo-Indian fiction finds its mythic brown-skinned rapist in the violence of 1857–8, which it repeats and embellishes into a pornographic fantasy of rape.[50]

There exists no other stereotype produced on the scale of the 'Sepoy fiend' that expresses an aggressive Indian male sexuality. In keeping with the perceived decadence of the Mogul Empire that sanctioned a British colonization of India, the sexuality of the 'Oriental type' was typically decadent – the licentious sensuality of an Aziz who visits prostitutes in Calcutta and offers to arrange 'a lady with breasts like mangoes' (*PI*, p. 120) for his friend Fielding. Standard colonial stereotypes of the 'Hindoo' depict him as licentious, but effeminate; cruel, yet physically weak; duplicitous rather than savage. His racial type of passivity explained the long history of India as a conquered nation even as it permitted the British to cast themselves as mere players in a prewritten script. According to this script, the European civilizers were saving the natives from Eastern despotism until a future time of self-government. When the violent rebellions of 1857 erupted upon the colonial scene, the British found themselves without a script on which they could rely. The popular basis to the uprisings was read as an attempt to restore the aging Mogul king of Delhi as sovereign over India. In the absence of a stereotype for the 'savage Hindoo', the 'blood-thirsty Musselman' was often identified as the instigator and perpetrator of its worst crimes. Like the men identified as the most savage mutineers, the man who stands accused of rape in *A Passage to India* is a Muslim, and one who indulges in orientalist fantasies about his Mogul ancestors at that.

When he began writing *A Passage to India* after a visit to India in 1913, Forster conceived of its plot as an illicit romance between an Indian man and an English woman.[51] By the time he completed the novel after a second trip in 1921, the story of an interracial love mired in cultural differences was out of step with the events of history. The story of an interracial rape, more volatile by far, plays out the tensions between a dissenting native population and a defensive European minority. The India of the 1920s, with its demonstrations, general strikes and civil disturbances, reminded the ruling white minority of those earlier crisis-ridden years of 1857–8. One event that especially revived the Mutiny memory was the 1919 massacre at Amritsar, where General Dyer ordered his men to fire on unarmed protesters attending a banned meeting. Approximately five hundred Indian men, women and children were killed and fifteen hundred wounded. The name of 'Amritsar' was for Indians synonymous with massacre much in the same way that 'Cawnpore' resonated with the murder of innocents within the Anglo-Indian community.[52] Although *A Passage to India* makes no explicit reference to the scandal of Amritsar, the shadowy presence of the massacre – and the martial law which sanctioned it – haunts the novel.[53] The major's uncontrollable outburst for the Chandrapore community to 'call in the troops and clear the bazaars' (*PI*, p. 187) is reminiscent of Dyer's directive at Amritsar. Mrs Turton's command that every Indian who dare look at an English woman should crawl from Chandrapore to the Marabar Caves echoes the law Dyer passed six days after the massacre, which forced Indians to crawl on all fours through the street on which an English woman had been attacked. In turn, General Dyer's 'crawling order' repeats Colonel Neill's 'strange law' of 1857.

The Amritsar massacre, which spoke of British soldiers firing mercilessly on defenceless Indian women and children, transformed the colonizers into the object of their own emblem of barbarism. As a consequence, the two discrete historical moments of 1857 and 1919 were read as continuous. On the one hand, there were the supporters of British imperialism who defended the events at Amritsar as a necessary measure against a bloodbath on the order of 1857. At an inquiry into the massacre eight months later, Dyer claimed that he had averted a second mutiny.[54] Several of the leading Anglo-Indian newspapers defended his actions by confirming that he did indeed face a situation as serious as the early stages of the Mutiny.[55] Critics, however, held the Mutiny memory itself responsible for the massacre. 'What is immediately relevant', writes historian Edward Thompson in *The Other Side of the Medal* (1925), 'is for us to note that at Jallianwalla [the Amritsar public square] and during the outcry which our people made afterwards we see the workings of imperfectly informed minds obsessed with the thought of Cawnpore and of merciless, unreasoning "devils" butchering our women.'[56] In *A Passage to India* Forster is also critical of a community obsessed with the racial memory of 1857.

The Anglo-Indians of Chandrapore turn to the Mutiny as a convenient proper name for characterizing the events surrounding Adela's accusation of rape and Aziz's subsequent arrest. The district superintendent of Police, Mr McBryde, advises Fielding to 'read any of the Mutiny records' (*PI*, p. 169) for understanding the psychology of the Indian criminal mind. As the court case draws nearer, the explosive atmosphere of 1857 is recreated in the club members who debate what they should do about the hostile Indian mobs demanding that Aziz be released. Their discussion centers on defending their 'women and children', a particularly charged phrase for eliciting cries of revenge. One young, golden-haired woman whose husband is away is afraid to go home 'in case the "niggers attacked"' (*PI*, p. 181). Her fellow Anglo-Indians invest the image of 'her abundant figure and masses of corn-gold hair' with the full value of colonialism; for them, 'she symbolized all that is worth fighting and dying for' (*PI*, p. 181). Parodies of this sort can be read as sobering reminders of colonial retributions against a rebellious Indian population committed in the name of English women.

A Passage to India recreates in the drama surrounding Aziz's arrest the precariousness of the imperialist mission under threat of insurrection. It is a vulnerability that necessitates the positing of a native desire for white women as the 'chief cause' for interracial conflict. In all those scenes that allude to Dyer's command at Amritsar and the racial memory of the Mutiny, the novel also shows the fear of a native assault on English women to be a screen for imperialist strategies of counterinsurgency. In other words, it draws attention to a discourse of rape deployed in the management of anticolonial rebellion. Such stagings, however, do not disrupt the dominant Mutiny narrative but simply question its premises. What does reveal the fictionality of colonial truth-claims is the element of doubt Adela introduces into the certainty of a crime confirming the native's depravity.

During the trial, Adela delivers a verdict that throws the place of imperial law into chaos. 'Dr Aziz never followed me into the cave' (*PI*, p. 229), she declares, 'I withdraw everything' (*PI*, p. 229). When situated within the racial memory of the Mutiny, her extension and withdrawal of her charge drives a wedge of doubt between a colonial discourse of rape and its object. In other words, Adela's declaration of Aziz's innocence undermines the racist assumptions underpinning an official discourse that represents anticolonial insurgency as the savage attack of barbarians on innocent women and children. Yet, Forster does not replace the certainty of an attack with its negation but rather with a narrative suspension that opens up the space for a mystery.[57] After the trial, Fielding explores with Adela four possible explanations for what happened: either Aziz did molest her, she claimed he did out of malice, she hallucinated the attack, or someone else followed her into the cave (the guide and a Pathan are offered as two likely assailants). Although Fielding rules out the first two possibilities, Adela gives no indication to him (or the reader, for that matter) whether she reacted to a real or imaginary assault. She finally admits that the only one who knows for sure is Mrs Moore, whom she claims to have acquired her knowledge through a telepathic communication. As he keeps forcing Adela to return to the question of what happened in the caves, Fielding soon realizes that the very multiplicity of explanations offer no easy resolution to the mystery: 'Telepathy? What an explanation! Better withdraw it, and Adela did so. . . . Were there worlds beyond which they could never touch, or did all that is possible enter their consciousness They could not tell. . . . Perhaps life is a mystery, not a muddle; they could not tell' (*PI*, p. 263). As readers, we are perhaps less satisfied than Fielding with the 'life is a mystery' response, for critics have, and still do, search their imaginations for an explanation. Forster himself imagined at least one possibility in a scene that does not appear in the published version of his novel.

The deleted scene contains such a detailed description of the assault in the cave that it would be practically impossible to read what transpired there as Adela's hallucination. Here we have no helpless woman seeking the protection of others, but one who calculates the right moment to make her move and manages to fight off her attacker:

> At first she thought that ⟨she was being robbed,⟩ he was ⟨holding⟩ \taking/ her hand \as before/ to help ⟨out⟩, then she realised, and shrieked at the top of her voice. 'Boum' ⟨went⟩ \shrieked[?]/ the echo. She struck out and he got hold of her other hand and forced her against the wall, he got both her hands in one of his, and then felt at her ⟨dress⟩ \breasts/. 'Mrs Moore' she yelled 'Ronny – don't let him, save me.' The strap

of her Field Glasses, tugged suddenly, was drawn across her throat. She understood –
it was to be passed once around her neck ⟨it was to⟩ she was to be throttled as far as
necessary and then … [Forster's suspension points] Silent, though the echo still raged
up and down, she waited and when the breath was on her wrenched a hand free, got
hold of the glasses and pushed them at \into/ her assailant's mouth. She could not push
hard, but it was enough to ⟨free her⟩ hurt him. He let go, and then with both hands
\on her weapon/ she smashed ⟨him to pieces⟩ \at him again/. She was strong and had
horrible joy in revenge. 'Not this time,' she cried, and he answered – or ⟨perhaps it
was⟩ the cave \did/.[58]

Like the Anglo-Indian women who survived the 1857 attacks, Adela's act of self-
defense is a odds with a dominant discourse that constructs the 'English Lady' as
a passive victim. As a consequence, one cannot help but notice a resemblance
between the absent text of her struggle and an official discourse which erases
colonial women's agency. In fact, feminist critics have submitted Forster's deletion
of this scene as the sign of a more pervasive silencing of women or the repression
of a misogyny that returns in subtler forms throughout the novel.[59] What these
readings cannot account for, however, is that the 'passive victim'[59] is recorded in
the deleted script as 'feminist England', but only at the risk of confirming the
attempted rape. A clearing up of the mystery in favor of Adela's guilt or innocence
consequently adheres to the terms of a discourse that displaces racial signification
away from colonial relations onto narratives of sexual violence. We see that a
restoration of the silenced stories of English women alone cannot disrupt a colonial
plotting on interracial rape.

The racial and sexual significance of rape in *A Passage to India* does not issue
from Adela's experience in the cave; the answer is not to be found there. To clear
up the mystery of what happened in the caves by searching our imagination for the
missing details involves reading Forster's novel according to the narrative demands
of the Mutiny reports. To read the mystery itself as an effect of that colonial history,
however, is to see in its indeterminacies the imprint of a racial memory and to 'trace
the path which leads from the haunted work to that which haunts it'.[60] In the place
of 'what happened in the caves', I offer a different kind of question, one suggested
by Adela's cry in the deleted assault scene. Managing to free herself from the grip
of her attacker, Adela screams – 'Not this time.' What are the other times, the other
assaults to which her triumphant cry alludes? I think that I have already answered
that question.

If we are to study literature for its disruption of an ideological production that
prevents social change, we can no longer afford to restrict our readings to the limits
of the literary text. Rather, we should regard the literature as working within, and
sometimes against, the historical limits of representation. *A Passage to India*
contends with a discourse of power capable of reducing anticolonial struggle to the
pathological lust of dark-skinned men for white women. Adela serves the narrative
function of undermining such racial assumptions but then, having served her
purpose, she is no longer of interest to the concerns of the novel. The 'girl's sacrifice'

(*PI*, p. 245) remains just that, a sacrifice for advancing a plot centered on the impossibility of a friendship between men across the colonial divide. As feminists, we should not reverse the terms of the 'sacrifice' but, rather, negotiate between the sexual and racial constructions of the colonial female and native male without reducing one to the other. Like Fielding and Adela who confront the mystery in the multiplicity of explanations, we should recognize that there are no easy resolutions.

Notes

1. E. M. Forster, *A Passage to India*, Harcourt, Brace & Jovanovich: New York, 1952. All further references to this work, abbreviated *PI*, will be included in the text.
2. Sepoys were the native soldiers in the British army. As an outcome of the 1857–8 rebellions, the East India Company was abolished and its administrative duties transferred to the British Crown. Since India was not consolidated as the Indian Empire until after the Revolt, I use the term colonialism for discussing Indo-British relations prior to 1858 and imperialism for the post-1858 era.
3. Ainslie Embree (ed.), *1857 in India: Mutiny or war of independence?*, D. C. Heath: Boston, MA, 1963, p. 39.
4. I read the racialization of colonial discourse as primarily a defensive strategy emeging in response to attacks on the moral and ethical grounds of colonialism.
5. The following select list offers some indication of the range of criticism that presumes Adela's accusation of rape to be a sign of her sexual desire and/or repression: Lionel Trilling, *E. M. Forster*, New Directions: New York, 1943, pp. 144–9; Wilfred Stone, *The Cave and the Mountain: A study of E. M. Forster*, Oxford University Press: London, 1966, p. 335; Louise Dauner, 'What happened in the cave? Reflections on *A Passage to India*', in V. A. Shanane (ed.), *Perspectives on E. M. Forster's 'A Passage to India'*, Barnes: New York, 1968, pp. 51–64; Benita Parry, *Delusions and Discoveries: Studies on India in the British imagination*, Allen Lane: London, 1972, pp. 294–5; Barbara Rosencrance, *Forster's Narrative Vision*, Cornell University Press: Ithaca, NY, 1982, p. 207; Abdul R. JanMohamed, 'The economy of Manichean allegory: the function of racial difference in colonialist literature', in Henry Louis Gates, Jr. (ed.), *'Race', Writing and Difference*, University of Chicago Press: Chicago, IL, 1986, pp. 94–5; David Rubin, *After the Raj: British novels of India since 1947*, University Press of New England: Hanover, ME, 1986, p. 66; Sara Suleri, 'The geography of *A Passage to India*', in Harold Bloom (ed.), *E. M. Forster's A Passage to India*, Chelsea House: New York, 1987, pp. 109–10.
6. Elaine Showalter, '*A Passage to India* as "marriage fiction": Forster's sexual politics', *Women & Literature*, 5, 2, 1977, pp. 3–16.
7. Brenda R. Silver, 'Periphrasis, power and rape in *A Passage to India*', *Novel*, 22, Fall 1988, p. 100. Reprinted in Lynn Higgins and Brenda R. Silver, *Rape and Representation*, Columbia University Press: New York, 1991.
8. Anglo-Indians, more commonly referred to as English or Europeans, were the British residents of India.
9. Showalter, *op. cit.*, p. 6.
10. Mrs Turton addresses Indian women in the third person, as if they do not exist, and Mrs Callendar stares right through Aziz when she takes his carriage. Forster has justifiably

been taken to task for situating the evils of imperialism in the attitudes of Anglo-Indian women. What I am attempting to do here, however, is to read the strategic deployment of 'the *memsahib*' in colonial discourse, one that demands her scapegoating in an anti-imperialist statement like *A Passage to India*.

11. The heroic image of colonial martyrdom is splendidly captured by Charlotte Brontë in the eulogy of St John with which *Jane Eyre* ends: 'As to St John Rivers, he left England: he went to India. . . . A more resolute, indefatigable pioneer never wrought amidst rocks and dangers. Firm, faithful, and devoted; full of energy, and zeal, and truth, he labours for his race; he clears their painful way to improvement; he hews down like a giant the prejudices of creed and caste that encumber it . . . and the toil draws near its close: his glorious sun hastens to its setting' (*Jane Eyre*, Norton: New York, 1971, p. 398).

12. The following statement, for instance, alludes to Aziz as a black man: 'However powerful the representation of the black man as penis, illustrated by Fanon, may appear to the English, it functions as well to reduce Aziz to a physicality that can then be subordinated to the authority vested in the greater power of the (phallic) legal system and the symbolic order that engenders and supports it' (Silver, *op. cit.*, p. 98).

13. Ida B. Wells-Barnett, On *Lynchings: Southern horrors, a red record, mob rule in New Orleans*, reprint edn, Ayer: Salem, NH, 1987.

14. Eugene Genovese, *Roll, Jordan, Roll: The world the slaves made*, Vintage: New York, 1976, p. 462.

15. Silver, *op. cit.*, p. 97.

16. *ibid.*, p. 88.

17. Edward Said, *Beginnings: Intention and method*, Columbia University Press: New York, 1985.

18. Pat Barr, *The Memsahibs: The women of Victorian India*, Secker & Warburg: London, 1976, p. 143.

19. In *Theories of the Indian Mutiny (1857–59)*, Sashi Bhusan Chaudhuri aptly captures the heterogeneity of the rebellion in his opening description of its popular base: 'The villagers impeded the march of the British avenging army by withholding supplies and information which they freely gave to the rebel forces; wage earners vented their rage on the system of foreign exploitation by a wholesale destruction of the British-owned factories; the social destitutes to whom borrowing was the only means of livelihood turned against the bankers, *mahajans* (capitalists) and usurers, the class protected by the British courts; the priests and prophets preached *jehad* against the *feringhis*; and attacked police and revenue establishments, destroyed govalgovernent records and court-buildings and telegraph poles, in fact everything which could remind them of the English' (Calcutta, 1965, p. 1).

20. Sir John Kaye, *Kaye's and Malleson's History of the Indian Mutiny of 1857–8*, vol. 2, Longmans, Green & Co: London, 1898, p. 299.

21. Barr, *op. cit.*, p. 113.

22. *The Times* (London), 6 August 1857.

23. *New of the World*, 19 July 1857.

24. The source of a news story was never identified as rumor. Rather, the term was reserved for the stories circulating among the Indian populace, which predicted the end of the British rule. As Ranajit Guha points out, the systematic dismissal of word of mouth transmissions as rumor and superstition negates the mobilizing power of oral reports in preliterate societies. See his *Elementary Aspects of Peasant Insurgency in Colonial India*, Oxford University Press: New Delhi, 1983, pp. 220–77.

25. Sir George Campbell, *Memoirs of My Indian Career*, vol. 1, ed. Sir Charles E. Bernard, Macmillan: London, 1893, p. 400; Christopher Hibbert, *The Great Mutiny, India 1857*, Penguin: London, 1980, p. 213.

26. It is perhaps worth noting that the Irish supported the Sepoys and criticized the British army for its attacks on the Indian peasantry. The London *Times* makes a point of expressing its disapproval of the 'foolish fanatics in Ireland who write Sepoy sentences, and paste Sepoy placards on walls and gate-posts, calling upon Ireland to awake, and rise up, and "give 3 cheers for old Ireland, and 3 more for the Sepoys"' (8 November 1857).

27. Letter from a clergyman dated July 4 and published in the *Times* (London), 25 August 1857.

28. Karl Marx, *Colonialism and Modernization*, ed. Shlomo Avineri, Anchor: Garden City, NY, 1969, p. 226.

29. Edward Lecky, *Fictions Connected with the Outbreak of 1857 Exposed*, Chesson & Woodhall: Bombay, 1858.

30. My discussion of rape as a violence that reproduces the gender roles of women is indebted to Monique Plaza's 'Our damages and their compensation, rape: the will not to know of Michel Foucault', *Feminist Issues*, 1, Summer 1981, pp. 25–35.

31. Sir Colin Campbell, *Narrative of the Indian Revolt from its Outbreak to the Capture of Lucknow*, George Vicers: London, 1858, p. 20.

32. This is the term that Plaza used for the sexual positioning of the rape victim, which can include men.

33. Letter dated 4 August 1857, in the letters of Colonel Hugh Pearce Pearson MSS Eur C231 (India Office Library: London).

34. *News of the World*, 22 November 1857. The term 'atrocity', which is so common in British accounts of 1857, condemns anticolonial insurgency to the morally reprehensible annals of the 'great crimes'. 'Atrocity', observes Michel Foucault, 'is a characteristic of some of the great crimes: it refers to the number of natural or positive, divine or human laws that they attack, to the scandalous openness or, on the contrary, to the secret cunning with which they have been committed, to the rank and status of those who are their authors and victims, to the disorder that they presuppose or bring with them, to the horror they arouse' (*Discipline and Punish: The birth of the prison*, trans. Alan Sheridan, Vintage: New York, 1979, p. 56).

35. Hibbert, *op. cit.*, 377–8, 385. For a study of the Rani as a heroic figure in Indian literature, see Joyce Lebra-Chapman. *The Rani of Jhansi: A study of female heroism in India*, University of Hawaii Press: Honolulu, 1986.

36. *The Times*, 16 October 1885, quoted in *India, Before and After the Mutiny* by an Indian Student, E. S. Livingstone: Edinburgh, 1886, p. 40.

37. *op. cit.*, *Bombay Times*, 31 March 1858, cited by Lecky, pp. 171–2.

38. Stuart Hall explains overdetermined instances as 'the product of an articulation of contradictions, not directly reduced to one another' ('Race articulation and societies structured in dominance', in UNESCO, *Sociological Theories: Race and colonialism*, Unesco Press: Paris, 1980, p. 326).

39. Elizabeth Cowie. 'Woman as sign', *m/f*, 1, 1978, pp. 49–63.

40. My observations are based on readings of journals, memoirs and diaries, primarily written by officers' wives. In keeping with their claims to be representing the viewpoints of 'a lady', they largely discuss domestic concerns such as the hardship of maintaining a civilized decorum in the absence of servants, most of whom ran away. The authority

with which these women speak reflects their class standing as much as a racial
superiority. I recognize, as a limitation to my reading, the class bias built into a reliance
upon written records. Despite the absence of working-class women's writings it is
possible to account for their subject positionings by reading the official discourse
symptomatically. I include such readings in the longer study to which this essay belongs.

41. *An Englishwoman in India: The memoirs of Harriet Tytler, 1828–1858*, ed. Anthony
    Sattin, Oxford University Press: Oxford, 1966, p. 160. This is one of the few women's
    diaries to have been recently reprinted.

42. An exception is Margaret Strobel's 'Gender and race in the nineteenth- and twentieth-
    century British Empire', which is attentive to the contradictions of the European
    woman's privileged yet subordinate role in colonial society (in Renate Bridenthal *et al.*
    (eds.), *Becoming Visible: Women in European history*, 2nd edn, Houghton Mifflin:
    Boston, MA, 1987, pp. 375–96).

43. Campbell, *Memoirs*, p. 231.

44. Sashi Bhusan Chaudhuri has chronicled instances in which the British reprisals identified
    as acts of revenge in *Kaye's and Malleson's History of the Indian Mutiny* often took place
    before the massacres to which Kaye alludes. See his *English Historical Writings on the
    Indian Mutiny, 1857–1859*, World Press: Calcutta, 1970, pp. 106–7.

45. In *Shamanism, Colonialism, and the Wild Man*, Michael Taussig explains reversals of
    this kind as 'a colonial mirroring of otherness that reflects back onto the colonists the
    barbarity of their own social relations, but as imputed to the savagery they yearn to
    colonize' (University of Chicago Press: Chicago, IL, 1987, p. 134).

46. Cited by Francis Cornwallis Maude and John Walter Sherer, in *Memoirs of the Mutiny*,
    vol. 1, Remington & Company: London, 1894, p. 71. Maude, a British officer who
    served during the Mutiny, writes: 'I believe our feeling was not so much of revenge as
    a desire to strike terror into the hearts of those natives who were in any way either
    sympathizing with or had been aiding and abetting in these horrors' (p. 70).

47. Cited by Kaye (*op. cit.*, vol. 2, p. 300). Tactics similar to the ones the British used
    against the Sepoys were deployed against Sikh rebels in 1872 and during the Second
    Afghan War of 1879. See Edward Thompson, *The Other Side of the Medal*, Hogarth:
    London, 1925, pp. 87–94. Edward Thompson, whose writings include novels and
    histories on India, served as an educational missionary in Bengal. He resigned from the
    ministry upon his return to England in 1923 and for the next ten years taught Bengali
    at Oxford. He was the father of the British cultural Marxist and pacifist E. P. Thompson.

48. Bernard Cohn, 'Representing authority in Victorian England', in Eric Hobsbawm and
    Terence Ranger (eds.), *The Invention of Tradition*, Cambridge University Press:
    Cambridge, 1984, p. 179.

49. Inscription on the well at Cawnpore, cited by Vincent Smith, *The Oxford History of
    India*, 2d edn, Clarendon Press: Oxford, 1923, p. 719. The plaque was removed along
    with other colonial historical markers after Independence.

50. The Mutiny is one of the most popular themes in Anglo-Indian fiction. For a nineteenth-
    century review of Mutiny literature, see 'The Indian Mutiny in fiction', *Blackwood's
    Edinburgh Magazine*, February 1897, pp. 218–31. For a more updated bibliographical
    study, see Sailendra Dhari Singh, *Novels on the Indian Mutiny*, Arnold-Heinemann:
    New Delhi, 1980. Patrick Brantlinger ends with a discussion of *A Passage to India* in
    his chapter, 'The well at Cawnpore: literary representations of the Indian Mutiny of
    1857', in *Rule of Darkness: British literature and imperialism, 1830–1914*, Cornell
    University Press: Ithaca, NY, 1988, pp. 199–224.

51. Forster's outline for the 1912–13 manuscript reads:

> Aziz & Janet [Adela's name in the early manuscript] drift into one another's arms – then apart \marriage impossible./ She – theoretically – immoral: he practically, but believes it impossible with an Englishwoman \she is ugly/ Discovers she loves him – less offensive \than Englishmen/
>
> As Horror of falling in love with Englishwomen – not due to natural reverence but since they could be only obtained on terms of marriage which is impossible & since of purity of blood.

Oliver Stallybrass, *The Manuscripts of A Passage to India*, Holmes & Meier: New York, 1978, p. 580.

52. The effects of the Amritsar massacre were not felt in England until several years later. In 1919, the events of Amritsar received little attention in the British press and were largely ignored by the intelligentsia. Upon examining the 'charges that have been brought against the English as a nation', however, Forster does refer to the massacre as one of those indefensible 'examples of public infamy' ('Notes on the English character' [1920], in *Abinger Harvest*, Edward Arnold: London, 1936, p. 13.

53. For a mapping of the historical events surrounding the 1919 Amritsar massacre onto the narrative of the novel, see G. K. Das, *E. M. Forster's India*, Methuen: London, 1977, pp. 46–54. Other studies that read *A Passage to India* as a comment on the political instability of the 1920s include Jeffrey Meyers, *Fiction and the Colonial Experience*, Rowan & Littlefield: Totawa, NJ, 1973, pp. 29–53; Molly Mahood, *The Colonial Encounter: A reading of six novels*, Rex Collings: London, 1977, pp. 65–91; Hunt Hawkins, 'Forster's critique of imperialism in *A Passage to India*', *South Atlantic Review*, 48, 1, 1983, pp. 54–65; Frances B. Singh, '*A Passage to India*, the national movement, and independence', *Twentieth Century Literature*, 35, 2/3, Sumer/Fall 1985, pp. 265–78.

54. *The Times* (London), 15 December 1919.

55. Reported in *News of the World*, 31 December 1919.

56. Thompson, *op. cit.*, p. 95.

57. Although it is possible to read such indecisiveness as an expression of Forster's liberalism, one must remember that he was writing out of a disillusionment with the failure of liberalism to bring about social change.

58. Stallybrass, *op. cit.*, pp. 242–3.

59. Silver, *op. cit.*, p. 86; Frances Restuccia, '"A cave of my own", the sexual politics of indeterminacy', *Raritan*, 2, Fall 1989, ix, pp. 110–28. For other citations of the deleted scene, see June Perry Levine, 'An analysis of the manuscripts of *A Passage to India*', *PMLA*, 85, March 1970, pp. 287–8, and Jo Ann Hoeppner Moran, 'E. M. Forster's *A Passage to India*: what really happened in the caves', *Modern Fiction Studies*, 34, Winter 1988, pp. 596–7.

60. Pierre Macherey, *A Theory of Literary Production*, trans. Geoffrey Wall, Routledge & Kegan Paul: London, 1978, p. 94.

13 □ *Woman Skin Deep: Feminism and the Postcolonial Condition*

Sara Suleri

Given the current climate of rampant and gleeful anti-intellectualism that has overtaken the mass media at the present time, both literary and cultural interpretive practitioners have more than ample reason to reassess, to reexamine, and to reassert those theoretical concerns that constitute or question the identity of each putatively marginal group. There are dreary reiterations that must be made, and even more dreary navigations between the Scylla and Charybdis so easily identified in journalism as a conflict between the 'thought police' on the one hand and the proponents of 'multiculturalism' on the other. As readers of mass culture, let us note by way of example the astonishing attention that the media has accorded the academy: the Gulf War took up three months of their time, whereas we have been granted over a year of headlines and glossy magazine newsworthiness. Is our anathema, then, more pervasive than that of Saddam Hussein? In what fashion is the academy now to be read as one of the greatest sources of sedition against the new world order? The moment demands urgent consideration of how the outsideness of cultural criticism is being translated into that most tedious dichotomy that pits the 'academy' against the 'real world'. While I am somewhat embarrassed by the prospect of having to contemplate such a simplistic binarism, this essay seeks to question its own cultural parameters by situating both its knowledge and its ignorance in relation to the devastating rhetoric of 'us and them' that beleaguers issues of identity formation today. Grant me the luxury, then, of not having to supply quotation marks around several of the terms employed, and – since the time of life is short – an acknowledgement that the 'we' to which I am forced to take recourse is indeed very, very wee.

The sustained and trivializing attack on what is represented as academic self-censorship cannot be segregated from current reformulations of cultural identities: the former will continue to misconstrue deliberately questions of marginality into solutions of frivolity, or cultural criticism into tyrannical clichés about the political correctness of the thought police. And, if the debate on multiculturalism simply

From *Critical Inquiry*, 18, Summer 1992, pp. 756–69.

degenerates into a misplaced desire for the institution of rainbow coalition curricula, its shadow will fall in all heaviness on those disciplines most responsible for producing the kind of rhetoric that is presently castigated for its political rectitude. Discursive formations that question canonical and cultural censors, in other words, are precisely the ones to be singled out as demonstrative of the academy's spinelessly promiscuous submission to 'correctness'. The list of public enemies thus produced is hardly surprising: our prostitution is repeatedly characterized by intellectual allegiances to the identity of postcolonialism, of gender, of gay and lesbian studies, and, finally, of the body. The academy has subcultured itself out of viable existence, we are told, and the subtextual moral that attends such journalistic cautionary tales is almost too obvious to merit articulation: if thy left hand offendeth thee, cut it off.

Since none of us are partial to being lopped, the only resort appears to be a two-tiered response to the anti-intellectualism that is our 'fin de siècle' fate. First – as has been clear for at least the last year – the world lies all before us; we have and must continue to respond. While much of the material that has appeared in the popular press is so low-grade as to disqualify itself as discourse, the academy must persist in making a resolute attempt to present some firm alternative opinions within those very columns. On a very simplistic and pragmatic level, if we must be freaks, let us be freaks with a voice. It may well be that this effort at articulation will yield some useful readings of the peculiar identity of the professional academic: how plural are we in our constructions of singularity; and how singular in our apprehensions of the plural? The second tier of any sustained response consists of an attempt to engender within the academy an overdue exchange about the excesses and the limitations that marginal discourses must inevitably accrue, even as they seek to map the ultimate obsolescence of the dichotomy between margin and center. For until the participants in marginal discourses learn how best to critique the intellectual errors that inevitably accompany the provisional discursivity of the margin, the monolithic and untheorized identity of the center will always be on them. The following readings seek an alignment with the second strategic tier to contain anti-intellectualism – that is, an essay into the methodology through which contemporary academic discourse seeks to decontaminate itself of territorial affiliations and attempts instead to establish the proliferating and shifting locations of the margins of cultural identities.

I

The specific margin that is my subject is one most virulently subjected to popular parodies and to the label of irrational rectitude: the work conducted around theoretical intersections of feminism and gender studies. It would be unproductive to demonstrate that journalists are shoddy readers, or that the 'elevation' of Camille Paglia's words to the pages of a soft-core porn magazine is in fact quite apposite with her discourse. An alternative margin might be found in the tensions incipient within the critical practice itself: are the easy pieties that emanate from the anti-thought-police press in any way implicit in academic discourse on this keen cultural problem?

Is girl talk with a difference, in other words, at all responsible for the parodic replays that it has engendered in the scurrilous imaginations of North American magazines? If the academy chooses to be the unseen legislator through which cultural difference is regulated into grouped identities of the marginal, then an urgent intellectual duty would surely be to subject not merely our others but ourselves to the rigors of revisionary scrutiny.

If you will allow me some further space-clearing generalizations, I would claim that while current feminist discourse remains vexed by questions of identity formation and the concomitant debates between essentialism and constructivism, or distinctions between situated and universal knowledge, it is still prepared to grant an uneasy selfhood to a voice that is best described as the property of 'postcolonial Woman'. Whether this voice represents perspectives as divergent as the African-American or the postcolonial cultural location, its imbrications of race and gender are accorded an iconicity that is altogether too good to be true. Even though the marriage of two margins should not necessarily lead to the construction of that contradiction in terms, a 'feminist center', the embarrassed privilege granted to racially encoded feminism does indeed suggest a rectitude that could be its own theoretical undoing. The concept of the postcolonial itself is too frequently robbed of historical specificity in order to function as a preapproved allegory for any mode of discursive contestation. The coupling of *postcolonial* with *woman*, however, almost inevitably leads to the simplicities that underlie unthinking celebrations of oppression, elevating the racially female voice into a metaphor for 'the good'. Such metaphoricity cannot exactly be called essentialist, but it certainly functions as an impediment to a reading that attempts to look beyond obvious questions of good and evil. In seeking to dismantle the iconic status of postcolonial feminism, I will attempt here to address the following questions: within the tautological margins of such a discourse, which comes first, gender or race? How, furthermore, can the issue of chronology lead to some preliminary articulation of the productive superficiality of race?

Before such questions can be raised, however, it is necessary to pay some critical attention to the mobility that has accrued in the category of postcolonialism. Where the term once referred exclusively to the discursive practices produced by the historical fact of prior colonisation in certain geographically specific segments of the world, it is now more of an abstraction available for figurative deployment in any strategic redefinition of marginality. For example, when James Clifford elaborated his position on travelling theory during a recent seminar, he invariably substituted the metaphoric condition of postcoloniality for the obsolete binarism between anthropologist and native.[1] As with the decentering of any discourse, however, this reimaging of the postcolonial closes as many epistemological possibilities as it opens. On the one hand, it allows for a vocabulary of cultural migrancy, which helpfully derails the postcolonial condition from the strictures of national histories, and thus makes way for the theoretical articulations best typified by Homi Bhabha's recent anthology *Nation and Narration*.[2] On the other hand, the current metaphorization of postcolonialism threatens to become so amorphous as to repudiate any locality for cultural thickness. A symptom of this terminological and theoretical dilemma is astutely read in Kwame Anthony Appiah's essay, 'Is the post- in postmodernism the post- in postcolonial?'[3] Appiah argues for a discursive space-clearing that allows postcolonial discourse a figurative flexibility and at the same time reaffirms its radical locality within historical exigencies. His discreet but firm segregation of the postcolonial from the postmodern is indeed pertinent to the dangerous democracy accorded the coalition between postcolonial and feminist theories, in which each term serves to reify the potential pietism of the other.

In the context of contemporary feminist discourse, I would argue, the category of postcolonialism must be read both as a free-floating metaphor for cultural embattlement and as an almost obsolete signifier for the historicity of race. There is no available dichotomy that could neatly classify the ways in which such a redefinition of postcoloniality is necessarily a secret sharer in similar reconfigurations of feminism's most vocal articulation of marginality, or the obsessive attention it has recently paid to the racial body. Is the body in race subject or object, or is it more dangerously an objectification of a methodology that aims for radical subjectivity? Here, the binarism that informs Chandra Mohanty's paradigmatic essay 'Under western eyes: feminist scholarship and colonial discourses', deserves particular consideration. Where Mohanty engages in a particular critique of 'Third World Woman' as a monolithic object in the texts of Western feminism, her argument is premised on the irreconcilability of gender as history and gender as culture. 'What happens', queries Mohanty, 'when [an] assumption of "women as an oppressed group" is situated in the context of Western feminist writing about third world women?' What happens, apparently, begs her question. In contesting what she claims is a 'colonialist move', Mohanty proceeds to argue that 'western feminists alone become the true "subjects" of this counter-history. Third-World women, on the other hand, never rise above the debilitating generality of their "object" status.'[4] A very literal ethic underlies such a dichotomy, one that demands attention to its very obviousness: how is this objectivism to be avoided? How will the ethnic voice of womanhood counteract the cultural articulation that Mohanty too easily dubs as the exegesis of Western feminism? The claim to authenticity – only a black can speak for a black; only a postcolonial subcontinental feminist can adequately represent the lived experience of that culture – points to the great difficulty posited by the 'authenticity' of female racial voices in the great game that claims to be the first narrative of what the ethnically constructed woman is deemed to want.

This desire all too often takes its theoretical form in a will to subjectivity that claims a theoretical basis most clearly contravened by the process of its analysis. An example of this point is Trinh Minh-ha's treatise, *Woman, Native, Other*,[5] which seeks to posit an alternative to the anthropological twist that constitutes the archaism through which nativism has been apprehended. Subtitled *Writing postcoloniality and feminism*, Trinh's book is a paradigmatic meditation that can be essentialized into a simple but crucial question: how can feminist discourse represent the categories of 'woman' and 'race' at the same time? If the languages of feminism and ethnicity are to escape an abrasive mutual contestation, what novel idiom can freshly articulate their radical inseparability? Trinh's strategy is to relocate her gendering of ethnic realities on the inevitable territory of postfeminism, which underscores her desire to represent discourse formation as always taking place after the fact of discourse. It further confirms my belief that had I any veto power over prefixes, *post-* would be the first to go – but that is doubtless tangential to the issue at hand. In the context of Trinh's methodology, the shape of the book itself illuminates what may best be called the endemic ill that effects a certain temporal derangement between the work's originary questions and the narratives that they engender. *Woman, Native, Other* consists of four loosely related chapters, each of which opens with an abstraction and ends with an anecdote. While there is a self-pronounced difference between the preliminary thesis outlined in the chapter 'Commitment from the mirror-writing box' to the concluding claims in 'Grandma's story', such a discursive distance is not matched with any logical or theoretical consistency. Instead, a work that is impelled by an impassioned need to question the lines of demarcation between race and gender concludes by falling into a predictable biological fallacy in which sexuality is reduced to the literal structure of the racial body, and theoretical interventions within this trajectory become minimalized into the naked category of lived experience.

When feminism turns to lived experience as an alternative mode of radical subjectivity, it only rehearses the objectification of its proper subject. While lived experience can hardly be discounted as a critical resource for an apprehension of the gendering of race, neither should such data serve as the evacuating principle for both historical and theoretical contexts alike. 'Radical subjectivity' too frequently translates into a low-grade romanticism that cannot recognize its discursive status as *pre-* rather than *post-*. In the concluding chapter of Trinh's text, for example, a section titled 'Truth and fact: story and history' delineates the skewed idiom that marginal subjectivities produce. In attempting to proclaim an alternative to male-identified objectivism, Trinh-as-anthropologist can only produce an equally objectifying idiom of joy:

> Let me tell you a story. For all I have is a story. Story passed on from generation to generation, named Joy. Told for the joy it gives the storyteller and the listener. Joy inherent in the process of storytelling. Whoever understands it also understands that a story, as distressing as it can be in its joy, never takes anything away from anybody. (*WNO*, p. 119)

Given that I find myself in a more acerbic relation both to the question of the constitution of specific postcolonialisms and of a more metaphoric postcolonial feminism, such a jointly universalist and individualist 'joy' is not a term that I would ordinarily welcome into my discursive lexicon. On one level, its manipulation of lived experience into a somewhat fallacious allegory for the reconstitution of gendered race bespeaks a transcendence – and an attendant evasion – of the crucial cultural issues at hand. On a more dangerous level, however, such an assumption serves as a mirror image of the analyses produced by the critics of political rectitude. For both parties, 'life' remains the ultimate answer to 'discourse.' The subject of race, in other words, cannot cohabit with the detail of a feminist language.

Trinh's transcendent idiom, of course, emanates from her somewhat free-floating understanding of 'postcoloniality': is it an abstraction into which all historical specificity may be subsumed, or is it a figure for a vaguely defined ontological marginality that is equally applicable to all 'minority' discourses? In either case, both the categories of 'woman' and 'race' assume the status of metaphors, so that each rhetoric of oppression can serve equally as a mirrored allegory for the other. Here, *Woman, Native, Other* is paradigmatic of the methodological blurring that dictates much of the discourse on identity formation in the coloring of feminist discourse. To privilege the racial body in the absence of historical context is indeed to generate an idiom that tends to waver with impressionistic haste between the abstractions of postcoloniality and the anecdotal literalism of what it means to articulate an 'identity' for a woman writer of color. Despite its proclaimed location within contemporary theoretical – not to mention post-theoretical – discourse, such an idiom poignantly illustrates the hidden and unnecessary desire to resuscitate the 'self.'

What is most striking about such discursive practices is their failure to confront what may be characterized best as a great enamorment with the 'real'. Theories of postcolonial feminism eminently lend themselves to a reopening of the continued dialogue that literary and cultural studies have – and will continue to have – with the perplexing category known as realism, but at present the former discourse chooses to remain too precariously parochial to recognize the bounty that is surely its to give. Realism, however, is too dangerous a term for an idiom that seeks to raise identity to the power of theory. While both may be windmills to the quixotic urge to supply black feminism with some version of the 'real', Trinh's musings on this subject add a mordantly pragmatic option to my initial question: 'what comes first, race or gender?' Perhaps the query would be more finely calibrated if it were rephrased to ask, 'What comes first, race, gender, or profession?' And what, in our sorry dealings with such realisms, is the most phantasmagoric category of all?

According to *Woman, Native, Other*, such a triple bind can be articulated only in order to declare that bonding is all. An opening section of that text is in fact titled 'The triple bind'; it attempts to outline the alternative realism still to be claimed by the postcolonial feminist mentality:

> Today, the growing ethnic-feminist consciousness has made it increasingly difficult for [the woman of color who writes] to turn a blind eye not only to the specification of the writer as historical subject ... but also to writing itself as a practice located at the intersection of subject and history – a literary practice that involves the possible knowledge (linguistical and ideological) of itself as such. (*WNO*, p. 6)

Here the text evades the threat of realism by taking recourse to the 'peaceable' territory of writing, on which all wars may be fought with each discursive contingency in deployment. While writing may serve as a surrogate for the distance between subject (read self) and history, Trinh unwittingly makes clear her academic appreciation of alterity: the female writer, or the third person 'she' that haunts her text, 'is made to feel she must choose from among three conflicting identities. Writer of color? Woman writer? Or woman of color? Which comes first? Where does she place her loyalties?' (*WNO*, p. 6). The hierarchy of loyalties thus listed illustrates the danger inherent in such cultural lists: the uneasy proclamation with which *Woman, Native, Other* sets out to be the 'first full-length study of post-feminism' (according to the book's jacket) is a self-defeating project, for feminism has surely long since laid aside the issue of an individualized female loyalty as its originating assumption. If race is to complicate the project of divergent feminisms, in other words, it cannot take recourse to biologism, nor to the incipient menace of rewriting alterity into the ambiguous shape of the exotic body.

The body that serves as testimony for lived experience, however, has received sufficient interrogation from more considered perspectives on the cultural problems generated by the dialogue between gender and race, along with the hyperrealist idiom it may generate. Hazel Carby helpfully advocates that

> black feminist criticism [should] be regarded critically as a problem not a solution, as a sign that should be interrogated, a locus of contradictions. Black feminist criticism has its source and its primary motivation in academic legitimation, placement within a framework of bourgeois humanist discourse.[6]

The concomitant question that such a problem raises is whether the signification of gendered race necessarily returns to the realism that it most seeks to disavow. If realism is the Eurocentric and patriarchal pattern of adjudicating between disparate cultural and ethnic realities, then it is surely the task of radical feminism to provide an alternative perspective. In the vociferous discourse that such a task has produced, however, the question of alternativism is all too greatly subsumed either into the radical strategies that are designed to dictate the course of situated experience, or into the methodological imperatives that impell a work related to *Woman, Native, Other* such as bell hooks's *Talking Back: Thinking feminist, thinking Black.*

While the concept of 'talking back' may appear to be both invigorating and empowering to a discourse interested in the reading of gendered race, the text *Talking Back* is curiously engaged in talking to itself; in rejecting Caliban's mode of protest, its critique of colonization is quietly narcissistic in its projection of what a black and thinking female body may appear to be, particularly in the context of its repudiation of the genre of realism. Yet this is the genre, after all, in which African-American feminism continues to seek legitimation: hooks's study is predicated on the anecdotes of lived experience and their capacity to provide an alternative to the discourse of what she terms patriarchal rationalism. Here the unmediated quality of a local voice serves as a substitute for any theoretical agenda that can make more than a cursory connection between the condition of postcolonialism and the question of gendered race. Where hooks claims to speak beyond binarism, her discourse keeps returning to the banality of easy dichotomies: 'Dare I speak to oppressed and oppressor in the same voice? Dare I speak to you in a language that will take us away from the boundaries of domination, a language that will not fence you in, bind you, or hold you? Language is also a place of struggle.'[7] The acute embarrassment generated by such an idiom could possibly be regarded as a radical rhetorical strategy designed to induce racial discomfort in its audience, but it more frequently registers as black feminism's failure to move beyond the proprietary rights that can be claimed by any oppressed discourse.

As does Trinh's text, hooks's claims that personal narrative is the only salve to the rude abrasions that Western feminist theory has inflicted on the body of ethnicity. The tales of lived experience, however, cannot function as a sufficient alternative, particularly when they are predicated on dangerously literal progressions of postcolonialism. *Yearning: Race, gender, and cultural politics*, hooks's more recent work, rehearses a postcolonial fallacy in order to conduct some highly misguided readings of competing feminisms within the context of racial experience. She establishes a hierarchy of color that depressingly segregates divergent racial perspectives into a complete absence of intellectual exchange. The competition is framed in terms of hooks's sense of the hostility between African-American and Third World feminisms:

> The current popularity of post-colonial discourse that implicates solely the West often obscures the colonizing relationship of the East in relation to Africa and other parts of the Third World. We often forget that many Third World nationals bring to this country the same kind of contempt and disrespect for blackness that is most frequently associated with white western imperialism. ... Within feminist movements Third World nationals often assume the role of mediator or interpreter, explaining the 'bad' black people to their white colleagues or helping the 'naive' black people to understand whiteness. ... Unwittingly assuming the role of go-between, of mediator, she re-inscribes a colonial paradigm.

What is astonishing about such a claim is its continued obsession with a white academy, with race as a professional attribute that can only reconfigure itself around an originary concept of whiteness. Its feminism is necessarily skin deep in that the pigment of its imagination cannot break out of a strictly biological reading of race. Rather than extending an inquiry into the discursive possibilities represented by the intersection of gender and race, feminist intellectuals like hooks misuse their status as minority voices by enacting strategies of belligerence that at this time are more divisive than informative. Such claims to radical revisionism take refuge in the political untouchability that is accorded the category of Third World Woman, and in the process sully the crucial knowledge that such a category has still to offer to the dialogue of feminism today.

The dangers represented by feminists such as hooks and Trinh is that finally they will represent the profession as both their last court of appeal and the anthropological ground on which they conduct their field work. The alternative that they offer, therefore, is conceptually parochial and scales down the postcolonial condition in order to encompass it within North American academic terms. As a consequence, their discourse cannot but fuel the criticism of those who police the so-called thought police, nor is it able to address the historically risky compartmentalization of otherness that masquerades under the title of multi-culturalism. Here it is useful to turn to one of the more brilliant observations that pepper Gayatri Spivak's *The Post-Colonial Critic*. In concluding an interview on multiculturalism, Spivak casually reminds her audience that

> if one looks at the history of post-Enlightenment theory, the major problem has been the problem of autobiography: how subjective structures can, in fact, give objective truth. During these same centuries, the Native Informant [was] treated as the objective evidence for the founding of the so-called sciences like ethnography, ethnolinguistics, comparative religion, and so on. So that, once again, the theoretical problems only relate to the person who knows. The person who *knows* has all of the problems of selfhood. The person who is *known*, somehow seems not to have a problematic self.[9]

Lived experience, in other words, serves as fodder for the continuation of another's epistemology, even when it is recorded in a 'contestatory' position to its relation to realism and to the overarching structure of the profession.

While cultural criticism could never pretend that the profession does not exist, its various voices must surely question any conflation of the professional model with one universal and world historical. The relation between local and given knowledge is obviously too problematic to allow for such an easy slippage, which is furthermore the ground on which the postcolonial can be abused to become an allegory for any one of the pigeonholes constructed for multiculturalism. Allow me to turn as a consequence to a local example of how realism locates its language within the postcolonial condition, and to suggest that lived experience does not achieve its articulation through autobiography, but through that other third-person narrative known as the law.

2

I proffer life in Pakistan as an example of such a postcolonial and lived experience. Pakistani laws, in fact, pertain more to the discourse of a petrifying realism than do any of the feminist critics whom I have cited thus far. The example at hand takes a convoluted postcolonial point and renders it nationally simple: if a postcolonial nation chooses to embark on an official program of Islamization, the inevitable result in a Muslim state will be legislation that curtails women's rights and institutes in writing what has thus far functioned as the law of the passing word. The Hudood Ordinances in Pakistan were promulgated in 1979 and legislated in 1980, under the military dictatorship of General Mohammad Zia-ul-Haq. They added five new criminal laws to the existing system of Pakistani legal pronouncements, of which the second ordinance – against *Zina* (that is, adultery as well as fornication) – is of the greatest import. An additional piece of legislation concerns the law of evidence, which rules that a woman's testimony constitutes half of a man's. While such infamous laws raise many historical and legal questions, they remain the body through which the feminist movement in Pakistan – the Women's Action Forum – must organize itself.

It is important to keep in mind that the formulation of the Hudood Ordinances was based on a multicultural premise, even though they were multicultural from the dark side of the moon. These laws were premised on a Muslim notion of *Hadd* and were designed to interfere in a postcolonial criminal legal system that was founded on Anglo-Saxon jurisprudence. According to feminist lawyer Asma Jahangir,

> the Hudood Ordinances were promulgated to bring the criminal legal system of Pakistan in conformity with the injunctions of Islam. ... Two levels of punishments are introduced in the Ordinances. Two levels of punishment and, correspondingly, two separate sets of rules of evidence are prescribed. The first level or category is the one called the 'Hadd' which literally means the 'limit' and the other 'Tazir', which means 'to punish'.[10]

The significance of the *Hadd* category is that it delineates immutable sentences: *Tazir* serves only as a safety net in case the accused is not convicted under *Hadd*. These fixed rules are in themselves not very pretty: *Hadd* for theft is amputation of a hand; for armed robbery, amputation of a foot; for rape or adultery committed by married Muslims, death by stoning; for rape or adultery committed by non-Muslims or unmarried Muslims, a hundred public lashes (see *HO*, p. 24). While I am happy to report that the *Hadd* has not yet been executed, the laws remain intact and await their application.

The applicability of these sentences is rendered more murderous and even obscenely ludicrous when the immutability of the *Hadd* punishments is juxtaposed with the contingency of the laws of evidence. If a man is seen stealing a thousand rupees by two adult Muslim males, he could be punished by *Hadd* and his hand would be amputated. If an adult Muslim stole several million rupees and the only available witnesses were women and non-Muslims, he would not qualify for a *Hadd* category and would be tried under the more free-floating *Tazir* instead. 'A gang of men can thus rape all the residents of a women's hostel,' claims Jahangir with understandable outrage, 'but [the] lack of ocular evidence of four Muslim males will rule out the imposition of a Hadd punishment' (*HO*, p. 49). Such a statement, unfortunately, is not the terrain of rhetoric alone, since the post-Hudood Ordinance application of the *Tazir* has made the definition of rape an extremely messy business indeed.

Here, then, we turn to *Zina*, and its implications for the Pakistani female body. The Hudood Ordinances have allowed for all too many openings in the boundaries that define rape. Women can now be accused of rape, as can children; laws of mutual consent may easily convert a case of child abuse into a prosecution of the child for *Zina*, for fornication. Furthermore, unmarried men and women can be convicted of having committed rape against each other, since a subsection of the *Zina* offense defines rape as 'one where a man or a woman have illicit sex knowing that they are not validly married to each other' (quoted in *HO*, p. 58). In other words, fornication is all, and the statistics of the past few years grimly indicate that the real victims of the Hudood Ordinances are women and children, most specifically those who have no access to legal counsel and whose economic status renders them ignorant of their human rights.

Jahangir cites the example of a fifteen-year-old woman, Jehan Mina, who, after her father's death, was raped by her aunt's husband and son. Once her pregnancy was discovered, another relative filed a police report alleging rape. During the trial, however, the accused led no defense, and Mina's testimony alone was sufficient to get her convicted for fornication and sentenced to one hundred public lashes. That child's story is paradigmatic of the untold miseries of those who suffer sentences in Muslim jails.

Let me state the obvious: I cite these alternative realisms and constructions of identity in order to reiterate the problem endemic to postcolonial feminist criticism. It is not the terrors of Islam that have unleashed the Hudood Ordinances on Pakistan, but more probably the United States government's economic and ideological support of a military regime during that bloody but eminently forgotten decade marked by the 'liberation' of Afghanistan. Jehan Mina's story is therefore not so far removed from our current assessment of what it means to be multicultural. How are we to connect her lived experience with the overwhelming realism of the law? In what ways does her testimony force postcolonial and feminist discourse into an acknowledgement of the inherent parochialism and professionalism of our claims?

I will offer a weak bridge between the two poles of my rhetorical question: a poem by the feminist Pakistani writer, Kishwar Nahreed. Her writing has been perceived as inflammatory, and she has been accused of obscenity more than once. The obscenity laws, or the Fahashi laws, are another story altogether. Once they were passed, they could not be put in print because the powers that be declared them to be too obscene. The poem below, however, is one that could easily earn the poet a prison sentence in contemporary Pakistan:

> It is we sinful women
> who are not awed by the grandeur of those who wear gowns
> who don't sell our lives
> who don't bow our heads
> who don't fold our hands together.

> It is we sinful women
> while those who sell the harvests of our bodies
> become exalted
> become distinguished
> become the just princes of the material world.

It is we sinful women
who come out raising the banner of truth
up against barricades of lies on the highways
who find stories of persecution piled on each threshold
who find the tongues which could speak have been severed.

It is we sinful women
Now, even if the night gives chase
these eyes shall not be put out
For the wall which has been razed
don't insist now on raising it again

It is we sinful women
who are not awed by the grandeur of those who wear gowns
who don't sell our bodies
who don't bow our heads
who don't fold our hands together.[11]

We should remember that there remains unseen legislation against such poetry, and that the *Hadd* – the limit – is precisely the realism against which our lived experience can serve as a metaphor, and against which we must continue to write. If we allow the identity formation of postcolonialism to construe itself only in terms of nationalism and parochialism, or of gender politics at its most narcissistically ahistorical, then let us assume that the media have won their battle, and the law of the limit is upon us.

Notes

1. James Clifford's course 'Travel and identity in twentieth-century interculture' was given as the Henry Luce Seminar at Yale University, fall 1990.
2. See Homi Bhabha (ed.), *Nation and Narration*, New York, 1990.
3. See Kwame Anthony Appiah, 'Is the post- in postmodernism the post- in postcolonial?', *Critical Inquiry*, 17, Winter 1991, pp. 336–57.
4. Chandra Talpade Mohanty, 'Under western eyes: feminist scholarship and colonial discourses', in Chandra Talpade Mohanty, Ann Russo and Lourdes Torres (eds.), *Third World women and the Politics of Feminism*, Bloomington, IN, 1991, p. 71. [See also p. 207 above.]
5. See Trinh T. Minh-ha, *Woman, Native, Other: Writing postcoloniality and feminism*, Bloomington, IN, 1989; hereafter abbreviated *WNO*.
6. Hazel V. Carby, *Reconstructing Womanhood: The emergence of the Afro-American woman novelist*, New York, 1987, p. 15.
7. bell hooks [Gloria Watkins], 'On self-recovery', in *Talking Back: Thinking feminist, thinking black*, Boston, MA, 1989, p. 28.
8. *idem*, *Yearning: Race, gender and cultural politics*, Boston, MA, 1990, pp. 93–4.

9. Gayatri Chakravorty Spivak, 'Questions of Multiculturalism', interview by Sneja Gunew (30 Aug. 1986), in *The Post-Colonial Critic: Interviews, strategies, dialogues*, ed. Sarah Harasym, New York, 1990, p. 66.
10. Asma Jahangir and Hina Jilani, *The Hudood Ordinances: A divine sanction?*, Lahore, Pakistan, 1990, p. 24; hereafter abbreviated *HO*.
11. Kishwar Naheed. 'We sinful women', in *Beyond Belief; Contemporary feminist Urdu poetry*, trans. Rukhsana Ahmad, Lahore, Pakistan, 1990, pp. 22–3.

14 □ *Speaking in Tongues: Dialogics, Dialectics and the Black Woman Writer's Literary Tradition*

Mae Gwendolyn Henderson

I am who I am, doing what I came to do, acting
upon you like a drug or a chisel to remind you of your me-ness, as
I discover you in myself.

Audre Lorde, Sister Outsider [emphasis mine]

There's a noisy feelin' near the cracks
crowdin' me . . : slips into those long, loopin' 'B's'
There's a noisy feelin' near the cracks
crowdin' me . . . slips into those long, loopin' 'B's'
of Miss Garrison's handwritin' class;
they become the wire hoops I must jump through.
It spooks my alley, it spooks my play,
more nosey now than noisy,
*   lookin' for a tongue*
*   lookin' for a tongue*
*   to get holy in.*
Who can tell this feelin' where to set up church?
Who can tell this noise where to go?
A root woman workin' . . . a mo-jo,
Just to the left of my ear.

Cherry Muhanji, 'Tight spaces'

From Henry Louis Gates, Jr. (ed.), *Reading Black, Reading Feminist: A critical anthology*, Meridian Press: New York, 1990, pp. 116–25, 136–40, 142.

Some years ago, three black feminist critics and scholars edited an anthology entitled *All the Women Are White, All the Blacks Are Men, But Some of Us Are Brave*,[1] suggesting in the title the unique and peculiar dilemma of black women. Since then it has perhaps become almost commonplace for literary critics, male and female, black and white, to note that black women have been discounted or unaccounted for in the 'traditions' of black, women's and American literature as well as in the contemporary literary-critical dialogue. More recently, black women writers have begun to receive token recognition as they are subsumed under the category of woman in the feminist critique and the category of black in the racial critique. Certainly these 'gendered' and 'racial' decodings of black women authors present strong and revisionary methods of reading, focusing as they do on literary discourses regarded as marginal to the dominant literary-critical tradition. Yet the 'critical insights' of one reading might well become the 'blind spots' of another reading. That is, by privileging one category of analysis at the expense of the other, each of these methods risks setting up what Fredric Jameson describes as 'strategies of containment', which restrict or repress different or alternative readings.[2] More specifically, blindness to what Nancy Fraser describes as 'the gender subtext' can be just as occluding as blindness to *the racial subtext* in the works of black women writers.[3]

Such approaches can result in exclusion at worst and, at best, a reading of part of the text as the whole – a strategy that threatens to replicate (if not valorize) the reification against which black women struggle in life and literature. What I propose is a theory of interpretation based on what I refer to as the 'simultaneity of discourse', a term inspired by Barbara Smith's seminal work on black feminist criticism.[4] This concept is meant to signify a mode of reading which examines the ways in which the perspectives of race and gender, and their interrelationships, structure the discourse of black women writers. Such an approach is intended to acknowledge and overcome the limitations imposed by assumptions of internal identity (homogeneity) and the repression of internal differences (heterogeneity) in racial and gendered readings of works by black women writers. In other words, I propose a model that seeks to account for racial difference within gender identity and gender difference within racial identity. This approach represents my effort to avoid what one critic describes as the presumed 'absolute and self-sufficient' *otherness* of the critical stance in order to allow the complex representations of black women writers to steer us away from 'a simple and reductive paradigm of "otherness"'.[5]

Discursive Diversity: Speaking in Tongues

What is at once characteristic and suggestive about black women's writing is its interlocutory, or dialogic, character, reflecting not only a relationship with the 'other(s)', but an internal dialogue with the plural aspects of self that constitute the matrix of black female subjectivity. The interlocutory character of black women's writings is, thus, not only a consequence of a dialogic relationship with an imaginary or 'generalized Other', but a dialogue with the aspects of 'otherness' within the self. The complex situatedness of the black woman as not only the 'Other' of the Same, but also as the 'other' of the other(s), implies, as we shall see, a relationship of difference and identification with the 'other(s)'.

It is Mikhail Bakhtin's notion of dialogism and consciousness that provides the primary model for this approach. According to Bakhtin, each social group speaks in its own 'social dialect' – possesses its own unique language – expressing shared values, perspectives, ideology and norms. These social dialects become the 'languages' of heteroglossia 'intersect[ing] with each other in many different ways. ... As such they all may be juxtaposed to one another, mutually supplement one another, contradict one another and be interrelated dialogically.'[6] Yet if language, for Bakhtin, is an expression of social identity, then subjectivity (subjecthood) is constituted as a social entity through the 'role of [the] word as medium of consciousness'. Consciousness, then, like language, is shaped by the social environment. ('Consciousness becomes consciousness only ... in the process of social interaction'.) Moreover, 'the semiotic material of the psyche is preeminently the word – *inner speech*'. Bakhtin in fact defines the relationship between consciousness and inner speech even more precisely: 'Analysis would show that the units of which inner speech is constituted are certain *whole entities ... [resembling] the alternating lines of a dialogue*. There was good reason why thinkers in ancient times should have conceived of inner speech as *inner dialogue*.'[7] Thus consciousness becomes a kind of 'inner speech' reflecting 'the outer word' in a process that links the psyche, language and social interaction.

It is the process by which these heteroglossic voices of the other(s) 'encounter one another and coexist in the consciousness of real people – first and foremost in the creative consciousness of people who write novels',[8] that speaks to the situation of black women writers in particular, 'privileged' by a social positionality that enables them to speak in dialogically racial and gendered voices to the other(s) both within and without. If the psyche functions as an internalization of heterogeneous social voices, black women's speech/writing becomes at once a dialogue between self and society and between self and psyche. Writing as inner speech, then, becomes what Bakhtin would describe as 'a unique form of collaboration with oneself' in the works of these writers.[9]

Revising and expanding Teresa de Lauretis's formulation of the 'social subject and the relations of subjectivity to sociality', I propose a model that is intended not only to address 'a subject en-gendered in the experiencing of race', but also what I submit is *a subject 'racialized' in the experiencing of gender*.[10] Speaking both to and from the position of the other(s), black women writers must, in the words of Audre Lorde, deal not only with 'the external manifestations of racism and sexism', but also 'with the results of those distortions internalized within our consciousness of ourselves and one another'.[11]

What distinguishes black women's writing, then, is the privileging (rather than repressing) of 'the other in ourselves'. Writing of Lorde's notion of self and otherness, black feminist critic Barbara Christian observes of Lorde what I argue is true to a greater or lesser degree in the discourse of black women writers: 'As a black, lesbian, feminist, poet, mother, Lorde has, in her own life, had to search long and hard for *her* people. In responding to each of these audiences, in which a part of her identity lies, she refuses to give up her differences. In fact she uses them, as woman to man, black to white, lesbian to heterosexual, as a means of conducting creative dialogue.'[12]

If black women speak from a multiple and complex social, historical and cultural positionality which, in effect, constitutes black female subjectivity, Christian's term 'creative dialogue' then refers to the expression of a multiple *dialogic of differences* based on this complex subjectivity. At the same time, however, black women enter into a *dialectic of identity* with those aspects of self shared with others. It is Hans-Georg Gadamer's 'dialectical model of conversation', rather than Bakhtin's dialogics of discourse, that provides an appropriate model for articulating a relation of mutuality and reciprocity with the 'Thou' – or intimate other(s). Whatever the critic thinks of Gadamer's views concerning history, tradition and the like, one can still find Gadamer's emphases – especially as they complement Bakhtin's – to be useful and productive. If the Bakhtinian model is primarily adversarial, assuming that verbal communication (and social interaction) is characterized by contestation with the other(s), then the Gadamerian model presupposes as its goal a language of consensus, communality, and even identification, in which 'one claims to express the other's claim and even to understand the other better than the other understands [him or herself]'. In the 'I–Thou' relationship proposed by Gadamer, 'the important thing is . . . to experience the 'Thou' truly as a 'Thou', that is, not to overlook [the other's] claim and to listen to what [s/he] has to say to us'. Gadamer's dialectic, based on a typology of the 'hermeneutical experience', privileges tradition as 'a genuine partner in communication, with which we have fellowship as does the "I" with a "Thou"'. For black and women writers, such an avowal of tradition in the subdominant order, of course, constitutes an operative challenge to the dominant order. It is this rereading of the notion of tradition within a field of gender and ethnicity that supports and enables the notion of community among those who share a common history, language and culture. If Bakhtin's dialogic engagement with the Other signifies conflict, Gadamer's monologic acknowledgment of the Thou signifies the potential of agreement. If the Bakhtinian dialogic model speaks to the other within, then Gadamer's speaks to *the same within*. Thus, 'the [dialectic] understanding of the [Thou]' (like the dialogic understanding of the other[s]) becomes 'a form of self-relatedness'.[13]

It is this notion of discursive difference and identity underlying the simultaneity of discourse which typically characterizes black women's writing. Through the multiple voices that enunciate her complex subjectivity, the black woman writer not only speaks familiarly in the discourse of the other(s), but as Other she is in contestorial dialogue with the hegemonic dominant and subdominant or 'ambiguously (non)hegemonic' discourses.[14] These writers enter simultaneously into familial, or *testimonial* and public, or *competitive* discourses – discourses that both affirm and challenge the values and expectations of the reader. As such, black women writers enter into testimonial discourse with black men as blacks, with white women as women, and with black women as black women.[15] At the same time, they enter into a competitive discourse with black men as women, with white women as blacks, and with white men as black women. If black women speak a discourse of racial and gendered difference in the dominant or hegemonic discursive order, they speak a discourse of racial and gender identity and difference in the subdominant discursive order. This dialogic of difference and dialectic of identity characterize both black women's subjectivity and black women's discourse. It is the complexity of these simultaneously homogeneous and heterogeneous social and discursive domains out of which black women write and construct themselves (as blacks and women and, often, as poor, black women) that enables black women writers authoritatively to speak to and engage both hegemonic and ambiguously (non)hegemonic discourse.

Janie, the protagonist in Zora Neale Hurston's *Their Eyes Were Watching God*, demonstrates how the dialectics/dialogics of black and female subjectivity structure black women's discourse.[16] Combining personal and public forms of discourse in the court scene where she is on trial and fighting not only for her life but against 'lying thoughts' and 'misunderstanding', Janie addresses the judge, a jury composed of 'twelve more white men', and spectators ('eight or ten white women' and 'all the Negroes [men] for miles around' [p. 274]). The challenge of Hurston's character is that of the black woman writer – to speak at once to a diverse audience about her experience in a racist and sexist society where to be black and female is to be, so to speak, 'on trial'. Janie not only speaks in a discourse of gender and racial difference to the white male judge and jurors, but also in a discourse of gender difference (and racial identity) to the black male spectators and a discourse of racial difference (and gender identity) to the white women spectators. Significantly, it is the white men who constitute both judge and jury, and, by virtue of their control of power and discourse, possess the authority of life and death over the black woman. In contrast, the black men (who are convinced that the 'nigger [woman] kin kill . . . jus' as many niggers as she please') and white women (who 'didn't seem too mad') read and witness/oppose a situation over which they exercise neither power nor discourse (pp. 225, 280).

Janie's courtroom discourse also emblematizes the way in which the categories of public and private break down in black women's discourse. In the context of Janie's courtroom scene, testimonial discourse takes on an expanded meaning referring to both juridical, public and dominant discourse as well as familial, private and nondominant discourse. Testimonial, in this sense, derives its meaning from both 'testimony' as an official discursive mode and 'testifying', defined by Geneva Smitherman as 'a ritualized form of . . . communication in which the speaker gives verbal witness to the efficacy, truth, and power of some experience in which [the group has] shared'. The latter connotation suggests an additional meaning in the context of theological discourse where testifying refers to a 'spontaneous expression to the church community [by whomever] feels the spirit'.[17]

Like Janie, black women must speak in a plurality of voices as well as in a multiplicity of discourses. This discursive diversity, or simultaneity of discourse, I call 'speaking in tongues'. Significantly, glossolalia, or speaking in tongues, is a practice associated with black women in the Pentecostal Holiness church, the church of my childhood and the church of my mother. In the Holiness church (or as we called it, the Sanctified church), speaking unknown tongues (tongues known only to God) is in fact a sign of election, or holiness. As a trope it is also intended to remind us of Alice Walker's characterization of black women as artists, as 'Creators', intensely rich in that spirituality which Walker sees as 'the basis of Art'.[18]

Glossolalia is perhaps the meaning most frequently associated with speaking in tongues. It is this connotation which emphasizes the particular, private, closed and privileged communication between the congregant and the divinity. Inaccessible to the general congregation, this mode of communication is outside the realm of public discourse and foreign to the known tongues of humankind.

But there is a second connotation to the notion of speaking in tongues – one that suggests not glossolalia, but heteroglossia, the ability to speak in diverse known languages. While glossolalia refers to the ability to 'utter the mysteries of the spirit', heteroglossia describes the ability to speak in the multiple languages of public discourse. If glossolalia suggests private, nonmediated, nondifferentiated univocality, heteroglossia connotes public, differentiated, social, mediated, dialogic discourse. Returning from the trope to the act of reading, perhaps we can say that speaking in tongues connotes both the semiotic, presymbolic babble (baby talk), as between mother and child – which Julia Kristeva postulates as the 'mother tongue' – as well as the diversity of voices, discourses and languages described by Mikhail Bakhtin.

Speaking in tongues, my trope for both glossolalia and heteroglossia, has a precise genealogical evolution in the Scriptures. In Genesis 11, God confounded the world's language when the city of Babel built a tower in an attempt to reach the heavens. Speaking in many and different tongues, the dwellers of Babel, unable to understand each other, fell into confusion, discord and strife, and had to abandon the project. Etymologically, the name of the city Babel sounds much like the Hebrew word for 'babble' – meaning confused, as in baby talk. Babel, then, suggests the two related, but distinctly different, meanings of speaking in tongues, meanings borne out in other parts of the Scriptures. The most common is that implied in 1 Corinthians 14 – the ability to speak in unknown tongues. According to this interpretation, speaking in tongues suggests the ability to speak in and through the spirit. Associated with glossolalia – speech in unknown tongues – it is ecstatic, rapturous, inspired speech, based on a relation of intimacy and identification between the individual and God.

If Genesis tells of the disempowerment of a people by the introduction of different tongues, then Acts 2 suggests the empowerment of the disciples who, assembled on the day of Pentecost in the upper room of the temple in Jerusalem, 'were filled with the Holy Spirit and began to speak in other tongues'. Although the people thought the disciples had 'imbibed a strange and unknown wine', it was the Holy Spirit which had driven them, filled with ecstasy, from the upper room to speak among the five thousand Jews surrounding the temple. The Scriptures tell us that the tribes of Israel all understood them, each in his own tongue. The Old Testament, then, suggests the dialogics of difference in its diversity of discourse, while the New Testament, in its unifying language of the spirit, suggests the dialectics of identity. If the Bakhtinian model suggests the multiplicity of speech as suggested in the dialogics of difference, then Gadamer's model moves toward a unity of understanding in its dialectics of identity.

It is the first as well as the second meaning which we privilege in speaking of black women writers: the first connoting polyphony, multivocality and plurality of voices, and the second signifying intimate, private, inspired utterances. Through their intimacy with the discourse of the other(s), black women writers weave into their work competing and complementary discourses – discourses that seek both to adjudicate competing claims and witness common concerns.[19]

Also interesting is the link between the gift of tongues, the gift of prophecy, and the gift of interpretation. While distingushing between these three gifts, the Scriptures frequently conflate or conjoin them. If to speak in tongues is to utter mysteries in and through the Spirit, to prophesy is to speak to others in a (diversity of) language(s) which the congregation can understand. The Scriptures would suggest that the disciples were able to perform both. I propose, at this juncture, an enabling critical fiction – that it is black women writers who are the modern-day apostles, empowered by experience to speak as poets and prophets in many tongues. With this critical gesture, I also intend to signify a deliberate intervention by black women writers into the canonic tradition of sacred/literary texts.[20]

A Discursive Dilemma

In their works, black women writers have encoded oppression as a discursive dilemma, that is, their works have consistently raised the problem of the black woman's relationship to power and discourse. Silence is an important element of this code. The classic black woman's text *Their Eyes Were Watching God* charts the female protagonist's development from voicelessness to voice, from silence to tongues. Yet this movement does not exist without intervention by the other(s) – who speak for and about black women. In other words, it is not that black women, in the past, have had nothing to say, but rather that they have had no say. The absence of black female voices has allowed others to inscribe, or write, and ascribe to, or read, them. The notion of speaking in tongues, however, leads us away from an examination of how the Other has written/read black women and toward an examination of how black women have written the other(s)' writing/reading black women.

[. . .]

Disruption and Revision

[...]

It is [the multivocal] quality of speaking in tongues [...] that accounts in part for the current popularity and critical success of black women's writing. The engagement of multiple others broadens the audience for black women's writing, for like the disciples of Pentecost who spoke in diverse tongues, black women, speaking out of the specificity of their racial and gender experiences, are able to communicate in a diversity of discourses. If the ability to communicate accounts for the popularity of black women writers, it also explains much of the controversy surrounding some of this writing. Black women's writing speaks with what Mikhail Bakhtin would describe as heterological or 'centrifugal forces' but (in a sense somewhat different from that which Bakhtin intended) also unifying or 'centripetal force'.[21] This literature speaks as much to the notion of commonality and universalism as it does to the sense of difference and diversity.

Yet the objective of these writers is not, as some critics suggest, to move from margin to center, but to remain on the borders of discourse, speaking from the vantage point of the insider/outsider. As Bakhtin further suggests, fusion with the (dominant) Other can only duplicate the tragedy or misfortune of the Other's dilemma. On the other hand, as Gadamer makes clear, 'there is a kind of experience of the "Thou" that seeks to discover things that are typical in the behaviour of [the other] and is able to make predictions concerning another person on the basis of [a commonality] of experience.'[22] To maintain this insider/outsider position, or perhaps what Myra Jehlen calls the 'extra-terrestrial fulcrum' that Archimedes never acquired, is to see the other, but also to see what the other cannot see, and to use this insight to enrich both our own and the other's understanding.[23]

As gendered and racial subjects, black women speak/write in multiple voices – not all simultaneously or with equal weight, but with various and changing degrees of intensity, privileging one *parole* and then another. One discovers in these writers a kind of internal dialogue reflecting an *intrasubjective* engagement with the *intersubjective* aspects of self, a dialectic neither repressing difference nor, for that matter, privileging identity, but rather expressing engagement with the social aspects of self ('the other[s] in ourselves'). It is this subjective plurality (rather than the notion of the cohesive or fractured subject) that, finally, allows the black woman to become an expressive site for a dialectics/dialogics of identity and difference.

Unlike Bloom's 'anxiety of influence' model configuring a white male poetic tradition shaped by an adversarial dialogue between literary fathers and sons (as well as the appropriation of this model by Joseph Skerrett and others to discuss black male writers), and unlike Gilbert and Gubar's 'anxiety of authorship' model informed by the white women writer's sense of 'dis-ease' within a white patriarchal tradition, the present model configures a tradition of black women writers generated less by neurotic anxiety or dis-ease than by an emancipatory impulse which freely engages both hegemonic and ambiguously (non)hegemonic discourse.[24] Summarizing [Toni] Morrison's perspectives, Andrea Stuart perhaps best expresses this notion:

> I think you [Morrison] summed up the appeal of black women writers when you said that white men, quite naturally, wrote about themselves and their world; white women tended to write about white men because they were so close to them as husbands, lovers and sons; and black men wrote about white men as the oppressor or the yardstick against which they measured themselves. Only black women writers were not interested in writing about white men and therefore they freed literature to take on other concerns.[25]

In conclusion, I return to the gifts of the Holy Spirit: 1 Corinthians 12 tells us that 'the [one] who speaks in tongues should pray that [s/he] may interpret what [s/he] says'. Yet the Scriptures also speak to interpretation as a separate gift – the ninth and final gift of the Spirit. Might I suggest that if black women writers speak in tongues, then it is we black feminist critics who are charged with the hermeneutical task of interpreting tongues?

Notes

1. Gloria Hull, Patricia Bell Scott and Barbara Smith (eds.), *All the Women Are White, All the Blacks Are Men, But Some of Us Are Brave*, Feminist Press: Old Harbury, NY, 1982.
2. Fredric Jameson, *The Political Unconscious: Narrative as a socially symbolic act*, Cornell University Press: Ithaca, NY, 1981, p. 53.
3. The phrase 'gender subtext' is used by Nancy Fraser (and attributed to Dorothy Smith) in Fraser's critique of Habermas in Nancy Fraser, 'What's critical about critical theory?', in Seyla Benehabib and Drucilla Cornell (eds.), *Feminism as Critique*, University of Minnesota Press: Minneapolis, 1987, p. 42.
4. See Barbara Smith (ed.), *Home Girls: A black feminist anthology*, Kitchen Table/Women of Color Press: New York, 1983, p. xxxii.
5. John Carlos Rowe, 'To live outside the law, you must be honest: the authority of the margin in contemporary theory', *Cultural Critique*, I, 2, pp. 67–8.
6. Mikhail Bakhtin, 'Discourse in the novel', reprinted in Michael Holquist (ed.), *The Dialogic Imagination: Four essays by M. M. Bakhtin*, University of Texas Press: Austin, 1981, p. 292. Bakhtin's social groups are designated according to class, religion, generation, region and profession. The interpretative model I propose extends and rereads Bakhtin's theory from the standpoint of race and gender, categories absent in Bakhtin's original system of social and linguistic stratification.
7. V. N. Vollosinov [Mikhail Bakhtin], *Marxism and the Philosophy of Language*, Seminar Press: New York, 1973, pp. 11, 29, 38. Originally published in Russian as *Marksizm I Filosofija Jazyka*, Leningrad, 1930. Notably, this concept of the 'subjective psyche' constituted primarily as a 'social entity' distinguishes the Bakhtinian notion of self from the Freudian notion of identity.
8. Bakhtin, 'Discourse in the novel', p. 292.

9. According to Bakhtin, 'The processes that basically define the content of the psyche occur not inside but outside the individual organism. ... Moreover, the psyche enjoys extraterritorial status ... [as] a social entity that penetrates inside the organism of the individual person (*Marxism and the Philosophy of Language*, pp. 25, 39). Explicating Caryl Emerson's position on Bakhtin, Gary Saul Morson argues that selfhood 'derives from an internalization of the voices a person has heard, and each of these voices is saturated with social and ideological values'. 'Thought itself', he writes, 'is but "inner speech", and inner speech is outer speech that we have learned to "speak" in our heads while retaining the full register of conflicting social values.' See Gary Saul Morson, 'Dialogue, monologue, and the social: a reply to Ken Hirschkop', in Morson (ed.), *Bakhtin: Essays and dialogues on his work*, University of Chicago Press: Chicago, IL, 1986, p. 85.

10. Teresa de Lauretis, *Technologies of Gender*, Indiana University Press: Bloomington, IN, 1987, p. 2.

11. Audre Lorde, 'Eye to eye', included in *Sister Outsider*, Crossing Press: Trumansburg, NY, 1984, p. 147.

12. Barbara Christian, 'The dynamics of difference: book review of Audre Lorde's *Sister Outsider*', in *Black Feminist Criticism: Perspectives in black women writers*, Pergamon Press: New York, 1985, p. 209.

13. While acknowledging the importance of historicism, I can only agree with Frank Lentricchia's conclusion that in some respects Gadamer's 'historicist argument begs more questions than it answers. If we can applaud the generous intention, virtually unknown in structuralist quarters, of recapturing history for textual interpetation, then we can only be stunned by the implication of what he has uncritically to say about authority, the power of tradition, knowledge, our institutions, and our attitudes.' See Frank Lentricchia, *After the New Criticism*, University of Chicago Press: Chicago, 1980, p. 153. Certainly, Gadamer's model privileges the individual's relation to history and tradition in a way that might seem problematic in formulating a discursive model for the 'noncanonical' or marginalized writer. However, just as the above model of dialogics is meant to extend Bakhtin's notion of class difference to encompass gender and race, so the present model revises and limits Gadamer's notion of tradition. See Hans-Georg Gadamer, *Truth and Method*, Seabury Press: New York, 1975, pp. 321–5. My introduction to the significance of Gadamer's work for my own reading of black women writers was first suggested by Don Bialostosky's excellent paper entitled 'Dialectic and anti-dialectic: a Bakhtinian critique of Gadamer's dialectical model of conversation', delivered at the International Association of Philosophy and Literature in May 1989 at Emory University in Atlanta, Georgia.

14. I extend Rachel Blau DuPlessis's term designating white women as a group privileged by race and oppressed by gender to black men as a group privileged by gender and oppressed by race. In this instance, I use 'ambiguously (non)hegemonic' to signify the discursive status of both these groups.

15. Black women enter into dialogue with other black women in a discourse that I would characterize as primarily testimonial, resulting from a similar discursive and social positionality. It is this commonality of history, culture and language which, finally, constitutes the basis of a tradition of black women's expressive culture. In terms of actual literary dialogue among black women, I would suggest a relatively modern provenance of such a tradition, but again, one based primarily on a dialogue of affirmation rather than contestation. As I see it, this dialogue begins with Alice Walker's response to Zora

Neale Hurston. Although the present article is devoted primarily to contestorial function of black women's writing, my forthcoming work (of which the present essay constitutes only a part) deals extensively with the relationships among black women writers.

16. Zora Neale Hurston, *Their Eyes Were Watching God*, 1937; reprint, University of Illinois Press: Urbana, IL, 1978. All subsequent references in the text.

17. Geneva Smitherman, *Talkin and Testifyin: The language of black America*, Wayne State University Press: Detroit, 1986, p. 58.

18. Alice Walker, 'In search of our mothers' gardens', in *In Search of Our Mothers' Gardens: Womanist prose*, Harcourt Brace Jovanovich: New York, 1984, p. 232.

19. Not only does such an approach problematize conventional categories and boundaries of discourse, but, most importantly, it signals the collapse of the unifying consensus posited by the discourse of universalism and reconstructs the concept of unity in diversity implicit in the discourse of difference.

20. The arrogant and misogynistic Paul tells us, 'I thank God that I speak in tongues more than all of you. But in church I would rather speak five intelligible words to instruct others [i.e. to prophesy] than ten thousand words in a tongue.' Even though we are perhaps most familiar with Paul's injunction to women in the church to keep silent, the prophet Joel, in the Old Testament, speaks to a diversity of voices that includes women: 'In the last days, God says, I will pour out my Spirit on all people. Your sons and *daughters* will prophesy. . . . Even on my servants, both men and *women*, I will pour out my Spirit in those days, and they will prophesy' (emphasis mine). I am grateful to the Rev. Joseph Stephens whose vast scriptural knowledge helped guide me through these and other revelations.

21. Bakhtin, 'Discourse in the novel', pp. 271–2.

22. Gadamer, *op. cit.*, p. 321.

23. Myra Jehlen, 'Archimedes and the paradox of feminist criticism', reprinted in Elizabeth Abel and Emily K. Abel (eds.), *The Signs Reader: Women, gender and scholarship*, University of Chicago Press: Chicago, 1983.

24. See Harold Bloom, *The Anxiety of Influence: A theory of poetry*, Oxford University Press: New York, 1973; Sandra M. Gilbert and Susan Gubar (eds.), *The Madwoman in the Attic: The woman writer and the nineteenth-century literary imagination*, Yale University Press: New Haven, CT, 1979; and Joseph T. Skerrett, 'The Wright interpretation: Ralph Ellison and the anxiety of influence', *Massachusetts Review*, 21, Spring 1980, pp. 196–212.

25. Andrea Stuart in an interview with Toni Morrison, 'Telling our story', *Spare Rib*, April 1988, pp. 12–15.

PART FOUR

Theorising Post-Coloniality: Intellectuals and Institutions

Introduction

The relation of intellectuals to progressive or emancipatory movements, and in particular to proletarian or revolutionary ones, has troubled thinkers at least from the time of Marx and Engels. Many Marxists have been unsure about the nature, or even the possibility, of links between broad sections of the population and that élite group which would seem on the face of it to have little to do with them. While intellectuals could be said properly to belong to the bourgeois revolutions, it was by no means obvious that they could hope for any such relation with working-class ones. Lenin's lack of faith in the utility of bourgeois intellectuals in a proletarian revolutionary situation is mirrored in Fanon's scepticism, in 'Pitfalls of the national consciousness', regarding the role of intellectuals from the national bourgeoisie in the struggle for independence and in the post-colonial situation – 'the bourgeois phase in the history of under-developed countries is a completely useless phase'[1] – and to the extent that intellectuals are part of the bourgeoisie then they tend towards a similar uselessness. Fanon does not, however, believe in class determinism, and acknowledges that some intellectuals do manage, against the odds, to adopt an oppositional stance. In the reading included in Part One, 'On national culture', Fanon takes a more nuanced and, we might say, historically aware view of intellectuals in the colonial and post-colonial situation, recognising various stages of assimilation and rejection of the culture of the coloniser, as well as foreseeing a much more active and politically committed function for the intellectual:

> If man is known by his acts, then we will say that the most urgent thing today for the intellectual is to build up his nation. . . . National consciousness, which is not the same as nationalism, is the only thing that will give us an international dimension.[2]

Another important analyst of colonial and post-colonial intellectuals is Edward Said. For a number of reasons, this is no surprise, not least because the two theorists on whom Said, as we saw in Part Two, draws extensively, namely Gramsci and Foucault, are also the most important theorists of the role of the intellectual in twentieth-century Marxism and post-structuralism. Both Gramsci and Foucault construct a bi-polar model of intellectual types: for Foucault, these are the 'universal' and the 'specific' intellectual; for Gramsci, the 'traditional' and the 'organic'. Although these distinctions are typological, they are also developmental and chronological, to the extent that each sees a particular relation – between the (traditional) intellectual and (aristocratic) social class in Gramsci's case, or between the (universal) intellectual and (dominant) regime of truth in Foucault's – and in each case this relation is seen as capable of being superseded or challenged (although, in the case of Foucault, Gayatri Chakravorty Spivak has voiced her scepticism about the apparent ease with which this transition from universal to specific can supposedly be achieved[3]). Each considers that intellectuals can emerge from potentially any social class. Foucault's 'specific' intellectuals perhaps operate in a more modest sphere – in keeping with his ideas of micro-politics – than Gramsci's organic intellectuals, but for each the new type of intellectual is also an acknowledgement that the mass of the people do not need to have understanding thrust on them from above. Fanon is entirely in agreement: 'we must above all rid ourselves of the very Western, very bourgeois, and therefore contemptuous, attitude that the masses are incapable of governing themselves. In fact, experience proves that the masses understand perfectly the most complicated problems.'[4]

Said's own position, as set out in articles such as 'Third World intellectuals and metropolitan culture' or 'Intellectuals in the post-colonial world', explicitly draws on Gramsci and Foucault, but also embraces a number of the writers and thinkers included in this volume: Césaire, Cabral, Fanon, Ngũgĩ. For Said, what Marx called 'the weapons of criticism' can be firmly grasped by post-colonial intellectuals and turned against the former colonisers (not least with regard to their neo-colonial pretensions). This does not, however, involve any automatic total repudiation of the West: Said describes intellectuals like the Caribbean/exile Marxist C. L. R. James as fiercely criticising Western domination or excesses, but doing so very much from a position located within the Western cultural tradition. (Something of the same process can be seen in Part Two in the reading where Césaire – though perhaps in a more radical way – uses Western values as the basis for a critique of the West.) That location within Western traditions disappears, however (according to Said's argument), in the case of a more recent generation of intellectuals such as Ranajit Guha.

If some critics, Said among them, seem to use post-colonialism in an unselfconscious, apparently common-sense manner, for others it is very much a contested term, or one in need of urgent clarification. From differing perspectives, Anne McClintock, Vijay Mishra and Bob Hodge undertake the rather thankless task of trying to theorise post-colonialism. While McClintock's discussion draws on political economy, Mishra and Hodge's analysis remains firmly located in the textual/theoretical, taking as its starting point the problems with the kind of approach represented by *The Empire Writes Back*. The latter's attempt to provide a model for post-colonial texts and theories is described by Mishra and Hodge as variously homogenising, totalising and post-modernist (which in this context at least is a negative phenomenon). They themselves offer a different model based on 'ideological orientations' in discourses: 'oppositional postcolonialism' and 'complicit postcolonialism'. In a manner reminiscent of *The Empire Writes Back*, these (unhyphenated) forms are taken to be 'an always present tendency in any literature of subjugation'. Continuing the point which was raised in the Introduction to this volume, Mishra and Hodge voice their unease at the inclusion of white settler colonies in models of post-colonialism, especially because of the post-modernist bias, both textual and theoretical, which this introduces. Not that post-modernism can be altogether avoided, since an increasing alliance between 'complicit post colonialism' and post-modernism is one of the trends which the authors identify. This kind of complicity and convergence is not what they would wish for, however: 'It must be possible to acknowledge difference and insist on a strongly-theorized oppositional postcolonialism as crucial to the debate, without claiming that this form is or has been everywhere the same wherever a colonizer's feet have trod.'

Anne McClintock's worries about post-colonialism are also to do with homogenising and the eliding of differences. For her, the term itself suggests a unified and universal condition of post-coloniality, and 're-orients the globe once more around a single, binary opposition: colonial/post-colonial'. It also risks being prematurely celebratory about a world which is scarcely uniformly post-colonial. In addition, post-colonialism apparently reproduces the very narratives of progress and development which were part of the problematic past from which it seeks to escape. The perceived universalism in the term means that for McClintock it is as 'historically voided' as other concepts dear to literary theorists such as 'the signifier' 'the subject' or 'the other', and as a result her argument moves away from such questions, drawing instead on history and political economy to provide the specificity she sees as lacking in the debate so far. In particular, the emphasis on political economy enables a discussion of neo-colonialism, which in certain respects possesses superior explanatory power or terminological accuracy to post-colonialism, though it is not necessarily easily substitutable for it, especially in the area of cultural theory.

While McClintock is interested, among other things, in global distributions of power as an aspect of neo-colonialism, the reading by Arjun Appadurai provides a different view of globalisation to hers, or to that offered by Giddens in Part Two, not least because of its emphasis on culture and on the disjuncture in the global institutions and processes in this field. As Appadurai argues, the globalisation of culture is not the same as its homogenisation, but the latter is nevertheless a central feature (along with heterogenisation) of the global cultural network. Appadurai proposes five 'landscapes' as a framework for understanding the contemporary economy of culture: 'ethnoscape' (people, especially groups in movement), 'technoscape' (the institutions of technology and its informational flows), 'finanscape' (the disposition of global capital), 'mediascape' (both the images produced and the mode of production) and 'ideoscape' (ideologies). While these obviously intersect in various ways, Appadurai regards them as increasingly disjunctive, following 'non-isomorphic paths'. As the formations of people and place which previously gave coherence and structure to cultural forms become more mobile and their links more tenuous, Appadurai suggests we conceptualise contemporary culture as 'fundamentally fractal, that is, as possessing no Euclidean boundaries, structures or regularities'. This resemblance to elements of chaos theory is not meant to suggest, however, that the relations between the components of global culture are purely arbitrary, for even in a model like this the forces of capitalism, militarism, even racism, drive the flows of the economy of culture.

The reading by Teshome H. Gabriel takes just one area of the global economy, the Third World, and one area of culture, film. It is a testimony to the power of Fanon's analysis of political and cultural institutions and intellectuals that Gabriel bases his study on Fanon, in particular the three-phase movement from assimilation to opposition. These phases are also related to theoretical questions concerning the text, its production and reception, but, as Gabriel says, the most important question is 'Precisely what kind of institution is cinema in the Third World?' He suggests a number of ways in which the institutions and practices of Third World cinema relate to social and psychological dimensions of Third World life in a way that Western cinema cannot – self-evidently, perhaps, but then universal applicability continues to be one of the (implicit) assumptions underlying much Western cultural production. Third World cinema is slowly forcing the West to acknowledge that in some areas at least neither its images nor its institutional practices have quite the global reach to which they might aspire.

For Ania Loomba, as for so many others, Fanon remains a point of reference, though perhaps in a less productive way than for Gabriel, for example, as she talks about the worn Fanonian tightrope between nativist revivalism and models of development which post-colonial activists and intellectuals have to negotiate. Her discussion unites both elements of this part's subtitle: intellectuals, insofar as she continues, though generally in a more temperate manner, Benita Parry's critique of certain aspects of post-colonial theorising (particularly the work of Homi Bhabha and Gayatri Chakravorty Spivak), and institutions, insofar as she juxtaposes this to an examination of Indian television and representations of nationalism. Analysing institutions allows her to advance an argument which she feels goes beyond both the dichotomised Manichean model favoured by Abdul JanMohamed and Benita Parry, and the complex hybridity theorised by Homi Bhabha and others, which blurs the structure of power in the colonial situation and seems to leave no room for indigenous resistance. Loomba's own favoured 'variegated' position lies between the two, neither rigidly polarised nor unhelpfully blurred, and allowing for the possible or actual presence of oppositional practices. The institutional/intellectual inter-action is examined in the context of education in English in India, and, as Loomba points out, 'The native intelligentsia certainly cannot be dismissed easily as *either* revivalist or "native informants".'

Jean Franco's discussion of Third World intelligentsia also takes Fanon as its point of departure, especially with regard to the destructive effects of the institutionalised division between the intellectuals and the bulk of the population. Franco analyses intellectuals as 'a systematically constituted group', and, like Ania Loomba, looks at the implications of this for the question of resistance. Importantly, her reading extends the discussion to the Latin American context, where social conditions which blocked contributions in the area of scientific thought meant that the intelligentsia's efforts were channelled into literature. Intellectual cultural production is analysed in relation to representations of gender, gendered positionality and the sexual division of labour. For Franco, the Latin American intelligentsia were in a 'feminised' position *vis-à-vis* metropolitan discourses (i.e. immobilised, rendered passive and relatively powerless), and moved from an acceptance of gendered positionality as natural to a reinterpretation of the meanings associated with such positions. This involved greater understanding of those other 'feminised' – silenced, disempowered – groups in society, while nevertheless, and contradictorily, retaining the traditional masculine role of creator. Faced with this situation, it is the subordinated groups themselves who, in a classically Fanonian manner, are breaking down the divisions, and, in Franco's words, recognising 'the importance of cultural politics in the creation of non-gendered solidarity groups' – the production of a united politics which is not split between intellectuals and the people.

Notes

1. Frantz Fanon, *The Wretched of the Earth*, trans. Constance Farrington, Penguin: Harmondsworth, 1967, p. 142.
2. *ibid.*, p. 199. See also p. 51 above.
3. Gayatri Chakravorty Spivak, 'Criticism, feminism and the institution', in *The Post-Colonial Critic: Interviews, strategies, dialogues*, ed. Sarah Harasym, Routledge: London, 1991.
4. Fanon, *op. cit.*, p. 153.

15 □ *What is Post(-)colonialism?*

Vijay Mishra and Bob Hodge

As the British Empire broke up and attempted to sustain an illusion of unity under the euphemistic title of 'Commonwealth', a new object appeared on the margins of departments of English Literature: 'Commonwealth literature'. The ambiguous politics of the term was inscribed in the field that it called into being. 'Commonwealth literature' did not include the literature of the centre, which acted as the impossible absent standard by which it should be judged. The term also occluded the crucial differences between the 'old' and the 'new' Commonwealth, between White settler colonies and Black nations that typically had a very different and more difficult route into a different kind of independence.

The struggling enterprise of 'Commonwealth literature' was jeopardized from the start by the heavily ideological overtones of its name. Now a new term has gained currency to designate the field: 'post-colonial'. Post-colonial(ism) has many advantages over the former term. It foregrounds a politics of opposition and struggle, and problematizes the key relationship between centre and periphery. It has helped to destabilize the barriers around 'English literature' that protected the primacy of the canon and the self-evidence of its standards. But in order to consolidate its place in the curriculum it needed a good, teachable text. With the publication of *The Empire Writes Back*[1] (hereinafter abbreviated to *EWB*) that need is now met. *EWB* is a lucid, judicious and representative text which is destined to play a decisive role in this emerging field. That importance is good reason for subjecting it to close critical scrutiny, as we propose to do.

The word post-colonialism (hyphenated) is not given an independent entry in the *OED* (1989). It is still a compound in which the 'post-' is a prefix which governs the subsequent element. 'Post-colonial' thus becomes something which is 'post' or after colonial. In the *OED* the compound exists alongside other compounds such as post-adolescent, post-cognitive, post-coital and so on. The first entry for the word is dated 12 December 1959: 'It was probably inevitable that India, in the full flush of post-colonial sensitivity, should fear that association with the America of that

From *Textual Practice*, 5, 3, 1991, pp. 399–414.

period might involve her necessarily in troubles which were little to do with Asia.'
Subsequent entries (1969; 1974) carry this meaning of post-colonial as something
which happened after colonization. Edward Said writes about a 'postcolonial field'[2]
to which modern anthropologists can no longer return with their erstwhile
certitudes. Here too 'post-colonial' is used in the sense in which the *OED* defines the
term.

EWB takes up as its central theme the relationship of the periphery to the
metropolitan centre in the context of post-colonial literature. Some of the problems
that it faces in positioning itself in relation to this theme can be seen in some
ambiguities in the title of the book itself, which makes connections with two
seemingly divergent moments in modern culture. The first is the intertext that the
title echoes, *The Empire Strikes Back*, the second film in the Star Wars Trilogy in
which the father and the Empire are momentarily on the ascendant as Darth Vader
all but incapacitates his son (Luke Skywalker) and the counter-insurgence of the
guerrillas is checked by the might of the Empire.

The second intertext is not so much a narrative as a personality around whom
a bizarre postmodern fiction has been constructed. The title is a quotation from
Salman Rushdie who, writing from within the centre as a critic of it, now finds
himself denounced for complicity with the values of the colonizer, the imperialist.
Saladin the 'chamcha' becomes Rushdie the 'chamcha' who, in Rushdie's own
definition, is someone who 'sucks up to powerful people, a yes-man, a sycophant'.
'The Empire', adds Rushdie, 'would not have lasted a week without such
collaborators among the colonized people.'[3] The condemnation of Rushdie by the
Islamic post-colonial world raises interesting questions about the category of the
post-colonial itself and whether one can ever totally remove the stains of complicity
with the Empire that come with the 'profession' of post-colonial writer. For the
Islamic post-colonial world the moral is clear and succinct: to write in the language
of the colonizer is to write from within death itself. As a result of all this, the title
of *EWB* begins to sound like a Freudian slip, announcing the inevitable triumph of
the Empire's counter-attack as the slogan for a book that celebrates post-colonial
subversion.

The Rushdie case is a parable that challenges the notion of post-colonial writing
as defined by Ashcroft, Griffiths and Tiffin. In the final analysis post-colonial writers
who write in the language of the Empire are marked off as traitors to the cause of
a reconstructive post-colonialism. The authors of *EWB* seem to be conscious of this
paradox, the paradox that the 'post' in 'post-colonialism' may well imply 'business
as usual, only *more* so'.[4] Consequently, they point to the dangers of writing in
English (spelt with a lower case whenever non-British English is being referred to)
and they know that the post-colonial writers compose in the shadow of 'death'.
Many years ago Frantz Fanon anticipated this paradox when he wrote that the
colonized is either doomed to be a mere reflection of his master (located in the
Imaginary) or he must fight his master through active struggle (so as to enter into
the realm of the Symbolic).[5] The withholding of legitimate consciousness, I-ness or
self-hood, the impossibility on the part of the colonized even to qualify for the

thingness of things (thingword), produces a radical politics in which violence is embraced. But as the ANC's own struggle for self-legitimation demonstrates, the colonizer never completely withholds 'I-ness' or 'self-hood' since to do so would make the colonized worthless. Thus there is always, in the colonial regime, a tantalizing offer of subjectivity and its withdrawal which, for the colonized, momentarily confirms their entry into the world of the colonizer only to be rejected by it. The colonized never know when the colonizers consider them for what they are, humans in full possession of a self, or merely objects.

In Fanon's version of the conditions under which the radical post-colonial might come into being, the colonial world must be strategically rendered as Manichean in its *effects*, since the system reduces the colonized to the status of permanent bondage. Consequently, it is in the nature of the Manichean world-order that violence should be seen as a cleansing force. This is a severe indictment of the imperialist since the withdrawal of subjectivity hits at the very core of the Enlightenment project, the civilizing values of modernity which the colonized (a V. S. Naipaul for instance) sees as imperialism's positive, reconstructive and basically humane face. The complexity of this essentially Hegelian problematic, the centrality of action in a retheorization of history as class struggle, is transformed by the authors of *EWB* into a broader, somewhat depoliticized category, the 'counter-discourse'. Political insurgency is replaced by discursive radicalism, for which the West Indian example is offered as paradigmatic.

The danger here is that the post-colonial is reduced to a purely textual phenomenon, as if power is simply a matter of discourse and it is only through discourse that counter-claims might be made. This move is clearly aimed at making the diverse forms of the post-colonial available as a single object on the curriculum of the centre. Since a *grand récit* is not available equally to the varieties of post-colonialism that *EWB* addresses, it is hardly surprising that the dominant tone in the book is the tolerant pluralism of liberal humanism. Difference is recognized but contained within a single pattern, the coexistence of two kinds of relationship to the language and culture of the centre: 'abrogation' or refusal, and 'appropriation'. The latter gathers under a single term a large and diverse set of strategies involving both accommodation and compromise, whose political meaning is highly dependent on specific historical circumstances.

Post-Orientalism and Counter-Discursivity

A grand theory of post-colonialism inevitably throws up comparisons with another totalizing form of scholarship, orientalism. This is not to say that *EWB* duplicates orientalism's political strategy or, more significantly, is unaware of its redemptive as well as damning characteristics. What *EWB*, however, ends up doing is something which is endemic to a project in which particularities are homogenized, perhaps unconsciously, into a more or less unproblematic theory of the Other. One remembers Edward Said's well-known warning that even with the best of intentions one might, and sometimes does, give the impression that through one's own discourses the Other is now representable without due regard to its bewildering complexity. Perhaps it is in the very nature of any totalizing enterprise that simplifications which are avoided elsewhere (as in individual articles by Ashcroft, Griffiths and Tiffin) make their way into the body of the text.

The paradox that surfaces – a paradox that we would call post-orientalism – is part of an historical process that grew out of Europe's reading of the Other. Orientalism's heavily skewed and ideologically marked discourses – the enterprise was never totally homogeneous, and often contradictory – haunt the post-colonial in ways that make, in places, the post-colonial itself post-oriental. Depending upon one's point of view, this might be a positive acknowledgement of a larger continuity. At the same time a more sophisticated orientalism (as post-orientalism) would take us back to Warren Hastings's astute observation in his panegyric on Charles Wilkins's path-breaking translation of the *Bhagavadgita* (1785):

> But such instances can only be obtained in their [the Hindus'] writings: and these will survive when the British dominion in India shall have long ceased to exist, and when the sources which it once yielded of wealth and power are lost to remembrance.[6]

What Hastings is anticipating here are the different forms of pre-english literatures which will have a very different relationship with the emergent literatures in English. When the power of the British is 'lost to remembrance', as is increasingly becoming evident in the new Indian *lebenswelt* for instance, indigenous literatures would again begin to show a resurgence and self-confidence which would question the self-evident primacy of a literature written in English. In jettisoning the almost auratic status given to the English language, the new reckoning with an imperial language both changes the form of the language itself and marginalizes it politically: the Shiv Sena uses Marathi, the Sikh militants Punjabi, and so on.

In this instance, a post-colonial theory becomes a radical form of orientalism (or post-orientalism) which insinuates, at every point, a dialectical process now under way between literature in English, and those written and oral non-english discourses which, in Hastings' words, 'will survive'. Where the early version of orientalism effectively reduced this multiplicity of languages and ideologies into a homogenized European discourse – E. Trump gave up his translation of the *Adi Granth* (1877) because it lacked a grand epic narrative – the *EWB* strategy, for very different reasons, can't hear the almost carnivalesque sounds of the non-english unconscious either. It is a price that *EWB*, like any other enterprise with totalizing ambitions, must inevitably pay. The failure to position author(s) into a culture so as to 'mediate between discrepant worlds of meaning'[7] led the orientalists back into the essentially European reconstructions of the Other. The authors of *EWB* do make a conscious attempt at this mediation, and bring together some of the best insights into post-orientalism of most contemporary theorists of the subject. However, there are intrinsic problems with any proposal to account, within a unitary scheme, for the unmanageable plethora of 'discrepant worlds of meaning' in contemporary post-colonial societies. *EWB* proposes the category of 'context' as the crucial source for the construction of meaning, but this solution has its own difficulties.

The scope of the 'context' that they mobilize in analysis is necessarily a closed frame, not an open-ended plenitude of meanings connecting unpredictability with other meanings and texts. For the authors of *EWB*, once the context of a text is understood, there is nothing terribly difficult about a Sanskrit compound or a hidden cultural text which might require specialized knowledge to identify. Thus if one were to read the song of Gibreel in Rushdie's *The Satanic Verses*[8] through *EWB*, its effect within the context is all that would really matter to the reader. The fact that beneath the song is an entire text of Bombay Cinema which, to the bilingual reader, would recall, more specifically, Raj Kapoor's *Shree 420* (1955) is knowledge that *EWB* must either ignore or relegate to the level of spurious or unnecessary footnote. This supplementarity, however, even in terms of *EWB*'s own design is counter-discursive in a radically different fashion. The supplement, the anecdotal invasion or culture-specific power, is, however, a form of intervention that questions, as supplements always do, the very adequacy of a theory of the centre and its periphery. At the very moment that the narrative is invaded by an intertext from a different centre – the centre and centrality of the Bombay commercial cinema, India's pre-eminent contemporary cultural form – the focus shifts from a fixed centre and its satellite system to a multiplicity of centres in the culture itself.

There is an intractable problem here for the syncretic enterprise of *EWB*. Actually to explore every 'pre-english' literature is clearly beyond its scope, but their mere existence, acknowledged or otherwise, makes the unitary post-colonial itself extremely problematic. Should one, therefore, acknowledge the impossibility of a comprehensive post-colonial literary theory without encroaching upon a multiplicity of other theories and disciplines? Can the post-colonial be anything other than a celebration of a specious unity rather than a critique? The political danger here is not that post-colonial literary theory might become post-oriental without orientalism's philosophical strengths; rather it might become not unlike the project of the raj historians of the 1960s who were totally bereft of any culture-specific know-how and effectively lost the chance to develop the study of Indian culture in universities.

With these other forms of knowledge ruled out as unnecessary because they are too difficult, a comprehensive theory of an uncanonized genre such as the novel is all that one needs to interpret post-colonial literature. Beneath the strategies of *EWB* is the dialogism of Bakhtin; and beneath post-colonial literature lies the might of the novel form. Absence of cultural specificity leads to cultural collapse, and cultural collapse takes us to the modern genre *par excellence*, the novel. The European bourgeois novel comes with a pre-existent philosophical apparatus that implicitly questions the representation of history to the extent that any counter-historical move must begin with a reading of the capacities of the novelistic genre itself. The extreme extension of this theory is that the post-colonial as a duplication of Bakhtin's essentially polyphonic reading of the novel form makes the post-colonial redundant. It is important that we meet this hypothesis half-way, accept that a European epic narrative mediated through the European bourgeois novel was an available discourse to the post-colonial writer, and then fill out the other half of the equation with those very precise, historically and culturally specific distinctions that mark off post-colonial difference without constructing, in turn, a post-colonial homogeneity that cancels out its own oppositions and fractures.

Those writers who use forms of 'appropriation' recognize that colonial discourse itself is a complex, contradictory mode of representation which implicates both the colonizer and the colonized. Nowhere is this more evident than in V. S. Naipaul, who is so very conscious of writing from within the shadow of an English master like Conrad, whose personal contact with England as a Polish émigré he finds echoes his own journey back to the centre. Years before, Romesh Dutt had translated sections from the *Ramayana* and *Mahabharata* in octametric lines. It is therefore not totally true that the post-colonial precursor discourse, the colonial, existed only in the hands of the colonizer. The Aboriginal writer Mudrooroo Narogin Noongah certainly recognizes the paradox of his writing in the language of the master, for the master, in novels and criticism that nevertheless insist upon the category of 'Aboriginality' as a defining feature of the Aboriginal postcolonial.[9]

Into this colonial discourse, into a discourse which has been identificatory, constructing the colonized as a fixed reality, the post-colonial makes its dramatic entry. But the post-colonial is nevertheless lumbered by the discourse of the colonized and is inexorably fissured. And it is not only fissured. It has also a political agenda that requires it to deconstruct an 'alien' subjectivity (a subjectivity growing out of a Hegelian master–slave relationship) but still hold on to the dominant genre through which it had been initially constituted, realism, that leads to the crossing over of post-colonialism into postmodernism.

The Postmodern Connection

Linda Hutcheon, whose reading of postmodernism as parody has been taken up by so many post-colonial writers, gets her own discussion of the two (postmodernism and post-colonialism) under way by emphasizing their distinct political agendas. Implicit in the diverging political agendas is the question of the definition of the *subject*. If for postmodernism the object of analysis is the subject as defined by humanism, with its essentialism and mistaken historical verities, its unities and transcendental presence, then for post-colonialism the object is the imperialist subject, the colonized as formed by the processes of imperialism. Hutcheon's warning is salutary and should be quoted in full:

> The current post-structuralist/postmodern challenges to the coherent, autonomous subject have to be put on hold in feminist and post-colonial discourses, for both must work first to assert and affirm a denied or alienated subjectivity: those radical postmodern challenges are in many ways the luxury of the dominant order which can afford to challenge that which it securely possesses.[10]

In spite of Linda Hutcheon's warning – one which she herself later in the same essay seems to forget in proclaiming the ambiguous post-colonialism of Canadian culture – the project of *EWB* is essentially postmodern. Admittedly, there is a whole section in *EWB* where postmodernism is treated agonistically, and earlier Tiffin[11] had subtly accused postmodernism of hegemonic tendencies driven by a European desire to dominate the field of post-colonialism as well, but *EWB*'s version of post-colonialism, it seems to us, cannot, as a unified field, function without it. The central problematic arises out of the status of settler cultures, and their place in this unified field.

The 'justifying' discourse which allows this settler incorporation into post-colonialism is clearly postmodernism. In someone as astute as Stephen Slemon[12] the strategies of modernism/postmodernism arise out of a European assimilation of the heterogeneous colonial Other into its own social and discursive practices. It is this reading of post-colonialism as already present in European thought, as well as, by extension, in colonial culture, which allows Slemon to shift gear and move into Canadian settler culture forthwith. He speaks of Canada and the other White dominions as second world societies in which the post-colonial is an anti-colonial discourse, a kind of counter-discursive energy. Through this counter-discursivity the settler colony acquires a political agenda which demonstrates its reaction against an imperial homogenizing tendency. How this happens, in Slemon's subtle argument, is clearly based upon a 'complicity' theory of post-colonialism. Though Slemon does not make it explicit, in the complicity theory, the literature of settler colonies, which did not have to go through a prolonged independence struggle, still has post-colonial tendencies embedded within it. In the age of the postmodern, the settler colonies' counter-discursive energy can now speak with greater assurance.

Like the authors of *EWB*, Slemon is at pains to avoid the collapse of the post-colonial and the postmodern. He must therefore insist upon the political strategy of post-colonialism, and argue that all post-colonial literatures demonstrate the recuperative work going on in marginalized societies. But it is salutary that the argument is developed not through, say Patrick White's *A Fringe of Leaves* but through Salman Rushdie's *Midnight's Children*. For postmodernism, Rushdie's questioning of historical certainties is exemplary of its own project; for the post-colonial what is important is the way in which another, lost master-narrative recalled through the creative power of *maya*, of illusion, is used to free the colonized. The narrative energy of Rushdie is to be found in the magical narratives of the *Mahabharata* and the *Kathasaritasagara*. Whereas a postmodern reading of *Midnight's Children* would emphasize play and deferral, a fully post-colonial reading will locate the meaning of the untranslated words and the special, culture-specific resonances of the text. It might even offer a radical reshaping or rethinking of what Habermas has called our 'communicative rationality'. The post-colonial text persuades us to think through logical categories which may be quite alien to our own. For a text to suggest even as much is to start the long overdue process of dismantling classical orientalism.

But the positions outlined above are not mutually exclusive. Pre-colonial Indian narratives too are all about deferral, and play; they are open-ended where meaning is constantly displaced.[13] That is, a post-colonial text in this case can draw on an indigenous precursor tradition that has some of the features of postmodernism. In Mammata's theory and poetics (which he borrowed from the *Dhvanyaloka* of Anandavardhana), *dhvani* theory is really a theory of the signifier where meaning is constantly deferred. *Dhvani* clearly stipulates that the referent is not available, only the suggested meanings are. Thus writes Mammata:

> This [the poem] is best when the suggested meaning far excels the expressed sense; it is called *dhvani* by the learned.[14]

Rushdie's *The Satanic Verses* is a case in point, since it has been (and can be) defended on aesthetic/postmodern grounds. Thus for John McLaren[15] *The Satanic Verses* offers the possibilities of alternative histories to the reader, since Rushdie cannot accept any history as fixed, especially through the *ipsissima verba*, God's exact words. Similarly Helen Watson-Williams[16] bypasses the political arguments completely by a universalist move: the text explores 'truth' and may be explained rationally. Fantasy is simply a metaphor which can be reduced to its realist origins. As it becomes clear in Amin Malak's[17] reading, *The Satanic Verses* is defensible on postmodern grounds, where everything is subjected to subversive parody, but this kind of reading is highly dangerous politically. And here is the crux of the matter. The moment the dominant culture itself begins to draw generic lines (fiction, history; politics and postmodern play), the text gets transformed into distinct objects, with distinct effects and meanings. In political terms *The Satanic Verses* ceases to be post-colonial and becomes postmodern. Srinivas Aravamudan's[18] suggestive essay shows how *The Satanic Verses* can be both postmodern and post-colonial at the same time. In it, pastiche, parody and history as unstable discourse, in short all the root-metaphors of postmodernism, are juxtaposed alongside culture-specific knowledges (the '420' reference requires no research for the Indian reader), the privileged position of the native reader, the absence of orientalist glossary and those obvious stylistic nuances which mark the text's post-coloniality.

By seeming to transform the post-colonial into an object of knowledge that might be critiqued through a postmodern/novelistic critical discourse, what *EWB* has done is to remove the post-colonial as a radical political act of self-legitimation and self-respect locked into practices which antedate the arrival of the colonizer, and bracket it with postmodern practices generally. It is not surprising, therefore, that the trope of metonymy becomes so decisive for the authors of *EWB*. Since metonymy bypasses the laws of censorship (Lacan called it the trope of the Unconscious), it enables the return of the repressed, the articulation of that which has become taboo in a colonized world. Thus in an example taken from Nkosi it is the power of the book, the pen, which is advanced: since writing is power, the pen, metonymically, is the displaced colonial phallus seeking a fulfilment of desire in its relationship with the absent Other. Occasionally, as in Chapter 3, where Nkosi is examined at some length, the political argument comes across decisively: 'only by denying the authenticity of the line [the apartheid line] and taking control of the means of communication can the post-colonial text overcome this silence' (p. 87).

Forms of Post-Colonialism

What emerges, especially past Chapter 4 of *EWB*, is the fact that we are really talking about not one 'post-colonialism' but many postcolonialisms. When we drop the hyphen, and effectively use 'postcolonialism' as an always present tendency in any literature of subjugation marked by a systematic process of cultural domination through the imposition of imperial structures of power, we can begin to see those aspects of the argument of *EWB* which could be profitably extended. This form of 'postcolonialism' is not 'post-' something or other but is already implicit in the discourses of colonialism themselves. We would then want to distinguish sharply between two kinds of postcolonialism, viewed as ideological orientations rather than as a historical stage. The first, and more readily recognizable, is what we call oppositional postcolonialism, which is found in its most overt form in post-independent colonies at the historical phase of 'post-colonialism' (with a hyphen). This usage corresponds to the *OED*'s definition of the 'post-colonial'. The second form, equally a product of the processes that constituted colonialism but with a different inflection, is a 'complicit postcolonialism', which has much in common with Lyotard's unhyphenated postmodernism: an always present 'underside' within colonization itself.[19] Thus Charles Harpur, Marcus Clarke, Christopher Brennan as well as V. S. Naipaul and Bibhutibhushan Banerji are postcolonial in this sense.

It would follow, therefore, that other theories such as feminism which are also predicated upon some definition of oppression would find points of contact with postcolonialism. Significant terms used by the authors of *EWB* such as 'other', 'subversion', 'marginalized' and 'linguistic difference' are all replicated in feminist discourses. But the analogy also gives rise to a problem within postcolonial women's writing which would require a different order of theorizing, since postcolonial women are like a fragment, an oppositional system, within an overall colonized framework. Women therefore function here as burdened by a twice-disabling discourse: the disabling master discourse of colonialism is then redirected against women in an exact duplication of the colonizer's own use of that discourse *vis-à-vis* the colonized in the first instance.

One finds a reaction against this twice-disabling discourse even in the context of someone who writes, essentially, within the *riti* ('love') and *bhakti* ('devotional') poetics of India.[20] In Mahadevi Varma's *chhayavad* poetry the metaphysical domains of both *riti* and *bhakti* are replaced by a search for an ennobling humanism, the discriminatory desire of a woman herself as she seeks fulfilment in love. Into the hegemonic world of traditional Sanskrit genres and discourses, Mahadevi Varma inserts the female body, its sensations and its self-identity as woman. In the 1920s and 1930s Mahadevi Varma, as a woman, was grasping the nettle of a poetics which had produced the great patriarchal figures of Nanak and Tulsidasa.

The homogenizing drive of *EWB* leads it to seek to establish a dominant field and not a set of heterogeneous 'moments' arising from very different historical processes. As we have said, it is especially important to recognize the different histories of the White settler colonies which, as fragments of the metropolitan centre, were treated very differently by Britain, which, in turn, for these settler colonies, was not the imperial centre but the Mother Country. What an undifferentiated concept of postcolonialism overlooks are the very radical differences in response and the unbridgeable chasms that existed between White and non-White colonies.

A difficult category which is in need of theorizing is, of course, *race*. The decisive role that race has played in all forms of colonial society over the past 500 years (and perhaps even before that) cannot be overestimated. At the same time since racial categories interweave with social classes at every point, they become much more complex in their uses and effects. There is certainly no essentialist meaning of race itself. It is what one does with the category and, more importantly, how it impinges upon power relations in the colonial/post-colonial world that is of concern to the cultural theorist. It is here that the concept itself, in a non-essential fashion, nevertheless needs a level of specificity which would identify its function as a category of analysis. Race is not part of an unproblematic continuum alongside discursive categories such as linguistic rupture, syncreticism, hybridity and so on. In all kinds of oppositional postcolonialism (within settler countries themselves and without) race was part of a larger struggle for self-respect. The post-colonial is the single most important phenomenon in which it played such a decisive role.

These difficulties disrupt the smooth and seamless surface of *EWB*'s definition of the 'post-colonial':

> We use the term 'post-colonial', however, to cover all the culture affected by the imperial process from the moment of colonization to the present day. This is because there is a continuity of preoccupations throughout the historical process initiated by European imperial aggression. (p. 2)

What is this 'continuity of preoccupations'? Is it purely aesthetic? What is the material basis of this aesthetic? How is the 'post-colonial experience' reconstructed? How does it become 'rich' and 'incisive' (p. 91) if we can't relativize this image of discursive wealth through some understanding of social conditions? The annual per capita income of an Indian, for instance, is around $150, that of an African is around $300. In the West Indies it is probably not much more. And social security is non-existent. An average Australian worker (though not an unemployed Aborigine) earns above these levels in a week. Perhaps it is only in the Indian diaspora of Britain, the US and Canada that the 'historical process initiated by European imperialist aggression' can be placed upon a uniform material footing. Without an adequate materialist theory of postcolonialism, *EWB*'s theory of 'post-coloniality' is a general hypothesis applicable to any text which dismantles power relations existing in an 'anterior' text. The problematic, extended and reformulated, finds centre and periphery in social structures as diverse as race, class, women's rights and so on.

In practice, therefore, for the authors of *EWB*, the postcolonial is a hermeneutic which is vindicated by the conditions in non-settler colonies, but is then used unchanged to apply to settler colonies, thus making strategic moves of these settler colonies towards greater political and economic autonomy within a capitalist world economy appear as heroic and revolutionary ruptures. 'The Empire strikes back' indeed, under the cover yet again of its loyal White colonies. From the base of this elision, the construction of meaning in these non-settler colonies takes up a highly postmodern resonance. Meaning resides in the 'slippage' of language; meaning is constantly deferred; meaning grows out of a dialectical process of a relationship between the margins and the centre (meaning arises out of a discourse of marginality); meanings are not culture-specific and in postcolonial texts are constructed metonymically, not metaphorically. Since metonymy defers meaning, it is repetitive, and returns to haunt us in a replay of a version of the Gothic. Not surprisingly, then, the postcolonial text is 'always a complex and hybridized formation' (p. 10).

The more we probe statements such as these, the more conscious we become of a model for the construction of meaning which advances metonymy over metaphor, hybridity over purity, syncretism over difference, pluralism over essentialism or pan-textualism, and diglossia over monoglossia. The paradigmatic postcolonial text is the West Indian novel which is elevated, implicitly, to the position of pre-eminence: all postcolonial literatures aspire to the condition of the West Indian, and the achievements of West Indian writers are read back into the settler traditions. But the West Indian paradigm is just not applicable to a country like Australia for instance, either historically or linguistically. Australian English is an almost exact duplication of Received Standard English and Australian colloquialisms (its most obvious anti-language) follow exactly the rules by which the language of the British underground comes into being. That crucial fracturing of the deep structure of a language found in non-settler 'englishes' just does not occur in Australia, a country which, historically, has always seen itself as part of the Empire, ever ready to follow, uncritically, in the footsteps of the Mother Country. Gallipoli, the Australian colonization of the Pacific, the White Australia Policy, Prime Minister Menzies' recitation of love-poetry for the departing Queen Elizabeth in 1953, may be explained simply in terms of a country which saw itself as an integral part of the White British Empire. The settler colonies provided the manpower, the support systems for colonialism to flourish.

At the heart of the oppositional post-colonial are three fundamental principles – principles which are as much points of difference between White settler colonies and the rest – which may be summarized as (a) racism, (b) a second language, (c) political struggle. For the category of the post-colonial to work in any other fashion it must become a 'complicit post-colonialism' and therefore effectively postmodern. It is the uneasy manner in which these three principles may be discussed with reference to the settler colonies which, to our mind, explains the pan-textualist bias within an otherwise mutually exclusive pluralist enterprise. Thus where subversion, for instance, is emphasized, this is done in largely non-political and non-racial terms. In short, subversion becomes a kind of an anti-language (the authors call it an inter-language) which largely defines the postcolonial experience. What is worrying is that the category of subversion applies without change to literary tendencies within the canon itself (Donne, Sterne, Mary Shelley, etc.) rather than specifying those material conditions which give rise to post-colonial difference.

All uncritical adulation of pluralism, which leads, finally, to post-colonialism becoming the liberal Australian version of multiculturalism, then produces concepts such as 'hybridity' and 'syncretism' as the theoretical 'dominants' of post-colonial society. In doing so the authors then implicitly argue that the post-colonial rejects a monocentric view of human experience: assimilation (monocentrism) is out, hybridity (multiculturalism) is in. John Lennon sings 'Imagine all the people ...'. Theories of syncretism/hybridization are essentially pluralistic, as they maintain a pluralism which encourages freedom and independence. Their parallel, as we have said, is to be found in Australian multiculturalism, a utopian view of the world which is so very recent in origin and reflects as much global economic policies as any concerted effort on the part of Anglo-Celtic Australian society to change itself.

The emphasis on hybridization leads to an uneasiness with social and racial theories of post-colonial literature. Though Sanskrit theories are given an extended gloss, their interest for the authors of *EWB* lies, it seems to us, in their affirmation, finally, of an ahistorical aesthetic. Sanskrit theories of reception (*rasa*) and suggestiveness (*dhvani*) after all keep the primacy of the literary object intact. Sanskrit theories are still individual-oriented and easier for a pluralist to handle than theories of negritude (Aimé Césaire, Léopold Senghor, Fanon) or Aboriginality (Narogin). The authors of *EWB* tend to use the word 'essentialism' for any mode of criticism that claims indigineity and avoids pluralism without in fact conceding that pluralism itself might be yet another version of what Achebe called 'colonialist criticism' (p. 127).

Furthermore, a related question may now be posed. Does the postcolonial exist only in English? The emphasis on language and 'englishes' in *EWB* seems to say so. But why are Premchand, Bannerjee (of *Pather Panchali* fame) and Satyajit Ray, and Raj Kapoor and Guru Dutt (the last three film-makers) not postcolonial? And what about the writings of the Indian diaspora not written in English, such as the Mauritian Abhimanyu Anat's *Lal Pasina* ('Blood and Sweat')?

For the authors of *EWB* it is syncretism ('syncretism is the condition within which post-colonial societies operate' [p. 180]) and hybridity ('hybridity ... is the primary characteristic of all post-colonial texts' [p. 185]) which are the hallmarks of postcolonial writing. As a consequence post-colonial literatures are 'constituted in counter-discursive rather than homologous practices' (p. 196). In the process, as we have argued, the post-colonial has adopted almost every conceivable postmodern theory as well as a number of propositions which are absolutely central to the rise of the bourgeois novel in Europe.

What is Post(-)colonialism?

The work of Bill Ashcroft, Gareth Griffiths and Helen Tiffin is a timely contribution to the post-colonial debate. The strategic moves they adopt in their unenviable task for a comprehensive post-colonial theory have paved the way for our own critique. What follows is, we hope, an extension, albeit in a slightly different form, of their own intrinsically difficult project. Firstly, there is, we feel, a need to make a stronger distinction between the postcolonialism of settler and non-settler countries. But within each of these there is a need to see greater continuities between the colonial and the post-colonial. In some ways the postcolonial is really a splinter in the side of the colonial itself and the kinds of rebellion that we find in the postcolonial are not unlike the reactions of the child against the law of the father.[21] Because of the indeterminacy of the fused postcolonial (in which oppositional and complicit forms coexist), theorization about it inevitably pushes us towards postmodernism. If we catalogue the crucial features of postcolonialism as advanced by *EWB* – fracture, interlanguage, polyglossia, subversion, and so on – we find that we are drawn, via the defining qualities of postmodernism, to propose a counter-literary history functioning as the underside of the dominant literary history. The postcolonial (unhyphenated) is a ghost that stalks the parent literary history just as vernacular literatures of Europe in Rome's former colonies challenged Latin, and Hindi-Urdu literature challenged Sanskrit/Persian. From this point of view it is then possible to claim that the postcolonial as a category subsumes the postmodern.

As the memory of independence struggles recedes and global capitalism in its latest avatar dominates our lives, and Hastings's prophecy is no longer simply a future hope but a living if still partial reality, we believe that postcolonialism, in its unhyphenated variety, will become the dominant 'post-colonial' practice. Though it seems highly unlikely that the difference between settler and non-settler countries will cease to exist – they will in fact become more marked – it is, nevertheless, possible to construct a theory which predicts the inevitable triumph of various complicit forms of postcolonialism in all late post-colonial societies. In order to explore the ramifications of this claim we would need further research into the nature of colonialism itself and the ways in which the struggle towards self-determination found expression. In doing so we should be able to acknowledge the quite radical differences in the 'colonial' relationship between the imperial centre and the colonized in the various parts of the former empires. It appears that the experience of colonialization was more similar across all the White settler colonies than in the non-settler colonies. In the Indian subcontinent the colonial experience seems to have affected the cities only, in Africa it worked hand in hand with evangelical Christianity, in Southeast Asia the use of migrant labour – notably Chinese and Indian – mediated between the British and the Malays. In the West Indies slave labour, and later indentured Indian labour, again made the relationship less combative and more accommodating. To use a non-literary marker, cricket triumphed in the British settler countries, on the Indian subcontinent and in the West Indies but not in non-settler Africa, the Middle East or Southeast Asia. Smaller *récits* must replace the *grand récit* of postcolonialism in all these instances so that we can know the historical background better. In these smaller *récits* it may well be that the term 'postcolonial' is never used.

Beyond that, in the present late stage of world capitalism, the complicit postcolonial is on the way to becoming the literary dominant of 'postcolonialism'. In this situation it is important to recognize its complex relationship with postmodernism, neither collapsing the two categories nor positing an absolute distinction. The postmodern has made some features of the postcolonial visible or speakable for the colonizers, reassuringly strange and safely subversive, just as orientalism did in an earlier stage of colonial ideology. In return, postcolonialism draws attention to the occluded politics and forgotten precursors of postmodernism.

Postcolonialism, we have stressed, is not a homogeneous category either across all postcolonial societies or even within a single one. Rather it refers to a typical configuration which is always in the process of change, never consistent with itself. In settler countries like Australia, for instance, writers such as Harpur, Brennan, Richardson and Patrick White can be read as aspirants to the canon, extending but not challenging the standards of the imperial centre. But even while this was going on, the indigenous peoples whom the settlers had silenced could not be ignored, and their ghosts began to invade the texts of the dominant tradition. The kind of parasitism found in the original settler literature *vis-à-vis* the Mother Country is at first a prominent feature of the emerging writings of the Australian Aborigine, the New Zealand Maori and the Canadian Indian. Then a distinctive form of the postcolonial arises, as defiant as oppositional postcolonialism but without political independence or autonomy ever a realistic option. This symbiotic postcolonial formation has many of the same features as the more exciting postcolonialism of the non-settler countries as they establish their national identity. From here it begins to affect the form of writing of the settlers themselves, leading to a shift of balance within a type of the fused postcolonial.

In the age of the postmodern, then, there is a double trend towards the complicit postcolonial: an increasing alliance with the postmodern at the level of theory, and an increasing predominance in political life. The echoes of guilty partnership in an illicit affair are set off by the word 'complicit', and these overtones hold back the difficult task of defining the 'new' postcolonialism which would take us beyond the oppositional postcolonialism of non-settler colonies that pivots around the moment of independence. It must be possible to acknowledge difference and insist on a strongly theorized oppositional postcolonialism as crucial to the debate, without claiming that this form is or has been everywhere the same wherever a colonizer's feet have trod. We can trace the creative process of cultural syncretism and its collapse of distinctions without having to overlook the contradictions and oppositions which still survive, and without disavowing the sometimes violent nature of colonial struggles in non-settler countries before and after independence. It is precisely if we acknowledge the pervasiveness but not universality of complicit forms of the postcolonial that we can trace the connections that go back to the settler experience and beyond, and forward to the new postcolonialism. Theory must be flexible and prudent enough to say: the post-colonial is dead; long live postcolonialism.

Notes

1. Bill Ashcroft, Gareth Griffiths and Helen Tiffin, *The Empire Writes Back: Theory and practice in post-colonial literatures*, Routledge: London, 1989. All quotations from this text are cited parenthetically.
2. Edward W. Said, 'Representing the colonized: anthropology's interlocutors', *Critical Inquiry*, 15, 2, Winter 1989, p. 209.
3. Salman Rushdie, 'The Empire writes back with a vengeance', *The Times*, 3 July 1980, p. 8.
4. Terry Eagleton, *The Ideology of the Aesthetic*, Basil Blackwell: Oxford, 1990, p. 381.
5. Frantz Fanon, *The Wretched of the Earth*, Penguin Books: Harmondsworth, 1961. See also Frantz Fanon, *Black Skin, White Masks*, Grove Press: New York, 1967.
6. Charles Wilkins (trans.), *The Bhagvat-Geeta or Dialogues of Kreeshna and Arjoon*, C. Nourse: London, 1785, p. 13.
7. James Clifford, *The Predicament of Culture: Twentieth-century ethnography, literature and art*, Harvard University: Cambridge, MA, 1988, p. 113.
8. Salman Rushdie, *The Satanic Verses*, Viking: London, 1988, p. 5.
9. Mudrooroo Narogin, *Writing from the Fringe: A study of modern Aboriginal literature*, Hyland House: Melbourne, 1990.
10. Linda Hutcheon, 'Circling the downspout of empire: post-colonialism and postmodernism', *Ariel*, 20, 4, October 1989, p. 151.
11. Helen Tiffin, 'Post-colonialism, post-modernism and the rehabilitation of post-colonial history', *Journal of Commonwealth Literature*, 23, 1, 1988, pp. 169–81.
12. Stephen Slemon, 'Modernism's last post', *Ariel*, 20, 4, October 1989, pp. 3–17.
13. Vijay Mishra, 'The centre cannot hold: Bailey, Indian culture and the sublime', *South Asia*, NS, 12, 1, June 1989, pp. 103–14.
14. Mammata, *Kavyaprakasha*, ed. Acharya Vishveshvar, Jñanamandala: Varanasi, 1960, IV, 39, 24, p. 91.
15. John McLaren, 'The power of the word: Salman Rushdie and *The Satanic Verses*', *Westerly*, 1, March 1990, pp. 61–5.
16. Helen Watson-Williams, 'Finding a father: a reading of Salman Rushdie's *The Satanic Verses*', *Westerly*, 1, March 1990, pp. 66–71.
17. Amin Malak, 'Reading the crisis: the polemics of Salman Rushdie's *The Satanic Verses*', *Ariel*, 20, 4, October 1989, pp. 175–86.
18. S. Aravamudan, 'Salman Rushdie's *The Satanic Verses*', *Diacritics*, 19, 2, Summer 1989, pp. 3–20.
19. See Jean-François Lyotard, *The Postmodern Condition*, Manchester University Press: Manchester, 1986.
20. See Karine Schomer, *Mahadevi Varma and the Chhayavad Age of Modern Hindi Poetry*, University of California Press: Berkeley, CA, 1983.
21. See Bob Hodge and Vijay Mishra, *The Dark Side of the Dream: Australian literature and the postcolonial mind*, Allen & Unwin: Sydney, 1991.

16 □ *The Angel of Progress: Pitfalls of the Term 'Post-colonialism'*

Anne McClintock

> His face is turned towards the past. . . . The angel would like
> to stay, awaken the dead, and make whole that which has
> been smashed. But a storm is blowing from Paradise; it has got
> caught in his wings with such violence that the angel can no
> longer close them. This storm irresistibly propels him into the
> future to which his back is turned, while the pile of debris
> before him grows skyward. This storm is what we call
> progress.
>
> Walter Benjamin

To enter the Hybrid State exhibit on Broadway, you enter The Passage. Instead of
a gallery, you find a dark antechamber, where one white word invites you forward:
COLONIALISM. To enter colonial space, you stoop through a low door, only to
be closeted in another black space – a curatorial reminder, however fleeting, of
Fanon: 'The native is a being hemmed in'.[1] But the way out of colonialism, it
seems, is forward. A second white word, POSTCOLONIALISM, invites you
through a slightly larger door into the next stage of history, after which you emerge,
fully erect, into the brightly lit and noisy HYBRID STATE.

I am fascinated less by the exhibit itself, than by the paradox between the idea
of history that shapes 'The Passage', and the quite different idea of history that
shapes the 'Hybrid State' exhibit itself. The exhibit celebrates 'parallel history':

> Parallel history points to the reality that there is no longer a mainstream view of
> American art culture, with several 'other', lesser important cultures surrounding it.
> Rather there exists a parallel history which is now changing our understanding of our
> transcultural understanding.[2]

From *Social Text*, Spring 1992, pp. 1–15.

Yet the exhibit's commitment to 'hybrid history' (multiple time) is contradicted by the linear logic of The Passage ('A Brief Route to Freedom'), which, as it turns out, rehearses one of the most tenacious tropes of colonialism. In colonial discourse, as in The Passage, space is time, and history is shaped around two, necessary movements: the 'progress' forward of humanity from slouching deprivation to erect, enlightened reason. The other movement presents the reverse: regression backwards from (white, male) adulthood to a primordial, black 'degeneracy' usually incarnated in women. The Passage rehearses this temporal logic: progress through the ascending doors, from primitive pre-history, bereft of language and light, through the epic stages of colonialism, post-colonialism and enlightened hybridity. Leaving the exhibit, history is traversed backwards. As in colonial discourse, the movement forward in space is backwards in time: from erect, verbal consciousness and hybrid freedom – signified by the (not very free) white rabbit called 'Free' which roams the exhibit – down through the historic stages of decreasing stature to the shambling, tongueless zone of the pre-colonial, from speech to silence, light to dark.

The paradox structuring the exhibit intrigues me, as it is a paradox, I suggest, that shapes the term 'post-colonialism'. I am doubly interested in the term, since the almost ritualistic ubiquity of 'post-' words in current culture (post-colonialism, post-modernism, post-structuralism, post-cold war, post-marxism, post-apartheid, post-Soviet, post-Ford, post-feminism, post-national, post-historic, even post-contemporary) signals, I believe, a widespread, epochal crisis in the idea of linear, historical 'progress'.

In 1855, the year of the first imperial Paris Exposition, Victor Hugo announced: 'Progress is the footsteps of God himself.' 'Post-colonial studies' has set itself against this imperial idea of linear time – the 'grand idea of Progress and Perfectability', as Baudelaire called it. Yet the *term* 'post-colonial', like the exhibit itself, is haunted by the very figure of linear 'development' that it sets out to dismantle. Metaphorically, the term 'post-colonialism' marks history as a series of stages along an epochal road from 'the pre-colonial', to 'the colonial', to 'the post-colonial' – an unbidden, if disavowed, commitment to linear time and the idea of 'development'. If a theoretical tendency to envisage 'Third World' literature as progressing from 'protest literature', to 'resistance literature', to 'national literature' has been criticized as rehearsing the Enlightenment trope of sequential, 'linear' progress, the term 'post-colonialism' is questionable for the same reason. Metaphorically poised on the border between old and new, end and beginning, the term heralds the end of a world era, but within the same trope of linear progress that animated that era.

If 'post-colonial' *theory* has sought to challenge the grand march of western historicism with its entourage of binaries (self–other, metropolis–colony, center–periphery, etc., the *term* 'post-colonialism' nonetheless re-orients the globe once more around a single, binary opposition: colonial/post-colonial. Moreover, theory is thereby shifted from the binary axis of *power* (colonizer/colonized – itself inadequately nuanced, as in the case of women) to the binary axis of *time*, an axis even less productive of political nuance since it does not distinguish between the beneficiaries of colonialism (the ex-colonizers) and the casualties of colonialism (the ex-colonized). The 'post-colonial scene' occurs in an entranced suspension of history, as if the definitive historical events have preceded us, and are not now in the making. If the theory promises a decentering of history in hybridity, syncreticism, multi-dimensional time, and so forth, the *singularity* of the term effects a re-centering of global history around the single rubric of European time. Colonialism returns at the moment of its disappearance.

The word 'post', moreover, reduces the cultures of peoples beyond colonialism to *prepositional* time. The term confers on colonialism the prestige of history proper; colonialism is the determining marker of history. Other cultures share only a chronological, prepositional relation to a Euro-centered epoch that is over (post-), or not yet begun (pre-). In other words, the world's multitudinous cultures are marked, not positively by what distinguishes them, but by a subordinate, retrospective relation to linear, European time.

The term also signals a reluctance to surrender the privilege of seeing the world in terms of a singular and ahistorical abstraction. Rifling through the recent flurry of articles and books on 'post-colonialism', I am struck by how seldom the term is used to denote *multiplicity*. The following proliferate: '*the* post-colonial condition', '*the* post-colonial scene', '*the* post-colonial intellectual', '*the* emerging disciplinary space of post-colonialism', 'post-coloniality', '*the* post-colonial situation', 'post-colonial space', '*the* practice of postcoloniality', 'post-colonial discourse', and that most tedious, generic hold-all: '*the* post-colonial Other'.

I am not convinced that one of the most important emerging areas of intellectual and political inquiry is best served by inscribing history as a single issue. Just as the singular category 'Woman' has been discredited as a bogus universal for feminism, incapable of distinguishing between the varied histories and imbalances in power among women, so the singular category 'post-colonial' may license too readily a panoptic tendency to view the globe within generic abstractions voided of political nuance. The arcing panorama of the horizon becomes thereby so expansive that international imbalances in power remain effectively blurred. Historically voided categories such as 'the other', 'the signifier', 'the signified', 'the subject', 'the phallus', 'the postcolonial', while having academic clout and professional marketability, run the risk of telescoping crucial geo-political distinctions into invisibility.

The authors of the recent book *The Empire Writes Back*, for example, defend the term 'post-colonial literature' on three grounds: it 'focuses on that relationship which has provided the most important creative and psychological impetus in the writing'; it expresses the 'rationale of the grouping in a common past' and it 'hints at the vision of a more liberated and positive future'.[3] Yet the inscription of history around a single 'continuity of preoccupations' and 'a common past' runs the risk of a fetishistic disavowal of crucial international distinctions that are barely understood and inadequately theorized. Moreover, the authors decided, idiosyncratically to say the least, that the term 'post-colonialism' should not be understood as everything that has happened *since* European colonialism, but rather everything that has happened from the very *beginning* of colonialism, which means turning back the clocks and unrolling the maps of 'post-colonialism' to 1492, and earlier.[4] Whereupon, at a stroke, Henry James and Charles Brockden Brown, to name only two on their list, are awakened from their tête-à-tête with time, and ushered into 'the post-colonial scene' alongside more regular members like Ngũgĩ wa Thiong'o and Salman Rushdie.

Most problematically, the historical rupture suggested by the preposition 'post-' belies both the continuities and discontinuities of power that have shaped the legacies of the formal European and British colonial empires (not to mention the Islamic, Japanese, Chinese, and other imperial powers). Political differences *between* cultures are thereby subordinated to their temporal distance *from* European colonialism. But 'post-colonialism' (like postmodernism) is unevenly developed globally. Argentina, formally independent of imperial Spain for over a century and a half, is not 'post-colonial' in the same way as Hong Kong (destined to be independent of Britain only in 1997). Nor is Brazil 'post-colonial' in the same way as Zimbabwe. Can most of the world's countries be said, in any meaningful or theoretically rigorous sense, to share a single 'common past', or a single common 'condition', called 'the post-colonial condition', or 'post-coloniality'? The histories of African colonization are certainly, in part, the histories of the collisions between European and Arab empires, and the myriad African lineage states and cultures. Can these countries now best be understood as shaped exclusively around the 'common' experience of European colonization? Indeed, many contemporary African, Latin American, Caribbean and Asian cultures, while profoundly effected by colonization, are not necessarily *primarily* preoccupied with their erstwhile contact with Europe.

On the other hand, the term 'post-colonialism' is, in many cases, prematurely celebratory. Ireland may, at a pinch, be 'post-colonial', but for the inhabitants of British-occupied Northern Ireland, not to mention the Palestinian inhabitants of the Israeli Occupied Territories and the West Bank, there may be nothing 'post' about colonialism at all. Is South Africa 'post-colonial'? East Timor? Australia? By what fiat of historical amnesia can the United States of America, in particular, qualify as 'post-colonial' – a term which can only be a monumental affront to the Native American peoples currently opposing the confetti triumphalism of 1992. One can also ask whether the emergence of Fortress Europe in 1992 may not signal the emergence of a new empire, as yet uncertain about the frontiers of its boundaries and global reach.

My misgivings, therefore, are not about the theoretical substance of 'post-colonial theory', much of which I greatly admire. Rather, I wish to question the orientation of the emerging discipline and its concomitant theories and curricula changes, around a singular, monolithic term, organized around a binary axis of time rather than power, and which, in its premature celebration of the pastness of colonialism, runs the risk of obscuring the continuities and discontinuities of colonial and imperial power. Nor do I want to banish the term to some chilly, verbal Gulag; there seems no reason why it should not be used judiciously in appropriate circumstances, in the context of other terms, if in a less grandiose and global role.

One might distinguish theoretically between a variety of forms of global domination. *Colonization* involves direct territorial appropriation of another geopolitical entity, combined with forthright exploitation of its resources and labor, and systematic interference in the capacity of the appropriated culture (itself not necessarily a homogeneous entity) to organize its dispensations of power. *Internal colonization* occurs where the dominant part of a country treats a group or region as it might a foreign colony. *Imperial colonization*, by extension, involves large-scale, territorial domination of the kind that gave late Victorian Britain and the European 'lords of humankind' control over 85% of the earth, and the USSR totalitarian rule over Hungary, Poland and Czechoslovakia in the twentieth century.

Colonization, however, may involve only one country. Currently, China keeps its colonial grip on Tibet's throat, as does Indonesia on East Timor, Israel on the Occupied Territories and the West Bank, and Britain on Northern Ireland. Since 1915, South Africa has kept its colonial boot on Namibia's soil, first by League of Nations mandate, and then later in defiance of a UN General Assembly Resolution and a 1971 World Court Order. Only in 1990, having stripped Namibia of most of its diamond resources, was South Africa content to hand back the economically empty shell to the Namibians. Israel remains in partial occupation of Lebanon and Syria, as does Turkey of Cyprus. None of these countries can, with justice, be called 'post-colonial'.

Different forms of colonization have, moreover, given rise to different forms of de-colonization. Where *deep settler colonization* prevailed, as in Algeria, Kenya, Zimbabwe and Vietnam, colonial powers clung on with particular brutality.[5] Decolonization itself, moreover, has been unevenly won. In Zimbabwe, after a seven-year civil war of such ferocity that at the height of the war 500 people were killed every month and 40% of the country's budget was spent on the military, the Lancaster House Agreement choreographed by Britain in 1979 ensured that one-third of Zimbabwe's arable land (12 million hectares) was to remain in white hands, a minute fraction of the population.[6] In other words, while Zimbabwe gained formal political independence in 1980 (holding the chair of the 103-nation Non-Aligned Movement from 1986–1989) it has, economically undergone only *partial decolonization*.

Break-away settler colonies can, moreover, be distinguished by their formal independence from the founding metropolitan country, along with continued control over the appropriated colony (thus displacing colonial control from the metropolis to the colony itself). The United States, South Africa, Australia, Canada and New Zealand remain, in my view, break-away settler colonies that have not undergone decolonization, nor, with the exception of South Africa, are they likely to in the near future.

Most importantly, orienting theory around the temporal axis colonial/post colonial makes it easier *not* to see, and therefore harder to theorize, the continuities in international imbalances in *imperial* power. Since the 1940s, the United States' imperialism-without-colonies has taken a number of distinct forms (military, political, economic and cultural), some concealed, some half-concealed. The power of US finance capital and huge multi-nationals to direct the flows of capital, commodities, armaments and media information around the world can have an impact as massive as any colonial regime. It is precisely the greater subtlety, innovation and variety of these forms of imperialism that makes the historical rupture implied by the term 'post-colonial' especially unwarranted.

'Post-colonial' Latin America has been invaded by the United States over a hundred times this century alone. Each time, the US has acted to install a dictatorship, prop up a puppet regime, or wreck a democracy. In the 1940s, when the climate for gunboat diplomacy chilled, United States' relations with Latin America were warmed by an economic imperial policy euphemistically dubbed 'Good Neighborliness', primarily designed to make Latin America a safer backyard for the US' virile agribusiness. The giant cold-storage ships of the United Fruit Company circled the world, taking bananas from poor agrarian countries dominated by monocultures and the marines to the tables of affluent US housewives.[7] And while Latin America hand-picked bananas for the United States, the United States hand-picked dictators for Latin America. In Chile, Allende's elected, socialist government was overthrown by a US-sponsored military coup. In Africa, more covert operations such as the CIA assassination of Patrice Lumumba in Zaire had consequences as far-reaching.

In the cold war climate of the 1980s, the US, still hampered by the Vietnam syndrome, fostered the more covert military policy of 'low intensity' conflicts (in El Salvador and the Philippines), spawning death squads and proxy armies (Unita in Angola, and the Contras in Nicaragua) and training and aiding totalitarian military regimes in anti-democratic, 'counter-insurgency' tactics (El Salvador, Honduras, South Africa, Israel, and so forth). In Nicaragua in February 1990 the 'vote of fear' of continuing, covert war with the US brought down the Sandinistas.

The US's recent fits of thuggery in Libya, Grenada and Panama, and most calamitously in Iraq, have every characteristic of a renewed military imperialism, and a renewed determination to revamp military hegemony in a world in which it is rapidly losing economic hegemony. The attacks on Libya, Grenada and Panama (where victory was assured) were practice runs for the new imperialism, testing both the USSR's will to protest, and the US public's willingness to throw off the Vietnam syndrome, permitting thereby a more blatant era of intervening in Third World affairs. At the same time, having helped stoke the first Gulf War, the US had no intention of letting a new boy on the block assert colonial dominance in the region.

For three years before the second Gulf War, the US arms trade had been suffering a slump. After what one military industrialist gloatingly called the Gulf War's 'giant commercial-in-the-sky', US arms sales have soared. Nonetheless, if the US had the political muscle to resuscitate a nearly defunct Security Council and strong-arm a consensus through the UN, and the military capacity to make short shrift of 150,000 Iraqi soldiers and an estimated 200,000 civilians in one month, it did not have the economic means to pay for the war. Saddled with its own vast debts, the US has been massively paid off in reimbursements (an estimated $50 billion) by Saudi Arabia, Kuwait, Japan and Germany, so that it now appears in fact to have profited from the war to the tune of $4–5 billion. At the same time, most of the estimated $20 billion necessary to restore Kuwait will go to western, largely US, companies. The war has thus made ever more likely a global security system based on military muscle, not political cooperation, policed by the US's high-tech, mercenary army (and perhaps NATO), moving rapidly around the world, paid for by Germany and Japan, and designed to prevent regional, Third World consensuses from emerging. Far from heralding the end of imperial intervention, the second Gulf War simply marks a new kind of interventionism. Not only is the term 'post-colonial' inadequate to theorize these dynamics, it actively obscures the continuities and discontinuities of US power around the globe.

While some countries may be 'post-colonial' with respect to their erstwhile European masters, they may not be 'post-colonial' with respect to their new colonizing neighbours. Both Mozambique and East Timor, for example, became 'post-colonial' at much the same time, when the Portuguese empire decamped in the mid-seventies, and both remain cautionary tales against the utopian promise and global sweep of the preposition 'post'. In East Timor, the beds of the Portuguese were scarcely cold before the Indonesians invaded, in an especially violent colonial occupation that has lasted nearly two decades. The colonial travail of the East Timoreans has gone largely unprotested by the UN – the familiar plight of countries whose pockets aren't deep, and whose voices don't carry.

In Mozambique, on the other hand, after three centuries of colonial drubbing, the Portuguese were ousted in 1975 by Frelimo, Mozambique's socialist independence movement. But across the border, white Rhodesians, resentful of Mozambique's independence and socialist promise, spawned the Mozambique National Resistance (MNR), a bandit army bent only on sowing ruin. After Zimbabwe itself became politically independent of Britain in 1980, the MNR has continued to be sponsored by South Africa. A decade of the MNR's killing-raids and South Africa's predations has subjected the country to a fatal blood-letting and displaced nearly two million people, in a war so catastrophic that Frelimo has been forced to renounce Marxism and consider shaking hands with the bandits. Now Mozambique is in every sense a country on its knees. What might have been a 'post-colonial' showpiece has instead become the killing-fields of Southern Africa.

Yet neither the term 'post-colonial' nor 'neo-colonial' is truly adequate to account for the MNR. Neo-colonialism is not simply a repeat performance of colonialism, nor is it a slightly more complicated, Hegelian merging of 'tradition' and 'colonialism' into some new, historic hybrid. In recent years, the MNR has become inextricably shaped around local inter-ethnic rivalries, distinct religious beliefs, and notions of time and causality (especially ancestral intervention) which cannot be reduced to a western schema of linear time. More complex terms and analyses, of alternative times, histories and causalities, are required to deal with complexities that cannot be served under the single rubric 'post-colonialism'.

Singular universals such as 'the post-colonial intellectual' obscure international disparities in cultural power, electronic technology and media information. The role of 'Africa' in 'post-colonial theory' is different from the role of 'post-colonial theory' in Africa. In 1987, UNESCO calculated that Africa was spending only 0.3% of the world's $207 billion allocated to scientific research and development.[8] In 1975 the entire continent had only 180 daily newspapers, compared with 1,900 for the US, out of a world total of 7,970. By 1984, the number of African dailies dropped to 150, then staggered back to 180 in 1987 (the same figure as in 1955). In 1980, the annual production of films in the continent was 70. In contrast, the production of long films in Asia was 2,300 in 1965, and 2,100 in 1987.[9] The film industry in India remains the largest in the world, while Africa's share of TV receivers, radio transmitters and electronic hardware is miniscule.

The term 'post-colonialism' is prematurely celebratory and obfuscatory in more ways than one. The term becomes especially unstable with respect to women. In a world where women do two-thirds of the world's work, earn 10% of the world's income, and own less than 1% of the world's property, the promise of 'post-colonialism' has been a history of hopes postponed. It has generally gone unremarked that the national bourgeoisies and kleptocracies that stepped into the shoes of 'post-colonial' 'progress', and industrial 'modernisation' have been overwhelmingly and violently male. No 'post-colonial' state anywhere has granted women and men equal access to the rights and resources of the nation-state. Not only have the needs of 'post-colonial nations' been largely identified with male conflicts, male aspirations and male interests, but the very representation of 'national' power rests on prior constructions of gender power. Thus even for Fanon, who at other moments knew better, both 'colonizer' and 'colonized' are unthinkingly male: 'The look that the native turns on the settler is a look of lust ... to sit at the settlers' table, to sleep in the settler's bed, with his wife, if possible. The colonized man is an envious man.'[10] Despite most anti-colonial nationalisms' investment in the rhetoric of popular unity, most have served more properly to institutionalize gender power. Marital laws, in particular, have served to ensure that for women citizenship in the nation-state is mediated by the marriage relation, so that a woman's *political* relation to the nation is submerged in, and subordinated to, her *social* relation to a man through marriage.

The global militarization of masculinity and the feminization of poverty have thus ensured that women and men do not live 'post-coloniality' in the same way, or share the same singular 'post-colonial condition'. In most countries, IMF and World Bank policy favoured cash-cropping and capital surplus in the systematic interests of men, and formed a predictable pattern where men were given the training, the international aid, the machinery, the loans and cash. In Africa, women farmers produce 65%–80% of all agricultural produce, yet do not own the land they work, and are consistently by-passed by aid programs and 'development' projects.

The blame for women's continuing plight cannot be laid only at the door of colonialism, or footnoted and forgotten as a passing 'neo-colonial' dilemma. The continuing weight of male economic self-interest and the varied undertows of patriarchal Christianity, Confucianism and Islamic fundamentalism continue to legitimize women's barred access to the corridors of political and economic power, their persistent educational disadvantage, the bad infinity of the domestic double day, unequal child care, gendered malnutrition, sexual violence, genital mutilation and domestic battery. The histories of these male policies, while deeply implicated in colonialism, are not reducible to colonialism, and cannot be understood without distinct theories of gender power.

Finally, bogus universals such as 'the post-colonial woman' or 'the post-colonial other' obscure relations not only between men and women, but among women. Relations between a French tourist and the Haitian woman who washes her bed linen are not the same as the relations between their husbands. Films like *Out Of Africa*, clothing chains like Banana Republic and perfumes like 'Safari' all peddle neo-colonial nostalgia for an era when European women in brisk white shirts and safari green supposedly found freedom in empire: running coffee plantations, killing lions and zipping about the colonial skies in airplanes – an entirely misbegotten commercialization of white women's 'liberation' that has not made it any easier for women of color to form alliances with white women anywhere, let alone parry criticisms by male nationalists already hostile to feminism.

How, then, does one account for the curious ubiquity of the preposition 'post' in contemporary intellectual life, not only in the universities, but in newspaper columns and on the lips of media moguls? In the case of 'post-colonialism', at least, part of the reason is its academic marketability. While admittedly another p-c word, 'post-colonialism' is arguably more palatable and less foreign-sounding to sceptical deans than 'Third World Studies'. It also has a less accusatory ring than 'Studies In Neo-colonialism', say, or 'Fighting Two Colonialisms'. It is more global, and less fuddy-duddy, than 'Commonwealth Studies'. The term borrows, moreover, on the dazzling marketing success of the term 'post-modernism'. As the organizing rubric of an emerging field of disciplinary studies and an archive of knowledge, the term 'post-colonialism' makes possible the marketing of a whole new generation of panels, articles, books and courses.

The enthusiasm for 'post-' words, however, ramifies beyond the corridors of the university. The recurrent, almost ritualistic incantation of the preposition 'post' is a symptom, I believe, of a global crisis in ideologies of the future, particularly the ideology of 'progress'.

The first seismic shift in the idea of 'progress' came with the abrupt shift in US Third World policy in the 1980s. Emboldened in the 1950s by its economic 'great leap forward' (space, again, is time), the US was empowered to insist globally that other countries could 'progress' only if they followed the US road to mass-consumption prosperity. W.W. Rostow's 'Non-Communist Manifesto' envisaged the so-called 'developing' nations as passing through similar stages of development, out of tradition-bound poverty, through an industrialized modernization overseen by the US, the World Bank and the IMF, to mass-consumer prosperity. Nonetheless, except for the Japanese 'miracle' and the Four Tigers (Taiwan, Singapore, Hong Kong and South Korea), the vast majority of the world's populations have, since the 1940s, come to lag even further behind the consumer standards set by the west.[11]

Then, between 1979 (the second oil shock) and 1982 (the Mexican default), the world economy began to creak. Increasingly, it became clear that the US was no longer destined to be the only economic power of the future. Hobbled by its phenomenal debts, and increasingly diminished by the twin shadows of Japan and Germany, the US summarily abandoned the doctrine of global 'progress' and 'development'. During the Reagan era, the US instituted instead a bullying debt-servicing policy towards poorer countries, bolstered by aggressive competition with them on the market, and defended by sporadic fits of military gangsterism, as in Grenada and Panama. The cataclysmic war in the Gulf served only to underscore the point.

For many poorer countries, the shift in US policy meant abandoning overnight the fata morgana of capitalist 'progress', and settling for chronically stricken positions in the global hierarchy. Henceforth, they could aspire only to tighten their belts, service their debts, and maintain some credit. In 1974, Africa's debt–service ratio was a manageable 4.6%. Thirteen years later it had rocketed to 25%.[12] But the collapse of the US model of 'progress' has also meant the collapse, for many regimes, of the legitimacy of their national policies, in the panicky context of world-wide economic crisis, ecological calamity and spiralling popular desperation. Indeed, perhaps one reason, at least, for the burgeoning, populist appeal of Islamic fundamentalism is the failure of other models of capitalist or communist 'progress'. As a senior Libyan aide, Major Abdel-Salam Jalloud, has said of the destiny of the FIS in Algeria: 'It's impossible to turn back. The FIS has an appointment with history; it will not miss it.'[13]

A monotonously simple pattern has emerged. Despite the hauling down of colonial flags in the 1950s, revamped economic imperialism has ensured that America and the former European colonial powers have become richer, while, with a tiny scattering of exceptions, their ex-colonies have become poorer.[14] In Africa before decolonization, World Bank projects were consistently supportive of the colonial economies. Since formal decolonization, contrary to the World Bank's vaunted technical 'neutrality' and myth of expertise, projects have aggressively favoured the refinement and streamlining of surplus extraction, cash crop exports, and large-scale projects going to the highest bidders, fostering thereby cartels and foreign operators, and ensuring that profits tumble into the coffers of the multi-nationals. During 1986, Africa lost $19 billion through collapsed export prices alone.[15] In 1988 and 1989, debt service payments from the Third World to the US were $100 billion.[16] At the same time, as Fanon predicted, Third World kleptocracies, military oligarchies and warlords have scrambled over each other to plunder the system. To protect these interests, the tiny, male elites of 'developing' countries have spent almost 2.4 trillion on the military between 1960 and 1987, almost twice the size of the entire Third World debt.[17] Now, after the 1980s' 'desperate decade' of debt, drought and destabilization, the majority of Third World countries are poorer than they were a decade ago.[18] Twenty-eight million Africans face famine, and in countries like Mozambique, Ethiopia, Zaire and the Sudan the economies have simply collapsed.

The US's 'development' myth has had a grievous impact on global ecologies. By 1989, the World Bank had $225 billion in commitments to poorer countries, on condition that they, in turn, endure the purgatory of 'structural adjustment', export their way to 'progress', cut government spending on education and social services (with the axe falling most cruelly on women), devalue their currencies, remove trade barriers and raze their forests to pay their debts.[19] Under the financial spell of the US (and now Japan), and in the name of the fairy-tale of unlimited technological and capital 'growth', the World Bank engineered one ecological disaster after another: the Indonesian Transmigrasi programme, the Amazonian Grande Carajas iron-ore and strip-mining project, and Tucurui Dam deforestation project, and so on. The Polonordeste scheme in Brazil carved a paved highway through Amazonia, luring timber, mining and cattle ranching interests into the region with such calamitous impact that in May 1987 even the President of the World Bank, Mr Barber Conable, confessed he found the devastation 'sobering'.[20]

The Four 'miracle' Tigers have paid for progress with landscapes pitted with poisoned water, toxic soil, denuded mountains and dead coral seas. In 'miracle' Taiwan, an estimated 20% of the country's farmland is polluted by industrial waste, and 30% of the rice crops contain unsafe levels of heavy metals, mercury and cadmium.[21] A World Bank report in 1989 concluded gloomily that 'adjustment programs' carry the by-product that 'people below the poverty line will probably suffer irreparable damage in health, nutrition and education'.[22] Now Japan, insatiably hungry for timber and raw resources, is the major foreign aid donor, to the tune of $10 billion. In short, the World Bank and IMF 'road to progress' has proven a short road to what Susan George has called 'a fate worse than debt'.

To compound matters, the collapse of the US myth of 'progress' was swiftly followed by the collapse of the Soviet Union, which dragged down with it an entire master narrative of communist 'progress'. The zig-zag of Hegelian-Marxist 'progress', managed by a bureaucratic, command economy, had been destined to arrive ineluctably at its own utopian destination. The toppling of the Soviet Empire has meant, for many, the loss of a certain privileged relation to history as the epic unfolding of linear, if spasmodic, progress, and with it the promise that the bureaucratic, communist economy could one day outstrip the US in providing consumer abundance for all. As a result, there has also been some loss of political certitude in the inevitable role of the male (and, as it turns out, white) industrial working class as the privileged agent of history. If the bureaucracy of the Soviet Union fell, it was not under the weight of popular, industrial mobilization, but rather under the double weight of its economic corruption and manic military spending. The irony is not lost that the ascendant economies of Japan and Germany were historically denied the unsupportable burden of the arms race. Thus, despite the fact that men are slaughtering each other around the globe with increased dedication, there has been a certain loss of faith in masculine militarism as the inevitable guarantee of historical 'progress'. For the first time in history, moreover, the idea of industrial 'progress' impelled by technocratic 'development' is meeting the limits of the world's natural resources.

Ironically, the last zone on earth to embrace the ideology of capitalist 'development' may be the one now controlled by Mr Yeltsin and his allies. The world has watched awestruck as Yeltsin and his fellow-travellers swerved dizzyingly off the iron road of the centralized, communist, command economy, and lurched bumpily onto the capitalist road of decentralization, powered no longer by the dialectic as the motor and guarantee of 'progress', but by tear-away competition and mad marketeering. Never mind that this swerve is likely to unleash a disaster on a scale comparable to the famines that followed the original Bolshevik revolution, nor that the rough beast that slouches out of the chaos may, indeed, not be western capitalism at all, but a particularly grisly form of fascism.

For both communism and capitalism, 'progress' was both a journey forward and the beginning of a return; for as in all narratives of 'progress', to travel the 'road of progress' was to cover, once again, a road already travelled. The metaphor of the 'road' or 'railway' guaranteed that 'progress' was a fait accompli. The journey was possible because the road had already been made (by God, the Dialectic, the Weltgeist, the Cunning of History, the Law of the Market, Scientific Materialism). As Hegel decreed, 'progress' in the realm of history was possible because it has already been accomplished in the realm of 'truth'. But now, if the owl of Minerva has taken flight, there is widespread uncertainty whether it will return.

The collapse of both capitalist and communist teleologies of 'progress' has resulted in a doubled and overdetermined crisis in images of future time. The uncertain global situation has spawned a widespread sense of historic abandonment, of which the apocalyptic, time-stopped prevalence of 'post-' words is only one symptom. The storm of 'progress' had blown for both communism and capitalism alike. Now the wind is stilled, and the angel with hunched wings broods over the wreckage at its feet. In this calm at 'the end of history', the millennium has come too soon, and the air seems thick with omen.

Francis Fukuyama has declared history dead. Capitalism, he claims, has won the grand agon with communism, and is now 'post-historic'. Third World countries lag behind in the zone of the 'historic', where matters are decided by force.[23] Far from the 'end of history' and the triumph of US consumer capitalism, however, the new order of the day is most likely to be multi-polar competition between the four currently decisive regions of the world: Japan, the United States, Fortress Europe and the Middle East. The arms trade will continue, as the military-industrial wizards of Armageddon turn their attention from cold war scenarios to multiple, dispersed wars of attrition, fought by the US mercenary army and other proxies, and paid for by Japan and Germany. Within the US, with the vanishing of international communism as a rationale for militarism, new enemies will be found: the drug war, international 'terrorism', Japan, feminists, the PC hordes and 'tenured radicals', lesbians and gays, and any number of international 'ethnic' targets.

For this reason, there is some urgency in the need for innovative theories of history and popular memory, particularly mass-media memory. Asking what *single* term might adequately replace 'post-colonialism', for example, begs the question of rethinking the global situation as a *multiplicity* of powers and histories, which cannot be marshalled obediently under the flag of a single theoretical term, be that feminism, marxism or post-colonalism. Nor does intervening in history mean lifting, again, the mantle of 'progress' or the quill-pen of empiricism. 'For the native', as Fanon said, 'objectivity is always against him.' Rather, a *proliferation* of historically nuanced theories and strategies is called for, which may enable us to engage more effectively in the politics of affiliation, and the currently calamitous dispensations of power. Without a renewed will to intervene in the unacceptable, we face being becalmed in an historically empty space in which our sole direction is found by gazing back, spellbound, at the epoch behind us, in a perpetual present marked only as 'post'.

Notes

1. Frantz Fanon, *The Wretched of the Earth*, Penguin: London, 1963, p. 29.
2. Gallery Brochure, 'The Hybrid State Exhibit', Exit Art, 578 Broadway, New York (2 Nov.–14 Dec. 1991).
3. Bill Ashcroft, Gareth Griffiths and Helen Tiffin, *The Empire Writes Back: Theory and practice in post-colonial literatures*, Routledge: London, 1989, p. 24.
4. 'We use the term "post-colonial", however, to cover all the culture affected by the imperial process from the moment of colonization to the present day.' *ibid.*, p. 2.
5. During the Algerian war of resistance, over a million Algerians died out of a total of about 9 million.
6. Andrew Meldrum, *The Guardian*, Thursday, 25 April 1991, p. 13.
7. Cynthia Enloe, *Bananas, Beaches and Bases: Making feminist sense of international politics*, University of Colorado Press: Berkeley, CA, 1989, ch. 6.
8. Davidson, *op. cit.*, p. 670.
9. Kinfe Abraham, 'The media crisis: Africa's exclusion zone', *SAPEM*, September 1990, pp. 47–9.
10. Fanon, *op. cit.*, p. 30.
11. See Giovanni Arrighi, 'World income inequalities and the future of socialism', *New Left Review*, 189, September/October 1991, p. 40.
12. Davidson, *op. cit.*, p. 669.
13. *The Guardian*, Tuesday, 14 January 1992, p. 9.
14. The international monetary system set up at the Bretton Woods Conference in 1944 excluded Africa (still colonized) and most of what is now called the Third World, and was designed to achieve two explicit objectives: the reconstruction of Europe after World War II, and the expansion and maintenance (especially after decolonization) of international trade in the interests of the colonial powers and America. The president of the World Bank and the deputy managing director are always American, while by tradition the managing director is European. See Cheryl Payer, *The Debt Trap: The International Monetary Fund and the Third World*, Monthly Review Press: New York, 1974, and *idem*, *The World Bank: A critical analysis*, Monthly Review Press: New York, 1982.
15. Davidson, *op. cit.*, p. 669.

16. Robin Broad, John Cavanagh and Walden Bello, 'Sustainable development in the 1990s', in Chester Hartman and Pedro Vilanova (eds.), *Paradigms Lost: The post cold war era*.

17. *ibid.*, p. 100. Calculations are based on figures in Ruth Leger Sivard, *World Military and Social Expenditures 1989*, World Priorities: Washington, DC, 1989, p. 6. A few African socialist states, like Angola and Mozambique, tried to dodge the IMF and WB's blandishments, until national economic mismanagement and South Africa's regional maulings forced them to bend the knee.

18. The World Bank has concluded that 'fifteen African countries were worse off in a number of economic categories after structural adjustment programs. ... A World Bank study found that the debt-ridden developing countries under structural adjustment programs performed as well as non-recipients less than half the time.' Broad *et al.*, *op. cit.*, p. 96.

19. See Susan George, 'Managing the global house: redefining economics', in Jeremy Legget (ed.), *Global Warming: The Greenpeace report*, Oxford University Press: Oxford and New York, 1990.

20. G. Hancock, *The Lords of Poverty*, Macmillan: London, 1989, p. 131, n. 14, citing Barber Conable's speech to the World Resources Institute, Washington, DC, 5 May 1987.

21. Broad *et al.*, *op. cit.*, p. 91.

22. p. 95.

23. Francis Fukayama, 'Forget Iraq – history is dead', *The Guardian*, 12 August 1990, p. 3.

17 □ *Overworlding the 'Third World'*

Ania Loomba

'Neocolonialism' cannot be discussed without the politics of that very discussion coming under scrutiny.[1] This despite the fact that colonialism and its aftermath are increasingly being discussed within the umbrella of 'theory' – literary or critical, whose political effects (or the very demand that literary theory have a politics) are being questioned.[2] As, in the first place, (a particular kind of) 'theory' gets institutionalized in the Western academy, and we enter what Stephen Heath has called 'the age of fictions, the end of truth'; and as, second, both the possibility of knowledge and its relation to the political are problematized; and as, third, recent events in Europe make it possible to think of the next few decades as those in which 'ideology' and 'commitment' will be unfashionable terms, it seems stubborn and naive to insist that the politics of colonialism and neocolonialism cannot be entirely dissociated from those of its various examinations·today.[3] Of course, 'the Third World' (and sometimes 'feminism') are politely bracketed, while it is alleged that the institutionalization of oppositional criticism has robbed it of its punch: on two separate occasions, influential Western academics, speaking in Delhi, distinguished between postcolonial and Western universities – in the latter, oppositional criticism allegedly had no socio-political reverberations.[4] Such token exclusions usually follow modest disclaimers to knowledge about postcolonial institutions, which themselves sanction continuing ignorance and vague generalizations about 'postcolonial'.

Whatever the nature of the 'metropolitan' academy, it continues to hold much influence over its counterparts in once-colonized societies, and this obliges us to engage with its debates. I say 'us' and 'its' because, despite the heterogeneity of and conflicts within academic structures at either end, and despite the obvious and growing overlaps between work done in 'first' and 'third' world universities and research institutions, as well as between issues of neocolonialism, racism and minority politics within Western countries, there remain important differences between them. Moreover, 'influence' does not suggest unmitigated dependence or mimicry,

From *Oxford Literary Review*, Special Issue 'Neocolonialism', 13, 1991, pp. 164–6, 170–91.

although some postcolonial intellectuals suggest that the hegemony of the 'humanist' academy has been exchanged by that of the poststructuralist one. In any case, the institutionalization of whatever we understand by 'influence', in the shape of publishing networks, funding agencies (including for example, the British Council and USIS), patronage networks, educational, research and 'development' institutions, needs to be underlined. Like all neocolonial scenarios, this one also implicates the internal politics of the 'Third World'.

There is no doubt that the concerns of current discussions of colonialism in Western academies (however sophisticated, and, some would argue, convoluted and obscure, they might have become after the influx of 'theory') remain that of dismantling not only imperialist and colonialist versions of history but also their contemporary effects. That is why they must be alert not only to the way in which 'postcolonial' issues and literatures can be accommodated within the neocolonial academy, but also to the nuances of the 'influence' referred to above.[5] Their own interrogation is both an example of, and is necessarily concerned with, the agency, voice, subjectivity of individual and collective colonized subjects; hence colonial discourse theories (like others) participate in the very process they seek to analyse.

Since Fanon and Tagore, the dichotomy of black skins/white masks, of native subjects having to choose between a regressive 'nativist' or equally questionable 'Westernized' position, remains an important object of inquiry. It can also become a paralysing dichotomy; in the case of debates around communalism or widow immolation in contemporary India, for example, it is invoked along with the accompanying polarity modernist/nativist to efface the real issues at stake, as will be discussed later. Gayatri Chakravorty Spivak draws a distinction between herself, Edward Said and other 'Third World' intellectuals working in the USA, and 'most postcolonials': 'in fact most postcolonials are not like us. Most postcolonials in fact are still quite interested either in proving that they are ethnic subjects and therefore the true marginals or that they are as good as the colonials.'[6] I don't know quite how one defines 'most', but will indicate a few of the many efforts made by some postcolonials (intellectuals, activists, and others), in the past and today, to negotiate the worn tightrope between revivalism and a Western model of development more productively. For all of us (perhaps particularly those of us who teach English literature in India, and who are therefore almost stereotypical 'postcolonial subjects'), to engage with current debates about the colonial subject and resistance is also to examine our own construction, and to reflect on the possibilities of our articulation. Such a personal stake in subaltern agency may be read as detrimental to 'true' analysis or, on the other hand, as making possible the connections between 'neo' and 'colonialism'. [. . .]

[. . .] Benita Parry accuses current theories of colonial discourse of an 'exorbitation of discourse and a related incuriosity about the enabling socio-economic and political institutions and other forms of social praxis'.[7] At one level, such a distinction, and indeed any demand to attend to 'the social' can be and is dismissed as subscribing to the traditional, and by now variously and thoroughly critiqued, model of the political as lying outside discourse, language and culture. But the dangers of a reverse crudity are always imminent. These are evident in sections of feminist theory as well as in writings on ideology, or language, or subjectivity wherein consciousness is prioritized to the point where it breaks with social existence; or ideology moves from being 'material in its effect' or 'structured like a language' to material *in itself* or *the same as* language; the ideological or discursive is narrowed down to mean simply the individual, and simultaneously, the entirely fruitful exercise of looking at the textuality of history turns on its head to collapse history into a privileged text.[8] I take it, then, that Parry, rather than subscribing to a reductive division between the discursive and the social, locates similar pitfalls in the emphasis of current theories, whereby the social realities of language fade as language replaces social and historical space.

This, she argues, is responsible for what these theories look for, and what they find, in the colonial encounter; they 'either erase the voice of the native or limit native resistance to the devices circumventing and interrogating colonial authority', so that there is a 'downgrading of the anti-imperialist texts written by national liberation movements; while the notion of epistemic violence and the occluding of reverse discourses have obliterated the role of the native as historical subject and combatant, possessor of an-other knowledge and producer of alternative traditions' (PCT, pp. 33–5). It might be useful to recall the political effects of another influential privileging of discourse and language in the work of Julia Kristeva and other French feminists, which, as Ann Jones has powerfully demonstrated, reduce 'revolution' to a linguistic and solitary act.[9] Jones also connects linguistic bias with the ethnocentricity of *l'écriture féminine*; this is crucial since so much of linguistic and semiotic theory brushes, often via psychoanalysis, perilously close to universalist assumptions about the nature of subversion and thereby about the repressed and rebellious subject. The specific inputs into protest need not be examined, hence woman becomes a category that need admit of little differentiation. Her agency as interrogator of patriarchal discourse often collapses into a romanticization of her biological difference and negates the rich histories of this interrogation, its successes and its failures. The charge that the privileging of discourse leads to a particular construction of the colonial subject wherein her history, various social positioning, and finally her agency in questioning colonialism are downgraded can fruitfully be read against these other debates. It is not entirely surprising that the neglect of histories surrounding native insubordination either devalues or romanticizes the latter, or worse, tends to read colonized subjects through linguistic or psychoanalytical theories which remain suspiciously and problematically shot through with ethnocentric assumptions whose transfer to all subalterns is unacceptable. This is not a crude dismissal of these ways of seeing, only a discomfort with their being mapped crudely (despite 'sophisticated' manoeuvres) onto all ways of being.[10]

Parry's third criticism is that emphasis on the hybridity of colonial discourse has the effect of obscuring what Fanon called the 'murderous and decisive struggle between two protagonists'. Abdul JanMohamed makes a related critique of the work of Homi Bhabha in particular, arguing that its notion of hybridity glosses over the economic and cultural plunder of the colonized and can therefore only be sustained by 'circumvent[ing] entirely the dense history of the material conflict between Europeans and natives and ... focus[ing] on colonial discourse as if it existed in a vacuum'.[11] He goes on to warn that, far from allowing the native to interrogate or seize power, hybridity may itself be a colonial strategy for repression (EMA, pp. 60–1). Both JanMohamed and Parry offer an alternative model for the colonial encounter wherein the starkness of what Thomas Cartelli elsewhere calls 'the master–slave configuration' is emphasized, in opposition to hybridity, as the defining characteristic of colonial dynamics. A Manichean dichotomy between colonizer/colonized is recommended as the means to recover (a) the socio-economic and historical referents of the colonial encounter and (b) the agency and oppositional impulses of the individual colonized subject and nationalist discourses and movements in general.

This essay will suggest that such recoveries are not possible by reverting to these polarizations in all histories of colonialism. The choice between stark oppositions of colonizer and colonized societies, on the one hand, and notions of hybridity that leave little room for a resistance outside that allowed by the colonizing power on the other, between romanticizing subaltern resistance or effacing it, is not particularly fertile. Parry's critique draws upon her reading of the African experience of colonialism, on which I am not qualified to comment, and its theoretician, Frantz Fanon. But she goes on to offer this as the only politically correct model for a theory of colonialism. It is difficult to accept that any notion of hybridity will dilute the violence of the colonial encounter; if we, following Benita Parry's own suggestion, scrutinize colonial *institutions* (as opposed to just discourse) and also look at the anti-colonial impulses of nationalism (in India in both cases) we will not necessarily find the starkness she hopes to recover, but a variegation. This hybridity, however, is different from the one which Parry finds unacceptable, in as much as it both draws upon indigenous traditions and is not entirely dependent upon the contradictions of colonial authority. As such, it also questions the idea that colonial power was completely effective in erasing native cultures with all their differences, shifts, evolutions and contradictions, which makes them irrecoverable in any pristine form. The paralysing dichotomy of black skin/white masks can be questioned without downgrading indigenous cultures and subjects: we can then move on to look at the relation between 'post' and 'colonial'.

Both Homi Bhabha and Gayatri Spivak are also critical of these binary oppositions. Parry has effectively taken apart the way in which such a denial works for Homi Bhabha (despite the slipperiness of his language and construction, which is itself open to criticism in work which purports to be political and interventionist). The technique of seizing upon a single event or anecdote as emblematic, revealing the intersection of 'behavioural codes, logics, and motives controlling a whole society', has of course been forcefully deployed in much recent and not so recent cultural criticism and historiography.[12] But it cannot be used to simply slide from particular to general, as does Bhabha's article 'Signs taken for wonders', which confidently moves from discussing the authority of the 'English book' in a particular situation to pronouncements about colonial authority *per se*.[13] Two problematic shifts are involved here – one, from a particular act of enunciation to a theory of all utterance, and two, from enunciation to positionality. Hence, 'colonial "positionality" – the division of self/other – and the question of colonial power – the differentiation of colonizer/colonized – ... is a *difference* produced within the act of enunciation' (STW, p. 150). The hybridity of enunciation spills over into becoming the definitive characteristic of *all* colonial authority, everywhere, at any time: 'the colonial presence is *always* ambivalent, split between its appearance as original and authoritative and its articulation as repetition and difference' (p. 150; my emphasis).

Nor does the notion of hybridity stop there – in a more recent article, Bhabha expands it to contend that it alone promises the possibility of 'committed' reading and political practices:

> The language of critique is effective not because it keeps for ever separate the terms of the master and the slave, the mercantilist and the Marxist, but the extent to which it overcomes the given grounds of opposition and opens up a space of 'translation': a place of hybridity, figuratively speaking, where the construction of a political object that is new, *neither the one nor the Other*, properly alienates our political expectations and changes, as it must, the very forms of our recognition of the 'moment' of politics. ... This must be a sign that history is *happening* – within the windless pages of theory, within the systems and structures that we construct to figure the passage of the historical.[14]

One cannot quarrel with a refusal to simply separate theory and practice (although it seems Bhabha is trying to assign the theoretician *the* central role). Nor can one deny that historical writing is both a political and historical act. But it must be equally obvious that history is happening *outside* as well as within 'the windless pages of theory', a history that despite occasional gestures Bhabha has little time for, and which may question the structures he constructs to figure the passage of the historical. First, his too easy shift from semiotic to social is repeated in this essay; secondly, 'hybridity' swells from its previous colonial context to become paradigmatic of all oppositional theory and politics – itself illustrative of how feebly it was grounded in the colonial encounter to begin with. As Suvir Kaul puts it:

> Bhabha is sanguine in his faith that the ambivalence, the splitting of 'the subject of culture' originates in phenomena explained by the general laws of semiotics. ... What authorizes [this subject], it seems to me, is not only its methodological and narrative paradigms ... but its genealogy, in which the congruent discourses of imperialism and humanism (to name only the big guns!) feature prominently. Their historical logic, in all its continuing institutional authority and transformative power, is at stake too, and that suggests to me that the play of self and other, or self as other, is not reducible, even as a heuristic, to the splitting of the subject at the moment of [its] enunciation. Indeed, it is strange to read Bhabha arguing hard against the prescriptive and predictive 'ruptures' of the teleological marxist social text by privileging the single rupture enshrined by semiotic theories of the general condition of language.[15]

Precisely. Even theories of reading should make it possible to attribute the inefficacy of the master text to more than the internal instabilities of the text itself, otherwise it follows that the doubting recipient subject is reduced to the effect of the text itself. Bhabha's final slide is from colonial authority to colonized subject, so that the same rules of ambivalent enunciation govern hegemonic and interrogative discourses and subjects. Naturally, then, 'resistance is not necessarily an oppositional act of political intention, nor is it the simple negation or exclusion of the "content" of another culture, as difference once perceived . . . [but] the effect of an ambivalence *produced within the rules of recognition of dominating discourses as they articulate the signs of cultural difference*' (STW, p. 153; my emphasis).

Ambivalence is also produced within different rules of recognition, by the placement of the recipient of the master text within other discourses, texts, cultures and social formations which prompt and shape questioning of received truths of the text, contradictory though these might be in themselves and in their 'enunciation'.[16] In other words, the reception of the text involves all that Bhabha does not care to see, not just in socio-economic terms but also finally, in native discourses themselves, which even colonial discourses engage with – mutilate, transform, appropriate – in their production of hegemony. By Bhabha's 'rules', alienation from the received readings of Shakespeare, or Shakespearean texts themselves, in the situation in which I and so many others teach them in India, is dependent on the contradictions within Shakespeare and the surrounding critical discourses. As I argue elsewhere, oppositional English literary pedagogy in India has to draw upon, even crudely – even stretching 'the rules' of comparison – our contemporary experiences. Even so, there comes a point when such appropriations or questionings become problematic in as much as they still engage with Shakespeare, or with the master texts of English literature, and perhaps boomerang to confirm the shaping power of the Western text.[17]

Readings of Western literature by nineteenth-century Indian nationalists reveal a similar double bind. They question, as does the history of the teaching of English literature in India, both Bhabha's notion of interrogation and the polarizations suggested by Parry. Such a history demands an analysis of *both* discourses and institutions; in the case of both we can locate the interplay of colonial and indigenous educational practices. Gauri Viswanathan's work uncovers the ways in which the history of English literature teaching in India can be read as one of the devices of imperial governance. It shows how the English literary text came to function 'as the surrogate Englishman in his highest and most perfect state'.[18] In a way, such studies serve as a vital and necessary insistence on 'the master/slave configuration' in an area where Western discussions of English pedagogy had for too long neglected its colonial deployment and where departments of English in India have been largely functioning as the last outposts of Leavisite criticism; their value lies in the connection Viswanathan makes between British education policy (which has been researched earlier), the humanistic claims of English literature, and the dominant critical paradigms within English studies: an interaction not hitherto noted by historians of colonial India.

But so far the focus has largely been, perhaps understandably, on the attempts of colonial educationalists to impose a certain pedagogical practice upon Indian subjects.[19] If such a focus is (mis)taken as a theoretical paradigm, it becomes exclusive and there is a danger of forgetting that English literature, like British education in general, was not inserted upon a colonial vacuum but entered into a lively interaction with indigenous educational practices and subjects, which both implicates them in the legitimization of the English text, and registers the subversive potential of the encounter. I do not mean to underplay the asymmetry of such an interaction or deny the locus of power in the colonial encounter, but to suggest that the spread of English literature teaching cannot be explained away as the simple *effectiveness* of British policies; neither can its persistence in contemporary institutions be understood as a straightforward indication of Indians' continued subjection, a neocolonial conspiracy or a simple nostalgia for the West. Both kinds of inquiry – into nineteenth-century or modern Indian interaction with English literature – cannot be usefully conducted within the parameters of either a theory which insists on the starkness of the colonial encounter, or another where native recipients are entirely conditioned or devastated by the master culture.

To begin with, colonial strategies evolved in the context of specific situations. Pedagogic methods that became central to the teaching of English language, and later English literature – such as its textual bias – were not crudely exported from the metropolis but actually developed in the process of interaction with Indian pedagogical traditions. Pattanayak suggests that:

> During the medieval period [in India], the study of language meant by and large the study of grammar or of literature. When the British took over the administration, it suited their purpose to continue this tradition as regards English education. Thus a study of English remained confined to the study of English literature and students were not prepared for the use of English as a medium of other sciences and humanistic subjects.[20]

Krishna Kumar also argues that 'the text-book culture was a joint product of the soil as it existed and the seed thrown in it by the missionary and the colonial administrator. The soil was of archaic pedagogical practices which treated memorization as a mode of achievement'; as he points out, memorization was 'a prized feature of ancient Brahminical pedagogy, though for different reasons which were related to the necessity of oral storage'.[21] But detailed researches, mapping the interaction between the evolution of a text-book culture (which was useful in homogenizing educational structures across the country, in imposing colonial choice of texts, in establishing a policy of impersonalized, centralized examinations) and English literary studies in particular are still to be undertaken.

Of course, interaction between English and indigenous education can also be seen as part of imperial strategy. For example, Viswanathan has indicated ways in which the apparently conflicting views of Anglicists and Orientalists converged to reinforce colonial hegemony in education. She also suggests, however, that, from the beginning, English enjoyed 'a different status, for there was a scrupulous attempt to establish separate colleges for its study. Even when it was taught within the same college, the English course of studies was kept separate from the course of Oriental study, and was attended by a different set of students' (BEL, p. 13). Such strategies of separation did not always work – partly because colonial educators desired the percolation of values and morals from English to vernacular education, and partly because many of the Indians who wanted to learn English literature were scholars in their own languages.

Sanskrit College, Calcutta, was established in 1824 with the objective of reviving Sanskrit language and literature and therefore initially an English curriculum was not envisaged. The 'General Report on Public Instruction in the Lower Provinces of the Bengal Presidency, from 27 January to 30 April, 1855' tells us that, three years after its establishment, 'the Committee of Public Instruction, deeming it highly desirable that the pupils of the Sanscrit College should acquire a competent knowledge of English literature and science, to be enabled to transfuse occidental ideas and occidental science into the Vernacular literature of Bengal, and forty of the pupils expressing a strong desire to study English simultaneously with Sanskrit, an English class was established'.[22] Henry Woodrow, Inspector of Schools, East Bengal, reported in 1859 that the effect of this on 'the learned Pundits of Sanscrit college' was one of making them speak a language others could understand:

> They have at last consented to cast away their . . . compounded words a line and a half long, and to write a language that ordinary people may read . . . only fifteen years ago, the Vernacularists might have been tempted to say, can any good thing come out of Sanscrit college? The pundits of that college then despised European science and literature as utterly as the Madrussa Moulavies do now. Yet during these last fifteen years they have awoken from the slumber of hundreds, or rather, thousands of years, and now again are appearing as instructors of their countrymen'. (ULV, p. 19)

Clearly, English education was meant to penetrate and inform vernacular instruction; the Rev. J. Lang noted with satisfaction that 'the men that are taking the lead in Bengali literature now, forming and moulding the language, are Sanskrit Pundits, who know sufficient English to acquire ideas from it' (ULV, p. 19). One evident result of this interpenetration is that today the critical orthodoxies prevailing in the departments of English literature and those of different Indian literatures are not entirely different – it would be erroneous to suppose that the latter are free of notions of the transcendent text or the literature teacher as the moral guru; the orthodoxies draw sustenance from different cultural objects but there is a shared way of seeing. The crisis of English literature is compounded of both the postcolonial crisis of English and the crisis of literature teaching in general.

All this is as noted by colonial authorities. What were the perceptions of Indians themselves? The much discussed native informant, who is obviously central to theories of the downward filtration of colonial ideologies, cannot be seen as the simple effect of Macaulay's Minute, just as nostalgia for the West cannot entirely explain the stances of contemporary departments of English in India. Equally, it would be reductive to search for subjects uncontaminated by the effects of colonial rule. In other words, strong impulses towards nationalism (read, as Parry does, as serious interrogation of colonial authority) and towards either chauvinism or revivalism and, certainly, patriarchalism, can be located within the same class, or groups of people, and individuals as well. In the case of English literature's encounter with Indians, perhaps no Indian, however subversive or nationalist, is free of such complexity: it has been suggested that the universal humanism put forward by institutionalized literary studies was useful in the task of hegemonizing native elite culture. The native intellectual in the nineteenth century used English literature to claim a place under the sun.[23] These attempts to appropriate the master-texts for radical and anti-colonial ends included both a re-enforcement of the claims of English literature to universal meaning and validity, and an erasure of difference between the Indians and the British, giving us room for pause in our contemporary efforts at appropriation. That we are all human beings is a slogan which can function in many contradictory ways at the same time.[24]

For example, Lala Hardayal, a self-proclaimed rationalist, and a founder of the anti-colonial Ghaddar Association (later Ghadder Society), writes a book in 1934 called *Hints for Self-Culture*.[25] Here prescriptions for the same are illustrated with references to Western as well as indigenous texts. Shakespeare repeatedly crops up to garnish and bolster all sorts of advice. Throughout the book universalism is used in the way suggested above – to claim equality. British rule is rarely referred to directly, yet universal humanity is used to question dominant British historiography and literary readings. In a section called 'History', Hardayal warns against

> dangerous guides, who suppose that 'History' only means the history of Europe. . . . Thus 'the world' is regarded as equivalent to 'Europe' and the part is unwisely taken for the whole. . . . History is a universal epic or it is nothing. If it is written and interpreted by narrow minded patriots or sectarians, it is changed into 'a tale told by an idiot, full of sound and folly, signifying nothing'. (p. 38)

In another section, devoted to 'the common humanity' of all men and women, Hardayal refers to the exclusion of blacks from public places in South Africa, elaborates on the oppression of the non-white American but makes no reference to his own specific context – British rule in India. He then goes on to quote at length from Shylock's speech from *The Merchant of Venice* beginning 'I am a Jew. Hath not a Jew eyes?' (III.i.51–7) to conclude: 'If you are ever tempted to scorn or wrong a brother man of another race or creed, remember the pathetic plaint of Shylock the Jew' (p. 238). This arguably legitimizes the validity of Shakespeare for all Indians; it also works against the grain of what British educationalists were propounding in the Indian classroom, and certainly against interpretations of the play then dominant in the Western world. What makes matters complex is that the radical potential of the nationalist invocation of universalism was severely undercut by the consolidation of a patriarchal and otherwise repressive authority that laid the groundwork for the India we live in today.

Of course, British historians had for long cheerfully attributed such oppositional impulses to Western education and literature: by this count Percival Spear reckons that Shakespeare schooled Indians in nationalism, and English education taught them 'rationalism, civil liberties, and constitutional self-government'.[26] Here, the word 'hybridity' is missing; the Western book is straightforward in its democratic impulses and thereby paradoxically undermines its own authority. Bhabha's theory works on far more sophisticated lines; his political intentions, I have no doubt, are the very opposite of Percival Spear's. But the similarities of their *effect*, where the interrogation of colonialism is shaped primarily by its own discourse, are disquieting. This theoretical bias is obviously detrimental to research on the culture of the colonized. Parry rightly seeks to redress it by correctly pointing out that 'the construction of a text disrupting imperialism's authorized version was begun long ago within the political and intellectual cultures of colonial liberation movements' (PCT, p. 27). As a polemical intervention, one cannot quarrel with it. However, such reminders can usefully function as corrective of the tendency to overdetermine the Third World only if they simultaneously acknowledge that nationalism 'rarely has that pure virginal quality about it in which its ideologues like to indulge themselves. Depending on the social forces and processes which articulate it, it can be defensive or imperialist, tolerant or chauvinist, universalist/humanist or racist'.[27]

Given the contemporary political configurations in countries such as India, it is certainly crucial to recover alternative versions of nationalism which could not be accommodated within and were drawing upon different traditions than the official one – which certainly received its share of ratification by the colonial masters. A growing body of work delineates the complex interface of nationalism and colonial authority, suggesting that sites of resistance are far from clearly demarcated and that particular subjects may contribute to diverse and even conflicting traditions of anti-colonialism, nativism and collaboration.[28] Moreover, since 'the colonial subject' is a heterogeneous category, particular positionings (for example, those of different categories of women within nationalist discourses) sharply question the notion of a single master/slave configuration. If current theory has the effect of neglecting the radical potential of nationalism, we cannot construct an alternative which will be in danger of romanticizing it. As I have already indicated, contemporary media appropriations of nationalism in India manage to do both simultaneously.

This problem is especially acute when it comes to colonial education whose recipients are not likely to be from the ranks of those who can provide 'ideal' revolutionaries. Bhabha's suggestion that we need to rethink Fanon's choice between turning white or disappearing is productive in this context. The native intelligentsia certainly cannot be dismissed easily as *either* revivalist or 'native informants'. One within their own ranks, Bipin Chandra Pal, could acknowledge both as reactive positions; the Indian reformer, inspired by the West, and the revivalist, harking back to a golden and mythical past, are both inspired, he says, 'the one consciously, the other unconsciously, by the spirit of Europe. Both have, more or less, imbibed the European temperament.'[29] His *The Soul of India*, written early in this century, anticipates contemporary critiques of Orientalist scholarship. In a passage that comes close to Edward Said's brief discussion of Orientalist responses to India, Pal says that although Orientalists

> know something, no doubt, of our past, and speak in terms almost of exaggerated admiration of that past ... almost invariably they leave the sad impression upon the reader's mind that all they say are matters of ancient history. ... Max Muller ... persistently refused ... to come to this country, lest his dream picture of our land and people should be cruelly destroyed. The fact of the matter really is that neither Max Muller nor any other European Orientalist has been ... able to grasp the truth that age after age, and epoch after epoch, there have been evolution and progress in India as elsewhere, that this process of progressive evolution was never stopped at any period of our history and it is going on as much today as it did at the time of the Vedas, the Upanishads or the Epics. (pp. 4–5)

In a passage that startlingly prefigures recent critiques of rationalism and the arrogance of European thought processes, he concedes that Orientalists, missionaries and English officials 'have tried faithfully to record what they have actually seen or heard'. But,

> they usually forget the common truth that what we see or hear are mere externals and appearances. ... When, therefore, the European scientist studies the physical features of our land, when he mensurates our fields, trigonometrates our altitudes and undulations, investigates our animal, our vegetable or our mineral kingdoms, the records of his study and investigations are accepted as true and authoritative. But the study of man belongs altogether to a different plane. The specific organs of truth in the domain of the psychological, the sociological and the spiritual sciences are not our senses. Here also the eye sees, the ear hears, but the real meaning of what is seen or heard is supplied not by the senses but by the understanding, which interprets what is seen or heard in the light of its own peculiar experiences and associations. (pp. 8–9)

Such insights do not preclude crude chauvinism or Hindu revivalism, or (especially) patriarchalism. Pal's interrogation of Western epistemology also ties in with nationalist splitting of material and spiritual worlds, which worked within and contributed to existing social differentials. As Partha Chatterjee argues, 'nationalism ... located its own subjectivity in the spiritual domain of culture, where it located itself superior to the West and hence undominated and sovereign'.[30] Hence it simultaneously conceded the claims of Western civilization in the material sphere, thereby arguing in favour of Western education, and asserted Indian cultural superiority. Chatterjee shows how this inner/outer distinction was mapped on that of the home and the world, and worked specifically to produce an accommodative ideal of the Indian woman, who was both educated in the Western mode and retained traditional Indian values – she was made to bear the burden of preserving the superior spirituality of India. In other words, the passages above contribute to an indigenous critique of Orientalism and *feed* into patriarchal and ultimately nativist discourse. To the extent that they are part of what Parry calls 'a text disrupting imperialism's authorised version', however, they are not exclusively prompted or shaped by the hybridity of colonial discourse.

Despite Bhabha's hybridity thesis, the colonial subject in his work is remarkably free of gender, class, caste or other distinctions. Other historians of colonial discourse, alert to all of these, and sensitive also to postcolonial politics, arrive at a very different notion of interaction and locate subaltern resistance within a population which cannot be homogenized even by virtue of its common subjection to colonialism.

I have been suggesting that the notion of interaction is not detrimental to the recovery of resistance to colonialism. I will briefly consider how it is employed by Gayatri Spivak and Lata Mani, especially in relation to *sati* or widow immolation in nineteenth-century India.[31] These are very different exercises: Spivak examines a single case-history, that of the Rani of Sirmur, to investigate the 'worldling' of 'the Third World' and the epistemic violence to which it was subjected, and to deny a nostalgic, revisionist recovery of this world. Mani uses the debate on *sati* in colonial India to question the concepts 'tradition' and 'modernity' by showing the ways in which colonial rulers and indigenous patriarchy constructed the issue of *sati*, how women become 'emblematic of tradition' – she then considers connections between colonial and postcolonial India. Both, however, deal with the difficulty in recovering the agency, subjectivity and voice of the colonized woman, who is caught within indigenous and colonial male constructions of her, each parading as her liberator from the other.

Parry quotes liberally from Spivak's repeated documentation of subaltern silence to show that she generalizes from the absence of Indian women's voices in the history of *sati* to suggest the disarticulation of all colonized men and women throughout the colonial encounter (PCT, p. 35). Spivak obliges one to read her otherwise extremely thought-provoking work as arguing for the impossibility of subaltern agency on several counts. She approaches this conclusion from several different directions. Her comments on the Subaltern group of Indian historians are relevant, since 'the most significant outcome' of their revision of colonial historiography, according to Spivak herself, is 'that the agency of change is located in the insurgent or the "subaltern"'.[32] In her critique, Spivak locates an inconsistency in their desire to locate 'the subaltern as the subject of history' and in 'their actual practice' which, she argues, 'is closer to deconstruction', documenting as it does the impossibility of agency or group consciousness in any pure sense. 'The language', she says, 'seems also to be straining to acknowledge that the subaltern's view, will, presence, can be no more than a theoretical fiction to entitle the project of reading. It cannot be recovered . . . in the work of this group, what had seemed the historical predicament of the colonial subaltern can be made to become the allegory of *all* thought, *all* deliberative consciousness' (DH, pp. 332, 340).

She maintains, in other words, that even as they work with a desire to locate agency, these historians actually come close to acknowledging what deconstructionists and

European critiques of humanism have always maintained: the impossibility of a sovereign and determining subject, philosophically and historically. She then reads 'the retrieval of subaltern consciousness as the charting of what in poststructuralist language would be called subaltern subject-effect', whereby an actual historical subject is posited by the historian in order to explain effects which are actually the result of 'an immense discontinuous network ... of strands that may be termed politics, ideology, economics, history, sexuality, language and so on' (DH, p. 341). In the different volumes of *Subaltern Studies*, Spivak argues, there is such a reading backwards of effects into subjects with a will. At the same time, she acknowledges, using Marx and Gramsci, the *political and strategic necessity of supposing such agency*, arguing that this pragmatic hypothesis can co-exist with a philosophical acknowledgement that no such agency is actually possible: 'I would read it, then, as a *strategic* use of positivist essentialism in a scrupulously visible political interest' (DH, p. 342).

Whether or not one agrees with her annexation of the Subaltern historians to deconstruction, the difficulty of establishing subject positions in history cannot be simply equated with denying the subaltern her positionings, which, it seems to me, is what Bhabha does: following this difference, he displays none of Spivak's interest in the diverse contexts in which colonial subjects are placed. At the same time, Spivak is explicitly interested in emphasizing the worldling of the 'Third World' by imperialist and colonial plunder and its intellectual co-ordinates, which, she explains, is meant to disallow a romanticizing of once colonized societies 'as distant cultures, exploited but with rich intact heritages waiting to be recovered, interpreted, and curricularized in English translation [which] helps the emergence of "Third World" as a convenient signifier that allows us to forget that "worldling" even as it expands the empire of the discipline' (ROS, p. 247). This is an entirely laudable impulse, especially in the context of her own institutional position. But it is at least as much a strategy as the one she detects in the Subaltern historians, and subject to comparable contradictions, because it is then offered as the definitive account of colonial history and of the subaltern subject. Moreover, her two positions – the deconstructive one detecting methodological and epistemological problems with charting subject positions, and the second one emphasizing epistemic and other violence of colonialism – so slide into each other that the force of the first one is borne entirely by the subaltern alone: she alone is silenced.

Jonathan Dollimore's point that 'if the emphasis on the excluded and on resistance is to be more than the simple substitution of the affirmative for the nihilistic, or the reading of texts for disruptions, we need to attend carefully to actual histories of in/subordination' is important.[33] But in the context of colonialism, these actual histories equally problematize a singular emphasis on 'worldling'. Spivak rightly criticizes the discourse of postmodernism, where a total 'emptying of the subject-position' accompanies an ignorance 'in the history of imperialism, in the epistemic violence that constituted/effaced a subject that was obliged to cathect (occupy in response to a desire) the space of the Imperialists' self-consolidating other. It is almost as if the force generated by their crisis is separated from its appropriate field by a sanctioned ignorance of that history' (DH, p. 348). But that is not the only history of the 'Third World' they are ignorant of, not if there is another history where resistance, however problematic, is present, and where precolonial history also needs to be rewritten, lifted from its nostalgic or Orientalist versions. From a different positioning, that other history is of strategic importance, not simply and romantically to sanction our own voices, but also to look at the pretexts of colonialism – Brahminism, different varieties of regional and class differentations, precolonial patriarchy – of which Spivak shows much knowledge but which are not worked into this schema of silence. Those who search for subaltern agency do not necessarily do so at the expense of acknowledging colonial plunder, violence, and savagery; Spivak's own emphasis results, as Parry puts it, in 'deliberate deafness to the native voice where it *is* to be heard' (PCT, p. 39, my emphasis).

In her article on the Rani of Sirmur, Spivak shows the imperial construction of the archives, pointing to the difficulty of reconstructing the life (let alone the subjectivity) of any nineteenth-century Indian woman: 'To retrieve her as information will be no disciplinary triumph. Caught in the cracks between the production of the archives and indigenous patriarchy, today distanced by waves of hegemonic "feminism", there is no "real Rani" to be found' (p. 271). This is fair enough. But the author informed me after an earlier presentation of this paper that she found out from the Pandas at Haridwar what she could not from the archives at London or Delhi – that her Rani did not commit *sati*.[34] Obviously, in this case, indigenous archives survived the epistemic violence of colonialism. I do not want to suggest, much less celebrate, such survival on a wide scale. But it seems necessary to interrupt equally easy conclusions where researches are still in their infancy.

Moreover, having spent twenty-five learned pages on the Rani, Spivak suddenly invokes a situation where 'the current crisis of capital . . . traces out the international division of labor' because 'the lives and deaths of the paradigmatic victims of that division, the women of the urban sub-proletariat and of unorganized peasant labor, are not going on record in the "humanist" academy even as we speak'. She says this works against her 'disciplinary satisfaction in retrieving the Queen of Sirmur' (ROS, p. 271) which comes close to suggesting that the working class, peasantry and any other of the 'most' victimized people should be the sole objects of inquiry. (Spivak's own researches hardly show such concentration.) Finally, other women who are trying, precisely, to record such voices within colonial and postcolonial history do not indicate the epistemic wasteland Spivak implies.[35] There have been attempts to locate contemporary Indian women's struggles for survival against colonial and indigenous structures of domination in the context of cultures that did not simply 'escape' colonialism but resisted its attempts to shape their epistemology. To take just one example: Vandana Shiva's recent book *Staying Alive: Women, ecology and survival in India* documents many grassroots struggles against Western, capitalist and colonial notions of 'development'.[36] Shiva suggests that in many communities these struggles are fed by an alternative understanding of nature, of development, and of community, which has survived – in resistance to, not just bypassed by – colonial violence. It is possible to quarrel with Shiva's notions of both feminism and tribal or peasant cultures. But the book cannot be simply dismissed as nostalgic revisionism since it meticulously documents alternative ways of being and seeing as the fuel of contemporary struggles and questions, especially by a theory which will then look for the repressive results of the interface between colonial and colonized cultures at the cost of subversive histories which were also sparked off by the encounter.

Admittedly, these are difficult questions, framed as they are by sophisticated attempts, in India, to feed such questioning into a crude opposition to what is regarded as Western science. And of course it would not do to romanticize the past, specially in the contemporary Indian situation where revivalism feeds into rampant communalism and patriarchalism. That is why the desire to reclaim the past is legitimate. But revivalism itself always reworks 'tradition' rather than simply adopts it. The practice of dowry-marriages in contemporary India, for instance, is not a simple remnant of feudalism but an aspect of contemporary commercial culture. Similarly, each incident of *sati* creates its own mythology and is bolstered by specific power groups. Since the practice was officially outlawed, the politics of *sati* have evolved and shifted: the latest one at Deorala, Rajasthan, in September 1987, revealed that 'a new configuration of caste/class social forces has appeared, but it is obfuscating its interests as it wears the mask of an "ancient" and "timeless" practice. ... In this it has raised the most dangerous of mythologies of femininity that the democratic movement in the post-1947 period has had to struggle against.'[37] Many feminists in India have been at pains to stress these evolutions, which cannot be ignored if we are to make connections between colonialism and current situations in the 'third' world, as colonial discourse theory seeks to do.

Lata Mani's meticulous researches into the production of an official discourse on *sati* perceptively problematize the terms 'tradition' and 'modernity' in the nineteenth-century context. But her excellent account of the interface between indigenous and colonial patriarchies on the 'ground of the discourse of *sati*' is marred precisely when she relaxes her grip on the contemporary scenario. Finding as she does that woman is hardly the subject of the entire discourse on *sati* and that it is extremely difficult to construct any idea of the woman's subjectivity, she is impelled to locate some notion of women's 'selfhood' in the notion of the voluntary *sati*: 'given the absence of women's voices and historical and cultural variability of such terms as "agency" and "subjecthood", it seems to me that the volition of some widows can justifiably be seen as equal to the resistance of others' (CT, p. 129). Although Mani avows that she is not in any way trying to endorse the practice of *sati*, the fact remains that similar views were expressed by defenders of the practice in the massive controversy following the September 1987 incident. Their arguments rest less on an invocation of the ancient texts, or scriptures, than on the notion of choice;[38] in such a situation, there is something very distasteful – our desire to problematize the notion of a unified female subjectivity notwithstanding – to locate female agency (entirely on conjecture) in a death-wish, simply (and also especially) because there is no other record of her voice. It is worth pointing out that analogous cases of violence against women, where young wives are killed for lack of adequate dowry, are also sought to be recorded and treated as cases of suicide. In most instances, the woman's testimony is either just not recorded, or manipulated by taking her dying declaration in the presence of her murderers. Still, there are many women who testify to suicide in order to protect their family honour, or children, or even the husbands who killed them. Despite this, we have to recognize that they are murders and not suicides; and over the last two years, women involved in the anti-*sati* campaigns have argued that this is true of that practice as well.

To reveal 'the continuing persistence of colonial discourse', 'to question the "post" in "postcolonial"', as Mani wishes to do, is important; at the same time, if we are contesting the stasis attributed to colonized societies by Orientalist discourse, the 'pre' and the 'post' of colonialism deserve equal attention. In contemporary communalism, tradition does not, as Mani contends, refer solely or even mainly to a textual tradition. In fact, appropriated and changed and newly-created traditions are sought to be sanctified by the creation of new texts. A Hindu fundamentalist organization, the Vishwa Hindu Parishad has, for the past two years, been seeking to build a temple to Rama at Ayodhya, his legendary birthplace. But it is no ordinary temple. It is proposed to be built after demolishing an existing Muslim masjid: the contention is that this is the precise birthplace of Rama where a temple originally existed but was destroyed by Muslims during the reign of the Mughal king Babar. There is no historical evidence for such a take-over; occasionally even fundamental organizations and journals will concede actual history has nothing to do with it – that it is a matter of 'faith' or 'Hindu sentiments'. But at the same time, there are frantic efforts to forge such a history – at Ayodhya itself (and elsewhere) a spate of literature is being produced, crassly but powerfully 'documenting' a fundamentalist history for mass consumption. These books (ludicrously crude at one level) provide 'textual' legitimacy for contemporary communalism.[39] Communalism was catalysed by colonialism, but it is clear that it has other roots as well, and therefore has contemporary manifestations – not all of which can be neatly telescoped backwards to British rule, although that governance necessarily interlocks with communal history.

The women's movement, the struggles against communalism, and for survival and land, deny an easy polarization of 'theory' and 'practice' or the assumption that what I earlier called the Fanonian tightrope remains the major postcolonial preoccupation. They are some of the spaces where many men and women have to intervene in structures worked through by colonialism, as well as earlier and later histories of domination. Such intervention is difficult, and, at the moment, often ineffective. It is also limited to relatively small sections of people, but is significant because it has to reclaim some earlier histories – such as those of secularism, or women's struggles, *while contesting* revisionism or nostalgia or the kind of state-sponsored nationalism revealed by the television films. To say that if the subaltern could speak she/he would not be a subaltern is a neat enough formulation, but somewhat inadequate if the 'Third World' is not to be, yet again, theorized into silence.[40]

Notes

1. This article was written in 1989, and unfortunately does not take into account the crucial developments in Indian political life since then: the entire tenure and fall of the V.P. Singh government, the assassination of Rajiv Gandhi, the violent agitations around caste-based reservations in 1990, and, especially, the escalation of communal violence and of the contest over 'nationalism' between various political forces. Despite this, I believe that the main arguments of the article are still pertinent.

2. Robert Young, 'The politics of "the politics of literary theory"', *Oxford Literary Review*, 10, 1988, pp. 131–57; Stephen Heath ('Modern literary theory', *Critical Quarterly*, 31, 2, 1990) remarks: 'It is significant . . . that we hear little in modern literary theory these days of *ideology*, so little so that it is tempting sometimes to see that as one of the very requirements of a *modern* theory: reference to ideology become old-fashioned, a concept of yesteryear' (p. 41).

3. Heath, *op. cit.*, p. 41.

4. Howard Felperin, giving a public lecture on *The Tempest* during a conference on 'Shakespeare for all time' organized by the Department of English, University of Delhi, December 1989, and Jonathan Culler speaking on 'Literary theory in America today' to the Association of College Teachers of English, Delhi University, in February 1990.

5. See Spivak's statement of the problem, below.

6. Gayatri Chakravorty Spivak, 'New historicism: political commitment and the postmodern critic', in H. Aram Veeser (ed.), *The New Historicism*, Routledge: New York, 1989, p. 290.

7. Benita Parry, 'Problems in current theories of colonial discourse', *Oxford Literary Review*, 9, 1987, p. 43; henceforth abbreviated as PCT.

8. Stuart Hall, 'Recent developments in theories of language and ideology: a critical note', in Hall *et al.* (eds.), *Culture, Media, Language: Working papers in cultural studies*, Hutchinson: London, 1980, p. 162; see also Michèle Barrett, 'Ideology and the cultural production of gender', in Judith Newton and Deborah Rosenfelt (eds.), *Feminist Criticism and Social Change*, Methuen: New York, 1985, p. 72; Jonathan Dollimore and Alan Sinfield, 'Culture and textuality: debating cultural materialism', *Textual Practice*, 4, 1, 1990, pp. 91–100.

9. Ann Rosalind Jones, 'Writing the body: towards an understanding of *l'écriture féminine*', Newton and Rosenfelt, *op. cit.*, pp. 86–101.

10. This is not to suspect the politics of all psychoanalytic theory; the work of Jacqueline Rose is especially thought-provoking with regard to the usefulness of psychoanalysis for feminist theory in particular and political analysis in general (see especially *Sexuality in the Field of Vision*, Verso: London, 1986). But how such a perspective can accommodate cultural difference still remains to be demonstrated.

11. Abdul R. JanMohamed, 'The economy of Manichean allegory: the function of racial difference in colonialist literature', *Critical Inquiry*, 12, 1985, p. 60; henceforth abbreviated as EMA.

12. H. Aram Veeser, 'Introduction', *The New Historicism*, p. xi.

13. Homi Bhabha, 'Signs taken for wonders: questions of ambivalence and authority under a tree outside Delhi, May 1817', *Critical Inquiry*, 12, 1985, 144–65; henceforth abbreviated as STW.

14. *idem*, 'The commitment to theory', *New Formations*, 5, 1988, pp. 10–11.

15. Suvir Kaul, 'The Indian academic and resistance to theory', paper presented at Jawaharlal Nehru University, March 1990, forthcoming in Rajeswari Sunder Rajan (ed.), *'The Lie of the Land': English Literature in the Indian University*, Oxford University Press: New Delhi.

16. Dave Morley, 'Texts, readers, subjects', in Hall *et al. op. cit.*, pp. 163–73.

17. Ania Loomba, *Race, Gender, Renaissance Drama*, Manchester University Press: Manchester and New York, 1989, pp. 31–5, 142–58.

18. Gauri Viswanathan, 'The beginnings of English literary studies in British India', *Oxford Literary Review*, 9, p. 23; this essay is henceforth abbreviated as BEL; see also Viswanathan, *Masks of Conquest: Literary study and British rule in India*, Faber & Faber: London, 1990, for a full version of her argument.

19. This is not to suggest that it is incumbent upon all studies dealing with colonial education to deal with its reception. Edward Said's work has been criticized for its omission of the native subject, but neither he nor Viswanathan suggests that either Orientalism or British education were uncritically received. However, it is time to flesh out the contexts of reception; in the case of English literary studies in India, the existing bias predictably results in looking at the current situation as simply a colonial remnant, or in suggesting the teaching of Indian literature as a corrective to the 'crisis' of English literature. For the suggestion that pedagogy in indigenous literatures may be shot through with analogous orthodoxies concerning the nature and function of literary texts and readings see Loomba, 'Criticism and pedagogy in the Indian classroom', in Rajan, *op. cit.* Some essays in this volume hope to begin the task of mapping the field of past and present reception of English literature in India.

20. D. P. Pattanayak, *Multi-lingualism and Mother-Tongue Education*, Oxford University Press: New Delhi, 1981, pp. 16–61.

21. Krishna Kumar, 'Origins of India's textbook culture', *Occasional Papers on History and Society*, XLVII, Nehru Memorial Museum and Library: New Delhi, 1987.

22. Arabinda Guha (ed.), *Unpublished Letters of Vidyasagar*, Ananda Publishers: Calcutta, 1971, pp. 16–17; henceforth cited as ULV.

23. Jasodhara Bagchi, 'Shakespeare in a loin-cloth: English literature and the early nationalist consciousness in Bengal' (paper presented at Miranda house, University of Delhi, April 1988).

24. Loomba, *op. cit.*, pp. 20–3.

25. Lala Hardayal, *Hints for Self-Culture*, Current Events: Dehra Dun 1934.

26. Percival Spear, *A History of India*, vol. 2, Penguin: Harmondsworth, 1966; reprinted 1984, p. 166.

27. Dilip Simeon, 'Communalism in modern India: a theoretical examination', *Social Science Probings*, 4, 1, 1987, p. 67.

28. See Kumkum Sangari and Sudesh Vaid (eds.), *Recasting Woman: Essays in colonial history*, Kali for Woman: New Delhi, 1989.

29. Bipin Chandra Pal, *The Soul of India: A constructive study of Indian thoughts and ideals*, Calcutta: Yugayatri Prakashak, 1958, p. 155.

30. Partha Chatterjee 'The nationalist resolution of the women's question', in Sangari and Vaid, *op. cit.*, p. 249.

31. Gayatri Chakravorty Spivak, 'The Rani of Sirmur: an essay in reading the archives', *History and Theory*, 24, 3, 1985, pp. 247–72, and Lata Mani, 'Contentious traditions:

the debate on *sati* in colonial India', *Cultural Critique*, 7, 1987, pp. 119–56; henceforth cited as ROS and CT respectively.

32. Gayatri Chakravorty Spivak, 'Subaltern Studies: deconstructing historiography', in Ranajit Guha (ed.), *Subaltern Studies IV: Writings on South Asian History and Society*, Oxford University Press: New Delhi, 1985, p. 330; henceforth DH.

33. Dollimore and Sinfield, *op. cit.*, p. 94.

34. At the 'Colonialism Now' conference, University of Southampton, July 1989.

35. See, for example, Vasantha Kannibiran and K. Lalitha, 'That magic time: women in the Telengana people's struggle', in Sangari and Vaid, *op. cit.*, pp. 180–203.

36. Vandana Shiva, *Staying Alive: Women, ecology and survival in India*, Kali for Woman: New Delhi, 1988.

37. Sudesh Vaid, 'Politics of widow immolation', *Seminar*, 342, 1988, pp. 20–3; cf. Madhu Kiswar and Ruth Vanita, 'The burning of Roop Kanwar', *Manushi*, 42–3, 1987, pp. 15–25.

38. Kumkum Sangari, 'Perpetuating the myth', *Seminar*, 342, 1988, pp. 24–30, discusses the myth of the voluntary *sati* and its politics in the post-Deorala debate.

39. Urvashi Butalia, 'The literature at Ram Janambhoomi', unpublished paper.

40. Spivak, 'New historicism', p. 283.

18 □ Disjuncture and Difference in the Global Cultural Economy

Arjun Appadurai

It takes only the merest acquaintance with the facts of the modern world to note that it is now an interactive system in a sense which is strikingly new. Historians and sociologists, especially those concerned with translocal processes[1] and with the world systems associated with capitalism,[2] have long been aware that the world has been a congeries of large-scale interactions for many centuries. Yet today's world involves interactions of a new order and intensity. Cultural transactions between social groups in the past have generally been restricted, sometimes by the facts of geography and ecology, and at other times by active resistance to interactions with the Other (as in China for much of its history and in Japan before the Meiji Restoration). Where there have been sustained cultural transactions across large parts of the globe, they have usually involved the long-distance journey of commodities (and of the merchants most concerned with them) and of travellers and explorers of every type.[3] The two main forces for sustained cultural interaction before this century have been warfare (and the large-scale political systems sometimes generated by it) and religions of conversion, which have sometimes, as in the case of Islam, taken warfare as one of the legitimate instruments of their expansion. Thus, between travellers and merchants, pilgrims and conquerors, the world has seen much long-distance (and long-term) cultural traffic. This much seems self-evident.

But few will deny that given the problems of time, distance and limited technologies for the command of resources across vast spaces, cultural dealings between socially and spatially separated groups have, until the last few centuries, been bridged at great cost and sustained over time only with great effort. The forces of cultural gravity seemed always to pull away from the formation of large-scale ecumenes, whether religious, commercial or political, towards smaller-scale accretions of intimacy and interest.

Sometime in the last few centuries, the nature of this gravitational field seems to have changed. Partly due to the spirit of the expansion of Western maritime interests

From *Public Culture*, 2, 2, Spring 1990, pp. 1–11, 15–24.

after 1500, and partly because of the relatively autonomous developments of large and aggressive social formations in the Americas (such as the Aztecs and the Incas); in Eurasia (such as the Mongols, and their descendants, the Mughals and Ottomans); in island South-East Asia (such as the Buginese); and in the kingdoms of pre-colonial Africa (such as Dahomey), an overlapping set of ecumenes began to emerge, in which congeries of money, commerce, conquest and migration began to create durable cross-societal bonds. This process was accelerated by the technology transfers and accelerations of the late eighteenth and nineteenth centuries,[4] which created complex colonial orders centered on European capitals and spread throughout the non-European world. This complex and overlapping set of Euro-colonial worlds (first Spanish and Portuguese, later principally English, French and Dutch) set the basis for a permanent traffic in ideas of peoplehood and selfhood, which created the imagined communities[5] of recent nationalisms throughout the world.

With what Benedict Anderson has called 'print capitalism', a new power was unleashed in the world, the power of mass literacy and its attendant large-scale production of projects of ethnic affinity that were remarkably free of the need for face-to-face communication or even of indirect communication between persons and groups. The act of reading things together set the stage for movements based on a paradox – the paradox of constructed primordialism. There is, of course, a great deal else that is involved in the story of colonialism and of its dialectically generated nationalisms,[6] but the issue of constructed ethnicities is surely a crucial strand in this tale.

But the revolution of print capitalism, and the cultural affinities and dialogues unleashed by it, were only modest precursors to the world we live in now. For in the last century, there has been a technological explosion, largely in the domain of transportation and information, which makes the interactions of a print-dominated world seem as hard-won and as easily erased as the print revolution made earlier forms of cultural traffic appear. For with the advent of the steamship, the automobile and the aeroplane, the camera, the computer and the telephone, we have entered into an altogether new condition of neighborliness, even with those most distant from ourselves. Marshall McLuhan, among others, sought to theorize about this world as a global village, but theories such as McLuhan's appear to have overestimated the communitarian implications of the new media order. We are now aware that with media, each time we are tempted to speak of the 'global village', we must be reminded that media create communities with 'no sense of place'.[7] The world we live in now seems rhizomic,[8] even schizophrenic, calling for theories of rootlessness, alienation and psychological distance between individuals and groups, on the one hand, and fantasies (or nightmares) of electronic propinquity on the other. Here we are close to the central problematic of cultural processes in today's world.

Thus, the curiosity which recently drove Pico Iyer to Asia, is in some ways the product of a confusion between some ineffable McDonaldization of the world and the much subtler play of indigenous trajectories of desire and fear with global flows of people and things. Indeed Iyer's own impressions are testimony to the fact that, if 'a' global cultural system is emerging, it is filled with ironies and resistances, sometimes camouflaged as passivity and a bottomless appetite in the Asian world for things Western.

Iyer's own account of the uncanny Philippine affinity for American popular music is rich testimony to the global culture of the 'hyper-real', for somehow Philippine renditions of American popular songs are both more widespread in the Philippines, and more disturbingly faithful to their originals, than they are in the United States today. An entire nation seems to have learned to mimic Kenny Rogers and the Lennon sisters, like a vast Asian Motown chorus. But Americanization is certainly a pallid term to apply to such a situation, for not only are there more Filipinos singing perfect renditions of some American songs (often from the American past) than there are Americans doing so, there is, of course, the fact that the rest of their lives is not in complete synchrony with the referential world which first gave birth to these songs.

In a further, globalizing twist on what Jameson has recently called 'nostalgia for the present',[10] these Filipinos look back to a world they have never lost. This is one of the central ironies of the politics of global cultural flows, especially in the arena of entertainment and leisure. It plays havoc with the hegemony of Euro-chronology. American nostalgia feeds on Filipino desire represented as a hyper-competent reproduction. Here we have nostalgia without memory. The paradox, of course, has its explanations, and they are historical; unpacked, they lay bare the story of the American missionization and political rape of the Philippines, one result of which has been the creation of a nation of make-believe Americans, who tolerated for so long a leading lady who played the piano while the slums of Manila expanded and decayed. Perhaps the most radical postmodernists would argue that this is hardly surprising, since in the peculiar chronicities of late capitalism, pastiche and nostalgia are central modes of image production and reception. Americans themselves are hardly in the present any more as they stumble into the mega-technologies of the twenty-first century garbed in the film noir scenarios of sixties 'chills', fifties diners, forties clothing, thirties houses, twenties dances, and so on ad infinitum.

As far as the United States is concerned, one might suggest that the issue is no longer one of nostalgia but of a social *imaginaire* built largely around re-runs. Jameson[11] was bold to link the politics of nostalgia to the postmodern commodity sensibility and surely he was right. The drug wars in Colombia recapitulate the tropical sweat of Vietnam, with Ollie North and his succession of masks – Jimmy Stewart concealing John Wayne concealing Spiro Agnew and all of them transmogrifying into Sylvester Stallone who wins in Afghanistan – thus simultaneously fulfilling the secret American envy of Soviet imperialism and the re-run (this time with a happy ending) of the Vietnam War. The Rolling Stones, approaching their fifties, gyrate before eighteen year-olds who do not appear to need the machinery of nostalgia to be sold on their parents' heroes. Paul McCartney is selling the Beatles to a new audience by hitching his oblique nostalgia to their desire for the new that smacks of the old. *Dragnet* is back in nineties drag, and so is *Adam-12*, not to speak of *Batman* and *Mission Impossible*, all dressed up technologically but remarkably faithful to the atmospherics of their originals.

The past is now not a land to return to in a simple politics of memory. It has become a synchronic warehouse of cultural scenarios, a kind of temporal central casting, to which recourse can be had as appropriate, depending on the movie to be made, the scene to be enacted, the hostages to be rescued. All this is par for the course, if you follow Baudrillard or Lyotard into a world of signs wholly unmoored from their social signifiers (all the world's a Disneyland). But I would like to suggest that the apparent increasing substitutability of whole periods and postures for one another, in the cultural styles of advanced capitalism, is tied to larger global forces, which have done much to show Americans that the past is usually another country. If your present is their future (as in much modernization theory and in many self-satisfied tourist fantasies), and their future is your past (as in the case of the Philippine virtuosos of American popular music), then your own past can be made to appear as simply a normalized modality of your present. Thus, although some anthropologists may continue to relegate their Others to temporal spaces that they do not themselves occupy,[12] post-industrial cultural productions have entered a post-nostalgic phase.

The crucial point, however, is that the United States is no longer the puppeteer of a world system of images, but is only one node of a complex transnational construction of imaginary landscapes. The world we live in today is characterized by a new role for the imagination in social life. To grasp this new role, we need to bring together: the old idea of images, especially mechanically produced images (in the Frankfurt School sense); the idea of the imagined community (in Anderson's sense); and the French idea of the imaginary (*imaginaire*), as a constructed landscape of collective aspirations, which is no more and no less real than the collective representations of Emile Durkheim, now mediated through the complex prism of modern media.

The image, the imagined, the imaginary – these are all terms which direct us to something critical and new in global cultural processes: *the imagination as a social practice*. No longer mere fantasy (opium for the masses whose real work is elsewhere), no longer simple escape (from a world defined principally by more concrete purposes and structures), no longer elite pastime (thus not relevant to the lives of ordinary people) and no longer mere contemplation (irrelevant for new forms of desire and subjectivity), the imagination has become an organized field of social practices, a form of work (both in the sense of labor and of culturally organized practice) and a form of negotiation between sites of agency ('individuals') and globally defined fields of possibility. It is this unleashing of the imagination which links the play of pastiche (in some settings) to the terror and coercion of states and their competitors. The imagination is now central to all forms of agency, is itself a social fact, and is the key component of the new global order. But to make this claim meaningful, it is necessary to address some other issues.

Homogenization and Heterogenization

The central problem of today's global interactions is the tension between cultural homogenization and cultural heterogenization. A vast array of empirical facts could be brought to bear on the side of the homogenization argument, and much of it has come from the left end of the spectrum of media studies,[13] and some from other perspectives.[14] Most often, the homogenization argument subspeciates into either an argument about Americanization, or an argument about commoditization, and very often the two arguments are closely linked. What these arguments fail to consider is that at least as rapidly as forces from various metropolises are brought into new societies they tend to become indigenized in one or another way: this is true of music and housing styles as much as it is true of science and terrorism, spectacles and constitutions. The dynamics of such indigenization have just begun to be explored systemically[15] and much more needs to be done. But it is worth noticing that for the people of Irian Jaya, Indonesianization may be more worrisome than Americanization, as Japanization may be for Koreans, Indianization for Sri Lankans, Vietnamization for the Cambodians, Russianization for the people of Soviet Armenia and the Baltic Republics. Such a list of alternative fears to Americanization could be greatly expanded, but it is not a shapeless inventory: for polities of smaller scale, there is always a fear of cultural absorption by polities of larger scale, especially those that are nearby. One man's imagined community is another man's political prison.

This scalar dynamic, which has widespread global manifestations, is also tied to the relationship between nations and states. [. . .] [The] simplification of these many forces (and fears) of homogenization can also be exploited by nation-states in relation to their own minorities, by posing global commoditization (or capitalism, or some other such external enemy) as more real than the threat of its own hegemonic strategies.

The new global cultural economy has to be seen as a complex, overlapping, disjunctive order, which cannot any longer be understood in terms of existing center–periphery models (even those which might account for multiple centers and peripheries). Nor is it susceptible to simple models of push and pull (in terms of migration theory), or of surpluses and deficits (as in traditional models of balance of trade), or of consumers and producers (as in most neo-Marxist theories of development). Even the most complex and flexible theories of global development which have come out of the Marxist tradition[16] are inadequately quirky and have failed to come to terms with what Lash and Urry have called disorganized capitalism.[17] The complexity of the current global economy has to do with certain fundamental disjunctures between economy, culture and politics which we have only begun to theorize.[18]

I propose that an elementary framework for exploring such disjunctures is to look at the relationship between five dimensions of global cultural flow which can be termed: (a) ethnoscapes; (b) mediascapes; (c) technoscapes; (d) finanscapes; and (e) ideoscapes.[19] The suffix -scape allows us to point to the fluid, irregular shapes of these landscapes, shapes which characterize international capital as deeply as they do international clothing styles. These terms with the common suffix -scape also indicate that these are not objectively given relations which look the same from every angle of vision, but rather that they are deeply perspectival constructs, inflected by the historical, linguistic and political situatedness of different sorts of actors: nation-states, multinationals, diasporic communities, as well as sub-national groupings and movements (whether religious, political or economic), and even intimate face-to-face groups, such as villages, neighborhoods and families. Indeed, the individual actor is the last locus of this perspectival set of landscapes, for these landscapes are eventually navigated by agents who both experience and constitute larger formations, in part by their own sense of what these landscapes offer.

These landscapes thus are the building blocks of what (extending Benedict Anderson) I would like to call *imagined worlds*, that is, the multiple worlds which are constituted by the historically situated imaginations of persons and groups spread around the globe.[20] An important fact of the world we live in today is that many persons on the globe live in such imagined worlds (and not just in imagined communities) and thus are able to contest and sometimes even subvert the imagined worlds of the official mind and of the entrepreneurial mentality that surround them.

By ethnoscape, I mean the landscape of persons who constitute the shifting world in which we live: tourists, immigrants, refugees, exiles, guestworkers and other moving groups and persons constitute an essential feature of the world and appear to affect the politics of (and between) nations to a hitherto unprecedented degree. This is not to say that there are no relatively stable communities and networks, of kinship, of friendship, of work and of leisure, as well as of birth, residence and other filiative forms. But it is to say that the warp of these stabilities is everywhere shot through with the woof of human motion, as more persons and groups deal with the realities of having to move or the fantasies of wanting to move. What is more, both these realities as well as these fantasies now function on larger scales, as men and women from villages in India think not just of moving to Poona or Madras, but of moving to Dubai and Houston, and refugees from Sri Lanka find themselves in South India as well as in Switzerland, just as the Hmong are driven to London as well as to Philadelphia. And as international capital shifts its needs, as production and technology generate different needs, as nation-states shift their policies on refugee populations, these moving groups can never afford to let their imaginations rest too long, even if they wish to.

By technoscape, I mean the global configuration, also ever fluid, of technology, and of the fact that technology, both high and low, both mechanical and informational, now moves at high speeds across various kinds of previously impervious boundaries. Many countries now are the roots of multinational enterprise: a huge steel complex in Libya may involve interests from India, China, Russia and Japan, providing different components of new technological configurations. The odd distribution of technologies, and thus the peculiarities of these technoscapes, are increasingly driven not by any obvious economies of scale, of political control, or of market rationality, but by increasingly complex relationships between money flows, political possibilities and the availability of both un- and highly skilled labor. So, while India exports waiters and chauffeurs to Dubai and Sharjah, it also exports software engineers to the United States – indentured briefly to Tata-Burroughs or the World Bank, then laundered through the State Department to become wealthy resident aliens, who are in turn objects of seductive messages to invest their money and know-how in federal and state projects in India.

The global economy can still be described in terms of traditional indicators (as the World Bank continues to do) and studied in terms of traditional comparisons (as in Project Link at the University of Pennsylvania), but the complicated technoscapes (and the stifling ethnoscapes) which underlie these indicators and comparisons are further out of the reach of the queen of the social sciences than ever before. How is one to make a meaningful comparison of wages in Japan and the United States or of real estate costs in New York and Tokyo, without taking sophisticated account of the very complex fiscal and investment flows that link the two economies through a global grid of currency speculation and capital transfer?

Thus it is useful to speak as well of finanscapes, since the disposition of global capital is now a more mysterious, rapid and difficult landscape to follow than ever before, as currency markets, national stock exchanges, and commodity speculations move mega-monies through national turnstiles at blinding speed, with vast absolute implications for small differences in percentage points and time units. But the critical point is that the global relationship between ethnoscapes, technoscapes and finanscapes is deeply disjunctive and profoundly unpredictable, since each of these landscapes is subject to its own constraints and incentives (some political, some informational and some techno-environmental), at the same time as each acts as a constraint and a parameter for movements in the others. Thus, even an elementary model of global political economy must take into account the deeply disjunctive relationships between human movement, technological flow and financial transfers.

Further refracting these disjunctures (which hardly form a simple, mechanical global infrastructure in any case) are what I call mediascapes and ideoscapes, though the latter two are closely related landscapes of images. Mediascapes refer both to the distribution of the electronic capabilities to produce and disseminate information (newspapers, magazines, television stations and film production studios), which are now available to a growing number of private and public interests throughout the world, and to the images of the world created by these media. These images of the world involve many complicated inflections, depending on their mode (documentary or entertainment), their hardware (electronic or pre-electronic), their audiences (local, national or transnational) and the interests of those who own and control them. What is most important about these mediascapes is that they provide (especially in their television, film and cassette forms) large and complex repertoires of images, narratives and ethnoscapes to viewers throughout the world, in which the world of commodities and the world of news and politics are profoundly mixed. What this means is that many audiences throughout the world experience the media themselves as a complicated and interconnected repertoire of print, celluloid, electronic screens and billboards. The lines between the realistic and the fictional landscapes they see are blurred, so that, the further away these audiences are from the direct experiences of metropolitan life, the more likely they are to construct imagined worlds which are chimerical, aesthetic, even fantastic objects, particularly if assessed by the criteria of some other perspective, some other imagined world.

Mediascapes, whether produced by private or state interests, tend to be image-centered, narrative-based accounts of strips of reality, and what they offer to those who experience and transform them is a series of elements (such as characters, plots and textual forms) out of which scripts can be formed of imagined lives, their own as well as those of others living in other places. These scripts can and do get disaggregated into complex sets of metaphors by which people live[21] as they help to constitute narratives of the Other and proto-narratives of possible lives, fantasies which could become prolegomena to the desire for acquisition and movement.

Ideoscapes are also concatenations of images, but they are often directly political and frequently have to do with the ideologies of states and the counter-ideologies of movements explicitly oriented to capturing state power or a piece of it. These ideoscapes are composed of elements of the Enlightenment worldview, which consists of a concatenation of ideas, terms and images, including 'freedom', 'welfare', 'rights', 'sovereignty', 'representation' and the master-term 'democracy'. The master-narrative of the Enlightenment (and its many variants in England, France and the United States) was constructed with a certain internal logic and presupposed a certain relationship between reading, representation and the public sphere.[22] But their diaspora across the world, especially since the nineteenth century, has loosened the internal coherence that held these terms and images together in a Euro-American master-narrative and provided instead a loosely structured synopticon of politics, in which different nation-states, as part of their evolution, have organized their political cultures around different keywords.[23]

As a result of the differential diaspora of these keywords, the political narratives that govern communication between elites and followings in different parts of the world involve problems of both a semantic and a pragmatic nature: semantic to the extent that words (and their lexical equivalents) require careful translation from context to context in their global movements; and pragmatic to the extent that the use of these words by political actors and their audiences may be subject to very different sets of contextual conventions that mediate their translation into public politics. Such conventions are not only matters of the nature of political rehtoric (viz., what does the aging Chinese leadership mean when it refers to the dangers of hooliganism? What does the South Korean leadership mean when it speaks of discipline as the key to democratic industrial growth?)

These conventions also involve the far more subtle question of what sets of communicative genres are valued in what way (newspapers versus cinema, for example) and what sorts of pragmatic genre conventions govern the collective readings of different kinds of text. So, while an Indian audience may be attentive to the resonances of a political speech in terms of some keywords and phrases reminiscent of Hindi cinema, a Korean audience may respond to the subtle codings of Buddhist or neo-Confucian rehtorical strategy encoded in a political document.

The very relationship of reading to hearing and seeing may vary in important ways that determine the morphology of these different ideoscapes as they shape themselves in different national and transnational contexts. This globally variable synaesthesia has hardly even been noted, but it demands urgent analysis. Thus democracy has clearly become a master-term, with powerful echoes from Haiti and Poland to the Soviet Union and China, but it sits at the center of a variety of ideoscapes (composed of distinctive pragmatic configurations of rough translations of other central terms from the vocabulary of the Enlightenment). This creates ever new terminological kaleidoscopes, as states (and the groups that seek to capture them) seek to pacify populations whose own ethnoscapes are in motion and whose mediascapes may create severe problems for the ideoscapes with which they are presented. The fluidity of ideoscapes is complicated in particular by the growing diasporas (both voluntary and involuntary) of intellectuals who continuously inject new meaning-streams into the discourse of democracy in different parts of the world.

This extended terminological discussion of the five terms I have coined sets the basis for a tentative formulation about the conditions under which current global flows occur: *they occur in and through the growing disjunctures between ethnoscapes, technoscapes, finanscapes, mediascapes and ideoscapes.* This formulation, the core of my model of global cultural flow, needs some explanation. First, people, machinery, money, images and ideas now follow increasingly non-isomorphic paths: of course, at all periods in human history, there have been some disjunctures between the flows of these things, but the sheer speed, scale and volume of each of these flows is now so great that the disjunctures have become central to the politics of global culture. The Japanese are notoriously hospitable to ideas and are stereotyped as inclined to export (all) and import (some) goods, but they are also notoriously closed to immigration, like Swiss, the Swedes and the Saudis. Yet the Swiss and Saudis accept populations of guestworkers, thus creating labor diasporas of Turks, Italians and other circum-Mediterranean groups. Some such guestworker groups maintain continuous contact with their home nations, like the Turks, but others, like high-level South Asian migrants, tend to desire lives in their new homes, raising anew the problem of reproduction in a deterritorialized context. [. . .]

Returning [. . .] to the ethnoscapes with which I began, the central paradox of ethnic politics in today's world is that primordia (whether of language or skin color or neighborhood or kinship) have become globalized. That is, sentiments whose greatest force is in their ability to ignite intimacy into a political sentiment and turn locality into a staging ground for identity, have become spread over vast and irregular spaces as groups move, yet stay linked to one another through sophisticated media capabilities. This is not to deny that such primordia are often the product of invented traditions[24] or retrospective affiliations, but to emphasize that because of the disjunctive and unstable interplay of commerce, media, national policies and consumer fantasies, ethnicity, once a genie contained in the bottle of some sort of locality (however large), has now become a global force, forever slipping in and through the cracks between states and borders.

But the relationship between the cultural and economic levels of this new set of global disjunctures is not a simple one-way street in which the terms of global cultural politics are set wholly by, or confined wholly within, the vicissitudes of international flows of technology, labor and finance, demanding only a modest modification of existing neo-Marxist models of uneven development and state-formation. There is a deeper change, itself driven by the disjunctures between all the landscapes I have discussed, and constituted by their continuously fluid and uncertain interplay, which concerns the relationship between production and consumption in today's global economy. Here I begin with Marx's famous (and often mined) view of the fetishism of the commodity and suggest that this fetishism has been replaced in the world at large (now seeing the world as one, large, interactive system, composed of many complex subsystems) by two mutually supportive descendants, the first of which I call production fetishism, and the second of which I call the fetishism of the consumer.

By production fetishism I mean an illusion created by contemporary transnational production loci, which masks translocal capital, transnational earning-flows, global management and often faraway workers (engaged in various kinds of high-tech putting-out operations) in the idiom and spectacle of local (sometimes even worker) control, national productivity and territorial sovereignty. To the extent that various kinds of Free Trade Zones have become the models for production at large, especially of high-tech commodities, production has itself become a fetish, masking not social relations as such, but the relations of production, which are increasingly transnational. The locality (both in the sense of the local factory or site of production and in the extended sense of the nation-state) becomes a fetish which disguises the globally dispersed forces that actually drive the production process. This generates alienation (in Marx's sense) twice intensified, for its social sense is now compounded by a complicated spatial dynamic which is increasingly global.

As for the fetishism of the consumer, I mean to indicate here that the consumer has been transformed, through commodity flows (and the mediascapes, especially of advertising, that accompany them), into a sign, both in Baudrillard's sense of a simulacrum which only asymptotically approaches the form of a real social agent; and in the sense of a mask for the real seat of agency, which is not the consumer but the producer and the many forces that constitute production. Global advertising is the key technology for the worldwide dissemination of a plethora of creative, and culturally well-chosen, ideas of consumer agency. These images of agency are increasingly distortions of a world of merchandising so subtle that the consumer is consistently helped to believe that he or she is an actor, where in fact he or she is at best a chooser.

The globalization of culture is not the same as its homogenization, but globalization involves the use of a variety of instruments of homogenization (armaments, advertising techniques, language hegemonies and clothing styles) which are absorbed into local political and cultural economies, only to be repatriated as heterogeneous dialogues of national sovereignty, free enterprise and fundamentalism in which the state plays an increasingly delicate role: too much openness to global flows, and the nation-state is threatened by revolt – the China syndrome; too little, and the state exits the international stage, as Burma, Albania and North Korea in various ways have done. In general, the state has become the arbitrater of this *repatriation of difference* (in the form of goods, signs, slogans and styles). But this repatriation or export of the designs and commodities of difference continuously exacerbates the internal politics of majoritarianism and homogenization, which is most frequently played out in debates over heritage.

Thus the central feature of global culture today is the politics of the mutual effort of sameness and difference to cannibalize one another and thus to proclaim their successful hijacking of the twin Enlightenment ideas of the triumphantly universal and the resiliently particular. This mutual cannibalization shows its ugly face in riots, in refugee flows, in state-sponsored torture and in ethnocide (with or without state support). Its brighter side is in the expansion of many individual horizons of hope and fantasy, in the global spread of oral dehydration therapy and other low-tech instruments of well-being, in the susceptibility even of South Africa to the force of global opinion, in the inability of the Polish state to repress its own working classes, and in the growth of a wide range of progressive, transnational alliances. Examples of both sorts could be multiplied. The critical point is that both sides of the coin of global cultural process today are products of the infinitely varied mutual contest of sameness and difference on a stage characterized by radical disjunctures between different sorts of global flows and the uncertain landscapes created in and through these disjunctures.

The Work of Reproduction in an Age of Mechanical Art

I have inverted the key terms of the title of Walter Benjamin's famous essay[25] to return this rather high-flying discussion to a more manageable level. There is a classic human problem which will not disappear however much global cultural processes might change their dynamics, and this is the problem today typically discussed under the rubric of reproduction (and traditionally referred to in terms of the transmission of culture). In either case, the question is as follows: how do small groups, especially families, the classical loci of socialization, deal with these new global realities as they seek to reproduce themselves, and in so doing, as it were by accident, reproduce cultural forms themselves? In traditional anthropological terms, this could be phrased as the problem of enculturation in a period of rapid culture change. So the problem is hardly novel. But it does take on some novel dimensions under the global conditions discussed so far in this essay.

In the first place, the sort of trans-generational stability of knowledge which was presupposed in most theories of enculturation (or, in slightly broader terms, of socialization) can no longer be assumed. As families move to new locations, or as children move before older generations, or as grown sons and daughters return from time spent in strange parts of the world, family relationships can become volatile, as new commodity patterns are negotiated, debts and obligations are recalibrated and rumors and fantasies about the new setting are maneuvred into existing repertoires of knowledge and practice. Often, global labor diasporas involve immense strains on marriages in general and on women in particular, as marriages become the meeting points of historical patterns of socialization and new ideas of proper behavior. Generations easily divide, as ideas about property, propriety and collective obligation wither under the siege of distance and time. Most important of all, the work of cultural reproduction in new settings is profoundly complicated by the politics of representing a family as 'normal' (particularly for the young) to neighbors and peers in the new setting. All this is, of course, not new to the cultural study of immigration.

What is new is that this is a world in which both points of departure and points of arrival are in cultural flux, and thus the search for steady points of reference, as critical life-choices are made, can be very difficult. It is in this atmosphere that the invention of tradition (and of ethnicity, kinship and other identity-markers) can become slippery, as the search for certainties is regularly frustrated by the fluidities of transnational communication. As group pasts become increasingly parts of museums, exhibits and collections, both in national and transnational spectacles, culture becomes less what Bourdieu would have called a habitus (a tacit realm of reproducible practices and dispositions) and more an arena for conscious choice, justification and representation, the latter often to multiple, and spatially dislocated audiences.

The task of cultural reproduction, even in its most intimate arenas, such as husband–wife and parent–child relations, becomes both politicized and exposed to the traumas of deterritorialization as family members pool and negotiate their mutual understandings and aspirations in sometimes fractured spatial arrangements. At larger levels, such as community, neighborhood and territory, this politicization is often the emotional fuel for more explicitly violent politics of identity, just as these larger politics sometimes penetrate and ignite domestic politics. When, for example, two offspring in a household split with their father on a key matter of political identification in a transnational setting, pre-existing localized norms carry little force. Thus a son who has joined the Hezbollah group in Lebanon may no longer get along with parents or siblings who are affiliated with Amal or some other branch of Shi'ite ethnic political identity in Lebanon. Women in particular bear the brunt of this sort of friction, for they become pawns in the heritage politics of the household, and are often subject to the abuse and violence of men who are themselves torn about the relation between heritage and opportunity in shifting spatial and political formations.

The pains of cultural reproduction in a disjunctive global world are, of course, not eased by the effects of mechanical art (or mass media, if you will) since these media afford powerful resources for counter-nodes of identity which youth can project against parental wishes or desires. At larger levels of organization, there can be many forms of cultural politics within displaced populations (whether of refugees or of voluntary immigrants), all of which are inflected in important ways by media (and the mediascapes and ideoscapes they offer). A central link between the fragilities of cultural reproduction and the role of the mass media in today's world is the politics of gender and of violence. As fantasies of gendered violence dominate the B-grade film industries that blanket the world, they both reflect and refine gendered violence at home and in the streets, as young men (in particular) come to be torn between the macho politics of self-assertion in contexts where they are frequently denied real agency, and women are forced to enter the labor force in new ways on the one hand, and continue the maintenance of familial heritage on the other. Thus the honor of women becomes not just an armature of stable (if inhuman) systems of cultural reproduction, but a new arena for the formation of sexual identity and family politics, as men and women face new pressures at work, and new fantasies of leisure.

Since both work and leisure have lost none of their gendered qualities in this new global order, but have acquired ever subtler fetishized representations, the honor of women becomes increasingly a surrogate for the identity of embattled communities of males, while their women, in reality, have to negotiate increasingly harsh conditions of work at home and in the non-domestic workplace. In short, deterritorialized communities and displaced populations, however much they may enjoy the fruits of new kinds of earning and new dispositions of capital and technology, have to play out the desires and fantasies of these new ethnoscapes, while striving to reproduce the family-as-microcosm of culture. As the shapes of cultures grow themselves less bounded and tacit, more fluid and politicized, the work of cultural reproduction becomes a daily hazard. Far more could, and should, be said about the work of reproduction in an age of mechanical art: the preceding discussion was meant to indicate the contours of the problems that a new, globally informed, theory of cultural reproduction will have to face.

Shape and Process in Global Cultural Formations

The deliberations of the arguments that I have made so far constitute the bare bones of an approach to a general theory of global cultural processes. Focusing on disjunctures, I have employed a set of terms (ethnoscape, finanscape, technoscape, mediascape and ideoscape) to stress different streams or flows along which cultural material may be seen to be moving across national boundaries. I have also sought to exemplify the ways in which these various flows (or landscapes, from the stabilizing perspectives of any given imagined world) are in fundamental disjuncture with respect to one another. What further steps can we take towards a general theory of global cultural processes, based on these proposals?

The first is to note that our very models of cultural shape will have to alter, as configurations of people, place and heritage lose all semblance of isomorphism. Recent work in anthropology has done much to free us of the shackles of highly localized, boundary-oriented, holistic, primordialist images of cultural form and substance.[26] But not very much has been put in their place, except somewhat larger if less mechanical versions of these images, as in Wolf's work on the relationship of

Europe to the rest of the world. What I would like to propose is that we begin to think of the configuration of cultural forms in today's world as fundamentally fractal, that is, as possessing no Euclidean boundaries, structures or regularities. Second, I would suggest that these cultural forms, which we should strive to represent as fully fractal, are also overlapping, in ways that have been discussed only in pure mathematics (in set theory for example) and in biology (in the language of polythetic classifications). Thus we need to combine a fractal metaphor for the shape of cultures (in the plural) with a polythetic account of their overlaps and resemblances. Without this latter step, we shall remain enmired in comparative work which relies on the clear separation of the entities to be compared, before serious comparison can begin. How are we to compare fractally shaped cultural forms which are also polythetically overlapping in their coverage of terrestrial space?

Finally, in order for the theory of global cultural interactions predicated on disjunctive flows to have any force greater than that of a mechanical metaphor, it will have to move into something like a human version of the theory that some scientists are calling 'chaos' theory. That is, we will need to ask how these complex, overlapping, fractal shapes constitute not a simple, stable (even if large-scale) system, but to ask what its dynamics are: Why do ethnic riots occur when and where they do? Why do states wither at greater rates in some places and times rather than others? Why do some countries flout conventions of international debt repayment with so much less apparent worry than others? How are international arms flows driving ethnic battles and genocides? Why are some states exiting the global stage while others are clamoring to get in? Why do key events occur at a certain point in a certain place rather than in others? These are, of course, the great traditional questions of causality, contingency and prediction in the human sciences, but in a world of disjunctive global flows, it is perhaps important to start asking them in a way that relies on images of flow and uncertainty, hence 'chaos', rather than on older images of order, stability and systemacity. Otherwise, we will have gone far towards a theory of global cultural systems but thrown out 'process' in the bargain. And that would make these notes part of a journey towards the kind of illusion of order that we can no longer afford to impose on a world that is so transparently volatile.

Whatever the directions in which we can push these macro-metaphors (fractals, polythetic classifications and chaos), we need to ask one other old-fashioned question out of the Marxist paradigm: is there some pre-given order to the relative determining force of these global flows? Since I have postulated the dynamics of global cultural systems as driven by the relationship between flows of persons, technologies, finance, information and ideology, can we speak of some structural-causal order linking these flows, by analogy to the role of the economic order in one version of the Marxist paradigm? Can we speak of some of these flows as being, for a priori structural or historical reasons, always prior to and formative of other flows? My own hypothesis, which can only be tentative at this point, is that the relationship of these various flows to one another, as they constellate into particular events and social forms, will be radically context-dependent. Thus, while labor flows and their loops with financial flows between Kerala and the Middle East may account for the shape of media flows and ideoscapes in Kerala, the reverse may be true of Silicon Valley in California, where intense specialization in a special technological sector (computers) and specific flows of capital may well profoundly determine the shape that ethnoscapes, ideoscapes and mediascapes may take.

This does not mean that the causal-historical relationship between these various flows is random or meaninglessly contingent, but that our current theories of cultural 'chaos' are insufficiently developed to be even parsimonious models, at this point, much less to be predictive theories, the golden fleeces of one kind of social science. What I have sought to provide in this essay is a reasonably economical technical vocabulary and a rudimentary model of disjunctive flows, from which something like a decent global analysis might emerge. Without some such analysis, it will be difficult to construct what John Hinkson [...] calls a 'social theory of postmodernity' that is adequately global.

Notes

1. M. Hodgson, *The Venture of Islam: Conscience and history in a world civilization*, University of Chicago Press: Chicago, IL, 1974.
2. J. Abu-Lughod, *Before European Hegemony: The world system AD 1250–1350*, Oxford University Press: New York, 1989; F. Braudel, *Civilization and Capitalism, 15th–18th Century* (3 vols.), Collins: London, 1981–4; P. Curtin, *Cross-Cultural Trade in World History*, Cambridge University Press: Cambridge, 1984; I. Wallerstein, *The Modern World-System* (2 vols.), Academic Press: New York and London, 1974; E. Wolf, *Europe and the People Without History*, University of California Press: Berkeley, CA, 1982.
3. M. W. Helms, *Ulysees' Sail: An ethnographic odyssey of power, knowledge, and geographical distance*, Princeton University Press: Princeton, NJ, 1988; E. Schafer, *Golden Peaches of Samarkand: A study of T'ang exotics*, University of California Press: Berkeley, 1963.
4. See, e.g., C. Bayly, *Imperial Meridian: The British Empire and the world, 1780–1830*, Macmillan: London and New York, 1989.
5. B. Anderson, *Imagined Communities: Reflections on the origin and spread of nationalism*, Verso: London, 1983.
6. P. Chatterjee, *Nationalist Thought and the Colonial World: A derivative discourse*, Zed Press: London, 1986.
7. J. Meyrowitz, *No Sense of Place: The impact of electronic media on social behavior*, Oxford University Press: New York, 1985.
8. G. Deleuze and F. Guattari, *A Thousand Plateaus: Capitalism and schizophrenia*, trans. B. Massumi, University of Minnesota Press: Minneapolis, 1987.
9. P. Iyer, *Video Night in Kathmandu*, Knopf: New York, 1988.
10. F. Jameson, 'Nostalgia for the present', *South Atlantic Quarterly*, 88, 2, Spring 1989, pp. 517–37.
11. *idem*, 'Postmodernism and consumer society', in H. Foster (ed.), *The Anti-Aesthetic: Essays on postmodern culture*, Bay Press: Port Townsend, Washington, 1983, pp. 111–25.
12. J. Fabian, *Time and the Other: How anthropology makes its object*, Columbia University Press: New York, 1983.

13. C. Hamelink, *Cultural Autonomy in Global Communications*, Longman: New York, 1983; A. Mattelart, *Transnationals and the Third World: The struggle for culture*, Bergin & Garvey: South Hadley, MA, 1983; H. Schiller, *Communication and Cultural Domination*, International Arts and Sciences: White Plains, NY, 1976.

14. E. Gans, *The End of Culture: Towards a generative anthropology*, University of California Press: Berkeley, CA, 1985; Iyer, *op. cit.*

15. K. Barber, 'Popular arts in Africa', *African Studies Review*, 30, 3, September 1987, pp. 1–78; S. Feld, 'Notes on world beat', *Public Culture*, 1, 1, 1988, pp. 31–7; U. Hannerz, 'The world in creolization', *Africa*, 57, 4, 1987, pp. 546–59, and 'Notes on the global ecumene', *Public Culture*, 1, 2, Spring 1989, pp. 66–75; M. Ivy, 'Tradition and difference in the Japanese mass media', *Public Culture*, 1, 1, 1988, pp. 21–9; F. Nicoll, 'My trip to Alice', *Criticism, Heresy and Interpretation (CHAI)*, 3, 1989, pp. 21–32; M. Yoshimoto, 'The postmodern and mass images in Japan', *Public Culture*, 1, 2, 1989, pp. 8–25.

16. S. Amin, *Class and Nation: Historically and in the current crisis*, Monthly Review Press: New York, 1980; E. Mandel, *Late Capitalism*, Verso: London, 1978; Wallerstein, *op. cit.*; Wolf, *op. cit.*

17. S. Lash and J. Urry, *The End of Organized Capitalism*, University of Wisconsin Press: Madison, WI, 1987.

18. One major exception is Fredric Jameson, whose work on the relationship between postmodernism and late capitalism has, in many ways, inspired this essay. However, the debate between Jameson and Ahmad in *Social Text* shows that the creation of a globalizing Marxist narrative, in cultural matters, is difficult territory indeed. My own effort, in this context, is to begin a restructuring of the Marxist narrative (by stressing lags and disjunctures) that many Marxists might find abhorrent. Such a restructuring has to avoid the dangers of obliterating difference within the third world, of eliding the social referent (as some French postmodernists seem inclined to do) and of retaining the narrative authority of the Marxist tradition, in favor of greater attention to global fragmentation, uncertainty and difference.

19. These ideas are argued more fully in a book I am currently working on, tentatively entitled *Imploding Worlds: Imagination and disjuncture in the global cultural economy*.

20. A. Appadurai, 'Global ethnoscapes: notes and queries for a transnational anthropology', in R. G. Fox (ed.), *Interventions: Anthropologies of the present*, in press.

21. G. Lakoff and M. Johnson, *Metaphors We Live By*, University of Chicago Press: Chicago, IL, and London, 1980.

22. For the dynamics of this process in the early history of the United States, see M. Warner, *The Letters of the Republic: Publication and the public sphere*, Harvard University Press: Cambridge, MA, in press.

23. See, e.g., R. Williams, *Keywords*, Oxford University Press: New York, 1976.

24. E. Hobsbawm and T. Ranger (eds.), *The Invention of Tradition*, Columbia University Press: New York, 1983.

25. W. Benjamin, 'The work of art in the age of mechanical reproduction', in *Illuminations*, ed. H. Arendt, trans. H. Zohn, Schocken Books: New York, 1969, pp. 217–51 (first published 1936).

26. Appadurai, 'Global ethnoscapes'; Hannerz, 'Notes on the global ecumene'; G. Marcus and M. Fisher, *Anthropology as Cultural Critique: An experimental moment in the human sciences*, University of Chicago Press: Chicago, IL, 1986; R. Thornton, 'The rhetoric of ethnographic holism', *Cultural Anthropology*, 3, 3, August 1988, pp. 285–303.

19 □ *Towards a Critical Theory of Third World Films*

Teshome H. Gabriel

Wherever there is a film-maker prepared to stand up against commercialism, exploitation, pornography and the tyranny of technique, there is to be found the living spirit of *New Cinema*. Wherever there is a film-maker, of any age or background, ready to place his cinema and his profession at the service of the great causes of his time, there will be the living spirit of *New Cinema*. This is the correct definition which sets *New Cinema* apart from the commercial industry because the commitment of industrial cinema is to untruth and exploitation.

Glauber Rocha (Brazil), *The Aesthetics of Hunger*

Insert the work as an original fact in the process of liberation, place it first at the service of life itself, ahead of art; *dissolve aesthetics in the life of society*: only in this way, as [Frantz] Fanon said, can decolonisation become possible and culture, cinema, and beauty – at least, what is of greatest importance to us – become *our culture, our films, and our sense of beauty*.

Fernando Solanas and Octavio Gettino (Argentina),
Towards a Third Cinema

Frantz Fanon, in his attempts to identify the revolutionary impulse in the peasant of the Third World, accepted that culture is an act of insemination upon history, whose product is liberation from oppression.[1] In my search for a methodological device for a critical inquiry into Third World films, I have drawn upon the historical works of this ardent proponent of liberation, whose analysis of the steps of the genealogy of Third World culture can also be used as a critical framework for the study of Third World films. This essay is, therefore, divided into two parts and

From Jim Pines and Paul Willeman (eds.), *Questions of Third World Cinema*, BFI: London, 1989, pp. 30–52.

focuses on those essential qualities Third World films possess rather than those they may seem to lack. The first part lays the formulation for Third World film culture and filmic institutions based on a critical and theoretical matrix applicable to Third World needs. The second part is an attempt to give material substance to the analytic constructs discussed previously.

From pre-colonial times to the present, the struggle for freedom from oppression has been waged by the Third World masses, who in their maintenance of a deep cultural identity have made history come alive. Just as they have moved aggressively towards independence, so has the evolution of Third World film culture followed a path from 'domination' to 'liberation'. This genealogy of Third World film culture moves from the First Phase in which foreign images are impressed in an alienating fashion on the audience, to the Second and Third Phases in which recognition of 'consciousness of oneself' serves as the essential antecedent for national and, more significantly, international consciousness. There are, therefore, three phases in this methodological device.

Phases of Third World Films

Phase I – The Unqualified Assimilation

The industry
Identification with the Western Hollywood film industry. The link is made as obvious as possible and even the names of the companies proclaim their origin. For instance, the Nigerian film company, Calpenny, whose name stands for California, Pennsylvania and New York, tries to hide behind an acronym, while the companies in India, Egypt and Hong Kong are not worried being typed the 'Third World's Hollywood', 'Hollywood-on-the-Nile', and 'Hollywood of the Orient' respectively.
The theme
Hollywood thematic concerns of 'entertainment' predominate. Most of the feature films of the Third World in this phase sensationalise adventure for its own sake and concern themselves with escapist themes of romance, musicals, comedies etc. The sole purpose of such industries is to turn out entertainment products which will generate profits. The scope and persistence of this kind of industry in the Third World lies in its ability to provide reinvestable funds and this quadruples their staying power. Therefore, in cases where a counter-cinematic movement has occurred the existing national industry has been able to ingest it. A good example is in the incorporation of the 'cinema nôvo' movement in the Brazilian Embrafilme.
Style
The emphasis on formal properties of cinema, technical brilliance and visual wizardry, overrides subject matter. The aim here is simply to create a 'spectacle'. Aping Hollywood stylistically, more often than not, runs counter to Third World needs for a serious social art.

Phase II – The Remembrance Phase

The industry
Indigenisation and control of talents, production, exhibition and distribution. Many Third World film production companies are in this stage. The movement for a social institution of cinema in the Third World such as 'cinema moudjahid' in Algeria, 'new wave' in India and '*engagé* or committed cinema' in Senegal and Mozambique exemplifies this phase.

The theme
Return of the exile to the Third World's source of strength, i.e. culture and history. The predominance of filmic themes such as the clash between rural and urban life, traditional versus modern value systems, folklore and mythology, identifies this level. Sembene Ousmane's early film *Mandabi* about a humble traditional man outstripped by modern ways characterises this stage. *Barravento* ('The Turning Wind'), a poetic Brazilian film about a member of a fishermen's village who returns from exile in the city, is a folkloric study of mysticism. The film from Burkina Faso (Upper Volta), *Wend Kûuni* ('God's Gift'), attempts to preserve the spirit of folklore in a brilliant recreation of an old tale of a woman who is declared a witch because of her conflicts with custom when she refused to marry after the disappearance of her husband. While the most positive aspect of this phase is its break with the concepts and propositions of Phase I, the primary danger here is the uncritical acceptance or undue romanticisation of ways of the past.

It needs to be stressed that there is a danger of falling into the trap of exalting traditional virtues and racialising culture without at the same time condemning faults. To accept totally the values of Third World traditional cultures without simultaneously stamping out the regressive elements can only lead to 'a blind alley', as Fanon puts it, and falsification of the true nature of culture as an act or agent of liberation. Therefore, unless this phase, which predominates in Third World film practices today, is seen as a process, a moving towards the next stage, it could develop into opportunistic endeavours and create cultural confusion. This has been brilliantly pointed out by Luis Ospina of Colombia in his self-reflexive film *Picking on the People*, in which he criticises the exploitative nature of some Third World film-makers who peddle Third World poverty and misery at festival sites in Europe and North America and do not approach their craft as a tool of social transformation. An excellent case in point is the internationally acclaimed film *Pixote* by Hector Babenco. According to a *Los Angeles Times* correspondent in Rio de Janeiro, Da Silva, the young boy who played the title role of the film, was paid a mere $320. The correspondent writes: 'In a real life drama a juvenile judge in Diadema, a suburb of Sao Paulo, last week released Da Silva, now 16, to the custody of his mother after his arrest on charges of housebreaking and theft.' According to Da Silva's mother, who sells lottery tickets for her living, 'after a trip to Rio when he got no work, he told me, "Mother, they have forgotten me, I am finished."' In the meantime Mr Babenco, the now famous film director, was about to shoot his next feature, *The Kiss of the Spider Woman*, in collaboration with producers in Hollywood.[2]

The style

Some attempts to indigenise film style are manifest. Although the dominant stylistic conventions of the first phase still predominate here, there appears to be a growing tendency to create a film style appropriate to the changed thematic concerns. In this respect, the growing insistence on spatial representation rather than temporal manipulation typifies the films in this phase. The sense of a spatial orientation in cinema in the Third World arises out of the experience of an 'endless' world of the large Third World mass. This nostalgia for the vastness of nature projects itself into the film form, resulting in long takes and long or wide shots. This is often done to constitute part of an overall symbolisation of a Third World thematic orientation, i.e. the landscape depicted ceases to be mere land or soil and acquires a phenomenal quality which integrates humans with the general drama of existence itself.

Phase III – The Combative Phase

The industry

Film-making as a public service institution. The industry in this phase is not only owned by the nation and/or the government, it is also managed, operated and run for and by the people. It can also be called a cinema of mass participation, one enacted by members of communities speaking indigenous language, one that espouses Julio García Espinosa's polemic of 'An Imperfect Cinema',[3] that in a developing world, technical and artistic perfection in the production of a film cannot be the aims in themselves. Quite a number of social institutions of cinema in the Third World, some underground like Argentina's 'Cine Liberacion' and some supported by their governments – for instance, 'Chile Films' of Allende's Popular Unity Socialist government – exemplify this phase. Two industrial institutions that also exemplify this level are the Algerian L'Office National pour le Commerce et l'Industrie Cinématographique (ONCIC) and Cuba's Institute of Film Art and Industry (ICAIC).

The theme

Lives and struggles of Third World peoples. This phase signals the maturity of the film-maker and is distinguishable from either Phase I or Phase II by its insistence on viewing film in its ideological ramifications. A very good example is Miguel Littin's *The Promised Land*, a quasi-historical mythic account of power and rebellion, which can be seen as referring to events in modern-day Chile. Likewise, his latest film *Alsino and the Condor* combines realism and fantasy within the context of war-torn Nicaragua. The imagery in *One Way or Another* by the late Sara Gómez Yara, of an iron ball smashing down the old slums of Havana, not only depicts the issue of women/race in present-day Cuba but also symbolises the need for a new awareness to replace the old oppressive spirit of *machismo* which still persists in socialist Cuba. The film *Soleil O*, by the Mauritanian film-maker Med Hondo, aided by the process of Fanonian theses, comes to the recognition of forgotten heritage in the display of the amalgam of ideological determinants of European 'humanism', racism and colonialism. The failure of colonialism to convert Africans into 'white-thinking blacks' depicted in the film reappears in a much wider symbolic form in his later film, *West Indies*, where the entire pantheon of domination and liberation unfolds in a ship symbolic of the slave-ship of yesteryear.

The style

Film as an ideological tool. Here, film is equated or recognised as an ideological instrument. This particular phase also constitutes a framework of agreement between the public (or the indigenous institution of cinema) and the film-maker. A Phase III film-maker is one who is perceptive of and knowledgeable about the pulse of the Third World masses. Such a film-maker is truly in search of a Third World cinema – a cinema that has respect for the Third World peoples. One element of the style in this phase is an ideological point-of-view instead of that of a character as in dominant Western conventions. *Di Cavalcanti* by Glauber Rocha, for instance, is a take-off from 'Quarup', a joyous death ritual celebrated by Amazon tribes.[4] The celebration frees the dead from the hypocritical tragic view modern man has of death. By turning the documentary of the death of the internationally renowned Brazilian painter Di Cavalcanti into a chaotic/celebratory montage of sound and images, Rocha deftly and directly criticised the dominant documentary convention, creating in the process not only an alternative film language but also a challenging discourse on the question of existence itself. Another element of style is the use of flashback – although the reference is to past events, it is not stagnant but dynamic and developmental. In *The Promised Land*, for instance, the flashback device dips into the past to comment on the future, so that within it a flash-forward is inscribed. Similarly, when a flash-forward is used in Sembene's *Ceddo* (1977), it is also to convey a past and future tense simultaneously to comment on two historical periods.

Since the past is necessary for the understanding of the present, and serves as a strategy for the future, this stylistic orientation seems to be ideologically suited to this particular phase.

It should, however, be noted that the three phases discussed above are not organic developments. They are enclosed in a dynamic which is dialectical in nature; for example, some Third World film-makers have taken a contradictory path. *Lucía*, a Cuban film by Humberto Solás, about the relations between the sexes, belongs to Phase III, yet Solás latest film, *Cecilia*, which concerns an ambitious mulatto woman who tries to assimilate into a repressive Spanish aristocracy, is a regression in style (glowing in spectacle) and theme (the tragic mulatto) towards Phase I. Moving in the opposite direction, Glauber Rocha's early Brazilian films like *Deus e O Diabo na Terra do Sol* (literally 'God and the Devil in the Land of the Sun', but advertised in the United States as 'Black God, White Devil'!) and *Terra em Transe* ('The Earth Trembles') reflect a Phase II characteristic, while his last two films, *A Idade da Terra* ('The Age of Earth') and *Di Cavalcanti*, both in their formal properties and subject matter, manifest a Phase III characteristic in their disavowal of the conventions of dominant cinema. According to Glauber Rocha, *A Idade da Terra* (which develops the theme of *Terra em Transe*) and *Di Cavalcanti* disintegrate traditional 'narrative sequences' and rupture not only the fictional and documentary cinema style of his early works, but also 'the world cinematic language' under 'the dictatorship of Coppola and Godard'.[5]

The dynamic enclosure of the three phases posits the existence of grey areas between Phases I and II, and II and III. This area helps to identify a large number of important Third World films. For instance, the Indian film *Manthan* ('The Churning'), the Senegalese film *Xala* ('Spell of Impotence'), the Bolivian film *Chuquiago* (Indian name for La Paz), the Ecuadorean film *My Aunt Nora*, the Brazilian film *They Don't Wear Black Tie* and the Tunisian film *Shadow of the Earth* occupy the grey area between Phase II and III. The importance of the grey areas cannot be over-emphasised, for not only do they concretely demonstrate the *process of becoming* but they also attest to the multi-faceted nature of Third World cinema and the need for the development of new critical canons.

Components of Critical Theory

From the above it can be seen that the development of Third World film culture provides a critical theory particular to Third World needs. I would like to propose at this stage an analytic construct consisting of three components that would provide an integrative matrix within which to approach and interpret the Three Phases drawn out from the Third World's cultural history. The components of critical theory can be schematised as follows:

Component 1: *Text*
> The intersection of codes and sub-codes; the chief thematic and formal characteristics of existing films and the rules of that filmic grammar. And the transformational procedures whereby new 'texts' emerge from old.

Component 2: *Reception*
> The audience: the active interrogation of images versus the passive consumption of films. The issue of alienated and non-alienated identity and the ideal/inscribed or actual/empirical spectatorship illustrates this component of critical theory.

Component 3: *Production*
> The social determination where the wider context of determinants informs social history, market considerations, economy of production, state governance and regulation composes this stage of the critical constructs. Here, the larger historical perspective, the position of the institution of indigenous cinema in progressive social taste, is contexted. The overriding critical issue at this juncture is, for instance, the unavoidable ultimate choice between the classical studio system and the development of a system of production based on the lightweight 16 mm or video technology. The pivotal concern and the single most significant question at this stage, therefore, is: 'Precisely what kind of institution is cinema in the Third World?'

Confluence of Phases and Critical Theory

Each phase of the Third World film culture can be described in terms of all the three components of critical theory, because each phase is necessarily engaged in all the critical operations. For instance, Phase I is characterised by a type of film that simply mirrors, in its concepts and propositions, the *status quo*, i.e. the text and the rules of the grammar are identical to conventional practices. The consequence of this type of 'mimicking' in the area of 'reception' is that an alienated identity ensues from it precisely because the spectator is unable to find or recognise himself/herself in the images. The mechanisms of the systems of 'production' also acknowledge the *status quo* – the reliance is on the studio systems of controlled production and experimentation.

If we apply the components of critical theory to Phase II only, a slight shift in the text and the rules of the grammar is noticeable. Although the themes are predominantly indigenised, the film language remains trapped, woven and blotted with classical formal elements, and remains stained with conventional film style. In terms of 'reception' the viewer, aided by the process of memory and an amalgam of folklore and mythology, is able to locate a somewhat diluted traditional identity. The third level of critical theory also composes and marks the process of indigenisation of the institution of cinema where a position of self-determination is sought.

Finally, the three components of critical theory find their dynamic wholeness in Phase III – the Combative Phase. Here, the text and sub-texts go through a radical shift and transformation – the chief formal and thematic concerns begin to alter the rules of the grammar. Another film language and a system of new codes begin to manifest themselves. With regard to 'reception' we discover that the viewer or subject is no longer alienated because recognition is vested not only in genuine cultural grounds but also in an ideological cognition founded on the acknowledgment of the decolonisation of culture and total liberation.

The intricate relationships of the three phases of the evolution of Third World film culture and the three analytic constructs for filmic institutions help to establish the stage for a confluence of a unique aesthetic exchange founded on other than traditional categories of film conventions (see Figure 1).

This new Third World cinematic experience, inchoate as it is, is in the process of creating a concurrent development of a new and throbbing social institution capable of generating a dynamic and far-reaching influence on the future socio-economic and educational course of the Third World.

I contend that the confluence obtained from the interlocking of the *phases* and the critical *constructs* reveals underlying assumptions concerning perceptual patterns and film viewing situations. For instance, with respect to fiction film showing in Third World theatres, rejection on cultural grounds forces incomplete transmission of meaning. That is, the intended or inscribed meaning of the film is deflected and acquires a unique meaning of its own – the mode of address of the film and the spectator behaviour undergo a radical alteration. Therefore, what has

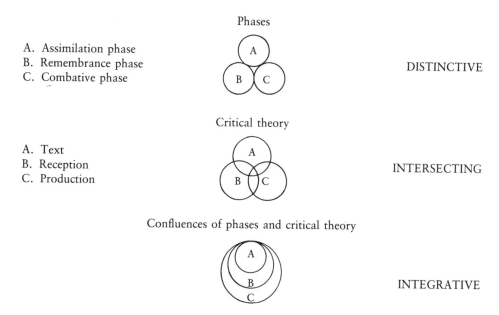

Phases

A. Assimilation phase
B. Remembrance phase
C. Combative phase

DISTINCTIVE

Critical theory

A. Text
B. Reception
C. Production

INTERSECTING

Confluences of phases and critical theory

INTEGRATIVE

Figure 1 Summary of the development of film culture and filmic institutions

Here, A and B find themselves in a larger historical perspective C. It is a wider context of indigenisation and self-determination which conditions levels A and B to give up their position of dominance to C, a stage which composes and marks the union of Third World film culture and the social institutions of cinema.

been presented as a 'fiction' film is received as if it were a 'documentary'. The same fiction film screened in its own country of origin, however, claims an ideal spectatorship because it is firmly anchored in its own cultural references, codes and symbols. A classic example of how films from one culture can be easily misunderstood and misinterpreted by a viewer from another culture is Glauber Rocha's *The Lion Has Seven Heads* (*Der Leone Have Sept Cabezas*). The film was extensively exhibited in the West, one catalogue compiled in 1974 crediting Rocha with bringing 'the Cinema Novo to Africa for this Third World assault on the various imperialisms represented in its multilingual title. Characters include a black revolutionary, a Portuguese mercenary, an American CIA agent, a French missionary, and a voluptuous nude woman called the Golden Temple of Violence.'[6] Again, a recent compendium of reviews, *Africa on Film and Videotape, 1960–1981*, dismisses the film completely with a one-liner, 'An allegorical farce noting the bond between Africa and Brazil'.[7]

Yet Glauber Rocha, in an interview given to a prominent film historian, Rachel Gerber (author of *Glauber Rocha, Cinema, Politica e a Estetica do Inconsciente*), in Rome, February 1973, and in a discussion with this author at UCLA in 1976, said that the film is a story of Che Guevara who is magically resurrected by Blacks through the spirit of Zumbi, the spiritual name of the late Amilcar Cabral. To Rocha, the film is in fact a homage to Amilcar Cabral. Thus, while the West looks at this film as an offering of clichéd images and an object of curiosity, the film-maker is only trying to affirm the continuity of the Third World's anti-imperialist struggle from Che to Cabral (and beyond), to initiate an awareness of their lives, and the relevance to use today of what they struggled and died for. To the extent that we recognise a history of unequal exchanges between the South and the North, we must also recognise the unequal 'symbolic' exchanges involved. The difficulty of Third World films of radical social comment for Western interpretation is the result (a) of the film's resistance to the dominant conventions of cinema, and (b) of the consequence of the Western viewers' loss of being the privileged decoders and ultimate interpreters of meaning.

The Western experience of film viewing – dominance of the big screen and the sitting situation – has naturalised a spectator conditioning so that any communication of a film plays on such values of exhibition and reception. The Third World experience of film viewing and exhibition suggests an altogether different route and different value system. For instance, Americans and Europeans hate seeing a film on African screens, because everybody talks during the showings; similarly, African viewers of film in America complain about the very strict code of silence and the solemn atmosphere of the American movie-theatres.

How the system of perceptual patterns and viewing situation varies with conditions of reception from one culture to another, or how changes in the rules of the grammar affect spectator viewing habits, is part of a larger question which solidifies and confirms the issue of cultural relativism and identity.

The confluence of the phases and the constructs also converges on the technologically mediated factors of needed production apparatuses, productive relations and the mechanisms of industrial operations. It needs to be stated outright that 'technology' as such does not in itself produce or communicate meaning; but it is equally true to say that 'technology' has a dynamic which helps to create ideological carry-overs that impress discourse language, i.e. ideological discourse manifests itself in the mechanisms of film discourse. By way of an example, it is possible that a film-maker might have the idea of 'filmic form' before having 'a content' to go along with it. Third World films are heterogeneous, employing narrative and oral discourse, folk music and songs, extended silences and gaps, moving from fictional representation to reality, to fiction – these constitute the creative part that can challenge the ideological carry-overs that technology imposes.

From the needs of Third World film criticism, contemporary film scholarship is criticised on two major fronts: first, contemporary film theory and criticism is grounded in a conception of the 'viewer' (subject or citizen) derived from psychoanalytic theory where the relation between the 'viewer' and the 'film' is determined by a particular dynamic of the 'familial' matrix. To the extent that Third World culture and familial relationships are not described through psychoanalytic theory, Third World filmic representation is open for an elaboration of the relation 'viewer'/'film' on terms other than those founded on psychoanalysis. The Third World relies more on an appeal to social and political conflicts as the prime rhetorical strategy and less on the paradigm of oedipal conflict and resolution.

Second, on the semiotic front, the Western model of filmic representation is essentially based on a literary or written conception of the scenario which implies a linear, cause/effect conception of narrative action.[8] However, Third World oral narratives, founded on traditional culture, are held in memory by a set of formal strategies specific to repeated, oral, face-to-face tellings.

It is no longer satisfactory to use existing critical criteria, which may be adequate for a film practice (Western in this case) now at a plateau of relevance,[9] to elucidate a new and dynamic film convention whose upward mobility will result in a totally new cinematic language. The Third World experience is thus raising some fundamental concerns about the methods and/or commitment of traditional film scholarship. The Third World filmic practice is, therefore, reorganising and refining the pictorial syntax and the position of the 'viewer' (or spectator) with respect to film. The Third World cinematic experience is moved by the requirements of its social action and contexted and marked by the strategy of that action. We need, therefore, to begin attending to a new theoretical and analytic matrix governed by other than existing critical theories that claim specific applications for universal principles.

Cultural contamination is a deeply rooted human fear: it smells of annihilation. Spiritual and traditional practices have a terrific hold on the Third World rural populace. This reminds us of the maxim which was enunciated by Confucius in the sixth century BC and still prevails: 'I'm a transmitter, not an inventor.' To the Third World, spirits, magic, masquerades and rituals, however flawed they may be, still constitute knowledge and provide collective security and protection from forces of evil. Unknown forces for the rural community can only be checked or controlled if they can be identified.

One way of readily understanding what Third World culture is, is to distinguish it from what it claims not to be.[10] We call at this juncture for a thorough and comparative analysis of 'oral' or 'folk' art form and 'literate' or 'print' art form to situate the foregoing discussion on critical theory into focused attention. I propose here to examine the centrifugal as well as the centripetal cultural forces that might determine not only film, but also the media, in the Third World. This dialectical, not differential or oppositional, conception of cultural forms takes into account the dynamics of their exchange.

Several factors ensue from the examination of the two modes of culture expression. While, for instance, the community issue is at the heart of Third World traditional culture, the issue of the individual is at the base of Western or print culture. With regard to performatory stage presentation, a Western actor interacting with the audience breaks the compact or marginal boundary. Because a special kind of magic enters a playing space, Western stage performance does not allow cross-over. While, therefore, a Western person feels his privacy violated with interactive drama, in the Third World context the understanding between the viewer and the performers is that their positions are interchangeable without notice.

Awe for the old in the Third World culture is very much in evidence. Several films reflect it. The old or the aged as repositories of Third World history is well documented in such films as *Emitai* from Senegal, *They Don't Wear Black Tie* from Brazil, *Shadow of the Earth* from Tunisia and *The In-Laws* from the People's Republic of China. The issue of the aged in Third World culture is beautifully illustrated in Safi Faye's film *Fad Jal*, where the opening sequence of the film states: 'In Africa, an old man dying is like a library burning down.'

A major area of misunderstanding (if we take into account the 'Cognitive Characteristics' of the 'Folk/Print Art' dichotomy in Table 1) is the definition and replacement of 'man', the individual, within Third World societies. For any meaningful dialogue centring on Third World developmental schemes the issue of 'man/woman' in a society must be carefully debated. As Julius K. Nyerere of Tanzania puts it, 'The Purpose is Man',[11] and as the Wolof saying goes, 'Man is the medicine of man.'

A cultural orientation of 'man', the individual, as changeable and capable of effecting change is a condition that reverberates in all advanced societies of the world, be they of capitalist or socialist persuasion. The idea that man, both in the singular and in the plural, has the capability of controlling his/her own destiny and effecting change by his/her own will is a dynamic force which can alter both the thought patterns and work habits of a people. This concept, it must be stated, is not the opposite of the Third World ideal of the primacy of the community over the individual. An excellent example is the film *Beyond the Plains* (where man is born) by Michael Raeburn, in which a young man from the Masai tribe in Tanzania was able to change his people's negative attitude towards education by not only doggedly pursuing it to the university level, but also never losing contact with his people. As he grew up he made sure he performed all the customary rites and fulfilled all the obligations demanded by his people, thus demonstrating that Western and tribal cultural education were not incompatible. From this, it can be seen that the major

Table I Comparison of folk and print art forms

Folk (or Oral) Art Form	Print (or Literate) Art Form
Conception of the Value and Evaluation of Art	
Deeper meaning of art held by cultural groups or community. Interpretive device: one needs to belong and/or understand cultural or folk nuances.	Deeper meaning of art held as the sole property of the artist. Interpretive device: the artist proclaims 'it is for me to know and for you to find, or art is what you mean it to be.'
Recognises general level of excellence, hence emphasis on group competence in the aesthetic judgment of art.	Recognises exceptions, hence emphasis on individual achievement and individual responsibility.

Table 1 (*continued*)

Master artist concept – gifted but normal, and so conforms to the group.	Master artist concept – gifted but eccentric and essentially nonconformist.
Art as occasion for collective engagement.	Art as occasion for 'escape' from normal routine.
Emphasis on contextual relevance.	Emphasis on conceptual interpretation.
Art defined in terms of context.	Art defined in terms of aesthetic.

Performatory Presentation

Held in fluid boundaries, churchyards, fields, marketplaces – operating in a 360° dimension.	Boxed-in theatres and elevated to a stage – operating in a 180° dimension.
A scene flows into another. Cyclical progression linked thematically.	Each scene must follow another scene in linear progression.

Performatory Effect

Expects viewer participation, therefore arouses activity and prepares for and allows participation.	Discourages viewer participation. Puts an end to activity. Inhibits participation.
Multiple episodes that have their own centres.	Singular episode extended through detail.

Cognitive Characteristics

Man defined as 'unchangeable' alone. Change emanates from the community.	Man defined as 'man', changeable and, by virtue of his person, capable of effecting change and progress.
Individual interlinked with total social fabric. Concept of human rather than concept of 'man' as such.	Individual perceived primarily as separated from general social fabric.
Strong tradition of suggestion in the cultural symbol and in the use of linguistic formulae.	Strong tradition of detail and minute (graphic) description.
Time assumed to be a subjective phenomenon, i.e. it is the outcome of conceptualising and experiencing movement.	Time assumed to be an 'objective' phenomenon, dominant and ubiquitous.
Wisdom is a state of intellectual maturity gained by experience. Cumulative process of knowledge, derived from the past. Characterised by slowness of judgment.	Wisdom is characterised by high degree of specialisation in a particular field or discipline. Characterised by quickness of judgment based on a vast accumulation of data and information.
Earth is not a hostile world; e.g. the cult of the ancestors is an attempt at unification with the past, present and future.	Earth is a hostile world and has to be subdued. Paradise is in the future or elsewhere.

difference between the Third World and the West with regard to changing the community from a passive to a dynamic entity is one of approach. Whereas the former aims at changing the individual through the community, the latter wants the community changed by the individual. Only time will tell which of the two approaches makes for sustained, beneficial social progress.

Manipulation of Space and Time in Cinema

A child born in a Western society is encased, from the initial moments of birth, in purposive, man-made fabricated objects. The visual landscape he experiences is dominated by man-made forms. Even the child's dolls reflect the high technology of the environment. Nowadays, a child who is beginning to learn to spell can have a computer that can talk to him and interact with him in a human way. All of these developments are based on the insistence of a society that puts a high price on individualism, individual responsibility and achievement as most necessary.

A child in a rural Third World setting is born in an unrestricted natural landscape. From the day he/she is born the child is dominated by untampered natural forms. Even the interior of the dwelling where the child is born is made to look like the natural environment: it is not unusual to see fresh grass and flowers lending nature's colour to the child's initial world setting. The child grows in this vast universe where his place within the family and in nature is emphasised. A child born and raised in this situation is taught to submerge his individuality and show responsibility to his extended family and his community. His accomplishments are measured not only by his individual achievements but by the degree to which they accomplish and contribute to the social good.

Culture, the terms on which films are based, also naturally grows from these environmental factors. An examination of oral and literate culture in terms of film brings to light two very crucial elements of cinema, namely the concepts of 'space' and 'time'. All cinema manipulates 'time' and 'space'. Where Western films manipulate 'time' more than 'space', Third World films seem to emphasize 'space' over 'time'. Third World films grow from folk tradition where communication is a slow-paced phenomenon and time is not rushed but has its own pace. Western culture, on the other hand, is based on the value of 'time' – time is art, time is money, time is most everything else. If time drags in a film, spectators grow bored and impatient, so that a method has to be found to cheat natural time. In film, this is achieved in the editing. It is all based on the idea that the more purely 'non-dramatic' elements in film are considered 'cinematic excess', i.e. they serve no unifying purpose. What is identified as 'excess' in Western cinematic experience is, therefore, precisely where we locate Third World cinema. Let me now identify those essential elements of cinematic practice that are considered cinematic excess in Western cinema but which in the Third World context seem only too natural.

The long take: It is not uncommon in Third World films to see a concentration of long takes and repetition of images and scenes. In the Third World films, the slow, leisurely pacing approximates the viewer's sense of time and rhythm of life. In addition, the preponderance of wide-angle shots of longer duration deal with a viewer's sense of community and how people fit in nature. Whereas when Michelanglo Antonioni and Jean-Luc Godard use these types of shot it is to convey an existential separation and isolation from nature and self.

Cross-cutting: Cross-cutting between antagonists shows simultaneity rather than the building of suspense. The power of images lies not in the expectation we develop about the mere juxtapositions or the collision itself, but rather in conveying the reasons for the imminent collision. Where, therefore, conventional cinema has too often reduced this to the collision of antagonists, on a scale of positive and negative characters, Third World films doing the same thing make it more explicitly an ideological collision.

The close-up shot: A device so much in use in the study of individual psychology in Western film-making practice is less used in Third World films. Third World films serve more of an informational purpose than as a study in 'psychological realism'. The isolation of an individual, in tight close-up shots, seems unnatural to the Third World film-maker because (i) it calls attention to itself; (ii) it eliminates social considerations; and (iii) it diminishes spatial integrity.

The panning shot: Since a pan shot maintains integrity of space and time, the narrative value of such a shot renders the 'cut' or editing frequently unnecessary. The emphasis on space also conveys a different concept of 'time', a time which is not strictly linear or chronological but co-exists with it. My own observation indicates that while Western films tend to pan right on a left–right axis, Middle Eastern films, for instance, tend to pan generally toward the left, as in *Alyam Alyam* (Morocco) and *Shadow of the Earth* (Tunisia). It is quite possible that the direction of panning toward left or right might be strongly influenced by the direction in which a person writes.

The concept of silence: The rich potential for the creative interpretation of sound as well as the effective use of its absence is enormous in Third World films. For instance, in *Emitai* there are English subtitles for drum messages, and a rooster crows as Sembene's camera registers a low-angle shot of a poster of General de Gaulle. A neat visual pun! Silence serves as an important element of the audio track of the same film. It is 'a cinema of silence that speaks'. Silences have meaning only in context, as in the Ethiopian film *Gouma* and the Cuban film *The Last Supper*, where they contribute to the suspension of judgment which one experiences in watching a long take. Viewers wonder what will happen, accustomed as they are to the incessant sound and overload of music of dominant cinema.

The concept of 'hero': Even if a Western viewer cannot help but identify and sympathise with the black labour leader in *They Don't Wear Black Tie*, the lunatic in *Harvest: 3000 years*, the crazy poet in *The Chronicle of the Years of Ember* and the militant party member in *Sambizanga*, the films nevertheless kill those characters. This is because wish-fulfilment through identification is not the films' primary objective; rather, it is the importance of collective engagement and action that matters. The individual 'hero' in the Third World context does not make history, he/she only serves historical necessities.

In summary, Table 2 brings into sharper focus the differences between the film conventions of the Third World and the West and shows the dynamics of their cultural and ideological exchange.

Table 2 Comparison of filmic conventions (these are tendencies, not absolutes)

Western Dominant Conventions	Non-Western Use of Conventions
Lighting	
High contrast and low key, mostly Rembrandt lighting in drama while comedy uses low contrast and high-key lighting.	Lighting as a convention in Third World films is less developed, with the exception of Cuban films, whose use of lighting as a language is manifest in *Lucía* and *The Last Supper*.
Camera Angle	
Mostly governed by eye-level perspective which approximates to our natural position in the world. Use of angle shots primarily for aesthetic look.	Deliberate choice of low/high-angle shots for purposes of political or social comment. Low/high-angle shots show dominance and power relations between the oppressed and oppressing classes.
Camera Placement	
Distance varies according to the emotional content of the scene. Emotion, e.g. anger, is portrayed in close-up.	There is minimal use of the convention of close-up shots. This is perhaps due to lack of emphasis on psychological realism.
Camera Movement	
Mostly a fixed perspective (tripod operation), promoting exposition and understanding. Often the camera moves to stay with the individual to study character development and psychological state.	Fixed perspective in African films. A moving perspective (hand-held camera in Latin American films) promotes experiential involvement and dramatic identification. If the camera moves it is to contain a scene or a sequence as a unit and not in response to individual psychology.
Set Design	
A studio set. Tightens manipulatory controls, enchances fictional reality.	A location set. Location shooting relaxes manipulatory controls, and enhances documentary reality.

Table 2 (*continued*)

Acting	
A Hollywood convention, actor as icon.	Mostly non-actors acting out their real-life roles.

Parallel Montage	
Shows the relations of conflicting characters/forces for dramatic and expository narrative purposes, i.e. suspense.	Cross-cutting serves an ideological purpose and denotes ironical contrast and class distinction. Consider the film *Mexico: The frozen revolution*.

Point of View	
Actors avoid looking directly at the camera. Actors are usually positioned or blocked so that their emotional state is easily observed by the camera.	It is not uncommon to see a look directed at the camera, hence a direct address to the audience. A shift to the conventions of oral narrative is evident. Consider the Algerian film *Omtar Gatlato*.

The sum total of what is listed above as technique or elements of the film-making process is what expresses ideology. Films that hide the marks of production are associated with the ideology of presenting 'film as reality', the film that announces its message as an objective reflection of the way things are; whereas films which do exhibit the marks of production are associated with the ideology of presenting 'film as message'. Predominant aspect or point of view in Third World film is film announcing itself as a polemic comment on the way things are in their 'natural' reflection.

Films, therefore, in their point of view and stylistic choices, are structured to evoke a certain ideology in their production. A consequence of this, quite logically, is their different use of the conventions of time and space in cinema.

Conclusion

The spatial concentration and minimal use of the conventions of temporal manipulation in Third World film practice suggest that Third World cinema is initiating a coexistence of film art with oral traditions. Non-linearity, repetition of images and graphic representation have very much in common with folk customs. Time duration, though essential, is not the major issue because in the Third World context the need is for films, in context, to touch a sensitive cultural chord in a society. To achieve this, a general overhaul of the parameters of film form is required. Should the reorganisation be successful and radical enough, a rethinking of the critical and theoretical canons of cinema would be called for, leading to a reconsideration of the conventions of cinematographic language and technique. The final result would tend towards a statement James Potts made in his article 'Is there an international film language?':

> So, far from there being an international language of cinema, an internationally agreed
> UN charter of conventions and grammatical rules, we are liable to be presented, quite

suddenly, with a new national school of film-making, which may be almost wholly untouched by European conventions and will require us to go back to square one in thinking about the principles and language of cinematography.[12]

Film-makers in the Third World are beginning to produce films that try to restructure accepted filmic practices. There is now a distinct possibility of James Potts' perceptive remarks coming true, and it is in anticipation of the emergence of the 'new national school of film-making ... untouched by European conventions' that this paper has been written.

Already, certain reactions from film critics may be regarded as a sign of this 'emergence'. For example, a general criticism levelled at Third World films is that they are too graphic. This spatial factor is part of a general rhythm of pictorial representation in most Third World societies. It is, therefore, precisely because graphic art creates symbols in space that it enables Third World viewers to relate more easily to their films. In the Chinese case, for example:

> The spiritual quality achieved in the supreme Chinese landscape and nature paintings is a feeling of harmony with the universe in which the inner psychic geography of the artist and the outer visual reality transcribed are fused through brush strokes into a new totality that ... resonates with the viewer.[13]

Both the Chinese contemporary photographers and cinematographers have attempted to create similar syntax and effects to enhance the people's appreciation of their art.

Again, the most inaccessible Phase III film, the one African film that drops a curtain in front of a Western audience, and at the same time a most popular and influential film in Africa, is *Emitai* ('The Angry God'). Shot in social space by the Senegalese film-maker Sembene, the film explores the spiritual and physical tension in a rural community. To begin with the film carries its viewers into the story without any credits, only for the entire credit to be provided some twenty-five minutes later. Spectators have been known to leave the screening room at this point, conditioned to read the credits as signalling the end of the film. What Sembene has provided before the credits is essentially the preface of the story like an African folktale. In addition, the ending of the film an hour and a half later is anticlimactic and this occurs at the moment the film is truly engaging – the film simply stops – what we hear is the staccato of bullet sounds against a screen gone dark. In this film the film-maker is forcing us to forget our viewing habits and attend to the film in context instead of the experienced, framed as artistic package. A lesson is thus learned; concern should be with the language of the 'film text' in its own terms and not with the skeletal structure and chronology of the film.

Cinema, since its creation, has beguiled spectators by its manipulation of time – it expands, contracts, is lost and found, fragmented and reassembled. The resultant multiple time-perspectives have conditioned film appreciation as pure entertainment. There is perhaps some justification for this objective in a society whose stabilising conditions can afford the use of the film medium solely for entertainment. The Third World, on the other hand, is still engaged in a desperate struggle for socio-political and economic independence and development and cannot afford to dissipate its meagre resources and/or laugh at its present political and historical situation.

The Combative Phase, in which the historical determinants of Third World culture occur, provides us with the final horizon of a cinema oriented toward a peaceful coexistence with folk-culture. That oral tradition reasserts itself in a new medium is a contribution not only to Third World societies but to the cinematic world at large.

Film is a new language to the Third World and its grammar is only recently being charted. Its direction, however, seems to be a discursive use of the medium and an appeal for intellectual appreciation. Tomás Gutiérrez Alea perhaps best exemplifies the new awareness when he says:

> if we want film to serve something higher, if we want it to fulfil its function more perfectly (aesthetic, social, ethical, and revolutionary), we ought to guarantee that it constitutes a *factor in spectators' development*. Film will be more fruitful to the degree that it pushes spectators toward a more profound understanding of reality and, consequently, to the degree that it helps viewers live more actively and incites them to stop being mere spectators in the face of reality. To do this, film ought to appeal not only to emotion and feeling but also to reason and intellect. In this case, both instances ought to exist indissolvably [sic] united, in such a way that they come to provoke as Pascal said, authentic 'shuddering and tremblings of the mind'.[14]

Notes

1. F. Fanon, *The Wretched of the Earth*, Grove Press: New York, 1963, pp. 207–48. See also A. Cabral, *Return to the Source*, African Information Service: New York, 1973, pp. 42–69.
2. J. DeOnis, '"Pixote" role proves all too real', *Los Angeles Times*, 5 June 1984.
3. J. Espinosa, 'For an imperfect cinema', in M. Chanan (ed.), *Twenty-five Years of the New Latin American Cinema*, BFI/Channel 4 Television: London, 1983, pp. 28–33.
4. R. Gerber, *Glauber Rocha, Cinema, Politica e a Esthetica do Inconsciente*, Editore Vozes: Brasil, 1982, p. 34 and *passim*.
5. G. Rocha, *Revolucão do Cinema Nôvo*, Alhambra/Embrafilme: Rio de Janeiro, 1981, p. 467.
6. From a film catalogue entitled *Films about Africa Available in the Midwest*, African Studies Program, University of Wisconsin: Maddison, WI, 1974, p. 37.
7. *Africa on Film and Videotape, 1960–81: A compendium of reviews*, African Studies Center, Michigan State University: East Lansing, MI, 1982, p. 219.
8. It must be freely acknowledged that the future of art criticism and appreciation no doubt lies in the domain of semiotic inquiry. Presently, while its greater virtue lies in the attention it gives to the role of the reader, its greatest weakness is its cultural fixation with Western thought. Third World aesthetics and cultures have been ignored, making it impossible for it to occupy its premier place in a unified human science. Since the works

of Lévi-Strauss and various essays and a book by Roland Barthes, nothing of substance regarding semiotic inquiry into cultural studies has been offered. For a general reading on the topic, see Edith Kurzweil, *The Age of Structuralism: Lévi-Strauss to Foucault*, Columbia University Press: New York, 1980, and R. Barthes, *Mythologies*, trans. Annette Lavers, Hill & Wang: New York, 1970. For the various contending factions in the semiotic camp – structuralists, deconstructionists, reader-response critics, theories of intertextuality and narratology – the following books will serve as introductions: R. Scholes, *Semiotics and Interpretation*, Yale University Press: New Haven, CT, 1982, and J. Culler, *The Pursuit of Signs*, Cornell University Press: Ithaca, NY, 1983.

 9. Recently Western film-makers, in a bid to revitalise their film world, have made 'realistic' forays into Third World themes: *Gandhi* on India's struggle for independence, *The Year of Living Dangerously* on Sukarno's fall from power, *Under Fire* on the Sandinista revolution in Nicaragua, and *Circle of Deceit* on the Lebanese civil war. The statement by one of the characters in *Circle of Deceit* – 'We are defending Western civilization' – is an ironic but true epigram for all the films. Far from being radical or new, therefore, these productions give us no more than Hollywood's version of the Third World. For an illuminating discussion on this recent fascination with 'the other', see John Powers, 'Saints and savages', *American Film*, January–February 1984, pp. 38–43.

10. Various sources were consulted, including but not limited to H. Arvon's *Marxist Esthetics*, Cornell University Press: Ithaca, NY, 1973, p. 71 and *passim*, and K. Gotrick, *Apidan Theatre and Modern Drama*, Graphic Systems AB: Gothenburg, 1984, pp. 140–63. For an elaboration of culture in the context of Third World films, see my book *Third Cinema in the Third World: The aesthetics of liberation*, UMI Research Press: Ann Arbor, MI, 1982.

11. J. K. Nyerere, *Ujamaa: Essays on socialism*, Oxford University Press: London, 1968, pp. 91–105.

12. J. Potts, 'Is there an international film language?', *Sight and Sound*, 48, 2, Spring 1979, pp. 74–81.

13. A. Goldsmith, 'Picture from China: the style and scope of photography are changing as outside influences mix with traditional values', *Popular Photography*, February 1984, pp. 45–50, 146 and 156.

14. T. G. Alea, *Dialéctica del Espectador*, Cuidad de la Habana, Sobre la presente edición, 1982, p. 21. The first part of the book has been translated by Julia Lesage and appears under the title 'The viewer's dialectic' in *Jump Cut*, 29, February 1984, pp. 18–21, from which this quotation is taken.

20 □ *Beyond Ethnocentrism: Gender, Power and the Third-World Intelligentsia*

Jean Franco

Anyone involved in Latin American studies knows what it is to be placed last on the program, when everyone else has left the conference. Latin America (and third-world societies) generally occupy some exceptional and therefore awkward position in mainstream scholarship. Indeed, they are not yet 'in' it at all. 'British intellectuals: Latin American revolutionaries' was the wording of an ad I once saw in the *New Statesman* in England. It summed up very nicely the separation of intellectual and manual labor along the axis of metropolis and periphery, as well as suggesting the flow of revolutionary action into areas where people know no better than to fight. The conclusion is that the Third World is not much of a place for theory; and if it has to be fitted into theory at all, it can be accounted for as exceptional or regional.

That is why it is worth beginning with Fanon, whose *Black Skin, White Masks* and *The Wretched of the Earth* snatched the leadership of revolution away from the first-world proletariat (grown fat on imperialism) and revived the metropolis's paranoid fears of the vengeance that pullulated in the ill-lit streets of the native quarters. For Fanon, the whole colonized world had to be shocked out of its bewitchment. It was a becalmed world whose inhabitants, 'wasted by fevers, obsessed by ancestral customs', formed an almost 'inorganic background for the innovating dynamism of colonial mercantilism'.[1] The colonized fantasies of action had to be converted into revolutionary potential. 'The first thing the native learns is to stay in his place and not go beyond certain limits. That is why the dreams of the native are always of muscular prowess; his dreams are of action and of aggression. I dream I am jumping, winning, running, climbing. I dream that I burst out laughing, that I span a river in one stride or that I am followed by a flood of motorcars that never catch up with me.'[2] Yet it is within the power of the wretched

From C. Nelson and L. Grossberg (eds.), *Marxism and the Interpretation of Culture*, Macmillan Education: Basingstoke, 1988, pp. 503–9, 512–15.

of the earth, the *fellahin,* to overcome immobility, to turn the relation of colonizer and colonized on its head, to cleanse themselves of inferiority through violence. The native intelligentsia, caught between the ambiguities of folklore and assimilation to the metropolis, will be dragged in the wake of the *fellahin,* forcibly immersed in the struggle.

Clearly, Fanon's blueprint is locked in the same mind/body polarity that separates metropolitan intellect from the sacrificial body of third-world peoples. The white mask woven and painted by the colonizer's discourse can only be broken apart by the confrontation with death. The colonized need recognition in order to know they exist but will only be recognized by the metropolis as a mask or a grinning skull.

From the standpoint of the present, it is easy to see that Fanon's existentialist psychology has its limitations; he understood the alienation of thinking in the foreign tongue of the metropolis but not the pervasive web of discourse in which he was enmeshed. Today, we know much more about the constitution of subjectivities within particular discursive formations; we are aware of the dissolution of the 'individual' or the 'self' in subjectivities, of the relation between power and knowledge. We can even arrive at a more materialist version of Foucault's theorizing of power by distinguishing between comparatively transient microexercises of power and the perpetuation of knowledge-power through institutions that reproduce both the machinery and the discourse of domination.[3] What makes Fanon's contribution of value is that he recognized that there was something distinct about the colonial struggle, that the separation between manual and mental labor was reproduced in the relationship between the *fellahin* and the intelligentsia and that this hierarchy had to be destroyed if the revolutionary struggle was to succeed.

This essay attempts to delineate the constitution of the intelligentsia in the Third World, their subordination of manual labor and women, and the consequences of this for the formation of counterhegemonic discourses. I am thus deliberately considering the intelligentsia not as individuals, nor as class factions, but rather as a systematically constituted group bound by a common *habitus* (to use Pierre Bourdieu's expression), that is by common perceptions, dispositions, practices and institutions that account for the systematized nature of their intellectual production while simultaneously allowing for different discursive strategies within the intellectual field.[4] Since I refer mainly to Latin America, it is necessary to emphasize the crucial and constitutive activity of the *literary* intelligentsia which is empowered by writing. Because it was blocked from making contributions to the development of scientific thought, the intelligentsia was forced into the one area that did not require professional training and the institutionalization of knowledge – that is, into literature. It is here, therefore, that the confrontation between metropolitan discourse and the utopian project of an autonomous society takes place.

Metropolitan discourses on the Third World have generally adopted one of three devices: (1) *exclusion* – the Third World is irrelevant to theory, (2) *discrimination* – the Third World is irrational and thus its knowledge is subordinate to the rational knowledge produced by the metropolis; and (3) *recognition* – the Third World is only seen as the place of the instinctual. In the discourse of exclusion, the Third World exists only as a scenario; it is the stage for the activities of *Nostromo* or worse: consider Werner Herzog, who broke down ancestral customs merely to provide *Fitzcaraldo* with a dramatic movie sequence. (The discourse of metropolitan power refuses to acknowledge the all too human smell of crushed bodies.) In this discourse, the oppressed and exploited are outside civilization and hence constitute its heart of darkness, the negativity against which the metropolitan project must be defined. When the nineteenth-century intelligentsia of Latin America attempted to occupy the first-person position in this discourse, to separate 'I', it could do so only by speaking as if the indigenous peoples had cause to exist, as if they already belonged to the past. This discourse was interrupted and thrown into confusion whenever the masses erupted as subjects of history, as they did during the Mexican Revolution.[5]

A second kind of metropolitan discourse, a discourse of discrimination, was structured as a hierarchy in which an irrational intelligentsia that tried to occupy the subject position in this discourse found itself forced to embody the rich heterogeneity of its own culture and to rationalize it. This was Alfonso Reyes's strategy when he described indigenous culture as red clay that would be washed by the pure waters of Latin culture, or Neruda's strategy when he invoked the dead laborers of the Inca empire and called on them to speak through his lips and mouth.[6] This representative discourse was subverted by some avant-garde writers (especially Vallejo) but was decisively challenged during and just after the Cuban revolution when the intelligentsia, wishing to speak for the masses, was asked to take up the gun and fight with them.

Finally, the discourse of recognition becomes possible when heterogeneity is valorized by the increasingly routinized metropolis. At this moment, the Third World becomes the place of the unconscious, the rich source of fantasy and legend recycled by the intelligentsia, for which heterogeneity is no longer a ghostly, dragging chain but material that can be loosened from any territorial context and juxtaposed in ways what provide a constant frisson of pleasure. The intelligentsia no longer speaks *for* the masses but productively transposes mythic material. But in order to do this, it must distinguish between its properly authorial activity and mere reproduction, between an essentially masculine form of creativity and the feminine reproductive activity. This discourse is only interrupted when the differentiation between male authorship and female reproduction is exposed as a socially constructed position; then women and indigenous peoples can take the production of meaning into their own hands.

Because gender is the last category to be deconstructed in this way, I shall concentrate on this third type of discursive formation. However, some preliminary points need to be made. In the first place, it is important to recognize that in Latin America there is a dislocation between the establishment of a capitalist-dominated economy and the institutionalization of what is generally thought to be its ideology – the work ethic, individualism, an epistemology based on exchange, and so on.

That is to say, capitalism in Latin America was articulated with the hacienda and the mine, both of which disciplined the work force not only through direct repression but also by using the paternalistic discourse of the Church. Furthermore, indigenous communes in which symbolic production (artisanry, dance, fiestas), economic production, and reproduction of the labor force were lodged in a single institution, namely, the family, coexisted with plantation and mining enclaves in which the family was often broken up altogether.[7] It is only very recently, with the incorporation of new sectors into the labor force and the instrumental use of the mass media, that there has been a concerted attempt to introduce 'modern' values. Thus, the belief systems of the indigenous, blacks, and women were *of necessity* archaic, for no other options were open to them. At the same time, this very anachronism provided them with 'regions of refuge', with traditions, moral rights and spiritual bonds to particular territories (often organized around devotion to saints) that could be explosive when the state encroached on them. In contrast, the intelligentsia was a secular group, empowered by writing and therefore isolated from the culture of the majority of the population. Unlike Samuel Richardson in eighteenth-century England who, according to Terry Eagleton, was 'locked into the economic infrastructure of bourgeois England' through his printing firm, which was also 'the nub of a whole discursive formation ... interlocked with every major ideological apparatus of English society',[8] the Latin American intelligentsia was interlocked only with a ghostly and somewhat abstract 'nation'. By providing the spiritual webbing of the national spirit, it hoped to soar to immortality.

In the second place, the analogous position of the intelligentsia – which was subordinated to metropolitan discourse at the same time it was constituting the discourse of nationalism – is indivisible from the sexual division of labor. Domination has traditionally been semanticized in sexual terms and power has traditionally been associated with masculinity. Social, political and economic power are represented through a lexicon that is drawn from sexual relations. Hence the social and the sexual have become intimately connected. In a famous essay published in 1950, Octavio Paz based an analysis of Mexican national character on the contrast between female 'openness' (and therefore vulnerability to rape and domination) and male closure (invulnerability). A critique of machismo elevated to the level of a national madness, Paz's *Labyrinth of Solitude* affirms rather than deconstructs these archetypal differences. Many novels written in the nineteenth and early twentieth centuries were disguised national allegories in which social forces were represented in terms of impotence, castration, domination and prostitution. In one well-known Puerto Rican story, the protagonist actually castrates himself.[9]

The significance of the semanticization of the social as the sexual has been discussed by Nancy Hartsock in *Money, Sex and Power: Towards a feminist historical materialism*.[10] This book sets out to show that there is an epistemology of reproduction, just as there is an epistemology of production (Marx) and exchange (capitalism). But there is a serious weakness in an approach that neglects social and discursive formations and the constitution of subjectivity. Ignoring the lesson of Foucault, Hartsock often slips into a history of ideas. Even so, her book shows how the sexual division of labor that subordinated reproduction to the lowest level of human creativity has led to the valorization of intellectual creations 'born to the minds of those not contaminated by the concerns or necessities of the body'.[11] Hartsock argues that from the Greeks onward public space has belonged to the warrior hero and to the hero-citizen; both have their paradigm in the Greek agonic hero. Intellectual life, too, follows this paradigm, since the search for immortality, conceived as domination within public life, has, since Plato, been associated with the distantiation of intellectual activities from the mortal body, and hence from the 'feminine', that have always been associated with the realm of necessity. 'Over and over again', Hartsock comments, 'the fear of ceasing to exist is played out',[12] and the possibility of fusion, and hence of the death of the self, are found to be at the source of theoretical production and political deeds. This has serious consequences since it subordinates not only the feminine but also all the positive aspects of eros that derive from the experience of reproduction – for instance, connectedness and community.

In the Third World, in which mortality is not only individual but affects entire social movements, which flourish, die and are forgotten like the ephemeral human body, we should expect this distantiation from the body to be most intense. Indeed, if we take Borges as an example, we find that the quest for immortality (which depends on metropolitan recognition) can only be realized by abstracting the fictional world from any local connotations and turning it into the paradigmatic confrontation of the pursuer and the pursued, the writer and the reader, which often culminates with a male bonding at the point of death.

In Latin America, the subordination of the feminine is aggravated by the rigid confinement of women to private spaces. The terms

     masculine   mobile (active)
     feminine   immobile (passive)

were interchangeable with

     masculine   public
     feminine   private

primarily because women were traditionally limited to the home, the convent or the brothel. From the colonial period until recent times, the meanings born by the feminine can thus be illustrated by a simple semiotic diagram (see Figure 1). The central term of the quadrangle is the phallus, which is the bearer of meaning and the active element that determines social reproduction. One term of the semiotic quadrangle is occupied by the mother, who is not a virgin but is the bearer of children and whose space is the home. Here we should keep in mind the privatized and inward-looking Hispanic house and the fact that the virtual confinement of married women to the home had not only been required by the Church but was also intended to ensure the purity of blood that Spanish society had imposed after the

mother		virgin
	phallus	
not virgin		mother
not mother		virgin
(whore)		(Mary)

Figure I

wars against the Moors. Thus the mother's immobility is related to racism and to the protection of inheritable property. The opposite term to the mother is the virgin – that is, the nun who is pure and uncontaminated and whose space is the convent. The negation of the mother and the virgin is the whore, whose body is open to all men. For example, in his novel *The Fox Above and the Fox Below*, José María Arguedas describes a brothel in the Peruvian port town of Chimbote where the women sit in small cubicles in the middle of a compound with their legs apart to show their openness. Yet the compound is also prisonlike; the 'public' women are immobile and privatized just as much as the mother or the nun.[13] Finally, there is the impossible other, the mother who is a virgin, the mother of God who is not only the unattainable ideal term but the woman who has given birth to the Creator. (Consider this ironic parallel: Fidel Castro visits Chile, and Mrs Allende states that the highest task of Chilean women is to give birth to sons who would be like Che Guevara.)

Certainly, what strikes us about this diagram of feminine meanings is the immobility and privacy that it implies. To understand how natural this disposition appears, even to the most sophisticated of the intelligentsia, we have only to read García Márquez's interview in *Playboy*, in which he declares that women 'stay at home, run the house, bake animal candies so that men can go off and make wars'.[14] Whether this was said in earnest or in jest is beside the point. It is along this axis that social meanings accrue so that the *madre patria* in nationalist discourse is productive or sterile, prostituted or sacred.

Yet in a society scarred by the violence and death that inevitably accompanied capitalist penetration of Latin America, it is not surprising to observe a certain 'femininization of values' (to use Terry Eagleton's phase). Thus, in a poem by Vallejo, the mother's body is depicted as a house, and the womb acquires the configuration of rooms and corridors: 'Your archway of astonishment expects me / The tonsured volume of your cares / That have eroded life. The patio expects me / The hallway down below with its indentures and its / feast-day decorations.' When the father enters this temple/house, it is on his knees. He has become the subordinate partner in the act of creation. The mother's body, on the other hand, offers the only unchanging territory in an uncertain world: 'Between the colonnade of your bones

/ That cannot be brought down even with lamentations / And into whose side not even Destiny / can place a single finger.'

This poem, written before Vallejo joined the Communist party, is in sharp contrast to his Soviet-inspired poems, in which the miners make history through work, or his poems of the Spanish Civil War, where the forging of history is in the hands of the male militia.[15] We also note that the mother can only (literally) *embody* certainty because of her immobility because she is related to physical territory. Indeed, it was the female territory of the house that allowed private and family memory to be stored; there, archaic values, quite alien to the modern world, continued to flourish.

In the fifties and sixties, for reasons that are too complex to examine here, there was a radical shift in the meanings attached to the feminine. This period was marred by two quite contrary trends. On the one hand, the Cuban revolution aroused hopes that other countries could adopt original versions of socialism. Marxist theory could be Latin Americanized. Yet, during this same period, the struggle for national liberation was countered by a massive onslaught of advanced capitalism. At the very moment Latin America was asserting its difference, the armies of metropolitan corporations – in the form of mass media advertising and consumer goods – were poised, ready to destroy those very structures (urban/rural, commune, plantation) that had for so long been an embarrassment and yet had become the very source of Latin American originality.

The rich heterogeneity that formerly had to be subordinated as irrational began to be proudly displayed by Latin American writers as proof of cultural vitality. Writers like Asturias, Arquedas, Carpentier, Roa Bastos and Rulfo undertook the recycling of ancient legends, traditional cultures and archaic ways of life, not as folklore but as literary models of autarkic societies. As the literary intelligentsia discovered the utopian elements in popular culture, it also discovered in that very carnivalesque pluralism the claim on metropolitan attention that had so long eluded it. Thus, when Mario Vargas Llosa, at the outset of his career, declared that the Latin American novel 'ceased to be Latin American', he meant that it had finally broken out of the backwater of provincialism and regionalism and had indeed, become 'recognizable'.[16] Like Evita Peron, the literary intelligentsia had finally entered into immortality.[17] It was not even necessary for it to follow in Borges's footsteps and abstract plot from all regional and local references so that it could circulate as the agonic confrontation of pursuer and pursued, unencumbered by referentiality. The 'new novelists' of the early sixties discovered the shock value of catachresis and juxtaposition in which those once embarrassing heterogeneous elements became positive devices for defamiliarization.

This valorization of heterogeneity was accompanied by the reinvention of a myth of authorship, which once again affirmed the difference between natural reproduction and the masculine province of creativity. The slogan of the sixties – liberation through the imagination, immortality through the invention of imaginary worlds or the real autonomous societies like Cuba – was underpinned by the resemanticization of the sexual division of labor:

mother   author

child   creation

In a masculine world dominated by death and violence, the space of the mother had come to seem utopian, the space of a community that does not reproduce agonal relationships. Yet instead of trying to understand what this might mean for the construction of a more humane society and for revolutionary politics, both political leaders and writers during this period felt compelled to reaffirm political and artistic creativity as an exclusively male activity. [. . .]

[I shall now discuss] the connection between the literary intelligentsia of the sixties and the oppositional politics of this same period, a politics dominated by the guerrilla movements and their hero, Che Guevara. No one will deny the heroism of these national liberation movements, many of which ended tragically. Yet the literature they produced, with its ideal of the 'new man' activated by nonmaterial incentives, bears out Nancy Hartsock's description of a left-wing theory that is trapped within a negative eros, one that values the violent confrontation with death over community and life. It is only recently that women who participated in these movements have begun to speak of their experiences and to criticize an ideal of the militant that suppressed feelings of weakness. A former Tupamara (of Uruguay) writes: 'Feminine sexuality, desire to have children or not to have them, the disposition of our bodies was not taken into account. For instance, maternity was lived by us as an obstacle that prevented us from continuing the struggle, especially the military struggle.'[18] Even when a woman managed to become a militant, she was often forced into a traditional gender role and classified as either butch or seductress. Women 'were not militants in the true sense'.[19] These comments were made by women who admire Che Guevara and neither regret nor reject armed struggle. Yet they are forced to recognize the unbalanced nature of a movement in which one gender constitutes revolutionary meaning and practice.

Before discussing some of the factors that have led to this kind of criticism, let me briefly summarize my argument up to this point. In its confrontation with metropolitan discourses that placed its members in a traditionally female position in the play of power and meaning, the Latin American intelligentsia attempted to speak on behalf of the nonliterate, the indigenous, and women who, through 'archaic' institutions and practices, maintained forms of symbolic production that allowed them to deal with and even resist capitalism. In the fifties and sixties this repressed material and the interesting incongruities that had arisen because of the coexistence of different modes of symbolic production led some writers – Asturias, Arguedas, Roa Bastos – to incorporate these subjectivities which were alien to capitalism into their narratives as utopian elements. In other writers, the critique of violence and machismo similarly led to a feminization of values. However, creativity – the active creation of real or imaginary societies that would perpetuate the originality of Latin America beyond the span of mortal life – was still regarded as a masculine province. Women's sole creative function was the lowly task of reproducing the labor force.

Clearly, this state of affairs, in which one sector of the population monopolizes creativity and makes it a quest for immortality, has been seriously challenged in recent years. The reinstallation of military governments and the breakdown of traditional political parties, as well as the establishment of revolutionary governments in Cuba and Nicaragua, has led to serious questioning of the past. Democratic participation has been reevaluated and is no longer regarded as a bourgeois deception but as the only practical basis for socialism. Such participation cannot be developed as long as one gender continues to be subordinate.

At the same time, the violence of military governments in the southern cone, the wars in Central America and the activities of death squads have all been directed at those places, like the home and the Church, that have harbored 'archaic' subjectivities. The murder of the archbishop in El Salvador, of priests and nuns, the attack on the cathedral, the uprooting of indigenous peoples from their homes in Guatemala, the resettlement of working-class populations in Argentina and Chile, the sterilization of Puerto Rican women, the rape of women in front of their husbands and children, all represent ferocious attacks on the family and the Church by the very forces (the military) that rhetorically invoke these institutions. By attacking them and by appealing to more deterritorialized forms of domination – 'mass media' and electronic religion or abstract notions of nationhood – the military governments have also unwittingly contributed to the subversion of these formerly 'sacred' categories. Moral rights, which formerly had been attached to particular territories or genders, are rapidly undergoing resemanticization, not only by the military, but also by new oppositional forces. The present stage of 'deterritorialization', which has separated women from their traditional regions of refuge in the home and the Church, and indigenous peoples from their communities, represents a cultural revolution brought about by imperialism.[20] But this conservative cultural revolution has been so radical that it has also opened up new areas of struggle; as a consequence of these social changes, new types of power, no longer solely identified with masculinity, have become increasingly important.

Let me give one example – the resistance of the 'madwomen' of the Plaza de Mayo in Argentina. These women have not only redefined public space by taking over the center of Buenos Aires on one afternoon every week but have also interrupted military discourse (and now the silence of the new government) by publicly displaying the photographs of sons and daughters who have 'disappeared'. This form of refusing a message of death is obviously quite different from the quest for immortality that has traditionally inspired the writer and the political leader. The women interrupted the military by wrestling meaning away from them and altering the connotations of the word 'mother'. To the military, they were the mothers of dead subversives, therefore, of monsters. But they have transformed themselves into the 'mothers of the Plaza de Mayo', that is, in the words of one of them, into 'mothers of all the disappeared', not merely their own children. They have thus torn the term 'mother' from its literal meaning as the biological reproducer of children and insisted on social connotations that emphasize community over individuality.

In using the term 'mother' in this way, these women show that mothering is not simply tied to anatomy but is a position involving a struggle over meanings and the history of meanings, histories that have been acquired and stored within unofficial institutions. While 'mothers of subversives' is univocal, stripped of any connotation but that of reproduction, 'mothers of the disappeared' signals an absence, a space that speaks through a lack – the lack of a child – but also a continuing lack within the government of any participatory dialogue, of any answer to the question of how their children disappeared.

The activities of the women of the Plaza de Mayo are symptomatic of many grass-root movements in Latin America, from the *comunidades de base* in Brazil to the popular song movements in Chile and Argentina. These are movements in which the so-called silent sectors of the population are forging politics in ways that no longer subordinate popular culture and women to the traditional view of culture determined by metropolitan discourse. In addition, the postrevolutionary societies of Cuba and Nicaragua have been forced to deal with the participation of women. Nicaragua has, indeed recognized that creativity is not exclusive to a male elite but is something that is dispersed among the entire population.

In countries under military dictatorship, there is a growing recognition of the importance of cultural politics in the creation of nongendered solidarity groups. To go back to Fanon, this involves transcending the traditional fear of the intelligentsia of immersing its members' individuality in the masses. It also entails realizing that violence, while necessary in self-defense, as in present-day Central America, is not the only way to be revolutionary. That is why an understanding of the socially constructed nature of sexual as well as class and racial divisions is so important, for it enables us to recognize the ethnocentricity of knowledge/power. The fact that the metropolis has always been the place in which knowledge is produced has reinforced the association of domination with masculinity in the Third World and has, therefore, restricted the balanced development of revolutionary movements.

Marx offered an epistemological position that allows us to understand the world *as if* we belonged to the proletariat. Fanon forces us to see the world *as if* we were people of color. One of the lessons of revolutionary movements of the last several years is that we have to resemanticize preconstructed gender categories by taking meaning into our own hands and overcoming the traditional associations of the feminine with nature and the immobile. For those of us living in the metropolis, there is another essential process of defamiliarization. We must step outside the display window of advanced capitalism and look through it from the point of view of societies of scarcity. Then it may appear not only replete but also grotesquely reified. And only then will we understand that the becalmed sea traps not the colonized but the colonizers.

Notes

1. Frantz Fanon, *The Wretched of the Earth*, Grove Press: New York, 1968, p. 51.
2. *ibid.*, p. 52.
3. For clarification of Foucault's theory and methodology, see 'Two Lectures', *Power/Knowledge: Selected interviews and other writings, 1972–77*, Pantheon: New York, 1981.
4. Pierre Bourdieu, *Le Sens pratique*, Les Editions de Minuit: Paris, 1980.
5. I am extending the notion of 'interruption' as it is developed by David Silverman and Brian Torode, 'Interrupting the "I"', in *The Material Word*, Routledge & Kegan Paul: London, 1980, pp. 3–19.
6. Alfonso Reyes, 'Discurso por Virgilio', *Antologia de la revista contempóranea*, Mexico, 1973, pp. 163–89. The reference to Neruda is to 'Alturas de Macchu Picchu', which is part of *Canto General*.
7. For the relation of this organization to indigenous culture, see Nesot García Canclini, *Las cultura populares en el capitalismo*, Nueva Imagen: Mexico, 1982.
8. Terry Eagleton, *The Rape of Clarissa*, University of Minnesota Press: Minneapolis, 1982, p. 7.
9. René Marques, 'En una ciudad llamada San Juan', *En una ciudad llamada San Juan*, UNAM: Mexico, 1960.
10. Nancy Hartsock, *Money, Sex and Power: Towards a feminist historical materialism*, Longman: New York, 1983.
11. *ibid.*, p. 203.
12. *ibid.*, p. 253.
13. José María Arguedas, *El zorro de arriba y el zorro de abajo*, Losada: Buenos Aires, 1971.
14. *Playboy Magazine*, 30, 2, 1983.
15. 'Madre, me voy mañana a Santiago', in *Trilce* (1922), my translation. The Spanish Civil War poems 'España, aparta de mi este caliz' ('Spain, Take This Cup from Me') were published posthumously.
16. Mario Vargas Llosa, 'Novela primitiva y novela de creación en América Latina', *Revista de la Universidad de México*, 23, 10, 1969, p. 31.
17. This refers to a phrase that radio announcers in Argentina repeated daily at the time of Eva Peron's death.
18. Ana Maria Auraujo, *Tupamaras, des femmes de Uruguay*, des femmes: Paris, 1980, p. 163.
19. *ibid.*, p. 145.
20. For terms such as 'overcoding' and 'deterritorialization', I am indebted to Gilles Deleuze and Felix Guattari, *Anti-Oedipus: Capitalism and schizophrenia*, Viking Press: New York, 1972.

PART FIVE

*Theorising Post-Coloniality:
Discourse and Identity*

Introduction

As in Part One, the theorisation of post-colonial cultural discourses and identities cannot escape a conflation (and sometimes confusion) of description and prescription of cultural processes and values. If Frantz Fanon's account, in *Black Skin, White Masks*, suggests the extreme complexity of colonised subjectivities, the readings here attest to the ongoing complexity of post-colonial subjectivities. The complexity for the reader arises as much from the immense geo-political range included in the category of the 'post-colonial' as from the inner dynamics of post-colonial selves: the category as used in this reader includes diasporic communities, 'ethnic minority' communities within the overdeveloped world as well as formerly colonised national cultures. Debates on identity continue and develop many of the nativist/essentialist, socialist, humanist and anti-foundationalist arguments found in historical debates on colonised cultures.

When it comes to issues of contemporary post-colonial discourse, the medium of printed literature needs to be seen as but one of many media; for many post-colonial constituencies, the media of music, visual art and film may be more compelling, accessible and popular expressions, equally in need of theorisation. Stuart Hall's discussion invokes cinema; that of bell hooks contrasts the reception of Black literature and music in the United States. Arguments for the greater popular accessibility of cinema over literature, for instance, have led the Senegalese artist Sembene Ousmane to turn to film-making in preference to fiction-writing (see the reading by Laura Mulvey in Part Six). There are a number of material questions which need to be asked of the production of post-colonial cultural discourse: Who controls its production and distribution? Who/what forms its intended and actual audience? As hooks suggests, US publishers play an instrumental role in determining the values and character of much Black writing. The relations between style, technology and economy require theorisation. In the very different context of modern Africa, the example of Chinua Achebe's and Ngũgĩ wa Thiong'o's debate over the usage of European languages in modern literary production raises similar questions about the politics and economics of publishing, about literacy, access to and distribution of literature, and implied and empirical audiences.

Theorisation of post-colonial identity is, of course, not gender-neutral. Drawing from theoretical and area social studies' debates on gender and nationalism, Deniz Kandiyoti focuses on historical and contemporary examples from South Asia and the Middle East. Charting the diversity of positions accorded and taken up by women in post-colonial and national cultures, Kandiyoti discerns certain common features in nationalist organisation, history, ideology and legislation. Whether women are constructed as guardians of traditional cultures or as icons of national modernity, they are consistently stationed as the ideological boundary markers and emblems of the nation, and as long as this continues their social, legal and economic rights will remain unstable.

The cultural dynamics of the Caribbean have received a variety of theorisations; the paradigm of William Shakespeare's *The Tempest* has excited the imagination of a number of thinkers, among them the Cuban writer Roberto Fernández Retamar, in his seminal 1974 essay 'Caliban: notes towards a discussion of culture'.[1] Whereas Retamar's discussion is concerned primarily with relations between the Caribbean and the Americas, the Afro-Caribbean/British critic Stuart Hall explores here the tripartite formations of Caribbean post-colonial cultural identity, given as the African, European and American presences.

Hall here takes culture on its own terrain (as is perhaps appropriate in a paper originally given to an audience of film specialists). Paul Gilroy, in the final chapter of his '*There Ain't No Black in the Union Jack*' (1987), reprinted here, focuses on the social and political identities of contemporary Black British communities. (Earlier chapters of his book deal directly with aesthetic expressions of black identities.) Drawing upon theories of recent social movements as set out by Alberto Melucci, Manuel Castells and Alain Touraine, Gilroy produces an analysis of contemporary black politics which offers a strong challenge to longstanding left-wing conceptions of the traditional industrial proletariat as the vanguard of anti-capitalist emancipation.

African-American critic bell hooks engages with current US academic debates on post-modernity, 'difference' and 'otherness', to critique dominant intellectual blindspots regarding Black ethnicity in a manner not unlike that of Gayatri Chakravorty Spivak in Part One. hooks simultaneously recuperates those aspects of post-modern theory and culture which offer opportunity for political empathy across social groupings of race, gender and class. Also, like Spivak, she refuses to honour boundaries separating 'objective' and 'subjective' discourses, or those between academic and political value. Problematising the category of the intellectual, and writing self-reflexively as a Black academic, she provides the prospect of a bridge between Black intellectuals and Black communities. Critical of the language of essentialism, she produces an important distinction between notions of Black 'authenticity' and notions of experience-based Black 'authority'.

Writing in 1964, within the first decade of political independence for a number of African nation-states, Nigerian writer and critic Chinua Achebe produces a controversial argument in favour of the adoption of the English language by African writers. His discussion combines an historical determinism and anti-foundationalism, realism and idealism: history, which imposed European languages and made them an inescapable fact of modern African culture, does not dictate the cultural values and forms which can attach to the language. Those are by definition heterogeneous and variable; African writers can Africanise European languages as a form of national self-determination and inter-ethnic communication.

The exiled Kenyan writer Ngũgĩ wa Thiong'o writes in the 1980s, a decade which had seen the intensification of economic neo-colonialism in many of those nation-states which had, in Achebe's 1960s, recently enjoyed independence. In a sense, his argument reverses Achebe's determinism and anti-foundationalism. Whereas Achebe sees language and culture as being primarily mobile, without fixed character, Ngũgĩ sees them as containing and conveying essential and unchangeable ideological values; whereas Achebe considers that the history of European colonisation represents an irreversible factor in contemporary culture and political organisation, not contradictory to national self-determination, Ngũgĩ sees the ongoing cultural hegemony of Europe in Africa as both a cause and reflection of neo-colonialism. Whereas Achebe claims realism in his argument for English as a necessary medium of national and international communication, Ngũgĩ claims a contrasting realism in his argument for English as the language of the ruling class minority, and ethnic languages as the primary language of the majority of African populations.

Note

1. Roberto Retamar, 'Caliban: notes towards a discussion of culture in our America', *Massachusetts Review*, 15, Winter-Spring 1974, pp. 7–72.

21 □ *Identity and its Discontents: Women and the Nation*

Deniz Kandiyoti

Introduction

The aim of this paper is to explore some contradictory implications of nationalist projects in post-colonial societies. It examines the extent to which elements of national identity and cultural difference are articulated as forms of control over women and which infringe upon their rights as enfranchised citizens.

Despite the extensive literature on nationalism, there are relatively few systematic attempts to analyse women's integration into nationalist projects. The little there is conveys seemingly contradictory messages. Like Jayawardena, those who link the rise of feminist movements to anti-colonial and nationalist struggles note its coincidence with a move towards secularism and a broader concern with social reform.[1] Nationalist aspirations for popular sovereignty stimulate an extension of citizenship rights, clearly benefiting women. Since the emergence of women as citizens is also predicated upon the transformation of institutions and customs that keep them bound to the particularistic traditions of their ethnic and religious communities, the modern state is assumed to intervene as a homogenising agent which acts as a possible resource for more progressive gender politics.

In contrast, others expose state interventions as a sham by drawing attention to the purely instrumental agenda of nationalist policies that mobilise women when they are needed in the labour force or even at the front, only to return them to domesticity or to subordinate roles in the public sphere when the national emergency is over. The apparent convergence between the interests of men and the definition of national priorities leads some feminists to suggest that the state itself is a direct expression of men's interests.[2]

Further, Yuval-Davis and Anthias convincingly argue that the control of women and their sexuality is central to national and ethnic processes.[3] Women bear the burden of being 'mothers of the nation' (a duty that gets ideologically defined to suit official priorities), as well as being those who reproduce the boundaries of

From *Millenium: Journal of International Studies*, 20, 3, 1991, pp. 429–43.

ethnic/national groups, who transmit the culture and who are the privileged signifiers of national difference. The demands of the 'nation' may thus appear just as constraining as the tyranny of more primordial loyalties to lineage, tribe or kin, the difference being that such demands are enforced by the state and its legal administrative apparatus rather than by individual patriarchs.

These superficially divergent points of view share an important commonality: a recognition that the integration of women into modern 'nationhood', epitomised by citizenship in a sovereign nation-state, somehow follows a *different* trajectory from that of men. Where do the sources of this difference reside?

According to some writers, women are relegated to the margins of the polity even though their centrality to the nation is constantly being reaffirmed. It is reaffirmed consciously in nationalist rhetoric where the nation itself is represented as a woman to be protected or, less consciously, in an intense preoccupation with women's appropriate sexual conduct. The latter often constitutes the crucial distinction between the nation and its 'others'.

For Pateman, modern civil society 'is constituted through the "original" separation and opposition between the modern, public-civil world and the modern, private or conjugal familial sphere'.[4] It emerges as a patriarchal category. Moreover, Pateman interprets the transition from the traditional to the modern world as 'a change from a traditional (paternal) form of patriarchy to a new *specifically modern* (or fraternal) form: patriarchal civil society'.[5] It follows that the concepts of 'citizen' and 'civil society' must be read in the masculine. Mann, on the other hand, suggests that since women have at least achieved legal rights, patriarchy has, in the modern nation-state, evolved into 'neo-patriarchy'.[6] This is a position echoed by Water's preference for the term 'viriarchy'.[7] Walby, who proposes a multi-factor account of patriarchy, distinguishes between two main forms – private and public. Private patriarchy is based on the relative exclusion of women from arenas of social life other than the household and the appropriation of their services by individual patriarchs within the confines of the home. Public patriarchy is based on employment and the state; women are no longer excluded from the public arena, but subordinated within it. More collective forms of appropriation of their services supersede the individual mode of private patriarchy. Walby argues that the twentieth century has witnessed a major shift from private to public patriarchy.[8]

From a perspective that links women's rights to historical changes in patriarchy, the national projects of most 'modernising' states may seem to introduce a tug-of-war between private and public patriarchy. Indeed, one finds battles over women's souls (exemplified in debates over educating women) and their bodies (seen in debates over fertility control) and between the bureaucrat or the district commissar versus the male household head, the tribal chief or the local *mullah*. The battles are crucial to secular nationalism and signal women's entry into the 'universal' realm of citizenship. However, as Yuval-Davis cautions, we should be wary of ethnocentric definitions of the private and the public and acknowledge the extent to which the boundaries of the so-called private domain are in fact structured by the state.[9]

The definition of household and kin-based controls over women as 'private' presupposes the existence of a central state apparatus that subordinates such entities to its own political ends. Likewise, it is an entirely different matter for a woman to be subject to the customary strictures of a community which happens to be Hindu or Muslim and quite another for her to live under a regime that has adopted one or another faith as a source of public policy, social legislation and national identity. A sphere marked out as 'private' at one stage of nation-building may reappear with the full trappings of the 'public' at another, their boundaries being fluid and subject to redefinition.[10]

Thus, while acknowledging women's differential and often tentative integration into national projects, I am reluctant to describe the diversity of their experiences with reference either to the public/private distinction or to types of patriarchy. I agree with Connell that the state is centrally implicated in gender relations and that each state embodies a definable 'gender regime'.[11] Moreover, I feel that the nationalist histories of states and their politics of national identity can shed considerable light on the nature and transformation of gender regimes. I shall, therefore, focus quite narrowly on the contradictions inherent in the gender agenda of some nationalist projects and examine how women can, at the same time, participate actively in, and become hostages to, such projects.

A feature of nationalist discourse that has generated considerable consensus is its Janus-faced quality. It presents itself both as a modern project that melts and transforms traditional attachments in favour of new identities and as a reaffirmation of authentic cultural values culled from the depths of a presumed communal past.[12] It therefore opens up a highly fluid and ambivalent field of meanings which can be reactivated, reinterpreted and often reinvented at critical junctures of the histories of nation-states. These meanings are not given, but fought over and contested by political actors whose definitions of *who* and *what* constitutes the nation have a crucial bearing on notions of national unity and alternative claims to sovereignty as well as on the sorts of gender relations that should inform the nationalist project.[13] In what follows, I will first examine how the vagaries of nationalist discourse are reflected in changing portrayals of women as victims of social backwardness, icons of modernity or privileged bearers of cultural authenticity. I shall then consider some of the tensions and contradictions in nationalist projects that ultimately limit women's claims to enfranchised citizenry. I will draw my illustrations primarily from the Middle East and South Asia where women's rights continue to occupy part of a violently contested ideological and political terrain.

Women, Nationalism and the Politics of Modernity

Debates about the nature of society within turn of the century modernist movements in the Middle East gave the position of women a prominent place. Just like Western colonisers who used the 'plight' of Oriental women as a hallmark of the savagery and depravity of the colonised and as a justification of the mission incumbent upon their own civilisational superiority, modernist reformers bemoaned the condition of women as a clear symptom of backwardness.[14] As Zubaida points out, the main enemy of early reformers was 'backwardness' rather than 'foreignness'. Although they were politically opposed to European domination, they were not culturally antagonistic to its civilisation.[15] At this stage, the emancipation of women could be presented as part and parcel of a national regeneration project articulated in the language of moral redemption. A pervasive feature of such 'feminism' was that rather than presenting itself as a radical break with the past, which it did in fact represent, it often harkened back to more distant and presumably more authentic origins. Islamic reformists could claim that early Islam had been corrupted by foreign accretions and bad government, and that early Islam was, in fact, totally compatible with progressivist ideals. Those who emphasised ethnic rather than Islamic sources of national identity invoked a pre-Islamic past (in Central Asia for the Turks, in the Pharaonic era for Egypt and in the pre-Islamic dynasties for Iran) as the repository of national values implying a higher status for women than was the rule in their current societies. Similar tendencies were apparent in India with the invocation of a golden age of Hinduism that was not oppressive to women. The 'modern' was thus often justified as the more 'authentic' and discontinuity presented as continuity.

Before concluding, as does Gellner, that this is an instance of the 'pervasive false consciousness' of nationalist ideology, we must pause to consider the particular perils of a 'modernist' position on women and gender relations in many post-colonial societies.[16] Nationalism and secularism principally appealed to a narrow stratum of the bourgeoisie and bureaucracy who, despite their political credentials as anti-imperialists, could nonetheless be accused of succumbing to Western cultural hegemony. Moreover, representatives of more traditional ideologies as the *ulama* (Muslim clergy) did not deny the need for technological progress, modern armies or more efficient administration. However, for the achievement of progress to proceed without undue dilution of national identity (a key dilemma of cultural nationalism), the central symbols of this identity must be preserved and safeguarded from contaminating foreign influences. Tensions between modernist and organicist, anti-modernist strands in nationalism found a natural focus around the personal status of 'modern' citizenry and, more particularly, around the place and conduct of women. Since they were operating essentially within the same symbolic universe, secular nationalists were at pains to establish the indigenous and patriotic credentials of their modernising projects. Women participating in nationalist movements were likewise prone to justify stepping out of their narrowly prescribed roles in the name of patriotism and self-sacrifice for the nation.[17] Their activities, be they civic, charitable or political, could most easily be legitimised as natural extensions of their womanly nature and as a duty rather than a right. Modernity was invested with different meanings for men, who were relatively free to adopt new styles of conduct, and women, who, in Najmabadi's terms, had to be 'modern-yet-modest'.[18]

Meanwhile, in what constituted an explicit reversal of Orientalist depictions of passive, veiled women, nationalist propaganda began portraying women unveiled, participating in athletic competitions, making public speeches and handling sophisticated technology. As Graham-Brown points out, these icons of modernity were less a comment on changing gender relations than a symbolic evocation of the dynamism of a 'new' nation.[19] Schick suggests that in such a context:

> a photograph of an unveiled woman was not much different from one of a tractor, an industrial complex, or a new railroad; it still merely symbolised yet another one of men's achievements. One again reduced to mere objects, women were, in these images, at the service of a political discourse conducted by men and for men.[20]

Yet women's stake in nationalism is far more complex than the foregoing suggests. On the one hand, nationalist movements invite women to participate more fully in collective life by interpellating them as 'national' actors: mothers, educators, workers and even fighters. On the other hand, they reaffirm the boundaries of culturally acceptable feminine conduct and exert pressure on women to articulate their gender interests within the terms of reference set by nationalist discourse. Feminism is not autonomous, but bound to the signifying network of the national context which produces it.

In countries where the most prominent form of cultural nationalism is Islamic, for instance, feminist discourse can legitimately proceed only in one of two directions: either denying that Islamic practices are necessarily oppressive or asserting that oppressive practices are not necessarily Islamic. The first strategy usually involves counterposing the dignity of the protected Muslim women against the commodified and sexually exploited Western woman. It is thus dependent on a demonified 'other'. The second depends on a 'golden age' myth of an uncorrupted original Islam against which current discriminatory gender practices may be denounced as actually not Islamic. Although the implications of the first strategy are conservative and those of the second clearly more radical, they share the same discursive space; a space delineated by a nationalist discourse reproduced by men and women alike. Changing the terms of this discourse exacts a heavy price: alienation from the shared meanings which constitute a language of identity, affiliation and loyalty.

It may well be argued that there is no particular reason to single women out as prisoners of a discourse they share with men. However, their gender interests may, at times, dictate their own demands and produce divided loyalties with men of their class, creed or nation. Women may choose to either openly express or to suppress such divergences of interest, which they generally do at their own cost in both cases.

There is a wealth of evidence to suggest that, for women, the 'modern' is always perilously close to the 'alien', particularly when contemplated codes of behaviour can be identified as an outright betrayal of the expectations of their own communities. In this connection, Hatem relates how during Napoleon's Egyptian expedition some middle-class Egyptian women saw it as in their interests to be allied with the French.[21] Impressed by the apparent courteousness of French husbands, a group of women in Rosetta petitioned Napoleon to enforce similar relations within Egyptian families. The patriarchal backlash against Egyptian women who consorted with the colonists was apparently fierce, with alleged massacres of collaborators serving, in Hatem's view, to discipline women.

The notion that women's gender interests could be used to turn women into political 'fifth columnists' was an explicit article of official policy in at least one well documented social experiment carried out by the Bolsheviks in Soviet Central Asia between 1919 and 1929. Massell's study of the Soviet-sponsored mobilisation of Muslim women is a classic case of a modernising state 'liberating' women as a means of undermining traditional solidarities and identities based on kinship, custom and religion.[22] Molyneux also documents several instances where the emancipation of women was used as a tool for socialist transformation.[23]

Ironically, the very structures defined as backward, feudal or patriarchal by the modernising state are the ones that get redefined as ethnic markers or as symbols of 'national' identity, especially if they are forcibly obliterated by an authoritarian statist project. Indeed, the *khudzhum* (assault) in Central Asia had a radicalising effect that produced a rally around the symbols of Muslim identity. There was a substantial rise in attendance at prayers and meetings in mosques, widespread withdrawal of Muslim children (especially girls) from Soviet schools and, more tragically, a terrible wave of violence and killing of women who transgressed communal norms. More significantly, even those men who had exhibited pro-Soviet leanings at an earlier stage recemented their alliance with traditional elites, and women themselves retreated into traditional practices since they felt vulnerable and exposed.

Lest we imagine that these tensions are peculiar to the encounter between 'foreign' ruling elites and native populations, Vieille extends his analysis to all 'modernising' states of the periphery. The state, in his view, seeks to repudiate the separate existence of civil society. It intervenes increasingly in society and 'turns on the routine of day-to-day existence, polices it tightly and symbolically devalues it'.[24] This suppression of the private may elicit active resistance. Vieille goes as far as to interpret the Iranian revolution as 'a surging back of the "private" into the public and the colonisation by the private of the State'.[25] Men's honour is invested in the 'private', which has women at its centre, and the state's interventions in this realm only aim 'to deprive the citizen of his honour and divest him of his right to political participation'.[26] Here, the 'private', defined as 'backward' or 'patriarchal' by modernist reformers, is redefined as a site of radical resistance against a despotic state. With typical oversight, the notion that women themselves may have an independent right to political participation is not even entertained by Vieille, nor does the fact that the symbol of resistance happens to be a veiled woman elicit any unease.

It is not my intention to vilify the 'private' as the nexus of patriarchal oppression or to glorify it as a site of cultural resistance against the coercive intrusions of the state.[27] I think, instead, that the identification of the private with the 'inner sanctum' of group identity has serious implications for how women of different class, religious or ethnic backgrounds fare through the ups and downs of secular nationalism, since it determines whether they emerge as enfranchised citizens or as wards of their immediate communities.

The very language of nationalism singles women out as the symbolic repository of group identity. As Anderson points out, nationalism describes its object using either the vocabulary of kinship (motherland, *patria*) or home (*heimat*), in order to denote something to which one is 'naturally' tied. Nationness is thus equated with gender, parentage, skin-colour – all those things that are not chosen and which, by virtue of their inevitability, elicit selfless attachment and sacrifice.[28] The association of women with the private domain reinforces the merging of the nation/community with the selfless mother/devout wife; the obvious response of coming to her defence and even dying for her is automatically triggered.

I argued earlier that the emancipation of women was equated with modernity by nationalist movements whose reforms were meant to serve as a tool for social 'progress'. Nonetheless, definitions of the 'modern' take place in a political field where certain identities are privileged and become dominant, while others are submerged or subordinated. In this process, certain ethnic, religious, linguistic or even spatial (urban versus rural or tribal) categories may be devalued or marginalised. Likewise, secular notions of modern nationhood subordinate and sometimes seek to destroy alternative bases for solidarity and identity. The fact that these submerged identities can become foci of cultural resistance and even lead to contested definitions of nationhood does not necessarily imply that they are uniformly emancipatory, nor does it guarantee that they will have a progressive gender agenda. Wherever women continue to serve as boundary markers between different national, ethnic and religious collectivities, their emergence as full-fledged citizens will be jeopardised, and whatever rights they may have achieved during one stage of nation-building may be sacrificed on the altar of identity politics during another.

Women may be controlled in different ways in the interests of demarcating and preserving the identities of national/ethnic collectivities. As Anthias and Yuval-Davis point out, regulations concerning who a woman can marry and the legal status of her offspring aim at reproducing the boundaries of the symbolic identity of their group.[29] Until recently, white South African women were not allowed to have sex with men of other groups, nor were women of higher castes in India. Similarly, Muslim societies do not normally condone their women marrying out of the faith, although no such strictures exist for men since Islam is transmitted through the male line.

Women are also considered to be the custodians of cultural particularisms by virtue of being less assimilated, both culturally and linguistically, into the wider society. Immigrant women reproduce their culture through the continued use of their native language, the persistence of culinary and other habits and the socialisation of the young. Even in their native land, women of minority communities retain their cultural separateness to a greater extent than men. For instance, a Kurdish woman in Turkey is less likely to learn Turkish than a Kurdish man who comes into more frequent contact with the dominant culture through compulsory military service, greater access to schooling, dealings with the state bureaucracy or work experiences. Finally, cultural difference is frequently signalled through the dress and deportment of women. Mandel, who analyses the 'headscarf debate' in Germany, suggests that Islamic dress has taken on an additional symbolic dimension among migrant Turks who feel threatened by the Christian, German milieu and its potentially corrupting influence: 'They see the headscarf as a symbolic border, delimiting two separate corporate groups, and affirming themselves as part of a moral community.'[30] Conversely, many Germans interpret the headscarf as a sign of the Turks' essential inability to assimilate into German society and a justification for denying them citizenship rights.

Drawing women out into variously defined 'national' mainstreams through mass education, labour force participation and formal emancipation has been a standard feature of secular projects. It should not surprise us to discover that the failure of such projects and the politicisation of religious and ethnic identities have direct consequences for women's rights.

Women, Secularism and the Politics of Personal Law

Nationalist projects often attempt to redefine, ethnically, religiously and linguistically, diverse collectivities as a single nation through several means: by virtue of citizenship in the state, formal equality before the law and resocialisation through mass education and the media into new forms of civic consciousness. In most countries of the Middle East and South Asia, this unifying secular impulse has foundered most clearly in the area of family legislation and personal law. The legal equality granted to women under the constitutions of modern states is more often than not circumscribed by family legislation privileging men in the areas of marriage, divorce, child custody, maintenance and inheritance rights.

Although the Indian constitution endorses the division between secular and personal law, it also contains the eventual commitment to creating a uniform civil code. In a climate of endemic communal strife, this goal seems further from realisation than ever. In 1985, a divorced Muslim woman, Shah Bano, pressed for her maintenance rights under the Indian Code of Criminal Procedure and won her case after many years of litigation. This judgement created a furor among Indian Muslims – a furor which threatened to have electoral consequences and resulted in the passing of a separate Muslim Women's Act in 1986. Shah Bano was finally forced to assert her Muslim loyalty by rejecting the Supreme Court judgement that was in her favour. Pathak and Rajan note that this episode was capitalised upon by Hindus, the majority community, whose concern for the welfare of Muslim women seemed merely a ploy to repress the religious freedom of the minority and so ensure its own dominance.[31]

This, not surprisingly, led some Muslim women's organisations to oppose the judgement and accept the perception that their community was being threatened. The authors also interpret this incident as a conflict between the state and the patriarchal family over the 'protection' of women. They argue that 'any rights granted to the woman as an individual citizen by the state can only be imperfectly enforced within that state-within-a-state.'[32] Note, however, that it was the Indian state itself which, through new legislation, ended up blocking Muslim women's recourse to secular law.

Oommen questions the claims made in the name of secularism in a comparative analysis of multi-religious nation-states in South Asia. He concludes that state policy is substantially moulded by the norms, values and lifestyles of the dominant religious collectivity, irrespective of the character of the state or the features of the religions involved.[33] Chhachhi further argues that Indian nationalism, despite its secular objectives, exploited communal consciousness and played upon an identification of nationalism with Hinduism.[34] She suggests that notions of femininity are intimately bound up in the construction of communal identities so that incidents like the Shah Bano trial or the case of *sati* (widow immolation) in Deorala, in 1987, signal the occasion for displays of communal militancy. The communalisation of political and civil life in India clearly encourages the growth of revivalist movements which do not further the rights of women of either majority or minority groups.

The duality between personal and secular law also persists throughout the Arab world, irrespective of the nature of the political regimes of specific countries. Family and personal laws generally derive from the *Shar'iah* (Muslim canonical law) even when other legal codes are fully secular. Hijab relates this to the divergent trends in Arab nationalism which have dominated the debate on women's rights since its earliest days.[35] Proponents and opponents of equality for women were divided into the liberal and conservative nationalist camps. The former, following Qasim Amin, argued that the Arab world had to emulate Europe in those respects that made it strong: democracy, freedom and equality of rights under the law. They also claimed that these goals could be achieved within an Islamic framework. The conservative nationalists, on the other hand, believed that the only way to resist foreign intrusion was to preserve traditions, and that the very concept of 'women's liberation' was a foreign implant aiming to weaken Arab society by attacking its very core, the family. Hijab argues that the more threatened the Arab world feels, the stronger the conservative nationalist trend becomes. As a result, the association between equal rights for women and the betrayal of cultural values shaped by Islamic tradition is reinforced, thereby blocking any further changes in the position of women. Several feminist theorists of the Arab world also place cultural resistance to women's emancipation within the context of relations with an imperialistic West.[36]

The fact that Islam acts as a communal identity marker against outsiders does not, however, mean that charges of 'foreignness' and alterity are reserved for those outside national boundaries. Communalist sentiments, as Zubaida notes, can be directed against local religious minorities who may become identified, in the popular mind, with European Christian powers.[37] Likewise, Westernised local elites may be denounced not merely as corrupt, but as morally tainted as was the *gharbzahdegi* (Westoxified) elite in Pahlavi Iran. Philipp, in his analysis of the relationship between nationalism and women's emancipation in Egypt, comments on the clear predominance of members of minority religious communities (Copts, Syrian and

Lebanese Christians, Jews) among female journalists publishing feminist women's magazines at the turn of the century.[38] This predominance confirmed the worst suspicions of conservative nationalists such as Mustafa Kamil, who concluded that the liberation of women could only represent an unpatriotic development. Thus, the question of what and who constitutes the 'West' often has less to do with the outside world than with class, religious or ethnic cleavages within the nation itself. Nader draws our attention to the fact that 'Occidentalism', and its related demonology (materialism, anomie, immorality, etc.), is used as a mechanism of social control over Middle Eastern women.[39] Conservatives, she suggests:

> instead of blaming the West for exporting its ills, are searching for the agencies that import them. This adds up to a kind of 'siege mentality' in which stripping Arab women of their rights has become well justified and condoned as a protective act.[40]

Al-Khalil raises an even more fundamental question by taking issue with the notion that Arab nationalism, at least in its Ba'thist version, ever embodied a secular project. He argues that pan-Arabism is doctrinally linked to Islam in that the demarcation of national identity was made possible through arguments about the primacy of the Arabs within Islam. In the words of Aflaq, the father of Arab nationalism, 'it was "the force of Islam" that had the "new appearance" of pan-Arabism.' Al-Khalil also points out that the religious group is still the raw material of politics in the Middle East, and that identification with the nation-state and social class remains at a disadvantage. The communal consciousness fostered under the Ottoman *millet* system (a combination of national and religious communities) intensified in the nineteenth century as the European powers assumed protectorships over different communities as a means of establishing their influence in the region. Al-Khalil suggests that the dissolution of many of communalism's traditional roles through nation-building and modernisation may rather have intensified its moral hold over the lives of otherwise modern Arabs.

Most modern states in the Arab world have nonetheless made attempts at legal reform in the areas of family and personal law. Although they remained within the framework of Islamic law, they sought to expand women's rights. This was also the case of the 1978 Personal Status law in Iraq. Joseph argues that the main aim of the partial emancipation of women was to tap their labour potential and to wrest their allegiance from more traditional foci of loyalty, such as the extended family, the tribe or ethnic group.[42] Al-Khalil interprets this legislation merely as an exercise in consolidating the power of the party and the Leader:

> It rankles to have fathers, brothers, uncles and cousins all lined up to exert varying degrees of real power and control over half of the Iraqi population. Thus if a new loyalty to the Leader, the party, and the state is to form, women must be 'freed' from the loyalties that traditionally bound them to their husbands and male kin.[43]

In this context, such legislation appears as part of a totalitarian project of social control over the 'private' and its subversive centrifugal potential. The same logic applies to the political organisation of children in the Pioneers, Vanguards and Youth Organisations. Their new value as social actors and the relative gain in status they may experience in their families is predicated upon their total allegiance to the party and state.

The case of Iraq, despite its specificity, does not stand alone. Reformist legislation affecting women was frequently sponsored by authoritarian and 'dirigiste' regimes whose ultimate aim was not to increase the autonomy of individual women, but to harness them more effectively to national developmental goals. Typically, women's independent attempts at political organisation were actively discouraged and considered divisive. This was the case in Turkey, where the Turkish Women's Federation was disbanded in 1935, a year after women got the vote and under Nasser in Egypt, who, in 1956, immediately after granting women suffrage, outlawed all feminist organisations. Regimes as diverse as those of Atatürk, Reza Shah and Nasser had in common their stress on national consolidation and unity and the development of a modern centralised bureaucracy. This emphasis was congruent with the mobilisation of women to aid the expansion of new cadres and the socialisation of a uniform citizenry. There were significant advances in the education of women and in their recruitment into the qualified labour force at all levels; their public visibility not only increased but was vested with a new legitimacy.

Most post-independence states were faced with contradictory developments that had an important bearing on family and gender relations. Processes of capitalist penetration led to the destructuring of local communities, fuelling massive rural to urban migration, aggravating social inequalities and weakening kin solidarities. The material bases of traditional authority relations within the family between the young and the old and between genders were substantially eroded by such processes.[44] Integration into capitalist markets probably did more to undermine 'private' patriarchy than any piece of reformist legislation. For instance the secular Turkish Civil Code, passed in 1926, was inoperative in the rural hinterland until such time that the countryside was substantially transformed by an expanding capitalist economy. Women who had been previously active in the domestic economy as unpaid family labourers now had to join the waged labour force in increasing numbers. Mernissi argues, using data from Morocco, that the growing gap between cultural ideals (male breadwinner/protected female) and actual reality created a situation of 'sexual anomie', making male–female relations an area of intense tension and conflict.[45] She suggests that the popular appeal of fundamentalist ideologies is enhanced by the profound unease of men who feel both threatened and humiliated by these contemporary developments.[46]

Indeed some successor regimes seem to have reversed what appeared as the steady expansion of women's rights in the early stages of nationalism by adopting 'Islamisation' programmes. This approach is most clear in Iran and Pakistan, where Islam is incorporated into official state policy. There are similar trends in countries ranging from Bangladesh to Algeria. The distributive and political failures of nationalist projects are often identified not as merely technical but as 'moral' failures which require a complete overhaul of the worldviews underpinning them.

There is an important literature on the problems of secular nationalism and the growing role of political Islam. Points of view vary. Badie contends that the idea of the nation is accommodated with difficulty and has limited mobilising potential in Muslim societies where the territorial state (as distinct from the *umma*, the religious collectivity) remains an alien concept.[47] Zubaida convincingly retorts that Islamist movements are modern developments clearly inscribed in the political field of the nation-state.[48] The failure of nation-formation resides, according to Zubaida, not on some essential property of political culture or ethnic composition, but on the lack of economic and political achievements which gives citizens a stake in the national entity and promotes national stability.[49] The failure of states to create and distribute resources adequately intensifies conflicts and cleavages expressed in religious, ethnic and regional terms. The importance and role of sectional allegiances increase as they assume a crucial role in mediating citizens' access to scarce resources and providing a more workable focus of solidarity. Since the state itself uses local patronage networks and sectional rivalries in its distributive system, citizens also turn to their primary solidarities both to protect themselves from the potentially repressive and arbitrary agencies of the state and to compensate for or take advantage of inefficient administration. With growing popular discontent and endemic legitimacy crises, governments may make the tactical choice of relinquishing the control of women to their immediate communities and families, thereby depriving their female citizens of legal protection.[50] It is against this background that the Shah Bano incident, referred to above, must be interpreted. Furthermore, in cases where the operation of state-sponsored religious fundamentalism is witnessed, the exercise of patriarchal authority may be extended to unrelated men, like the clergy, the police or 'concerned' citizens, who are given a free hand in monitoring women's dress and conduct in public places.[51] Such developments reveal both the fragility of women's citizenship rights and the fact that women are the weakest link in national projects.

Conclusion

The integration of women into nationalist projects has been rich in paradoxes and ambiguities in most post-colonial societies. As Rowbotham points out, nationalist and anti-colonialist movements opened an important theoretical space for questioning women's position and the prevailing religious doctrines which legitimise their subordination.[52] The emancipation of women became a central tenet of liberal nationalist ideology. Reformers often engaged in a selective process of backward-looking nationalism in search of 'indigenous' models to legitimise women's emancipation. Although many were influenced by the ideas of the Enlightenment and were of secular persuasion, they unwittingly endorsed the notion that any changes in the position of women could only be condoned in the national interest. Moreover, the proponents of conservative, anti-modernist cultural nationalism had an even stronger hand to play by insisting on an interpretation of cultural integrity that was coterminous with the patriarchal control of women. This interpretation was facilitated by the equation between changes in gender relations and capitulation to Western cultural imperialism. Throughout these ideological battles, women were variously portrayed as the victims of their societies' backwardness, symbols of the nation's newly found vigour and modernity or the privileged repository of uncontaminated national values. Women, who were also active participants in nationalist movements, felt compelled to articulate their gender interests within the parameters of cultural nationalism, sometimes censoring or muting the radical potential of their demands.

The political and distributive failures which plagued the post-independence trajectories of many states called into question the secular pretensions of earlier nationalist projects. The increasing politicisation of ethnic and religious identities fuelled new conflicts, challenging existing definitions of national unity and promoting the rise of new cultural revivalist and religious fundamentalist movements.

I have argued throughout this paper that the regulation of gender is central to the articulation of cultural identity and difference. The identification of women as privileged bearers of corporate identities and boundary markers of their communities has had a deleterious effect on their emergence as full-fledged citizens of modern nation-states. This is nowhere more evident than in the fact that women's hard-won civil rights become the most immediate casualty of the breakdown of secularist projects. Discourses valorising the 'private' as a site of resistance against repressive states, or as the ultimate repository of cultural identity, should not let us overlook the fact that, in most instances, the integrity of the so-called 'private' is predicated upon the unfettered operations of patriarchy. We should search, instead, for a language of identity which allows for difference and diversity without making women its hostages.

Notes

1. K. Jayawardena, *Feminism and Nationalism in the Third World*, Zed Press: London, 1988; and M. Molyneux, 'Family reform in socialist states: the hidden agenda', *Feminist Review*, 21, Winter 1985, pp. 47–64.
2. C. MacKinnon, 'Feminism, Marxism, method and the state: an agenda for theory', *Signs*, 7, 3, 1989, pp. 515–44; V. Burstyn, 'Masculine dominance and the state', *Socialist Register*, 1983, pp. 45–89; M. Mies, *Patriarchy and Accumulation on a World Scale*, Zed Press: London, 1986. This perspective is found wanting by Connell, who criticises its 'categorialism' (see n. 11) and Yuval-Davis and Anthias (see n. 3), who discuss the limitations of reductionist approaches to the state.
3. N. Yuval-Davis and F. Anthias (eds.), *Woman-Nation-State*, Macmillan: London, 1989.
4. C. Pateman, 'The fraternal social contract', in J. Keane (ed.), *Civil Society and the State*, Verso: London, 1988, p. 102.

5. *ibid.*, p. 104, emphasis in the original.

6. M. Mann, 'A crisis in stratification theory? Persons, households/families/lineages, gender, classes and nations', in R. Crompton and M. Mann (eds.), *Gender and Stratification*, Polity Press: Oxford, 1986, pp. 40–56.

7. M. Waters, 'Patriarchy and viriarchy: an exploration and reconstruction of concepts of masculine domination', *Sociology*, 23, 2, 1989, pp. 193–211.

8. B. S. Walby, *Theorising Patriarchy*, Blackwell: Oxford, 1990.

9. N. Yuval-Davis, 'Woman, the state and ethnic processes – the citizenship debate', forthcoming in *Feminist Review*.

10. I would consider it a serious misjudgement to interpret state-sponsored attempts at policing women's conduct, even when they are religiously inspired as in Iran, as a return to or extension of the 'private'. For such a point of view, see P. Vieille, 'The state of the periphery and its heritage', *Economy and Society*, 17, 1, 1988, p. 66.

11. R. W. Connell, 'The state, gender and sexual politics: theory and appraisal', *Theory and Society*, 19, 5, 1990, pp. 507–44.

12. A. D. Smith, *Theories of Nationalism*, Duckworth: London, 1971; E. Gellner, *Nations and Nationalism*, Blackwell: Oxford, 1983; B. Anderson, *Imagined Communities*, Verso: London, 1983; and H. K. Bhabha (ed.), *Nation and Narration*, Routledge: London, 1990.

13. The national projects of modern states may involve a denial of the separate existence of ethnically and culturally distinct collectivities (such as the Kurds in Turkey). The collectivities whose identities are thus subordinated may evolve their own national projects with attendant claims to sovereignty. Definitions may also change over time. The current political struggle in India partly centres on a redefinition of 'Indianness' as coterminous with Hinduism, the Muslims being cast as 'foreigners' in the midst of the Hindu nation.

14. For an excellent account of Orientalist depictions of women see, S. Graham-Brown, *Images of Women*, Quartet Books: London, 1988.

15. S. Zubaida, 'Islam, cultural nationalism and the left', *Review of Middle East Studies*, 4, 1988, p. 7.

16. Gellner, *op. cit.*, p. 124.

17. The memoirs of the Turkish and Egyptian feminists Halide Edib and Huda Sharaawi confirm this view. A broader assessment of women's nationalist activities may be found in B. Baron, 'Women's nationalist rhetoric and activities in early twentieth-century Egypt', in L. Anderson *et al.* (eds.), *The Origins of Arab Nationalism*, Columbia University Press: New York, 1991.

18. A. Najmabadi, 'The hazards of modernity and morality: women, state and ideology in contemporary Iran', in D. Kandiyoti (ed.), *Women, Islam and the State*, Macmillan: London, 1991, p. 49.

19. Graham-Brown, *op. cit.*, p. 220.

20. I. C. Schick, 'Representing Middle Eastern women: feminism and colonial discourse', *Feminist Studies*, 16, 2, 1990, p. 369.

21. M. Hatem, 'The politics of sexuality and gender in segregated patriarchal systems: the case of eighteenth and nineteenth-century Egypt', *Feminist Studies*, 12, 2, 1986, pp. 250–73.

22. G. J. Massell, *The Surrogate Proletariat*, Princeton University Press: Princeton, NJ, 1974.

23. M. Molyneux, 'Women in socialist societies: problems of theory and practice', in K. Young *et al.* (eds.), *Of Marriage and the Market*, CSE Books: London, 1981,

pp. 167–202; and M. Molyneux, 'The law, the state and socialist policies with regard to women: the case of the People's Democratic Republic of Yemen, 1967–1990', in Kandiyoti, *op. cit.*, pp. 237–71.

24. Vieille, *op. cit.*, p. 66.
25. *ibid.*, p. 67.
26. *ibid.*
27. This is the subject of an ongoing feminist debate. As key divergent texts, see J. Elshtain, *Public Man, Private Women*, Princeton University Press: Princeton, NJ, 1981; and M. Barrett and M. McIntosh, *The Anti-Social Family*, Verso: London, 1982.
28. Anderson, *op. cit.*, p. 131.
29. F. Anthias and N. Yuval-Davis, *op. cit.*, pp. 1–15.
30. R. Mandel, 'Turkish headscarves and the "foreigner problem": constructing difference through emblems of identity', *New German Critique*, 46, Winter 1989, p. 42.
31. Z. Pathak and R. S. Rajan, 'Shahbano', *Signs*, 14, 3, 1989, pp. 558–82.
32. *ibid.*, p. 569.
33. T. K. Oommen, 'State and religion in multi-religious nation states', *South Asia Journal*, 4, 1, 1990, pp. 17–33.
34. A. Chhachhi, 'Forced identities: the state, communalism, fundamentalism and women in India' in Kandiyoti, *op. cit.*, pp. 144–75.
35. N. Hijab, *Womanpower*, Cambridge University Press: Cambridge, 1988.
36. L. Ahmed, 'Early feminist movements in Turkey and Egypt', in F. Hussain (ed.), *Muslim Women*, Croom Helm: London, 1984; F. Mernissi, Beyond the Veil, Al Saqi Books: London, 1985; N. El Saadawi, 'The political challenges facing Arab women at the end of the 20th century' in N. Toubia (ed.), *Women of the Arab World*, Zed Press: London, 1988.
37. S. Zubaida, *Islam, the People and the State*, Routledge: London, 1988.
38. T. Philipp, 'Feminism and nationalist politics in Egypt' in L. Beck and N. Keddie (eds.), *Women in the Muslim World*, Harvard University Press: Cambridge, MA, 1978, pp. 277–94.
39. L. Nader, 'Orientalism, occidentalism and the control of women', *Cultural Dynamics*, 2, 3, 1989, pp. 324–55.
40. *ibid.*, p. 327.
41. S. Al-Khalil, *The Republic of Fear*, Hutchinson: London, 1989, p. 211.
42. S. Joseph, 'Elite strategies for state-building: women, family, religion and the state in Iraq and Lebanon', in Kandiyoti, *op. cit.*, pp. 176–200.
43. Al-Khalil, *op. cit.*, p. 92.
44. D. Kandiyoti, 'Bargaining with patriarchy', *Gender & Society*, 2, 3, 1988, pp. 274–90.
45. Mernissi, *op. cit.*
46. *idem*, 'Muslim women and fundamentalism', *MERIP Reports*, 153, July–August 1988, pp. 8–11.
47. B. Badie, *Les Deux États: Pouvoir et société en occident et en terre d'Islam*, Fayard: Paris, 1986.
48. Zubaida, *Islam, the People and the State*.
49. *idem*, 'Nations: old and new', *Ethnic and Racial Studies*, 12, 3, 1989, pp. 329–39.
50. R. Jahan, 'Hidden wounds, visible scars: violence against women in Bangladesh', in B. Agarwal (ed.), *Structures of Patriarchy*, Zed Press: London, 1988, pp. 199–227; D. Kandiyoti, 'Islam and patriarchy: a comparative perspective', in N. Keddie and B. Baron

(eds.), *Shifting Boundaries: Women and gender in Middle Eastern history*, Yale University Press: New Haven, CT, forthcoming.

51. A. Chhachhi, 'The state, religious fundamentalism and women: trends in South Asia', *Economic and Political Weekly*, 18 March 1989, pp. 567–78.

52. S. Rowbotham, *Women in Movement: Feminism and social action*, Routledge: London, forthcoming.

22 □ *Cultural Identity and Diaspora*

Stuart Hall

A new cinema of the Caribbean is emerging, joining the company of the other 'Third Cinemas'. It is related to, but different from, the vibrant film and other forms of visual representation of the Afro-Caribbean (and Asian) 'blacks' of the diasporas of the West – the new post-colonial subjects. All these cultural practices and forms of representation have the black subject at their centre, putting the issue of cultural identity in question. Who is this emergent, new subject of the cinema? From where does he/she speak? Practices of representation always implicate the positions from which we speak or write – the positions of *enunciation*. What recent theories of enunciation suggest is that, though we speak, so to say 'in our own name', of ourselves and from our own experience, nevertheless who speaks, and the subject who is spoken of, are never identical, never exactly in the same place. Identity is not as transparent or unproblematic as we think. Perhaps instead of thinking of identity as an already accomplished fact, which the new cultural practices then represent, we should think, instead, of identity as a 'production' which is never complete, always in process, and always constituted within, not outside, representation. This view problematises the very authority and authenticity to which the term 'cultural identity' lays claim.

We seek, here, to open a dialogue, an investigation, on the subject of cultural identity and representation. Of course, the 'I' who writes here must also be thought of as, itself, 'enunciated'. We all write and speak from a particular place and time, from a history and a culture which is specific. What we say is always 'in context', *positioned*. I was born into and spent my childhood and adolescence in a lower-middle-class family in Jamaica. I have lived all my adult life in England, in the shadow of the black diaspora – 'in the belly of the beast'. I write against the background of a lifetime's work in cultural studies. If the paper seems preoccupied with the diaspora experience and its narratives of displacement, it is worth remembering that all discourse is 'placed', and the heart has its reasons.

From J. Rutherford (ed.), *Identity: Community, culture, difference*, Lawrence & Wishart: London, 1990, pp. 222–37.

There are at least two different ways of thinking about 'cultural identity'. The first position defines 'cultural identity' in terms of one, shared culture, a sort of collective 'one true self', hiding inside the many other, more superficial or artificially imposed 'selves', which people with a shared history and ancestry hold in common. Within the terms of this definition, our cultural identities reflect the common historical experiences and shared cultural codes which provide us, as 'one people', with stable, unchanging and continuous frames of reference and meaning, beneath the shifting divisions and vicissitudes of our actual history. This 'oneness', underlying all the other, more superficial differences, is the truth, the essence, of 'Caribbeanness', of the black experience. It is this identity which a Caribbean or black diaspora must discover, excavate, bring to light and express through cinematic representation.

Such a conception of cultural identity played a critical role in all post-colonial struggles which have so profoundly reshaped our world. It lay at the centre of the vision of the poets of 'Negritude', like Aimé Césaire and Léopold Senghor, and of the Pan-African political project, earlier in the century. It continues to be a very powerful amd creative force in emergent forms of representation amongst hitherto marginalised peoples. In post-colonial societies, the rediscovery of this identity is often the object of what Frantz Fanon once called a

> passionate research ... directed by the secret hope of discovering beyond the misery of today, beyond self-contempt, resignation and abjuration, some very beautiful and splendid era whose existence rehabilitates us both in regard to ourselves and in regard to others.

New forms of cultural practice in these societies address themselves to this project for the very good reason that, as Fanon puts it, in the recent past,

> Colonisation is not satisfied merely with holding a people in its grip and emptying the native's brain of all form and content. By a kind of perverted logic, it turns to the past of oppressed people, and distorts, disfigures and destroys it.[1]

The question which Fanon's observation poses is, what is the nature of this 'profound research' which drives the new forms of visual and cinematic representation? Is it only a matter of unearthing that which the colonial experience buried and overlaid, bringing to light the hidden continuities it suppressed? Or is a quite different practice entailed – not the rediscovery but the *production* of identity. Not an identity grounded in the archaeology, but in the *re-telling* of the past?

We should not, for a moment, underestimate or neglect the importance of the act of imaginative rediscovery which this conception of a rediscovered, essential identity entails. 'Hidden histories' have played a critical role in the emergence of many of the most important social movements of our time – feminist, anti-colonial and anti-racist. The photographic work of a generation of Jamaican and Rastafarian artists, or of a visual artist like Armet Francis (a Jamaican-born photographer who has lived in Britain since the age of eight) is a testimony to the continuing creative power of this conception of identity within the emerging practices of representation. Francis's photographs of the peoples of The Black Triangle, taken in Africa, the Caribbean, the USA and the UK, attempt to reconstruct in visual terms 'the underlying unity of the black people whom colonisation and slavery distributed across the African diaspora'. His text is an act of imaginary reunification.

Crucially, such images offer a way of imposing an imaginary coherence on the experience of dispersal and fragmentation, which is the history of all enforced diasporas. They do this by representing or 'figuring' Africa as the mother of these different civilisations. This Triangle is, after all, 'centred' in Africa. Africa is the name of the missing term, the great aporia, which lies at the centre of our cultural identity and gives it a meaning which, until recently, it lacked. No one who looks at these textural images now, in the light of the history of transportation, slavery and migration, can fail to understand how the rift of separation, the 'loss of identity', which has been integral to the Caribbean experience only begins to be healed when these forgotten connections are once more set in place. Such texts restore an imaginary fullness or plentitude, to set against the broken rubric of our past. They are resources of resistance and identity, with which to confront the fragmented and pathological ways in which that experience has been reconstructed within the dominant regimes of cinematic and visual representation of the West.

There is, however, a second, related but different view of cultural identity. This second position recognises that, as well as the many points of similarity, there are also critical points of deep and significant *difference* which constitute 'what we really are'; or rather – since history has intervened – 'what we have become'. We cannot speak for very long, with any exactness, about 'one experience, one identity', without acknowledging its other side – the ruptures and discontinuities which constitute, precisely, the Caribbean's 'uniqueness'. Cultural identity, in this second sense, is a matter of 'becoming' as well as of 'being'. It belongs to the future as much as to the past. It is not something which already exists, transcending place, time, history and culture. Cultural identities come from somewhere, have histories. But, like everything which is historical, they undergo constant transformation. Far from being eternally fixed in some essentialised past, they are subject to the continuous 'play' of history, culture and power. Far from being grounded in mere 'recovery' of the past, which is waiting to be found, and which when found, will secure our sense of ourselves into eternity, identities are the names we give to the different ways we are positioned by, and position ourselves within, the narratives of the past.

It is only from this second position that we can properly understand the traumatic character of 'the colonial experience'. The ways in which black people, black experiences, were positioned and subject-ed in the dominant regimes of representation were the effects of a critical exercise of cultural power and normalisation. Not only, in Said's 'Orientalist' sense, were we constructed as different and other within the categories of knowledge of the West by those regimes. They had the power to make us see and experience *ourselves* as 'Other'. Every regime of representation is a regime of power formed, as Foucault reminds us, by the fatal couplet 'power/knowledge'. But this kind of knowledge is internal, not external. It is one thing to position a subject or set of peoples as the Other of a dominant discourse. It is quite another thing to subject them to that 'knowledge', not only as a matter of imposed will and domination, by the power of inner compulsion and subjective con-formation to the norm. That is the lesson – the sombre majesty – of Fanon's insight into the colonising experience in *Black Skin, White Masks*.

This inner expropriation of cultural identity cripples and deforms. If its silences are not resisted, they produce, in Fanon's vivid phrase, 'individuals without an anchor, without horizon, colourless, stateless, rootless – a race of angels'.[2] Nevertheless, this idea of otherness as an inner compulsion changes our conception of 'cultural identity'. In this perspective, cultural identity is not a fixed essence at all, lying unchanged outside history and culture. It is not some universal and transcendental spirit inside us on which history has made no fundamental mark. It is not once-and-for-all. It is not a fixed origin to which we can make some final and absolute Return. Of course, it is not a mere phantasm either. It is *something* – not a mere trick of the imagination. It has its histories – and histories have their real, material and symbolic effects. The past continues to speak to us. But it no longer addresses us as a simple, factual 'past', since our relation to it, like the child's relation to the mother, is always-already 'after the break'. It is always constructed through memory, fantasy, narrative and myth. Cultural identities are the points of identification, the unstable points of identification or suture, which are made, within the discourses of history and culture. Not an essence but a *positioning*. Hence, there is always a politics of identity, a politics of position, which has no absolute guarantee in an unproblematic, transcendental 'law of origin'.

This second view of cultural identity is much less familiar, and more unsettling. If identity does not proceed, in a straight unbroken line, from some fixed origin, how are we to understand its formation? We might think of black Caribbean identities as 'framed' by two axes or vectors, simultaneously operative: the vector of similarity and continuity; and the vector of difference and rupture. Caribbean identities always have to be thought of in terms of the dialogic relationship between these two axes. The one gives us some grounding in, some continuity with, the past. The second reminds us that what we share is precisely the experience of a profound discontinuity: the peoples dragged into slavery, transportation, colonisation, migration, came predominantly from Africa – and when that supply ended, it was temporarily refreshed by indentured labour from the Asian subcontinent. (This neglected fact explains why, when you visit Guyana or Trinidad, you see, symbolically inscribed in the faces of their peoples, the paradoxical 'truth' of Christopher Columbus's mistake: you *can* find 'Asia' by sailing west, if you know where to look!) In the history of the modern world, there are few more traumatic ruptures to match these enforced separations from Africa – already figured, in the European imaginary, as 'the Dark Continent'. But the slaves were also from different countries, tribal communities, villages, languages and gods. African religion, which has been so profoundly formative in Caribbean spiritual life, is precisely *different* from Christian monotheism in believing that God is so powerful that he can only be known through a proliferation of spiritual manifestations, present everywhere in the natural and social world. These gods live on, in an underground existence, in the hybridised religious universe of Haitian voodoo, pocomania, Native pentacostalism, Black baptism, Rastafarianism and the black Saints Latin American Catholicism. The paradox is that it was the uprooting of slavery and transportation and the insertion into the plantation economy (as well as the symbolic economy) of the Western world that 'unified' these peoples across their differences, in the same moment as it cut them off from direct access to their past.

Difference, therefore, persists – in and alongside continuity. To return to the Caribbean after any long absence is to experience again the shock of the 'doubleness' of similarity and difference. Visiting the French Caribbean for the first time, I also saw at once how different Martinique is from, say, Jamaica: and this is no mere difference of topography or climate. It is a profound difference of culture and history. And the difference *matters*. It positions Martiniquains and Jamaicans as *both* the same *and* different. Moreover, the boundaries of difference are continually repositioned in relation to different points of reference. Vis-à-vis the developed West, we are very much 'the same'. We belong to the marginal, the underdeveloped, the periphery, the 'Other'. We are at the outer edge, the 'rim', of the metropolitan world – always 'South' to someone else's *El Norte*.

At the same time, we do not stand in the same relation of the 'otherness' to the metropolitan centres. Each has negotiated its economic, political and cultural dependency differently. And this 'difference', whether we like it or not, is already inscribed in our cultural identities. In turn, it is this negotiation of identity which makes us, vis-à-vis other Latin American people, with a very similar history, different – Caribbeans, *les Antilliennes* ('islanders' to their mainland). And yet, vis-à-vis one another, Jamaican, Haitian, Cuban, Guadeloupean, Barbadian, etc. . . .

How, then, to describe this play of 'difference' within identity? The common history – transportation, slavery, colonisation – has been profoundly formative. For all these societies, unifying us across our differences. But it does not constitute a common *origin*, since it was, metaphorically as well as literally, a translation. The inscription of difference is also specific and critical. I use the word 'play' because the double meaning of the metaphor is important. It suggests, on the one hand, the instability, the permanent unsettlement, the lack of any final resolution. On the other hand, it reminds us that the place where this 'doubleness' is most powerfully to be heard is 'playing' within the varieties of Caribbean musics. This cultural 'play' could not therefore be represented, cinematically, as a simple, binary opposition – 'past/present', 'them/us'. Its complexity exceeds this binary structure of representation. At different places, times, in relation to different questions, the boundaries are re-sited. They become, not only what they have, at times, certainly been – mutually excluding categories, but also what they sometimes are – differential points along a sliding scale.

One trivial example is the way Martinique both *is* and *is not* 'French'. It is, of course, a *department* of France, and this is reflected in its standard and style of life:

Fort de France is a much richer, more 'fashionable' place than Kingston – which is not only visibly poorer, but itself at a point of transition between being 'in fashion' in an Anglo-African and Afro-American way – for those who can afford to be in any sort of fashion at all. Yet, what is distinctively 'Martiniquais' can only be described in terms of that special and peculiar supplement which the black and mulatto skin adds to the 'refinement' and sophistication of a Parisian-derived *haute couture*: that is, a sophistication which, because it is black, is always transgressive.

To capture this sense of difference which is not pure 'otherness', we need to deploy the play on words of a theorist like Jacques Derrida. Derrida uses the anomalous 'a' in his way of writing 'difference' – *differance* – as a marker which sets up a disturbance in our settled understanding or translation of the word/concept. It sets the word in motion to new meanings without erasing the *trace* of its other meanings. His sense of *differance*, as Christopher Norris puts it, thus

> remains suspended between the two French verbs 'to differ' and 'to defer' (postpone), both of which contribute to its textual force but neither of which can fully capture its meaning. Language depends on difference, as Saussure showed ... the structure of distinctive propositions which make up its basic economy. Where Derrida breaks new ground ... is in the extent to which 'differ' shades into 'defer' ... the idea that meaning is always deferred, perhaps to this point of an endless supplementarity, by the play of signification.[3]

This second sense of difference challenges the fixed binaries which stabilise meaning and representation and show how meaning is never finished or completed, but keeps on moving to encompass other, additional or supplementary meanings, which, as Norris puts it elsewhere,[4] 'disturb the classical economy of language and representation'. Without relations of difference, no representation could occur. But what is then constituted within representation is always open to being deferred, staggered, serialised.

Where, then, does identity come in to this infinite postponement of meaning? Derrida does not help us as much as he might here, though the notion of the 'trace' goes some way towards it. This is where it sometimes seems as if Derrida has permitted his profound theoretical insights to be reappropriated by his disciples into a celebration of formal 'playfulness', which evacuates them of their political meaning. For if signification depends upon the endless repositioning of its differential terms, meaning, in any specific instance, depends on the contingent and arbitrary stop – the necessary and temporary 'break' in the infinite semiosis of language. This does not detract from the original insight. It only threatens to do so if we mistake this 'cut' of identity – this *positioning*, which makes meaning possible – as a natural and permanent, rather than an arbitrary and contingent 'ending' – whereas I understand every such position as 'strategic' and arbitrary, in the sense that there is no permanent equivalence between the particular sentence we close, and its true meaning, as such. Meaning continues to unfold, so to speak, beyond the arbitrary closure which makes it, at any moment, possible. It is always either over- or under-determined, either an excess or a supplement. There is always something 'left over'.

It is possible, with this conception of 'difference', to rethink the positioning and repositioning of Caribbean cultural identities in relation to at least three 'presences', to borrow Aimé Césaire's and Léopold Senghor's metaphor: *Présence Africaine, Présence Européenne*, and the third, most ambiguous, presence of all – the sliding term, *Présence Americaine*. Of course, I am collapsing, for the moment, the many other cultural 'presences' which constitute the complexity of Caribbean identity (Indian, Chinese, Lebanese, etc). I mean America, here, not in its 'first-world' sense – the big cousin to the North whose 'rim' we occupy, but in the second, broader sense: America, the 'New World', *Terra Incognita*.

Présence Africaine is the site of the repressed. Apparently silenced beyond memory by the power of the experience of slavery, Africa was, in fact, present everywhere: in the everyday life and customs of the slave quarters, in the languages and patois of the plantations, in names and words, often disconnected from their taxonomies, in the secret syntactical structures through which other languages were spoken, in the stories and tales told to children, in religious practices and beliefs in the spiritual life, the arts, crafts, musics and rhythms of slave and post-emancipation society. Africa, the signified which could not be represented directly in slavery, remained and remains the unspoken unspeakable 'presence' in Caribbean culture. It is 'hiding' behind every verbal inflection, every narrative twist of Caribbean cultural life. It is the secret code with which every Western text was 're-read'. It is the ground-bass of every rhythm and bodily movement. *This* was – is – the 'Africa' that 'is alive and well in the diaspora'.[5]

When I was growing up in the 1940s and 1950s as a child in Kingston, I was surrounded by the signs, music and rhythms of this Africa of the diaspora, which only existed as a result of a long and discontinuous series of transformations. But, although almost everyone around me was some shade of brown or black (Africa 'speaks'!), I never once heard a single person refer to themselves or to others as, in some way, or as having been at some time in the past, 'African'. It was only in the 1970s that this Afro-Caribbean identity became historically available to the great majority of Jamaican people, at home and abroad. In this historic moment, Jamaicans discovered themselves to be 'black' – just as, in the same moment, they discovered themselves to be the sons and daughters of 'slavery'.

This profound cultural discovery, however, was not, and could not be, made directly, without 'mediation'. It could only be made *through* the impact on popular life of the post-colonial revolution, the civil rights struggles, the culture of Rastafarianism and the music of reggae – the metaphors, the figures or signifiers of a new construction of 'Jamaican-ness'. These signified a 'new' Africa of the New World, grounded in an 'old' Africa: a spiritual journey of discovery that led, in the Caribbean, to an indigenous cultural revolution; this is Africa, as we might say, necessarily 'deferred' – as a spiritual, cultural and political metaphor.

It is the presence/absence of Africa, in this form, which has made it the privileged signifier of new conceptions of Caribbean identity. Everyone in the Caribbean, of whatever ethnic background, must sooner or later come to terms with this African presence. Black, brown, mulatto, white – all must look *Présence Africaine* in the face, speak its name. But whether it is, in this sense, an *origin* of our identities, unchanged by four hundred years of displacement, dismemberment, transportation, to which we could in any final or literal sense return, is more open to doubt. The original 'Africa' is no longer there. It too has been transformed. History is, in that sense, irreversible. We must not collude with the West which, precisely, normalises and appropriates Africa by freezing it into some timeless zone of the primitive, unchanging past. Africa must at last be reckoned with by Caribbean people, but it cannot in any simple sense be merely recovered.

It belongs irrevocably, for us, to what Edward Said once called an 'imaginative geography and history', which helps 'the mind to intensify its own sense of itself by dramatising the difference between what is close to it and what is far away'. It 'has acquired an imaginative or figurative value we can name and feel'.[7] Our belongingness to it constitutes what Benedict Anderson calls 'an imagined community'.[8] To *this* 'Africa', which is a necessary part of the Caribbean imaginary, we can't literally go home again.

The character of this displaced 'homeward' journey – its length and complexity – comes across vividly, in a variety of texts. Tony Sewell's documentary archival photographs, 'Garvey's Children: the Legacy of Marcus Garvey' tell the story of a 'return' to an African identity which went, necessarily, by the long route through London and the United States. It 'ends', not in Ethiopia but with Garvey's statue in front of the St Ann Parish Library in Jamaica: not with a traditional tribal chant but with the music of Burning Spear and Bob Marley's 'Redemption Song'. This is our 'long journey' home. Derek Bishton's courageous visual and written text, *Black Heart Man* – the story of the journey of a *white* photographer 'on the trail of the promised land' – starts in England, and goes, through Shashemene, the place in Ethiopia to which many Jamaican people have found their way on their search for the Promised Land, and slavery; but it ends in Pinnacle, Jamaica, where the first Rastafarian settlements were established, and 'beyond' – among the dispossessed of 20th-century Kingston and the streets of Handsworth, where Bishton's voyage of discovery first began. These symbolic journeys are necessary for us all – and necessarily circular. This is the Africa we must return to – but 'by another route': what Africa has *become* in the New World, what we have made of 'Africa': 'Africa' – as we re-tell it through politics, memory and desire.

What of the second, troubling, term in the identity equation – the European presence? For many of us, this is a matter not of too little but of too much. Where Africa was a case of the unspoken, Europe was a case of that which is endlessly speaking – and endlessly speaking *us*. The European presence interrupts the innocence of the whole discourse of 'difference' in the Caribbean by introducing the question of power. 'Europe' belongs irrevocably to the 'play' of power, to the lines of force and consent, to the role of the *dominant*, in Caribbean culture. In terms of colonialism, underdevelopment, poverty and the racism of colour, the European presence is that which, in visual representation, has positioned the black subject within its dominant regimes of representation: the colonial discourse, the literatures of adventure and exploration, the romance of the exotic, the ethnographic and travelling eye, the tropical languages of tourism, travel brochure and Hollywood and the violent, pornographic languages of *ganja* and urban violence.

Because *Présence Européenne* is about exclusion, imposition and expropriation, we are often tempted to locate that power as wholly external to us – an extrinsic force, whose influence can be thrown off like the serpent sheds its skin. What Frantz Fanon reminds us, in *Black Skin, White Masks*, is how this power has become a constitutive element in our own identities.

> The movements, the attitudes, the glances of the other fixed me there in the sense in which a chemical solution is fixed by a dye. I was indignant; I demanded an explanation. Nothing happened. I burst apart. Now the fragments have been put together again by another self.[9]

This 'look', from – so to speak – the place of the Other, fixes us, not only in its violence, hostility and aggression, but in the ambivalence of its desire. This brings us face to face with the dominating European presence not simply as the site or 'scene' of integration where those other presences which it had actively disaggregated were recomposed – re-framed, put together in a new way; but as the site of a profound splitting and doubling – what Homi Bhabha has called 'this ambivalent identification of the racist world ... the "Otherness" of the Self inscribed in the perverse palimpsest of colonial identity'.[10]

The dialogue of power and resistance, of refusal and recognition, with and against *Présence Européenne* is almost as complex as the 'dialogue' with Africa. In terms of popular cultural life, it is nowhere to be found in its pure, pristine state. It is always-already fused, syncretised, with other cultural elements. It is always-already creolised – not lost beyond the Middle Passage, but ever-present: from the harmonics in our musics to the ground-bass of Africa, traversing and intersecting our lives at every point. How can we stage this dialogue so that, finally, we can place it, without terror or violence, rather than being forever placed by it? Can we ever recognise its irreversible influence, whilst resisting its imperialising eye? The enigma is impossible, so far, to resolve. It requires the most complex of cultural strategies. Think, for example, of the dialogue of every Caribbean filmmaker or writer, one way or another, with the dominant cinemas and literature of the West – the complex relationship of young black British filmmakers with the 'avant-gardes' of European and American filmmaking. Who could describe this tense and tortured dialogue as a 'one way trip'?

The Third, 'New World' presence, is not so much power, as ground, place, territory. It is the juncture-point where the many cultural tributaries meet, the 'empty' land (the European colonisers emptied it) where strangers from every other part of the globe collided. None of the people who now occupy the islands – black, brown, white, African, European, American, Spanish, French, East Indian, Chinese, Portuguese, Jew, Dutch – originally 'belonged' there. It is the space where the creolisations and assimilations and syncretisms were negotiated. The New World is the third term – the primal scene – where the fateful/fatal encounter was staged between Africa and the West. It also has to be understood as the place of many, continuous displacements: of the original pre-Columbian inhabitants, the Arawaks, Caribs and Amerindians, permanently displaced from their homelands and decimated; of other peoples displaced in different ways from Africa, Asia and Europe; the displacements of slavery, colonisation and conquest. It stands for the endless ways in which Caribbean people have been destined to 'migrate'; it is the signifier of migration itself – of travelling, voyaging and return as fate, as destiny; of the Antillean as the prototype of the modern or postmodern New World nomad, continually moving between centre and periphery. This preoccupation with movement and migration Caribbean cinema shares with many other 'Third Cinemas', but it is one of our defining themes, and it is destined to cross the narrative of every film script or cinematic image.

Présence Americaine continues to have its silences, its suppressions. Peter Hulme, in his essay on 'Islands of enchantment'[11] reminds us that the word 'Jamaica' is the Hispanic form of the indigenous Arawak name – 'land of wood and water' – which Columbus's renaming ('Santiago') never replaced. The Arawak presence remains today a ghostly one, visible in the islands mainly in museums and archeological sites, part of the barely knowable or usable 'past'. Hulme notes that it is not represented in the emblem of the Jamaican National Heritage Trust, for example, which chose instead the figure of Diego Pimienta, 'an African who fought for his Spanish masters against the English invasion of the island in 1655' – a deferred, metonymic, sly and sliding representation of Jamaican identity if ever there was one! He recounts the story of how Prime Minister Edward Seaga tried to alter the Jamaican coat-of-arms, which consists of two Arawak figures holding a shield with five pineapples, surmounted by an alligator. 'Can the crushed and extinct Arawaks represent the dauntless character of Jamaicans. Does the low-slung, near extinct crocodile, a cold-blooded reptile, symbolise the warm, soaring spirit of Jamaicans?' Prime Minister Seaga asked rhetorically.[12] There can be few political statements which so eloquently testify to the complexities entailed in the process of trying to represent a diverse people with a diverse history through a single, hegemonic 'identity'. Fortunately, Mr Seaga's invitation to the Jamaican people, who are overwhelmingly of African descent, to start their 'remembering' by first 'forgetting' something else, got the comeuppance it so richly deserved.

The 'New World' presence – America, *Terra Incognita* – is therefore itself the beginning of diaspora, of diversity, of hybridity and difference, what makes Afro-Caribbean people already people of a diaspora. I use this term here metaphorically, not literally: diaspora does not refer us to those scattered tribes whose identity can only be secured in relation to some sacred homeland to which they must at all costs return, even if it means pushing other people into the sea. This is the old, the imperialising, the hegemonising, form of 'ethnicity'. We have seen the fate of the people of Palestine at the hands of this backward-looking conception of diaspora – and the complicity of the West with it. The diaspora experience as I intend it here is defined, not by essence or purity, but by the recognition of a necessary heterogeneity and diversity; by a conception of 'identity' which lives with and through, not despite, difference; by *hybridity*. Diaspora identities are those which are constantly producing and reproducing themselves anew, through transformation and difference. One can only think here of what is uniquely – 'essentially' – Caribbean: precisely the mixes of colour, pigmentation, physiognomic type; the 'blends' of tastes that is Caribbean cuisine; the aesthetics of the 'cross-overs', of 'cut-and-mix', to borrow Dick Hebdige's telling phrase, which is the heart and soul of black music. Young black cultural practitioners and critics in Britain are increasingly coming to acknowledge and explore in their work this 'diaspora aesthetic' and its formations in the post-colonial experience:

> Across a whole range of cultural forms there is a 'syncretic' dynamic which critically appropriates elements from the master-codes of the dominant culture and 'creolises' them, disarticulating given signs and re-articulating their symbolic meaning. The subversive force of this hybridising tendency is most apparent at the level of language itself where creoles, patois and black English decentre, destabilise and carnivalise the linguistic domination of 'English' – the nation-language of master-discourse – through strategic inflections, re-accentuations and other performative moves in semantic, syntactic and lexical codes.[13]

It is because this New World is constituted for us as place, a narrative of displacement, that it gives rise so profoundly to a certain imaginary plentitude, recreating the endless desire to return to 'lost origins', to be one again with the mother, to go back to the beginning. Who can ever forget, when once seen rising up out of that blue-green Caribbean, those islands of enchantment. Who has not known, at this moment, the surge of an overwhelming nostalgia for lost origins, for 'times past'? And yet, this 'return to the beginning' is like the imaginary in Lacan – it can neither be fulfilled nor requited, and hence is the beginning of the symbolic, of representation, the infinitely renewable source of desire, memory, myth, search, discovery – in short, the reservoir of our cinematic narratives.

We have been trying, in a series of metaphors, to put in play a different sense of our relationship to the past, and thus a different way of thinking about cultural identity, which might constitute new points of recognition in the discourses of the emerging Caribbean cinema and black British cinemas. We have been trying to theorise identity as constituted, not outside but within representation; and hence of cinema, not as a second-order mirror held up to reflect what already exists, but as that form of representation which is able to constitute us as new kinds of subjects, and thereby enable us to discover places from which to speak. Communities, Benedict Anderson argues in *Imagined Communities*, are to be distinguished, not by their falsity/genuineness, but by the style in which they are imagined.[14] This is the vocation of modern black cinemas: by allowing us to see and recognise the different parts and histories of ourselves, to construct those points of identification, those positionalities we call in retrospect our 'cultural identities'.

We must not therefore be content with delving into the past of a people in order to find coherent elements which will counteract colonialism's attempts to falsify and harm. . . . A national culture is not a folk-lore, nor an abstract populism that believes it can discover a people's true nature. A national culture is the whole body of efforts made by a people in the sphere of thought to describe, justify and praise the action through which that people has created itself and keeps itself in existence.[15]

Notes

1. Frantz Fanon, 'On national culture', in *The Wretched of the Earth*, London, 1963, p. 170. [See also p. 37 above.]
2. *ibid.*, p. 176.
3. Christopher Norris, *Deconstruction: Theory and practice*, London, 1982, p. 32.
4. *idem*, *Jacques Derrida*, London, 1987, p. 15.
5. Stuart Hall, *Resistance Through Rituals*, London, 1976.
6. Edward Said, *Orientalism*, London, 1985, p. 55.
7. *ibid.*
8. Benedict Anderson, *Imagined Communities: Reflections on the origin and rise of nationalism*, London, 1982.
9. Frantz Fanon, *Black Skin, White Masks*, London, 1986, p. 109.
10. Homi Bhabha, 'Foreword' to Fanon, *ibid.*, pp. xiv–xv. [See also p. 116 above.]
11. In *New Formations*, 3, Winter 1987.
12. *Jamaica Hansard*, 9, 1983–4, p. 363. Quoted in Hulme, *ibid.*
13. Kobena Mercer, 'Diaspora culture and the dialogic imagination', in M. Cham and C. Watkins (eds), *Blackframes: Critical perspectives on black independent cinema*, 1988, p. 57.
14. Anderson, *op. cit.*, p. 15.
15. Fanon, *Black Skin, White Masks*, p. 188.

23 □ *Urban Social Movements, 'Race' and Community*

Paul Gilroy

It is directly at the level of the production of social relations
that capitalism is vulnerable and en route to perdition. Its fatal
malady is not its incapacity to reproduce itself economically
and politically, but its incapacity to reproduce itself
symbolically.

Jean Baudrillard

As an analysis of the mode of capitalist production, Marxism
defines the conditions under which the system enters a state of
crisis. As a theory of revolution, it lacks the analytic
instruments required for defining the actors and political
forms of socio-economic transformation.

Alberto Melucci

The expressive culture [of black society] has been loosely described as the voice of
social movement. It provides an opportunity to gauge the character, scope and
orientation of a movement among British blacks and their inner-city associates
which is encouraged and enabled by the [specific] patterns of cultural creation
[. . .]. However, the collective action which that culture marks out, and the
interpretive and participative community which is produced in the process of
consuming it, is not confined to the dance-halls, parties and clubs which constitute
an alternative public sphere beyond the colour line.

The counter-cultures and sub-cultures of black Britain may have held the
movement together at certain crucial moments. They provide, among other things,
important rituals which allow its affiliates to recognize each other and celebrate their
coming together. But culture, though integral to the social movement, is not
its totality. It is therefore necessary [. . .] to explore [the movement's] social

Conclusion to Paul Gilroy, *'There Ain't No Black in the Union Jack'*, Hutchinson: London,
1987, pp. 223–36, 245–8.

and political position. Analysis of black Britain must be able to address the synchronic, structural aspects of the movement as well as its diachronic, historical dimension.

The first chapter of [*'There Ain't No Black in the Union Jack'*] raised the question of historical agency and, as part of its critique of class theory, argued that class analysis of contemporary Britain could be reconceptualized in the light of an extended exploration of 'race'. [Here I suggest] that social movement theory can provide a valuable starting point from which this analytical and political transformation might be accomplished. The problem of agency is addressed again, this time in the context of a study of disorderly protest. We focus directly on the kind of collective political action which 'racial' subjectivities allow people to execute. Links between 'race' and the urban environment are discussed at length as are the language and politics of community which have been a notable feature of this relationship.

The term 'social movement' is used here in a way which derives from the theoretical elaboration which the concept has received in the works of Alain Touraine, Manuel Castells and Alberto Melucci.[1] All have used it to examine new patterns of political action and organization, which have emerged in the overdeveloped countries as their old industrial order has begun to decompose and social and political collectivities based away from the workplace have become as vocal, militant and politically significant as the residues of the workers' movement.[2] Touraine and his collaborators link the appearance of the new anti-industrial and anti-bureaucratic political forces – the women's movements, youth movements, anti-nuclear and peace movements, ecological movements, and various urban or citizen movements – with changes in the mode of production. In particular with the growth of large-scale structural unemployment, the expansion of nuclear power, the rise of new technologies, and new communicative networks.

> in a society where the larger investments no longer serve to transform the organisation of labour, as in industrial society, but to create new products, and beyond that, new sources of economic power through the control of complex systems of communication, then the central conflict has shifted. It no longer opposes manager and worker, subjected to the rationalising apparatuses which have acquired the power to impose patterns of behaviour on people according to their own interests.[3]

These new movements may challenge the mode of production and struggle for control of the ways in which a society appropriates scarce resources, but this is not their primary orientation. They are struggling not only for the reappropriation of the material structure of production, but also for collective control over socio-economic development as a whole. Their goals involve the transformation of new modes of subordination located outside the immediate processes of production and consequently require the reappropriation of space, time, and of relationships between individuals in their day to day lives. All these are perceived to be the results of social action. The struggle over production is broadened, and spreads into new areas: 'The defense of identity, continuity and predictability of personal experience is beginning to constitute the substance of new conflicts.'[4] Thus for Touraine and Melucci the new social movements are not phenomena of class politics in any simple sense. Both argue that society should be understood as a self-creating process rather than a finished edifice or structure. The distinctive feature of these movements, diverse as they are, rests on their potential for universalizing the issue of emancipation beyond the particularistic interests of industrial workers employed full time in work that produces surplus value. It is located in their common struggle for the social control of historicity: 'the symbolic capacity that enables [society] to construct a system of knowledge together with the technical tools which it can use to intervene in its own functioning.'[5]

[In] contemporary Britain the symbols associated with 'race', nation, national culture, patriotism and belonging have acquired potent new meanings which are deeply implicated in the way in which national crisis is represented and mediated. In a sense, these symbols and the various meanings attached to them suggest that the painful experiences of crisis and decline can be reversed if not postponed.

Contrasting it with the political and cultural vitality of the new social movements, Touraine identifies the decline of the workers' movement in the overdeveloped countries as an important part of a 'far more general disintegration of the culture of industrial society'.[6] The decomposition of this culture has been articulated to the appearance of a 'modernising cultural critique' which emanates in part from the new social movements and, in turn, encourages their development. These new movements are part of a new phase of class conflict so far removed from the class struggles of the industrial era that the vocabulary of class analysis created during that period must itself be dispensed with, or at least ruthlessly modernized. It must be replaced with or reformed into a theory capable of linking analysis of new social, economic and political structures with analysis of the new social actors who inhabit and create them.[7]

The accumulation of capital is no longer fed by the mere exploitation of the labour force. It depends increasingly on manipulation of complex organizational and informational systems, 'on control over the processes and institutions of symbol formation, and by intervention in interpersonal relations'.[8] This change lends cultural politics an additional cutting edge, particularly where advanced capitalism has developed a

> capacity for intervention and transformation which extends beyond the natural environment and exerts an influence on social systems, on interpersonal relations and on the very structure of the individual (personality, the unconscious, biological identity).[9]

Melucci expands on Touraine's view that Marxism has wrongly separated the analysis of social systems from the analysis of social actors, individual and collective. He goes further than Touraine in suggesting several core characteristics which connect the disparate social movements and allow analysts to perceive their novelty and common identity. He begins by comparing their modes of collective action with those of class politics and observes that the new movements tend to refuse mediation of their demands by the political system against which they have defined themselves. The sociology of these social movements cannot therefore centre, as class analysis has done, on the study of the articulation of class behaviours in the political system. The first characteristic which unites the new movements is the resolutely non-negotiable nature of their demands. This relates directly to a second characteristic feature visible in the extent to which the new movements are not primarily oriented towards instrumental objectives, such as the conquest of political power or state apparatuses, but rather towards 'control of a field of autonomy or independence vis-á-vis the system' and the *immediate* satisfaction of collective desires. Acknowledging that this quality has been criticised as a weakness, particularly by Marxian writers, Melucci instead interprets it as an indication of the movements' potential strength. He argues that it manifests the specificity of the new forms of collective action they have developed. The very refusal to accept mediation by the existing frameworks and institutions of the political system, or to allow strategy to be dominated by the task of winning power within it, provides these movements with an important focus of group identity.

The creation of solidarity from a sense of particularity is an objective for these groups and their political behaviour is not exclusively directed towards the outside. Their characteristic rejection of a politics of representative delegation and their enthusiasm for direct participation and direct action also distinguishes these new social movements from the ossified practices of corporatist class politics.[10]

Melucci identifies two further issues which play a fundamental definitive role in the new movements. The first is the central place they give to the body, and through it to an understanding of human beings as part of the natural world. Blacks who live 'in the castle of their skin' and have struggled to escape the biologization of their socially and politically constructed subordination are already sensitive to this issue. The attempt to articulate blackness as an historical rather than as a natural category confronts it directly. The escape from bestial status into a recognized humanity has been a source of both ethics and politics since the slave system was first instituted and there is an extensive literature which surrounds the absurdities of racial biology and the difficulties associated with its overcoming.[11] Black artists have thus identified the body as a seat of desires and as a nexus of interpersonal relationships in a special way which expresses the aspiration that skin colour will one day be no more significant than eye pigment and, in the meantime, announces that black is beautiful. Whether it is anti-racist universality or spurious racial classification which is being invoked, the black body bears some potent meanings. However, a similar concern and fascination with the body has been expressed by the women's movement, the gay movement and sections of the peace movement where the body has become, in various different ways, a cultural locus of resistances and desires. A sense of the body's place in the natural world can provide, for example, a social ecology and an alternative rationality that articulate a cultural and moral challenge to the exploitation and domination of 'the nature within us and without us'.[12]

A homology has also been identified between care of the body and care of the planet and its biosphere. In black cultures, the themes of bodily control and care emerge most strongly in relation to dance and martial arts. George *et al.* 1985 support this view by pointing persuasively to the similarity between breakdancing and Capoeira, the martial art of Brazilian slaves.[13] However, the same themes are present in the eschatological notion of reconciliation with nature which is central to Rastafari ideology. They have been refined into a holistic concern with ital (natural) eating and physical fitness[14] which has remained in the 'good sense' of the community even where some of the movement's more antiquated or theological concepts have been de-emphasized.

A religious or spiritual component is the second fundamental element which Melucci identifies as connecting the diverse new social movements. Spirituality is more than just a consistent factor in the origins of these various movements. It has acquired powerful radical dimensions not only because religious language can express an intensity of aspirations for which no secular alternative is available but because the political order which these movements criticize and oppose is itself increasingly secular in its rationalizations. In these circumstances, religion may become detached from the institutional life of the official church. Its moral authority increases where the instrumental, secular rationality which informs the operations of the dominant order can be shown to be pragmatic rather than principled. Where the new movements have kept their distance from the institutions of the political system, the moral and metaphysical attributes of religious language can provide a legitimacy which significantly appears to be above politics. The distinction between authentic human emancipation and the formal freedoms guaranteed by politics is constantly underlined.

Britain's social movement around 'race' exhibits all the characteristics suggested by Touraine and Melucci. Its demands around work, law and racism are non-negotiable and where they are not openly hostile to the institutions of the political system, its organizational forms fit only loosely and partially into it. There is [...] a degree of hostility to these institutions and the types of politics they promote. This feeling – 'A terrifying sense of powerlessness which is easily mistaken for apathy'[15] – has been identified as a problem and as an object of state intervention by inner-city local governments. The anti-racist programmes [of 1980s Britain] are aimed directly at alleviating it. The campaign for 'black sections' in the Labour Party is similarly designed to show that the discredited political institutions of the working class retain an importance for blacks. [16] Both campaigns have had only limited success in countering the idea that being political now requires complete disassociation from the corporate structures of formal politics which are in need of drastic re-politicization. Authentic politics is thought to recommence with this act of withdrawal.[17]

The importance of local factors and local state initiatives as well as the intersection of territoriality and identity in urban black cultures provide a further clue to the character of contemporary 'race' politics. It demands that the role of distinctively urban processes and experiences are recognized. [...] Britain's 'race' politics are quite inconceivable away from the context of the inner city which provides such firm foundations for the imagery of black criminality and lawlessness. We must therefore confront the extent to which the cultural politics of 'race' reveals conflict over the production of urban meanings and situate the meanings which have already been identified as constitutive of 'race' in their proper place as contending definitions of what city life is about.

[The] image of black and white neighbours living side by side yet estranged from each other is a recurrent theme in the discourse of contemporary racism. [There] is a sense in which Powell's 'wide grinning piccanninies' tormenting the aged white woman have metamorphosed into a riotous mob energized by the deviant impulses of their pathological alien culture. The *Daily Express* version of the Tottenham riot of October 1985 reveals the enduring potency of these images in its account of 'Old folk left helpless as looters strip their homes. . . . Elderly couples told how they were pulled from their flats and had to stand and watch as youths looted their homes.'[18] These and similar images derive their power partly from what they convey about the incompatibility of black and white people and their respective 'ethnic' cultures conceived along absolutely separate lines. They are also highly significant for what they communicate about the city in which blacks and whites encounter each other with such negative results.

The idea of the city as a jungle where bestial, predatory values prevail preceded the large-scale settlement of Britain by blacks in the post-war period.[19] It has contributed significantly to contemporary definitions of 'race', particularly those which highlight the supposed primitivism and violence of black residents in inner-city areas. This is the context in which 'race' and racism come to connote the urban crisis as a whole and that crisis to embody racial problems even where they are not overtly acknowledged or defined.

'Race' has become a marker for the activity of urban social movements and their conflict with urban political systems and state institutions. This connection between contemporary British racism and the city is an important reminder that 'race' is a relational concept which does not have fixed referents. The naturalization of social phenomena and the suppression of the historical process which are introduced by its appeal to the biological realm can articulate a variety of different political antagonisms. They change, and bear with them no intrinsic or constant political effects.

[The] local state has been especially prominent in recent 'race' politics as a key source of anti-racist activity. This prominence is a further sign of the importance of the urban context in shaping racial meanings. The municipal anti-racism discussed above has become an important issue in its own right, separate from the struggles of black city dwellers. The Labour councils who have set out to 'attack' racism and win active support from their black citizens by changing 'Britannia Walk' to 'Shaheed E Azam Bhagot Singh Avenue'[20] or by telling environmental health officers who monitor noise on their estates to be lenient with noisy parties which are the product of black ethnicity, while prosecuting white infringers whose anti-social behaviour lacks any comparable cultural explanation,[21] have been severely criticized in the popular press. Their initiatives have been presented as the inevitably disastrous effect of a mistaken desire to secure racial equality by means of an active policy. The true tyranny revealed by the 'race' issue is thus no longer the oppression of blacks by whites that is institutionalized in Britain's social and political life. It is defined instead as the anti-racist autocracy which blacks and their socialist allies are able to practise on a tolerant population by means of their hold on the local state. This is demonstrated in the reporting of anti-racist policies which have been described as a 'sinister attempt to first curb and then destroy freedom of speech'.[22]

The popular opposition to municipal anti-racism also constructs a version of the national past which directly challenges the emphasis on slavery [...] emerging [...] from the expressive culture of Britain's blacks: 'British people are not and have never been, racist. This country has always involved a reputation as a tolerant, welcoming haven for refugees and immigrants.'[23] Racism has been redefined as the product of black and anti-racist zeal that is both destructive of democracy and subversive of order. The right to be prejudiced is claimed as the heritage of the freeborn Briton and articulated within the discourses of freedom, patriotism and democracy while despotic anti-racism is associated with authoritarianism, statism and censorship.

The power which this ideological package has acquired can lead to its municipal context being overlooked. However tokenistic, ill-considered and poorly presented to the public, recent attempts to rename and unname streets, areas and public facilities at least express something of the fundamental connection between 'race' and the city. They seek to make visible the consonance of social and physical space and this becomes all the more important because ethnic absolutism appears to have forsaken the distinctively urban dimensions of 'race' altogether. The supposed cultural essences of Britain's black populations have been accorded a determining role irrespective of their surroundings. Concern with the relationship between 'race' and the urban environment which was an important feature of the early sociology of 'race relations' has faded.[24]

Manuel Castells has developed a theory of the distinctively urban dimensions of the new social movements which can contribute to the theorization of contemporary 'race' politics in this country.[25] He argues that urban social movements share some basic characteristics in spite of their obvious diversity. They consider themselves to be urban, citizen or related to the city in their self-denomination; they are locally based, territorially defined and they tend to mobilize around three central goals: (1) collective consumption; (2) cultural identity; (3) political self-management. Collective consumption refers to the goods and services directly or indirectly provided by the state; cultural identity becomes an issue where it is closely associated with a specific territory and is defended on that basis; and political self-management relates to the attempt by urban groups to win a degree of autonomy from the local governments which directly oversee their immediate environments providing use values, income and services.

Each of these features can be found in the recent history of Britain's black communities: struggles over the services provided by the state, particularly the quality of educational opportunities for black children, have been intense;[26] the cultural dimensions to the struggle of black inner-city dwellers have already been examined; and the demands of community organizations have repeatedly focused on the need to gain a degree of control over the processes which shape day to day experience. Local campaigns for police accountability, prompted by concern about the organization and role of the force in inner-city areas, perfectly illustrate the type of issue which falls in Castells's last category.[27]

There are good grounds on which to argue that the language of community has displaced both the language of class and the language of 'race' in the political activity of black Britain. Though blacks identify themselves as an exploited and subordinated group, there are marked and important differences between the political cultures and identities of the various black communities which together make up the social movement. Local factors, reflecting the class, ethnic and 'racial' composition of any particular area, its political traditions, the local economy and residential structure, may all play a decisive part in shaping precisely what it means to be black. [The] relationship between Afro-Caribbean and Asian descended populations is the most obvious factor of this type. The forms of racism which develop in areas where the two groups are closely associated are quite different from those which obtain where there is a measure of antipathy or even conflict between them. Some inner-city whites, particularly the young, may find much in 'West Indian' culture which they can evaluate positively. If black culture appears in syncretised Afro-Caribbean forms which are relatively desirable and attractive when contrasted to the more obviously 'alien' Asian varieties, the white racist may be faced with considerable problems.[28]

According to Castells, it is only when all three of these goals combine in the practice of an urban movement that social change can occur. The separation of any one goal from the others reduces the potential of the social movement and recasts it in the role of an interest group that may be 'moulded into the established institutions of society, so losing its impact'.[29] He views these social movements as precarious, fragile collectivities which may be unable to fully accomplish all the projects promised by their organizational rhetoric. Their specific appeal and the popular power they represent cannot necessarily survive contact with the agencies of the state against which they struggle: 'they lose their identity when they become institutionalised, the inevitable outcome of bargaining for social reform within the political system.'

The theory of urban social movements correctly emphasizes that they are not ready-made agents for structural change but rather 'symptoms of resistance to domination'. They have their roots in a radical sense of powerlessness and though their resistances may have important effects on cities and societies, they are best understood as defensive organizations which are unlikely to be able to make the transition to more stable forms of politics. This lends these movements certain strengths as well as the obvious weaknesses. The utopian strands in their ideology, which demand the immediate satisfaction of needs, require totalizing, historically feasible plans for economic production, communication and government. The movements are unlikely to be unable to supply these without losing the very qualities which make them dynamic and distinct. Their orientation towards local governments and political institutions, on the immediate conditions in which exploitation and domination are experienced, is a result of the simple fact that those whose grievances give the movements momentum have no other choice. They lack any sense of credible democracy other than the grassroots variety practised in their own organizations. As Castells puts it, 'When people find themselves unable to control the world, they simply shrink the world to the size of their community.' The 'politricks' of the system is replaced by an authentic, immediate politics.

Like Touraine, Castells lays great stress on the decline of the workers' movement which has been apparent in inverse proportion to the rise of the new social movements.[30] This decline has been hastened by the fact that the parties and organizations of Labour operate an obsolete analysis which privileges industrial work and depends ultimately on a mystical view of the proletariat as a 'universal class' which, in liberating itself, is expected to liberate everybody. Further problems have arisen where the idea of socialism has itself been discredited by the barbarities practised in its name by the 'actually existing socialist' states. Castells sums up the situation thus:

> the philosophical rationalism of the political left and the one dimensional culture of the Labour movement lead the social movements of industrial capitalism to ignore sub-cultures, gender specificity, ethnic groups, religious beliefs, national identities and personal experiences. All human diversity was generally considered a remnant of the past, and class struggle and human progress would help to supersede it until a universal fraternity was arrived at that would provide, paradoxically, the ideal stage for both bourgeois enlightenment and proletarian marxism. Between times, people continued to speak their languages, pray to their saints, celebrate their traditions, enjoy their bodies and refuse just to be labour or consumers.

André Gorz also discusses these issues.[31] He points to several problems in Marxist theory which have a direct bearing on the relationship between the new social movements and industrial class politics. His central proposition is that the large-scale, structural unemployment produced by crisis and technological change combines with a related loss of ability to identify with work among those who remain employed. Together these patterns are bringing about a complete transformation of work in the overdeveloped countries.

> Just as work has become a nondescript task carried out without any personal involvement, which one may quit for another equally contingent job, so too has class membership come to be lived as a contingent and meaningless fact.[32]

By the same remorseless logic with which earlier forms of capitalism created the proletariat, the crises of late capitalism are creating a 'non-class of non-workers' from the unemployed, part-timers, and those who work with no security – 'all the supernumeraries of present day social production'. This historical and structural problem is compounded in Marxist theory by the idealist residues of Hegelianism which are concentrated in Marx's analysis of the proletariat. Gorz argues that rather than being confined to Marx's early writings, metaphysical, ontological views of the origin and mission of the proletariat pervade Marx's mature work.

This thesis has been stated in a more circumspect manner by other authors, particularly Murray Bookchin and Rudolf Bahro.[33] It rests on a contentious reading of Marx with which I have considerable sympathy even though it has been described by one critic as 'trivializing'.[34] It can supply an important corrective to Marxian theories of 'race' which have sought [. . .] to use outmoded criteria as a means to measure the activities of the new social movements and find them wanting. Gorz suggests that the Hegelian philosophy which constructs the proletariat as a universal class has encouraged a 'mythologized proletarian ideal' which can never be matched by the composite, fractured and heterogeneous actions of the empirical working class.

The same Hegelian traces, described by Gorz as a 'theology translated as a theophany', also lead Marxists to deny the necessary space between individual autonomy, freedom and happiness and *social* being, which is allocated pride of place in their theory. Individuals will not necessarily find their self-realization congruent with the socialization of their needs and Gorz insists that there are some aspects of life which are not in any case amenable to socialization. He argues forcefully that socialists have abandoned this area of individual autonomy to the right with disastrous results. Yet it is precisely this sphere of autonomous self-realization which is addressed by many of the new social movements.

[Black] expressive cultures which prize non-work time and space have articulated a political and philosophical critique of work and productivism – the ideology which sees the expansion of productive forces as an indispensable precondition of the attainment of freedom. The critique of work in general and the capitalist division of labour in particular described by these forms involves a more modest formulation of the project which Gorz describes as 'the abolition of work'. It can be more accurately summarized in his three points for a utopian political programme: work less; consume better; and reintegrate culture with everyday life.

There are considerable difficulties in Gorz's analysis. Not least of these are his inability to see beyond Europe and an unsatisfactory attempt to unify the disparate forces which share an ambiguous relationship to the world of work, in the non-class of non-workers category. However, his post-industrial utopia finds a resonance that cannot be overlooked in many of the themes and preoccupations which have emerged spontaneously from the political culture of black Britain.

Operating in a similar but less rhetorical vein to Gorz, Rudolf Bahro has also sketched the elements of a utopian vision which combines a critique of productivism with an ethical dimension and some explicit concern with the necessary realization of individual autonomy. Bahro's definition of Cultural Revolution is encapsulated in a single desire: 'to create that new organisation of labour and social life on which it will be possible to base a community that deserves the old name of a free association of individuals in solidarity.'[35] The overcoming of racial segmentation and ethnic absolutism is implicit in this formula, since for Bahro 'this is a society in which there is no longer any domination of man by man [*sic*].' He reduces this maximum programme to five essential demands which also find echoes in the expressive culture [of Black society].

1. The goal of production as rich individuality.
2. A new determination of the need for material goods and the availability of living labour from the standpoint of the optimization of conditions of development for fully socialized individuals.
3. A more harmonious form of reproduction.
4. Accounting for a new economy of time.
5. Individual initiative and genuine communality.

Bahro recognizes that the emancipatory potential signalled in these demands is 'already in train spontaneously'. He argues that the insights they contain must be expanded and developed through an extensive educational process.

For the social movement of blacks in Britain, the context in which these and other similar demands have been spontaneously articulated has been supplied by a political language premised on notions of community. Though it reflects the concentration of black people, the term refers to far more than mere place or population. It has a moral dimension and its use evokes a rich complex of symbols surrounded by a wider cluster of meanings. The historical memory of progress from slave to citizen actively cultivated in the present from resources provided by the past endows it with an aura of tradition. Community, therefore, signifies not just a distinctive political ideology but a particular set of values and norms in everyday life: mutuality, co-operation, identification and symbiosis. For black Britain, all these are centrally defined by the need to escape and transform the forms of subordination which bring 'races' into being. Yet they are not limited by that objective. The disabling effects of racial categorization are themselves seen as symbols of the other unacceptable attributes of 'racial capitalism'. The evident autonomy of racism from production relations demands that the reappropriation of production is not pursued independently of the transformation of capitalist social relations as a whole. The social bond implied by use of the term 'community' is created in the practice of collective resistance to the encroachments of reification, 'racial' or otherwise. It prefigures that transformation in the name of a radical, democratic, anti-racist populism. This is not so much

> a distinct set of political opinions as a mobilisation of people who [share] a common understanding of how life ought to be. Not all of the people are mobilised at any one time but the mode of understanding [is] widespread.[36]

The generalization of this mode of understanding coincides with the formation of what has already been called an interpretive community. It has been spread through the distinctive [literary and musical] networks. [...]

The cultural focus [I have adopted] requires that attention be paid to the symbolic dimensions of community. It is necessary, therefore, to briefly discuss the means by which community is constructed symbolically as part of or in support of the collective actions of a social movement. As Anthony Cohen points out:

> community might not have the structure or direction which we associate with social movements, it may nevertheless serve a similar need. It is a largely mental construct, whose 'objective' manifestations in locality or ethnicity give it credibility. It is highly symbolized, with the consequence that its members can invest it with their selves. Its character is sufficiently malleable that it can accommodate all of its members' selves without them feeling their individuality to be overly compromised. Indeed, the gloss of commonality which it paints over its diverse components gives to each of them an additional referent for their identities.[37]

This definition of community depends on the distinction between symbols and meanings. The former are flexible vehicles for a variety of potentially contradictory readings which may be held by a movement's adherents. The idea of a social movement as an interpretive community should not lead to an undifferentiated monadical view of the group from which it wins active support. The strength of symbols is their multi-accentuality and malleability. Sharing a common body of symbols created around notions of 'race', ethnicity or locality, common history or identity does not dictate the sharing of the plural meanings which may become attached to those symbols and cluster around them.

Community is as much about difference as it is about similarity and identity. It is a relational idea which suggests, for British blacks at least, the idea of antagonism – domination and subordination between one community and another. The word directs analysis to the boundary between these groups. It is a boundary which is presented primarily by symbolic means and therefore a broad range of meanings can co-exist around it reconciling individuality and commonality and competing definitions of what the movement is about. The political rhetoric of leaders is, after all, not a complete guide to the motivations and aspirations of those who play a less prominent role. In Cohen's words again:

> just as the common form of the symbol aggregates the various meanings assigned to it, so the symbolic repertoire of a community aggregates the individualities and other differences found within the community and provides the means for their expression, interpretation and containment. . . . It continuously transforms the reality of difference into the appearance of similarity with such efficacy that people can still invest [their] community with ideological integrity. It unites them in their opposition, both to each other and to those 'outside'.[38]

[The] points at which closures have been introduced into the symbolic repertoire of black Britain [. . .] can be identified where particular definitions of 'race' and nation or of the meaning attributed to skin colour have been invested with special significance by a group which tries to fix their reading of these symbols as a universal one capable of binding the whole community together. It bears repetition that these tensions are part of a political struggle inside the black communities over what 'race' adds up to.

Such conflicts are possible because black Britain's repertoire of symbols is relatively unfixed and still evolving. It includes the languages of Ethiopianism and Pan-Africanism and the heritage of anti-colonial resistances as well as the inputs from contemporary urban conflicts. These diverse elements combine syncretically in struggles to reconstruct a collective historical presence from the discontinuous, fractured histories of the African and Asian diasporas. Multiple meanings have grouped around the central symbol of racial alterity – the colour black – and it is difficult to anticipate the outcome of the political struggle between the different tendencies they represent – ethnic absolutism on the one hand and a utopian, democratic populism on the other. Yet despite their differences, the 'black professional' in a local authority social services department, the Afro-Caribbean ancillary in a hospital and the hip-hopping Asian youth of West London may all discover within that colour a medium through which to articulate their own experiences and make sense of their common exclusion from Britain and Britishness. The actions of organizations of the urban social movement around 'race' may themselves assume symbolic significance. Particularly where people are mobilized to protest, innumerable political and ethical grievances, desires and aspirations may be condensed and unified in the symbolism which dissent provides. [. . .]

[. . .] In the representation of recent riots, it is possible to glimpse a struggle, a sequence of antagonisms which has moved beyond the grasp of orthodox class analysis. Unable to control the social relations in which they find themselves, people have shrunk the world to the sise of their communities and begun to act politically on that basis. The politics of the urban social movements supply an answer to the question of historical agency [. . .].

[Forms] of political calculation ordered by the priorities and experiences of the dwindling industrial proletariat find it difficult to make sense of these new social struggles. They are written off as mere deviancy or marginality. This dismissal is the penalty for disappointing the teleology of economistic socialism.[39]

[If] these struggles (some of which are conducted in and through 'race') are to be called class struggles, then class analysis must itself be thoroughly overhauled. I am not sure whether the labour involved in doing this makes it either a possible or a desirable task. The liberatory rationality which informs these struggles has found new modes of expression which stress what can be called neo-populist themes. They appeal directly to 'the people'. By contrast, the political languages of class and socialism have been so thoroughly discredited by Labourism at home and 'actually existing socialism' abroad that they may be completely beyond resuscitation. The dynamism and cultural vitality of the neo-populist social movements, of which struggles around 'race' are only one example, contrasts sharply with the decadent corporate organizations and political styles from which the new movements tell us we must disengage if authentic politics is to be re-born. Whether such disengagement leads to an enhancement of radical, democratic politics is likely to depend to a considerable degree on local factors. In examining the demand for tactical withdrawal, I hope to have shown that the organizational possibilities provided by 'race' and the forms of consciousness which have emerged with the rejection of racism by urban communities are now at least as likely to provide strong foundations for radical collective action as the equivalent appeal derived from narrowly-based class politics – Labourist or Leninist, 'Eurocommunist' or Fundamentalist.[40]

I believe that this argument can also be sustained at a more general level. As Craig Calhoun has shown in *The Question of Class Struggle*, rootedness in tradition and immediate social relations is the essential basis of a radical response to social change.[41] This sense of rootedness is powerfully expressed today in the politics of the inner-city communities, particularly where locality, ethnicity or 'race' grounds them in potent historical memories. The significance of this general point has evaded Marxism whether it has made 'class consciousness the pre-requisite of class struggle' (Lenin) or 'class consciousness largely the outcome of that struggle' (Gramsci).

If, as Gorz has argued, class membership is increasingly being lived out as a 'contingent and meaningless fact',[42] the ground on which the whole productivist, Marxian edifice has been erected is in jeopardy. The proletariat of yesterday, classically conceived or otherwise, now has rather more to lose than its chains. The real gains which it has made have been achieved as the cost of a deep-seated accommodation with capital and the political institutions of corporatism. Its will, as Calhoun has also pointed out 'is apt to be a reformist will' and this prompts a further question: Where is radical collective action to come from in the miserable years of crisis and crisis management which await Britain?

The answer [...] is that it is likely to arise from those groups who find the premises of their collective existence threatened. In earlier phases of capitalist development and in peripheral states these may have been workers tied to pre-capitalist modes of production locked into the capitalist system in a subordinate position or those whose traditional social relations were displaced by its consolidation.

These groups, who were not and are not still classes in the Marxian sense, responded to their situation, not as isolated individuals but as social actors. Their histories point to fundamental problems in Marxist theory which has rested for far too long on an idealized view of the modern proletariat.[43] The Marxist view has been criticized above for being based on Hegel's notion of a universal class and on a loose analogy with 'the emergence of the bourgeoisie out of feudalism' as a class for itself.[44]

In the present, studying the potency of racism and nationalism and observing the capability of movements formed around 'racial' subjectivities involves an examination of the social relations within which people act and their junctions with forms of politics which articulate themselves through historical memory's 'traditional' roots. 'Race', and its attendant imaginary politics of community, affect and kinship, provide a contemporary example of how 'traditional' ties are created and re-created out of present rather than past conditions.

Taking on board C. L. R. James's important observation that 'there is nothing more to organize' because 'organization as we have known it is at an end',[45] it is possible to comprehend how people act socially and cohesively without the structures provided by formal organizations. Collective identities spoken through 'race', community and locality are, for all their spontaneity, powerful means to co-ordinate action and create solidarity. The constructed 'traditional' culture becomes a means [...] to articulate personal autonomy with collective empowerment focused by a multi-accented symbolic repertoire and its corona of meanings.

The world 'radical' carries with it connotations of rootedness which [...] are once again becoming highly significant for British political culture. 'Race' must be retained as an analytic category not because it corresponds to any biological or epistemological absolutes, but because it refers investigation to the power that collective identities acquire by means of their roots in tradition. These identities, in the forms of white racism and black resistance, are the most volatile political forces in Britain today.

Notes

1. See Alain Touraine, *Anti-nuclear Protest, the Opposition to Nuclear Energy in France*, Cambridge University Press: Cambridge, 1983; *Solidarity Poland 1980–81*, Cambridge University Press: Cambridge, 1983; *The Voice and the Eye: An analysis of social movements*, Cambridge University Press: Cambridge, 1981; *The Self-Production of Society*, University of Chicago Press: London, 1977. See also Manuel Castells, *The City and the Grassroots*, Edward Arnold: London, 1983. See also Alberto Melucci, 'Ten hypotheses for the analysis of new movements', in D. Pinto (ed.), *Contemporary Italian Sociology*, Cambridge University Press: Cambridge, 1981; 'New movements, terrorism and political system: reflections on the Italian case', *Socialist Review* (US), 56, March-April 1981; 'The new social movements: a theoretical approach', *Social Science Information*, 19, 2, 1980.
2. See J. Freeman (ed.), *Social Movements of the Sixties and Seventies*, Longman: New York, 1983.
3. Touraine, *Anti-nuclear Protest*, p. 4.
4. Melucci, 'The new social movements'.
5. Touraine, *The Self-Production of Society*.
6. *Idem, The Voice and the Eye*.
7. See M. Bookchin, 'Beyond Neo-Marxism', *Telos*, 36, Summer 1978.
8. Melucci, 'The new social movements'.
9. *ibid.*, p. 218
10. See Z. Bauman, *Memories of Class: The pre-history and after-life of class*, Routledge and Kegan Paul: London, 1982. See also L. Panitch, 'Trades unions and the State', *New Left Review*, 25, 1981.
11. See N. Larsen, *Passing*, Negro Universities Press: New York, 1929 (reissue 1969). See also J. Weldon Johnson, *The Autobiography of an Ex-Coloured Man*, Avon Books: New York, 1965.

12. See S. Ben-Habib, 'Modernity and the aporias of critical theory', *Telos*, 49, 1981. See also M. Daly, *Gyn/Ecology: The meta-ethics of radical feminism*, The Women's Press: London, 1979.
13. See N. George *et al.*, *Fresh Hip Hop Don't Stop*, Random House: New York, 1985.
14. Freddie McGregor's song 'Jogging' exemplifies this theme.
15. Bookchin, 'Beyond Neo-Marxism'.
16. See D. Howe, *Black Sections in the Labour Party*, Race Today Publications: London, 1985.
17. Stafford Scott, leader of Broadwater Farm Youth Association, addressing a public meeting in Haringey Town Hall, 10.11.85.
18. *Daily Express*, 7.10.85. See also Charles Moore's *The Old People of Lambeth*, Salisbury Papers, 9, 1982.
19. See P. Langer, 'Sociology – four images of organised diversity: bazaar, jungle, organism and machine', in Rodwin and Hollister (eds.), *Cities of the Mind: Images and themes of the city in social science*, Plenum Press: London, 1984.
20. *Sun*, 7.9.85.
21. *Standard*, 17.6.83.
22. *Sun*, 24.10.58.
23. *ibid*.
24. See, for example, John Rex's 'The sociology of a zone of transition' and Ruth Glass's 'Conflict in cities', both in Raynor and Harden (eds.), *Cities, Communities and Young*, Routledge & Kegan Paul: London/Open University Press: Milton Keynes, 1973.
25. Castells, *op. cit.*
26. A good account of community struggles around education is included in the CARF study of Southall, *Southall: The birth of a black community*, IRR: London, 1981, pp. 33–4. A useful overview of Afro-Caribbean community activism emerges from David Pearson's *Race, Class and Political Activism: A study of West Indians in Britain*, Gower: Farnborough, 1981.
27. See P. Scraton, *The State of the Police*, Pluto Press: London, 1985.
28. See P. Gilroy and E. Lawrence, 'Two-tone Britain, black youth white youth and the politics of anti-racism', in P. Cohen and H. S. Bains (eds.), *Youth in Multi-Racist Britain*, MacMillan: Basingstoke, 1988.
29. Castells, *op. cit.*
30. See I. Wallerstein, 'Eurocommunism: its roots in European working class history', *Contemporary Marxism*, 2, Winter 1980.
31. See A. Gorz, *Farewell to the Working Class*, Pluto: London, 1982.
32. *ibid.*, p. 67.
33. 'It seems to me that the entire concept of the proletariat was never completely free from the Hegelian antithesis between (rational, essential) reality and (merely empirical, accidental) existence, and this for reason of their own subjective needs. The actual empirical proletariat, even though summoned by them to represent the whole of humanity in its progress, is a class that, left to its own devices, only attains trade-union expression of its interests. As the result of an overwhelming structure of historical reality, the same as formerly affected church organisations concerned with the saving of souls, consciousness of its "true", world-historical goals had to be brought into the workers' movement from outside' (Rudolph Bahro, p. 195).
34. See Richard Hyman's 'André Gorz and the disappearing proletariat', in Ralph Miliband and John Saville (eds.), *The Socialist Register 1983*, Merlin: London, 1983.

35. Bahro, *op. cit.*
36. Craig Calhoun, 'Community: Toward a variable conceptualisation for comparative research', *Social History*, 5, 1, January 1980. See also C. Calhoun, *The Question of Class Struggle*, Basil Blackwell: Oxford, 1982.
37. See A. P. Cohen, *The Symbolic Construction of Community*, Tavistock: London, 1985, p. 109.
38. *ibid.*, p. 21.
39. See J. Lea and J. Young, *What is to be done about law and order?*, Penguin/Socialist Society: London, 1984. See also I. Taylor, 'Against crime and for socialism', *Crime and Social Justice*, 18, 1982.
40. See B. Fine *et al.*, *Class Politics: An answer to its critics*, Leftover Pamphlets: London, 1984.
41. See n. 36 above.
42. Gorz, *op. cit.*
43. See M. Adas, *Prophets of Rebellion: Millenarian protest movements against the European colonial order*, University of North Carolina Press: Chapel Hill, NC, 1979.
44. See M. Bookchin, 'Finding the subject: notes of Whitebook and Habermas Ltd', *Telos*, 52, Summer 1982.
45. C. L. R. James, *Notes on Dialectics*, Allison and Busby: London, 1980.

24 □ *Postmodern Blackness*

bell hooks

Postmodernist discourses are often exclusionary even as they call attention to, appropriate even, the experience of 'difference' and 'Otherness' to provide oppositional political meaning, legitimacy and immediacy when they are accused of lacking concrete relevance. Very few African-American intellectuals have talked or written about postmodernism. At a dinner party I talked about trying to grapple with the significance of postmodernism for contemporary black experience. It was one of those social gatherings where only one other black person was present. The setting quickly became a field of contestation. I was told by the other black person that I was wasting my time, that 'this stuff does not relate in any way to what's happening with black people'. Speaking in the presence of a group of white onlookers, staring at us as though this encounter were staged for their benefit, we engaged in a passionate discussion about black experience. Apparently, no one sympathized with my insistence that racism is perpetuated when blackness is associated solely with concrete gut level experience conceived as either opposing or having no connection to abstract thinking and the production of critical theory. The idea that there is no meaningful connection between black experience and critical thinking about aesthetics or culture must be continually interrogated.

My defense of postmodernism and its relevance to black folks sounded good, but I worried that I lacked conviction, largely because I approach the subject cautiously and with suspicion.

Disturbed not so much by the 'sense' of postmodernism but by the conventional language used when it is written or talked about and by those who speak it, I find myself on the outside of the discourse looking in. As a discursive practice it is dominated primarily by the voices of white male intellectuals and/or academic elites who speak to and about one another with coded familiarity. Reading and studying their writing to understand postmodernism in its multiple manifestations, I appreciate it but feel little inclination to ally myself with the academic hierarchy and exclusivity pervasive in the movement today.

From bell hooks, *Yearning: Race, gender, and cultural politics*, Turnaround: London/South End Press: Boston, MA, 1991, pp. 23–31.

Critical of most writing on postmodernism, I perhaps am more conscious of the way in which the focus on 'Otherness and difference' that is often alluded to in these works seems to have little concrete impact as an analysis or standpoint that might change the nature and direction of postmodernist theory. Since much of this theory has been constructed in reaction to and against high modernism, there is seldom any mention of black experience or writings by black people in this work, specifically black women (though in more recent work one may see a reference to Cornel West, the black male scholar who has most engaged postmodernist discourse). Even if an aspect of black culture is the subject of postmodern critical writing, the works cited will usually be those of black men. A work that comes immediately to mind is Andrew Ross's chapter 'Hip, and the long front of color' in *No Respect: Intellectuals and popular culture*; while it is an interesting reading, it constructs black culture as though black women have had no role in black cultural production. At the end of Meaghan Morris' discussion of postmodernism in her collection of essays *The Pirate's Fiancé: Feminism and postmodernism*, she provides a bibliography of works by women, identifying them as important contributions to a discourse on postmodernism that offer new insight as well as challenging male theoretical hegemony. Even though many of the works do not directly address postmodernism, they address similar concerns. There are no references to works by black women.

The failure to recognize a critical black presence in the culture and in most scholarship and writing on postmodernism compels a black reader, particularly a black female reader, to interrogate her interest in a subject where those who discuss and write about it seem not to know black women exist or even to consider the possibility that we might be somewhere writing or saying something that should be listened to, or producing art that should be seen, heard, approached with intellectual seriousness. This is especially the case with works that go on and on about the way in which postmodernist discourse has opened up a theoretical terrain where 'difference and Otherness' can be considered legitimate issues in the academy. Confronting both the absence of recognition of black female presence that much postmodernist theory re-inscribes and the resistance on the part of most black folks to hearing about real connection between postmodernism and black experience, I enter a discourse, a practice, where there may be no ready audience for my words, no clear listener, uncertain, then, that my voice can or will be heard.

During the sixties, the black power movement was influenced by perspectives that could easily be labeled modernist. Certainly many of the ways black folks addressed issues of identity conformed to a modernist universalizing agenda. There was little critique of patriarchy as a master narrative among black militants. Despite the fact that black power ideology reflected a modernist sensibility, these elements were soon rendered irrelevant as militant protest was stifled by a powerful, repressive postmodern state. The period directly after the black power movement was a time when major news magazines carried articles with cocky headlines like 'Whatever happened to Black America?' This response was an ironic reply to the aggressive, unmet demand by decentered, marginalized black subjects who had at least momentarily successfully demanded a hearing, who had made it possible for black liberation to be on the national political agenda. In the wake of the black power movement, after so many rebels were slaughtered and lost, many of these voices were silenced by a repressive state; others became inarticulate. It has become necessary to find new avenues to transmit the messages of black liberation struggle, new ways to talk about racism and other politics of domination. Radical postmodernist practice, most powerfully conceptualized as a 'politics of difference', should incorporate the voices of displaced, marginalized, exploited and oppressed black people. It is sadly ironic that the contemporary discourse which talks the most about heterogeneity, the decentered subject, declaring breakthroughs that allow recognition of Otherness, still directs its critical voice primarily to a specialized audience that shares a common language rooted in the very master narratives it claims to challenge. If radical postmodernist thinking is to have a transformative impact, then a critical break with the notion of 'authority' as 'mastery over' must not simply be a rhetorical device. It must be reflected in habits of being, including styles of writing as well as chosen subject matter. Third world nationals, elites and white critics who passively absorb white supremacist thinking, and therefore never notice or look at black people on the streets or at their jobs, who render us invisible with their gaze in all areas of daily life, are not likely to produce liberatory theory that will challenge racist domination, or promote a breakdown in traditional ways of seeing and thinking about reality, ways of constructing aesthetic theory and practice. From a different standpoint, Robert Storr makes a similar critique in the global issue of *Art in America* when he asserts:

> To be sure, much postmodernist critical inquiry has centered precisely on the issues of 'difference' and 'Otherness'. On the purely theoretical plane the exploration of these concepts has produced some important results, but in the absence of any sustained research into what artists of color and others outside the mainstream might be up to, such discussions become rootless instead of radical. Endless second guessing about the latent imperialism of intruding upon other cultures only compounded matters, preventing or excusing these theorists from investigating what black, Hispanic, Asian and Native American artists were actually doing.

Without adequate concrete knowledge of and contact with the non-white 'Other', white theorists may move in discursive theoretical directions that are threatening and potentially disruptive of that critical practice which would support radical liberation struggle.

The postmodern critique of 'identity', though relevant for renewed black liberation struggle, is often posed in ways that are problematic. Given a pervasive politic of white supremacy which seeks to prevent the formation of radical black subjectivity, we cannot cavalierly dismiss a concern with identity politics. Any critic exploring the radical potential of postmodernism as it relates to racial difference and racial domination would need to consider the implications of a critique of identity for oppressed groups. Many of us are struggling to find new strategies of resistance. We must engage decolonization as a critical practice if we are to have meaningful chances of survival even as we must simultaneously cope with the loss of political grounding which made radical activism more possible. I am thinking here about the postmodernist critique of essentialism as it pertains to the construction of 'identity' as one example.

Postmodern theory that is not seeking to simply appropriate the experience of 'Otherness' to enhance the discourse or to be radically chic should not separate the 'politics of difference' from the politics of racism. To take racism seriously one must consider the plight of underclass people of color, a vast majority of whom are black. For African-Americans our collective condition prior to the advent of postmodernism and perhaps more tragically expressed under current postmodern conditions has been and is characterized by continued displacement, profound alienation and despair. Writing about blacks and postmodernism, Cornel West describes our collective plight:

> There is increasing class division and differentiation, creating on the one hand a significant black middle-class, highly anxiety-ridden, insecure, willing to be co-opted and incorporated into the powers that be, concerned with racism to the degree that it poses constraints on upward social mobility; and, on the other, a vast and growing black underclass, an underclass that embodies a kind of walking nihilism of pervasive drug addiction, pervasive alcoholism, pervasive homicide, and an exponential rise in suicide. Now because of the deindustrialization, we also have a devastated black industrial working class. We are talking here about tremendous hopelessness.

This hopelessness creates longing for insight and strategies for change that can renew spirits and reconstruct grounds for collective black liberation struggle. The overall impact of postmodernism is that many other groups now share with black folks a sense of deep alienation, despair, uncertainty, loss of a sense of grounding even if it is not informed by shared circumstance. Radical postmodernism calls attention to those shared sensibilities which cross the boundaries of class, gender, race, etc., that could be fertile ground for the construction of empathy – ties that would promote recognition of common commitments, and serve as a base for solidarity and coalition.

Yearning is the word that best describes a common psychological state shared by many of us, cutting across boundaries of race, class, gender and sexual practice. Specifically, in relation to the postmodernist reconstruction of 'master' narratives, the yearning that wells in the hearts and minds of those whom such narratives have silenced is the longing for critical voice. It is no accident that 'rap' has usurped the primary position of rhythm and blues music among young black folks as the most desired sound or that it began as a form of 'testimony' for the underclass. It has enabled underclass black youth to develop a critical voice, as a group of young black men told me, a 'common literacy'. Rap projects a critical voice, explaining, demanding, urging. Working with this insight in his essay 'Putting the pop back into postmodernism', Lawrence Grossberg comments:

> The postmodern sensibility appropriates practices as boasts that announce their own – and consequently our own – existence, like a rap song boasting of the imaginary (or

real – it makes no difference) accomplishments of the rapper. They offer forms of empowerment not only in the face of nihilism but precisely through the forms of nihilism itself: an empowering nihilism, a moment of positivity through the production and structuring of affective relations.

Considering that it is as subject one comes to voice, then the postmodernist focus on the critique of identity appears at first glance to threaten and close down the possibility that this discourse and practice will allow those who have suffered the crippling effects of colonization and domination to gain or regain a hearing. Even if this sense of threat and the fear it evokes are based on a misunderstanding of the postmodernist political project, they nevertheless shape responses. It never surprises me when black folks respond to the critique of essentialism, especially when it denies the validity of identity politics, by saying, 'Yeah, it's easy to give up identity, when you got one'. Should we not be suspicious of postmodern critiques of the 'subject' when they surface at a historical moment when many subjugated people feel themselves coming to voice for the first time. Though an apt and oftentimes appropriate comeback, it does not really intervene in the discourse in a way that alters and transforms.

Criticisms of directions in postmodern thinking should not obscure insights it may offer that open up our understanding of African-American experience. The critique of essentialism encouraged by postmodernist thought is useful for African-Americans concerned with reformulating outmoded notions of identity. We have too long had imposed upon us from both the outside and the inside a narrow, constricting notion of blackness. Postmodern critiques of essentialism which challenge notions of universality and static over-determined identity within mass culture and mass consciousness can open up new possibilities for the construction of self and the assertion of agency.

Employing a critique of essentialism allows African-Americans to acknowledge the way in which class mobility has altered collective black experience so that racism does not necessarily have the same impact on our lives. Such a critique allows us to affirm multiple black identities, varied black experience. It also challenges colonial imperialist paradigms of black identity which represent blackness one-dimensionally in ways that reinforce and sustain white supremacy. This discourse created the idea of the 'primitive' and promoted the notion of an 'authentic' experience, seeing as 'natural' those expressions of black life which conformed to a pre-existing pattern or stereotype. Abandoning essentialist notions would be a serious challenge to racism. Contemporary African-American resistance struggle must be rooted in a process of decolonization that continually opposes re-inscribing notions of 'authentic' black identity. This critique should not be made synonymous with a dismissal of the struggle of oppressed and exploited peoples to make ourselves subjects. Nor should it deny that in certain circumstances this experience affords us a privileged critical location from which to speak. This is not a re-inscription of modernist master narratives of authority which privilege some voices by denying voice to others. Part of our struggle for radical black subjectivity is the quest to find ways to construct self and identity that are oppositional and liberatory. The unwillingness to critique essentialism on the part of many African-Americans is rooted in the fear that it will cause folks to lose sight of the specific history and experience of African-Americans and the unique sensibilities and culture that arise from that experience. An adequate response to this concern is to critique essentialism while emphasizing the significance of 'the authority of experience'. There is a radical difference between a repudiation of the idea that there is a black 'essence' and recognition of the way black identity has been specifically constituted in the experience of exile and struggle.

When black folks critique essentialism, we are empowered to recognize multiple experiences of black identity that are the lived conditions which make diverse cultural productions possible. When this diversity is ignored, it is easy to see black folks as falling into two categories: nationalist or assimilationist, black-identified or white-identified. Coming to terms with the impact of postmodernism for black experience, particularly as it changes our sense of identity, means that we must and can rearticulate the basis for collective bonding. Given the various crises facing African-Americans (economic, spiritual, escalating racial violence, etc.), we are compelled by circumstance to reassess our relationship to popular culture and resistance struggle. Many of us are as reluctant to face this task as many non-black postmodern thinkers who focus theoretically on the issue of 'difference' are to confront the issue of race and racism.

Music is the cultural product created by African-Americans that has most attracted postmodern theorists. It is rarely acknowledged that there is far greater censorship and restriction of other forms of cultural production by black folks – literary, critical writing, etc. Attempts on the part of editors and publishing houses to control and manipulate the representation of black culture, as well as the desire to promote the creation of products that will attract the widest audience, limit in a crippling and stifling way the kind of work many black folks feel we can do and still receive recognition. Using myself as an example, that creative writing I do which I consider to be most reflective of a postmodern oppositional sensibility, work that is abstract, fragmented, non-linear narrative, is constantly rejected by editors and publishers. It does not conform to the type of writing they think black women should be doing or the type of writing they believe will sell. Certainly I do not think I am the only black person engaged in forms of cultural production, especially experimental ones, who is constrained by the lack of an audience for certain kinds of work. It is important for postmodern thinkers and theorists to constitute themselves as an audience for such work. To do this they must assert power and privilege within the space of critical writing to open up the field so that it will be more inclusive. To change the exclusionary practice of postmodern critical discourse is to enact a postmodernism of resistance. Part of this intervention entails black intellectual participation in the discourse.

In his essay 'Postmodernism and Black America', Cornel West suggests that black intellectuals 'are marginal – usually languishing at the interface of Black and white cultures or thoroughly ensconced in Euro-American settings'. He cannot see this group as potential producers of radical postmodernist thought. While I generally agree with this assessment, black intellectuals must proceed with the understanding that we are not condemned to the margins. The way we work and what we do can determine whether or not what we produce will be meaningful to a wider audience, one that includes all classes of black people. West suggests that black intellectuals lack 'any organic link with most of Black life' and that this 'diminishes their value to Black resistance'. This statement bears traces of essentialism. Perhaps we need to focus more on those black intellectuals, however rare our presence, who do not feel this lack and whose work is primarily directed towards the enhancement of black critical consciousness and the strengthening of our collective capacity to engage in meaningful resistance struggle. Theoretical ideas and critical thinking need not be transmitted solely in written work or solely in the academy. While I work in a predominantly white institution, I remain intimately and passionately engaged with black community. It's not like I'm going to talk about writing and thinking about postmodernism with other academics and/or intellectuals and not discuss these ideas with underclass non-academic black folks who are family, friends and comrades. Since I have not broken the ties that bind me to underclass poor black community, I have seen that knowledge, especially that which enhances daily life and strengthens our capacity to survive, can be shared. It means that critics, writers and academics have to give the same critical attention to nurturing and cultivating our ties to black community that we give to writing articles, teaching and lecturing. Here again I am really talking about cultivating habits of being that reinforce awareness that knowledge can be disseminated and shared on a number of fronts. The extent to which knowledge is made available, accessible, etc., depends on the nature of one's political commitments.

Postmodern culture with its decentered subject can be the space where ties are severed or it can provide the occasion for new and varied forms of bonding. To some extent, ruptures, surfaces, contextuality, and a host of other happenings create gaps that make space for oppositional practices which no longer require intellectuals to be confined by narrow separate spheres with no meaningful connection to the world of the everyday. Much postmodern engagement with culture emerges from the yearning to do intellectual work that connects with habits of being, forms of artistic expression and aesthetics that inform the daily life of writers and scholars as well as a mass population. On the terrain of culture, one can participate in critical dialogue with the uneducated poor, the black underclass who are thinking about aesthetics. One can talk about what we are seeing, thinking or listening to; a space is there for critical exchange. It's exciting to think, write, talk about and create art that reflects passionate engagement with popular culture, because this may very well be 'the' central future location of resistance struggle, a meeting place where new and radical happenings can occur.

25 □ *The African Writer and the English Language*

Chinua Achebe

In June 1952, there was a writers' gathering at Makerere, impressively styled: 'A Conference of African Writers of English Expression'. Despite this sonorous and rather solemn title, it turned out to be a very lively affair and a very exciting and useful experience for many of us. But there was something which we tried to do and failed – that was to define 'African literature' satisfactorily.

Was it literature produced *in* Africa or *about* Africa? Could African literature be on any subject, or must it have an African theme? Should it embrace the whole continent or south of the Sahara, or just *Black* Africa? And then the question of language. Should it be in indigenous African languages or should it include Arabic, English, French, Portuguese, Afrikaans, et cetera?

In the end we gave up trying to find an answer, partly – I should admit – on my own instigation. Perhaps we should not have given up so easily. It seems to me from some of the things I have since heard and read that we may have given the impression of not knowing what we were doing, or worse, not daring to look too closely at it.

A Nigerian critic, Obi Wali, writing in *Transition* 10 said: 'Perhaps the most important achievement of the conference . . . is that African literature as now defined and understood leads nowhere.'

I am sure that Obi Wali must have felt triumphantly vindicated when he saw the report of a different kind of conference held later at Fourah Bay to discuss African literature and the University curriculum. This conference produced a tentative definition of African literature as follows: 'Creative writing in which an African setting is authentically handled or to which experiences originating in Africa are integral.' We are told specifically that Conrad's *Heart of Darkness* qualifies as African literature while Graham Greene's *Heart of the Matter* fails because it could have been set anywhere outside Africa.

From Chinua Achebe, *Morning Yet on Creation Day*, Anchor Press/Doubleday: New York, 1975, pp. 91–103.

A number of interesting speculations issue from this definition which admittedly is only an interim formulation designed to produce an indisputably desirable end, namely, to introduce African students to literature set in their environment. But I could not help being amused by the curious circumstance in which Conrad, a Pole, writing in English could produce African literature while Peter Abrahams would be ineligible should he write a novel based on his experiences in the West Indies.

What all this suggests to me is that you cannot cram African literature into a small, neat definition. I do not see African literature as one unit but as a group of associated units – in fact the sum total of all the *national* and *ethnic* literatures of Africa.

A national literature is one that takes the whole nation for its province and has a realized or potential audience throughout its territory. In other words a literature that is written in the *national* language. An ethnic literature is one which is available only to one ethnic group within the nation. If you take Nigeria as an example, the national literature, as I see it, is the literature written in English; and the ethnic literatures are in Hausa, Ibo, Yoruba, Efik, Edo, Ijaw, etc., etc.

Any attempt to define African literature in terms which overlook the complexities of the African scene at the material time is doomed to failure. After the elimination of white rule shall have been completed, the single most important fact in Africa in the second half of the twentieth century will appear to be the rise of individual nation-states. I believe that African literature will follow the same pattern.

What we tend to do today is to think of African literature as a newborn infant. But in fact what we have is a whole generation of newborn infants. Of course, if you only look cursorily, one infant is pretty much like another; but in reality each is already set on its own separate journey. Of course, you may group them together on the basis of anything you choose – the color of their hair, for instance. Or you may group them together on the basis of the language they will speak or the religion of their fathers. Those would all be valid distinctions; but they could not begin to account fully for each individual person carrying, as it were, his own little, unique lodestar of genes.

Those who in talking about African literature want to exclude North Africa because it belongs to a different tradition surely do not suggest that Black Africa is anything like homogeneous. What does Shabaan Robert have in common with Christopher Okigbo or Awoonor-Williams? Or Mongo Beti of Cameroun and Paris with Nzekwu of Nigeria? What does the champagne-drinking upper-class Creole society described by Easmon of Sierra Leone have in common with the rural folk and fishermen of J. P. Clark's plays? Of course, some of these differences could be accounted for on individual rather than national grounds, but a good deal of it is also environmental.

I have indicated somewhat offhandedly that the national literature of Nigeria and of many other countries of Africa is, or will be, written in English. This may sound like a controversial statement, but it isn't. All I have done has been to look at the reality of present-day Africa. This 'reality' may change as a result of deliberate, e.g. political, action. If it does, an entirely new situation will arise, and there will be plenty of time to examine it. At present it may be more profitable to look at the scene as it is.

What are the factors which have conspired to place English in the position of national language in many parts of Africa? Quite simply the reason is that these nations were created in the first place by the intervention of the British, which, I hasten to add, is not saying that the peoples comprising these nations were invented by the British.

The country which we know as Nigeria today began not so very long ago as the arbitrary creation of the British. It is true, as William Fagg says in his excellent new book *Nigerian Images*, that this arbitrary action has proved as lucky in terms of African art history as any enterprise of the fortunate Princess of Serendip. And I believe that in political and economic terms too this arbitrary creation called Nigeria holds out great prospects. Yet the fact remains that Nigeria was created by the British – for their own ends. Let us give the devil his due: colonialism in Africa disrupted many things, but it did create big political units where there were small, scattered ones before. Nigeria had hundreds of autonomous communities ranging in size from the vast Fulani Empire founded by Usman dan Fodio in the north to tiny village entities in the east. Today it is one country.

Of course there are areas of Africa where colonialism divided up a single ethnic group among two or even three powers. But on the whole it did bring together many peoples that had hitherto gone their several ways. And it gave them a language with which to talk to one another. If it failed to give them a song, it at least gave them a tongue, for sighing. There are not many countries in Africa today where you could abolish the language of the erstwhile colonial powers and still retain the facility for mutual communication. Therefore those African writers who have chosen to write in English or French are not unpatriotic smart alecks with an eye on the main chance – outside their own countries. They are by-products of the same process that made the new nation-states of Africa.

You can take this argument a stage further to include other countries of Africa. The only reason why we can even talk about African unity is that when we get together we can have a manageable number of languages to talk in – English, French, Arabic.

The other day I had a visit from Joseph Kariuki of Kenya. Although I had read some of his poems and he had read my novels, we had not met before. But it didn't seem to matter. In fact I had met him through his poems, especially through his love poem 'Come away my love', in which he captures in so few words the trials and tensions of an African in love with a white girl in Britain:

> Come away, my love, from streets
> Where unkind eyes divide
> And shop windows reflect our difference.

By contrast, when in 1960 I was traveling in East Africa and went to the home of the late Shabaan Robert, the Swahili poet of Tanganyika, things had been different. We spent some time talking about writing, but there was no real contact. I knew from all accounts that I was talking to an important writer, but of the nature of his work I had no idea. He gave me two books of his poems which I treasure but cannot read – until I have learned Swahili.

And there are scores of languages I would want to learn if it were possible. Where am I to find the time to learn the half dozen or so Nigerian languages, each of which can sustain a literature? I am afraid it cannot be done. These languages will just have to develop as tributaries to feed the one central language enjoying nationwide currency. Today, for good or ill, that language is English. Tomorrow it may be something else, although I very much doubt it.

Those of us who have inherited the English language may not be in a position to appreciate the value of the inheritance. Or we may go on resenting it because it came as part of a package deal which included many other items of doubtful value and the positive atrocity of racial arrogance and prejudice which may yet set the world on fire. But let us not in rejecting the evil throw out the good with it.

Some time last year I was traveling in Brazil meeting Brazilian writers and artists. A number of the writers I spoke to were concerned about the restrictions imposed on them by their use of the Portuguese language. I remember a woman poet saying she had given serious thought to writing in French! And yet their problem is not half as difficult as ours. Portuguese may not have the universal currency of English or French but at least it is the national language of Brazil with her eighty million or so people, to say nothing of the people of Portugal, Angola, Mozambique, etc.

Of Brazilian authors I have only read, in translation, one novel by Jorge Amado, who is not only Brazil's leading novelist but one of the most important writers in the world. From that one novel, *Gabriella*, I was able to glimpse something of the exciting Afro-Latin culture which is the pride of Brazil and is quite unlike any other culture. Jorge Amado is only one of the many writers Brazil has produced. At their national writers' festival there were literally hundreds of them. But the work of the vast majority will be closed to the rest of the world forever, including no doubt the work of some excellent writers. There is certainly a great advantage to writing in a world language.

I think I have said enough to give an indication of my thinking on the importance of the world language which history has forced down our throats. Now let us look at some of the most serious handicaps. And let me say straightaway that one of the most serious handicaps is *not* the one people talk about most often, namely, that it is impossible for anyone ever to use a second language as effectively as his first. This assertion is compounded of half truth and half bogus mystique. Of course, it is true that the vast majority of people are happier with their first language than with any other. But then the majority of people are not writers. We do have enough examples of writers who have performed the feat of writing effectively in a second language. And I am not thinking of the obvious names like Conrad. It would be more germane to our subject to choose African examples.

The first name that comes to my mind is Olauda Equiano, better known as Gustavus Vassa, the African. Equiano was an Ibo, I believe from the village of Iseke in the Orlu division of Eastern Nigeria. He was sold as a slave at a very early age and transported to America. Later he bought his freedom and lived in England. In 1789 he published his life story, a beautifully written document which, among other things, set down for the Europe of his time something of the life and habit of his people in Africa, in an attempt to counteract the lies and slander invented by some Europeans to justify the slave trade.

Coming nearer to our times, we may recall the attempts in the first quarter of this century by West African nationalists to come together and press for a greater say in the management of their own affairs. One of the most eloquent of that band was the Honorable Casely Hayford of the Gold Coast. His presidential address to the National Congress of British West Africa in 1925 was memorable not only for its sound common sense but as a fine example of elegant prose. The governor of Nigeria at the time was compelled to take notice and he did so in characteristic style: he called Hayford's Congress 'a self-selected and self-appointed congregation of educated African gentlemen'. We may derive some amusement from the fact that British colonial administrators learned very little in the following quarter of a century. But at least they *did* learn in the end – which is more than one can say for some others.

It is when we come to what is commonly called creative literature that most doubt seems to arise. Obi Wali, whose article 'Dead end of African Literature' I referred to, has this to say:

> until these writers and their Western midwives accept the fact that any true African literature must be written in African languages, they would be merely pursuing a dead end, which can only lead to sterility, uncreativity and frustration.

But far from leading to sterility, the work of many new African writers is full of the most exciting possibilities.

Take this from Christopher Okigbo's 'Limits':

> Suddenly becoming talkative
>   like weaverbird
> Summoned at offside of
>   dream remembered
> Between sleep and waking
> I hand up my egg-shells
> To you of palm grove,
> Upon whose bamboo towers hang
> Dripping with yesterupwine
> A tiger mask and nude spear. ...
>
> Queen of the damp half light,
>   I have had my cleansing.
> Emigrant with air-borne nose,
>   The he-goat-on-heat.

Or take the poem, 'Night Rain', in which J.P. Clark captures so well the fear and wonder felt by a child as rain clamors on the thatch roof at night and his mother, walking about in the dark, moves her simple belongings

> Out of the run of water
> That like ants filing out of the wood
> Will scatter and gain possession
> Of the floor. . . .

I think that the picture of water spreading on the floor 'like ants filing out of the wood' is beautiful. Of course if you had never made fire with faggots, you may miss it. But Clark's inspiration derives from the same source which gave birth to the saying that a man who brings home ant-ridden faggots must be ready for the visit of lizards.

I do not see any signs of sterility anywhere here. What I do see is a new voice coming out of Africa, speaking of African experience in a world-wide language. So my answer to the question *Can an African ever learn English well enough to be able to use it effectively in creative writing*? is certainly yes. If on the other hand you ask: *Can he ever learn to use it like a native speaker*? I should say, I hope not. It is neither necessary nor desirable for him to be able to do so. The price a world language must be prepared to pay is submission to many different kinds of use. The African writer should aim to use English in a way that brings out his message best without altering the language to the extent that its value as a medium of international exchange will be lost. He should aim at fashioning out an English which is at once universal and able to carry his peculiar experience. I have in mind here the writer who has something new, something different to say. The nondescript writer has little to tell us, anyway, so he might as well tell it in conventional language and get it over with. If I may use an extravagant simile, he is like a man offering a small, nondescript routine sacrifice for which a chick, or less, will do. A serious writer must look for an animal whose blood can match the power of his offering.

In this respect Amos Tutuola is a natural. A good instinct has turned his apparent limitation in language into a weapon of great strength – a half-strange dialect that serves him perfectly in the evocation of his bizarre world. His last book, and to my mind, his finest, is proof enough that one can make even an imperfectly learned second language do amazing things. In this book, *The Feather Woman of the Jungle*, Tutuola's superb storytelling is at last cast in the episodic form which he handles best instead of being painfully stretched on the rack of the novel.

From a natural to a conscious artist: myself, in fact. Allow me to quote a small example from *Arrow of God*, which may give some idea of how I approach the use of English. The Chief Priest in the story is telling one of his sons why it is necessary to send him to church:

> I want one of my sons to join these people and be my eyes there. If there is nothing in it you will come back. But if there is something there you will bring home my share.

> The world is like a Mask, dancing. If you want to see it well you do not stand in one place. My spirit tells me that those who do not befriend the white man today will be saying *had we known* tomorrow.

Now supposing I had put it another way. Like this for instance:

> I am sending you as my representative among these people – just to be on the safe side in case the new religion develops. One has to move with the times or else one is left behind. I have a hunch that those who fail to come to terms with the white man may well regret their lack of foresight.

The material is the same. But the form of the one is *in character* and the other is not. It is largely a matter of instinct, but judgment comes into it too.

You read quite often nowadays of the problems of the African writer having first to think in his mother tongue and then to translate what he has thought into English. If it were such a simple, mechanical process, I would agree that it was pointless – the kind of eccentric pursuit you might expect to see in a modern Academy of Lagado; and such a process could not possibly produce some of the exciting poetry and prose which is already appearing.

One final point remains for me to make. The real question is not whether Africans *could* write in English but whether they *ought* to. Is it right that a man should abandon his mother tongue for someone else's? It looks like a dreadful betrayal and produces a guilty feeling.

But for me there is no other choice. I have been given this language and I intend to use it. I hope, though, that there always will be men, like the late Chief Fagunwa, who will choose to write in their native tongue and insure that our ethnic literature will flourish side by side with the national ones. For those of us who opt for English, there is much work ahead and much excitement.

Writing in the London *Observer* recently, James Baldwin said:

> My quarrel with the English language has been that the language reflected none of my experience. But now I began to see the matter another way. . . . Perhaps the language was not my own because I had never attempted to use it, had only learned to imitate it. If this were so, then it might be made to bear the burden of my experience if I could find the stamina to challenge it, and me, to such a test.

I recognize, of course, that Baldwin's problem is not exactly mine, but I feel that the English language will be able to carry the weight of my African experience. But it will have to be a new English, still in full communion with its ancestral home but altered to suit its new African surroundings.

26 □ *The Language of African Literature*

Ngũgĩ wa Thiong'o

[...]

II

[...]

As a writer who believes in the utilization of African ideas, African philosophy and African folklore and imagery to the fullest extent possible, I am of the opinion the only way to use them effectively is to translate them almost literally from the African language native to the writer into whatever European language he is using as medium of expression. I have endeavoured in my words to keep as close as possible to the vernacular expressions. For, from a word, a group of words, a sentence and even a name in any African language, one can glean the social norms, attitudes and values of a people.

In order to capture the vivid images of African speech, I had to eschew the habit of expressing my thoughts first in English. It was difficult at first, but I had to learn. I had to study each Ijaw expression I used and to discover the probable situation in which it was used in order to bring out the nearest meaning in English. I found it a fascinating exercise.[1]

Why, we may ask, should an African writer, or any writer, become so obsessed by taking from his mother-tongue to enrich other tongues? Why should he see it as his particular mission? We never asked ourselves: how can we enrich our languages? How can we 'prey' on the rich humanist and democratic heritage in the struggles of other peoples in other times and other places to enrich our own? Why not have Balzac, Tolstoy, Sholokov, Brecht, Lu Hsun, Pablo Neruda, H. C. Anderson, Kim Chi Ha, Marx, Lenin, Albert Einstein, Galileo, Aeschylus, Aristotle and Plato in African languages? And why not create literary monuments in our own languages?

From Ngũgĩ wa Thiong'o, *Decolonising the Mind: The politics of language in African literature*, James Currey: London, 1986, pp. 5, 8–33.

Why in other words should [Gabriel] Okara [quoted above] not sweat it out to create in Ijaw, which he acknowledged to have depths of philosophy and a wide range of ideas and experiences? What was our responsibility to the struggles of African peoples? No, these questions were not asked. What seemed to worry us more was this: after all the literary gymnastics of preying on our languages to add life and vigour to English and other foreign languages, would the result be accepted as good English or good French? Will the owner of the language criticise our usage? Here we were more assertive of our rights! Chinua Achebe wrote:

> I feel that the English language will be able to carry the weight of my African experience. But it will have to be a new English, still in full communion with its ancestral home but altered to suit new African surroundings.[2]

Gabriel Okara's position on this was representative of our generation:

> Some may regard this way of writing English as a desecration of the language. This is of course not true. Living languages grow like living things, and English is far from a dead language. There are American, West Indian, Australian, Canadian and New Zealand versions of English. All of them add life and vigour to the language while reflecting their own respective cultures. Why shouldn't there be a Nigerian or West African English which we can use to express our own ideas, thinking and philosophy in our own way?[3]

How did we arrive at this acceptance of 'the fatalistic logic of the unassailable position of English in our literature', in our culture and in our politics? What was the route from the Berlin of 1884 via the Makerere of 1962 to what is still the prevailing and dominant logic a hundred years later? How did we, as African writers, come to be so feeble towards the claims of our languages on us and so aggressive in our claims on other languages, particularly the languages of our colonisation?

Berlin of 1884 was effected through the sword and the bullet. But the night of the sword and the bullet was followed by the morning of the chalk and the blackboard. The physical violence of the battlefield was followed by the psychological violence of the classroom. But where the former was visibly brutal, the latter was visibly gentle, a process best described in Cheikh Hamidou Kane's novel *Ambiguous Adventure* where he talks of the methods of the colonial phase of imperialism as consisting of knowing how to kill with efficiency and to heal with the same art.

> On the Black Continent, one began to understand that their real power resided not at all in the cannons of the first morning but in what followed the cannons. Therefore behind the cannons was the new school. The new school had the nature of both the cannon and the magnet. From the cannon it took the efficiency of a fighting weapon. But better than the cannon it made the conquest permanent. The cannon forces the body and the school fascinates the soul.[4]

In my view language was the most important vehicle through which that power fascinated and held the soul prisoner. The bullet was the means of the physical subjugation. Language was the means of the spiritual subjugation. Let me illustrate this by drawing upon experiences in my own education, particularly in language and literature.

III

I was born into a large peasant family: father, four wives and about twenty-eight children. I also belonged, as we all did in those days, to a wider extended family and to the community as a whole.

We spoke Gĩkũyũ as we worked in the fields. We spoke Gĩkũyũ in and outside the home. I can vividly recall those evenings of storytelling around the fireside. It was mostly the grown-ups telling the children but everybody was interested and involved. We children would re-tell the stories the following day to other children who worked in the fields picking the pyrethrum flowers, tea-leaves or coffee beans of our European and African landlords.

The stories, with mostly animals as the main characters, were all told in Gĩkũyũ. Hare, being small, weak but full of innovative wit and cunning, was our hero. We identified with him as he struggled against the brutes of prey like lion, leopard, hyena. His victories were our victories and we learnt that the apparently weak can outwit the strong. We followed the animals in their struggle against hostile nature – drought, rain, sun, wind – a confrontation often forcing them to search for forms of co-operation. But we were also interested in their struggles amongst themselves, and particularly between the beasts and the victims of prey. These twin struggles, against nature and other animals, reflected real-life struggles in the human world.

Not that we neglected stories with human beings as the main characters. There were two types of characters in such human-centred narratives: the species of truly human beings with qualities of courage, kindness, mercy, hatred of evil, concern for others; and a man-eat-man two-mouthed species with qualities of greed, selfishness, individualism and hatred of what was good for the larger co-operative community. Co-operation as the ultimate good in a community was a constant theme. It could unite human beings with animals against ogres and beasts of prey, as in the story of how dove, after being fed with castor-oil seeds, was sent to fetch a smith working far away from home and whose pregnant wife was being threatened by these man-eating two-mouthed ogres.

There were good and bad story-tellers. A good one could tell the same story over and over again, and it would always be fresh to us, the listeners. He or she could tell a story told by someone else and make it more alive and dramatic. The differences really were in the use of words and images and the inflexion of voices to effect different tones.

We therefore learnt to value words for their meaning and nuances. Language was not a mere string of words. It had a suggestive power well beyond the immediate and lexical meaning. Our appreciation of the suggestive magical power of language was reinforced by the games we played with words through riddles, proverbs, transpositions of syllables, or through nonsensical but musically arranged words.[5] So we learnt the music of our language on top of the content. The language, through images and symbols, gave us a view of the world, but it had a beauty of its own. The home and the field were then our pre-primary school but what is important, for this discussion, is that the language of our evening teach-ins, and the language of our immediate and wider community, and the language of our work in the fields were one.

And then I went to school, a colonial school, and this harmony was broken. The language of my education was no longer the language of my culture. I first went to Kamaandura, missionary run, and then to another called Maanguuũ run by nationalists grouped around the Gĩkũyũ Independent and Karinga Schools Association. Our language of education was still Gĩkũyũ. The very first time I was ever given an ovation for my writing was over a composition in Gĩkũyũ. So for my first four years there was still harmony between the language of my formal education and that of the Limuru peasant community.

It was after the declaration of a state of emergency over Kenya in 1952 that all the schools run by patriotic nationalists were taken over by the colonial regime and were placed under District Education Boards chaired by Englishmen. English became the language of my formal education. In Kenya, English became more than a language: it was *the* language, and all the others had to bow before it in deference.

Thus one of the most humiliating experiences was to be caught speaking Gĩkũyũ in the vicinity of the school. The culprit was given corporal punishment – three to five strokes of the cane on bare buttocks – or was made to carry a metal plate around the neck with inscriptions such as I AM STUPID or I AM A DONKEY. Sometimes the culprits were fined money they could hardly afford. And how did the teachers catch the culprits? A button was initially given to one pupil who was supposed to hand it over to whoever was caught speaking his mother tongue. Whoever had the button at the end of the day would sing who had given it to him and the ensuing process would bring out all the culprits of the day. Thus children were turned into witch-hunters and in the process were being taught the lucrative value of being a traitor to one's immediate community.

The attitude to English was the exact opposite: any achievement in spoken or written English was highly rewarded; prizes, prestige, applause; the ticket to higher realms. English became the measure of intelligence and ability in the arts, the sciences, and all the other branches of learning. English became *the* main determinant of a child's progress up the ladder of formal education.

As you may know, the colonial system of education in addition to its apartheid racial demarcation had the structure of a pyramid: a broad primary base, a narrowing secondary middle and an even narrower university apex. Selections from primary into secondary were through an examination, in my time called Kenya African Preliminary Examination, in which one had to pass six subjects ranging from Maths to Nature Study and Kiswahili. All the papers were written in English.

Nobody could pass the exam who failed the English language paper no matter how brilliantly he had done in the other subjects. I remember one boy in my class of 1954 who had distinctions in all subjects except English, which he had failed. He was made to fail the entire exam. He went on to become a turn boy in a bus company. I who had only passes but a credit in English got a place at the Alliance High School, one of the most elitist institutions for Africans in colonial Kenya. The requirements for a place at the University, Makerere University College, were broadly the same: nobody could go on to wear the undergraduate red gown, no matter how brilliantly they had performed in all the other subjects, unless they had a credit – not even a simple pass! – in English. Thus the most coveted place in the pyramid and in the system was only available to the holder of an English language credit card. English was the official vehicle and the magic formula to colonial elitedom.

Literary education was now determined by the dominant language while also reinforcing that dominance. Orature (oral literature) in Kenyan languages stopped. In primary school I now read simplified Dickens and Stevenson alongside Rider Haggard. Jim Hawkins, Oliver Twist, Tom Brown – not Hare, Leopard and Lion – were now my daily companions in the world of imagination. In secondary school Scott and G. B. Shaw vied with more Rider Haggard, John Buchan, Alan Paton, Captain W. E. Johns. At Makerere I read English: from Chaucer to T. S. Eliot with a touch of Graham Greene.

Thus language and literature were taking us further and further from ourselves to other selves, from our world to other worlds.

What was the colonial system doing to us Kenyan children? What were the consequences of, on the one hand, this systematic suppression of our languages and the literature they carried, and on the other the elevation of English and the literature it carried? To answer those questions, let me first examine the relationship of language to human experience, human culture and the human perception of reality.

IV

Language, any language, has a dual character: it is both a means of communication and a carrier of culture. Take English. It is spoken in Britain and in Sweden and Denmark. But for Swedish and Danish people English is only a means of communication with non-Scandinavians. It is not a carrier of their culture. For the British, and particularly the English, it is additionally, and inseparably from its use as a tool of communication, a carrier of their culture and history. Or take Swahili in East and Central Africa. It is widely used as a means of communication across many nationalities. But it is not the carrier of a culture and history of many of those nationalities. However in parts of Kenya and Tanzania, and particularly in Zanzibar, Swahili is inseparably both a means of communication and a carrier of the culture of those people to whom it is a mother-tongue.

Language as communication has three aspects or elements. There is first what Karl Marx once called the language of real life,[6] the element basic to the whole notion of language, its origins and development: that is, the relations people enter into with one another in the labour process, the links they necessarily establish among themselves in the act of a people, a community of human beings, producing wealth or means of life like food, clothing, houses. A human community really starts its historical being as a community of co-operation in production through the division of labour; the simplest is between man, woman and child within a household; the more complex divisions are between branches of production such as those who are sole hunters, sole gatherers of fruits or sole workers in metal. Then there are the most complex divisions such as those in modern factories where a single product, say a shirt or a shoe, is the result of many hands and minds. Production is co-operation, is communication, is language, is expression of a relation between human beings and it is specifically human.

The second aspect of language as communication is speech and it imitates the language of real life, that is communication in production. The verbal signposts both reflect and aid communication or the relations established between human beings in the production of their means of life. Language as a system of verbal signposts makes that production possible. The spoken word is to relations between human beings what the hand is to the relations between human beings and nature. The hand through tools mediates between human beings and nature and forms the language of real life: spoken words mediate between human beings and form the language of speech.

The third aspect is the written signs. The written word imitates the spoken. Where the first two aspects of language as communication through the hand and the spoken word historically evolved more or less simultaneously, the written aspect is a much later historical development. Writing is representation of sounds with visual symbols, from the simplest knot among shepherds to tell the number in a herd or the hieroglyphics among the Agĩkũyũ gicaandi singers and poets of Kenya, to the most complicated and different letter and picture writing systems of the world today.

In most societies the written and the spoken languages are the same in that they represent each other: what is on paper can be read to another person and be received as that language which the recipient has grown up speaking. In such a society there is broad harmony for a child between the three aspects of language as communication. His interaction with nature and with other men is expressed in written and spoken symbols or signs which are both a result of that double interaction and a reflection of it. The association of the child's sensibility is with the language of his experience of life.

But there is more to it: communication between human beings is also the basis and process of evolving culture. In doing similar kinds of things and actions over and over again under similar circumstances, similar even in their mutability, certain patterns, moves, rhythms, habits, attitudes, experiences and knowledge emerge. Those experiences are handed over to the next generation and become the inherited basis for their further actions on nature and on themselves. There is a gradual accumulation of values which in time become almost self-evident truths governing their conception of what is right and wrong; good and bad, beautiful and ugly, courageous and cowardly, generous and mean in their internal and external relations. Over a time this becomes a way of life distinguishable from other ways of life. They develop a distinctive culture and history. Culture embodies those moral, ethical and aesthetic values, the set of spiritual eyeglasses, through which they come to view themselves and their place in the universe. Values are the basis of a people's identity, their sense of particularity as members of the human race. All this is carried by language. Language as culture is the collective memory bank of a people's experience in history. Culture is almost indistinguishable from the language that makes possible its genesis, growth, banking, articulation and indeed its transmission from one generation to the next.

Language as culture also has three important aspects. Culture is a product of the history which it in turn reflects. Culture in other words is a product and a reflection of human beings communicating with one another in the very struggle to create wealth and to control it. But culture does not merely reflect that history, or rather it does so by actually forming images or pictures of the world of nature and nurture. Thus the second aspect of language as culture is as an image-forming agent in the mind of a child. Our whole conception of ourselves as a people, individually and collectively, is based on those pictures and images which may or may not correctly correspond to the actual reality of the struggles with nature and nurture which produced them in the first place. But our capacity to confront the world creatively is dependent on how those images correspond or not to that reality, how they distort or clarify the reality of our struggles. Language as culture is thus mediating between me and my own self; between my own self and other selves; between me and nature. Language is mediating in my very being. And this brings us to the third aspect of language as culture. Culture transmits or imparts those images of the world and reality through the spoken and the written language, that is through a specific language. In other words, the capacity to speak, the capacity to order sounds in a manner that makes for mutual comprehension between human beings is universal. This is the universality of language, a quality specific to human beings. It corresponds to the universality of the struggle against nature and that between human beings. But the particularity of the sounds, the words, the word order into phrases and sentences, and the specific manner, or laws, of their ordering is what distinguishes one language from another. Thus a specific culture is not transmitted through language in its universality but in its particularity as the language of a specific community with a specific history. Written literature and orature are the main means by which a particular language transmits the images of the world contained in the culture it carries.

Language as communication and as culture are then products of each other. Communication creates culture: culture is a means of communication. Language carries culture, and culture carries, particularly through orature and literature, the entire body of values by which we come to perceive ourselves and our place in the world. How people perceive themselves affects how they look at their culture, at their politics and at the social production of wealth, at their entire relationship to nature and to other beings. Language is thus inseparable from ourselves as a community of human beings with a specific form and character, a specific history, a specific relationship to the world.

V

So what was the colonialist imposition of a foreign language doing to us children?

The real aim of colonialism was to control the people's wealth: what they produced, how they produced it, and how it was distributed; to control, in other words, the entire realm of the language of real life. Colonialism imposed its control of the social production of wealth through military conquest and subsequent political dictatorship. But its most important area of domination was the mental universe of the colonised, the control, through culture, of how people perceived themselves and their relationship to the world. Economic and political control can never be complete or effective without mental control. To control a people's culture is to control their tools of self-definition in relationship to others.

For colonialism this involved two aspects of the same process: the destruction or the deliberate undervaluing of a people's culture, their art, dances, religions, history, geography, education, orature and literature, and the conscious elevation of the language of the coloniser. The domination of a people's language by the languages of the colonising nations was crucial to the domination of the mental universe of the colonised.

Take language as communication. Imposing a foreign language, and suppressing the native languages as spoken and written, were already breaking the harmony previously existing between the African child and the three aspects of language. Since the new language as a means of communication was a product of and was reflecting the 'real language of life' elsewhere, it could never as spoken or written properly reflect or imitate the real life of that community. This may in part explain why technology always appears to us as slightly external, *their* product and not *ours*. The word 'missile' used to hold an alien far-away sound until I recently learnt its equivalent in Gĩkũyũ, *ngurukukĩ*, and it made me apprehend it differently. Learning, for a colonial child, became a cerebral activity and not an emotionally felt experience.

But since the new, imposed languages could never completely break the native languages as spoken, their most effective area of domination was the third aspect of language as communication, the written. The language of an African child's formal education was foreign. The language of the books he read was foreign. The language of his conceptualisation was foreign. Thought, in him, took the visible form of a foreign language. So the written language of a child's upbringing in the school (even his spoken language within the school compound) became divorced from his spoken language at home. There was often not the slightest relationship between the child's written world, which was also the language of his schooling, and the world of his immediate environment in the family and the community. For a colonial child, the harmony existing between the three aspects of language as communication was irrevocably broken. This resulted in the disassociation of the sensibility of that child from his natural and social environment, what we might call colonial alienation. The alienation became reinforced in the teaching of history, geography, music, where bourgeois Europe was always the centre of the universe.

This disassociation, divorce, or alienation from the immediate environment becomes clearer when you look at colonial language as a carrier of culture.

Since culture is a product of the history of a people which it in turn reflects, the child was now being exposed exclusively to a culture that was a product of a world external to himself. He was being made to stand outside himself to look at himself. *Catching Them Young* is the title of a book on racism, class, sex and politics in children's literature by Bob Dixon. 'Catching them young' as an aim was even more true of a colonial child. The images of this world and his place in it implanted in a child take years to eradicate, if they ever can be.

Since culture does not just reflect the world in images but actually, through those very images, conditions a child to see that world in a certain way, the colonial child was made to see the world and where he stands in it as seen and defined by or reflected in the culture of the language of imposition.

And since those images are mostly passed on through orature and literature it meant the child would now only see the world as seen in the literature of his language of adoption. From the point of view of alienation, that is of seeing oneself from outside oneself as if one was another self, it does not matter that the imported literature carried the great humanist tradition of the best in Shakespeare, Goethe, Balzac, Tolstoy, Gorky, Brecht, Sholokhov, Dickens. The location of this great mirror of imagination was necessarily Europe and its history and culture and the rest of the universe was seen from that centre.

But obviously it was worse when the colonial child was exposed to images of his world as mirrored in the written languages of his coloniser. Where his own native languages were associated in his impressionable mind with low status, humiliation, corporal punishment, slow-footed intelligence and ability or downright stupidity, non-intelligibility and barbarism, this was reinforced by the world he met in the works of such geniuses of racism as a Rider Haggard or a Nicholas Monsarrat; not to mention the pronouncement of some of the giants of western intellectual and political establishment, such as Hume ('the negro is naturally inferior to the whites'),[7] Thomas Jefferson ('the blacks ... are inferior to the whites on the endowments of both body and mind'),[8] or Hegel with his Africa comparable to a land of childhood still enveloped in the dark mantle of the night as far as the development of self-conscious history was concerned. Hegel's statement that there was nothing harmonious with humanity to be found in the African character is representative of the racist images of Africans and Africa such a colonial child was bound to encounter in the literature of the colonial languages.[9] The results could be disastrous.

In her paper read to the conference on the teaching of African literature in schools held in Nairobi in 1973, entitled 'Written literature and black images',[10] the

Kenyan writer and scholar Professor Mĩcere Mũgo related how a reading of the description of Gagool as an old African woman in Rider Haggard's *King Solomon's Mines* had for a long time made her feel mortal terror whenever she encountered old African women. In his autobiography *This Life* Sydney Poitier describes how, as a result of the literature he had read, he had come to associate Africa with snakes. So on arrival in Africa and being put up in a modern hotel in a modern city, he could not sleep because he kept on looking for snakes everywhere, even under the bed. These two have been able to pinpoint the origins of their fears. But for most others the negative image becomes internalised and it affects their cultural and even political choices in ordinary living.

Thus Léopold Sédar Senghor has said very clearly that although the colonial language had been forced upon him, if he had been given the choice he would still have opted for French. He becomes lyrical in his subservience to French:

> We express ourselves in French since French has a universal vocation and since our message is also addressed to French people and others. In our languages [i.e. African languages] the halo that surrounds the words is by nature merely that of sap and blood; French words send out thousands of rays like diamonds.[11]

Senghor has now been rewarded by being appointed to an honoured place in the French Academy – that institution for safe-guarding the purity of the French language.

In Malawi, Banda has erected his own monument by way of an institution, The Kamuzu Academy, designed to aid the brightest pupils of Malawi in their mastery of English.

> It is a grammar school designed to produce boys and girls who will be sent to universities like Harvard, Chicago, Oxford, Cambridge and Edinburgh and be able to compete on equal terms with others elsewhere.
>
> The President has instructed that Latin should occupy a central place in the curriculum. All teachers must have had at least some Latin in their academic background. Dr Banda has often said that no one can fully master English without knowledge of languages such as Latin and French.[12]

For good measure no Malawian is allowed to teach at the academy – none is good enough – and all the teaching staff has been recruited from Britain. A Malawian might lower the standards, or rather, the purity of the English language. Can you get a more telling example of hatred of what is national, and a servile worship of what is foreign even though dead?

In history books and popular commentaries on Africa, too much has been made of the supposed differences in the policies of the various colonial powers, the British indirect rule (or the pragmatism of the British in their lack of a cultural programme!) and the French and Portuguese conscious programme of cultural assimilation. These are a matter of detail and emphasis. The final effect was the same: Senghor's embrace of French as this language with a universal vocation is not so different from Chinua Achebe's gratitude in 1964 to English – 'those of us who have inherited the English language may not be in a position to appreciate the value of the inheritance.'[13] The assumptions behind the practice of those of us who have abandoned our mother-tongues and adopted European ones as the creative vehicles of our imagination are not different either.

Thus the 1962 conference of 'African Writers of English Expression' was only recognising, with approval and pride of course, what, through all the years of selective education and rigorous tutelage, we had already been led to accept: the 'fatalistic logic of the unassailable position of English in our literature'. The logic was embodied deep in imperialism; and it was imperialism and its effects that we did not examine at Makerere. It is the final triumph of a system of domination when the dominated start singing its virtues.

VI

The twenty years that followed the Makerere conference gave the world a unique literature – novels, stories, poems, plays written by Africans in European languages – which soon consolidated itself into a tradition with companion studies and a scholarly industry.

Right from its conception it was the literature of the petty-bourgeoisie born of the colonial schools and universities. It could not be otherwise, given the linguistic medium of its message. Its rise and development reflected the gradual accession of this class to political and even economic dominance. But the petty-bourgeoisie in Africa was a large class with different strands in it. It ranged from that section which looked forward to a permanent alliance with imperialism in which it played the role of an intermediary between the bourgeoisie of the western metropolis and the people of the colonies – the section which in my book *Detained: A writer's prison diary* I have described as the comprador bourgeosie – to that section which saw the future in terms of a vigorous independent national economy in African capitalism or in some kind of socialism, what I shall here call the nationalistic or patriotic bourgeoisie. This literature by Africans in European languages was specifically that of the nationalistic bourgeoisie in its creators, its thematic concerns and its consumption.[14]

Internationally the literature helped this class, which in politics, business and education, was assuming leadership of the countries newly emergent from colonialism, or of those struggling to so emerge, to explain Africa to the world: Africa had a past and a culture of dignity and human complexity.

Internally the literature gave this class a cohesive tradition and a common literary frame of references, which it otherwise lacked with its uneasy roots in the culture of the peasantry and in the culture of the metropolitan bourgeoisie. The literature added confidence to the class: the petty-bourgeoisie now had a past, a culture and a literature with which to confront the racist bigotry of Europe. This confidence –

manifested in the tone of the writing, its sharp critique of European bourgeois civilisation, its implications, particularly in its negritude mould, that Africa had something new to give to the world – reflects the political ascendancy of the patriotic nationalistic section of the petty-bourgeoisie before and immediately after independence.

So initially this literature – in the post-war world of national democratic revolutionary and anti-colonial liberation in China and India, armed uprisings in Kenya and Algeria, the independence of Ghana and Nigeria with others impending – was part of that great anti-colonial and anti-imperialist upheaval in Asia, Africa, Latin America and Caribbean islands. It was inspired by the general political awakening; it drew its stamina and even form from the peasantry: their proverbs, fables, stories, riddles and wise sayings. It was shot through and through with optimism. But later, when the comprador section assumed political ascendancy and strengthened rather than weakened the economic links with imperialism in what was clearly a neo-colonial arrangement, this literature became more and more critical, cynical, disillusioned, bitter and denunciatory in tone. It was almost unanimous in its portrayal, with varying degrees of detail, emphasis and clarity of vision, of the post-independence betrayal of hope. But to whom was it directing its list of mistakes made, crimes and wrongs committed, complaints unheeded, or its call for a change of moral direction? The imperialist bourgeoisie? The petty-bourgeoisie in power? The military, itself part and parcel of that class? It sought another audience, principally the peasantry and the working class or what was generally conceived as the people. The search for new audience and new directions was reflected in the quest for simpler forms, in the adoption of a more direct tone, and often in a direct call for action. It was also reflected in the content. Instead of seeing Africa as one undifferentiated mass of historically wronged blackness, it now attempted some sort of class analysis and evaluation of neo-colonial societies. But this search was still within the confines of the languages of Europe whose use it now defended with less vigour and confidence. So its quest was hampered by the very language choice, and in its movement toward the people, it could only go up to that section of the petty-bourgeoisie – the students, teachers, secretaries for instance – still in closest touch with the people. It settled there, marking time, caged within the linguistic fence of its colonial inheritance.

Its greatest weakness still lay where it has always been, in the audience – the petty-bourgeois readership automatically assumed by the very choice of language. Because of its indeterminate economic position between the many contending classes, the petty-bourgeoisie develops a vacillating psychological make-up. Like a chameleon it takes on the colour of the main class with which it is in the closest touch and sympathy. It can be swept to activity by the masses at a time of revolutionary tide; or be driven to silence, fear, cynicism, withdrawal into self-contemplation, existential anguish, or to collaboration with the powers-that-be at times of reactionary tides. In Africa this class has always oscillated between the imperialist bourgeoisie and its comprador neo-colonial ruling elements on the one hand, and the peasantry and the working class (the masses) on the other. This very lack of identity in its social and psychological make-up as a class was reflected in the very literature it produced: the crisis of identity was assumed in that very preoccupation with definition at the Makerere conference. In literature as in politics it spoke as if its identity or the crisis of its own identity was that of society as a whole. The literature it produced in European languages was given the identity of African literature as if there had never been literature in African languages. Yet by avoiding a real confrontation with the language issue, it was clearly wearing false robes of identity: it was a pretender to the throne of the mainstream of African literature. The practitioner of what Janheinz Jahn called neo-African literature tried to get out of the dilemma by over-insisting that European languages were really African languages or by trying to Africanise English or French usage while making sure it was still recognisable as English or French or Portuguese.

In the process this literature created, falsely and even absurdly, an English-speaking (or French or Portuguese) African peasantry and working class, a clear negation or falsification of the historical process and reality. This European-language-speaking peasantry and working class, existing only in novels and dramas, was at times invested with the vacillating mentality, the evasive self-contemplation, the existential anguished human condition, or the man-torn-between-two-worlds-facedness of the petty-bourgeoisie.

In fact, if it had been left entirely to this class, African languages would have ceased to exist – with independence!

VII

But African languages refused to die. They would not simply go the way of Latin to become the fossils for linguistic archaeology to dig up, classify, and argue about at international conferences.

These languages, these national heritages of Africa, were kept alive by the peasantry. The peasantry saw no contradiction between speaking their own mother-tongues and belonging to a larger national or continental geography. They saw no necessary antagonistic contradiction between belonging to their immediate nationality, to their multinational state along the Berlin-drawn boundaries, and to Africa as a whole. These people happily spoke Wolof, Hausa, Yoruba, Ibo, Arabic, Amharic, Kiswahili, Gĩkũyũ, Luo, Luhya, Shona, Ndebele, Kimbundu, Zulu or Lingala without this fact tearing the multinational states apart. During the anti-colonial struggle they showed an unlimited capacity to unite around whatever leader or party best and most consistently articulated an anti-imperialist position. If anything it was the petty-bourgeoisie, particularly the compradors, with their French and English and Portuguese, with their petty rivalries, their ethnic chauvinism, which encouraged these vertical divisions to the point of war at times. No, the peasantry had no complexes about their languages and the cultures they carried!

In fact when the peasantry and the working class were compelled by necessity or history to adopt the language of the master, they Africanised it without any of the respect for its ancestry shown by Senghor and Achebe, so totally as to have created new African languages, like Krio in Sierra Leone or Pidgin in Nigeria, that owed their identities to the syntax and rhythms of African languages. All these languages were kept alive in the daily speech, in the ceremonies in political struggles, above all in the rich store of orature – proverbs, stories, poems and riddles.

The peasantry and the urban working class threw up singers. These sang the old songs or composed new ones incorporating the new experiences in industries and urban life and in working-class struggle and organisations. These singers pushed the languages to new limits, renewing and reinvigorating them by coining new words and new expressions, and in generally expanding their capacity to incorporate new happenings in Africa and the world.

The peasantry and the working class threw up their own writers, or attracted to their ranks and concern intellectuals from among the petty-bourgeoisie, who all wrote in African languages. It is these writers like Heruy Wäldä Sellassie, Germacäw Takla Hawaryat, Shabaan Robert, Abdullatif Abdalla, Ebrahim Hussein, Euphrase Kezilahabi, B. H. Vilakazi, Okot p'Bitek, A. C. Jordan, P. Mboya, D. O. Fagunwa, Mazisi Kunene and many others rightly celebrated in Albert Gérard's pioneering survey of literature in African languages from the tenth century to the present, called *African Language Literatures* (1981), who have given our languages a written literature. Thus the immortality of our languages in print has been ensured despite the internal and external pressures for their extinction. In Kenya I would like to single out Gakaara we Wanjaũ, who was jailed by the British for the ten years between 1952 and 1962 because of his writing in Gĩkũyũ. His book, *Mwandĩki wa Mau Mau Ithaamĩrioinĩ*, a diary he secretly kept while in political detention, was published by Heinemann Kenya and won the 1984 Noma Award. It is a powerful work, extending the range of the Gĩkũyũ language prose, and it is a crowning achievement to the work he started in 1946. He has worked in poverty, in the hardships of prison, in post-independence isolation when the English language held sway in Kenya's schools from nursery to University and in every walk of the national printed world, but he never broke his faith in the possibilities of Kenya's national languages. His inspiration came from the mass anti-colonial movement of Kenyan people, particularly the militant wing grouped around Mau Mau or the Kenya Land and Freedom Army, which in 1952 ushered in the era of modern guerrilla warfare in Africa. He is the clearest example of those writers thrown up by the mass political movements of an awakened peasantry and working class.

And finally from among the European-language-speaking African petty-bourgeoisie there emerged a few who refused to join the chorus of those who had accepted the 'fatalistic logic' of the position of European languages in our literary being. It was one of these, Obi Wali, who pulled the carpet from under the literary feet of those who gathered at Makerere in 1962 by declaring in an article published in *Transition* (10, September 1963), 'that the whole uncritical acceptance of English and French as the inevitable medium for educated African writing is misdirected, and has no chance of advancing African literature and culture', and that until African writers accepted that any true African literature must be written in African languages, they would merely be pursuing a dead end.

> What we would like future conferences on African literature to devote time to, is the all-important problem of African writing in African languages, and all its implications for the development of a truly African sensibility.

Obi Wali had his predecessors. Indeed people like David Diop of Senegal had put the case against this use of colonial languages even more strongly.

> The African creator, deprived of the use of his language and cut off from his people, might turn out to be only the representative of a literary trend (and that not necessarily the least gratuitous) of the conquering nation. His works, having become a perfect illustration of the assimilationist policy through imagination and style, will doubtless rouse the warm applause of a certain group of critics. In fact, these praises will go mostly to colonialism which, when it can no longer keep its subjects in slavery, transforms them into docile intellectuals patterned after Western literary fashions which, besides, is another more subtle form of bastardization.[15]

David Diop quite correctly saw that the use of English and French was a matter of temporary historical necessity.

> Surely in an Africa freed from oppression it will not occur to any writer to express, otherwise than in his rediscovered language, his feelings and the feelings of his people.[16]

The importance of Obi Wali's intervention was in tone and timing: it was published soon after the 1962 Makerere conference of African writers of English expression; it was polemical and aggressive, poured ridicule and scorn on the choice of English and French, while being unapologetic in its call for the use of African languages. Not surprisingly it was met with hostility and then silence. But twenty years of uninterrupted dominance of literature in European languages, the reactionary turn that political and economic events in Africa have taken, and the search for a revolutionary break with the neo-colonial status quo, all compel soul-searching among writers, raising once again the entire question of the language of African literature.

VIII

The question is this: we as African writers have always complained about the neo-colonial economic and political relationship to Euro-America. Right. But by our continuing to write in foreign languages, paying homage to them, are we not on the cultural level continuing that neo-colonial slavish and cringing spirit? What is the difference between a politician who says Africa cannot do without imperialism and the writer who says Africa cannot do without European languages?

While we were busy haranguing the ruling circles in a language which automatically excluded the participation of the peasantry and the working class in the debate, imperialist culture and African reactionary forces had a field day: the Christian bible is available in unlimited quantities in even the tiniest African language. The comprador ruling cliques are also quite happy to have the peasantry and the working class all to themselves: distortions, dictatorial directives, decrees, museum-type fossils paraded as African culture, feudalistic ideologies, superstitions, lies, all these backward elements and more are communicated to the African masses in their own languages without any challenges from those with alternative visions of tomorrow who have deliberately cocooned themselves in English, French and Portuguese. It is ironic that the most reactionary African politician, the one who believes in selling Africa to Europe, is often a master of African languages; that the most zealous of European missionaries who believed in rescuing Africa from itself, even from the paganism of its languages, were nevertheless masters of African languages, which they often reduced to writing. The European missionary believed too much in his mission of conquest not to communicate it in the languages most readily available to the people: the African writer believes too much in 'African literature' to write it in those ethnic, divisive and underdeveloped languages of the peasantry!

The added irony is that what they have produced, despite any claims to the contrary, is not African literature. The editors of the Pelican Guides to English literature in their latest volume were right to include a discussion of this literature as part of twentieth-century English literature, just as the French Academy was right to honour Senghor for his genuine and talented contribution to French literature and language. What we have created is another hybrid tradition, a tradition in transition, a minority tradition that can only be termed as Afro-European literature; that is, the literature written by Africans in European languages.[17] It has produced many writers and works of genuine talent: Chinua Achebe, Wole Soyinka, Ayi Kwei Armah, Sembene Ousmane, Agostino Neto, Sédar Senghor and many others. Who can deny their talent? The light in the products of their fertile imaginations has certainly illuminated important aspects of the African being in its continuous struggle against the political and economic consequences of Berlin and after. However, we cannot have our cake and eat it! Their work belongs to an Afro-European literary tradition which is likely to last for as long as Africa is under this rule of European capital in a neo-colonial set-up. So Afro-European literature can be defined as literature written by Africans in European languages in the era of imperialism.

But some are coming round to the inescapable conclusion articulated by Obi Wali with such polemical vigour twenty years ago: African literature can only be written in African languages, that is, the languages of the African peasantry and working class, the major alliance of classes in each of our nationalities and the agency for the coming inevitable revolutionary break with neo-colonialism.

IX

I started writing in Gĩkũyũ language in 1977 after seventeen years of involvement in Afro-European literature, in my case Afro-English literature. It was then that I collaborated with Ngũgĩ wa Mĩriĩ in the drafting of the playscript *Ngaahika Ndeenda* (the English translation was *I Will Marry When I Want*). I have since published a novel in Gĩkũyũ, *Caitaani Mũtharabainĩ* (English translation: *Devil on the Cross*), and completed a musical drama, *Maitũ Njugĩra* (English translation: *Mother Sing for Me*), three books for children, *Njamba Nene na Mbaathi i Mathagu*, *Bathitoora ya Njamba Nene*, *Njamba Nene na Cibũ Kĩng'ang'i*, as well as another novel manuscript: *Matigari Ma Njirũũngi*. Wherever I have gone, particularly in Europe, I have been confronted with the question: why are you now writing in Gĩkũyũ? Why do you now write in an African language? In some academic quarters I have been confronted with the rebuke, 'Why have you abandoned us?' It was almost as if, in choosing to write in Gĩkũyũ, I was doing something abnormal. But Gĩkũyũ is my mother tongue! The very fact that what common sense dictates in the literary practice of other cultures is being questioned in an African writer is a measure of how far imperialism has distorted the view of African realities. It has turned reality upside down: the abnormal is viewed as normal and the normal is viewed as abnormal. Africa actually enriches Europe: but Africa is made to believe that it needs Europe to rescue it from poverty. Africa's natural and human resources continue to develop Europe and America: but Africa is made to feel grateful for aid from the same quarters that still sit on the back of the continent. Africa even produces intellectuals who now rationalise this upside-down way of looking at Africa.

I believe that my writing in Gĩkũyũ language, a Kenyan language, an African language, is part and parcel of the anti-imperialist struggles of Kenyan and African peoples. In schools and universities our Kenyan languages – that is the languages of the many nationalities which make up Kenya – were associated with negative qualities of backwardness, underdevelopment, humiliation and punishment. We who went through that school system were meant to graduate with a hatred of the people and the culture and the values of the language of our daily humiliation and punishment. I do not want to see Kenyan children growing up in that imperialist-imposed tradition of contempt for the tools of communication developed by their communities and their history. I want them to transcend colonial alienation.

Colonial alienation takes two interlinked forms: an active (or passive) distancing of oneself from the reality around; and an active (or passive) identification with that which is most external to one's environment. It starts with a deliberate disassociation of the language of conceptualisation, of thinking, of formal education, of mental development, from the language of daily interaction in the home and in the community. It is like separating the mind from the body so that they are occupying two unrelated linguistic spheres in the same person. On a larger social scale it is like producing a society of bodiless heads and headless bodies.

So I would like to contribute towards the restoration of the harmony between all the aspects and divisions of language so as to restore the Kenyan child to his environment, understand it fully so as to be in a position to change it for his collective good. I would like to see Kenyan peoples' mother-tongues (our national languages!) carry a literature reflecting not only the rhythms of a child's spoken expression, but also his struggle with nature and his social nature. With that harmony between himself, his language and his environment as his starting point, he can learn other languages and even enjoy the positive humanistic, democratic and revolutionary elements in other people's literatures and cultures without any complexes about his own language, his own self, his environment. The all-Kenya national language (i.e. Kiswahili); the other national languages (i.e. the languages of the nationalities like Luo, Gĩkũyũ, Maasai, Luhya, Kallenjin, Kamba, Mijikenda, Somali, Galla, Turkana, Arabic-speaking people, etc.); other African languages like Hausa, Wolof, Yoruba, Ibo, Zulu, Nyanja, Lingala, Kimbundu; and foreign languages – that is foreign to Africa – like English, French, German, Russian, Chinese, Japanese, Portuguese, Spanish will fall into their proper perspective in the lives of Kenyan children.

Chinua Achebe once decried the tendency of African intellectuals to escape into abstract universalism in the words that apply even more to the issue of the language of African literature:

> Africa has had such a fate in the world that the very adjective *African* can call up hideous fears of rejection. Better then to cut all the links with this homeland, this liability, and become in one giant leap the universal man. Indeed I understand this anxiety. *But running away from oneself seems to me a very inadequate way of dealing with an anxiety* [italics mine]. And if writers should opt for such escapism, who is to meet the challenge?[18]

Who indeed?

We African writers are bound by our calling to do for our languages what Spenser, Milton and Shakespeare did for English; what Pushkin and Tolstoy did for Russian; indeed what all writers in world history have done for their languages by meeting the challenge of creating a literature in them, which process later opens the languages for philosophy, science, technology and all the other areas of human creative endeavours.

But writing in our languages per se – although a necessary first step in the correct direction – will not itself bring about the renaissance in African cultures if that literature does not carry the content of our people's anti-imperialist struggles to liberate their productive forces from foreign control; the content of the need for unity among the workers and peasants of all the nationalities in their struggle to control the wealth they produce and to free it from internal and external parasites.

In other words writers in African languages should reconnect themselves to the revolutionary traditions of an organised peasantry and working class in Africa in their struggle to defeat imperialism and create a higher system of democracy and socialism in alliance with all the other peoples of the world. Unity in that struggle would ensure unity in our multi-lingual diversity. It would also reveal the real links that bind the people of Africa to the peoples of Asia, South America, Europe, Australia and New Zealand, Canada and the USA.

But it is precisely when writers open out African languages to the real links in the struggles of peasants and workers that they will meet their biggest challenge. For to the comprador-ruling regimes, their real enemy is an awakened peasantry and working class. A writer who tries to communicate the message of revolutionary unity and hope in the languages of the people becomes a subversive character. It is then that writing in African languages becomes a subversive or treasonable offence with such a writer facing possibilities of prison, exile or even death. For him there are no 'national' accolades, no new year honours, only abuse and slander and innumerable lies from the mouths of the armed power of a ruling minority – ruling, that is, on behalf of US-led imperialism – and who see in democracy a real threat. A democratic participation of the people in the shaping of their own lives or in discussing their own lives in languages that allow for mutual comprehension is seen as being dangerous to the good government of a country and its institutions. African languages addressing themselves to the lives of the people become the enemy of a neo-colonial state.

Notes

1. Gabriel Okara, *Transition* 10, September 1963, reprinted from *Dialogue*, Paris.
2. Chinua Achebe, 'The African writer and the English language', in *Morning Yet on Creation Day*, London, 1975, p. 103. [See also p. 426 above]
3. Okara, *op. cit.*
4. Cheikh Hamidou Kane, *L'aventure Ambiguë*, (English translation: *Ambiguous Adventure*). This passage was translated for me by Bachir Diagne.
5. Example from a tongue twister: 'Kaana ka Nikoora koona koora koora: na ko koora koona kaana ka Nikoora koora koora.' I'm indebted to Wangui wa Goro for this example. 'Nicola's child saw a baby frog and ran away: and when the baby frog saw Nichola's child it also ran away.' A Gĩkũyũ speaking child has to get the correct tone and length of vowel and pauses to get it right. Otherwise it becomes a jumble of *k*'s and *r*'s and *na*'s.
6. 'The production of ideas, or conceptions, of consciousness, is at first directly interwoven with the material activity and the material intercourse of men, the language of real life. Conceiving, thinking, the mental intercourse of men, appear at this stage as the direct efflux of their material behaviour. The same applies to mental production as expressed in the language of politics, laws, morality, religion, metaphysics, etc., of a people. Men are the producers of their conceptions, ideas etc. – real, active men, as they are conditioned by a definite development of their productive forces and of the intercourse corresponding to these, up to its furthest form'. Marx and Engels, *German Ideology*, the first part published under the title, *Feuerbach: Opposition of the materialist and idealist outlooks*, London, 1973, p. 8.

7. Quoted in Eric Williams, *A History of the People of Trinidad and Tobago*, London, 1964, p. 32.

8. *ibid.*, p. 31.

9. In references to Africa in the introduction to his lectures in *The Philosophy of History*, Hegel gives historical, philosophical, rational expression and legitimacy to every conceivable European racist myth about Africa. Africa is even denied her own geography where it does not correspond to the myth. Thus Egypt is not part of Africa; and North Africa is part of Europe. Africa proper is the especial home of ravenous beasts, snakes of all kinds. The African is not part of humanity. Only slavery to Europe can raise him, possibly, to the lower ranks of humanity. Slavery is good for the African. 'Slavery is in and for itself *injustice*, for the essence of humanity is *freedom*; but for this man must be matured. The gradual abolition of slavery is therefore wiser and more equitable than its sudden removal'. (Hegel, *The Philosophy of History*, Dover edition, New York, 1956, pp. 91–9) Hegel clearly reveals himself as the nineteenth-century Hitler of the intellect.

10. The paper is now in Akivaga and Gachukiah's *The Teaching of African Literature in Schools*, published by Kenya Literature Bureau.

11. Senghor, Introduction to his poems, 'Ethiopiques, le 24 Septembre 1954', in answering the question: 'Pourquoi, dès lors, écrivez-vous en français?' Here is the whole passage in French. See how lyrical Senghor becomes as he talks of this encounter with French language and French literature.

> Mais on me posera la question: 'Pourquoi, dès lors, écrivez-vous en français?' parce que nous sommes des métis culturels, parce que, si nous sentons en nègres, nous nous exprimons en français, parce que le français est une langue à vocation universelle, que notre message s'adresse *aussi* aux Français de France et aux autres hommes, parce que le français est une langue 'de gentillesse et d'honnêteté'. Qui a dit que c'était une langue grise et atone d'ingénieurs et de diplomates? Bien sûr, moi aussi, je l'ai dit un jour, pour les besoins de ma thèse. On me le pardonnera. Car je sais ses ressources pour l'avoir goûté, mâché, enseigné, et qu'il est la langue des dieux. Ecoutez donc Corneille, Lautréamont, Rimbaud, Péguy et Claudel. Ecoutez le grand Hugo. Le français, ce sont les grandes orgues qui se prêtent à tous les timbres, à tous les effets, des douceurs les plus suaves aux fulgurances de l'orage. Il est, tour à tour ou en même temps, flûte, hautbois, trompette, tamtam et même canon. Et puis le français nous a fait don de ses mots abstraits – si rares dans nos langues maternelles –, où les larmes se font pierres précieuses. Chez nous, les mots sont naturellement nimbés d'un halo de sève et de sang; les mots du français rayonnent de mille feux, comme des diamants. Des fusées qui éclairent notre nuit.

See also Senghor's reply to a question on language in an interview by Armand Guiber, and published in *Présence Africaine* 1962 under the title Léopold Sédar Senghor:

> Il est vrai que le français n'est pas ma langue maternelle. J'ai commencé de l'apprendre à sept ans, par des mots comme 'confitures' et 'chocolat'. Aujourd'hui, je pense naturellement en Français, et je comprend le Français – faut-il en avoir honte? Mieux qu'aucune autre langue. C'est dire que le Français n'est plus pour moi un 'véhicule étranger' mais la forme d'expression naturelle de ma pensée.
> Ce qui m'est étrange dans le français, c'est peut-être son style:
> Son architecture classique. Je suis naturellement porté à gonfler d'image son cadre étroit, sans la poussée de la chaleur émotionelle.

12. *Zimbabwe Herald*, August 1981.
13. Achebe, 'The African writer and the English language', p. 59.
14. Most of the writers were from Universities. The readership was mainly the product of schools and colleges. As for the underlying theme of much of that literature, Achebe's statement in his paper 'The novelist as a teacher' is instructive:

    > If I were God I would regard as the very worst our acceptance − for whatever reason − of racial inferiority. It is too late in the day to get worked up about it or to blame others, much as they may deserve such blame and condemnation. What we need to do is to look back and try and find out where we went wrong, where the rain began to beat us.
    >
    > Here then is an adequate revolution for me to espouse − to help my society regain belief in itself and put away the complexes of the years of denigration and self-abasement. (*Morning Yet on Creation Day*, p. 44)

    Since the peasant and the worker had never really had any doubts about their Africanness, the reference could only have been to the 'educated' or the petty-bourgeois African. In fact if one substitutes the words 'the petty-bourgeois' for the word 'our' and 'the petty-bourgeois class' for 'my society' the statement is apt, accurate, and describes well the assumed audience. Of course, an ideological revolution in this class would affect the whole society.
15. David Diop, 'Contribution to the debate on national poetry', *Présence Africaine*, 6, 1956.
16. *ibid*.
17. The term 'Afro-European literature' may seem to put too much weight on the Europeanness of the literature. Euro-African literature? Probably, the English, French and Portuguese components would then be 'Anglo-African literature', 'Franco-African literature' or 'Luso-African literature'. What is important is that this minority literature forms a distinct tradition that needs a different term to distinguish it from *African literature*, instead of usurping the title *African literature* as is the current practice in literary scholarship. There have even been arrogant claims by some literary scholars who talk as if the literature written in European languages is necessarily closer to the Africanness of its inspiration than similar works in African languages, the languages of the majority. So thoroughly has the minority 'Afro-European literature' (Euro-African literature?) usurped the name 'African literature' in the current scholarship that literature by Africans in African languages is the one that needs qualification. Albert Gérard's otherwise timely book is titled *African Language Literatures*.
18. Chinua Achebe, 'Africa and her writers', in *Morning Yet on Creation Day*, p. 27.

PART SIX
Reading from Theory

Introduction

The focus of the material included in the preceding parts has been largely, though not exclusively, the elaborating of theoretical and/or political points, rather than the production of an extensive reading of a text on the basis of a particular theoretical perspective. While there would be no justification for suggesting any simplistic dichotomy between theory and its 'application' to literature, there is, nevertheless, a particular value in the inclusion of pieces which undertake a sustained engagement with one or more texts which in a sense demonstrate the practical possibilities for intervention or analysis in the disciplinary area where so much current post-colonial work takes place, namely departments of literature and cultural studies. The readings included here range from those which could be considered classic colonial discourse analysis, to others which are clearly post-colonial in their theoretical and textual focus.

Three of the readings in this part are concerned with texts from the turn of the century, since, if we are to take seriously Said's argument about the way texts have effects, repercussions, in the 'real' world, there would seem to be a particular importance in examining that moment of greatest colonial domination, the moment when, because of the nature and extent of colonialism, the 'effects' were arguably the most direct and the most extensive. Concentrating on different areas of colonial control, the three readings suggest a variety of ways in which the cultural products of the period might be understood or analysed. In addition, each is written in dialogue with, or in opposition to, particular theoretical perspectives or critical traditions.

'The construction of woman in three popular texts of Empire', by Rosemary Hennessy and Rajeswari Mohan, continues a debate which has existed within Western feminism for a number of years over the relative merits of materialist feminism and Marxist feminism. Defenders of materialist feminism see it as an improvement on Marxist feminism since it avoids a number of problems associated with Marxism, such as gender blindness or economism, not to mention the tainted (Stalinist) past. Opponents of materialist feminism argue that its abandoning of Marxism deprives it of a powerful analytical tool, and, indeed, of the best means of understanding what is happening in the contemporary world.

Hennessy and Mohan's starting point is the perceived shortcomings of materialist feminism – especially its continued privileging of gender over other areas of exploitation. This narrowness of focus, they feel, diminishes the ability either to intervene politically or to provide an adequate analysis of forms of oppression. Hennessy and Mohan are not simply calling for a reinstatement of Marxism, however. Their approach is much bolder, as they lay claim to 'a globalizing reading strategy' capable both of teasing out the links between different forms of oppression in a particular example or historical moment, and of locating that example within global relations of power. This reading strategy they then apply to three texts from the 1890s (the analysis of one of which is included in the reading here). In addition, they feel that concepts of the Other have hitherto been insufficiently theorised (for instance in the work of Julia Kristeva, the *Screen* group, or Homi Bhabha) and aim to redress that also. In the section of the article included here, they read an apparently unlikely 'text of Empire', Conan Doyle's 'The Speckled Band' through the range of positions of alterity which it establishes, and the way in which these connect with questions of imperial or domestic power relations.

Patrick Williams's examination of *Kim* takes a text which might seem clearly, irredeemably imperialist, but which nevertheless has contrived to convince many critics, even contemporary post-colonial ones such as Abdul JanMohamed, that it somehow manages to escape, to a remarkable degree, the categories and constraints of colonial discourse – above all, perhaps, in terms of the quality of its representations of Indians and Indian culture. This has an obvious importance, since much of the force of Said's dissection of Orientalism derives from his emphasis on the politics of representation, and the ability of a text like *Kim* to overturn Orientalist norms – contrary to all expectations – would have clear implications for the applicability of Said's theory. Williams uses Said and the Marxist critic Pierre Macherey to read against this particular critical consensus surrounding *Kim* and to argue that, in spite of the subtlety of the strategies which the text adopts, Kipling's representation of Indians, their country and culture, is overwhelmingly negative in the best Orientalist manner.

Laura Chrisman's 'The imperial unconscious? Representations of imperial discourse' argues both against a powerfully endorsed critical position (in this instance the Gilbert and Gubar reading of Rider Haggard, praised by Spivak and Said, among others) and against a growing tendency to privilege *post*-colonial analyses at the expense of a necessary attention to the texts of Empire. As Chrisman points out, we neglect these at our peril, since 'Such imperialism, in remaining unanalysed, also remains, unwittingly albeit, hegemonic'. Chrisman is critical of the kinds of elisions which are all too frequently operative even in the work of writers like Spivak, and which obscure important differences and specificities in the colonial situation, for instance between women in India and in the Caribbean. This risks, on the one hand, repeating imperialism's general homogenising of its Others, while, on the other, ignoring the fact that imperialism could equally foster or exaggerate differences for political ends. Such lack of attention to detail and difference is what Chrisman finds in Gilbert and Gubar's study of Rider Haggard, and her own reading offers a more nuanced textual analysis, as well as a more historically grounded sense of the range of imperialism's strategies.

The other selections examine post-colonial authors from East and West Africa. Despite apparent shared features of post-coloniality, they are very differently located with regard to the choices surrounding language and text form. For Sembene Ousmane, for example, working in formerly French Senegal, which is still francophone at an official level, the use of film in order to communicate, in (non-written) Wolof, with as many of the population as possible is a particularly political act, whereas for Tayib Salih, in the formerly British Sudan, producing a novel in Arabic – the majority (written) language – is a very different sort of intervention.

Laura Mulvey takes Teshome Gabriel as the starting point for her discussion of *Xala*, one of the most obviously post-colonial of Ousmane's films. Ousmane himself is a paradigmatic Gramscian organic intellectual: working class, self-taught, unrepentantly Marxist, a soldier, turned docker, turned trades union organiser, turned novelist, and, eventually, turned film-maker in a search for the best means of communicating to his people the truth, as he sees it, of their colonial past and post-colonial present. *Xala* exemplifies many of Fanon's prescient worries about the nature and role of the national black bourgeoisie, notionally post-colonial, but still ideologically and economically shackled to the West – a view which is echoed in the novels and essays of African writers such as Ngũgĩ wa Thiong'o and Chinua Achebe. Mulvey's discussion concentrates on the question of fetishism, especially the anthropological and Marxist inflections, to which the film specifically alludes, but also the Freudian/sexual one. The anthropological and the economic come together surprisingly in Mulvey's demonstration of the way in which Western discourse around fetishism arose out of a particular attitude to Africans and trade, and, in turn, in a classically Orientalist manner, legitimated colonial exploitation. The two areas continue to interact in a neo-colonial setting, as when the film's central character compares the authenticity of his 'primitive' fetish to the economic and technical fetishism indulged in by his former government colleagues, which signals the fact that they continue to be controlled by the former colonising power.

In 'The Empire renarrated' Saree Makdisi looks at one of the great contemporary East African novels, al-Tayib Salih's *Season of Migration to the North*. For Makdisi, the book is an intervention both in the process of 'writing back' to the imperial centre, and in the post-colonial discourse of the Arab world. The novel figures the question of the frequently uneasy position of the post-colonial intellectual at the level of both authorship and characterisation. Problems of the relation to change and tradition are foregrounded in the responses of two different types of intellectual, the narrator and the 'migrant' central character, Mustafa Said. This relation remains unresolved as the approach of each ends in a different kind of uncertain failure. The narrator's nostalgia (and future hope) for some unsullied traditional culture is shown to be impossible in a post-colonial world, while Mustafa Said's more energetic and subversive attempt symbolically to reverse the flow, even the history, of European colonialism proves equally unworkable, ultimately as ahistorical as the position of the narrator.

27 □ The Construction of Woman in Three Popular Texts of Empire: Towards a Critique of Materialist Feminism

Rosemary Hennessy and Rajeswari Mohan

In the late 1970s materialist feminism emerged in the west from a feminist critique within Marxism. Annette Kuhn and Anne Marie Wolpe in Britain and Christine Delphy in France were among the promoters of 'materialist feminism', favouring that term over 'Marxist feminism' on the basis of an argument that Marxism cannot adequately address women's exploitation and oppression unless the Marxist problematic itself is transformed so as to be able to account for the sexual division of labour.[1] With its class bias, its emphasis on economic determinism, and its focus on a history exclusively formulated in terms of the laws of motion and transformation of capitalist production, classic Marxism had barely begun to analyse and critique patriarchal systems of exploitation. At the same time, there was a marked tendency in feminist theory to conceptualize woman in essentialist and idealist terms. In this context, materialist feminism provided an historically urgent ground from which to launch a critical counter-knowledge to mainstream feminism and classic Marxism.

While it has continued to be a source of powerful critiques of liberal and essentialist feminisms, materialist feminism's radical edge has blunted over time in the arenas of oppositional political struggles. As multinational capitalism systematically expands its network of exploitative relations of production and consumption, patriarchal and capitalist relations become even more securely imbricated – witness the growing disciplinary violence against third-world women by multinational corporate research, the increasing sexualization of women by an all-pervasive commodity aesthetics, and the intensified contestation over woman's

From *Textual Practice*, 3, 3, Winter 1989, pp. 323–37, 354–7.

body as the site of reproduction in the first world and of production in the third world. How we make sense of these disparate instances of women's oppression in our historical present will affect their perpetuation or elimination. It has therefore become urgent to adopt theoretical frames that can account for the complex interconnections between the various axes along which exploitation and oppression take place. A philosophy of praxis capable of directing a globally articulated revolutionary struggle gains a certain urgency as the confinement of oppositional struggles to regional and isolated sites becomes a widely deployed strategy of crisis management. In this respect, what was once materialist feminism's greatest strength is now being pressured by increasing calls to recognize difference within the category 'woman'. From the beginning, materialist feminism gave priority to the social construction of gender while simultaneously avowing commitment to the analysis of gender in its intersection with class. It is only recently that race and sexuality have become part of materialist feminist concerns, but the articulation of class, race, gender and sexuality has for the most part merely been used as the legitimizing cliché of a leftist discourse.

Early second-wave feminist critiques within Marxism produced at best a dual systems theory acknowledging women's positioning within patriarchal and capitalist systems, but often relegating patriarchy exclusively to ideological practice or explaining it only in terms of a specific social formation.[2] One consequence of this theoretical impasse was the inability to draw out the complex interrelations of support and opposition between capitalism and patriarchy.[3] More recent developments in an increasingly loosely defined materialist feminist project indicate a continued propensity toward regional analysis enhanced by an uncritical appropriation of postmodern discourses. For example, *Female Sexualization*, edited by Frigga Haug and produced collectively by feminists working on the editorial board of the German socialist journal *Das Argument*, takes up Foucauldian and Marxist problematics in an effort to address the historicity of the feminine for an emancipatory agenda but constructs both history and the feminine through the individualized white western woman.[4] Roberta Hamilton and Michèle Barrett's recent anthology *The Politics of Diversity* similarly gestures toward 'Racism, Ethnicity, and Nationalism' in re-thinking 'feminist marxism' in Canada but consistently subsumes these issues under (western white) women's interests.[5] Because materialist feminism's emphasis on gender has involved the backgrounding of other modalities of exploitation, the project is fraught with an ideologically charged discrepancy between its political desires and its effectivity. Judith Newton and Deborah Rosenfelt's 'Introduction' to their anthology *Feminist Criticism and Social Change* exemplifies this contradiction.[6] Although they define materialist feminist criticism as 'a criticism combining feminist, socialist and anti-racist perspectives' (p. xxvii), the analysis throughout both the essay and the volume privileges gender, at some points even explicitly. 'Materialist-feminist criticism', they claim, 'differs from traditional marxist criticism in its emphasis on gender relations and on the transforming potential of white middle-class female desire' (p. xxv). If materialist feminism 'differs from other feminisms in its refusal to valorize that desire *almost to the exclusion of other values*' (p. xxv; emphasis added), how can it do so and still emphasize gender over other subject positions? This contradiction in materialist feminist praxis supports the broader tendency to privilege gender over other subjectivities in the field of literary criticism where feminist theory has often provided the last haven for ethnocentric and class-biased ideologies. Materialist feminist and/or socialist feminist interventions into literary studies (the work of Cora Kaplan is one noteworthy British example) have involved the recuperation of the most radical features of their critiques by maintaining a privileged status for gender, by failing to extend the materialist understanding of history beyond attention to ideological practice and western culture, and by extending the inclusiveness of 'materialism' so broadly that its radical intervention is diffused into an acceptable eclecticism.[7]

As we live out the postmodern moment under the crisis conditions of multinational capitalism, materialist feminism does not have the same historical urgency it had at its inception. However, in arguing that the materialist feminist project has lost its radical edge we are in no way making the postfeminist argument that feminist struggles are irrelevant.[8] Our critique is a critique *for* feminism. Only it is directed as much against new imperialism, white supremacy, homophobia and class exploitation as it is against patriarchy. In doing so we argue for a globalizing reading strategy. Such a strategy attends to the interconnection between various modalities of oppression and exploitation at any one instance of the social while situating that instance in the global deployment of capitalist power relations.

Calling for such a strategy requires a particular understanding of feminism and a way of distinguishing between the point of entry of critique and its aims. Feminism is a discourse that critiques hegemonic constructions of woman as a social subject, advances an understanding of the historical factors that necessitate these constructions and the interests they serve, and in doing so seeks to end the self-perpetuating circuit of relations that alienate women from their labour, their sexuality, their comrades in struggle. So long as patriarchal and capitalist arrangements maintain a system of hegemonic relations wherein constructions of the feminine enable and support global exploitation and domination, feminism's point of entry to critique of those relations is urgent. In trying to destabilize mutually imbricated systems of exploitation and domination, however, feminism is just one oppositional discourse. It has to develop strategies to follow through all the lines of force that radiate from the category 'woman' to other categories and vice versa. In doing so feminism works toward change wrought through overdetermination, change which is the effect of a collective, not just a feminist, subject.

Implicit in a global reading strategy is a theory of history contrary to the understanding of history as distinct from theory that runs like a fault line through much materialist feminist criticism. (For instance, the organizational scheme of Newton and Rosenfelt's anthology – Part I Theory; Part II Applied Criticism – indicates this split.) This separation of the way of knowing from the object of knowledge is itself ideologically produced and serves to re-secure an idealist understanding of theory as meta-discourse and an empiricist notion of history as data. Even new historicist notions of theory as mediating the relationship between historical object and investigating subject often implicitly posit history or the body as existing outside of ways of knowing.[9]

Any understanding of history entails a theory of reading. Because 'history' in the sense of actual events is always and only intelligible to us through historically available ways of making sense, history is never accessible outside its production through reading in and for the ideological problems posed in the present. In this sense, reading is a material practice, contributing to the construction of the social real; any reading of any text of culture is first of all an ideological intervention in the available ways of making sense of 'history' in the subject's historical present. A global reading of history, then, does not seek to recover a past that has been silenced, but to investigate the cultural currency of the past in the present and critique the interests served by historical narratives as material practices shaping contemporary social arrangements. In re-narrating three texts of the nineteenth century – 'The Adventure of the Speckled Band' (1892) by Arthur Conan Doyle, 'Mussumat Kirpo's Doll' (1894) by Flora Annie Steel, and a cartoon from *Punch* entitled 'A Divided Duty' (1895)– our essay intervenes in current understandings of alterity, sexuality and patriarchal control.[10]

I

As responses to and interventions in the transition into monopoly capitalism that was building up slowly and unevenly across the social formation through the latter part of the nineteenth century, the texts we study are part of the general work of crisis containment performed by ideology. Competition from Germany, Russia and Japan, and nationalist struggles in the colonies, undermined the global reach of British imperial might, while domestic social order was threatened by a burgeoning feminist movement, working-class insurgency and the growing power of socialist movements. While all these crises were affected and made possible by the global reach of capitalism, part of the work of crisis containment has been directed toward reading them as isolated phenomena, thereby mystifying their systemic implication in capitalist and patriarchal relations. In Britain, the transition into monopoly capitalism took place under the pressures generated by the Great Depression (1873–96) and the adventures of New Imperialism (1870–1902). The enormity and obviousness of the economic benefits accompanying the Great Depression and Britain's New Imperialism in the last two decades of the nineteenth century have often resulted in an exclusive emphasis on the economic sphere in theories of imperialism. This tendency has been further sanctioned by a long tradition of economism in Marxist theory – where the economic level of a social formation is seen to determine or express its political and ideological practices. Because economic determinism understands the social formation as a homogeneous and monolithic expression of economic forces, it cannot explain the unevenness of a social formation nor account for the strong cross-currents impelling social change.

Furthermore, locating the economic sphere as the prime mover of social change ignores the crucial work performed by ideology in reproducing existing modes of production through its work of interpellating or constituting subjects.

From a post-Althusserian understanding of the social, popular culture can be seen as not just a reflection of economic and political forces, but as a site where ideological work is continuously produced out of diverse political and economic interests to disrupt or to re-secure existing social arrangements.[11] In this sense, popular culture is a terrain of contestation. The ideological struggles waged in popular texts of the late nineteenth century were crucial in constituting the modalities of the relations between the dominant and subordinate sectors of the social formation. It is important to locate these struggles in the global logic of capitalism in order to understand the containment of subaltern interests on which the western 'democratic way of life' is secured.[12]

In nineteenth-century Britain, popular culture was an influential site for the circulation of discourses of alterity and served as a powerful medium through which a re-articulated array of subject positions necessary for an emerging social order could be established. Narratives celebrating imperial and patriarchal authority were immensely popular in music halls, popular fiction, sensationalist 'new' journalism and advertising. As reading became a leisure-time activity to be slipped into the daily routine of travel and work, the long triple-decker novel lapsed from its privileged position into the cultural margin. Its place was taken by such popular productions as the 'railway novel' and variety magazine. Developments in printing and paper technology which made books cheaper than ever, greater access to education, increasing literacy levels after the Education Act of 1870, and the emergence of the advertisement-supported magazine, all greatly enhanced the influence of popular narratives. In the colonies – particularly in India, after Macaulay's infamous minutes of 1835 – teaching English, studying English literature and reading popular British texts were integral elements in the maintenance of imperial control.

Popular culture mediates between restricted 'specialized' discourses and the commonsense and circulates emergent knowledges. In so doing it performs the task of constructing subjectivities on a culturally pervasive scale. In addition, popular narratives from the late nineteenth century circulate tropes that maintain their ideological force to this day, defining the terms in which alterity is understood and setting the agenda for their deployment. It is with this understanding of the influence of nineteenth-century popular texts that our essay focuses on two short stories and a cartoon to draw out the regional and global interests served by the discourses of alterity circulating in them.

As a category that constitutes, consolidates and confirms the *self-in-relation*, alterity or otherness is integral to the demarcation of the limits of acceptability – even intelligibility – that are necessary for the constitution of cultural identities along the lines of race, gender and class. Discourses of alterity are therefore crucial factors in the division and hierarchization of the social necessary for the deployment of political power and the extraction of surplus value. In other words, the ideology of alterity permits relations of exploitation and domination to exist not just between individuals but between populations of individuals. The most influential of recent theories of alterity, deriving in various ways from Lacan's theoretical elaborations of subject constitution, have been unable rigorously to locate alterity in relation to exploitative relations of production. The importance given to the other in the work of the *Screen* group and of French feminists like Kristeva is adequate only to a limited elaboration of the power relations within which the subject is situated.[13] For instance, Homi Bhabha's appropriation of *Screen* theory to explain colonial and race relations has extended the Lacanian narrative of the ambivalence and fragmentation that accompany subject formation to produce a compelling account of the colonial subject oscillating between identification with and alienation from the colonized other.[14] But like the *Screen* theorists in general, Bhabha's careful insistence that the subject–other relation is culturally constituted still does not make it urgent for him to inquire into the historical specificity of that constitution. In other words, the historical pressures necessitating the subject–other axis to be cut at particular points – for instance, the coalescing of the feminine and the colonized subject under imperialism – and the material consequences at the conjunctural and global level of this demarcation of subjectivities elude his investigation. In this manner, most theories of alterity have consistently elaborated subjectivity in ahistorical terms because of their propensity to generalize and universalize accounts of subject formation from a configuration of psychosexual relations unique to western bourgeois family arrangements. Furthermore, in spite of their gestures towards radical political practice, these theories are unable to escape a dualism that separates the oppressive effects of sexual difference from exploitative economic practices enabling and enabled by it. As differences get conjugated in terms of sexuality in Lacanian derivatives, attempts to take into account other modalities of alterity – such as differences brought about by class and race divisions – inevitably lead to a rearticulation of those differences in sexual terms. As sexuality is understood solely in terms of pleasure and desire, the question of exploitation – the appropriation of surplus value under conditions where the exploiter maintains complete control over the means of production at the expense of the exploited – completely drops out.

To wrest the discussion of alterity away from its current focus on the individual subject and bring it to bear upon the constitution of collectivities, collectivities produced by the deployment of discursive mechanisms and necessary in exploitative capitalist relations, alterity must be seen as an ideological construct. To view alterity in this way is to insist that capitalist relations of production build up historically specific contradictions that shift the boundaries within which the subject is situated. In other words, alterity is continually re-articulated in terms dictated by its economic and political conditions of emergence.

The periodically recurring crises that marked the second half of the nineteenth century signalled the re-articulation of alterity as previously prevalent ideologies of otherness disintegrated against the force of the contradictions accompanying the global shift to monopoly capitalism. This shift required a redefinition of alterity around the issue of discipline to help produce the good subject necessary under the emergent conditions of production, exchange and consumption, and to serve as the ideological foundation for new laws marking increased state control over the family, sexuality and labour in both the colonies and the metropole. The re-articulation of alterity and its systemic recruitment to justify new forms of control and exploitation was aided by emergent knowledges of the nineteenth century. While the same discourses of social Darwinism, eugenics, civic health, medicine and secular morality were drawn upon in the articulation of racial, class and gender difference, the location of the subject across several positions often resulted in contradictions that required the important but local and contingent work of crisis containment carried out by popular narratives such as the stories of Conan Doyle and Steel.

'The Adventure of the Speckled Band' is one of several stories Conan Doyle published in *The Strand Magazine* in the 1890s which negotiates these contradictions through a variety of narrative strategies: the construction of Holmes as rational protector, the resolution of the narrative's enigma, and the positioning of the reader. The problem presented in the case involves a father's control over his unmarried daughter's property. Thirty-year-old Helen Stoner turns to Holmes for help in solving the riddle of her twin sister Julia's death a fortnight before her marriage. Helen's anxiety is based on vague suspicions sparked by the recurrence before her own impending marriage of a series of events similar to those surrounding Julia's death. The Stoner sisters live in a decaying ancestral manor with their step-father, Dr Grimsby Roylott, the last son of a pauperized aristocratic family. In India where he practiced medicine, Roylott married the Stoners's widowed mother who bequeathed a considerable sum of money ('not less than £1,000 a year') entirely to Roylott so long as the twins lived with him, with a provision that a certain annual sum should be allowed to each daughter in the event of her marriage (p. 196). Holmes's detection discloses Roylott as his daughter's murderer, motivated by greed for the money he would lose when she married. In staging the murder as symbolic rape (Roylott kills Julia by means of a poisonous snake sent through a vent connecting his bedroom to hers) the narrative dramatizes the sexual economy of patriarchy: the equation of woman and property. At the same time, it presents Holmes as woman's protector, rescuing her from the villainous patriarch's domination and defending her right to control over her own property and person.

In the construction of Holmes as hero, the narrative draws upon the codes of otherness, such as irrationality, lack of control, and dissipation, set by the discourses of alterity, and in so doing redefines subjectivities in ways historically necessitated by the regional and global rearrangements taking place in the late nineteenth century. Holmes's heroic status is constructed relationally in the narrative through a semic code that links various subject positions. Examining these links makes visible a network of gaps and contradictions which are suppressed in the interests of the narrative's coherent resolution. These gaps, associated with both Roylott and Helen, are details which 'exceed' the solution to the crime – details the solution does not and can not explain – specifically, Roylott's association with the gypsies, his possession of an excessive number of Indian animals, and Helen's silencing. As we will show, Holmes's status as hero depends on the down-played existence of these details.

Holmes's opposition to and complicity with the villainous patriarch, Roylott, indicates the articulation of a 'new' masculine subject. Roylott is coded as a failed aristocrat whose decline is owing to a weakness of both moral fibre and blood, a hereditary mania that translates into lack of self-control and results ultimately in his criminal fall from respectability. His friendship with the gypsies upon his return from India is related to this fall, and is presented as simultaneously self-explanatory and suspicious. Helen's suggestion that the 'band' of gypsies are linked to her sister's death draws on a commonly held suspicion of gypsies, but it does not explain the association between them and the lapsed aristocrat, Roylott. None the less, this unexplained contradictory class coding of Roylott helps valorize Holmes's status by positioning him in opposition to the negative upper- and lower-class alternatives associated with the villain. Holmes's amateur detective work (bearing the marks of an emergent professionalism: wage work as skilled yet artful dedication) takes on its value in opposition to Roylott's association with both aristocratic squandering and lower-class shiftlessness.[15]

In conjunction with his contradictory class location, Roylott's links to the Orient encode him with multiple semes for otherness in overdetermined opposition to the western, rational, middle-class Holmes. Semically marked for aristocratic dissipation, lower-class un-respectability, and eastern irrationality, Roylott presents a profile of the criminal as all that Holmes, the middle-class restrained gentleman, is not. The semic association of Roylott with the wild Orient is also in excess of the requirements of the solution – Holmes's disclosure of the phallic murder weapon. Roylott has lived in Calcutta, has access to knowledge of poisons available only to 'a clever and ruthless man with an Eastern training' (p. 209), keeps a baboon and a cheetah as well as the deadly swamp adder, and in his death scene is wearing turkish slippers. Like the gypsies, the Indian animals are decoys in the untangling of the enigma, possible suspects that establish a false lead but which ultimately are not required by the logic of the solution. However, Roylott's association with the East blurs with his ties to the gypsies – long figures of alterity in the west– and qualifies *as explanation* for his violence. The hereditary mania blamed for his outbursts 'had been intensified by residence in the tropics' (p. 196), and it is his robbery by a native in Calcutta that incites Roylott to beat his butler to death, an act that lands him in prison. While Roylott's violence is associated causally with the East, its enactment in relation to three significant figures – the colonial servant, the white daughter and the village blacksmith he assaults – constructs him in opposition to a series of 'others' arranged along race, gender and class lines. However, Holmes's privileged position in the narrative as subject of knowledge with which the reader identifies serves to dissociate him from these scenes of violence and to down-play any possible connections among imperial domination, patriarchal control and class privilege.

Still, as opposed as Roylott and Holmes are made to appear, the narrative resolution that valorizes Holmes as hero depends on his links to Roylott in a system of patriarchal gender relations that set both of them apart from woman as other. It is the threatened disruption of this system that occasions the murder constituting the narrative's enigma. In his daughter's murder and symbolic rape Roylott enacts the ultimate patriarchal privilege: control over women *as* property that simultaneously denies them access *to* property and to sexual consent. The narrative makes use of the twin sisters to negotiate woman's contradictory positioning as subject and object within capitalist patriarchal arrangements simultaneously cancelling and affirming woman's claim to and status as property as she shifts positions from daughter to wife. It is the management of the 'moment' of transition between these two highly controlled positions that comprises the ideological work of the story as it eliminates the threatening position of the independent, propertied female subject by means of the band of paternal protectors.

Questions about woman's status as subject in relation to property and sexual consent that are raised and quickly resolved in the narrative are symptomatic of the contest over woman's ambiguous social position, a struggle waged in the long campaign for reform of married women's property rights. The Married Women's Property Act (1882) overturned the common law of coverture according to which a wife forfeited all property upon marriage to her husband because husband and wife were one person and that person was the husband. While the formal arrangement of the family remained the same, legalized in the heterosexual monogamous Christian marriage, profound changes in property during industrialization – from land to money – created entirely new forms of wealth. By the late nineteenth century a transformation of entrepreneurial activity, brought about by the development of finance capital exemplified in the creation of the Stock Exchange and the legal recognition of limited liability companies, encouraged the investment of risk capital. These changes in economic practice meant that landed property inherited through a family line was no longer the sole source of wealth, a shift which paved the way for legal reforms relating to the family.[16] These legal reforms were also part of a process in the late nineteenth century by which the state, mediated by voluntary organizations, gradually intervened further in the private sphere in response to demands for civil equality from trade unions and women. These demands provided the state with opportunities to control and direct the emergence of an expanded and reconstructed middle-class workforce whose social position was grounded on education and business skills rather than inheritance. As a result, the division between public and private domains which undergirded the development of industrialization was re-articulated as the private family was gradually permeated by the disciplinary apparatuses of state intervention. In the process patriarchal gender relations were reshaped.

The Married Women's Property Act exemplifies the dynamics of this rearrangement. The contest over property rights simultaneously constituted and managed a crisis in woman's social position brought on by changes across the social formation which made visible woman's contradictory social status, spanning positions as property and property owner. Legal reforms addressed this crisis by giving women control over their property; but by doing so in terms of male protection, the law kept in place woman's position as non-rational other.[17]

Because feminist histories of the Married Women's Property Act have been based on a liberal humanist understanding of social relations, they leave unquestioned the notions of equity, property and the market-place western women struggled to gain access to. In opposition, our reading suggests a radical rethinking of these unquestioned categories in terms of the global exploitative relations they help to sustain. From this position, property reforms can be seen to readjust the patriarchal family alliance in Britain by perpetuating women's exclusion from full social participation. But this exclusion was only a regional aspect of the global social relations these reforms both depended on and affected. Reform of women's property rights also contributed to a shift in productive relations which would allow middle-class women in Britain to be recruited into a newly structured market-place. In turn, the emergence of the tertiary sector in Britain depended on the shift to the colonies of production and exploitable labour no longer viable in the metropole.

As the campaign for property reform made clear, the subject position most endangering the patriarchy – both sexually and economically – was the *femme sole*, a position made available by the shift in productive relations and threatening to elude the discourses of male protection that secured the feminine as other. Like all men, the single woman had legal control over her property. But because the skills thought to be needed for the administration of her property were locked in the male professions, the single woman's ability to exercise that control was curtailed.[18] Women's increasing demands in the late nineteenth century for access to the professions threatened the Victorian ideology of separate spheres by transgressing the paternalistic management of the division between the subject *of* property and the subject *as* property that constituted the feminine as other. The unusual terms of Mrs Stoner's will in 'The Speckled Band' – foreclosing the possibility that either daughter will occupy the position of *femme sole* – functions to suppress the availability of this dangerous feminine subject position, one that by the 1890s – when large numbers of single middle-class women were recruited into a newly formed clerical workforce – was becoming increasingly available.[19]

The same discourse of protection used in the law to justify women's limited liability and mystify the operation of patriarchal control underlies Holmes's defence of Helen's property right in 'The Speckled Band', and to a similar end. Holmes's opposition to Roylott's control over his daughter's sexual and economic power might seem at first glance to define a position that opposes traditional patriarchal domination. However, Holmes's inclusion in a circuit of exchange that enables Helen's passage from father to husband makes his role as protector problematic. As the go-between from the father who symbolically strangles his daughter with his poisoned phallic band to the fiancé whose power is encoded in his silencing of the daughter-wife's secret rape, the position of Holmes is in collusion with a 'band' of patriarchs implicated in suppressing that which poses an economic and sexual threat to patriarchal gender relations. Holmes's position as opponent to the traditional patriarch defines him as a 'new' man, but, as we will show, this 'newness' is more a re-articulation than a transformation of the sexual economy of patriarchy.

The construction of Helen as 'silent' provides the premise for Watson's narrative and allows Holmes the last word on it: Helen has pledged Watson to secrecy and he can only tell her story now because she is dead. Like Roylott's association with the gypsies and Oriental beasts, this detail – that Helen's story must be suppressed until after her death – is not explained. In this sense it lies outside the logic of the solution to the case. Moreover, Helen's version of events is suppressed as soon as Holmes takes over the case, and it never features in the official report. In the absence of her narrative after Roylott's death, Holmes's 'protection' of Helen elides easily with both the patriarch's phallic poisoning of his daughter until she 'choked her words' (p. 198) and could not name her murderer, and the 'protection' of her husband-to-be who censors Helen's narrative as 'the fancies of a nervous woman' (p. 195). Silencing the rescued daughter effectively protects patriarchy's privileged 'play': the inquest simply 'came to the conclusion that the Doctor met his fate while indiscreetly playing with a dangerous pet' (p. 208). Firmly situated within a protective circle of male kin, Helen's position as consenting subject is so overwritten by paternal authority that it is virtually effaced. Thus, she serves the function of the feminine 'other' in the economy of patriarchy: the conduit through which the phallus can be passed from father to son.[20]

The sexualization of the female body that serves as the symbolic ground for the narrative's enigma manages woman's contradictory position as property and property owner, a contradiction simultaneously being managed in the legal sphere by property reform and reform in the age of consent. Passed on the heels of the Married Woman's Property Act, the Criminal Law Amendment Act (1885) legislated a complementary shift in patriarchal arrangements affecting the status of woman outside the home.[21] In raising the age of consent for girls from 13 to 16, the act and its supporters purported to defend and protect the interests of girls from sexual offenders. However, as with property reform, the discourse of protection, which threads its way through the reform campaign and the law, conceals the class and gender interests served by the amendment. The passage of the Criminal Law Amendment Act was punctuated by one of the first and most effectively waged campaigns of sensationalist journalism and inaugurated a broad-based social purity movement that would extend through the next few decades. The 'Maiden Tribute of Modern Babylon', a series of stories written and published in *The Pall Mall Gazette* by its editor, W. T. Stead, provided the catalyst for passage of the Criminal Law Amendment Act by purportedly exposing extensive white slave trade between Britain and the continent as well as pervasive child prostitution in London. The exposé demonstrates the class lines along which the age of consent battle was fought and indicates the historical conditions of possibility for the overdetermined network of sexual and class codes in 'The Speckled Band'.[22] In targeting the foreign aristocrat as procurer and the 'daughters of the poor' as his victims, the campaign for raising the age of consent used one of the most familiar themes of popular melodrama – the seduction of the poor girl by the wealthy lecher – to sexualize threats to capitalist production: foreign competition, collective unrest fueled by feminist and socialist reform movements, and the destablization of gender arrangements by the recruitment of 'redundant' single middle-class women into the workforce. The patriarchal gender ideology that commodified bourgeois woman as ornament of the home was thereby re-articulated in age of consent legislation and the social purity campaigns that this reform movement spawned. By constructing woman outside the home as sexual commodity in need of state protection, the law addressed the increasing numbers of single middle-class women working outside the home and helped contain the threat they posed. In the name of protecting girls against sexual abuse, the law went a long way in re-securing the destablized patriarchal family: severely undermining the position of female 'consenting' subject outside the private sphere by constituting it as a position in which woman was still encircled by patriarchal controls, *subject* to the 'reasonable beliefs' of both her legal representative and her violator.[23]

Like the Married Women's Property Act, the age of consent law focused on issues central to patriarchal control – 'protection' and 'possession' – extending the protective arm of the state to girls and women outside the possessive claims of father or husband. But while the Married Women's Property Act emphasized woman as *subject* of property, age of consent legislation foregrounded woman *as* property. Both reforms managed complementary adjustments in the contradictory position of woman as the relationship between public and private spheres and middle-class women's place in both was gradually shifting. Most historical studies have treated one or the other of these reforms, but not both in conjunction.[24] Seeing them in adjacency rather than in isolation makes visible the mutual determination of woman's position as married property owner and as sexualized subject outside the home. Taken together, they comprise two sides of the same coin of patriarchal control under capitalism.

The symbolic appearance of the incest motif in 'The speckled band' is symptomatic of the contradictions which produced this de-securing of the patriarchal gender system from one set of social arrangements and its re-securing in another. As it is encoded in the story, the daughter's seduction demonstrates the class interests this sexualization of the family alliance served by dis-articulating the masculine subject from aristocratic aspirations and re-articulating it as the rational professional. Furthermore, the daughter's seduction enacts cultural anxiety about incest which helped reinforce the mutually supporting feminine subject of property – bound as non-person to patriarchal protection/possession within a father–daughter or a husband–wife relationship – and the non-subject of consent subjected to the state's (read Holmes's) protection in lieu of adequate protection from the father-husband.

The sexualization of woman through the narrative of the daughter's seduction took place in multiple sites of culture from sensationalist newspaper accounts of spoiled maidens to the theoretical discourses of Freudian psychoanalysis. Crucial to the elaboration of this narrative in the discourses of psychology and psychoanalysis is the construction of the bourgeois family romance as a universal arrangement. Postmodern feminist appropriations of the narrative of the daughter's seduction developed in various ways in the work of the French feminists – Luce Irigaray, Hélène Cixous, Catherine Clément – and their American and British commentators – among them Jane Gallop, Juliet Mitchell, Jacqueline Rose – leave unquestioned this trans-historical economy of the Freudian problematic reread through Lacan.[25] So long as the rewriting of the daughter's seduction in postmodern feminist discourses continues to close out the historicity of this construction of the feminine subject and its accompanying concepts of the family and of sexuality, it helps sustain the ideological function of the sexualization of the feminine in capitalist production. The consequences of this practice are evident in the discourses of French feminism where the narrative of the daughter's seduction by the law of the father generates a continual slippage between the claim that 'woman' signifies those processes that disrupt the symbolic order and the figuration of this symbolic excess by the female sex organs.[26] The slippage constitutes a contradictory explanation of feminine resistance as both constructed by psychosexual arrangements and inherent in the female body. The problem with this contradiction is that it forecloses any elaboration of the historically specific meaning of the female body as inscribed by/against the symbolic order. Furthermore, a sexualized, biologized concept of textuality undermines French feminists' forceful critique of logocentrism by duplicating the binarism of an oppressive gender hierarchy in which one term is privileged over the other and by failing to explain the relation between the social construction of gender difference and other hierarchized subjectivities.

Like the Freudian, Lacanian and French feminist theories, Foucault's reading of the intersection of family alliance and sexuality is based on a theory of the social which constitutes an ideological intervention in the contemporary moment.[27] The Foucauldian project emerged during the ideological crisis accompanying capital's transition to its late phase and was shaped in part by a critical opposition to Marxism which Foucault understood as a totalizing theory. Foucault's concept of the social as a diffused set of force relations implicitly contests the Althusserian understanding of the social as an ensemble of productive practices which work together to sustain historically determined class, race and gender interests.[28] Because the Foucauldian project is committed to a micro-analysis of institutional power, it does not allow for and cannot explain connections between systems of exploitation or oppression – between imperialism and patriarchy, for example – or between the sexualized feminine subject of the metropole and the feminized colonial producer, connections that a global reading practice will draw out and insist on. By forestalling explanation of systemic relations, Foucauldian micro-analysis helps to sustain their proliferation under late capitalism. Merely 'using' Foucault's historical analysis without making visible the political implications of its problematic helps to conceal its material force as ideological practice. Foucault's important contributions to understanding the relations between knowledge, power, and subject formation on a micro (regional) level of analysis, however, can be re-articulated within a postmodern Marxist problematic to advance a global reading practice. It is to this end that we take up Foucault's reading of the cultural anxiety over incest in nineteenth-century Britain as a defensive measure against the deployment of sexuality, but elaborate this event within the conjunctural movement of late-nineteenth-century Britain in terms of the global relations of capitalism during the high noon of British imperialism.

The sexualized subject of the late nineteenth century, inscribed by the disciplinary interventions of the state, did not supplant the subject of familial alliance. Rather, as Foucault has argued, the family provided an anchor of sorts whereby alliance and sexuality could be interchanged.[29] Universalizing the incest taboo made the law of the patriarch secure even in the new mechanics of power.[30] At the same time, the proliferation of incest motifs in the discourses of the social sciences – in particular, through the hystericization of the middle-class daughter – signalled a reformation of patriarchal gender arrangements that loosened the bonds of family alliance in order to construct an individualized, sexualized feminine subject. The symbolic encoding of the daughter's seduction in 'The Speckled Band', including Holmes's complicity with Roylott, is an instance of the ideological function of incest motifs: managing the threat to family alliance posed by the individualized, single, middle-class daughter by re-installing her within patriarchal control through a narrative of the family romance.

The narrative handling of the daughter's seduction in 'The Speckled Band' demonstrates the alliance between the re-articulation of woman as other and the discourses of scientific rationalism. The daughter's seduction, along with the race, class and gender hierarchies it supports, is silenced by the narrative's coherent solution, a coherence which depends on the reader taking up the position of the subject of knowledge offered by Holmes. Holmes's ability to 'explain it all' by pointing to the perfectly obvious 'elementary' details that have passed before the reader's unwitting eyes (as well as the reader's stand-in, Watson's) explains the enigma and gives Holmes his status as genius of detection. Holmes's authority as rational, scientific investigator works with the narrative movement toward resolution to seal over contradictions and gaps undermining both the coherence of the explanation and the obviousness of Holmes's authority as subject of knowledge.

If read from the subject position the story invites the reader to take up, these contradictory links and the fissures they open in Holmes's air-tight explanation are invisible. This invisibility is in itself a clue to the ideological force of both this position and the deductive logic it offers as an obviously enlightened way of seeing. Reason is presented simultaneously as a universal human attribute and a gratuitous gift of birth available only to a fortunate few. While the qualifications for those 'few' are not overtly explained – in this sense they are invisible – they are none the less encoded in Holmes, the consummate rational subject. The reader is invited to 'identify' with this subject through Watson, the classic participant-observer, in awe of Holmes's superior reasoning power and yet similarly qualified in terms of class, race and gender positions. Holmes's empiricist emphasis on the visible as self-explanatory mystifies the ways the narrative's endorsement of deductive logic naturalizes the visible marks of difference in order to sustain a social hierarchy. Thus, Roylott's association with the Orient and with the gypsies serve as obvious clues – visible signals to the reader – of his un-reasonableness just as mud splashes on a sleeve are visible evidence that Helen has ridden in a dog cart.

The ratiocination that employs an empiricist mode of knowing as a weapon for criminal justice explicitly sets the rational subject of knowledge apart not only from the criminal (who, as Roylott's overdetermined encoding indicates, is often a collective outlaw) but also from the pedestrian masses: 'Crime is common, logic is rare,' Holmes tells Watson. 'What do the public, the great unobservant public, who could hardly tell a weaver by his tooth or a compositor by his left thumb, care about the finer shades of analysis and deduction?'[31] This subject position endowed with heroic stature recruits the discourse of scientific rationalism increasingly taken up for state intervention into various domains of the social, to present as obvious and natural a hierarchy that protects the interests of the middle-class, western, white male. By privileging this subject position through Watson's narration, the narrative offers the reader a way of making sense by which the contradictory links between the science of deduction and the interests of patriarchy and imperialism are glossed over. [...]

Notes

1. Annette Kuhn and Ann Marie Wolpe, 'Feminism and materialism', in *Feminism and Materialism: Women and modes of production*, Routledge & Kegan Paul: London, 1978, pp. 1–10; Christine Delphy, *Close to Home: A materialist analysis of women's oppression*, trans. Diana Leonard, Hutchinson: London, 1984.
2. The debates between Christine Delphy on the one side and Michèle Barrett and Mary McIntosh on the other indicate two versions of dual systems theory from England and the continent. See Delphy, *op. cit.*, pp. 154–81; Barrett, *Women's Oppression Today: Problems in Marxist feminist analysis*, Verso: London, 1980; Barrett and Mary McIntosh, 'Christine Delphy: towards a materialist feminism?', *Feminist Review*, Jan. 1979, pp. 95–106.
3. Lydia Sargent (ed.), *Women and Revolution: A discussion of the unhappy marriage of Marxism and feminism*, South End: Boston, MA, 1981.
4. Frigga Haug (ed.), *Female Sexualization: A collective work of memory*, trans. Erica Carter, Verso: London, 1987.
5. Roberta Hamilton and Michèle Barrett (eds.), *The Politics of Diversity: Feminism, Marxism, and nationalism*, Verso: London, 1987.
6. Judith Newton and Deborah Rosenfelt, 'Introduction: toward a materialist feminist criticism', in J. Newton and D. Rosenfelt (eds.), *Feminist Criticism and Social Change*, Methuen: New York, 1985, pp. xv–xxxix.
7. Cora Kaplan, *Sea Changes: Culture and feminism*, Verso: London, 1987.
8. The retrenchment in the eighties among western feminists from a political agenda aimed at wide-ranging social transformation has begun to be addressed critically by feminists on the left (see, for example, Winnie Breines *et al.*, 'Social biology, family studies, and anti-feminist backlash', *Feminist Studies*, 4, 1, 1978, pp. 43–67; Barbara Ehrenreich *et al.*, *Re-making Love: The feminization of sex*, Anchor: New York, 1986; Katha Pollitt, 'Being wedded is not always bliss', *The Nation*, 20 Sept. 1986, pp. 239–42; Judith Stacy, 'Sexism by a subtler name?: postindustrial conditions and postfeminist consciousness in the Silicon Valley', *Socialist Review*, 96, 6, 1987, pp. 7–28. However, because these critiques of postfeminism treat it as a regional phenomenon, they fail to demonstrate the ways the simultaneous professionalization of western women and the

increased emphasis on marriage and the nuclear family are possible because of the shift on to third-world women of modes of exploitation under which first-world women had previously suffered. The conditions of exploitation have not disappeared, they have simply been displaced. The privilege of postfeminism depends on the invisibility of this displacement.

9. Examples of new historicist readings of the nineteenth century include Thomas Laqueur, 'Orgasm, generation, and the politics of reproductive biology', *Representations*, 14, 1986, pp. 1–41; Mary Poovey, 'Scenes of an indelicate character: the medical "treatment" of Victorian women', *Representations*, 14, 1986, pp. 137–56.

10. [...] All quotations from Conan Doyle will be taken from *The Complete Sherlock Holmes*, Omega: Ware, 1986. [The analyses of 'Mussumat Kirpo's Doll' and 'A Divided Duty' are not included in this extract.]

11. For a critique and overview of post-Althusserian developments in Marxist theory see Terry E. Boswell, Edgar Kiser and Kathryn A. Baker, 'Recent developments in Marxist theories of ideology', *Insurgent Sociologist*, 13, 4, 1986, pp. 5–22; and the Student Marxist Collective, 'Postmodern marxist theories of ideology: a critical bibliography', in Teresa Ebert and Mas'ud Zavarzadeh (eds.), *Theories of Ideology: Althusser and after*, Indiana University Press: Bloomington, IN, forthcoming.

12. Stuart Hall, 'Notes on deconstructing "the popular"', in Raphael Samuel (ed.), *People's History and Social Theory*, London, 1981, pp. 227–40.

13. For an overview of recent theories of alterity see Mandy Merk, 'Difference and its discontents', *Screen*, 28, 1, 1987, pp. 2–9. For a materialist critique of French feminism see Gayatri Chakravorty Spivak, 'French feminism in an international frame', *Yale French Studies*, 62, 1981, pp. 154–84.

14. Homi Bhabha, 'The other question', *Screen*, 24, 6, 1983, pp. 18–36.

15. Watson's introduction to Holmes in 'A Study in Scarlet' makes clear Holmes's new professional class position (p. 15). Unlike the 'armchair lounger who evolves all those neat little paradoxes in the seculsion of his own study', Holmes's theories are so practical that he depends upon them for his 'bread and cheese' (p. 18). The kinds of knowledge he commands indicate a fairly 'new' middle-class position. He has mastered the new natural sciences – chemistry and geology – is familiar with sensational literature (gained from sources like the *Daily Telegraph*), and also dabbles in genteel and manly leisure-time activities. As the skilled detective who applies practical scientific knowledge to protecting the social order, Holmes typifies a re-articulated masculine subject position which emerged with the transformation of the state accompanying Britain's transition to monopoly capitalism. The criminology Holmes both studies and advances exemplifies one feature of this transformation: the recruitment of science for increased state intervention in civil society, deployed through the free entrepreneurial subject who spontaneously serves the interests of the state by striving to maintain law and order.

16. Abie Sachs and Joan Hoff Wilson, *Sexism and the Law: A study of male beliefs and legal bias in Britain and the United States*, Free Press: New York, 1978.

17. Feminist histories of this legislation have either applauded the reform as a landmark victory in feminist struggles for equality or in a more critical mode pointed to the ways equality under the new law was undermined by other legal and economic structures. For an example of the former see Lee Holcombe, *Victorian Ladies at Work: Middle-class working women in England and Wales, 1850–1914*, Archon: Hamden, CT, 1973; the latter position is exemplified in Dorothy M. Stetson, *A Woman's Issue: The politics of family law reform in England*, Greenwood: Westport, CT, 1982; Sachs and Wilson,

op. cit., point out that although the act gave women the right to their separate earnings and property, it did not grant them legal status as persons.

18. Women were not granted legal status as persons in British law until 1928 when an act of Parliament granted all adult women the vote: for an overview of the long struggle in the courts to grant women legal status as 'persons' following the Second Reform Act (1867), see Sachs and Wilson, *op. cit.*, pp. 22ff.

19. For an overview of the conditions under which middle-class women were recruited into the workforce see Holcombe, *Victorian Ladies at Work*, Jane Lewis, *Women in England, 1870–1950: Sexual divisions and social change*, Wheatsheaf: Brighton, 1984, pp. 145–205; Joan W. Scott and Louise A. Tilly, 'Women's work and the family in nineteenth-century Europe', in Alice Amsden (ed.), *The Economics of Women and Work*, St Martin's Press: New York, 1980, pp. 91–124.

20. Several other examples of the containment of this figure in the Sherlock Holmes stories include 'A Scandal in Bohemia' (1891) – the first of Conan Doyle's stories published in *The Strand Magazine* and one of the few in which Holmes is outwitted, and by a woman no less; 'A Case of Identity' (1891); and 'The Adventure of the Solitary Cyclist' (1903).

21. For an annotated version of the law see Earl of Halsbury, *The Laws of England*, vol. 10, 3rd edn, Butterworth: London, 1955, pp. 750ff.

22. Deborah Gorham, 'The maiden tribute of modern Babylon re-examined: child prostitution and the idea of childhood in late Victorian England', *Victorian Studies*, 21, 1978, pp. 353–79.

23. Two features of the consent law that bypass the state's 'protective' role demonstrate how the law's 'protection' of women actually safeguarded patriarchal privilege: the reasonable claim to possession – a husband could not be guilty of rape (upon marriage a woman forfeited her position as subject of consent to her husband's conjugal rights); and a 'reasonable cause to believe' that the girl was over 16 in effect sanctioned child prostitution for first offenders under 23, granting them the chance to sow their youthful wild oats (Halsbury, *op. cit.*, pp. 746, 751).

24. See, for example, Lee Holcombe, *Wives and Property: Reform of the Married Women's Property Law in nineteenth-century England*, University of Toronto Press: Toronto, 1983; Mary Poovey, 'Covered but not bound: Caroline Norton and the 1857 Matrimonial Causes Act', in *Uneven Developments: The ideological work of gender in mid-Victorian England*, University of Chicago Press: Chicago, IL, 1988, pp. 5–88; Sachs and Wilson, *op. cit.*, and Stetson, *op. cit.*, on property. On reform of consent law see Edward J. Bristow, *Vice and Vigilance: Purity movements in Britain since 1700*, Gill and Macmillan: Dublin, 1977; and Gorham, *op. cit.*

25. Jane Gallop, *The Daughter's Seduction: Feminism and psychoanalysis*, Cornell University Press: Ithaca, NY, 1982; Juliet Mitchell and Jacqueline Rose, *Feminine Sexuality: Jacques Lacan and the Ecole Freudienne*, Norton: New York, 1982.

26. Catherine Clément's work, 'Sorceress and hysteric', in Hélène Cixous and Catherine Clément, *The Newly Born Woman*, trans. Betsy Wing, University of Minnesota Press: Minneapolis, 1986, may seem a notable exception because she deals with woman as a historical construction. However, by failing to attend to the historical specificity of various constructions of the feminine – she equates the medieval sorceress and the nineteenth-century hysteric, 'in the same scene, caught in the same networks of language' (p. 10) – Clément posits a generic feminine subject whose resistance, much like the feminine body in Irigaray and Cixous, derives from a transcendent, ahistorical position.

27. Michel Foucault, *The History of Sexuality. Vol. 1: An introduction*, trans. Robert Hurley, Vintage: New York, 1980.

28. For a critique of Foucault from a Marxist position see Alex Callinicos, *Is There a Future for Marxism?*, Macmillan: London, 1982; and Dominique Lecourt, *Marxism and Epistemology: Bachelard, Canguilhem, Foucault*, trans. Ben Brewster, New Left Books: London, 1975.

29. Foucault, *op. cit.*, p. 109.

30. Incest was not penalized under civil law in Britain until 1908; prior to that time it was handled by the ecclesiastical courts. But it was a cultural preoccupation throughout the late nineteenth century, serving as a symbolic index of the vices of the lower-class residium. See Shiela Jeffreys, *The Spinster and Her Enemies: Feminism and sexuality, 1880–1930*, Pandora: London, 1985, p. 77.

31. Conan Doyle, 'The Copper Beeches', p. 253.

28 □ Kim *and* Orientalism

Patrick Williams

It might appear modish to be writing on *Kim* and Orientalism so soon after the publication of a book on the subject of 'Kipling and "Orientalism"'[1] but this essay is in some respects born of a double dissatisfaction with that book: first, because although the author confines himself to Kipling's Indian material, *Kim* receives very little consideration, and secondly, because in spite of the fact that the concept of Orientalism as elaborated by Edward Said[2] does have its problems, Moore-Gilbert's treatment of it is unnecessarily reductive.

There are, of course, other important reasons for choosing to write on *Kim*, foremost among which is the fact that it has been and continues to be regarded as in some way central, special, even unique, not only within Kipling's *oeuvre*, but also within the entire range of colonial literature. Among more traditional critics, Mark Kinkead-Weekes, for example, has insisted that it is

> the answer to nine-tenths of the charges levelled against Kipling and the refutation of most of the generalisations about him . . . a whole kaleidoscope of race, caste, custom, and creed, all seen with a warm affection that is almost unique in Kipling.[3]

What is more interesting is that recent critics, even radical ones, are prepared to accord it special status. (Not that Kipling's attraction for the Left is a recent phenomenon: Gramsci – to whom we shall return later – was an admirer of Kipling's work and wanted his sons to read it.) John McClure is representative of recent critics when he argues that *Kim* not only repudiates racist modes of characterisation, but also dramatises the repudiation, that it is a Utopian portrayal of future racial harmony, and that it is perhaps a more effective antidote to racial antipathies than any of Conrad's works (which he has already praised for their attacks on racist forms of representation).[4] A more radical critic, Abdul JanMohamed, in a recent article on colonial (or as he prefers to call it, colonialist)

From P. Mallett (ed.), *Kipling Considered*, Macmillan: London, 1989, pp. 33–35.

fiction, sees *Kim* as the novel which, above all others, explores the possibilities of bridging the gap which separates coloniser and colonised. More than this,

> We are thus introduced to a positive, detailed and nonstereotypic portrait of the colonized that is unique in colonialist literature. . . . What may initially seem like a rapt aesthetic appreciation of Indian cultures turns out, on closer examination, to be a positive acceptance and celebration of difference.[5]

The force of this assessment lies in the fact that Said and those critics who have followed him, such as JanMohamed and Homi Bhabha, have located the stereotype as perhaps the principal mechanism in ideologies of discrimination and domination at work in colonialism. To assert, therefore, that *Kim* offers the representation free of stereotypes is to make a very large claim indeed. It is claims of this nature which the present essay intends to examine. Another reason for continuing to scrutinise works such as *Kim* is that, although clearly neither Kipling the author nor the range of positions offered by his texts is reducible to the merely imperialist, it is nevertheless important to achieve as precise a notion as possible of the ways in which the texts were involved in the process of the Empire. As Said reminds us, texts may have very substantial material effects, be they social, political or economic, and nowhere, one might argue, is this more the case than within imperialism. Said also talks about the

> rather complex dialectic of reinforcement by which the experiences of readers in reality are determined by what they have read, and this in turn influences writers to take up subjects defined in advance by readers' experiences. . . . Most important, such texts can *create* not only knowledge but also the very reality they appear to describe.[6]

This is very much what one might call the Kipling effect, seen, for instance, in Leonard Woolf's inability to distinguish whether the people he met in the Empire were living their lives as Kipling characters, or whether Kipling was 'simply' describing the normal behaviour of the imperial ruling class. Another example of the interaction of text and 'reality' is the case of Lord Birkenhead, Secretary of State for India 1924–8, and vigorous imperialist. An inflexible opponent of concessions to the Indians, he considered it 'inconceivable' that India would ever be fit for self-government. We are told, nevertheless, that

> He had the 'feel' of the country in a manner unusual in one who had never visited it, and he attributed this to an intensive reading of Kipling's Indian books with their wonderful descriptive passages.[7]

Although the adjective is clearly used here in an approbatory sense, it is not difficult to see how profoundly 'unusual' both such a 'feel', and, more importantly, the far-reaching policy decisions based on it would be.

The theoretical assumptions behind this essay are partly those elaborated in Pierre Macherey's *A Theory of Literary Production*,[8] and partly those of Said in *Orientalism*. Macherey says, among other things, that we need to look both at the text and beyond it: at it, in order to see how it attempts to create its own unity, to establish the 'class of truth' which determines its meaning; beyond it, because it is not an isolated object, but part, and product, of a combination of socio-historical forces. Regarding the latter point, he says that the (inevitable) incorporation of ideology into a text results in certain textual silences, contradictions and inconsistencies which allow the reader to perceive the workings of that ideology, and that what ideology remains silent about is the reality of the historical situation.

Orientalism as defined by Said is

> the corporate institution for dealing with the Orient – dealing with it by making statements about it, authorizing views of it, describing it, by teaching it, settling it, ruling over it; in short, Orientalism is a Western style for dominating, restructuring and having authority over the Orient.[9]

It is particularly concerned with the production of knowledge as power, and with the representation of the Orient and its inhabitants as static, unchanging, incapable of change. With these points in mind, I hope to be able to interrogate some of the impressive claims made for *Kim*, and also to show something of the way in which the text relates to the larger Orientalist and imperialist projects. In doing so, I am aware that I am reading somewhat against the grain of critical consensus on *Kim*.

Turning to look at the text in more detail, I propose to examine three positions which it offers, attitudes which may be taken as exemplary by virtue of being held by characters to which the text gives credence, and through them to reveal the ways in which ideology works in the text.

I

> but thou art a Sahib and the son of a Sahib. Therefore do not
> at any time be led to contemn the black man.
> (Colonel Creighton to Kim)[10]

One of the principal reasons for the large amounts of praise bestowed on the book is its perceived sympathy for the Indians – as noted, for example, in the quotations from JanMohamed and Kinkead-Weekes. Within the context of Kipling's *oeuvre*, there is some truth in this: there would, for instance, appear to be nothing in *Kim* to equal the overt racism with which 'Beyond the Pale' opens. In addition, there is a significant increase in the proportion of the work devoted to Indians, and there are even a number of derogatory remarks made about white men. Demands for the fair treatment of Indians, such as that made by Creighton, are, however, undermined by what happens in the text, as are both the apparently improved representations of the Indians and the anti-British sentiments. Indeed, there is a sense in which the attitude is undermined before it is voiced: Creighton's command occurs half way through the book, but there have already been a number of opposing actions or assertions, one of which forms the opening to the story. Here, Kim has just kicked his Hindu and Muslim playmates off the cannon outside the Lahore Museum. This is justified, we are told, because whoever holds the cannon holds the Punjab; *Kim* is English (*sic*) and holds the cannon, and the English hold the Punjab. It is also acceptable for Kim to kick Chota Lal off the cannon, because, even though his father is worth half a million sterling, India is 'the only democratic land in the world' (*Kim*, p. 5). Given Kipling's unflattering views on democracy, this is a strange sort of compliment, carrying as it does the added implication that democracy is a licence for the poor to kick the rich, but in essence it is simply one more restatement of the (democratic) right of the white man to kick the native, however rich he may be.

More insidious than this, because less immediately visible, and more damning because more all-pervasive, is the depiction of Indians. While it is true that some – Hurree, the Sahiba, and, above all, Mahbub – are treated with a certain amount of sympathy, particularly as individuals, the cumulative picture, operating as it does almost subliminally, makes any stated intent not to 'contemn' look rather hollow. The ability of texts and larger discourses to cope with this particular type of apparent contradiction between the individual and the general is by no means unusual, and, as Said points out, the disparity in no way disrupts the certainties of Orientalism:

> For the general category in advance offers the specific instance a limited terrain in which to operate: no matter how deep the specific exception, no matter how much a single Oriental can escape the fences placed around him, he is *first* an Oriental, *second* a human being, and *last* again an Oriental.[11]

Indians are particularly 'contemned' as incompetent apers of the English: students from the university smoke cigars to try to appear like the English, but their cigars are cheap and rank-smelling; groups of pretentious long-coated natives gather to discuss philosophy with Lurgan; babus all speak English in order to show off (and inevitably do it badly). It will be noted that these are particularly middle-class failings, and the fact that it was the British who had encouraged the Indian middle class to copy them in the first place was an irony not lost on the Indians, even though it was something which the British preferred to forget.

Kim, however, is said to be the book in which Kipling's regard for Indian religions is most clearly displayed. According to Noel Annan,

> Kipling . . . implied that the Indians were as superior to the British in matters of religion as the British were to them in material power.[12]

Certainly, there is very little that is positive in the portrayal of the representatives of Christianity in *Kim*: Reverend Bennett, in particular, deserves the uncomprehended insults which Kim lavishes on him, and, compared to the lama, both he and Father Victor lack dignity and tolerance. It is the figure of Teshoo lama which makes claims on behalf of Kipling's attitude to religion possible, and yet even he, most sympathetic of holy men, is seen as childish, unthinking, incapable – to the point of self-destruction – of existence in the real world. Despite the supposed sympathy for the lama, and Kim's growing affection for him, none of the characters seems to have the slightest qualms about abusing his spiritual quest by turning it into the cover for a counter-espionage mission, and, moreover, keeping him in the dark about the fact. Also, the moral of the quest would seem to be that without the help of the white man, the native has no hope of reaching enlightenment, salvation, full human status, or whatever: note the lama's insistence that 'the Search is sure' once Kim returns to him, and his equal conviction of the impossibility of success in his absence. Also, much has been made by critics of the fact that when, at the end of the book, Teshoo achieves enlightenment, he renounces Nirvana at the cost of great spiritual suffering, purely for Kim's sake (the implication no doubt being that this is only right, since he would not have got there without Kim's help), whereas, in fact, as a Tibetan – and therefore Mahayana – Buddhist, there is no question of his going to Nirvana until all sentient beings are ready to go, and in this cosmic perspective Kim is almost entirely irrelevant.

More than this, however, and rather than any positive attitude, there is a widespread negativity in the text towards Indian religion in general, and its practitioners in particular. Its priests, no matter what their allegiance, are described as relentlessly greedy for money, demanding large sums in exchange for inefficacious prayers and charms, and prepared even to go to the extent of robbing other priests. Not only is the country priest-ridden, however, but, being India, it is seen as unable to do anything about it:

All India is full of holy men stammering gospels in strange tongues; shaken and consumed in the fires of their own zeal; dreamers, babblers and visionaries: as it has been from the beginning and will continue to the end. (*Kim*, p. 43)

In addition, all Indians are profoundly superstitious and endlessly gullible in matters of religion and its cognate, magic. The Jat farmer, whose child Kim cures, is a good example – willing to believe not only that Kim can bodily transmute a trader from one part of the country into a religious mendicant from another, but also that if he dares to speak of what he has glimpsed, his house, fields, cattle and crops will all be blighted. Even a good Western-style education is not proof against racial characteristics of this sort, as we see when Hurree Babu (MA Calcutta) watches, trembling, Huneefa's ceremony of protection for Kim, vainly attempting to convince himself of the unreality of what he is witnessing.

Another universal characteristic of religion in India is the lack of discrimination of its practitioners. Benares is a microcosm of this:

Benares struck him [Kim] as a peculiarly filthy city, though it was pleasant to see how his cloth was respected. At least one-third of the population prays eternally to some group or other of the many million deities, and so reveres every sort of holy man. (p. 252)

A concomitant to this indiscriminateness is a lack of adherence to one's own religion, which is even enshrined in proverbs, as Kim quotes to Mahbub Ali: 'I will change my faith and my bedding, but *thou* must pay for it' (p. 176). Christianity may be a debased thing in Kipling's eyes, but the corresponding idea of a white man becoming a Hindu or Buddhist, and particularly for money, is unthinkable.

II

> 'The more one knows about natives the less one can say what they will or won't do.'
> 'That's consolin' – from the head of the Ethnological Survey'.
> (Colonel Creighton to Father Victor, p. 151)

This is an interesting exchange: Creighton utters what seems a classic formulation of Kipling-style Orientalism, but Father Victor's rejoinder adds a curious note of ambiguity. Is Father Victor in fact consoled that, like himself, the head of the Ethnological Survey cannot understand Indians, or is he ironically observing that the summation of the knowledge of the head of the Survey amounts to no more than this? Also, are we to assume that Creighton's ignorance is merely a function of his Ethnological persona, rather than his (undisclosed) Secret Service one? Regardless of how we interpret the conversation, Creighton's authoritative statement of one of the basic tenets of the white man's creed is contradicted by the events of the book.

In both of his guises, Creighton is in charge of collecting information, and it is obviously no small irony that the Survey, which is supposed to be concerned with scientific – and therefore, it would be claimed, disinterested – information, is in fact a spy network, and that the 'disinterested' information which is collected about the country is used for improved political control. Even such knowledge as is gathered by Creighton and Hurree and not specifically used in the maintenance of British power can hardly be said to be disinterested, since for both of them it represents the possibility of prestige in future membership of the Royal Society. (The slightly desperate air surrounding Hurree's efforts to succeed indicates the presence of yet another inadequate Indian attempt to emulate the British.) Further, the idea that, regardless of the way in which they operated in conjunction with colonialism, the new nineteenth-century sciences of ethnology and anthropology might aspire to a 'pure', impartial form will not stand scrutiny. As Christine Bolt points out, both racist bias and the desire for knowledge as socio-political control were built into them from the very first. Speaking of the newly-formed Anthropological Institute of Great Britain and Ireland, Bolt says:

Rejecting the Enlightenment stress on the similarity of men's bodies, the new society's president, Dr James Hunt, and his followers endeavoured (not without opposition) to prove the inferiority of blacks by means of craniology and comparative anatomy. This element clearly wished to see some practical application for their findings, challenged propositions in favour of the equality of the races, and advanced a racist position regarding the behaviour and condition of blacks in the United States and West Indies.[13]

And lest craniology should appear a rather flimsy foundation on which to base such important classifications, consider the case of H. H. Risley, member of the Viceroy's executive council and acknowledged authority on race, who used measurements of people's noses as evidence of the social and racial status of their ancestors.

However much it may represent acceptable, and accepted, ideology, Creighton's assertion must be wrong, especially in the case of those like himself whose Secret Service operations are to a large extent predicated on the use of acquired knowledge precisely to anticipate and forestall the various plots and contemplated treacheries. Like Creighton, then, the statement plays a double game (and perhaps more than one). On the one hand, it is a gesture of disavowal and concealment; it is Creighton in disguise, Creighton 'the father of fools', and as such is a lie; yet it is also one of the great (ideological) 'truths' of Empire, with the power to determine innumerable decisions and actions. At the same time, while it suggests the pointlessness of acquiring knowledge about natives – made famous in the lines like these from 'One Viceroy Resigns':

> You'll never plumb the Oriental mind,
> And if you did, it isn't worth the toil,[14]

– it also identifies that apparent resistance of Indians to Western attempts to 'know' them, which makes it all the more imperative that such attempts be repeated and extended.

As well as being contradicted by what Creighton is and does, this position is undercut by the forms of knowledge circulated in the text. Orientalism, as adjunct of colonial control, is pre-eminently involved in the production of various categories of knowledge about 'the native': historical, linguistic, religious, moral, political. This knowledge is most frequently presented in the form of bold syntheses, universal norms, invariant truths about Orientals, and one of its most obvious effects is the ability to say with enormous certainty exactly how they will or will not behave, which, being products of their eternally unchanging Oriental society, is exactly the same as the way they have behaved for centuries. If it is not already so, such knowledge is all too easily converted into stereotypes, and it is in this form that it most easily circulates in colonial literature. Interestingly enough, it is this fault which, as mentioned earlier, Abdul JanMohamed feels that Kipling spectacularly avoids, managing to produce 'a positive, detailed, non-stereotypic portrait of the colonized that is unique in colonialist literature'. However, despite the apparent air of benevolence which envelops the text, the more one reads it, the more derogatory stereotypes come to light, and although the narrative voice which enunciates them speaks as if from personal experience, thereby lending added weight to the condemnation, there is no sense of individualised observation, rather the mere reiteration of the already-known truths of Oriental degeneracy.

Foremost among such truths is that of the duplicitous, perpetually untruthful Oriental. It is no doubt a measure of the effect of India on him that 'Kim could lie like an Oriental' (p. 31) and that he and Mahbub Ali lie to everyone except one another. We also learn that natives never tell the truth to strangers – unlike their rulers, who are 'open-spoken English folk' (p. 199). This opposition occurs more than once: 'The English do eternally tell the truth,' he said, 'therefore we of this country are eternally made foolish' (p. 188). Even the westernised Hurree finds the English habit of demanding a straight and honest answer very unsettling. (It is perhaps worth setting beside these 'truths' the fact that in the book it is the English who are involved in the perpetration of deception and lies on a massive scale, in the shape of the Secret Service.)

According to Orientalist categorization, one of the principal attributes of Orientals is that they are deficient or abnormal *vis-à-vis* the English, no matter what the context. In *Kim* we are told that Indians lack a proper sense of time: 'All hours of the twenty four are alike to Orientals' (p. 35); 'Even an Oriental, with an Oriental's views of the value of time' (p. 30); of motion: 'Swiftly – as Orientals understand speed' (p. 191); of order: 'the happy Asiatic disorder' (p. 86); of sound: 'he had all the Oriental's indifference to mere noise' (p. 188) – no doubt because they make so much of it; of organisation: 'so he abandoned the project and fell back, Oriental fashion, on time and chance' (p. 143); and of correct speech, so that when they are not using 'what to a European would have been bad language' (p. 88), they are indulging in 'the usual aimless babble that every low-caste native must raise on every occasion' (p. 184). The list is very long, but these may serve as an indication of just how stereotypically Indians are represented.

There are other ways in which knowledge functions in the text. One of the staples of Orientalism is that it is Europeans who provide Orientals with the first accurate descriptions and proper explanations of their history, religion, language, and so on. Despite infrequent remarks such as 'The Sahibs have not *all* the world's wisdom' (p. 259) their control of its knowledge is so undisputed that a great Buddhist sage (Teshoo is one of only three men alive who can both draw and explicate the Wheel of Life) must come to an English museum curator for information about his own religion. He also appeals to the curator as the 'Fountain of Wisdom' and is astonished at how much white men know about Buddhism. Also, it is another white man, Lurgan, who teaches Kim the little he does not already know about things Indian.

Kim himself represents the apogee of a particular incarnation of Orientalism – the Englishman who has such a mastery of Oriental culture that he can pass for one of 'them'. This figure has its origins in travellers like Sir Richard Burton and Edward William Lane, whose accounts of their exploits begat a textual lineage particularly gratifying to the English sensibility. It was obvious at the time that England's technological and military superiority could forcibly subdue other countries, but

Burton and Lane were proof that an Englishman could meet the Orient on its own terms and outwit it. The ideological power of the figure is no doubt also a function of its compensatory force, given that the English in India were aware of the fact that they were extraordinarily visible, culturally ignorant and linguistically maladroit.

It is noticeable that when this figure makes its appearance in Kipling's fiction, as it does in stories like 'Miss Youghal's Sais' and 'The Mark of the Beast' in the shape of Strickland, the mastery and the knowledge it provides are specifically used for the purpose of social and political control. Kim, of course, is more than Strickland: like the almost mythical and unnamed individual on whom Strickland models himself, Kim can pass for a member of any religion, class or caste, and when Strickland makes his guest appearance in *Kim*, his part in the Great Game seems very much that of a white man in contrast to Kim's role. Despite the characterization of Kim and Strickland as anti-authoritarian figures, or at least disturbers of official procedures by their individualism, their abilities serve to maintain British rule just as surely as if they did everything by the book, perhaps even more so.

It is perhaps only to be expected that a text so concerned with disguise, appearance and reality, magic and illusion should be so singularly adept at operating its own forms of textual disguise and illusion. One manifestation of the illusion has already been mentioned; namely, that whereby the text convinces critics of all persuasions that it is in fact presenting a positive, non-stereotypical view of Indians. The illusion extends even to factual details, so that critics are led to assert that, for example,

> The action of the book encompasses much of India, moving the reader from west to east along the Great Trunk Road, and from the sweltering south to the superb Himalayan north[15]

when in fact the action takes place in a restricted area in northern India and never gets near the 'sweltering south' at all.

More importantly, the text itself is a dialogue, even a dialectical interaction, between the 'real' on the one hand, and, on the other, the world of magic, dreams, illusion and fable. Moore-Gilbert mentions the way in which those colonial texts which used the conventions of the Gothic, apparently the most unreal of modes, were still liable to be read as works of almost photographic realism, and this is another way in which the illusion of *Kim* functions, with this eminently fabular work consistently being read as the supreme example of realist fiction on India.

The interaction of 'real' and 'unreal' operates in other ways. Thus, for example, we find the text creating the sort of reality effect described by Barthes, advertising itself as 'the real' through its accumulation of detail, particularly of Indian life (and almost in the spirit of an ethnologist), yet at the same time, these details which supposedly ground the text in the real are likely to concern magic, prophecy or elements of the supernatural. Similarly, the text, in a manner reminiscent of Kipling's early stories but with greater force, claims an extra-textual veracity (asserting, for example, that Kim and the lama are real people outside the confines of the narrative[16]), while simultaneously abolishing reality within the text, in its denial of the political and historical realities of the Indian situation. This interplay is evident in the way that *Kim* addresses the principal British source of obsessive imperial anxiety in the late nineteenth century – Russian territorial ambitions in Asia – and yet manages to neutralise it at a stroke. There is also a definite dreamlike quality about the ease with which the bugbear can be knocked down (by Kim's little adventure) and yet always spring up again – the Great Game ceaselessly repeating itself, and only ending, as Hurree points out, when everyone is dead.

III

> How can a man follow the Way or the Great Game when he is eternally pestered by women? ... When I was a child it was well enough, but now I am a man and they will not regard me as a man.
>
> (Kim to himself, p. 348)

> Nevertheless, *Kim* is a triumph of exploratory vision. ... Only in one respect, the attitude to woman, does the myopia remain, and it is marginal. ... He has oddly, because so irrelevantly, touched once or twice on Kim's sexual attractiveness, and several times preached the old doctrine of the nuisance of women. On the other hand, the irrelevance shows how marginal the fault is.[17]

The text tries to marginalise women; the critic tries to marginalise the fault ...

Certainly, the position of women in *Kim* is unusual. The first thing to notice is that, apart from a disembodied voice telling Creighton that the commander-in-chief has arrived, and a soldier's wife who asks Kim if he thinks her husband will come back from the war, there are no white women in the book at all. Although Kipling, in a letter, attributed the absence to a reluctance to portray the memsahibs who, he felt (and current ideology concurred), were responsible for unsatisfactory racial relations, it is possible, as we shall see later, to regard such an absence as ideologically determined in other ways. The lack of white women may, for example, function as a potential escape clause by allowing, within the terms of the text, the unspoken displacement of the condemnation of women from women in general to Indian women in particular, since the latter are the only ones we see. Certainly, too, the text preaches 'the old doctrine of the nuisance of women' with great consistency. Whatever path a man chooses for himself in life, whether action (the Great Game) or contemplation (the Way), women are there to hinder him, we are told, with their ceaseless talk, or their sexual importuning, or both.

It may at first sight seem incongruous, in a book where all the major male characters are celibate, to lay as much stress as the text does on Kim's sexual attractiveness, but it is not, *pace* Kinkead-Weekes, irrelevant, nor is it 'once or twice'. This world of male celibacy inscribes rejection of women in the very form of the text, and creates the value-laden opposition: female = uncontrolled language (chatter, babble) = uncontrolled sexuality (prostitution, sexual propositioning) *vs* male = control of language (silence, secrets) = sexual control (abstention, celibacy).

Also, although Kim, the lama, and others may say that women are a nuisance and a hindrance, this is belied by the way that, throughout the book, Kim actively seeks them out, generally in order to manipulate or exploit them in some fashion. As Kim has discovered, 'few could resist' his charms, and he uses them on the Mohammedan girl (to get cigars), the vegetable seller (to get food), the Amritsar courtesan (to get money and a ticket), the cultivator's wife (to get food, and later, a bed for the night), the Sahiba on pilgrimage (to get money and food), the prostitute in Lucknow (for the means of disguise), and the Woman of Shamlegh (for information-carrying, food, money, porters) – apart, that is, from 'the girl at Akrola of the Ford and . . . the scullion's wife behind the dovecot – not counting the others' (p. 348). It is no doubt a measure both of Kim's powers of attraction and her own preternatural powers of perception that the magic-working Huneefa declares – before we realise that she is blind – that he 'is very good to look upon' (p. 240) – a sentiment echoed by Mahbub Ali and those women characters who call him a heart-breaker.

'[T]here are but two sorts of women . . . those who take the strength out of a man and those who put it back' (p. 374), says the Sahiba, acknowledging that she was previously one of the former, as – the inference is plain – are all the other women encountered in the book, with their endless wearying chatter and their exhausting sexuality. Even though this does at least allow the possibility of there being good women, its dichotomy can no more stand up to scrutiny in the face of the evidence already cited than can Kim's simple denunciation. For, once again, how far would Kim have got in his travels or in the Great Game without the strength that these supposedly debilitating women put into him in the shape of food, shelter, money and numerous forms of assistance? This is particularly true in the case of the Woman of Shamlegh, without whose help Kim and the lama (both exhausted, it should be noted, not through the fault of women, but through following their respective manly pursuits) could not possibly have returned to the safety of the Sahiba's house; and the crisis which she, the Woman of Shamlegh, represents helps to elucidate the type of ideology at work in the text.

Critics like John McClure have pointed to the importance of the fact that the Woman of Shamlegh is in fact Lispeth, from the story of that name, the first of the *Plain Tales from the Hills*, making a reappearance, but the conclusions they draw are in general unsatisfactory. It is clear – as she herself points out – that Lispeth is not like other women. Hitherto, it has hardly seemed to matter how many hearts Kim breaks, since their owners are doubly insignificant, being not only female but too old, like the Sahiba and her cousin, or too young, like the girls in the rissaldar's village; socially unacceptable – scullion's wives, and so on; morally unacceptable – a variety of prostitutes; or totally unacceptable – the hill women are 'unlovely and unclean, wives of many husbands, and afflicted with goitre' (p. 315). Now, however, we have a woman with power who is 'aught but unlovely' (p. 345), 'no common bearer of babes' (p. 348), and who calmly and boldly propositions Kim, offering not only herself but the village and all it contains. She is thus revealed as Kim's last and greatest temptation, and the anomaly of Kim's being the only white character who is obviously sexual is resolved: Kim is allowed sexuality so that he may triumph over it, in the unacceptable shape in which it presents itself, as part of his rites of passage to (proper) manhood.

McClure suggests that the situation of Kim and Lispeth parallels that in the earlier story, but that, unlike the first Englishman who deceives and rejects Lispeth, 'Kim deals with the Woman of Shamlegh frankly, fairly and generously'.[18] It is difficult to see how such an interpretation can be justified however, when Kim knowingly deceives her (since despite the clearly acknowledged understanding between them, he presumably has no intention of sleeping with her as the reward for her work as messenger), and then, when she asks for what he has promised, rejects her. The fact that Lispeth, having been not only rejected but also insulted by Kim as a 'woman of ill-omen' (p. 358), still provides Kim and the lama with all manner of assistance, makes her all the more remarkable, and in many ways superior to Kim. Twice now, however, she has been sufficiently foolish or forgetful of her position to harbour designs on a Sahib, and twice she has been spurned. The lesson to be learned from her treatment is clearly that what Kim has to avoid is not the tedious timewasting of chattering women, but the snares of inter-racial sex. Far from there being, as McClure says, a 'symbolic union' between Kim and Lispeth, there is, I would suggest, what in the text's terms is a properly irrevocable sundering. Lispeth's final question, 'you will come back again?' (p. 361), which McClure sees as somehow marking the difference between Kim and the first Englishman, nevertheless – and significantly – goes unanswered. No doubt Kim has had enough of perjuring himself for one day.

As well as carrying reminders of the cautionary tales of Trejago and Bisesa, and Holden and Ameera in *Plain Tales* and *Life's Handicap*, this situation helps to explain a certain silence or omission in one of the remarks quoted earlier. When Creighton tells Kim not to 'contemn the black man', he neglects to say anything about people of mixed race – the Eurasians – and it is these whom Kim most viciously 'contemns', as in the following, oddly tautological, remark on his schoolfellows, which manages to cast a slur on both Indians and Eurasians:

'Their eyes are blued and their nails are blackened with low-caste blood, many of them. Sons of *metheeranees* [sweeper women] – brothers-in-law to the *bhungi* [sweeper].'
    We need not follow the rest of the pedigree, but Kim made his little point clearly and without heat, chewing a piece of sugar-cane the while. (p. 194)

Also, in the 'do not be led to contemn' conversation, Kim attributes racist attitudes in the school solely to Eurasian boys, and yet he accounts for this by making a racist remark himself. The silence on the question of Eurasians is paralleled by that on the Western-educated Indian middle class, a group which, like the Eurasians, was deliberately created by the British and then systematically denounced and discriminated against by them.

Although the dangers of sexual contact form a recurrent theme in Kipling's work, particularly in the early stories, the way in which the point is remade here, using the repetition of Lispeth for added emphasis, can be seen as an indication of the current state of racial ideology. In the final years of the century, the pressures to avoid miscegenation were greater than ever. Particularly during Curzon's viceroyalty (1899–1905), the penalties for taking a native wife or mistress included not only loss of social position, but also frequently the loss of professional position too, and this applied even more in India itself than in other parts of the greater Indian empire such as Burma. Curzon became especially worried about the dangers of contact between white women and Indian men, and for this reason often refused permission for Indian princes to go to Britain. The original justification for this was so that the princes could not corrupt Englishwomen, but it was later changed, this time in order that the princes might not be corrupted by white women. The official view of the situation is given in the correspondence of Curzon and Lord George Hamilton:

> Strange as it may seem, English women of the housemaid class, and even higher, do offer themselves to these Indian soldiers, attracted by their uniforms, enamoured of their physique, and with a sort of idea that the warrior is also an oriental prince.
> (Curzon to Hamilton)

> Apparently it pervades all classes of society: the smartest peeresses were only too ready to make a fuss with Bikaner and the other Indian chiefs, and as you go lower in the social scale, so does this tendency manifest itself more strongly and in a way characteristic of the habits and lives of the respective classes of the community. At Hampton Court the great difficulty of the officers was in keeping white women away from our Native soldiers.
> (Hamilton to Curzon)[19]

Once again, then, the purity of the race was in danger, but that this time it was the ideologically most sensitive element – English womanhood, which had been the most powerful rallying cry ever since the Indian Mutiny in 1857 (and was not to stop being so now) – which posed the threat, called for a correspondingly forceful ideological counter-offensive in terms of the condemnation of inter-racial sex, and of blaming female sexuality for a supposedly deteriorating situation. Racial superiority was, by the end of the century, one of the few remaining justifications for British rule, and the perceived threat from uncontrolled female sexuality (here rendered as uncontrolled *Indian* female sexuality, the truth being literally unspeakable), was a grave one indeed.

The problem of race is also posed by the text in another way – in Kim himself, his search for personal identity being also a realisation of racial identity. On the surface at least, there is a fascinating amount of playing with the boundaries of race and of mixing of categories: for example, much is made of Kim's apparent racial indefiniteness; as he says to Mahbub Ali, 'What am I? Mussulman, Hindu, Jain, or Buddhist?' (p. 193), and people he meets never seem to suspect that he is other than he wishes to appear. At the same time, running through the text as a sort of counterpoint, is the statement 'Once a Sahib, always a Sahib'. The situation is nevertheless presented as if there were a choice for Kim, in which case a determining factor would no doubt be the nature of the races he might elect to join. We have already seen something of the available knowledge about Indians. Juxtaposed to this we are given a (restrained) amount of information about what it means to be a Sahib: Sahibs tell the truth; Sahibs cannot steal; Sahibs must act; Sahibs must obey; no Sahib would follow a Bengali's advice; Sahibs are a strong-backed breed who never grow old; Sahibs are the right ones to oversee justice because they know the land.

Apart from any racial determinism implied in 'Once a Sahib, always a Sahib', it would be astonishing, given these two sets of 'knowledge' about the races, if Kim chose to be an Indian. And of course he does not. The real problem in textual terms is how to make him black enough to fool everyone, but white enough to be recuperable as a Sahib – a recurrent difficulty for those colonial texts which wished to appear to question racial norms without really doing so. The usual unsophisticated solution was to allow the reader to assume that a particular character was black and then, by way of denouement, discover a respectable white parentage for them, as, for instance, in E. M. Hull's *The Sheik*. Here, the problem is resolved by making Kim *culturally* Indian and *naturally* British, and in such a contest the power of Nature is bound to win. Although, therefore, *Kim* gives the appearance of greater honesty in this respect, we might wish to question just how honest such an over-determined 'choice' or contest really is.

Another related but perhaps more genuine choice is not made until late in the book. Although Kim's fate as a Sahib might appear to be sealed from the time he enters St Xavier's, it is not until his second identity crisis at the end of the book that he opts for the 'real' world of materiality and common sense, which is *par excellence* that of the Englishman, rather than the morally superior but practically useless world of the lama.

The revealing/significant silence of the text in this respect concerns the extent to which Kim can really be a Sahib, even after his choice. It is not at all clear how far Kim, as 'a poor white of the very poorest' (p. 1) and Irish to boot, fits the image of the Sahib, which is very much more that of Colonel Creighton, *pukka* Englishman of the ruling class. There is a sense in which Kim's masters are playing a deceitful (great) game with him – much as the text plays with the readers – in suggesting that someone of his background can truly be a Sahib, other than in the spuriously levelling context of simple racial categories.

As a poor white, Kim is the inheritor of the most contradictory attitudes to the Indians – which may go some way towards explaining his being the Little Friend of all the World, but also being so unsuccessful at not 'contemning'. Along with the working class, the Irish were the group most frequently conflated with blacks by imperialists, as, for example, in the remark by Lord Salisbury, three times Prime Minister between 1886 and 1902, that the Irish were as fitted for self-government as the Hottentots. Both Irish and working class were held to be responsible for the worst excesses of racism, but they also showed the greatest solidarity with other oppressed groups – as when Irish people working in Scotland Yard helped Indian nationalists to smuggle documents. (The fact that this represents one of the best examples of collaboration shows how limited a scope the solidarity of the oppressed had.)[20]

Although there has been a certain amount of blurring of racial distinctions in the book – in Kim's relationship with the lama and with Mahbub Ali; in the figure of Strickland; in Kim himself – the effect is of *reculer pour mieux sauter*: distinctions are blurred in order to be more strictly redefined, in the same way that Kim is offered temptation so that correct sexual behaviour may be reasserted. Whatever doubts are created, whatever edges temporarily blurred, the central tenet, that Sahibs can and must continue to rule India, goes unquestioned, and it is only in Kim's contradictory relation to his status as Sahib, of which the text does not/cannot speak, that any questioning of whether the nature and function of Sahibs are such self-evident things can begin.

Another issue which the text treats in a less than straightforward manner is that of British political power in India. It is sufficiently present not to constitute one of the textual silences, the 'not-said' in Macherey's terms, but it is subject to another ideological operation, the attempt to make it appear as much a part of the natural order of things as possible. Thus, it is simply taken for granted that foreigners are wicked and must be kept out of India since any actual discussion of the rightness of British rule would risk exposing its shaky foundations (not to mention its foreignness). Similarly, the political reasons for opposition to the Russians are shifted to the 'natural' plane of the racial and/or personal: they are not proper white men because they follow the advice of a Bengali, because they do not understand natives or treat them correctly as 'we' do, and because they are not merry slaughterers of animals like Yankling Sahib. British control is similarly naturalised by the fact that spying (on Indians) is done by Indians, making it seem as if it were done in their interests, even as if they might be controlling their own political destiny. Linked to this is the way in which much of the pro-British propaganda – about the Sahibs being a strong-backed breed, the proper overseers of justice, and so on – is put in the mouths of Indian characters, making it seem, once again, more right and natural.

It remains, by way of conclusion, to suggest in a little more detail how *Kim* as aesthetic object forms part of the socio-historical processes of its period, in line with the second part of Macherey's approach. In the context of Orientalism, Said talks of the way in which the discourse aspires to the production of a vision of a static, unchanging Orient, for which its truths would have permanent validity, and of how this state is disturbed by narrative, the representation of historical process. In *Kim* there is the contradiction between the movement of the picaresque form and the stasis of the dehistoricised vision of an India free of internal conflict and about which the classic Orientalist generalisations can be uttered. This contradiction may be more apparent than real, however, since we are presented with a curiously circumscribed and non-disruptive picaresque, the end of whose journeying is to uphold rather than to disturb the existing order. In the struggle between action and contemplation, it would seem that Kim's choice of the former is vindicated, but it is an action whose aim is stasis, the maintenance of the status quo, rather than change of any sort. As Lord Salisbury said a year or two previously:

> Whatever happens will be for the worse, and therefore it is in our interests that as little should happen as possible.[21]

In aesthetic terms, this relates to the way in which the text produces the state of the Empire as an object for contemplation, a defused, dehistoricised spectacle, in much the same way as, for example, contemporary showmen were producing elements of imperial history as spectacle, with conflict contained and contradictions removed.[22] Empire as spectacle is also the appropriate aesthetic object for the period of Victoria's Jubilee celebrations, whose central message – we are all one big happy imperial family – finds its echo in Kim's India, where everyone would coexist so peacefully were it not for the trouble-making of foreigners jealous of Britain's achievements.

Finally, in producing this vision of the happy imperial family, *Kim* can be seen as both registering and participating in an important historical development. McClure makes the interesting suggestion that the book is a plea on behalf of the country-born Englishman (that is, born and bred in India), as the rightful ruler, rather than the 'genuine imported Sahib from England' (p. 204). However, far from being, as McClure then goes on to describe it, an elegy for imperial power about to decay, *Kim*, I would suggest, is a refracted image of political realignment, the ruling class in the process of transition, but manoeuvring to strengthen its hold rather than bidding farewell to its power; in other words, nothing less than the change from a form of government based on domination to one which used those strategies of hegemony (leadership and consent) which characterise more complex, essentially bourgeois, political systems.

According to Gramsci, in order for a class to become hegemonic it has to create a 'collective national-popular will', to take into account (to a certain extent) the needs of other classes, and to exercise power based on a series of strategic alliances with the other classes or elements within them. This is very much the situation both within Britain and in the Empire towards the end of the nineteenth century. In the wake of the electoral reforms of 1867, the Tory government, worried that the extended franchise would result in 'anarchy' – loss of power for the Tory government – set out deliberately to make itself more 'national-popular' and to create alliances, and the Empire was of central importance in both of these. The coincidence of ruling-class and working-class interests, which, according to the Tories, the Empire represented, became such a powerful force in late nineteenth-century politics that a change of government did not result in a change of policy, and thus, for example, the Liberal retreat from Empire, which was expected to occur with Gladstone's fourth ministry in 1892, did not materialise.

In India, different sorts of alliances had to be created to meet the changing conditions. Why the suggestion from McClure mentioned above is interesting is that it implicitly recognises one of the important aspects of *Kim*, the production of a new version of rulers and ruled. It is noticeable that this no longer consists of the old favourite of prince and peasant as the natural and proper combination; indeed, the princes in *Kim* are disaffected and rebellious. Instead, we have the country-born Englishman (as close to a mixture of English and Indian as racial ideology would permit), and the good Indian (more or less all of them, in the text's rosy vision). McClure's suggestion carries the unspoken but intriguing implication of the country-born English working to become a more autonomous colonial ruling class, like the *pieds noirs* in Algeria, and to that end attempting to forge an alliance with the Indians they would continue to rule. A text which not only figures such an alliance but also provides (a convincing illusion of) the sort of improved representations which might generate consent among the ruled is clearly at the heart of such a hegemonic project. It is entirely in keeping with what we have already seen of the visionary strategies at work within *Kim* that it says nothing of the real realignments occurring in Indian politics – for example, the admitting of Indian politicians to consultative positions in the 1890s – and instead offers this hypothetical alliance as not only right and natural but already in place, a combination which inevitably reveals it for the ideological construct it is.

Notes

1. B. J. Moore-Gilbert, *Kipling and 'Orientalism'*, London, 1986.
2. See particularly Edward Said, *Orientalism*, London, 1978; reprint Penguin: Harmondsworth, 1985, and an article, 'Orientalism reconsidered', in Francis Barker, Peter Hulme, Margaret Iversen and Diane Loxley (eds.), *Europe and its Others*, Proceedings of the Essex Conference on the Sociology of Literature, vol. 1, University of Essex: Colchester, 1985, pp. 14–27. My dissatisfaction with Moore-Gilbert's book also extends to Said's introduction to the new Penguin edition of *Kim*, though for rather different reasons. Unfortunately, it is beyond the scope of this article to address the issues they raise.
3. Mark Kinkead-Weekes, 'Vision in Kipling's novels', in Andrew Rutherford (ed.), *Kipling's Mind and Art*, Edinburgh and London, 1964, pp. 233, 216.
4. John McClure, 'Problematic presence: the colonial other in Kipling and Conrad', in David Dabydeen (ed.), *The Black Presence in English Literature*, Manchester, 1985, pp. 154–67.
5. Abdul JanMohamed, 'The economy of Manichean allegory: the function of racial difference in colonialist literature', *Critical Inquiry*, 12, Autumn 1985, p. 78.
6. Said, *Orientalism*, p. 94.
7. Frederick Smith, 2nd Earl of Birkenhead, *F. E.: The Life of F. E. Smith, First Earl of Birkenhead*, London, 1960, p. 506.
8. Pierre Macherey, *A Theory of Literary Production*, London, 1978.
9. Said, *Orientalism*, p. 3.
10. Kipling, *Kim*, p. 160 in the Sussex Edition; all subsequent page references will accompany the quotation.

11. Said, *Orientalism*, p. 102.
12. Noel Annan, 'Kipling's place in the history of ideas', in Rutherford, *op. cit.*, p. 109.
13. Christine Bolt, 'Race and the Victorians', in C. C. Eldridge, *British Imperialism in the 19th Century*, London, 1984, p. 129.
14. Kipling, 'One Viceroy Resigns', in *Rudyard Kipling's Verse: Definitive edition*, London, 1942, p. 69.
15. J. McClure, *Kipling and Conrad: The colonial fiction*, Cambridge, MA, 1981, p. 71.
16. See, for example, pp. 206, 233, 242–3, 274–5.
17. Kinkead-Weekes, *op. cit.*, p. 233.
18. McClure, *op. cit.*, p. 75.
19. Curzon–Hamilton correspondence, quoted in K. Ballhatchet, *Race, Sex and Class under the Raj*, London, 1981, pp. 119–20.
20. On this, see V. G. Kiernan, *The Lords of Humankind*, London, 1969, ch. 1, and Bolt, *op. cit.*.
21. Quoted in B. Porter, *The Lion's Share: A short history of British imperialism, 1850–1983*, London, 1984, p. 153.
22. See Ben Shepherd, 'Showbiz imperialism', in J. Mackenzie (ed.), *Imperialism and Popular Culture*, Manchester, 1986, pp. 94–112.

29 □ *The Imperial Unconscious? Representations of Imperial Discourse*

Laura Chrisman

The Empire Writes Back is the title of a recent critical work devoted to, in its subtitle's words 'theory and practice in post-colonial literatures'.[1] The title derives from a phrase of Salman Rushdie, which is the book's epigraph 'the Empire writes back *to the Centre ...*' This phrase is, of course, a palimpset, its original serving as a leitmotif for US cultural imperialism, as represented in and by the blockbuster movie *Star Wars*. Such an irony is surely deliberate; the very act of rewriting 'the Empire Strikes Back' constitutes a non-Western subversion and appropriation of the media of modern Western Empire. But this strategic and symbolic gain is also something of a conceptual loss. What happens to the imperial power – (either the US of *Star Wars* or the Europe of the Age of Empire) – which has generated this post-colonial retaliation? It remains, paradoxically, frozen in power, and repressed, an absent 'centre', a hidden referent. Through conferring its name (Empire) to its 'peripheries' it remains intact by virtue of its very invisibility. This might stand as a metaphor for the current invisibility of imperial discourse within critical theory and practice, an invisibility both historical and geographical. On the one hand, as the subtitle of the volume implies, recent critical interest has centred mostly on issues of post-World War Two, that is, on *post*-colonial literary activities and theory. This privileging of contemporary discourses is salutary and important, but it also risks being premature and misleading, if it suggests that the present can be analysed in isolation from the imperialism which formally produced it, and which is only arguably a matter of history. Such imperialism in remaining unanalysed also remains, unwittingly albeit, hegemonic.

If this near-exclusive attention to the 'post'-colonial represents one form of imperialism's historical/geographical exclusion, such work as does continue to be done on 'colonial discourse' represents another. As Benita Parry remarks, in such work 'colonialism as a specific, and the most spectacular, mode of imperialism's

From *Critical Quarterly*, 32, 3, 1990, pp. 38–58.

many and mutable states ... is treated as identical with all the variable forms.'[2] The result of such an equation is at least threefold: (1) analysis of colonial discourse becomes self-contained, even hypostatised, a scene devoted solely to the supreme encounter with the Other, removed from the network of domestic/metropolitan and imperial discourses which informed it and which were informed by it; (2) imperialism, in becoming subsumed into colonialism, or alternatively reduced to a synonym for the vague totality of 'Western power' and the conditions of possibility of Western discourse itself, is denied any self-representation through discourse, implicitly rendered homogeneous, unproblematic, no more in need of definition or explanation than 'power' itself; (3) as Parry suggests, colonialism becomes allegorised, 'a notion applicable to all situations of structural domination' in which Self is constituted through and against an Other.[3]

Even the exemplary criticism of Gayatri Spivak is not immune from these tendencies. Two of her essays, 'Imperialism and sexual difference' and 'Three women's texts and a critique of imperialism' have as their focus the discursive ramifications of imperialism for an analysis of a variety of nineteenth-century writing.[4] But, even when the analysis deals with specifically domestic/metropolitan texts, such as *Jane Eyre* (in 'Three women's texts'), imperial themes and tropes take on a highly colonial character. More particularly, one colony, India, inadvertently begins to occupy a privileged site of representativeness, of conceptual supremacy for imperial 'worlding', at the expense of other colonies such as those in Africa and the Caribbean. It is true that the explicit recipient of St John Rivers's missionary imperialism is India. But when Spivak extends this to suggest that proper analysis of the self-immolation of Bertha Mason, the first Mrs Rochester, requires a knowledge of the imperial discourses attached to the *Indian practice of sati*, she unwittingly implies that the Caribbean, colonial origin of the Mason family is unlikely to carry any such discursive imperial resonance of its own. (That the Caribbean islands held a particular, materially based ideological and economical colonial representativeness for the Brontës, and mid-nineteenth-century Yorkshire society, some members of which were plantation owners, is argued by Christopher Haywood.[5] Discourses of slavery derived from Caribbean practice are likely to be as operative in the presentation of Bertha Mason as are those of sati.)

The indirect elision of the 'black' presence happens again, most ironically, in the analysis of Baudelaire's use of the term 'negress', which is given an intertextual gloss by Spivak through an earlier poem's formulation of a *'malabaraise'*, a native of Malabar on the Indian coast, the original woman of that poem being, according to Spivak, 'one of two women Baudelaire encountered in Mauritius and the island of Reunion respectively'.[6] The grounding of the allusion to the 'negress' in the Indian woman is partly a strategic one; Spivak prefers this textual/historical line over the more obvious one, that the 'negress' in question might 'of course "be" Jeanne Duval, Baudelaire's famous Afro-European mistress' (she is rightly wary of the incorrect intrusion of biographical material into criticism when it serves to override attention to the details of formal representation).[7] Spivak's purpose is to reveal the degree to which imperialist discourse homogenises and misnames its others, disregards the specificity and propriety of their own cultural identities, in this case by subsuming Malabarians into the trope of Africa/blackness. But here the strategy risks the very carelessness for which it indicts Baudelaire, when it grants textual and epistemological priority to the Indian (for whom, by virtue of the Malabarians' earlier textual articulation, the 'negress' can only be a displacement, she suggests, a figure capable of signifying nothing but generalised otherness).

One effect of this is, paradoxically, a collusion with an Oriental/Occidental binarism, in which continents and colonies which do not belong to this West/East axis are nonetheless absorbed into it. Also, in emphasising the ways in which imperialism homogenises and generalises others, there is a risk of overlooking the ways in which imperial and colonial discourses often deploy strategies of exaggerating and playing off differences among diverse others.

If critical attention might profitably be devoted to the uses of imperial differentiation strategies, the same goes for analyses of imperial discourse itself. It is just as important to observe differences between imperial practices – whether it be geographical/national (for example, the differences between the French imperialism of Baudelaire and the English imperialism of Kipling) or historical (say, the differences between early-nineteenth-century imperialism, prior to its formal codification, and late-nineteenth-century imperialism) – as it is to emphasise what these formations all have in common.

It is time then to acknowledge that the Empire itself did 'write back'; that imperial discourses of self-representation not only did indeed exist but were often complex and heterogeneous; that the co-ordinates of colonial discourse analysis need to be broadened, removed from the risk of its own stasis, circularity and essentialism. In literary critical terms, what this amounts to is, in part, a shift away from a focus on 'images/allegories/tropes' of Others to an analysis of narrative structures and processes, attending to the diverse, overdetermined and contradictory formal dynamics and ideological codes which produce certain forms of Othering but which are not reducible to it. In more general terms, this means, among other things, that 'racism' and 'sexism' are not the sole causes, effects or definitions of 'imperialism' and 'colonialism'; nor is 'political domination' the sole goal of, or synonym for, these processes. It should be possible for critical analysis of imperial/colonial discourse to begin to address questions of capitalism and political economy. This is not in the name of positive discrimination on behalf of a neglected and beleaguered imperialism, to achieve its 'equal representation' with its objects/others, but in order to radically revise the construction and analysis of the latter; to suggest not only the imbalances of an isolated attention to Othering but also the conceptual and historical inaccuracies of such a critical enterprise. From metaphysics to dialectics, from accidental collusion with the antinomies of essential oppositions (self/other) to a stress on mediations, contradictions, the dynamics of relationality – whatever such critical shifts are called, they involve some further engagement with 'history' on one hand and 'narrative form' on the other.

I will suggest some of the complexities of imperial self-representation through an examination of a small portion of the work of H. Rider Haggard. Haggard is an apologist of Empire, a writer not noted for his sophistication. Precisely because of this he serves as an example of how imperialism even at its most basic is capable of constructing itself as a contradictory process, of commenting upon its own self-mythologising, and economic, imperatives, while in the course of pursuing them; is able, in sum, to reveal a great deal of self-knowledge but doesn't know what to do with this knowledge. I will look first at one example of Haggardian imperial discourse analysis, that of feminist critics Sandra Gilbert and Susan Gubar, in order to illustrate some of the problems of contemporary criticism.[8] Not least of the problems of Gilbert and Gubar's critical analysis is its hegemony; critics of imperialism no less luminary than Edward Said and Gayatri Spivak have given it an unqualified commendation.[9]

Imperialism as Sexual Allegory?

For Gilbert and Gubar, the imperial romance is no more and no less than an allegory for the penetration and fear of the (eternal and white) feminine. More particularly, the emergence in the late nineteenth century of the frighteningly independent New Woman in the British metropole, together with the development of (frequently female-associated) spiritualism (representing, it is argued, an Other form of knowledge, mysterious and destabilising to patriarchal/imperial masculinity), and Egyptology (ditto) – all these converge to constitute the immediate context and object of Haggard's anxieties, expressed in the figure of She/Ayesha herself, a compound of all (it is argued) that is alien and threatening to imperial masculinity.

What is so extraordinary about this reading is that, in the name of a critique of imperialism, it overlooks entirely the topoi of 'race', black Africa, and the processes of imperialism, as matrices and themes in Haggard's discourse; it ignores the fact that the romance itself is not identical with its eponymous female. That its setting, Southern Africa, might have had any historical and imperial significance for Haggard, in addition to its usability as a site of sexual metaphor, is unacknowledged; although they plunder aspects of Haggard's biography such as his love affairs in order to speculate about his constructions of the feminine, they omit to consider the relevance of the many years he spent involved in South African imperial administration. That there is a distinction to be made between Orientalism and discourse about sub-Saharan Africa is also overlooked by them, despite the fact that the romance clearly differentiates between the 'Oriental' and the black 'savagery'. Further contextualisation might here have alerted them to the fact that Haggard, far from producing the 'supernatural', spiritual and mythical, as oppositional to imperialism (in the figure of Ayesha), himself harnesses these modes throughout the text: even battles between animals, for example, have a double signification, both as expressions of an evolutionary and 'scientific' Darwinian naturalism and as articulations of a mythic mode; Haggard carefully utilises animals that are known to represent totems among Southern African people. As Patrick Brantlinger has pointed out, many imperialist writers, among them Haggard, were not automatically antagonistic to the new spirituality and to things occult, but were on the contrary attracted to them and saw their usability for imperialism, so much so that an 'Imperial Gothic' genre emerged.[10]

Consideration of any one of these aspects would have necessitated a different hermeneutics, based not on the explanation of the text through the isolated mistress-narrative of a hypostatised feminine (Gilbert and Gubar's method is based on a form of mythic essentialism, overlaid with a layer of selective 'new historicism') but on a premise of the multiple dynamics within the text, of gender, 'race', and a variety of social science discourses, whose intersections are overdetermined by the dictates of a highly problematic imperialism. To privilege the feminine in the way that Gilbert and Gubar do is to foreclose any analysis of these overdeterminations; instead of assuming that they all converge into a neatly homogeneous set of othernesses, it is useful to presume that they are constitutively contradictory. Two instances of the text's refusal of a schematic gender reading – the representation of the Amahagger people and the representation and structuration of She/Ayesha herself – illustrate this.

For Gilbert and Gubar, the Amahagger people over whom Ayesha rules are an expression of matriarchal power; quoting Herodotus on Egypt as evidence, they suggest such an inversion of female misrule is to be read as a sign of typical cultural alterity, profoundly oppositional to Western civilisation, and that such alterity has as its racial articulation the sign of Egypt.[11] A look at contemporary discourses, however, challenges the interpretation of the Amahagger as a simple, collective manifestation of the same gynocentric power that is, it is claimed, represented by Ayesha. By the time Haggard was writing, the idea that matriarchy was the original mode of social organisation (as had been suggested by Bachofen and McLennan) was discredited. Distinctions began to be made between descent and authority: a system of matrilinearity did not indicate an elevation of female status in political terms, for contemporary anthropologists; these writers (including Darwin, Westermarck, Tylor) consolidated a definition of 'power' as constituted by political rights and property ownership.[12] As women in most 'primitive' societies appeared to them to lack this form of power, it could be argued that they had no power at all. Accompanying this reformulation, of a patriarchal basis of originary primitive society, was a notion that the status of women had improved under Western civilisation. 'Progress' was construed as a consolidation and increased 'appreciation' of women's domestic status; in contrast, the system of 'primitive' culture turned women into 'drudges' by forcing them to undertake 'social'/manual labour. Therefore it is highly significant that the Amahagger women are excluded from the labour force; as the narrator states:

> the labour of digging is very great. It is, however, all done by the men, the women, *contrary to the habits of most savage races*, being entirely exempt from manual toil. (italics added)

Their function is reproduction rather than 'production' (to use a distinction made by the political economists and anthropologists in question). The fact that their society is matrilinear should not be taken to imply that women are dominant throughout that system, or that this is a matriarchy, but rather as a sign of the recognition and enforcement of this domestic function alone.

On the one hand, then, Haggard's construction of the Amahagger could be said to align them with a Western 'civilised' standard; they are more civilised than other savage tribes in their exaggerated association of women with the domestic sphere. But the fact that the Amahagger women are also in charge of selection of mates is evidence of the society's proximity to civilisation's 'opposite', the animal/natural world. For Darwin, sexual selection in animal systems was the responsibility of the female; it was only in the human species that the male took over this role. And so if on the one hand the Amahagger are encoded as aligned with Western civility, in their veneration of the feminine domestic space, on the other, this cultural 'progress' is revealed to be identical with an increased emphasis on animal naturalism. As a tribal 'Father' explains, women are worshipped 'because without them the world could not go on; they are the source of life'; but their worship only continues until the women became 'unbearable, which . . . happens about every second generation' and then 'we rise, and kill the old ones as an example to the young ones, and to show them that we are the strongest'.[14] A parodic evolutionism entails the systematic elimination of the 'weaker' sex, or rather those elements of it which are past child-bearing and therefore have outlived their natural function.

To add to the complexity, it is probable that Haggard based the Amahaggers on the 'Lovedu' people of southeast Africa, and Ayesha on their ruler, who was thought to be an inaccessible and immortal queen, 'the greatest magician of the north'.[15] If this is so, then Haggard has completely reversed the position of the Lovedu women, for whom patrilinearity not matrilinearity formed the descent system, but who enjoyed the public and practical representational power which Haggard denies them. At the least what this suggests is that the ideological scheme into which Haggard wished the Amahagger to fit was one which removed from the women the kind of representative power which their 'originals' possessed.

Far from the Amahagger being an obvious illustration of an inverted (to the West) system of feminine power, they are a compound of contradictory codes. The Amahagger are rendered both 'not-quite' Western and the opposite, 'not-quite' human, through respectively their *domestic* division of labour and their system of sexual selection. If they are viewed in terms of racial codification, the same oxymoronic hybridity presents itself as the Amahagger trait. To suggest that the Amahagger are synonymous with Egyptian people is to preclude any exploration of what it is that should make imperial discourse so bivalent in its desires and fears about racial otherness. The Amahagger are a degenerate example of the ancient and *imperial* Kor (an imaginary people); crucially, what it is that they are a hybrid of is unclear – Ayesha explains that either 'barbarians from the south' (sub-Saharan black/Zulu peoples) or 'my people, the Arabs' mated with the remnants of Kor to produce this 'bastard brood of the mighty sons of Kor'.[16] Either way, through adulteration with the superior Oriental or with the savage black other, this once great imperial culture is now degenerate. What is important is not only the structural principle of indeterminacy here; it is also the fact that this indeterminacy stems from possibilities that are precisely opposed to each other. Imperialism is covering all options and in the process, here with regard to racial determinations as above with gender politics, it manages to posit those antinomies as self-cancelling (deconstructive of each other) *and* identical at the same time. Here, for example, is upheld the possibility that both culture (in the form of the Arabs of the culturally supreme Ayesha) and barbarism (the black Africans) are equally or identically negative to imperialism, responsible for its decline.

Ayesha/She functions not simply as imperialism's other but as its double, antithesis and supplement. Her presence – and her gruesome extinction – are necessary for imperial self-legitimation. But this is an imperialism already in crisis. The *necessity* for its legitimation is equalled by its inability to determine what it is that is legitimate. Instead of starting from the premise that Ayesha, as a female monarch, is necessarily the polar opposite of and constitutive threat to masculine imperialism, it is better to see the selection of a female here as a symptom of how far imperialism is already profoundly split in its identity and value-scheme, utilising an other in order to dramatise its ambiguities, ambivalences and indeterminacies. Through Ayesha imperialism is able to acknowledge and disavow, simultaneously, its own dominatoriness, its systems of knowledge, its contradictions, by displacing them on to the figure of a female. Ayesha, in the narration of Western imperial history presented here (and condensed in the genealogy of the male protagonist Leo), has been repressed by and made marginal to this history. But contemporary imperialism doesn't know how to locate itself in this historical trajectory.

An imperialism which doesn't know to what extent to see itself as feudal/authoritarian or alternatively as capitalist/'democratic' can exploit these through the representation of political practice, and the ideologies, attached to Ayesha. She is in one sense a reiteration of Oriental despotism. Perhaps this is an opportune moment to dispel any errors concerning the status of the Orient within this imperialist discourse which Gilbert and Gubar's reading (of Orient as ultimate Other) may give rise to. Egypt is construed here not as antithetical to the narrative of Westernism, but literally, as an integral part of it. The genealogy of Leo, his foremother an Egyptian princess, his father a Greek priest – and the pattern of their geographical migration – renders them a sign for the inauguration of Western civilisation itself, achieved at the expense of Ayesha who herself desires to be the mate of the Greek.[17] If the Egyptian princess Amenartas represents one Orient, Ayesha represents another, a 'pure' Arabia, uncontaminated by assimilation into a Western genealogy. Orientalism is already therefore a divided and flexible construct here, not a monolith of otherness. And, perhaps, precisely because of her exclusion from the West, Ayesha in her very abstract Orientality can serve as the West's effective proxy in this discourse. Her despotism functions as imperialism's inadmissibly absolutist fantasy of its own power, exercised over a hybrid – possibly 'savage' – sub-Saharan Africa, *and* as admission of imperialism's actual authoritarianism.

Ayesha's oxymoronic knowledge serves to articulate imperialism's own bad faith, or negative self-knowledge. Her 'amazing' wisdom is, significantly, occult and scientific in equal degree; her experiments in breeding, for example, an expression of imperial eugenics, her supernatural clairvoyancy an expression of a principle of magic or myth (just as important to imperialism in its quest for self-affirmation). Her political ideology is contradictory: at times a Nietzschean materialism bordering on fascism, at others, a revolutionary–idealist philosophy of transcendental love. In and through all these contradictions, imperialism asserts and refutes itself. It can identify itself, for example, with the principles of social Darwinisim espoused by Ayesha, or in the same way oppose them (through locating Ayesha as other); similarly, and alternatively, it can align itself with a principle of romantic idealism, or oppose it. Ayesha is encoded, simultaneously and for the same reasons, as both subject and object of the imperial mode, both self and other.

Ayesha resists reduction to one principle vis-à-vis imperialism; similarly principles resist reduction to her. It is difficult (although Gilbert and Gubar attempt it) to ascribe to her the monopoly on symbolic eternal femininity, when Haggard gives another female – Ustane, the imperial Leo's Amahagger wife and reincarnation of his foremother – equal rights to the claim of feminine representativeness. This dualism is symptomatic; the whole text is structured upon strategies and devices of doubles and splits, both inviting and refusing a choice between two opposed possibilities, each claiming equal weight and priority over the other. Thus, as we have already seen, the origins of the Amahaggers' hybrid origins are given two possible definitions; thus, femininity is given two conflicting representatives (Leo has quite literally to choose between them). This formal principle extends too to the plotting of the imperial subject itself. For both Leo and Ayesha are invested with imperial iconic signification. Both are pursuing parallel imperial quests, she for her beloved, he for power/knowledge/revenge, in which the other is the object. Even if, as above, we can talk of Ayesha in isolation, as projection of imperialist negative knowledge, such a focus must be acknowledged as partial. For what is so significant is that imperialism cannot articulate itself through any one agent, representative or identity: either both Leo and Ayesha constitute, respectively, the imperial sign, or neither does; a third possibility is that it is the space between them, the fact of their formal interrelation, that marks imperialism's dynamics of definition. Questions of the actual possibility of imperial monologism, of autotelism, of absolutism, of a single centre of narrative and ideological value, are raised here through the dilemmas of an imperialism which is uncomfortable with the idea of an identity defined through displacement, meditation through others, but equally troubled by the alternative, an absolute and untouchable, autochthonous existence.

The scene of Ayesha's accidental self-immolation is crucial to an understanding of the imperial problematic, its enactment of an impossibility. Ayesha has been awaiting the return of her love, the Greek priest, for millennia; now he has returned in the form of his descendant Leo. Preparing for the life together they now anticipate, she steps into the eternal flame which had, when she first entered it, granted her eternal life, tremendous powers, beauty and knowledge; this second time, she dies. The narrator then ponders this:

Ayesha locked up in her living tomb, waiting from age to age for the coming of her lover, worked but a small change in the order of the World. But Ayesha strong and happy in her love, clothed with immortal youth, godlike beauty and power, and the wisdom of the centuries, would have revolutionised society, and even perchance have changed the destinies of Mankind. Thus she opposed herself to the eternal law, and, strong though she was, by it was swept back into nothingness.[18]

The crux here centres on the 'thus'; at the very point of explanation, the text falls prey to a semantic ambiguity which generates entirely opposite readings. It is usually assumed that Ayesha's transgression of the law lies in her aspirations to greatness, her revolutionary potential. But a closer look suggests that her violation of the law consists in her *failure* to revolutionise the world; either she has not gone far enough, wilfully underachieving in her abdication of the universal power that is hers, or she has gone too far, appropriating nature's gifts. In the former, Ayesha's initial act of transgression (her original bath in the flames) established an identity with the Law which she failed to sustain, while in the second, her act broke a mythic law and definition. This is then a double structure, in which both interpretive possibilities, logically exclusive, not only coexist but both equally and formally oppose each other.

Again, autochthony versus rationality, being versus becoming, for imperial self-definition emerges here. To what extent Ayesha's power was threatening and punishable because she did *not* share it (with the world and/or a fellow male ruler) or because she *wished* to share it, saw its expression as conditional upon a conjunction with her lover's presence, is indeterminate.

It really isn't very useful to see this scene, as Gilbert and Gubar do – and Freud, Jung and Henry Miller too – as a simple demonstration of the vanquishing of the threat of the feminine force, represented both as an elemental/mythic principle and as a human female in Ayesha, through the exercise of an equally autonomous primordial law identified as patriarchy/the phallus. It isn't useful because what the scene implies is the inability to determine the limits and contents of 'representativeness', of Law and legitimacy; it also problematises any notion of a conflation of the mythic and the human levels of signification (as implied by the equation of human female with cosmic femininity) by showing those levels to be literally in a state of conflict. To take this mythic interpretation on board is in one sense to collude with imperialism's desire to mythify itself; it is also to overlook the obvious ambiguities of the scene.

To see this as a contest by male and female for authority, for occupation of a primary site, for claim to possession of the origin, law of the life-force, is (as with the 'gynocentric' reading of the Amahagger society) to collapse biological oppositions (male–female) with political systems of representation, or rather to subsume the latter into the former. It overlooks, indeed, the fact that biology involves not only 'essences' but processes; it overlooks too the incredible intensity with which imperialism invested in questions of biology. To risk stating the obvious, imperialist discourse in its reversion from the discourse of political economy begins to invest instead in an economy centred on the physical body, to construct society as a biological organism. The life-force associated with the feminine, a foregrounding of 'womb-power', became not necessarily (as Gilbert and Gubar imply) a threat to masculinism/patriarchy but incorporated into it.

What this means is that, at the very least, questions of gender become inextricable from questions of generation, of racial reproduction, familial relations of power. In terms of an analysis of imperialist discourse in general, this means that it is not enough to focus on defining political relations exclusively according to terms of male–female; whether this be applied to women, or to 'natives', what needs to be included is some illumination of the range of familial definitions and processes through which the male and female are articulated. The matrix of discourse in which allusions are made to 'motherland' versus 'fatherland', to colonies as 'daughters' or 'dependencies', to natives as 'children' – these need attention. What this means for an analysis of this scene of Ayesha's destruction, at the least, is that such a confrontation with the 'law' of life is imbued with all sorts of questions about reproductive power and control, determined by imperial obsessions with race, genealogy, its own 'laws' of existence and perpetuation. Imperialism is confronted here with an ambivalent desire for an absolute status, to be the Law of nature/life/evolution, rather than sanctioned by it. It doesn't know, however, whether to locate power in the capacity to control life, or in the capacity to reproduce it; whether power lies in the ability to represent itself through and as history, or as that which transcends and causes history (myth, that is). In a sense these oppositions are rendered meaningless by the impasse of Ayesha's revolutionary extinction. Darwinism instead of working together with mythology to enforce imperialism destroys both, suggesting that the 'law' which imperialism cannot decide whether to identify itself with is one of arbitrary and 'lawless' physical materialism, cold comfort for imperialist desire for legitimation and affirmation.

Through the figure of Ayesha we witness the ideological bankruptcy of the imperialist enterprise, and receive a lesson not so much about the dangers of female imperial overreachers but the emptiness or fragility of imperial discourse itself. Whether Ayesha represents that which opposes Empire or is on the contrary the (empty) sign of its ideality and supremacy, forever unrealised (she is both), neither She nor a masculine imperialism can find anything to affirm.

The Economy of Imperial Discourse: Mining and Myth

If in *She* imperialist economy articulates itself through issues of biology and knowledge, Haggard's earlier *King Solomon's Mines* explicitly confronts issues surrounding one material practice of imperialism – namely, the mining of mineral wealth (gold and diamonds) that began in late-nineteenth-century South Africa.[19] It is rare for a fictional text of imperial discourse to engage so directly, on a thematic level, with the embarrassment – and symbolic recuperation – of political economy. Perhaps the fictional blatancy, emerging in the formative moment of an imperial cartography of Africa (the Berlin Conference of 1884–5), and more specifically in the inaugural foment of imperial capitalism in Southern Africa, was possible only as Haggard's own inauguration into imperial romance. The literal and figurative feature of the mines so foregrounds the issue of the processes of economic production, and value, that it should not be possible to read the concept of imperialism here as one exclusively concerned with *political* domination, with the physical conquest of the Other. It is tempting to read Haggard's text as a simple exercise in the ideological exoneration, a fantastic mythologising of contemporary mineral mining. But the text testifies less to a desire to constitute Africa as a site of colonial pastoral fantasy, in reaction against (and naturalisation of) the reality of imperial exploitation, than to a desire to render the capitalistic and the romantic-anti-capitalistic, the mythic/fantastic and the rational, the ideal and the material, the ancient and the contemporary, as *identical*.

This is suggested by the title itself. Archaeologists at the time were hoping to establish the ruins of Great Zimbabwe as being those of biblical antiquity, gold mines and fortresses constructed by King Solomon himself.[20] What is going on is an attempt to verify the myth of the Bible, by giving it material evidence; also, and equally, to give biblical sanction to contemporary mineral practice. The Zimbabwe ruins subsequently began to be featured within a variety of late-nineteenth-century texts, as a point of juncture for many imperialist fantasies and anxieties. For our purposes, what is important is the way in which the obsession with the ruins reveals just how determined imperialist discourse was to provide a historical justification for its own operations, to see itself both as the mythic repetition or reincarnation of an ancient mining system and as an evolutionary progression beyond that system.

But as much is either deliberately or unconsciously repressed and suppressed in this anxiety/fantasy as is acknowledged. The quest to find a 'rational' explanation for the existence of the ruins mirrors imperial discourse's attempts to find a rationality for its own operation, but the quest is also to mystify these ruins, to inscribe them as a vacant site of indeterminacy. In other words, three issues (at least) are intertwined here: imperialism's interrogation of its own historical origins, and of the relations between exploitation and civilisation; imperialism's desire to displace black Africans as the possible originators of civilisation, and as the original inhabitants of Africa itself. Haggard himself gives a 'non-fictional' interpretation of the ruins, in his introduction to A. Wilmot's book on *Monomotapa (Rhodesia): Its monuments, and its history from the most ancient times to the present century* (1896). Haggard supports the view that the ruins are undoubtedly of Phoenician origin, and argues that the neighbouring gold mines were worked by the Phoenicians also:

> Gain and slaves were the objects of the voyaging of this crafty, heartless, and adventurous race, who were the English of the ancient world without the English honour. ... A mere trading expedition [to Eastern Africa] was impossible; for it will be remembered that the servants of Solomon could not accomplish their visit to Ophir and return thence with merchandise ... in less than three years. *Moreover, as is the case to-day, the development and working of the inland mines by the help of native*

labour must have necessitated the constant presence of large numbers of armed and civilised men. It was therefore necessary that these adventurers, sojourning in the midst of barbarous tribes, should build themselves fortresses for their own protection, as it was natural that in their exile they should follow the rites and customs of their fathers. (italics added)

As is typical of contemporary accounts, the text concludes by instilling mystery:

At what date this Phoenician occupation began, for how many centuries or generations it endured, and when it closed, no man can say for certain, and it is probable that no man ever will be able to say. The people came, they occupied and built, they passed away, perhaps in some violent and sudden fashion such as might well have been brought about by a successful insurrection of their slaves, or by the overwhelming incursion of Arabian or more savage races.[21]

Haggard then postulates a Zimbabwe in which, as in his present, the imperial mining company requires the exploitation of native labourers but also fears the potential power of the force. The threat of the African is both internal – a slave insurrection – and external – an incursion of 'barbarians'. Frequently this overthrow is conjectured to be a sudden interruption. A. H. Keane, for example, makes the suddenness a central feature:

It is to the irruption of these Bantu hordes into Rhodesia that is to be attributed the sudden suspension of the mining operations, the expulsion or extermination of the Semitic prospectors and settlers. . . . There was unquestionably a total interruption of the works, and of the traffic in gold.[22]

King Solomon's Mines reveals a fascination for the idea of interruption, inscribed in the ruins themselves. In terms of ethnography, interruption here serves to indicate the violence of the African attack, a violence which reflects, even as it suppresses, the force of imperialist violence against the African. The situation serves both as outlet for real fears of African resistance, and as a wish-fulfilment: black Africans are blamed for erasing imperial history, rather than the reverse (the ruins were, as is now known, built by black Africans; this discourse reveals the violence of the repression of a repression, in a sense, the epistemological violence of the unconscious determination to deny such a possibility). For the contemporary imperial agent, summarised in *King Solomon's Mines*, the ancient Phoenicians are a flexible Oriental signifier, serving, just like Ayesha, both as proxy and as an inferior imperial presence, a slippery third term mediating imperialism's relation to black Africa. Again, through this device contemporary imperialism is able to acknowledge and disavow itself. The use of the Phoenicians as third term (imperial self and other) is balanced by the construction of another third term, the violent invading Africans, who similarly function to disrupt imperial self-adequation. To this third term is then attributed the very coercive force which has been exercised against it, materially and epistemologically. Barbaric Africans are responsible for creating the mystery of Zimbabwe, not the imperialists.

The mystery prevails; to Haggard, the Bantu barbarians who take over 'stamped out whatever civilisation . . . still flickered . . . so completely that even native tradition is silent concerning it, and once more oblivion covered the land and its story.'[23] Imperial history is given an unconscious, and the imperial unconscious is given a history, which can, like gold, be mined. The appeal of interrupted operations in Zimbabwe is as psychological as it is ethnographical: positing interruption invites completion.

When Haggard writes a romance whose heroes penetrate to the hidden treasure of the mines, but this time without being party to the exploitation of mining labour, the production of the mineral wealth itself, such heroes get to have mythical and historical backing. They fulfil the mandate created by the curtailed mining of the past, to complete, and capitalise on, its interrupted process, to get both a symbolic and a material purchase on the scene without dirtying their record.

Even the process of mining lends itself to a certain anti-capitalist fantasy of the natural not the constructed commodity. It can present the illusion of standing outside some of the definitions, determinants and relations of capitalist production, the minerals as 'natural' wealth, accordingly holding a given not produced value, the labour of their extraction one of midwifery, not itself constitutive of their value. Similarly, as Hannah Arendt suggests.

> Gold hardly has a place in human production and is of no importance compared with iron, coal, oil, and rubber; instead, it is the most ancient symbol of mere wealth. In its uselessness in industrial production it bears an ironical resemblance to the superfluous money that financed the digging of gold and to the superfluous men who did the digging. To the imperialists' pretense of having discovered a permanent savior for a decadent society . . . it added its own pretense of apparently eternal stability and independence of all functional determinants. It was significant that a society about to part with all traditional absolute values began to look for an absolute value in the world of economics where, indeed, such a thing does not and cannot exist since everything is functional by definition.[24]

It is a crucial irony that this 'unmediated' and 'absolute' value has to be mediated for the imperialist heroes of *King Solomon's Mines*, through a black female figure, Gagool, who is supremely antagonistic to the imperialist project, and who forces them to acknowledge simultaneously the relative not absolute value of the treasure, and the truth of their own economistic cupidity. Gagool brings the men to the treasure – she alone knows the secret.

It is through Gagool that imperialism's ambivalence about rationality and knowledge, as well as about Africa and the feminine, are best dramatised. The ancient seemingly omniscient Gagool is constructed as a figure whose supreme knowledgeability is necessary but intrinsically threatening; she must be both instrumentalised for imperialism and then killed off as a potential obstacle to its success. A figure who has witnessed ancient white/Oriental imperial civilisation (the Phoenicians) first hand, and 'learnt her art' from it, she is a necessary guarantor of imperialist history and destiny, affirming the 'fact' of an original imperial civilisation's authenticity and temporal priority. Gagool occupies the sites both of perverter and preserver of African custom, as epitome or aberration. While it may seem that this contradiction stems from a primary ambivalence of imperialism towards its African other, it is more accurate to see this as symptomatic of a confusion within imperialism about its own identity in relation to Africa. Imperialism seems to require a 'good' Africa (here represented by the figures of Umbopa and Foulata) which is instinctively pro-imperial, in which imperialism is a matter of natural law. But imperialism also needs a cognitive affirmation, conscious and not instinctive acknowledgement of its necessity. As the good Africa by definition cannot provide this, the bad knowledgeable Africa must. Gagool's knowledge is essential but of necessity evil; it matches imperialism's own, in this text exposing imperialism as the conscious process it claims not to be. Imperialism's mythical pretensions (primeval and absolute rightfulness of occupation of Africa) are belied by the very fact that it needs a Gagool to testify to, and bring into representation (and therefore into question) its 'mythical' origin. Gagool may, like Ayesha, be seen as a product of imperial discourse's own bad faith. She is its bad mirror, engendered by the conflicting desires, fears and self-knowledges that imperialism cannot acknowledge to itself.

Gagool leads the men to the treasure and then traps them, telling the men to 'eat of them, hee! hee! drink of them, ha! ha!', these 'bright stones that ye love'. When the men learn that they are trapped, they learn the value of the necessities of life over against the illusory value of treasure:

> There around us lay treasures enough to pay off a moderate national debt, or to build a fleet of ironclads, and yet we would gladly have bartered them all for the faintest chance of escape. Soon, doubtless, we should be glad to exchange them for a bit of food or a cup of water, and, after that, even for the privilege of a speedy close to our sufferings. Truly wealth, which men spend all their lives in acquiring, is a valueless thing at the last.[25]

What is set up here is a seemingly intransigent opposition, between one kind of 'materialism' – the physical matter of life itself, both as condition and absolute end of value itself, biologically defined – and another – capital wealth. But such an opposition – which is the crisis of 'value' itself in the imperialist 'economy' of this text – is soon resolved, through some deft textual manoeuvring. Even here, the persistence of an economistic terminology – as in the references to the 'bartering' and the 'exchange' of terms (i.e. 'exchange-value' is surreptitiously upheld even while 'use-value' is propounded) – should alert us to the ulterior motives and strategies of Haggard's discourse: a desire to recuperate materialism through a double system of conversion into transcendentalism and through preservation. Utilitarianism and romanticism, idealism and materialism, intertwine.

Haggard later provided an interesting illumination of the doubletake of this economy. In an interview on 'Land settlement and Empire' (1916), Haggard remarks: 'We know now that it is population which is the real wealth of a nation ... Germany, with her organised millions, has taught us that it is Man-Power which is the world's master' and continues:

> It is not the slightest use having all the riches in the world unless there are people to develop and use them. It is like the story I wrote in 'King Solomon's Mines' of three men who were shut in a treasure cave with enough wealth to build a fleet or run an Empire ... twelve hours later they would have bartered the lot for a piece of bread and a sup of water. Apply the parable to the Empire, with its enormous potential wealth, and regard it as the treature-house.[26]

The discourse slides easily away from its original premise – that people/life constitutes itself the real 'wealth' of the empire, life as an end in itself, not a means – to an instrumental view, in which people are necessary to 'develop and use' wealth. (Wealth, it should be noted, is always for Haggard something already out there, not produced – again, there is a repression of the knowledge of human agency and exploitation in its very production; nonetheless it is covertly acknowledged in the logic of the 'development' of capital.) So long as the metaphorical economy of the 'people' continues to be privileged, it seems, the literal financial economy can continue to exist. People can even serve it, provided that it pretends to be serving them.

In *King Solomon's Mines*, the contest between these two types of economic value is accompanied and assisted by two types of black Africa, racial others are auxiliary to (rather than the goal of) the imperial process. The imperial heroes are accompanied to the treasure not only by Gagool but also by an adoring, beautiful and servile African woman, Foulata, for whom one of the imperial trio, Captain Good, harbours erotic feelings. Foulata reciprocates these feelings, and the threat of miscegenation is foregrounded. Gagool however stabs Foulata; the men find her in her death throes. The men's grief is interrupted by their realisation that they are trapped. They decide to return to the treasure chamber.

> We turned and went, and as we did so I perceived by the unfinished wall across the passage the basket of food which poor Foulata had carried. I took it up, and brought it with me back to that accursed treasure chamber that was to be our grave. Then we went back and reverently bore in Foulata's corpse, laying it on the floor by the boxes of coin.[27]

The men succeed in leaving – of course they do, thanks to technological astuteness. They also succeed in taking a considerable quantity of treasure with them – an instinct leads one of them to stuff his pockets with as much as he can gather. By basing the theft in instinct rather than rational calculation or conscious volition, and by making the gesture a by-product rather than a goal of the situation (the goal now being the departure from the trap), Haggard removes the men from any risk of contamination by economic materialism. Once the men succeed in leaving, Foulata's remains become an essential component of the treasure chamber:

> If ever it should be entered again by living men, which I do not think it will be, he will find a token of our presence in the open chests of jewels, the empty lamp, and the white bones of poor Foulata. . . . Somehow, I seem to feel that the millions of pounds' worth of gems that lie in the three stone coffers will never shine round the neck of an earthly beauty. They and Foulata's bones will keep cold company till the end of all things.[28]

Here is an instance of the implicit instrumentalisation of that 'absolute' value, life; Foulata's fate when dead – and the necessity of her death in the first place – reveal just how instrumental the scheme is in the first place, towards 'live' people. Her death neatly transforms a literal threat to imperialism – miscegenation – into a symbolic affirmation – eternal devotion of a submissive Africa to her master. It is no accident that Foulata's final conflict with Gagool should occur in the treasure caves. Although Gagool's knowledge was necessary to get the men into the chamber, it has to be replaced by a force more positive to imperialism, and so Foulata's servility gets the last word. Gagool's eternal African evil is exchanged and displaced by Foulata's eternal African Love. This exchange can only really take place once Foulata has herself been transmuted from the sphere of the material to that of the ideal (emblem). This drama of economic exchange is evident in the textual operation upon the treasure itself. From being a signifier of capitalistic materialism (of cupidity as base and degrading as Good's erotic desire for Foulata) the treasure becomes, with the men's departure, fully transcendental and absolute (as Foulata now is), standing beyond the capitalist economy as an inaccessible and infinitely desirable idea, 'aesthetic' rather than material. Just as Foulata's love had to be physically unconsummated in order to have eternal symbolic force, so the treasure will now have to remain perpetually untapped.

Conclusion

Haggard's discourse suggests that it is impossible to identify a sole popular writer as the author of his mythologies. Contemporary readers while appreciating the singularity of Haggard, would also have been equipped (if only subliminally) to read the co-ordinates of that general ideology termed imperialism here. It is an important project to theorise the place of this readership. For a community whose experience of actual imperialism was profound and asymmetrical (people were both British subjects and objects of the political and economic complex), the fantasies produced by this popular form may well have seemed to promise more 'knowledge' of the race's destiny than journalistic reports from the Boer War front.

Imperialism is productive of a discourse that can testify neither to belief nor disbelief in its own archaism and fictionality, thus inviting and refusing questions of authenticity and legitimacy. As Theodor Adorno suggests:

> the question of authenticity is as fruitless here as elsewhere. Just as the overwhelming power of high capitalism forms myths that tower above the collective conscious, in the same way the mythic region in which the modern consciousness seeks refuge bears the marks of that capitalism: what subjectively was the dream of dreams is objectively a nightmare.[29]

It is fruitful to see in the formal Age of Empire something of the crisis of Enlightenment reasoning to which Adorno and Max Horkheimer, in *Dialectic of Enlightenment*, ascribe the phenomena both of late capitalism and fascism.[30] To be overly programmatic, if late-nineteenth-century imperial capitalism is defined as the (bad dialectic of the) simultaneous culmination and cancellation of mid-nineteenth-century laissez-faire capitalism, its transformation into a monopolistic, 'parasitic', 'decadent' form (to use Lenin's Hegelian schema), it is possible to see a similar pattern both in formal epistemologies and in patterns of subjectivity themselves: a crisis of Enlightenment scientific-instrumental reasoning in which ends and means become indistinguishable, rational and 'mythic' thought interchangeable; imperialism as idealism/civilisation ideology becomes structurally conjoined with an imperialism articulated as primitivism and romantic anti-capitalism; the 'laws' of social organisation and the source of economic value are constructed, as those of biology and the human body itself, in a rejection of the mid-nineteenth-century discourse of political economy which centred upon the 'laws' of capitalism.

Such a historical positioning and characterisation of imperialist discourse lends support to Spivak's notion of imperialism as a form of 'epistemic violence', a violence against the other produced by the inevitably dominatory systems of knowledge which constitute that figure of the other. But it also suggests that such a destructiveness through ideation and idealisms is historically structured and therefore variable; with the late-nineteenth-century formalisation of Empire (coincident with the formalisation of Imperial control over Africa) comes a formalisation of the crises, oxymorons and violence of an imperial (un)conscious.

Notes

1. Bill Ashcroft, Gareth Griffiths and Helen Tiffin, *The Empire Writes Back: Theory and practice in post-colonial literatures*, Routledge: London, 1989.
2. Benita Parry, 'Problems in current theories of colonial discourse', *Oxford Literary Review*, 9, 1–2, 1987, p. 34.

3. *ibid.*, p. 52.

4. Gayatri Chakravorty Spivak, 'Imperialism and sexual difference', *Oxford Literary Review*, 8, 1–2, 1986; 'Three women's texts and a critique of imperialism', in Henry Louis Gates Jr (ed.), *'Race, writing and difference*, University of Chicago Press: Chicago, IL, 1986.

5. Christopher Heywood, 'Yorkshire slavery in *Wuthering Heights*', *Review of English Studies*, XXXVIII, 150, 1987.

6. Spivak, 'Imperialism and sexual difference', p. 230.

7. *ibid.*, p. 230.

8. H. Rider Haggard, *King Solomon's Mines* (1885) – subsequent references are to the edition of 1972 (Harmondsworth: Penguin); *She* (1887) – subsequent references are to the 1980 edition (Sevenoaks: Hodder & Stoughton). The original article, by Sandra M. Gilbert, 'Rider Haggard's heart of darkness', *Partisan Review*, L, 3, 1983, appears in expanded form as the first chapter of Sandra M. Gilbert and Susan Gubar, *No Man's Land: The place of the woman writer in the twentieth century*, vol. 2: *Sexchanges*, Yale University Press: New Haven, CT, 1989.

9. Spivak's commendation comes in note 27 of her 'Three women's texts and a critique of imperialism', p. 280. Said's praise of Sandra Gilbert's piece occurs in his 'Orientalism reconsidered', in Francis Baker, Peter Hulme, Margaret Iversen and Diana Loxley (eds.), *Europe and Its Others*, vol. 1, Proceedings of the Essex Sociology of Literature Conference, University of Essex: Colchester, 1985, p. 23.

10. Patrick Brantlinger, 'Imperial gothic: atavism and the occult in the British adventure novel, 1880–1914', in his *Rule of Darkness: British literature and imperialism, 1830–1914*, Cornell University Press: Ithaca, NY, 1988.

11. Gilbert and Gubar, *op. cit.*, p. 13.

12. Rosalind Coward's *Patriarchal Precedents: Sexuality and social relations*, Routledge & Kegan Paul: London, 1983, gives a thorough account of these transformations within nineteenth-century social anthropology.

13. *She*, p. 77.

14. *ibid.*, p. 96.

15. E. and J. Krige, *The Realm of the Rain-Queen: A study of the pattern of Lovedu society*, Oxford University Press: Oxford, 1943, pp. 1–2. For Haggard's disclaimer of any relationship between the Lovedu and the Amahagger, see 'The death of "Majajie"', *The African Review*, 19 September 1896.

16. *She*, p. 149.

17. Evelyn J. Hinz in 'Rider Haggard's *She*: an archetypal "history of adventure"', *Studies in the Novel*, 4, 1972, gives an interesting analysis of the ways in which Leo's origins signify simultaneously those of 'Western civilisation'.

18. *She*, p. 238.

19. See, for example, Shula Marks and Richard Rathbone (eds.), *Industrialisation and Social Change in South Africa: African class formation, culture and consciousness 1870–1930*, Longman: London, 1982, for analyses of the mining industries in the late nineteenth century.

20. See Edward Bacon (ed.), *The Great Archaeologists: The modern world's discovery of ancient ruins as originally reported in the pages of the Illustrated London News from 1840 to the Present Day*, Secker & Warburg: London, 1976, p. 43.

21. London: T. Fisher Unwin, 1896, pp. xvii–xix. Wilmot was a member of the Legislative Council, Cape of Good Hope. The book's dedicatee, unsurprisingly is

> The Right Honourable Cecil J. Rhodes ... who has been principally the means of giving a new Empire to Britain, and by whose advice and aid the researches into the history of Monomotapa were undertaken.

22. A. H. Keane, *The Gold of Ophir: Whence brought and by whom?*, Edward Stanford: London, 1901.
23. Wilmot, *op. cit.*, pp. xiv–xv.
24. Hannah Arendt, *The Origins of Totalitarianism*, André Deutsch: London, 1986 (first published 1951).
25. *King Solomon's Mines*, pp. 230–1.
26. *Lloyd's Weekly News*, 26 November 1916, p. 3.
27. *King Solomon's Mines*, p. 228.
28. *ibid.*, pp. 236 and 242.
29. Theodor Adorno, *In Search of Wagner*, Verso: London, 1985, p. 123 (first published 1952).
30. Max Horkheimer and Theodor Adorno, *Dialectic of Enlightenment*, Continuum: New York, 1972 (first published 1944).

30 □ Xala, Ousmane Sembene 1976: The Carapace That Failed

Laura Mulvey

The film language of *Xala* can be constructed on the model of an African poetic form called 'semenna-worq' which literally means 'wax and gold'. The term refers to the 'lost wax' process in which a goldsmith creates a wax form, casts a clay mold around it, then drains out the wax and pours in pure molten gold to form the valued object. Applied to poetics, the concept acknowledges two levels of interpretation, distinct in theory and representation. Such poetic form aims to attain maximum ideas with minimum words. 'Wax' refers to the most obvious and superficial meaning, whereas the 'gold' embedded in the art work offers the 'true' meaning, which may be inaccessible unless one understands the nuances of folk culture.[1]

TESHOME H. GABRIEL

This quotation illuminates succinctly the intense interest that recent African cinema holds for any film theory concerned with the 'hieroglyphic' tradition, and potential, of cinema. The catch-all phrase 'hieroglyph' is useful in that it evokes three processes: a code of composition, the encapsulation of an idea in an image which is on the verge of writing; a mode of address that asks that an audience apply its ability to decipher the poetics of the 'screen script'; and, finally, the work of criticism as a means of articulating the poetics that an audience recognises, but leaves implicit. The critical perspective of this article cannot include the 'nuances of folk culture' or, indeed, other important aspects of African culture and history, but attempts to present *Xala* as a film of theoretical importance and interest beyond its immediate cultural context. African cinema should not be seen as a 'developing' cinema, but as a cinema which, in spite of the enormous difficulties presented by the post-colonial context, is now making an original and significant contribution to the aesthetics of contemporary cinema. Ironically, or appropriately, this is particularly so, as cinema in the West goes further into decline.

From *Third Text*, 16–17, Autumn/Winter 1991, pp. 19–37.

The germinal ground in which the African cinema developed in the post-colonial period was francophone sub-Sahara, above all Senegal, and first of all, Ousmane Sembene. It was not until independence in 1960, and the aftermath of the French defeat in the Algerian war, that the conditions for an African cinema came into being. During the Fifties, Sembene had made his name as a writer and published his first novel while working as a docker and a union organiser in Marseilles. His novel, *Les Bouts de Bois de Dieu*, based on his experiences during the famous 1947–8 strike on the Bamako–Dakar railway, was published in 1960. Then, in 1961, immediately after independence, he went to the Soviet Union to study at the Moscow Film School, and his first short film, *Borom Sarret*, was shown at the Tours film festival in 1963. *La Noire de* ..., released in 1966, was the first full length feature from the sub-Sahara. As a Wolof, Sembene came from an oral tradition in which the *griot* functioned as poet and storyteller. As the son of a fisherman, he was self-educated. Although he was writing during the period that African poets, novelists, Marxist theorists and intellectuals in Paris were grouped around the journal *Présence Africaine*, Sembene was critical of the Negritude[2] movement with which they were identified. He considered the concept to be irrelevant to the popular resistance that grew into the independence movement. He identified himself with, and was part of, the anti-colonial struggle in Senegal rather than intellectual circles in Paris. While his novels were, of course, written in French, Sembene's cinema is more the product of popular, Senegalese traditions and his films are directed towards the cultural needs of the Senegalese people through the specific possibilities offered by the cinema:

> Often the worker or the peasant don't have time to pause on the details of their daily lives; they live them and do not have time to tie them down. The film-maker, though, can link one detail to another to put a story together. There is no longer a traditional story-teller in our days and I think the cinema can replace him.[3]

This last observation is characteristic of Sembene's commitment to promoting and transforming traditional culture, to using the cultural developments of Western society in the interests of Africa. Sembene was more interested in finding a dialectical relationship between the two cultures than in an uncritical nostalgia for pre-colonial pure African-ness.

The cinema can speak across the divisions created by illiteracy and language and is, therefore, a perfect mechanism for a cultural dialectic. It can participate in the oral cultural tradition; it can produce a culture in which the Wolof language plays a major role; and it can bring Wolof culture into the modernity of the post-colonial. In 1968 Sembene made *Mandabi* simultaneously in French and Wolof, and in *Xala* the question of language is at the political centre of the drama. The economic division between the entrepreneurial elite and the people is reflected in a division between French and Wolof. The elite use French exclusively to communicate among themselves and as their official language. They speak Wolof only across class and gender lines and it is considered to be inferior and archaic. In the novel *Xala*, which

Sembene wrote up from his script while searching for funds for the film, the young people of the left have developed a written equivalent for the Wolof language and are publishing a journal in their native language for the first time. In the film, Sembene sets up a parallel between two figures, who are quite marginal to the story but significant for its politics. One is a young student selling a magazine written in the new Wolof script; the other is a peasant, robbed of his village's savings which he had brought to town to buy seed. Both get caught in the police round-up of beggars that forms the film's central tableau and become integrated into the beggar community. Any moves towards cultural and economic advance and self-sufficiency from the people themselves are dashed in the polarisation between the entrepreneurial elite and the underclass it creates.

In *Xala*, Sembene uses the language of cinema to create a kind of poetics of politics. He gives visibility to the forms, as opposed to the content, of colonialism. He deciphers links between underlying structures and the symptoms that are stamped, as it were, onto the surface of the colonised's existence, across all classes. The film is set in Senegal after independence, so colonialism's presence is concealed behind a façade of self-government. The underlying structures mark the lives of the ruling elite as well as the people, and signs and symptoms signal an insistent return of the repressed. The repression is both political, of the people by the ruling elite, and psychological, of the ruling elite by their relation to Frenchness, and the two spheres become increasingly interlinked throughout the course of the film. While Sembene's analysis of signs is always historical and, in the last resort, materialist, he also acknowledges the place of sexuality and the structure of the psyche in the symptomology of neo-colonialism. There are shades of Franz Fanon's *Black Skin, White Masks*.

I have chosen the word 'carapace', rather than 'mask', to evoke the central poetic and political themes in *Xala* in order to introduce the image of vulnerable flesh covered by a protecting shell. The carapace doubles as a mask behind which the ruling elite camouflages itself, adopting the clothes, language and behaviour of its former colonial masters. The carapace also evokes the social structure of neo-colonialism. The entrepreneurial bourgeoisie live the life of an upper-crust, floating and parasitical on the lives of the people. In *Xala* the carapace conceals not simply vulnerable flesh, but flesh that is wounded by class exploitation and rotting away with corruption. Whereas a scab indicates that a wound has developed its own organic means of protection, the carapace of neo-colonialism denies and disavows the wound and prevents healing. The elite encase themselves in expensive Western consumer goods, while the beggars are crippled by deformed or missing limbs. The plot of the film focuses on El Hadji, a member of the entrepreneurial elite, who finds he is impotent when he marries his third wife. A tension then runs through the film between the vulnerability of his body, his failed erection, and his outward carapace made up of European props. In the end, his sexual vulnerability has forced him to realise, as he stands naked and covered with spit in the beggars' ritual, that the carapace has failed.

Sembene weaves a series of reflections on fetishism into these themes. A fetish is something in which someone invests a meaning and a value beyond or beside its actual meaning and value. Why an object should take on this special significance is mysterious, but adds to its fascination in the eye of its beholder. This process involves the willing surrender of knowledge to belief but, however intensely invested, belief is vulnerable, always partly acknowledging what it simultaneously disavows. While the fetish object is mysterious and fascinating to the fetishist, it is also a primitive sign, signalling a meaning outside, unavailable to, consciousness and language. While supporting the suspension of disbelief, it also materialises the unspeakable, the disavowed, the repressed. Like a red-flag at the point of danger, the fetish object calls attention to a nodal point of vulnerability, whether within the psychic structure of an individual or the cultural structure of a social group. The fetish is a symptom. It has a semiotic aspect, but one that is wrapped up in the obscurity of a cipher. So, while fetishism may disavow a personal or collective pain or anxiety, it also, by elevating an object to the status of a symptom, allows access to its own decoding.

The cinema, too, appropriates objects, turns them into images and wraps them in connotations and resonances that are collectively understood, or elevates them to a specific significance on a single, one-off, basis. Sembene makes use of the language of cinema, its hieroglyphic or pictographic possibilities, and creates a text which is about the meaning of objects and objects as symptoms. His use of cinematic rhetoric is the key to *Xala*. The form of the film engages the spectators' ability to read the signs that emanate from colonialism and its neocolonialist off-spring. And, because the film shows an African ruling elite accepting and appropriating the fetishisms of European capitalism, it allows a double reading. As a comedy of fetishistic manners *Xala* uses signs, objects and the rhetoric of cinema to allow its audience direct engagement with, and access to solving, the enigmas represented on the screen. But *Xala* also sets off a kind of chain reaction of theoretical reflections on fetishism, linking together otherwise diverse ideas, and highlighting the age-old function of fetishism as a conduit for the to and fro of cultural and economic exchange between Europe and Africa.

In a scene towards the end of *Xala*, El Hadji is being hounded out of the Chamber of Commerce by his equally corrupt colleagues. His most vindictive antagonist seizes his attaché case, and opens it to find it empty except for the magic object with which El Hadji had attempted to ward off the curse of impotence, the *xala*, that had afflicted him. His enemy holds it up for public ridicule. El Hadji seizes it and waves it defiantly in the faces of the others, shouting 'This is the true fetish, not the fetishism of technology'. At this moment, Sembene brings into the open the theoretical theme of his film, that is, the different discourses of fetishism. Up until that point, these different discourses had been woven into the story implicitly, creating the complex semiotic system that makes the experience of watching the film into something like visual detective work. At this point, three strands are conjoined in one climactic moment: a signifier of the pre-colonial, pre-Islamic belief system, which is also a signifier of El Hadji's sexual impotence, and the attache case, a key signifier in the chain of objects that refer to commodity fetishism.

There's a double temporality hidden in Sembene's use of the discourses of fetishism in *Xala*. There's another, extra-diegetic, history that the film invokes. This history, quite appropriately, is not visible in the film. But any consideration of fetishism in Senegal today raises 'ghosts' from the past. These are reminders that the word first came into existence in the proto-colonial exchanges beginning in the mid 15th century, between Portuguese merchant traders and the inhabitants of the West African coast, part of which is now known as Senegal. Sembene depicts an entrepreneurial, pre-capitalist economy in contemporary Senegal and the film is about the function, within that economy, of fetishised objects as signifiers of unequal exchange. The film inevitably draws the attention of anyone interested in the history of the concept of fetishism to its origins in that earlier period of pre-capitalist, mercantile, economic exchange. Before analysing the theme of fetishism in the film itself, I would like to use it as an excuse to raise some of these ghosts and make some introductory points about the history of the concept of fetishism. Marcel Mauss first pronounced the epitaph on the anthropological use of the word fetishism as a compromised relic of 19th-century imperialist ethnography:

> When the history of the science of religions and ethnography comes to be written, the undeserved and fortuitous role played by concepts such as fetishism in theoretical and descriptive works will be considered astonishing. The concept represents nothing but an enormous misunderstanding between two cultures, the African and the European, and is based purely on a blind obeisance to colonial usage.[4]

The 'enormous misunderstanding between two cultures' provides a clue to the recent revival of interest in the origins of the term *fetishism*, and its significance for the development of a polarisation between primitive and civilised thought as a moral and intellectual justification for imperialism.

William Pietz has discussed the origins of both the word and the concept in a series of articles in the journal *Res*.[5] He shows how the word emerged in the cross-cultural encounter between West African and European Christian cultures in the 16th and 17th centuries. It was a 'novel word that appeared as a response to an unprecedented type of situation', of relations between 'cultures so radically different as to be mutually incomprehensible'. Pietz argues that the term bears witness to its own history. To reject the term completely, as purely and simply a relic of colonialism and imperialist anthropology, is to ignore its historical specificity and the cultural implications that go with it. Pietz demonstrates that fetishism is a debased derivation of the Portuguese *feitiço*, which means witchcraft, in turn derived from the Latin *facticium* which means artificial. *Feitiço* was applied by the Portuguese wholesale to beliefs and practices which they neither could nor would interpret, but encountered in their commercial relations. In the pidgin of middlemen, who settled in West Africa and became the *soi disant* experts on native customs, the word became *fetisso*. Pietz says:

> it brought a wide array of African objects and practices under a category that, for all its misrepresentation of cultural facts, enabled the formation of more or less non-coercive commerical relations between members of bewilderingly different cultures.[6]

The lore and practices that developed around the concept of the *fetisso* were then inherited, wholesale and to a second degree, by the Dutch traders who arrived on the West Coast in the very late 16th century and who had gradually ejected the Portuguese by 1641. The Dutch Calvinists brought the Reformation's deep hatred of, and anxiety at, the superstitious and idolatrous practices of Catholicism. To them, the idolatry of the Portuguese and the fetishism of the Africans became enmeshed. It was the Dutch merchants of this period, Pieter Marees and William Bosman in particular, who wrote down their experience and observation of African customs. Pietz argues that the implications of the concept 'fetishism' took shape during this period. It was during the late 17th century, with West African trade efficiently organised by the Dutch East India Company, that conceptual problems of value began to be theorised as 'a problematic concerning the capacity of the material object to embody values'. The concept of the fetish emerged alongside and in conjunction with 'the emergent articulation of the commodity form'. It was, for instance, during the second part of the 17th century that William Petty, an influence on Adam Smith, described by Marx as 'the father of Political Economy and to some extent the founder of statistics', was evolving an early version of the labour theory of value.

To the Europeans, the Africans' attribution of talismanic and prophylactic powers to inanimate objects was the basis for their false economic valuation to material objects. They would exchange gold for what the Europeans considered to be worthless 'trifles'. The overestimation, on the one hand, was the source of an underestimation on the other, blocking 'natural reason' and 'rational market activity'. At the same time, the *fetisso* became deeply imbricated in commercial relations. It was the practice to guarantee transactions by getting Africans to take 'fetish oaths', which, while ensuring the efficacity of the transactions, also confirmed the innately superstitious nature of the indigenous people.

> For the European merchant, the *fetisso* posed a double problem, a double perversion. First, the status of commercially valuable objects as *fetissos* complicated his ability to acquire them as commodities and seemed to distort their relative exchange value. This often led to transactions with an exceptionally high rate of profit, but it also caused difficulties since the locals regarded the desired objects in a personal, social, or religious register rather than an economic one. Second, to effect economic transactions merchants had to accept the preliminary swearing of oaths upon *fetissos* – a perversion of the natural processes of economic negotiation and legal contract. Desiring a clean economic interaction, seventeenth-century merchants unhappily found themselves

entering into social relations and quasi-religious ceremonies that should have been irrelevant to the conduct of trade were it not for the perverse superstitions of their trade partners. The general theory of fetishism that emerged in the eighteenth century was determined by the problematic specific to this novel historical situation.[7]

The beliefs and practices surrounding *fetissos* were described, exotically and derogatorily, by travellers, merchants and priests above all, during the 17th and early 18th century, culminating in the publication of William Bosman's *New and Accurate Account of the Coast of Guinea* in 1704. It was this descriptive work that was used as the basis for President de Brosses' general theorisation of fetishism published in 1760. De Brosses used the concept of fetishism to describe the culture of Africa as essentially childish and that 'what is today the religion of African Negroes and other barbarians, was once upon a time the religion of the ancients, everywhere on earth'. Writing at the time of the Encyclopaedia, de Brosses' account of fetishism began to become integrated into intellectual discourse. Pietz comments:

> This sanctioning power through magical belief and violent emotion was understood to take the place of the rational institutional sanctions that empowered the legal systems of European states ... social order was dependent on psychological facts rather than political principles.[8]

It is in this sense that the concept and discourse of fetishism has itself played an important part in justifying the colonisation, exploitation and oppression of Africa. The concept of fetishism allowed the Enlightenment to define the ability to conceptualise abstractly as an effect of the evolution of religion. August Comte used de Brosses to argue that fetishism constituted an infancy in the history of human spiritual belief, a moment through which, once upon a time, all religions have passed. He argues that the lack of priests as intermediaries and the personal and domestic nature of the cults blocked the development of belief in an invisible, abstract godhead.

> It is above all a belief in the invisibility of the gods and their essential distinction from the bodies under their discipline, that must determine, in the polytheistic period, the rapid and significant development of a true priesthood, able to acquire a high social authority, constituting, in a permanent and ordered manner, an indispensable intermediary between the worshipper and his god. Fetishism, on the other hand, does not involve this inevitable intervention, and thus tends to prolong indefinitely the infancy of social organisation, which must depend, for its first step, on the distinctive formation of a class of speculative thinkers, that is to say, a priesthood.[8]

Jean Pouillon argues that Hegel, however, saw the fetishism of the African not as a stage on the path towards civilisation but inherent: the 'African' being unable to 'move beyond a first antithesis between man and nature'. From the perspective of this logic, colonisation and civilisation became synonymous. Pouillon comments: 'Le fétichisme ne débouche sur rien et les colonialisateurs pourront avoir bonne conscience.'[10]

The concept of the fetish provides an antinomy for the rational thought of the post-Enlightenment period. It gives a new form and historic twist to the long-standing and familiar spirit-body and abstraction/materiality polarisations. It coincides with the iconoclastic purification of Christianity from the trappings of idolatrous Catholicism, in which a return to the Old Testament and the precedent of the Jewish, monotheistic rejection of Egyptian iconology was influential. Pietz emphasises that the coming into being of the concept of the fetish was necessarily in conjunction with 'the emergent articulation of the ideology of the commodity form'. W. J. Mitchell points out: 'If Adam Smith is Moses he is also Martin Luther.'[11] It was this discourse of fetishism ('the mist enveloped regions of the religious world') that Marx turned back onto his own society and that Freud used to define the furthest limits of the psyche's primitive (in)credulity. In both their uses of the analogy, however, they gave the concept of the fetish a new life, turning it away from its anthropological roots towards questions of signification. The fetish raises questions of meaning quite apart from its constructed antinomy with abstraction. It epitomises the human ability to project value onto a material object, repress the fact that the projection has taken place, and then interpret the object as the autonomous source of that value. Thus the process has become invisible, and the object acquires a meaning that denies its historical specificity. It is, then, an enigma and it is up to the critic or analyst to reveal its significance. The fetish is a sign rather than an idea and it can be analysed semiologically rather than philosophically. It announces the presence of an invisible structure as 'to be analysed' (whether psychoanalytically or politically). This process is central to *Xala*.

The opening, pre-credit, sequence of *Xala* shows a crowd celebrating as a group of African businessmen expel the French from the Chamber of Commerce and take control of their own economy. The people in the crowd are depicted in such a way as to evoke 'African-ness', with bare breasts, dancing and drums. These connotative images never appear again in the film; the depiction of the characters' clothes and appearance are appropriate for the Islamic sub-Sahara. The businessmen are dressed in loose shirts and trousers made out of 'African' type materials. They appear at the top of the steps, ejecting a few objects that evoke the colonising culture (including a bust of Marie-Antoinette). The camera is placed at the bottom of the steps. As the men turn to go into the building the camera dips slightly to change its angle and the steps suddenly resemble a stage on which a performance has just taken place. When the camera joins the men back in the Chamber, they are dressed in the dark European business suits that they will wear for the rest of the film. While the crowds are still celebrating, a posse of police start to push them back at the command of one of the recently expelled Frenchmen. The other two Frenchmen then enter the Chamber and place a black attaché case in front of each African businessman. Each case is full of money. The two men step backwards with the silent subservience they maintain, as 'advisers', for the rest of the film. The sequence closes as El Hadji

Abdou Kader Beye invites his colleagues to the wedding party celebrating his marriage to a third wife. All the speeches are in French.

The film opens with El Hadji collecting his two other wives to go to the party. The elder wife, Adja Awa Astou, is traditional and religious. Sembene says: 'He got his first wife before becoming a somebody.' The second wife, Oumi N'Doye, is Westernised and mercenary. Sembene says: 'Along with his economic and social development, he takes a second who corresponds, so to speak, to a second historical phase.' Awa's daughter Rama, who stands up to her father throughout the film, synthesises progressive elements in both African and Western cultures. She has posters of Amilcar Cabral and Charlie Chaplin in her room; she dresses in African style and rides a motor scooter; she is a student at the University and she will only speak Wolof. N'gone, El Hadji's new wife, is dressed for a white, Western wedding and her face is covered with a bridal veil. Sembene says: 'The third, his daughter's age but without her mind, is only there for his self-esteem.' Then, on the wedding night, El Hadji finds he is impotent. During the rest of the film he tries to work out who could have cursed him and visits two *marabouts* to cure him. His financial affairs unravel, unable to sustain the cost of three households and the lavish wedding, until he is finally expelled from the Chamber of Commerce.

The central enigma in *Xala* cannot be deciphered until the very last scene, when the beggars, who have gradually come to figure more significantly throughout the film, invade El Hadji's house. Then the different clues that have been signalled by Sembene throughout the film fall into place and complete the picture. El Hadji does not function as a knowing narrator and the only character with whom the spectator is given any identification, personally and ideologically, is Rama, who plays only a small part in the film. El Hadji is a didactic hero. He is made into an example, rather as Brecht makes an example out of Mother Courage. He only engages sympathy through the disaster he has brought on himself, and, like a tragic hero of the cathartic theatre, he is stripped literally to nakedness. On a more significant level, he cannot command the narration because he refuses to understand his own history. This creates a narrational structure that deprives the audience of the safety and security of a hero who will guide them through events, and provide them with an appropriate moral perspective. More importantly, the spectator realises, at the end, that the film itself has held the clues to the enigma of El Hadji's *Xala*, and these linked images and figurations can, retrospectively, be deciphered. Sembene's use of cinema demands a spectator who is actively engaged with reading and interpreting the sounds and images unrolling on the screen.

There are certain parallels between *Xala*'s narrational strategy and that of *Citizen Kane*. Both films are constructed around a central enigma, and tell the story of a man's relationship to money, fetishised objects and sexuality. In *Citizen Kane*, the audience's investigation of the enigma is conducted by a surrogate, the journalist, Thompson. However, he is unable to see or interpret the clues contained in the visual discourse of the film. These clues act as signifiers, building up concentrations of possible significance like the clustering of iron filings on a magnetic field. While they indicate an area of sensitivity, explanation or interpretation, as also in *Xala*, is denied until the end of the film. The pieces finally fall into place when the camera allows the audience a privileged look at the little sled as it is thrown on the flames. Thompson cannot see how these signifiers link together like the rings of a chain and mark the movement of associated ideas, objects and images that map out the process of displacement. The camera, or rather the rhetoric of the cinema, assumes the position of master narrator, and directly addresses the audience.

As in *Xala* the audience of *Citizen Kane* then has to think back over the whole course of the film to translate the 'sensitive areas', retrospectively, and solve the enigma by deciphering the sliding of the signifiers. Just as the glass snow-storm allows a 'reference back' to the log-cabin, so the name 'rosebud' on the sled at the end of the film returns the missing signified to the enigma, seeming to halt and restore order to the slippage of signifiers. But the signified 'Rosebud' then sets off on another journey, as a signifier for the lost mother and a memorial to that loss. As Jacques Lacan points out in his essay 'Agency of the letter in the unconscious', a signifier's ability to suggest multiple signifieds creates the leap of association that allows the unconscious mind to displace one idea onto another. Where the conscious mind has set up an impenetrable wall of censorship, the unconscious disguises its ideas through displacement, but not so completely that the link between the original idea and the disguised idea will be lost. Psychoanalysis tries to trace the process backwards, following the links and deciphering the clues in reverse, restoring the links between the signifier lodged, but indecipherable, in the conscious mind to the unconscious idea they represent. Describing the language of dreams, Freud used the image of a rebus and compared dream interpretation to the decipherment of the clues in a pictogram.

In *Xala* the visual coding of ideas is even more marked and further emphasised by the absence of a surrogate narrator. This mode of cinematic address is perfectly suited to the film's subject matter: fetishism. El Hadji and his colleagues have lost touch with their own history and society through adopting Frenchness as a sign of superior class position. There is an unbridgeable gap between the elite's own origins, the condition of the people and their present masquerade of Westernised, entrepreneurial modernity. The gap is demonstrated by the elite's use of French, rather than Wolof, and safeguarded by a fetishisation of European objects. Those things, like, for instance, El Hadji's Mercedes, are the literal materials of the carapace, his defence against political and economic reality, and the outward manifestations of a corruption that sucks the life blood of the people. When the Mercedes is repossessed, Modu, the chauffeur, carries a wooden stool as he guides his employer along the street. The stool is like a shrunken, or wizened, version of the proud object of display. It is a trace of, or a memorial to, the Mercedes and its meaning for El Hadji. Because Modu has been so closely identified with the car and its welfare, his presence links the two objects ironically together. Sembene consistently links people with things, things substitute for people or for each other, things acquire associations and resonances that weave like threads of meaning through the film. At the same time, he raises the issue of substitution and exchange in a social and economic sphere. The *marabout* who cures El Hadji's *xala*, Sereen

Mada, restores it when the cheque that El Hadji gave him in payment is bounced by the bank.

As the members of the Chamber of Commerce arrive at El Hadji's wedding party, the camera is positioned so that, as each man walks past, his attaché case is framed in close-up. On the outside, the attaché case is emblematic of the power of the international business community, but inside, as only the audience can know, is the secret evidence of corruption and collaboration with the old colonial masters. While seeming to be signs of power and authority, the attaché cases represent the real impotence of the entrepreneurial elite in relation to neo-colonialism. Once the film has established these associations, the image of the attaché case evokes them whenever it appears. So that when El Hadji walks dejectedly away, carrying his attaché case, from N'gone's house after his failed wedding night, he seems to be bowed down with a double impotence. And, in his final confrontation with his colleagues, his case is empty apart from the fetish given to him by the phoney *marabout*. The failed fetish is found in the place formally occupied by the fetishism of the banknotes.

Although the particular discourse of sexuality, on which Freud's theory of fetishism depends, cannot be imposed carelessly on another culture, Sembene's juxtaposition of the psycho-sexual with the socio-economic is explicit. He uses the sexual as the point of fissure, or weakness, in the system of economic fetishism. El Hadji's impotence is a symptom of something else, a sign of the eruption of the unconscious onto the body itself. For Freud, the fetish enables the psyche to live with the castration anxiety; it contributes to the ego's mechanisms of defence; it keeps the truth, which the conscious mind represses, concealed. When the fetish fails to function effectively, the symptoms it holds in check start to surface. In *Xala*, the fragile carapace collapses under pressure from class politics and economics but these pressures are expressed through, and latch on to, sexuality and work on the body's vulnerability to the psyche. For Sembene, class politics determine over and above sexuality. Sexuality plays its part in the drama as the site of the symptom, the first sign of a return of the repressed. In his representation of repression, he makes full use of the *double entendre* that can condense its political and psychological connotations.

The morning after the wedding El Hadji's secretary opens his shop. Modu delivers El Hadji in the Mercedes. El Hadji asks his secretary to telephone the President of the Chamber of Commerce who then comes over to see him at once. Interspersed and separate from these events, the beggars are slowly collecting and taking up their usual positions outside in the street. A theme of dirt versus cleanliness had been established in the opening moments of the sequence. As the local women empty their slops into the drain outside the shop, the secretary runs out with her disinfectant spray to ward off infection. As El Hadji's car appears, so do the beggars and their music; as the President's car appears, so do the cripples. In the back office, El Hadji tells the President about the *xala*. The President reacts with horror saying 'Who? Who could have done this to you?' At that moment the beggars' music drifts into the room. El Hadji gets up from his chair without answering and goes through to the front office and closes the window. He asks the President to call the police and remove this 'human refuse', adding that 'it's bad for tourism'. The police arrive, and under the direction of their French commander, load the beggars into a lorry and drive them out of town. They are left miles away, in the middle of nowhere, and start their slow, painful, trek back into town.

When watching this scene, the spectator cannot but be conscious of a figuration of 'repression'. The President orders that the beggars be removed from sight and from consciousness. And their return then figures a 'return of the repressed'. To the mutilated limbs of the cripples is now added a baton wound on the head of the boy who guides the blind man and whom Modu employs to clean the car. The repression is both physical and social and the bodies of the beggars are symptoms of social and economic injustice. But this scene also contains a clue to the enigma, to the source of the *xala*, to its source in El Hadji's social and historical position. This other, psychic, dimension is not revealed until the final scene in the film. When El Hadji's fall is complete, Oumi has left him, N'gone's *Badyen* (her father's sister) has repudiated the marriage, his cheque to the *marabout* had bounced so the *xala* returned, his bank has refused to extend his loans, and his colleagues have voted unanimously to expel him from the Chamber of Commerce for embezzling thirty tons of rice destined for the country people. As Modu takes him to Awa's house, he tells El Hadji that the blind man can cure the *xala*. The scene builds up to the final revelation as the beggars invade the house under the blind man's leadership. While some of the beggars loot the kitchen, the blind man sits as it were in judgement. He says to El Hadji:

> 'Do you recognize me? . . . Our story goes back a long way'. He tells how El Hadji had taken his clan's land. 'What I have become is your fault. You appropriated our inheritance. You falsified our names and we were expropriated. I was thrown in prison. I am of the Beye family. Now I will get my revenge. I arranged your xala. If you want to be a man you will undress nude in front of everyone. We will spit on you'.

It was this first act of oppression that had set El Hadji on the road towards entrepreneurial success and had taken him from the country to the town, away from loyalty to family to individualism, from traditional modes of inheritance to falsified, written, legal documents, away from the continuity of his own history into a charade of Frenchness. His failure to recognise the beggar indicates that he had covered his tracks by 'forgetting'. But when the President asked who had cursed him, his response was to shut out the sound of the beggar's song. This gesture signified both an acknowledgement of the truth and the need, quickly, to re-enact its repression.

During the final scene with the beggars, the tailor's dummy with N'gone's wedding veil, returned contemptuously to El Hadji by the *Badyen*, stands clearly visible in the corner. The presence of these objects sets off a chain of associations that run back through the film as the links between them begin to emerge. N'gone acts as a pivot between the two fetishistic systems the economic and the sexual. She is woman as commodity, woman as fetish and woman as consumer of commodities. This sphere of capitalist consumption has been traditionally the province of women and Luce Irigaray, in her essay 'Women on the market', traces the genealogy of the anthropological exchange of women to women as both consumers and consumed in modern, urban society. N'gone's marriage to El Hadji was based on exchange. At the wedding his gifts are displayed including, most prominently, a car key. The car which stands on the back of a truck, decked out with ribbons, outside the gate of the villa, is El Hadji's present to her in exchange for her virginity. As he leaves the villa after his unconsummated wedding night, he stops by the car and touches it mournfully, so that the car seems to substitute for N'gone's unattainable sexuality. The car's fetishistic quality, its elevation out of ordinary use, the ribbons, is displaced onto her figure. She is first seen concealed behind her wedding veil, packaged like a valuable commodity, and she speaks only once throughout the film. To emphasise this 'thing-ness' and 'to-be-looked-at-ness', Sembene places her next to a large, nude but tasteful, photograph of her as the *Badyen* prepares her for her wedding night. As she is undressed and her wedding veil placed on the tailor's dummy, the camera pans up from her naked back to her body in the photograph. In a later scene the same camera movement reiterates this juxtaposition.

N'gone's sexual attraction is in contrast to Oumi's immediate, vital, demanding and corporeal sexuality. N'gone is image and commodity and, half concealed behind the wedding veil, she evokes the double nature of commodity fetishism. The commodity, to circulate and realise the capital invested in it, must seduce its consumer and, in its very seductiveness, its 'packagedness', disguise the secret of its origins. That is, the inherent unglamorousness of the production process should be invisible, and, most of all, class relations, the extraction of surplus value, must be concealed by seductive surface. N'gone's image as fetish evokes the processes of veiling, disguise and substitution necessary to commodity fetishism. It is perhaps significant that when El Hadji, temporarily cured of his *xala* by Sereen Mada, goes triumphantly to his new bride, she has her period and is 'not available'. Her perfect surface is tarnished by menstrual blood. Although the depiction of N'gone suggests links with the appearance and circulation of the commodity under capitalism, the story is taking place in a non-industrialised and 'underdeveloped' country. The money El Hadji needed to acquire her as commodity, in the specific economic conditions of neo-colonialism, came from financial corruption and exploitative entrepreneurial capitalism. He paid for the wedding and N'gone's gifts by embezzling and illegally selling the quota of rice intended for the country people. The secret corruption is displaced onto the little car that N'gone will receive in exchange for her virginity, the car's fetishistic qualities are displaced onto N'gone for whom a photograph and a tailor's dummy become substitutes and metaphors.

Karl Marx evolved his theory of commodity fetishism in the process of developing his theory of value. The problem Marx perceived to be at stake in the theory of value is connected to the question of visibility and invisibility of labour power and of value. Here the question of materiality and abstraction returns, in the context of a capitalist system of thought that Marx can show to be deeply imbricated with fetishism, its phobic other. W. J. Mitchell says:

> Marx's turning the rhetoric of iconoclasm on its principal users was a brilliant tactical manoeuvre; given nineteenth-century Europe's obsession with primitive, oriental, 'fetishistic' cultures that were the prime object of imperialist expansion, one can hardly imagine a more effective rhetorical move.[12]

Marx identified commodity fetishism as emerging out of the gap between a belief in the commodity as its own autochthonous. as it were, source of value and knowledge of its true source in human labour. This gap is finally papered over and disguised under capitalism, as the labour market necessary for mass industrial production can only function by transforming individual labour power into abstract and generalised wage labour. There are issues of representation at stake here that can be rendered in a semiotic system, using Charles Peirce's tripartite division of the sign into index, icon and symbol. This approach would go as follows. If it is human labour that creates the value of a commodity, as some of Marx's bourgeois economist predecessors had already determined, the problem is how that value is represented in the commodity produced. As Marx pointed out, labour has no means of self-expression. Its first effacement is due to the failure of labour power to inscribe itself indexically on its product, the index being the sign that has a physical link to the object it represents. Labour power fashions the commodity, alters its formal structure, but cannot impose any signification of value on the object. Marx continues with his argument: value can only be signified through exchange, when one commodity measures itself against another and the differential can then be quantified. At this stage, the use value of the commodity falls into abeyance in relation to a new signifier, its exchange value. Marx's argument, at this point, illustrates the inadequacy of the icon, the sign that is based on resemblance. Although you can establish one commodity as a reflection of the value of others, the system is clumsy and, more importantly, insufficiently flexible for capitalism to function efficiently. The circulation of commodities in a capitalist market demanded a symbolic representation of value, enabling a generalised system of exchange. The articulation of value through literal equations of commodity against commodity is effaced, in its turn, under a new signifier, money as a general equivalent. This is a 'joint action of the whole world of commodities'. Value is now realised in an abstract form, as labour power itself is generalised into an abstraction. Labour power, under capitalism, is itself a commodity and measured by an undifferentiated and socially determined standard for the amount of time and effort necessary for a generalised system of production to function. And, in order to function, the extraction of surplus value from the labour power of the worker has to be rendered invisible, alongside labour power as the source of value. The commodity's glamour, verging into sex appeal, seals these complicated processes into a fixation on seeing, believing and not understanding.

Money, the means of expression of value as a symbolic equivalent, is comparable, Marx said, to language. The disavowal characteristic of fetishism is due to misunderstandings of the complex stages inherent in an abstract, symbolic system and the political need to disavow the worker labour power as source of the commodity's value. Just as a religious believer refuses to accept the human origin of his object of worship, so capitalism refuses to accept that value originates in the labour of the working class. The more abstract the process, the more utterly fundamental is the denial of human origin.

While belief in a fetish may be obviously a disavowal of its intractable materiality, belief in an abstract god creates a gap between man and spirit that is harder to materialise. 'A commodity is therefore a mysterious thing, because in it, the social character of men's labour appears to them as an objective character stamped on the product of that labour.' It was at this point that Marx invoked, in a famous phrase 'the mist enveloped regions of the religious world'. In that world

> the productions of the human brain appear as independent beings endowed with life and entering into relations both with one another and the human race. [And then] value does not stalk about with a label describing what it is. It is value that converts every product into a social hieroglyphic. . . . The determination of the magnitude of value by labour time is therefore a secret, hidden in the apparent fluctuations of the relative values of commodities. . . . It is the ultimate money form of the world of commodities that actually conceals instead of disclosing the social character of private labour and the social relations between the individual producers.[13]

The hieroglyph of value is like a trompe l'oeil. It appears on the surface to be intrinsic to its commodity but, with a move to another perspective, from the visible to the theoretical, its structure may be made accessible to knowledge. In capitalist society, the gap between the commodity's appearance and the labour power that originally produced it also masks and conceals the social reality of production, the sphere of the worker, of the factory, of toil and exploitation, of exhaustion and dirt. This property of the commodity then comes in useful in the sphere of circulation. The commodity has to realise its value in exchange. Someone must buy it. And so it has to present a seductive and attractive surface to the world of consumers, dressing up in a shiny, glittering packaging that in itself both adds consumer allure and the last fetishistic touch to its make-up.

The commodity thus seals its enigmatic self-sufficiency behind a masquerade, a surface that disavows both the structure of value and its origin in working-class labour. Instead it is inscribed with a different kind of semiotic, one that is directed towards the market place, which further disguises, or papers over, the semiotic that originated in its production. Baudrillard argues in *The Political Economy of the Sign*[14] that, increasingly in the consumer societies of advanced capialism, both the object form (use value) and the commodity form (exchange value) are transfigured into sign value. This is partly the function of advertising, which is expert in the creation of sign values, weaving an intricate web of connotation, as Roland Barthes describes in his analysis of the Panzani advertisement in the essay 'The rhetoric of the image'.[15] Baudrillard then argues that spending, or perhaps one should say 'shopping', elevates the commodity form into sign value, so that the economic is then transfigured into sign systems, and economic power becomes visibly transmuted into the trappings of social privilege. Consumer objects can then create needs in advance of the consumer's awareness of a need, bearing out Marx's point that 'production not only produces goods but it produces people to consume them and corresponding needs'.

The circulation of European commodity in a society of the kind depicted in *Xala* caricatures and exaggerates the commodity fetishism inherent in capitalism. Rather than representing an enigma that may be deciphered, politically and theoretically, to reveal its place in the historical and economic order of things, the commodity's ties with history are thus effectively severed. The chain of displacements that construct the concept of value are attenuated to the point that all connection with the source of value, basic to fetishism, are irredeemably lost in the movement from capitalism to colonialism. Floating freely outside its own economy, the gulf between luxury objects monopolised by a Third World elite and the labour power of the working class in the producing country seems vast. Belief in the commodity's supposedly self-generated value does not demand the process of disavowal it depends on at home, so that it can live out its myth as an object of cult. In *Xala*, Sembene uses the neo-colonial economy to show the capitalist commodity 'super fetishised'. Modu, for instance, only puts imported bottled water into the Mercedes. These things take on pure 'sign value' (as Baudrillard would put it). However, the objects enable another process of disavowal. Sembene suggests that these fetishised objects seal the repression of history and of class and colonial politics under the rhetoric of nationhood. His use of the concept of fetishism is not an exact theoretical working through of the Marxist or Freudian concepts of fetishism, however, his use is *Marxist* and *Freudian*. Furthermore, the interest of the film lies in its inextricable intermeshing of the two.

In the final images of the film, its class and psychological themes are suddenly polarised into a new pattern. Sembene invokes horror of the body and its materiality through the desperate and degraded condition of the beggars and cripples. As El Hadji is denounced by the blind man, their wounds and their missing limbs demonstrate the political fact that financial corruption and profit are manifested on the bodies of the poor. The Western objects that the entrepreneurial elite fetishise inflict not impotence but castration on those they impoverish. The wounded body, the source of horror in the Freudian concept of castration anxiety, returns in the wounded bodies of the beggars and the hunger of the peasants. These bodies break through the barriers maintained by the French language and symbolised, for instance, by El Hadji's cult of Evian water. The otherness of Africa which horrified the Europeans is perpetuated into a real horror for the ordinary people by colonialism, and grotesquely more so, by the irresponsible greed of the new ruling class.

For Freud, the site of castration anxiety is the mother's body. For Julia Kristeva, the mother's body is the site of abjection.[16] The child's relation to its mother was a time of boundarilessness and a time when the body and its fluids were not a source of disgust. For Kristeva, the ego defines itself by a demarcation of its limits through mastering its waste and separating itself from those of the mother. It establishes itself as an individual, in its oneness. This concept of individualism is, it has been extensively argued, a crucial basis for the ideology of entrepreneurial capitalism. And, as has also been extensively argued, the residue of disgust, bodily waste, are the matter of ritual. In the last moments of *Xala*, the beggars take their revenge on El Hadji in a role reversal of power and humiliation. As El Hadji stands naked, in front of his wife and daughter, the beggars crowd around and spit on him. This is the price that the blind man exacts for lifting the *xala*. And as the scene seems to continue beyond endurance, the film ends with a freeze frame.

Sembene's film, opening with the theatre of politics, moves through a ceremonial celebration of marriage, and closes with a ritual of rebirth. The prophylactic rituals of fetishised manhood fail, both financial and sexually. Teshome Gabriel says:

> The spitting on El Hadji helps reincorporate him into the people's fold. In other words, the ritual becomes a folk method of purgation which makes El Hadji a literal incarnation of all members of the class or group that spit on him and consequently reintegrates him into folk society.[17]

In submitting to the body, and to everything that fetishism disavows, psychic and political, El Hadji signals a lifting of amnesia and an acceptance of history. The freeze frame resur-erects a man, whole through community, stripped of the trappings of colonialism and fetishised individualism.

Teshome Gabriel draws attention to a scene between El Hadji and Rama in which words, emblems and the film image weave an intricate pattern of meanings at different levels of visibility:

> Before Rama stands up to walk out of the frame Sembene makes us take note, once again, of the map of Africa behind her. We notice too that the colour of the map reflects the exact same colours of Rama's traditional boubou, native costume – blue, purple, green and yellow – and it is not divided into boundaries and states. It denotes pan-Africanism;

> El Hadji: My child. do you need anything? (He searches his wallet).
> Rama: Just my mother's happiness. (She walks out of frame as the camera lingers on the map.)

> What Sembene is saying here is quite direct and no longer inaccessible. On one level Rama shows concern for her mother. . . . On another level . . . her concern becomes not only her maternal mother, but 'mother Africa'. This notion carries an extended meaning when we observe the shot of El Hadji – to his side we see a huge colonial map of Africa. The 'wax' and the 'gold' are posited jointly by a single instance of composition. Two realities fight to command the frame, but finally the 'gold' meaning leaps out and breaks the boundaries of the screen.

Notes

1. Teshome H. Gabriel' '*Xala*: cinema of wax and gold', in P. Stevens (ed.), *Jump Cut: Hollywood, politics and counter cinema*, Between the Lines: Toronto, 1985.

2. Noureddine Ghali says: 'The concept of "negritude" was developed by a group of French speaking black intellectuals studying in Paris during the 1930s and 1940s, among them Léopold Senghor later to be the first president of Senegal after colonial rule. It denoted a view of black people as particularly gifted in the art of immediate living, of sensual experience, of physical skill and prowess, all of which belonged to them by birthright. It was an attempt at the time to combat the racist view of African civilisation as a null quality, and the ideology that French colonial rule was providing otherwise worthless culture-less beings with the opportunity to assimilate themselves to French culture.... Sembene is one of the many later African writers who have criticised the concept vigorously, among other things for underpinning the view that the European contribution to global culture to be technological and rational, while Africa can continue in economic disarray because it is happy just "being"'. 'An interview with Ousmane Sembene', in J. Downing (ed.), *Film and Politics in the Third World*, Autonomedia: Brooklyn, 1987.

3. *ibid.*

4. Marcel Mauss, *Oeuvres II*, Editions de Minuit: Paris, 1969, p. 245.

5. William Pietz, 'The problem of the fetish', Part I, *Res*, 9, Spring 1985; Part IIIa, Peabody Museum, Harvard University, Cambridge, MA, Autumn 1988.

6. *ibid.*

7. *ibid.*

8. *ibid.*

9. From *Cours de philosophie positive*. Extracted in Pontalis (ed.), 'Objets du fétichisme', *Nouvelle Revue de Psychoanalyse*, 2, Autumn 1970.

10. 'Fetishism leads to nowhere and the colonisers can have a good conscience', Jean Pouillon, 'Fetiches sans fétichisme', in Pontalis, *op. cit.*

11. W. J. Mitchell, *Iconology: Image, text, ideology*, University of Chicago Press, Chicago, IL, 1986.

12. *ibid.*

13. Karl Marx, *Capital*, vol. 1, ch. 1, passim.

14. Jean Baudrillard, *For a Critique of the Political Economy of the Sign*, trans. Charles Levin, Telos Press: St Louis, MI, 1981.

15. Roland Barthes, 'The rhetoric of the image', in *Image-Music-Text*, essays selected and trans. Stephen Heath, Fontana: London, 1982, p. 32.

16. Julia Kristeva, *Powers of Horror: An essay on abjection*, trans. Leon S. Roudiez, Columbia University Press: New York, 1982.

17. Gabriel, *op. cit.*

31 □ *The Empire Renarrated:* Season of Migration to the North *and the Reinvention of the Present*

Saree S. Makdisi

The old river in its broad reach rested unruffled at the decline of day after ages of good service done to the race that peopled its banks, spread out in the tranquil dignity of a waterway leading to the uttermost ends of the earth.

JOSEPH CONRAD, *Heart of Darkness*

I

The serenity and majesty of the Thames as it is described at the beginning of *Heart of Darkness* are only too appropriate for this waterway down which had sailed, long before Joseph Conrad's time, vessels carrying with them the seeds of the British Empire. Conrad's Thames flows in remarkable contrast to the Nile that rages through al-Tayyib Salih's *Season of Migration to the North* (1969). Far from resting in 'tranquil dignity', the Nile and the people inhabiting its banks are shown undergoing violent transfigurations. If *Heart of Darkness* narrates the history of modern British imperialism from a position deep within its metropolitan centre, *Season of Migration* presents itself as the counternarrative of the same bitter history. Just as Conrad's novel was bound up with Britain's imperial project, Salih's participates (in an oppositional way) in the afterlife of the same project today, by 'writing back' to the colonial power that once ruled the Sudan.

But *Season of Migration* is also a radical intervention in the field of postcolonial Arab discourse, which has long been centered on the debate between 'traditionalism'

From *Critical Inquiry*, 18, Summer 1992, pp. 804–20.

and 'Westernism'. This debate has its origins in the nineteenth century, when the ideology of modernity (which sustained the emerging European empires) began to be imposed on Arab social formations, in many cases long before the actual arrival of the European armies.[1] From the very beginning, this ideology had to compete with the residual (but still very powerful) ideological structures of traditionalism, and the interaction of these ideologies has shaped the whole process of modernization in Arab societies from the nineteenth century until the present day. Modernity, in the Arab world, has been inextricably associated with Europe itself.[2] In the face of this association, however, some Muslim and Arab intellectuals tried to reform the traditional structures of Islamic society in order to contest modernity as it was presented by Europe. Jamal al-Din Afghani and Muhammad Abduh, for instance, argued that Islam embodied the principles of modernity within its own doctrine and therefore that the confrontation between traditionalism and modernity was a false one since the latter is immanent in the former.[3] Against this position many other Arab intellectuals insisted on the absolute identity of modernity and Europe. Rifaah al-Tahtawi, whose work has had tremendous influence on cultural production in the Arab world, emphasized the role of science as the basis for modern civilization and insisted that Arabs could modernize their societies by 'adopting' the European sciences. For Tahtawi, the European states (particularly France) became standards to which Arabs could aspire, although in order to 'be modern', one had somehow to 'become European'. The goal of the process of modernization, as it was formulated by Tahtawi, is therefore impossible; it means becoming Other.

The ideology of modernity, following Tahtawi, is at the center of the movement in the Arab world that came to be called the *Nahda* – literally a rebirth or reawakening.[4] The crisis of modernization, as it was formulated immediately before the *Nahda*, has emerged as one of double alienation. Abdallah Laroui and others maintain that Arab intellectuals still experience this crisis; in addition to the obvious alienation from Western culture, Laroui argues, there is another form of alienation, more prevalent but veiled, due to the 'exaggerated medievalization obtained through quasi-magical identification with the great period of classical Arabian culture'.[5] The Lebanese-Syrian critic Adunis argues that the Arab cultural heritage has been projected as something 'absolutely exemplary, timeless, and outside of history', and has been used as such to maintain what he identifies as a still-powerful 'religiofeudal' social order that bases itself on this heritage, especially in religious terms.[6] Against this sort of traditionalism, which has been sustained by the educational and cultural policies of the Arab states, the Westernizing rationale of the *Nahda* has been adopted by many twentieth-century intellectuals. Taha Hussein, one of the most admired novelists in the Arab world, renewed many of the arguments that had been made in the previous century by Tahtawi, declaring that 'we must follow the path of the Europeans so as to be their equals and partners in civilization, in its good and evil, its sweetness and bitterness, what can be loved or hated, what can be praised or blamed.'[7] The adherents of Hussein's position have engaged traditionalism in cultural production and educational institutions throughout the Arab world.

A compromise has, however, been reached between these ideological positions, out of which has emerged an institutionalized Manichaeism. This bifurcation permits, on the one hand, the preservation of a certain social, cultural and religious traditionalism, and, on the other, the adoption of certain 'modern' principles, especially in science, technology and economy. It is precisely this Manichaeism that has perpetuated the double alienation described by Laroui, which by now has institutionalized a permanent crisis of modernization in Arab societies.

2

If postcolonial Arabic discourse has been centered on the debate between traditionalism and Westernism, *Season of Migration to the North* shatters the very terms of this opposition and explodes the dualism developed before and during the *Nahda*. The novel lies between the traditional categories of East and West – that confusing zone in which the culture of an imperial power clashes with that of its victims – the antithetical relationship between which provides much of its driving force. This is the same dynamic that has generated many of the contradictions now characteristic of other postcolonial societies that manifest themselves in the clash between such categories as the 'modern' and the 'traditional', the new and old ways of life, and of course between Western and native cultures and values. Native intellectuals, as they have been called, often (though not always) feel trapped between some traditional culture (or its residual traces) and the now-dominant culture associated with imperialism, which forces itself on them.[8] In response to the alienation from the colonial and precolonial pasts there have been widespread efforts throughout the Third World at returning to and coming to terms with the past by revising it and renarrating it, often by literally rewriting the histories of imperialism.[9]

Often, however, the engagement with imperialism by postcolonial intellectuals centers on a reaffirmation of the traditional cultures and ways of life that were disrupted by it. They are thus led in search of alternatives to the present dominant culture that exist only in isolated images or practices that are taken as reaffirmations of traditional, precolonial cultures. Opposition to imperialism can therefore be diverted into a futile search for traditions, through which the postcolonial intellectual attempts (if only symbolically) to reembrace his or her own people and 'their' culture. Having adopted the vestiges (or outer trappings) of these traditions, these intellectuals soon discover their emptiness; having tried to grasp hold of 'the people', they are left clutching the now-barren symbols of the past.[10]

Rather than groping blindly for what is gone, however, *Season of Migration* sprawls not only between the past, the present and the future; it fans out, through and across the different registers of textuality, narrative, form, chronology and history, none of which remain stable, and each of which is wrapped up in a series of endless and constantly expanding contradictions. It shuns the straightforward narratives taken by some of Salih's earlier works (such as *The Wedding of Zein*) and presents itself as the narrative of a vast puzzle of which it is also one small part, and its reader another; it is therefore a narrative that necessarily will be incomplete. *Season of Migration* should be seen as a highly complex and multilayered event rather than as a 'simple' text.[11] It is caught in the turbulence that is at the heart of the contradictions it reflects not only in that it chronicles two attempts to resolve them (as we shall see), but above all in that it is itself composed of these contradictions. It does not pretend to propel its readers out of its own turbulent time; rather, it leaves us floating uneasily in the present, waiting for a resolution that does not come.

3

One of the threads around which the narrative is twined is the narrator's own attempt to close the gap between himself and his people, which had opened with his departure from the Sudan to study at a British university. The novel opens with his jubilant claim, 'I returned to my people, gentlemen, after a long absence: seven years, to be precise, during which time I was studying in Europe.'[12] Although he feels, at first, alienated from the other villagers, he eventually convinces himself that he has been able to reattach himself to his childhood roots. Having felt, while abroad, like a 'storm-tossed feather', he now feels like 'a being with an origin, roots, and a purpose' (*S*, p. 6). He reinforces this feeling with many visits to his grandfather, Hajj Ahmad, whom he upholds as the enduring image of an immutable past, 'something stable in a dynamic world' (*S*, p. 52). Indeed, Hajj Ahmad becomes his link to a precolonial past that he tries to construct, and to which he would like to escape.[13] Having thus 'secured' himself, the narrator renounces his immersion in British culture and tries to reengage his Arab heritage; although he had earned a doctorate in English literature, he goes to Khartoum to teach pre-Islamic Arabic poetry at the secondary school level. He tries to convince himself that the alternative heritage being presented to him and to his people through colonialism can simply be shrugged off. While he acknowledges the physical changes that have taken place in his village, he nevertheless reassures himself that 'life is good, and the world remains the same, unchanged' (*S*, p. 6).

In making this claim, however, he does so not just for himself, but for all of his people. He assures himself in a key passage:

> I am from here, just like the palm tree planted in the courtyard of our house grew in our courtyard and did not grow in some one else's. And if [the British] came to our villages, I don't know why, does this mean that we must poison our present and our future? They will leave our country sooner or later, just as other people have left other countries throughout history. The railways and the ships, the hospitals and the factories, will be ours; and we will use their language without feeling guilt or gratitude. We shall be as we are: normal people; and if we shall be lies, we shall be lies of our own making. (*S*, p. 53)

Unfortunately, the present and the painful realities of colonialism eventually intrude on the narrator's dream of a future devoid of the traces of British rule. A number of events (the disappearance of Mustafa Said, the discovery of his secret room, the murder of Wad Rayyes, and the suicide of Hosna Bint Mahmoud) precipitate his sudden awareness that things really have changed, and that he and his people remain fixed in the present. Even Hajj Ahmad, through whom he had tried to reattach himself to the past, suddenly seems less immutable. The narrator asks himself, 'My grandfather, with his thin voice and that mischievous laugh of his when he is in a good mood, where is his place in all this? Is he really as I assert and as he appears to be? Is he above this chaos? I don't know' (*S*, p. 111). His doubts multiply, and, no longer able to maintain his construction of a past and future that bypass the present, his alienation returns. 'No escape,' he finally realises, 'no place of safety, no safeguard. My world had been wide on the outside: now it has collapsed on itself, so that I have become the world and there is no world other than me. Where, then, are the roots striking into the past?' (*S*, p. 135). He walks, stunned, down to the banks of the river, and starts swimming to the north shore (the village is situated, symbolically, at a bend, where, 'after having flowed from south to north, [the Nile] suddenly bends at an almost right angle, and flows from west to east' [*S*, p. 66]). At a point halfway between north and south, he finds himself exhausted, unable to return and unable to continue. After almost losing hope, he finds strength:

> All my life I never chose or made decisions. Now I choose. I choose life. I shall live because there are a few people that I want to stay with for as long as possible, and because I have responsibilities to take care of. It does not matter to me whether life has meaning or not. If I cannot forgive, then I shall try to forget. I shall live by strength and cunning. And I moved my hands and feet violently and with difficulty, until my torso was above water. With all the strength remaining to me, I screamed, as if I were a comic actor acting on stage: 'Help. Help.' (*S*, p. 171)

The novel ends with darkness engulfing the narrator. Trapped between north and south and east and west, his screams for help are absorbed by the immensity of the Nile.

4

There is, however, another main character in *Season of Migration*. But while the narrator represses the realization and the knowledge that the precolonial world has been irrevocably changed, Mustafa Said acknowledges these changes and incorporates them into himself. If the narrator tries to retrieve the precolonial past while dreaming of the postcolonial future, Mustafa tries to bind together the past and the present. This leaves him in a closed circuit between the two, in which the possibility of an escape to the future is locked out.

Mustafa was born in Khartoum in 1898, the year of the bloody defeat of the Mahdist forces by Kitchener's army in the battle of Omdurman, which signalled the final collapse of Sudanese resistance to British encroachment.[14] Rather than passively accepting this defeat, however, Mustafa's life is spent trying to symbolically 'reverse' the history of modern European colonialism. As a child he quickly absorbs a Western education, pursuing it from a local school in the Sudan, to a British school in Cairo, to a university in England. After his appointment as a lecturer in economics at the University of London, he begins his campaign to throw colonialism back on the colonisers.

Mustafa carries out this self-appointed mission by inflicting pain and suffering on British women. Just as imperialism had violated its victims, Mustafa violates his, and his unwitting lovers become sacrifices in his violent campaign. The acts of finding lovers and engaging with them sexually become scouting operations and skirmishes in a war fought on the personal level. The descriptions used by Mustafa for his conquests are couched not only in terms of military operations in general, but in terms of traditional *Arab* military campaigns in particular: going to meet new victims is described in terms of saddling his camels; the process of courtship is compared to laying siege, involving tents, caravans, the desert, and so forth. The imagery associated with sexual acts are those of battle: bows, axes, spears and especially swords and knives. He compares his exploits to those of Tarik ibn-Ziyad, the commander of the Arab army that conquered Spain in the eighth century, as he tells the narrator, 'I imagined the Arab soldiers' first meeting with Spain. Like me at this moment, sitting opposite Isabella Seymour, a southern thirst being quenched in the northern mountain passes of history' (*S*, p. 46).

Not satisfied with only reenacting the ancient Arab victory over Europeans, Mustafa sees himself undoing the modern European victory over the Arabs. He claims to be the diametrical opposite of Kitchener and Allenby, reversing or at least superceding Kitchener's victories at Omdurman and Atbara, and Allenby's at Jerusalem (see *S*, p. 97). He dreams of telling the English, 'Yes, gentlemen, I have come to you as a conqueror within your very house, as a drop of the poison which you have injected into the veins of history' (*S*, p. 98). The connection in Mustafa's mind between his sexual actions and the fight against colonialism is thus all too clear; to several friends, he announces: 'I'll liberate Africa with my ———' (*S*, p. 122).

Mustafa's campaign is not carried out strictly in terms of physical violence, however. Indeed, most of the damage he does is psychological, and he drives all but one of his victims to suicide (he murders the last, Jean Morris). At the same time, however, he does violence to himself, willingly becoming for his victims the incarnation of the great Orientalist myth-fantasy; and his apartment in London, packed with incense, Persian rugs, mirrors, ointments and perfumes, becomes 'a den of lethal lies'. He weaves 'intricate and terrifying threads of fantasy', so that each victim 'would tell me that in my eyes she saw the shimmer of mirages in hot deserts, that in my voice she heard the screams of wild beasts in the jungles' (*S*, p. 147).[15] Soon, however, his lies turn into 'truths' that he himself begins to believe, so that he gets caught in his own Orientalist phantasmagoria.

Mustafa starts living a lie, and in doing so he 'becomes' a lie. There is an ongoing comparison in his own narrative between himself and Shakespeare's Othello, one of the best-known European literary misrepresentations of the Arab, as he alternately claims that 'I am no Othello: I am a lie', and that 'I am no Othello: Othello was a lie' (S, p. 37, 98).[16] During his trial for the murder of Jean Morris, Mustafa is tempted to stand up and shout, 'This Mustafa Said has no existence. He is an illusion, a lie. And I ask you to rule for the killing of the lie' (S, p. 36). He becomes, however, a bundle of contradictory selves, known to various people as Richard, Hassan, Charles, Amin and Mustafa.

After serving seven years in jail (for the murder he committed and to which he confessed) and then traveling all over the world, Mustafa Said, the child of colonialism, returns to his native Sudan and takes up residence in the narrator's village. Here his contradictions no longer manifest themselves violently or openly, as they had done in England. To everyone in the village, he presents himself as he does to the narrator: 'I am this person that is before you, as he is known to everyone in the village. I am nothing other than that, and I have nothing to hide' (S. p. 19). A lapse, however, reveals his hidden secrets. He drunkenly recites a poem in English, even though he denies any knowledge of the language of the imperialists.

His deepest, darkest secret, though, is his hidden room. The room, discovered late in the novel by the narrator, is a preserve for Mustafa's British self. It is a life-sise replica of the salon in his London apartment, complete with fireplace, chairs, Persian rugs and a vast library of books. When the narrator discovers the room, he is stunned:

> Imagine it – an English fireplace with all its accessories, above it a brass hood, and in front of it a square area tiled in green marble, with the mantelpiece of blue marble; on either side of the fireplace were two Victorian chairs covered in silk material, and between them was a round table with books and notebooks on it. (S, p. 137)

The bookshelf, not surprisingly, contains not a single Arabic book; even the Koran is in English. It does, however, hold a number of books by Mustafa (in English) on the economics of colonialism. The narrator is shocked by this, calling the library and the room itself 'a graveyard. A mausoleum. An insane idea. A prison. A huge joke' (S, p. 139). The photographs scattered throughout the room preserve intact various times in Mustafa's British life:

> Mustafa Said laughing, Mustafa Said writing, Mustafa Said swimming, Mustafa Said somewhere in the country, Mustafa Said in cap and gown, Mustafa Said rowing on the Serpentine, Mustafa Said in a Nativity play, a crown on his head, as one of the Three Kings who brought perfumes and myrrh to Christ; Mustafa Said between a man and a woman. Mustafa Said had not let a moment pass without recording it for memory and history. (S, p. 140)

The bundle of contradictions that Mustafa had become ('normal' Sudanese peasant farmer on the outside, sophisticated London intellectual on the inside) cannot be undone. He disappears one day, presumably drowned in the Nile, either by accident or by suicide.[17] To the narrator and to those who will uncover his room, he leaves his 'Life Story', which contains a one-line dedication: 'To those who see with one eye, talk with one tongue, and see things as either black or white, either Eastern or Western' (S, p. 152).

5

Mustafa's life story is dedicated to a nonbeing, a being that could not possibly exist; and, indeed, the rest of its pages are entirely empty. To see the world in the way it prescribes would, precisely, require one to be entirely Eastern or entirely Western, entirely black or entirely white. Mustafa's problem – and the narrator's – is that they are neither black nor white, but grey; neither wholly Eastern nor wholly Western, neither completely European nor completely Arab (furthermore, given Sudan's situation, neither entirely Arab nor entirely African). They are trapped between cultures (and here, as intellectuals, they are not exceptions to a social norm; rather, the contradictions of the rest of society are made explicit and even brought to their logical extremes in Mustafa and the narrator). The narrator responds to the trap by trying, unsuccessfully, to wish it away. Having embraced British culture, he tries to abandon it and to reembrace his native culture, the culture of his childhood.[18] Mustafa's response is no more successful. Rather than simply wishing away his experiences, he tries to maintain them, while completely separating them from each other. He does so not by becoming entirely European or entirely Arab, but by becoming *both*, but never at the same time, in the same place, or with the same people.

The contradictions that mold the characters of the narrator and Mustafa are also evident in the structure and form of *Season of Migration to the North*. The narrative is presented through a number of often conflicting voices, which flow through an extremely unstable chronological framework, moving in quick and apparently random succession through the past, present and future. Moreover, that the narrator is himself a main character in the novel also generates uncertainties; as the narrative voice breaks down, the reader is increasingly denied a stable reference point from which to assess other developments.

Even its form is a contradiction. As a novel, it has its origins in western Europe, but the style in which it is presented at the opening is that of the old *hakawati* of the Arabic oral tradition (it is addressed to an audience of 'gentlemen'). However, it moves away from this rigidly defined style – and hence from all of its traditional components, including a resolution at the end of the tale – to an indeterminate ending more characteristic of European modernist novels.[19] *Season of Migration* makes constant reference, both in terms of content and of structure, to Western literary works – *Othello*, *King Lear*, *Heart of Darkness* – and deliberately confronts these texts from within. Barbara Harlow argues that the novel has many of the elements of the Arabic literary techniques of *mu'arada*, which literally means opposition or contradiction, and which involves at least two writers, the first of whom writes a poem that the second will undo by writing along the same lines but reversing the meaning.[20] Salih's text, then, is and is not a novel; it is and is not a *hakawati* oral tale; it is like *Heart of Darkness* as much as it is unlike it; it draws its formal inspirations from Europe as much as it seeks to distort and undermine them; it remains, finally, an unstable synthesis of European and Arabic forms and traditions.

Rather than representing some imaginary resolution of the contradictions of form and content, *Season of Migration* leaves them gaping open. Ironically, it has been interpreted by many critics (particularly in the Arab world) as an affirmation of life, as a resolution of conflicts, as the representation of the final closure of imperialism. Such interpretations generally hinge on a positive reading of the closing chapter. Issa Boullata, for instance, concludes that

> gradually as [the narrator] is swimming across the river, he begins to feel he is being pulled downwards by the water and for an indeterminate period [surrenders] to its destructive force. Then suddenly he regains his desire for life, and for the first time in his life he chooses and he makes a decision. He fights the water and screams for help.
> With this affirmation of life, al-Tayyib Salih ends his novel.[21]

While the novel itself lacks any firm conclusion or resolution, these critics try – desperately and unconvincingly – to close it, to supply what is missing. They try to determine and fix those aspects of the plot, such as the fate of the narrator, that are left ambiguous by the flow of events through an unstable framework. While the novel gradually moves away from and finally abandons the traditional *hakawati* style, such critics remain imprisoned by the limitations of this older form and the neat resolutions it offers. While it moves continually between different registers and frameworks, they try to reduce it to a one-dimensional narrative with a beginning, a middle and an end. Its power as an ideological form is, ironically, demonstrated by these critics who try to supply it with a narrative closure that will 'make sense' within a certain ideological framework marked and governed by the existence of fundamental categories and rigid absolutes.

6

But *Season of Migration* defies and deconstructs such categories as it undermines many of the traditional dualisms that are associated with postcolonial discourse. What appears at first to be neatly divisible into black and white is dialectically broken down and synthesised into an endless variety of shades of grey. The existence of pure and unaffected traditional cultures to which postcolonial intellectuals can 'escape' is exposed as an illusion. Indeed, the very existence of any culture in some sort of absolute isolation from others is shown to be impossible in the postcolonial world; the very existence of *Season of Migration* is proof of this. The novel, in this sense, takes place in the twilight between cultures, for which the eerie dawn at the end of the narrative is a metaphor; the narrator is left not just between east and west and north and south, but also between day and night, so that 'the objects on the two shores [are] half visible, appearing and disappearing, shimmering between light and darkness' (*S*, p. 168).

At the beginning, however, the narrator views his return to his people as a return to his proper place, the place to which he can be attached, and in relation to which his life has meaning. When he first meets Mustafa, his immediate reaction is curiosity: 'Where is he from? Why has he taken up residence in this village? What is his story'? (*S*, p. 13). He is unable to place Mustafa, however, and hence unable to understand him; but he is amazed that Mustafa considers himself a part of the village and the narrator an outsider. Angered by the way Mustafa mocks his English degree ('we here have no need for poetry'), the narrator is outraged: 'Look at how he says "we" and does not include me, despite the fact that the village is my village, and it is he – not I – who is the stranger' (*S*, p. 13). Later, after Mustafa's disappearance, the narrator starts doubting his own position; 'Is it possible', he asks himself, 'that what happened to Mustafa Said could happen to me? He said that he was a lie. So am I also a lie'? He answers himself by insisting that 'I am from here. Is that not sufficient truth? I too lived with [the British], but I lived with them superficially, neither loving nor hating them. I used to carry this small village within myself, seeing it with the eye of my imagination wherever I went' (*S*, pp. 52–3). But the novel unfolds with his gradual realization that he has lost his proper place, and indeed that there is no longer any place that can be sealed off from others so that people can be identified by it. The rigid distinction between East and West to which the narrator originally clings has eroded by the end of the novel.

The dualism (between Eastern and Western) developed by Abduh, Tahtawi and others in the nineteenth century is thus broken down and destroyed in Salih's novel. While such dualisms have led to a whole series of inescapable dilemmas, *Season of Migration* negates them as well as the ideological framework they represent. The colonial project, as Johannes Fabian has argued, developed a scale of 'progress', so that 'all living societies were irrevocably placed on a temporal slope, a stream of Time – some upstream, others downstream. Civilization, evolution, development, acculturation, modernization (and their cousins, industrialization, urbanization) are all terms whose conceptual content derives, in ways that can be specified, from evolutionary Time.'[22] While the program of the *Nahda* was itself a formulation of this ideology, the world it mapped out is reconfigured in *Season of Migration*. If there is any sense of historical flow at all, as symbolized by the Nile itself, the crucial point is that, from the narrator's perspective at the end of the novel, the river's symbolic edges (north or south, east or west) are unattainable. There is no going north or west to become European, as Tahtawi and his followers would have insisted; and there is no going south or east to return to tradition, as Abduh would have had it.

Season of Migration points away from the traditionalism of the Arab past – as well as from the future that imperial Europe, through the ideology of modernity, once held out to its victims – and in an entirely new direction, finally escaping the narrow and tightly defined orbit of the debates surrounding the *Nahda*. Through this double negation, it offers tremendous liberating potential, allowing entirely new conceptualizations of social realities, and drawing an entirely different map of the present.

7

In a certain sense, then, *Season of Migration* 'reinvents' the present, bringing into sharp focus many of the issues that have long remained repressed in Arab cultural production. The ideological bulwark of religion, for instance, so prevalent in traditional writing, is absent here. If in *The Wedding of Zein*, one of Salih's earlier stories, the lives of the villagers center on the imam,[23] in the world of *Season of Migration* such a stable system of signification is inconceivable. Along with other novels of Arabic modernism – such as the later novels of Naguib Mahfouz (*Miramar*, for instance, or even *The Thief and the Dogs*), or the recent work of the Lebanese novelist Elias Khoury (such as *Little Mountain* and [forthcoming in English translation] *The Journey of Little Ghandi*), or that of the Palestinian Emile Habibi (author of *The Secret Life of Said, the Ill-Fated Pessoptimist*) – *Season of Migration to the North* challenges the literary and ideological principles of the *Nahda*.[24] Even beyond this, though, Salih, Khoury, Mahfouz and others situate themselves in opposition to Arabic cultural and ideological production long preceding the *Nahda* itself.

In *Season of Migration* this is perhaps nowhere clearer than in the novel's gender dynamics. It is not, of course, a coincidence that Mustafa conducts his misogynistic campaign of revenge against colonialism in sexual terms. This opens up a new register through which the novel runs, and the intersection of gender, sexuality, violence, male hegemony and colonialism is a central concern of this work. Even in Mustafa's narrative, such connections are revolutionary in terms of previous Arabic cultural production; *Season of Migration* brings them home much more forcefully in the violent and catastrophic clash between Hosna Bint Mahmoud and Wad Rayyes.

This clash forms the final blow for the narrator. If previously he had been able to convince himself that he could flee the contradictions of imperialism and modernity by clinging to his proper place, Hosna's murder and suicide drive home the realization that this place was never really what it had seemed. It is only after this double event that the narrator can say that 'the world has suddenly turned upside down' (*S*, p. 135). Earlier, when he questions whether Hosna wanted to be married to Wad Rayyes, Mahjoub cuts him off, saying,' You know how life is organized here. The woman belongs to the man, and a man is a man even if he gets old and decrepit.' The narrator protests, 'In this age . . .', but Mahjoub cuts him off again, saying, 'The world has not changed as much as you think' (S, pp. 102–3).

Later on, Hosna's own actions change the world, or, rather, change the villagers' awareness of their world. In defying her husband, Hosna defies tradition; in actually killing him, she aims her blows not only at Wad Rayyes as a person but at him as the embodiment of tradition. For if Hosna, as Mustafa's wife, had become in some measure Westernized through contact with him, Wad Rayyes, on the contrary, represents the extreme side of traditionalism.[25] While Mustafa's project of reversing colonialism, which had been encoded in sexual terms, serves in the novel as the first dramatic link between sexuality and violence, the marriage of Hosna and Wad Rayyes makes the connections even clearer. The villagers, however, are not willing to view Hosna's actions in terms of the tradition against which she rebels, but as a demented abberation that should never have happened; in this sense, they place the blame on her rather than on Wad Rayyes.[26] Even Bint Majzoub, the most important woman in the village, tells the narrator, 'A person cannot speak easily of Bint Mahmoud's action. It is something the likes of which we have neither seen nor heard of in past times or present' (S, p. 126). The villagers bury the bodies of Hosna and Wad Rayyes before dawn on the night of the killings with no funeral and no mourning; as Bint Majzoub says, they bury the story along with the corpses. But the narrator knows that despite the village's continuing and seemingly timeless routine, 'the world has changed' (S, p. 131). In making these connections in the way it does, *Season of Migration* goes against the standards and conventions of traditional Arabic literature; it comes as no surprise, then, that the original has only been published in Beirut.

8

Season of Migration to the North does not merely reinvent the present, it opens up new possibilities for the future. The process of cultural production not only shapes perceptions but constitutes a lived system of beliefs, values and realities. Artists like Salih, in struggling to create a new culture, are at the same time, however gradually, creating new ways of seeing and feeling reality. In rewriting imperialism, Arab modernism, including *Season of Migration*, necessarily looks away not only from the premodern but beyond imperialism and toward some alternative future that it is in the process of inventing.[27] If, in other words, European modernism can be seen as the narration of imperialism from a European perspective, *Season of Migration* and other works of Arab modernism emerge as counternarrations of the thoroughly intertwined histories of imperialism and modernization from a non-European perspective, a 'writing back' to Europe.

One cannot, however, as Fanon so brilliantly argues in *The Wretched of the Earth*, address imperialism only by addressing its victims, for in doing so one is already addressing the colonizers themselves.[28] In struggling for the creation of a postimperial Arab society, then, a novelist like Salih is struggling for the creation of a genuinely postimperial world. While Mustafa Said's life story is dedicated to a reader who could not possibly exist, *Season of Migration to the North* is dedicated to readers who do not yet exist; those who can simultaneously see with two eyes, talk with two tongues, and see things both as black *and* as white.

Notes

1. This is especially the case in the Levant. In North Africa, much of which came under direct rule earlier than the areas to the east, European empires often imposed their ideologies by force, as when the French tried to introduce private property in Algeria by forcibly breaking up and expropriating family-run farmland in 1873. This policy, according to one French deputy, was 'but the crowning touch to an edifice well-founded on a whole series of ordinances, edicts, laws and decrees of the Senate which together and severally have as the same object: the establishment of private property among the Arabs' (quoted in Rosa Luxemburg, *The Accumulation of Capital*, trans. Agnes Schwarzschild, London, 1951, p. 380).

2. This is true not just of the Arab societies but also of the Ottoman Turks who ruled them and acknowledged what they saw as a need to 'modernize'. They tried to address this problem by turning to western European societies: the sultan opened embassies in Europe at the end of the eighteenth century, and a major bureau was opened in Istanbul to translate documents and cultural artefacts from western European languages. See Albert Hourani, *Arabic Thought in the Liberal Age, 1798–1939*, 1962; Cambridge, 1983, pp. 40–9.

3. Jamal al-Din Afghani (1839–97) argued that Muslims should strictly obey the teachings of the Koran and follow the *Sunna* in order to revitalize the strength they had lost by straying off the Prophet's path. Muhammad Abduh (1849–1905) was an Egyptian student of his who elaborated some of his positions.

4. *Nahda* is thus used to describe the literary and cultural 'renaissance' that took place in the Arab world in the nineteenth century and culminated in the movements of Arab nationalism. See George Antonious, *The Arab Awakening: The story of the Arab national movement*, Philadelphia, PA, 1939. Even the term *Nahda*, however, derives from a European concept.

5. Abdallah Laroui, *The Crisis of the Arab Intellectual: Traditionalism or historicism?*, trans. Diarmid Cammell, 1974; Berkeley, CA, 1976, p. 156.

6. Adunis, *Al-thabat wa al-tahawwul: sadmal al-hadatha*, Beirut, 1979, p. 276.

7. Quoted in Hourani, *op. cit.*, p. 330. He goes on to say that 'Egypt has always been part of Europe', and blames the four centuries of Ottoman rule for the fall of the Arabs behind the Europeans in terms of modernity (*ibid.*; Hourani is paraphrasing Hussein here).

8. See, for example, Eqbal Ahmad, 'From potato sack to potato mash: the contemporary crisis of the Third World', *Arab Studies Quarterly*, 2, Summer 1980, pp. 223–34; Ngũgĩ wa Thiong'o, *Homecoming: Essays on African and Caribbean literature, culture, and politics*, London, 1972; Amilcar Cabral, 'National liberation and culture', in *Unity and Struggle: Speeches and writings*, trans. Michael Wolfers, New York, 1979, pp. 138–54 [see also pp. 53–65 above]; and of course Frantz Fanon, *The Wretched of the Earth*, trans. Constance Farrington, 1961; London, 1983, pp. 166–99 [see also pp. 36–52 above for an abridged version].

9. See Edward W. Said, 'Intellectuals in the post-colonial world', *Salmagundi*, 70/71, Spring–Summer 1986, pp. 44–64, and 'Third World intellectuals and metropolitan culture', *Raritan*, IX, 3, Winter 1990, pp. 27–50. The Subaltern Studies project in India is also an excellent example of this; see Ranajit Guha and Gayatri Chakravorty Spivak (eds.), *Selected Subaltern Studies*, New York, 1988. But 'writing back' to the metropolitan centers, of course, goes beyond historical and political analyses and into fiction, drama, poetry, and so on. On this point see Bill Ashcroft, Gareth Griffiths and Helen Tiffin (eds.), *The Empire Writes Back: Theory and practice in post-colonial literatures*, London, 1989.

10. See Fanon, *op. cit.*, p. 180. [See also pp. 41–2 above.]

11. To examine any aspect of this event necessarily involves unwrapping it, separating its elements, cutting it off from other aspects, and laying it in artificially reassembled fragments under close examination. My own analysis of *Season of Migration* will therefore require partial dis- and reassemblies of the text.

12. Al-Tayyib Salih, *Mawsim al-hijra ila al-Shimal* [*Season of Migration to the North*], 1969; Beirut, 1987, p. 5; hereafter abbreviated *S*. The English translation is by Denys Johnson-Davies, under the title *Season of Migration to the North*, London, 1969.

13. The narrator says of his grandfather: his 'thin tranquil voice forms a bridge between myself and that anxious time that has not yet been formed, the times whose events have taken place and passed, and become bricks in an edifice with dimensions and depth' (*S*, p. 77).

14. See John Gallagher and Ronald Robinson, *Africa and the Victorians: The climax of imperialism in the dark continent*, New York, 1961, pp. 339–78.

15. Earlier we learn of his meeting with Isabella Seymour: 'She asked me, as we drank tea, about my country. I told her that the streets of my country's capital were crowded with elephants and lions, and that crocodiles crawled through it during the afternoon nap-time' (*S*, p. 41).

16. Mustafa is, at another level, exactly like Othello. When Isabella Seymour asks him, 'Are you African or Asian?' he responds, 'I am like Othello: Arab-African' (*S*, p. 41). Moreover, the novel itself takes us back to *Othello* when a secret lover comes to Jean Morris's apartment and accidentally drops his handkerchief.

17. I've been told that if one keeps very careful account of the dates and time frames of the novel (which is very difficult to do), it emerges that Mustafa disappears at the age of fifty-eight, or in 1956, the year of Sudan's independence – that is, his life coincides with the period of direct British occupation of the Sudan.

18. His situation is strikingly similar to the native intellectual described by Fanon: 'In the second phase we find the native is disturbed; he decides to remember what he is. ... But since the native is not a part of his people, since he only has exterior relations with his people, he is content to recall their life only. Past happenings of the byegone days of his childhood will be brought up out of the depths of his memory; old legends will be reinterpreted in the light of a borrowed estheticism and of a conception of the world which was discovered under other skies' (Fanon, *op. cit.*, p. 179). [See also pp. 40–1 above]

19. *Heart of Darkness*, for example, closes as follows:

> Marlow ceased and sat apart, indistinct and silent, in the pose of a meditating Buddha. Nobody moved for a time. 'We have lost the first of the ebb,' said the director, suddenly. I raised my head. The offing was barred by a black bank of clouds, and the tranquil waterway leading to the uttermost ends of the earth

flowed somber under an overcast sky – seemed to lead into the heart of an immense darkness. (Joseph Conrad, *Heart of Darkness*, 1902; Harmondsworth, 1989, p. 121)

20. See Barbara Harlow, 'Sentimental Orientalism: *Season of Migration to the North and Othello*', in Mona Takieddine-Amyuni (ed.), *Tayeb Salih's 'Season of Migration to the North': A casebook*, Beirut, 1985, pp. 75–9.

21. Issa J. Boullata, 'Encounter between East and West: a theme in contemporary Arabic novels', in Boullata (ed.), *Critical Perspectives on Modern Arabic Literature*, Washington, DC, 1980, pp. 56–7. Another example of this is from an essay on *Season of Migration* by Takieddine-Amyuni, in her analysis of the final few lines:

> Symbolically, the Narrator finds himself halfway between North and South, the river's destructive forces pulling him downwards. But life is stronger in the Narrator after all. He chooses it whether it has meaning or not, for he has duties to perform and people to love. His daughter is called 'Hope' and he looks forward to the future. He has ceased to be the romantic young man we encountered at the beginning of the novel. He has grown into a realistic human being, fully aware of the mediocrity of his position in Khartoum and of all the pitfalls in which the newly independent Sudan was caught. (Takieddine-Amyuni, 'Tayeb Salih's *Season of Migration to the North*: an interpretation', *Arab Studies Quarterly*, 2, Winter 1980, pp. 16–17)

See also Takieddine-Amyuni's introduction to *Tayeb Salih's 'Season of Migration to the North'*. Joseph John and Yosif Tarawneh reach a similar conclusion:

> While, on the literal level, this statement [the narrator's last few words] denotes a sudden awareness of the need to strive for survival, at the symbolic level it is a re-enactment of his disengagement, his final liberation, from the ghost of Mustafa Sa'eed, laid to rest forever in the rectangular [secret] room. It is important to note that the river episode forms a richly symbolic finale to the narrator's moral pilgrimage. His final cry, 'Help! Help!' is a resounding repudiation of the Sa'eedian world of death; it is his everlasting 'yes' to life. (Joseph John and Yosif Tarawneh, 'Quest for identity: the I–Thou imbroglio in Tayeb Salih's *Season of Migration to the North*', *Arab Studies Quarterly*, 8, Spring 1986, p. 175)

22. Johannes Fabian, *Time and the Other: How anthropology makes its object*, New York, 1983, p. 17.

23. Here, we are told, 'the village was divided into clear camps in relation to the Imam (the villagers did not call him by name: he was, in their eyes, not a person but an institution)' (Salih, '*Urss al Zein*', Beirut, 1966, p. 75; trans. Johnson-Davies, under the title *The Wedding of Zein*, London, 1969.

24. To speak of an Arab 'modernism' is not to imply that this in any way follows in the path of European modernism. If the term is to be used at all – and it already has been – it should be used guardedly. Even while drawing connections between present-day Arabic novels and European novels of seventy years ago, one must not posit any sort of scale of progress on which Europeans would be placed at a more advanced level than Arabs. Such a notion would be consistent not only with the program of the *Nahda*, but with the ideology of modernity itself. See Fabian, *op. cit.*, p. 17.

25. Their clash further problematizes the binary oppositions of East and West, colonizer and colonized, male and female, oppressor and oppressed, even as it binds them together.
26. Hosna, by the way, is usually identified in the novel as 'Bint Mahmoud' – that is, the daughter of Mahmoud – so that her very being, her identity, is encoded in terms of a patriarchal structure.
27. Fredric Jameson has argued that European modernism celebrates the premodern. See the conclusion to his *Postmodernism, or, The Cultural Logic of Late Capitalism*, Durham, NC, 1991, pp. 297–318. Postmodernism arises, in Jameson's terms, out of a condition of completed modernization in which the premodern has finally been liquidated. In the situation of incomplete modernization in which the Arab world finds itself, the premodern has not yet been liquidated. One cannot speak of an Arab postmodernism in the same sense as Jameson speaks of, say, American postmodernism.
28. See Fanon, *op. cit.*, p. 254.

Bibliography

Achebe, Chinua, *Morning Yet on Creation Day*, Anchor Press/Doubleday: New York, 1975

Achebe, Chinua, *Hopes and Impediments*, Heinemann: London, 1988

Adam, Ian, and Tiffin, Helen (eds.), *Past the Last Post*, Harvester Wheatsheaf: Hemel Hempstead, 1991

Adorno, Theodor W., 'Progress', *The Philosophical Forum*, XV, 1–2, Fall–Winter 1983–4, pp. 55–70

Ahmad, Aijaz, 'Between Orientalism and anti-historicism: anthropological knowledge of India', *Studies in History*, 7, 1, 1991, pp. 135–63

Ahmad, Aijaz, *In Theory: Classes, nations, literatures*, Verso: London, 1992

Alloula, Malek, *The Colonial Harem*, trans. M. and W. Godzich, Manchester University Press: Manchester, 1986

Amuta, Chidi, *Theory of African Literature: Implications for practical criticism*, Zed Press: London, 1989

Anderson, Benedict, *Imagined Communities: Reflections on the origins and spread of nationalism*, Verso: London, 1983

Appadurai, Arjun, 'Disjuncture and difference in the global cultural economy', *Public Culture*, 2, 2, Spring 1990, pp. 1–24

Appiah, Anthony, *In My Father's House*, Methuen: New York, 1992

Appiah, Anthony, 'Is the post- in postmodernism the post- in postcolonial?', *Critical Inquiry*, 17, Winter 1991, pp. 336–57

Appiah, Anthony, 'Out of Africa: Topologies of nativism', *Yale Journal of Criticism*, 1, 2, 1988, pp. 153–78

Arendt, Hannah, *The Origins of Totalitarianism*, André Deutsch: London, 1986

Ashcroft, Bill, Griffiths, Gareth, and Tiffin, Helen, *The Empire Writes Back: Theory and practice in post-colonial literatures*, Routledge: London, 1989

Balibar, Etienne, and Wallerstein, Immanuel, *Race, Nation, Class: Ambiguous identities*, Verso: London, 1991

Barker, Francis, Hulme, Peter, Iversen, Margaret, and Loxley, Diane (eds.), *Europe and Its Others* (2 vols.), Proceedings of the Essex Sociology of Literature Conference, University of Essex: Colchester, 1985

Barone, Charles A., *Marxist Thought on Imperialism: Survey and critique*, Macmillan: London, 1985

Barrell, John, *The Infection of Thomas de Quincey: A Psychopathology of Imperialism*, Yale University Press: New Haven, CT, 1991

Benjamin, Walter, 'Theoretics of knowledge; theory of progress', *The Philosophical Forum*, XV, 1–2, Fall–Winter 1983–4, pp. 1–40

Benjamin, Walter, 'Theses on the philosophy of history', in *Illuminations*, trans. Harry Zohn, Fontana: London, 1973

Bhabha, Homi, 'Articulating the archaic: notes on colonial nonsense', in P. Collier and H. Geyer-Ryan (eds.), *Literary Theory Today*, Polity Press: Cambridge, 1990, pp. 203–18

Bhabha, Homi (ed.), *Nation and Narration*, Routledge: London, 1990

Bhabha, Homi, 'Of mimicry and man: the ambivalence of colonial discourse', *October*, 28, Spring 1984, pp. 125–33

Bhabha, Homi, 'The other question – the stereotype and colonial discourse', *Screen*, 24, 6, 1983, pp. 18–36

Bhabha, Homi, 'Remembering Fanon: self, psyche and the colonial condition', Foreword to Frantz Fanon, *Black Skin, White Masks*, Pluto Press: London, 1985, pp. xii–xxv

Bhabha, Homi, 'Representation and the colonial text: a critical exploration of some forms of mimeticism', in Frank Gloversmith (ed.), *Theory of Reading*, Harvester: Brighton, 1984, pp. 93–122

Bhabha, Homi, 'Signs taken for wonders: questions of ambivalence and authority under a tree outside Delhi, May 1817', in Henry Louis Gates, Jr. (ed.), *'Race', Writing and Difference*, University of Chicago Press: Chicago, IL, 1986, pp. 163–84

Biko, Steve, *I Write What I Like*, Heinemann: London, 1979

Blyden, Edward Wilmot, *Christianity, Islam and the Negro Race*, V. B. Whittingham: London, 1887

Boal, Augusto, *Theatre of the Oppressed*, Pluto Press: London, 1979

Boehmer, Elleke, Chrisman, Laura and Parker, Kenneth (eds.), *Altered State? Writing and South Africa*, Dangaroo Press: Aarhus, 1993

Brantlinger, Patrick, *Rule of Darkness: British literature and imperialism, 1830–1914*, Cornell University Press: Ithaca, NY, 1988

Brathwaite, Edward Kamau, *Contradictory Omens: Cultural diversity and integration in the Caribbean*, Savacou Press: Mona, Jamaica, 1974

Brathwaite, Edward Kamau, *History of the Voice: The development of nation language in anglophone Caribbean poetry*, New Beacon Books: London, 1984

Brennan, Timothy, *Salman Rushdie and the Third World*, Macmillan: London, 1989

Brewer, Anthony, *Marxist Theories of Imperialism: A critical survey*, Routledge: London, 1980

Bristow, Joseph, *Empire Boys*, Harper Collins: London, 1991

Brydon, Diana, 'Commonwealth or common poverty? The new literatures in English and the new discourse of marginality', *Kunapipi*, XI, 1, 1989, pp. 1–16

Cabral, Amilcar, 'National liberation and culture', in *Return to the Source: Selected speeches of Amilcar Cabral*, Monthly Review Press: New York, 1973, pp. 39–56

Cabral, Amilcar, *Unity and Struggle*, Heinemann: London, 1980

Carby, Hazel, 'White woman listen! Black feminism and the boundaries of sisterhood', in CCCS, *The Empire Strikes Back: Race and racism in 70s Britain*, Hutchinson: London, 1982

Cartey, Wilfred and Kilson, Martin (eds.), *The Africa Reader: Independent Africa*, Vintage Books: New York, 1970

Casely-Hayford, Joseph, *Ethiopia Unbound: Studies in race emancipation*, C. K. Phillips: London, 1911

Castillo, Debra, *Talking Back: Toward a Latin American feminist literary criticism*, Cornell University Press: Ithaca, NY, and London, 1992, pp. 1–33

Césaire, Aimé, *Discourse on Colonialism*, Monthly Review Press: New York, 1972

Chrisman; Laura, 'The imperial unconscious? Representations of imperial discourse', *Critical Quarterly*, 32, 3, 1990, pp. 38–58

Chrisman, Laura, 'Theorising "race", racism and culture: some pitfalls in idealist critiques', *Paragraph*, 16, 1, 1993, pp. 78–90

Chrisman, Laura, 'Feminism, race and empire in the fin de siècle: the work of George Egerton and Olive Schreiner', in Scott McCracken and Sally Ledger (eds.), *Cultural Politics in the Fin de Siècle*, Cambridge University Press: Cambridge, 1993

Chrisman, Laura, 'Gender and colonialism: the case of Olive Schreiner', *English in Africa*, 20, 1, May 1993

Chrisman, Robert, and Hare, Nathan (eds.), *Contemporary Black Thought: The best from the black scholar*, Bobbs-Merrill: New York, 1973

Chrisman, Robert and Hare, Nathan (eds.), *Pan-Africanism*, Bobbs-Merrill: New York, 1974

Christian, Barbara, *Black Feminist Criticism*, Pergamon: New York, 1986

Christian, Barbara, 'The race for theory', in Linda Kaufmann (ed.), *Gender and Theory: Dialogues on feminist criticism*, Basil Blackwell: Oxford, 1989, pp. 225–37

Clifford, James, 'On *Orientalism*', in *The Predicament of Culture: Twentieth-century ethnography, literature and art*, Harvard University Press: Cambridge, MA, 1988, pp. 255–76

Clifford, James, and Marcus, George (eds.), *Writing Culture: The poetics and politics of ethnography*, University of California Press: Berkeley, 1986

Coetzee, J. M., *White Writing: On the culture of letters in South Africa*, Yale University Press: New Haven, CT, 1988

Coetzee, J. M., *Doubling the Point*, ed. David Atwell, Harvard University Press: Cambridge, MA., 1993

Collins, Patricia, 'The social construction of black feminist thought', *Signs*, 14, pp. 745–73

Collins, Patricia Hill, *Black Feminist Thought: Knowledge, consciousness and the politics of empowerment*, Unwin Hyman: Boston, MA, 1990

Cooper, Brenda, *To Lay These Secrets Open: Evaluating African literature*, David Philip: Cape Town, 1992

Dabydeen, David (ed.), *The Black Presence in English Literature*, Manchester Univerity Press: Manchester, 1985

Dash, Michael, 'In search of the lost body: redefining the subject in Caribbean literature', *Kunapipi*, XI, 1, 1989, pp. 17–26

Davies, Carole Boyce, and Fido, Elaine Savory (eds.), *Out of the Kumbla: Caribbean women and literature*, Africa World Press: Trenton, NJ, 1990

Davis, Angela, *Women, Race and Class*, Women's Press: London, 1981

Davis, Angela, *Women, Culture and Politics*, Women's Press: London, 1990

De Kok, Ingrid, and Press, Karen (eds.), *Spring is Rebellious: Arguments about cultural freedom by Albie Sachs and respondents*, Buchu Press: Cape Town, 1990

Decker, Jeffrey Louis, 'Terrorism (un)veiled: Frantz Fanon and the women of Algiers', *Cultural Critique*, 17, Winter 1990–1, pp. 177–95

Dhareshwar, Vivek, 'Towards a narrative epistemology of the postcolonial predicament', *Inscriptions*, 5, 1989, pp. 135–58

Diawara, Manthia, *African Cinema: Politics and culture*, Indiana University Press: Bloomington, IN, 1992

Diawara, Manthia, 'The nature of mother in "Dreaming Rivers"', *Third Text*, 13, Winter 1990–1, pp. 73–84

Docherty, Thomas (ed.), *Postmodernism: A reader*, Harvester: Hemel Hempstead, 1992

Donald, James, and Rattansi, Ali (eds.), *'Race', Culture and Difference*, Sage/Open University Press: London, 1992

Dorfman. Ariel, and Mattelart, Armand, *How to Read Donald Duck: Imperialist ideology in the Disney comic*, trans. David Kunzle, International General: New York, 1984

Downing, J. D. H. (ed.), *Film and Politics in the Third World*, Autonomedia: New York, 1987

Du Bois, W. E. B., *The Souls of Black Folk*, Penguin: Harmondsworth, 1989

During, Simon, 'Postmodernism or postcolonialism?', *Textual Practice*, 1, 1, Spring 1987, pp. 32–47

Eagleton, Terry, Jameson, Fredric, and Said, Edward, *Nationalism, Colonialism, and Literature*, University of Minnesota Press: Minneapolis, 1990

Emberley, Julia V., '"A gift for languages": native women and the textual economy of the colonial archive', *Cultural Critique*, 17, Winter 1990–1, pp. 21–50

Fabian, Johannes, 'Presence and representation: the Other and anthropological writing', *Critical Inquiry*, 16, Summer 1990, pp. 753–72

Fanon, Frantz, *Toward the African Revolution*, Penguin: Harmondsworth, 1970

Fanon, Frantz, *Black Skin, White Masks*, Pluto Press: London, 1986

Fanon, Frantz, *The Wretched of the Earth*, trans. Constance Farrington, Penguin: Harmondsworth, 1967

Fanon, Frantz, *Studies in a Dying Colonialism*, Earthscan: London, 1988

Ferguson, Moira, *Subject to Others: British women writers and colonial slavery, 1670–1834*, Routledge: London, 1992

Franco, Jean, 'Beyond ethnocentrism: gender, power and the Third-World Intelligentsia', in C. Nelson and L. Grossberg (eds.), *Marxism and the Interpretation of Culture*, Macmillan Education: Basingstoke, 1988, pp. 503–15

Freire, Paulo, *A Pedagogy for Liberation: Dialogues on transforming education*

Fryer, Peter, *Black People in the British Empire*, Pluto: London, 1987

Fryer, Peter, *Staying Power: The history of black people in Britain*, Pluto: London, 1984

Gabriel, Teshome H., 'Towards a critical theory of Third World films', in Jim Pines and Paul Willeman (eds.), *Questions of Third World Cinema*, BFI: London, 1989, pp. 30–52

Gates, Henry Louis, Jr. 'Critical Fanonism', *Critical Inquiry*, 17, Spring 1991, pp. 457–70

Gellner, Ernest, *Nations and Nationalism*, Blackwell: Oxford, 1983

Giddens, Anthony, *Modernity and Self-identity*, Polity Press: Cambridge, 1991

Giddens, Anthony, *The Consequences of Modernity*, Polity Press: Cambridge, 1990

Giddings, Robert (ed.), *Literature and Imperialism*, Macmillan: London, 1991

Gilman, Sander, *Difference and Pathology: Stereotypes of sexuality, race and madness*, Cornell University Press: Ithaca, NY, and London, 1985

Gilroy, Paul, 'Cultural studies and ethnic absolutism', in L. Grossberg, C. Nelson and P. Treichler (eds.), *Cultural Studies*, Routledge: London, 1992, pp. 187–98

Gilroy, Paul, 'It ain't where you're from, it's where you're at. . . .: the dialectics of diasporic identification', *Third Text*, 13, Winter, 1990–1, pp. 3–16

Gilroy, Paul, *There Ain't No Black in the Union Jack*, Hutchinson: London, 1987

Giroux, Henry A., 'Post-colonial ruptures and democratic possibilities: multiculturalism as anti-racist pedagogy', *Cultural Critique*, 21, Spring 1992, pp. 5–40

Glissant, Edouard, *Caribbean Discourse*, trans. Michael J. Dash, University of Virginia Press: Lexington, VA, 1989

Goldberg, David (ed.), *Anatomy of Racism*, University of Minnesota Press: Minneapolis, 1990

Griffiths, Gareth, and Moody, David, 'Of Marx and missionaries: Soyinka and the survival of universalism in post-colonial literary theory', *Kunapipi*, XI, 1, 1989, pp. 74–85

Gugelberger, Georg M., 'Decolonizing the canon: considerations of Third World literature', *New Literary History*, 22, 1991, pp. 505–24

Gugelberger, Georg M. (ed.), *Marxism and African Literature*, James Currey: London, 1985

Guha, Ranajit, 'On some aspects of the historiography of colonial India', in Ranajit Guha (ed.), *Subaltern Studies I: Writings on South Asian history and society*, Oxford University Press: New Delhi, 1982, pp. 1–8

Guha, Ranajit, 'The prose of counter-insurgency', in Ranajit Guha (ed.), *Subaltern Studies II: Writings on South Asian history and society*, Oxford University Press: New Delhi, 1986

Hall, Stuart, 'Cultural identity and diaspora', in J. Rutherford (ed.), *Identity: Community, culture, difference*, Lawrence & Wishart: London, 1990, pp. 222–37

Hall, Stuart, 'Minimal selves', in *Identity: The real me*, ICA Documents: London, 1987, pp. 44–6

Harlow, Barbara, *Resistance Literature*, Methuen: New York and London, 1987

Harris, Wilson, *The Womb of Space: The cross-cultural imagination*, Greenwood Press: Westport, CT, 1983

Hawes, Clement, 'Three times round the globe: Gulliver and colonial discourse', *Cultural Critique*, 18, Spring 1991, pp. 187–214

Henderson, Mae Gwendolyn, 'Speaking in tongues: dialogics, dialectics and the black woman writer's literary tradition', in Henry Louis Gates Jr. (ed.), *Reading Black, Reading Feminist: A critical anthology*, Meridian Press: New York, 1990, pp. 116–42

Hennessy, Rosemary, and Mohan, Rajeswari, 'The construction of woman in three popular texts of empire: towards a critique of materialist feminism', in *Textual Practice*, 3, 3, Winter 1989, pp. 323–59

Hobsbawm, E. J., *The Age of Empire*, Weidenfeld & Nicolson: London, 1987

Hobsbawm, E. J., *Nations and Nationalism since 1780: Programme, myth, reality*, Cambridge University Press: Cambridge, 1990

Holmlund, Christine, 'Displacing limits of difference: gender, race, and colonialism in Edward Said and Homi Bhabha's theoretical models and Marguerite Duras's experimental films', *Quarterly Review of Film and Video*, 13, 1–3, 1991, pp. 1–22

Holst-Petersen, K., and Rutherford, A. (eds.), *A Double Colonisation: Colonial and post-colonial women's writing*, Dangaroo Press: Aarhus, 1985

hooks, bell, *Talking Back: Thinking feminist, thinking black*, South End Press: London, 1989

hooks, bell, 'Representing whiteness in the black imagination', in L. Grossberg, C. Nelson and P. Treichler (eds.), *Cultural Studies*, Routledge: London, 1992, pp. 338–46

hooks, bell, *Yearning: Race, gender, and cultural politics*, Turnaround: London, South End Press: Boston, MA, 1991

Horkheimer, Max, and Adorno, Theodor W., *Dialectic of Enlightenment*, trans., John Cumming, Allen Lane: London, 1973

Horton, James Africanus, *West African Countries and Peoples, British and Native; with the Requirements Necessary for Establishing that Self-government recommended by the Committee of the House of Commons, 1865; and a Vindication of the African Race*, W. J. Johnson: London, 1868

Hulme, Peter, *Colonial Encounters: Europe and the native Caribbean, 1492–1797*, Methuen: London, 1986

Hulme, Peter and Whitehead, Neil, *Wild Majesty: Encounters with Caribs from Columbus to the present day*, Oxford University Press: Oxford, 1992

Hyam, Ronald, *Empire and Sexuality*, Manchester University Press: Manchester, 1990

Irele, Abiola, *The African Experience in Literature and Ideology*, Heinemann: London, 1981

James, C. L. R., *The C. L. R. James Reader*, ed. Anna Grimshaw, Basil Blackwell: Oxford, 1992

Jameson, Fredric, 'Third World literature in the era of multinational capitalism', *Social Text*, 15, 1986, pp. 65–88

JanMohamed, Abdul, R., *Manichean Aesthetics: The politics of literature in colonial Africa*, University of Massachusetts Press: Amherst, MA, 1983

JanMohamed, Abdul R., 'The economy of Manichean allegory: the function of racial difference in colonialist literature', in *Critical Inquiry*, 12: 1 (1985), pp. 59–87

JanMohamed, Abdul R., and Lloyd, David (eds.), *The Nature and Context of Minority Discourse*, Oxford University Press: New York, 1990

John, Mary, 'Postcolonial feminists in the western intellectual field: anthropologists *and* native informants?', *Inscriptions*, 5, 1989, pp. 49–74

Johnson, Hazel, and Bernstein, Henry (eds.), *Third World Lives of Struggle*, Heinemann/Open University: Oxford, 1982

Jordan, June, *Technical Difficulties: Selected political essays*, Virago: London, 1992

Kandiyoti, Deniz, 'Identity and its discontents: women and the nation', *Millennium: Journal of International Studies*, 20, 3, 1991, pp. 429–43

Kapur, Geeta, 'The centre–periphery model or how are we placed? Contemporary cultural practice in India', *Third Text*, 16/17, Autumn/Winter 1991, pp. 9–18

Katrak, Ketu, 'Decolonizing culture: toward a theory for postcolonial women's texts', *Modern Fiction Studies*, 35, 1, Spring 1989, pp. 157–79

Kaye, Jacqueline, 'Islamic imperialism and the question of some ideas of "Europe"', in Francis Barker, Peter Hulme, Margaret Iversen and Diane Loxley (eds.), *Europe and Its Others*, vol. 1, Proceedings of the Essex Sociology of Literature Conference, University of Essex: Colchester, 1984

Lichtheim, George, *Imperialism*, Penguin: Harmondsworth, 1974

Loomba, Ania, 'Overworlding the "Third World"', *Oxford Literary Review*, Special Issue 'Neocolonialism', 13, 1991, pp. 164–91

Lorde, Audre, *Sister Outsider: Essays and speeches*, Crossing Press: Trumansburg, NY, 1984

Low, Gail Ching-Liang, 'His stories? Narratives and images of imperialism', *New Formations*, 12, Winter 1990, pp. 97–123

Low, Gail Ching-Liang, 'White skins/black masks: the pleasures and politics of imperialism', *New Formations*, 9, Winter 1989, pp. 83–104

Lowe, Lisa, 'Rereadings in Orientalism: Oriental inventions and inventions of the Orient in Montesquieu's *Lettres persanes*', *Cultural Critique*, 15, Spring 1990, pp. 115–44

McClintock, Anne, 'The angel of progress: pitfalls of the term "post-colonialism"', *Social Text*, Spring, 1992, pp. 1–15

Mackenzie, John M., *Propaganda and Empire*, Manchester University Press: Manchester, 1984

Maharaj, Sarat, 'The Congo is flooding the acropolis: art in Britain of the immigration', *Third Text*, 15, Summer 1991, pp. 77–90

Majeed, Javed, *Ungoverned Imaginings: James Mills' 'The History of British India' and Orientalism*, Clarendon Press: Oxford, 1992

Makdisi, Saree, S. 'The Empire renarrated: *Season of Migration to the North* and the reinvention of the present', *Critical Inquiry*, 18, Summer 1992, pp. 804–20

Mandela, Nelson, *The Struggle is My Life*, International Defence and Aid Fund: London, 1978

Mani, Lata, 'Cultural theory, colonial texts: reading eyewitness accounts of widow burning', in L. Grossberg, C. Nelson and P. Treichler (eds.), *Cultural Studies*, Routledge: London, 1992, pp. 392–405

Mani, Lata, 'The production of an official discourse on *sati* in early nineteenth-century Bengal', in Francis Barker, Peter Hulme, Margaret Iversen and Diane Loxley (eds.), *Europe and Its Others*, vol. 1, Proceedings of the Essex Sociology of Literature Conference, University of Essex: Colchester, 1984, pp. 107–27

Mattelart, Armand, *Multinational Corporations and the Control of Culture: The ideological apparatuses of imperialism*, Harvester Wheatsheaf: Brighton, 1979

Mattelart, Armand, *Transnationals and the Third World: The struggle for culture*, Bergin and Garvey: South Hadley, MA, 1983

Maughan-Brown, David, *Land, Freedom and Fiction: History and ideology in Kenya*, Zed Press, London, 1985

Mbembe, Achille, 'The banality of power and the aesthetics of vulgarity in the postcolony', *Public Culture*, 4, 2, Spring 1992, pp. 1–30

Memmi, Albert, *The Colonizer and the Colonized*, Earthscan: London, 1990

Mills, Sara, *Discourses of Difference*, Routledge: London, 1991

Minh-ha, Trinh T., *When the Moon Waxes Red: Representation, gender and cultural politics*, Routledge: London, 1991

Minh-ha, Trinh, T., *Woman, Native, Other: Writing postcoloniality and feminism*, Indiana University Press: Bloomington, IN, 1989

Mishra, Vijay, and Hodge, Bob, 'What is post(-)colonialism?', *Textual Practice*, 5, 3, 1991, pp. 399–414

Mohanty, Chandra, 'Under western eyes: feminist scholarship and colonial discourses', *Feminist Review*, 30, Autumn 1988, pp. 61–88

Moody, David, 'Marx meets masque: the play of history in African theatre', *World Literature Written in English*, 31, 1, 1991, pp. 93–102

Morrison, Toni, *Playing in the Dark*, Harvard University Press: Cambridge, MA, 1992

Mudimbe, V. Y., *The Invention of Africa: Gnosis, Philosophy and the Order of Knowledge*, James Currey: London, 1988

Mudimbe, V. Y. (ed.), *The Surreptitious Speech: Présence Africaine and the politics of otherness, 1947–87*, University of Chicago Press: Chicago, IL, 1992

Mukherjee, Arun P., 'The exclusions of postcolonial theory and Mulk Raj Anand's *Untouchable*: a case study', *Ariel*, 22, 3, July 1991, pp. 27–48

Mulvey, Laura, '*Xala*, Ousmane Sembene 1976: the carapace that failed', *Third Text*, 16–17, Autumn/Winter 1991, pp. 19–37

Nairn, Tom, *The Break-up of Britain*, New Left Books: London, 1977

Nasta, Susheila (ed.), *Motherlands*, The Women's Press: London, 1991

Ndebele, Njabulo, *Rediscovery of the Ordinary: Essays on South African literature and culture*, Congress of South African Writers: Johannesburg, 1991

Nederveen Pieterse, J. P., *Empire and Emancipation: Power and liberation on a world scale*, Pluto: London, 1989

Nederveen Pieterse, J. P., *White on Black: Images of Africa and blacks in western popular culture*, Yale University Press: London, 1992

Ngũgĩ wa Thiong'o, *Barrel of a Pen: Resistance to repression in neo-colonial Kenya*, New Beacon: London, 1985

Ngũgĩ wa Thiong'o, *Decolonising the Mind: The politics of language in African literature*, James Currey: London, 1986

Ngũgĩ wa Thiong'o, *Homecoming: Essays on African and Caribbean literature, culture and politics*, Heinemann: London, 1972

Ngũgĩ wa Thiong'o, *Moving the Centre: The struggle for cultural freedom*, James Currey: London, 1993

Ngũgĩ wa Thiong'o, *Writers in Politics*, Heinemann: London, 1981

Nkrumah, Kwame, *Consciencism, Philosophy and Ideology for De-Colonization*, Panaf: London, 1964

Nkrumah, Kwame, *Revolutionary Path*. Panaf: London, 1973

Noyes, J. K., *Colonial Space*, Harwood Academic: Chur, Switz., 1992

Nyerere, Julius K., *Ujamaa: Essays on socialism*, Oxford University Press: Dar-es-Salaam, 1968

Parker, A., Russo, M., Sommer, D., and Yaeger, P. (eds.), *Nationalisms and Sexualities*, Routledge: New York, 1992

Parmer, Pratibha, 'Black feminism: the politics of articulation', in J. Rutherford (ed.), *Identity: Community, culture, difference*, Lawrence & Wishart: London, 1990, pp. 101–26

Parry, Benita, 'Problems in current theories of colonial discourse', *Oxford Literary Review*, 9, 1–2, 1987, pp. 27–58

Parry, Benita, 'Resistance theory/theorising resistance or two cheers for nativism', in Peter Hulme (ed.), *Post-Colonial Theory and Colonial Discourse*, Manchester University Press: Manchester, 1993

Pathak, Z., Sengupta, S., and Purkayastha, S., 'The prisonhouse of Orientalism', *Textual Practice*, 5, 2, Summer 1991, pp. 195–218

Pechey, Graham, 'On the borders of Bakhtin: dialogization, decolonization', *Oxford Literary Review*, 9, 1–2, 1987, pp. 59–84

Plaatje, Sol T., *Native Life in South Africa Before and Since the European War and the Boer Rebellion*, P. S. King & Son: London, 1916

Plaatje, Sol T., *Native Life in South Africa*, Longman: Harlow, 1987

Porter, Dennis, *Haunted Journeys: Desire and transgression in European travel writing*, Princeton University Press: Princeton, NJ, 1991

Porter, Dennis, '*Orientalism* and its problems', in Peter Hulme, Margaret Iversen, and Diane Loxley (eds.), *The Politics of Theory*, Proceedings of the Essex Sociology of Literature Conference, University of Essex: Colchester, 1983

Pratt, Mary Louise, *Imperial Eyes: Travel writing and transculturation*, Routledge: London 1992

Rao, Venkat, 'Self-formations: speculations on the question of postcoloniality', *Wasafiri*, Spring 1991, pp. 7–10

Reid, Mark A., 'Dialogic modes of representing Africa(s): womanist film', *Black American Literature Forum*, 25, 2, Summer 1991, pp. 375–88

Retamar, Roberto, 'Caliban: notes towards a discussion of culture in our America', *Massachusetts Review*, 15, Winter–Spring 1974, pp. 7–72

Rice, Laura, '"Nomad Thought": Isabelle Eberhardt and the colonial project', *Cultural Critique*, 17, Winter 1990–1, pp. 151–76

Roberts, Sheila, '"Post-colonialism, or the House of Friday" – J. M. Coetzee's *Foe*', *World Literature Written in English*, 31, 1, 1991, pp. 87–92

Rodney, Walter, *How Europe Underdeveloped Africa*, Zimbabwe Publishing House: Harare, 1972

Rosen, Phillip, 'Making a nation in Sembene's *Ceddo*', *Quarterly Review of Film and Video*, 13, 1–3, 1991, pp. 147–72

Said, Edward, 'Representing the colonized: anthropology's interlocutors', *Critical Inquiry*, 15, Winter 1989, pp. 205–25

Said, Edward, *Culture and Imperialism*, Chatto & Windus: London, 1993

Said, Edward, 'Intellectuals in the post-colonial world', *Salmagundi*, 70/71, Spring–Summer 1986, pp. 44–64

Said, Edward, *Orientalism*, Routledge & Kegan Paul: London, 1978

Said, Edward, 'Orientalism reconsidered', in Francis Barker, Peter Hulme, Margaret Iversen and Diane Loxley (eds.), *Europe and Its Others*, vol. 1, Proceedings of the Essex Sociology of Literature Conference, University of Essex: Colchester, 1985, pp. 14–27

Said, Edward, 'Third World intellectuals and metropolitan culture', *Raritan*, IX, 3, Winter 1990, pp. 27–50

Sandoval, Chela, 'US Third World feminism: the theory and method of oppositional consciousness in the postmodern world', *Genders*, 10, Spring 1991, pp. 1–23

Sangari, Kumkum, 'The politics of the possible', *Cultural Critique*, Fall 1987, pp. 157–86

Sanjines, Jorge, 'Problems of form and content in revolutionary cinema', in Michael Chapman (ed.), *Twenty-Five Years of the New Latin American Cinema*, BFI: London, 1983

Seme, Pixley, 'The regeneration of Africa', in Brian Filling and Susan Stuart (eds.), *The End of a Regime?*, Aberdeen University Press: Aberdeen, 1991

Senghor, Léopold Sédar, 'Negritude: a humanism of the twentieth century', in Wilfred Cartey and Martin Kilson (eds.), *The Africa Reader: Independent Africa*, Vintage Books (Random House): New York, 1970

Sharpe, Jenny, 'The unspeakable limits of rape: colonial violence and counter-insurgency', *Genders*, 10, Spring 1991, pp. 25–46

Shohat, Ella, 'Gender and culture of empire: toward a feminist ethnography of the cinema', *Quarterly Review of Film and Video*, 13, 1–3, 1991, pp. 45–84

Sivanandan, A., *A Different Hunger: Writings on Black resistance*, Pluto Press: London, 1982

Sivanandan, A., *Communities of Resistance*, Verso: London, 1992

Slemon, Stephen, 'Post-colonial allegory and the transformation of history', *Journal of Commonwealth Literature*, 23, 1, 1988, pp. 157–68

Slemon, Stephen, 'Monuments of Empire: Allegory/counter-discourse/post-colonial writing', *Kunapipi*, 9, 3, 1987, pp. 1–16

Smith, Anthony D., *The Ethnic Origins of Nations*, Blackwell: Oxford, 1984

Soja, Edward, *Postmodern Geographies*, Verso: London 1989

Spivak, Gayatri Chakravorty, 'Can the subaltern speak?', in C. Nelson and L. Grossberg (eds.), *Marxism and the Interpretation of Culture*, Macmillan Education: Basingstoke, 1988, pp. 271–313

Spivak, Gayatri Chakravorty, 'Feminism in decolonization', *differences: A Journal of Feminist Cultural Studies*, 3, 3, 1991, pp. 139–70

Spivak, Gayatri Chakravorty, 'Imperialism and sexual difference', *Oxford Literary Review*, 8, 1–2, 1986, pp. 225–40

Spivak, Gayatri Chakravorty, *In Other Worlds: Essays in cultural politics*, Methuen: London, 1987

Spivak, Gayatri Chakravorty, 'Neocolonialism and the secret agent of knowledge', *Oxford Literary Review*, Special Issue 'Neocolonialism', 13, 1–2, 1991, pp. 220–51

Spivak, Gayatri Chakravorty, *The Post-Colonial Critic: Interviews, strategies, dialogues*, ed. Sarah Harasym, Routledge: London, 1991

Spivak, Gayatri Chakravorty, 'Poststructuralism, marginality, postcoloniality and value', in P. Collier and H. Geyer-Ryan (eds.), *Literary Theory Today*, Polity Press: Cambridge, 1990, pp. 219–44

Spivak, Gayatrti Chakravorty, 'The Rani of Sirmur', in Frances Barker, Peter Hulme, Margaret Iversen and Diane Loxley (eds.), *Europe and Its Others*, vol. 1, Proceedings of the Essex Sociology of Literature Conference, University of Essex: Colchester, 1984, pp. 128–51

Spivak, Gayatri Chakravorty, 'Three women's texts and a critique of imperialism', *Critical Inquiry*, 12, 1, 1985, pp. 262–80

Sprinker, Michael (ed.), *Edward Said: A critical reader*, Blackewell: Oxford, 1992

Stam, Robert, and Spence, Louise, 'Colonialism, racism and representation', *Screen*, 24, 2, 1983, pp. 2–20

Stott, Rebecca, 'The dark continent: Africa as female body in Haggard's adventure fiction', *Feminist Review*, 32, Summer 1989, pp. 69–89

Suleri, Sara, *The Rhetoric of English India*, University of Chicago Press: Chicago, IL, 1992

Suleri, Sara, 'Woman skin deep: feminism and the postcolonial condition', *Critical Inquiry*, 18, Summer 1992, pp. 756–69

Tandeciarz, Silvia, 'Reading Gayatri Spivak's "French feminism in an international frame": a problem for theory', *Genders*, 10, Spring 1991, pp. 75–90

Tiffin Helen, 'Post-colonialism, post-modernism and the rehabilitation of post-colonial history', *Journal of Commonwealth Literature*, 23, 1, 1988, pp. 169–81

Tiffin, Helen, 'Post-colonial literatures and counter-discourse', *Kunapipi*, 9, 3, 1987, pp. 17–34

Tomlinson, John, *Cultural Imperialism*, Pinter: London, 1991

Trump, Martin (ed.), *Rendering Things Visible: Essays on South African literary culture*, Raven Press: Johannesburg, 1990

Viswanathan, Gauri, *Masks of Conquest: Literary study and British rule in India*, Faber & Faber: London, 1990

Walker, Alice, *In Search of Our Mothers' Gardens: Womanist prose*, The Women's Press: London 1984

Wallace, Michele, *Invisibility Blues*, Verso; London 1990

Wallace, Michele, 'Negative images: towards a black feminist cultural criticism', in L. Grossberg, C. Nelson and P. Treichler (eds.), *Cultural Studies*, Routledge: London 1992, pp. 654–64

Wallerstein, Immanuel, *Historical Capitalism*, Verso: London, 1983

Ward, Cynthia, 'What they told Buchi Emecheta: oral subjectivity and the joys of "Otherhood"', *PMLA*, 105, 1, January 1990, pp. 83–97

Ware, Vron, *Beyond the Pale: White women, racism and history*, Verso: London, 1992

West, Cornel, 'The postmodern crisis of the black intellectuals', in L. Grossberg, C. Nelson and P. Treichler (eds.), *Cultural Studies*, Routledge: London, 1992, pp. 689–96

Williams, Patrick, '*Kim* and Orientalism', in P. Mallett (ed.), *Kipling Considered*, Macmillan: London, 1989, pp. 35–55

Williams, Patrick, 'Problems of post-colonialism', *Paragraph*, 16, 1, 1993, pp. 91–102

Woodhull, Winifred, 'Unveiling Algeria', *Genders*, 10, Spring 1991, pp. 112–31

Wynter, Sylvia, 'Beyond Miranda's meanings: un/silencing the "demonic ground" of Caliban's "woman"', in Carole Boyce Davis and Elaine Savoy Fido (eds.), *Out of the Kumbla: Caribbean women and literature*, Africa World Press: Trenton, NJ, 1990

Young, Robert, *White Mythologies: Writing History and the West*, Routledge: London, 1990

Yuval-Dais, Nira, and Anthias, Floya (eds.), *Woman-Nation-State*, Macmillan: London, 1989

Zamora, Marguerite, 'Abreast of Columbus: gender and discovery', *Cultural Critique*, 17, Winter 1990–1, pp. 127–50

Index